KU-574-392

LIVERPOOL
JOHN MOORES UNIVERSITY
AVRIL ROBARTS LRC
THE BARN STREET
LIVERPOOL L2 2ER
TEL 0151 231 4022

WITHDRAWN

VERPOOL JMU LIBRARY

3 1111 01210 9235

Globalization, Uncertainty and Youth in Society

Globalization, Uncertainty and Youth in Society is one of a series of books which presents the results of the international and multidisciplinary research program 'GLOBALIFE - Life Courses in the Globalization Process'. The program was based at the Otto-Friedrich University of Bamberg, and ran from 1999-2005, including experts from eleven different countries who studied the implications of the globalization process for individuals in industrialized societies. The research presents a systematic empirical examination of how global developments impact the life courses of individuals in a range of modern societies. Unlike much of the literature on globalization the GLOBALIFE project findings are not limited to the economic dimension but include a multi-causal intersection of economic, technological, cultural and political changes.

This collection of essays examines how youths in 14 different industrialized societies make the important transition from youth to adulthood in an era of globalization and rising uncertainty. It investigates how the institutions that operate on social groups of youths impact on their ability to make decisions that will determine their life course as an adult. *Globalization, Uncertainty and Youth in Society* takes an empirical approach to the topic, bringing the individual and nation-specific institutions back into the discussion on globalization.

Hans-Peter Blossfeld is the director of the GLOBALIFE program and is the Professor and Chair in Comparative Sociology at the Otto-Friedrich University of Bamberg. He has been Editor of European Sociological Review and is Associate Editor of International Sociology.

Erik Klijzing is the Executive Director of the International Union for the Scientific Study of Population in France. He has worked internationally as a population expert including positions with the United Nations.

Melinda Mills is Assistant Professor in the Department of Socio-Cultural Sciences at the Vrije University, Amsterdam.

Karin Kurz is Assistant Professor in the Faculty of Social and Economic Sciences at the Otto-Friedrich University of Bamberg. Her research interests include social inequality, social stratification, housing, the labor market and the life course.

LIVERPOOL
JOHN MOORES UNIVERSITY
AVRIL ROBARTS LRC
TITHEBARN STREET
LIVERPOOL L2 2ER

Routledge advances in sociology

This series aims to present cutting-edge developments and debates within the field of sociology. It will provide a broad range of case studies and the latest theoretical perspectives, while covering a variety of topics, theories and issues from around the world. It is not confined to any particular school of thought.

Globalization, Uncertainty and Youth in Society

Edited by Hans-Peter Blossfeld,
Erik Klijzing, Melinda Mills and
Karin Kurz

Routledge
Taylor & Francis Group

LONDON AND NEW YORK

GL BALIFE

Life Courses in the Globalization Process

First published 2005 by Routledge
2 Park Square, Milton Park, Abingdon, Oxon OX14 4RN

Simultaneously published in the USA and Canada
by Routledge
270 Madison Ave, New York, NY 10016

Routledge is an imprint of the Taylor & Francis Group

Transferred to Digital Printing 2006

© 2005 editorial matter and selection, Hans-Peter Blossfeld, Erik Klijzing, Melinda Mills and Karin Kurz; individual chapters, the contributors

All rights reserved. No part of this book may be reprinted or reproduced or utilised in any form or by any electronic, mechanical, or other means, now known or hereafter invented, including photocopying and recording, or in any information storage or retrieval system, without permission in writing from the publishers.

British Library Cataloguing in Publication Data
A catalogue record for this book is available from the British Library

Library of Congress Cataloging in Publication Data
A catalog record for this book has been requested

ISBN 0-415-35730-6

CONTENTS

TABLES

FIGURES

CONTRIBUTORS

Fabrizio Bernardi is an Assistant Professor in the Department of Sociology II of the Universidad Nacional de Educación a Distancia (UNED), Madrid, Spain. From 1998 to 2001 he worked as Assistant Professor of Sociology at the University of Bielefeld, Germany and within the GLOBALIFE project. His main research interests focus on social inequality, the relationship between labour market and family dynamics but also on quantitative methods for longitudinal analysis.
Address: Departamento de Sociología II, U.N.E.D.,c/ Obispo Trejo s/n, 28040 Madrid, Spain. [email:fbernardi@poli.uned.es]

Hans-Peter Blossfeld is a Professor of Sociology at the Department of Social and Economic Sciences, Bamberg University, Germany. He was Professor of Sociology at the European University in Florence and the Universities in Bremen and Bielefeld. He is editor of the *European Sociological Review*. He is the Director of the GLOBALIFE project and of the Staatsinstitut für Familienforschung an der Universität Bamberg (ifb) (Institute for Family Research at Bamberg University). His research interests include social inequality, youth, family, and educational sociology, labor market research, demography, social stratification and mobility, cross-national comparative research, modern methods of quantitative social research and statistical methods for longitudinal data analysis. He has published 16 books and over 100 articles.
Address: Lehrstuhl für Soziologie I, Otto-Friedrich-Universität Bamberg, Postfach 1549, D-96045 Bamberg, Germany.
[email: hans-peter.blossfeld@sowi.uni-bamberg.de]

Erzsébet Bukodi is Head of the Section of Social Stratification within the Department of Social Statistics of the Hungarian Central Statistical Office, Budapest, Hungary. Her research interests involve educational inequalities and different aspects of life-course analysis. She is a participant of a research project aiming to develop a new social indicator system in Hungary. Recently she published a book (her PhD dissertation) on marriage timing and educational homogamy of couples. Further publications examine career differences of married couples and the main features of regional and social stratification based on the Hungarian Census data.

Address: Hungarian Central Statistical Office, Keleti Károly utca 5-7. 1024. Budapest, Hungary. [email: Erzsebet.Bukodi@office.ksh.hu]

Magnus Bygren is an Assistant Professor in the Department of Sociology, Stockholm University, Sweden. His research interests are in the field of labour sociology, segregation and reference group theory. He is currently doing research on the causes of ethnic segregation and sex segregation in Swedish workplaces, and has recently published studies on how organizational factors affect the demographic composition of the in- and outflow of employees.

Address: Department of Sociology, Stockholm University, 10691 Stockholm, Sweden. [email: magnus.bygren@sociology.su.se]

Teresa Castro Martín is a Researcher at the Department of Demography, Institute of Economics and Geography, Spanish Council for Scientific Research, Spain. Her research interests include causes and consequences of lowest-low fertility in Southern Europe, changing family patterns in Spain and linkages between educational, work and family biographies of young adults. She is also interested on sexual and reproductive health issues in less developed countries. Recent publications examine union formation in Southern Europe, contraceptive patterns in Spain, consensual unions in Latin America and adolescent sexual behaviour in Brazil.

Address: Instituto de Economia y Geografia, CSIC, Pinar 25, 28006 Madrid, Spain. [email: tcastro@ieg.csic.es]

Ann-Zofie Duvander is a Senior Researcher at the Research Division, Department of Research, Statistics and Analysis, Swedish National Social Insurance Board, Sweden. Her research interests revolve around family dynamics, family policy and the interaction between work life and family life. She has recently published studies on the income effect on childbirth intensities, the gender division of parental leave and the connection between childcare characteristics and continued childbearing.

Address: Department of Research, Statistics and Analysis, National Social Insurance Board, 103 51 Stockholm, Sweden.
[email: ann-zofie.duvander@rfv.sfa]

Tony Fahey is a Research Professor in the Economic and Social Research Institute, Dublin, Ireland. His research interests include quality of life and social exclusion in the EU, family, the elderly and housing. Recent publications examine the relationship between home ownership, pensions and poverty among the elderly in Europe, quality of life in Europe, and housing in Ireland.

Address: The Economic and Social Research Institute, 4 Burlington Road, Dublin 4, Ireland. [email: Tony.Fahey@esri.ie]

Marco Francesconi is a Principal Research Officer at the Institute for Social and Economic Research at the University of Essex, United Kingdom. His research interests are on intergenerational links, family and household economics, and evaluations of labor market programs. Recent publications examine the effects of childhood parental behavior on children's later outcomes, educational homogomy and its effects on partners' labor market performance, intergenerational mobility and social capital, and gender pay gap.
Address: Institute for Social and Economic Research, University of Essex, Wivenhoe Park, Colchester CO4 3SQ, United Kingdom.
[email: mfranc@essex.ac.uk]

Katrin Golsch is currently a Lecturer and Senior Researcher at the Faculty of Economics, Business Administration and Social Sciences, University of Cologne, Germany. During the completion of this paper she was a researcher in the GLOBALIFE project and a lecturer in the Department of Sociology, Bielefeld University, Germany. She received her doctorate in Sociology in 2004 about labour market insecurity and its impact on work and family life of men and women in Germany, Britain and Spain. Her core interests include statistical methods for the analysis of survey data and longitudinal data analysis in particular, life-course analysis, social structure, labor market research and comparative sociological research.
Address: The Faculty of Economics, Business Administration and Social Sciences, University of Cologne, Herbert-Lewin-Str. 2, 50931 Cologne, Germany. [email: golsch@wiso.uni-koeln.de]

Mia Hultin was an Assistant Professor at the Swedish Institute for Social Research, Stockholm University, Sweden while working on the contribution to this book. Her doctoral thesis *Consider Her Adversity: Four Essays on Gender Inequality in the Labor Market* (2001) includes empirical studies of processes generating gender inequality in wages, internal career prospects and supervisory attainment. Mia Hultin passed away in October 2002.

Annick Kieffer is a Research Fellow at CNRS, and a member of Lasmas in Paris. Her research interests include education and training, transition in youth and women relations to labor force, in a comparative approach, as well as methodology of comparative indicators on these topics. She has published several articles on democratization of education, on the socioeconomic categories in Europe and more recently on low-skilled work.
Address: CNRS Lasmas, Iresco, 59-61 rue Pouchet, 75849 Paris Cedex 17.
[email: kieffer@iresco.fr]

Kalev Katus is a Professor and Director at the Estonian Interuniversity Population Research Centre, Estonia. His main research interests include long-term population development, particularly analysis of fertility and reproductive behaviour, as well as national statistical systems. Recent publications examine parity-specific fertility development, childbearing and reproductive careers in life course perspective. He is currently a member of editorial board of the *European Population Studies*.
Address: Estonian Interuniversity Population Research Centre, P.O.Box 3012, Tallinn 10504, Estonia. [email: kalev@ekdk.estnet.ee]

Rosalind B. King is a Health Scientist Administrator at the National Institute of Child Health and Human Development of the National Institutes of Health, USA. Her research interests include adolescent social and physical development, the transition to adulthood, romantic relationships and union formation, and women's fertility. Recent publications examine the relationship between body mass index and dating, clustering of healthy sleep and dietary habits, childbearing patterns in developed nations, and the interrelations between work, family, health, and well-being.
Address: 6100 Executive Blvd., Room 8B07, MSC 7510, Bethesda, MD, 20892-7510, USA. [email: rozking@mail.nih.gov]

Erik Klijzing is Executive Director of the Office of the International Union for the Scientific Study of Population (IUSSP) in Paris, France. His research interests include family demography, survey research, social statistics, and life course analysis. Recent publications examine unmet family planning needs, transitions to adulthood and the dynamics of fertility and partnership in Europe. He was Deputy Director of the GLOBALIFE project from 1999-2003.
Address: International Union for the Scientific Study of Population (IUSSP), 3-5 rue Nicolas, 75980 Paris cedex 20, France. [email: klijzing@iussp.org]

Karin Kurz is an Assistant Professor of Sociology at the Department of Social and Economic Sciences, Bamberg University, Germany. She was also a member of the GLOBALIFE project and Assistant Professor at the University of Bielefeld, Germany. Her research interests include the cross-national comparison of life course transitions, social inequality, the family and the labor market. Recent publications focus on the effects of labor market insecurities on long-term commitments, trends in employment mobility, and home-ownership and social inequality in a comparative perspective.
Address: Fakultät für Sozial- und Wirtschaftswissenschaften, Otto-Friedrich Universität Bamberg, Postfach 1549, 96045 Bamberg, Germany.
[email: karin.kurz@sowi.uni-bamberg.de]

Richard Layte is a researcher at the Economic and Social Research Institute Dublin. His main research interest is the interaction between households, individuals and the labour market and the implications this has for their social mobility, standard of living and health status. His recent publications have included papers on poverty dynamics and the impact of vocational education on unemployment risk across the life course.

Address: The Economic and Social Research Institute, 4 Burlington Road, Dublin 4, Ireland. [email: Richard.Layte@esri.ie]

Aart C. Liefbroer is Head of the Department of Social Demography at the Netherlands Interdisciplinary Demographic Institute (NIDI). His research focusses on demographic behaviour of young adults. Recent topics of interest are the impact of values, norms and attitudes on demographic decisions of young adults, the importance of intergenerational transmission for demographic behaviour and the explanation of cross-national differences in patterns of entry into adulthood.

Address: Netherlands Interdisciplinary Demographic Institute, PO Box 11650, 2502 AR The Hague, The Netherlands. [email: liefbroer@nidi.nl]

Selina McCoy, working within the Educational Policy Research Centre of the Economic and Social Research Institute, carries out research on a range of educational issues of concern in Ireland and internationally. Among the issues of particular interest are school effectiveness and process, school-to-work transitions and issues of educational equality. Most recently, she has published *Moving Up: The experiences of First Year Students in Post-Primary Education* (with E. Smyth and M. Darmody, 2004) and *Expanding Post-School Learning Opportunities* (with D.F. Hannan and A. Doyle, 2003), with a study on the effects of part-time employment among second-level students (*At Work in School*) soon to be published.

Address: The Economic and Social Research Institute, 4 Burlington Road, Dublin 4, Ireland. [email: selina.mccoy@esri.ie]

Catherine Marry is a Sociologist and Director of Research at CNRS. Her research concerns the relationship between school and employment as related to gender with cross-country comparisons. She has published extensively on women in science and technology. Since 1999, she is the coordinator of an European workgroup on labor market and gender (the Groupement de recherche Mage -Marché du travail et genre).

Address: LASMAS-IdL, IRESCO-CNRS, 59 rue Pouchet, 75849 Paris cedex 17. [email: marry@iresco.fr]

Monique Meron is a Statistician and Head of the Department 'Métiers et qualifications' at the Direction of Research and Statistics, Ministry of Work in Paris, France. During the completion of this paper, she worked at the National Institute of Demographic Studies (INED). Her research interests include interactions between employment and family life, gender studies on the job market,

employment and unemployment and occupational characteristics. She belongs to the Editoral board of the journal *Travail, genre, et sociétés*.
Address: Monique Meron, Chef du Département des métiers et qualifications, Dares-Ministère du travail, 39-43 quai André Citroën, 75902 Paris cedex 15.
[email: monique.meron@dares.travail.gouv.fr]

Melinda Mills is an Assistant Professor at the Department of Social-Cultural Sciences, Faculty of Social Sciences, Vrije Universiteit Amsterdam, The Netherlands. She is currently an Editor of the journal *International Sociology*. During the completion of this paper, she was a member of the GLOBALIFE project and Assistant Professor at the University of Bielefeld, Germany. Her research interests include cross-national comparative research, demography, youth, family sociology, time and causality, and quantitative and qualitative methods of social research. Recent publications examine globalization, partnership histories, labor market flexibility, time, and interdependent processes using event history models.
Address: Faculty of Social Sciences, Vrije Universiteit Amsterdam, De Boelelaan 1081, 1081 HV Amsterdam, The Netherlands.
[email: mc.mills@fsw.vu.nl]

Øivind Anti Nilsen is Associate Professor at the Norwegian School of Economics and Business Administration, Department of Economics, Norway. His research interests are applied microeconometrics and labour economics with a focus on areas such as the establishment of youth in the labour market, adjustment of the labour stock in firms, and early retirement, together with sickness absence. Nilsen has published in journals such as *Oxford Bulletin of Economics and Statistics*, *Review of Economics and Statistics*, but also in sociological journals such as *European Sociological Review*.
Address: Norwegian School of Economics and Business Administration, Department of Economics, Hellevn. 30, N-5045 Bergen, Norway.
[email: oivind.nilsen@nhh.no]

Tiziana Nazio is an Assistant Professor at the Department of Political and Social Sciences, Pompeu Fabra University in Barcelona, Spain. Formerly she worked in the FENICs and GLOBALIFE projects at the University of Bielefeld, Germany. Her research interests include family formation, labour force participation and fertility. Her methodological interests include event history analysis, diffusion models and interdependent processes. Recent publications examine the diffusion process of cohabitation in Europe. She is currently working on low fertility issues for the BBVA funded project FAMRISK.
Address: Universitat Pompeu Fabra, Departament de Ciències Polítiques i Socials, Edifici Jaume I - Ramon Trias Fargas, 25-27, E-08005 Barcelona.
[email: tiziana.nazio@upf.edu]

Philip J. O'Connell is Research Professor at the ESRI, Dublin. Much of his work focuses on education, training and the labour market. He has written several books on the effects of work-related education and training. Papers on this and other labour market issues have been published in *Work, Employment and Society, The Economic and Social Review, The European Sociological Review, The Industrial and Labour Relations Review,* and *The British Journal of Industrial Relations.* Current research interests include the impact of active labour market programmes and workplace change.
Address: The Economic and Social Research Institute, 4 Burlington Rd., Dublin 4, Ireland. [email: philip.oconnell@esri.ie]

Emilio A. Parrado is an Assistant Professor at Duke University, USA. His main research interests include migration, family and fertility behavior, educational inequality and Latin America. Publications include articles in *Journal of Marriage and the Family, Population and Development Review, Demography, Social Problems, Comparative Education Review* and *Social Science Quarterly.*
Address: Department of Sociology, 277B Soc/Psych Bldg, Box 90088, Duke University, Durham, NC 27708-0088. [email: eparrado@soc.duke.edu]

Allan Puur is a Researcher at the Estonian Interuniversity Population Research Centre, Estonia. His main research interests include economic activity of the population, interactions between employment and family life, and harmonisation of demographic data. Recent publications address labour market experience of the population during economic transition, women's employment careers in life course perspective and data quality issues.
Address: Estonian Interuniversity Population Research Centre, P.O.Box 3012, Tallinn 10504, Estonia. [email: allan@ekdk.estnet.ee]

Péter Róbert is an Associate Professor at the Department of Sociology, Faculty of Social Sciences, ELTE University, Budapest, Hungary. He is also a senior researcher at the TÁRKI Social Research Center. His research interests include social stratification and mobility with special focus on educational inequalities and life-course analysis. He also does research on lifestyle differentiation and on attitudes toward social inequalities. Recent publications examine career differences of married couples, educational transition from secondary to tertiary school, comparison of students' performance in state-owned and church-run schools.
Address: Faculty of Social Sciences, ELTE University, Pázmány Péter sétány 1/A. 1112. Budapest, Hungary. [email: robert@tarki.hu]

Luule Sakkeus is a Researcher at the Estonian Interuniversity Population Research Centre, affiliated with the Ministry of Social Affairs, Estonia. Her main research interests include long-term trends in migration processes, immigrant population and national minorities and corresponding data sources. Recent publications examine demographic development of foreign-origin population, migration careers of the population and national system of health statistics.

Address: Estonian Interuniversity Population Research Centre, P.O.Box 3012, Tallinn 10504, Estonia. [email: luule@ekdk.estnet.ee]

Carles Simó Noguera is a Researcher at the Department of Sociology and Social Anthropology, Universitat de València Estudi General, Spain. His research interests include ageing, divorce, fertility, early labor market careers, adulthood transitions, and job mobility. Recent publications examine the transition to parenthood and adulthood, globalization and immigrant care of the elderly in Spain.

Address: Departament de Sociologia i Antropologia Social, Universitat de València Estudi General, Edifici Departamental Oriental, Campus dels tarongers. Av. dels Tarongers s/n, 46022 València, Spain. [email:carles.simo@uv.es]

Anne Solaz is a Researcher at the Department of Demography Economics of INED (the French National Institute of Demographic Studies) Paris, France. Her research interests include the links between the demographic events (family formation and dissolution) and the labor market history of individuals. She is also working on the allocation of time (parental time, domestic time, common leisure) between partners. She is currently constructing a survey on interactions between work and family patterns, where interviews are held with both the household members and their employers.

Address: INED, 133 Bld Davout 75 985 Paris cedex 20, France. [email: solaz@ined.fr]

Asunción Soro Bonmatí is a Research Fellow at the Faculty of Economics, University of Alicante and external researcher at the Instituto Valenciano de Investigaciones Económicas (IVIE), Spain. Her research interests include comparative cross-country studies of the transition from education to the labour market and other life course events such as the entry into partnership and parenthood. Recent publications focus on job careers of young people. She has contributed to the book *Transitions from Education to Work in Europe* recently published in Oxford University Press.

Address: Faculty of Economics, University of Alicante, Apart. Correos, 99, E-03080, Alicante, Spain. [email: asuncion.soro@ivie.es]

Nikolei Steinhage was a member of the GLOBALIFE project, University of Bielefeld, Germany, where he was the webmaster and responsible for data storage, data organization, and data analysis. He has also worked at the Centre of Social Policy, University of Bremen, where he was responsible for making a complete dataset of German life insurance available for social research and building tools for data preparation of large, complex datasets with a focus on longitudinal morbidity research. In September 2002, he left the GLOBALIFE project to take up a tenured job in the public sector as Assistant Director of Network Security. His current profession is building firewalls, intrusion detection systems and hardend server based on open source.

Address: Blücherstr. 27, 65195 Wiesbaden, Germany.
[email: nikolei@linuxsecure.de]

Preface

This volume emanates from the international and multidisciplinary research program '*GLOBALIFE*' – *Life Courses in the Globalization Process*, funded by the Volkswagen Foundation (Hannover, Germany). GLOBALIFE studies the implications of the globalization process for the life courses of individuals in various OECD-type societies. The project examines how globalization impacts four aspects of the life course: 1) the transition to adulthood, 2) men's mid-career mobility, 3) women's mid-career mobility and the work/family link; and, 4) late careers and retirement. This volume represents the completion of the first phase of this project.

This volume examines how youth in 14 different industrialized societies make the transition into adulthood in an era of globalization and rising uncertainty. Globalization is an inherently complex concept, yet in recent years has become a central point of reference for media, politicians, academics and policy-makers to understand change. Globalization entails a series of significant macro-processes that are common to all modern societies: 1) internationalization of markets and subsequent decline in national borders, 2) intensification of competition and growth in discourse on deregulation, liberalization and privatization, 3) spread of global networks of people and firms linked by new technologies, and, 4) a rise in the importance of markets. Together these developments create an atmosphere of increasing uncertainty that is 'filtered' through country-specific institutions and perceptions. The institutions of welfare regimes, employment, education and family systems that operate during the transition to adulthood channel uncertainty to specific social groups of youth which in turn impacts their opportunity or ability to make decisions during the transition to adulthood. Yet youth are in a life course phase where they need to make vital and long-term binding decisions about entering the labor market and forming a partnership or family. This volume takes an empirical approach to the topic, brings the individual and nation-specific institutions back into the globalization discussion and examines the impact of globalization on social and gender inequalities.

The GLOBALIFE project, established and directed by Hans-Peter Blossfeld, began in September 1999 at the University of Bielefeld, Germany and will end in early 2005. Since September 2002, the project has been located at the Otto-Friedrich University in Bamberg, Germany. During the preparation of this volume, the project consisted of core project members located at the University of Bielefeld, including: Fabrizio Bernardi, Hans-Peter Blossfeld, Katrin Golsch, xxiv

Erik Klijzing, Karin Kurz, Melinda Mills, Tiziana Nazio, Carles Simó, Thorsten Sommer, and Nikolei Steinhage. Many of these researchers have now moved to take academic positions in various countries, perhaps a reflection of the 'globalized' nature of the project itself and our occupations. We thank all project members for their energy, persistence and contribution to the many lively 'globalization' debates during this period. We also thank Ingeborg McIntyre for competent administrative support. In particular, in the stage of preparing the typescript we received invaluable help from our student assistants Monique Antler, Katrin Busch, Cathrin Conradi, Kathrin Kolb, Jens Kratzmann, Wolfgang Kraus, Kerstin Künsebeck, Corinna Mergner, Robert Stephan, and Susanne Stedtfeld. We like to thank all of them.

Another important goal of the GLOBALIFE project was to create, expand, and utilize an international research network, in which specific substantive and methodological issues in the analysis of life courses in the globalization process could be developed and executed. The completion of this volume is therefore also attributed to the individual contributors to this volume who are experts in their respective countries who devoted time and energy into the project. We thank all of the contributors for their time and patience. Our condolences are extended to the family and friends of Mia Hultin, one of the contributors to this volume, who passed away in 2002. We would also like to thank the many individuals who responded to our work when it was presented at various conferences. Our appreciation goes to Terry Clague and Routledge in London for supporting the publication of the volume. Finally, we would like to thank the Volkswagen Foundation in Hannover for their continued financial support that made this ambitious project possible.

Hans-Peter Blossfeld
Otto-Friedrich University Bamberg

Erik Klijzing
IUSSP, Paris

Melinda Mills
Vrije Universiteit Amsterdam

Karin Kurz
Otto-Friedrich University Bamberg

Foreword

I have long been interested in the role of economic factors in influencing marriage behavior as economic change is a continuing feature of modern industrial, as well as industrializing, societies. As such it usually affects large numbers of people, although often differentially. Hence, economic factors could potentially be playing an important role in the substantial changes in marriage and fertility behavior that have characterized most industrial societies in recent years. To this end, I have been studying the impact of economic factors on American marriage and cohabitation behavior and am especially pleased to write a preface to this collection of studies because they partially build on and extend my own work to other societies.

Beginning some time in the early 1970s, the American age at marriage started its long-term rise. For many years, demographers thought this was due to women's increasing economic independence resulting from the large post-war rise in married women's employment. I did not think this was a particularly convincing explanation for a variety of theoretical and empirical reasons and recent research has borne out the weakness of this argument. More importantly, while demographers were so intent on the presumed consequences of *women's* rising employment, not much attention was being directed to the changes in *men's* economic status–and these were substantial. During the 1980s, labor economists started to document a sharp increase in economic inequality among American males. Most affected were less educated men, especially African Americans, but even *within* educational groups, there was a rise in inequality among those with less as compared to more labor market experience– i.e., the young. Labor economists were not particularly concerned with the likely impact of these changes on marriage and family behavior, and most social demographers did not seem to be noticing them, but warning bells definitely went off in my mind.

The increasing economic difficulties were not just characteristic of the least educated socioeconomic groups (high school dropouts) but also of the far more numerous group of moderately educated men (high school graduates) and of the young in particular. The question was how to get a handle on investigating the impact of economic inequality on marriage behavior. I conceptualized the problem from a career-development perspective as young men tend to be particularly vulnerable to changes in the economy–they have less work experience and hence less on-the-job training and low tenure at any particular job they may currently have. One well-known result of these vulnerabilities is that during recessions, the unemployment rates of young men rise much more than those of older men. What the labor market analyses indicated, however, was that the inherent career-entry problems of young American workers had increased over time. This, in turn, has accentuated a number of impediments to marriage formation. On the one hand, their earnings are low and often unstable, which makes it very difficult to set up an independent household. Their low income and job insecurity also raises considerable uncertainty about their current ability and willingness to make a stable commitment to adult family roles. Uncertainty about their long-term socioeconomic characteristics and life style also impedes assortative mating because marriages are supposed to last. Hence people not only sort on their *current* characteristics but also on their expected *future* characteristics as well and these can be heavily influenced by the ultimate nature of their occupational careers. In short, low earnings and high levels of career uncertainties should lead to marriage delays while such difficulties are being experienced.

I was fortunate in investigating these issues to have available a large longitudinal data set, the National Longitudinal Survey of Youth, first interviewed in 1979 when they were aged 14-22 and which I followed annually thereafter until 1990 for my analysis of marriage formation and 1993 for the cohabitation and marriage study (Oppenheimer *et al.*, 1997; Oppenheimer, 2003). Very detailed data were collected each year on economic and marital behavior. Hence, it was possible to develop measures of career-entry status for males (earnings, time out of school, amount worked each year, school enrollment, job type) and likely long-term socioeconomic characteristics (educational attainment). Discrete time logit analysis was used to assess whether evidence of career "immaturity" discouraged marriage formation in any given year. And indeed I found that it did.

Because of the longitudinal nature of the NLSY data, it was also possible to assess inequalities in the *pace* of these young men's career-entry process. This showed the persistence, over several years after they left school, of poverty-level earnings for a sizable proportion of moderately to less educated men, especially blacks. Furthermore, compared to those with a college degree, it also took several years for a sizable proportion to have worked full-time full-year for even one year and much longer to have worked full-time for two consecutive years. In short, there were considerable race and educational differences in the length of time it took these young NLSY cohorts to achieve a stable work career paying an above-poverty wage. This implied that the lowered risk of marrying due to economic difficulties in any given year would persist over some time for many of them. Using these data on educational and race differences in the pace of career development plus the logit analysis of the effect of the economic variables on marriage formation in any given year, it was possible to construct simulations of the pace of marriage formation for people with difficult vs. easier career transitions by education and race. The differences in marriage formation between difficult and easier transitions within race-education groups as well as between groups were dramatic. Hence, although a crude approximation, I thought this was telling evidence of the role of men's career-development difficulties in marriage delays in the United States.

Recently, I have extended the analysis of marriage formation among NLSY males to include cohabitation behavior. I used a multinomial logit analysis of, first, the effect of career-related factors on the entry into either a cohabiting or marital union and then, if a cohabitation has occurred, the effect of these same factors on whether the couple split up or married. In general, the analysis indicated that entering a marriage rather than a cohabitation is far more likely for those with the best long-term prospects (i.e., the more educated). However, if such men did enter a cohabitation, they were also more likely to marry out of it compared to the less educated, suggesting that their cohabitations might represent engagements. The evidence also suggests that those with a recent unstable employment record may have been using cohabitation as an adaptive strategy while their careers were still in flux. They were far more likely than the stably employed to enter a cohabitation and, once in a cohabitation, they were also far less likely to marry out of it.

My studies of the role of career-entry difficulties and the likely uncertainties they create for young people, along with the ensuing effects on cohabitation and marriage, have been limited to American society. Nor have I attempted to investigate the role of these factors in delayed childbearing. Yet increases in both cohabitation and delayed marriage and childbearing have also been occurring among many other developed countries. Hence, this volume makes an important contribution to our understanding of these issues by investigating them for 14 diverse but mostly European, societies. Furthermore, it broadens the scope of the studies in two other important ways as well. First it places the difficulties young people are experiencing within the context of the globalization phenomenon, thereby providing a single hypothesized cause or cluster of causes for young people's economic difficulties. Second, there is a clear recognition that the possibly negative effects of globalization will be mediated by specified differences in the institutional structure of the various societies. Hence, uniformity in the nature of the impact of globalization on young people's economic position or in their response to economic difficulties is not preordained in societies impacted by globalization shifts. All in all, this collection of different country studies raises important questions in marriage and family behavior and sets the stage for even more work to come.

Valerie Oppenheimer
University of California at Los Angeles

BIBLIOGRAPHY

Oppenheimer, V.K. (2003) 'Cohabiting and Marriage During Young Men's Career-Development Process', *Demography*, 40: 127-149.
Oppenheimer, V.K., Kalmijn, M. and Lim, N. (1997) 'Men's Career Development and Marriage Timing During a period of Rising Inequality', *Demography*, 3: 311-330.

1 Globalization, uncertainty and the early life course

A theoretical framework[1]

Melinda Mills and Hans-Peter Blossfeld

INTRODUCTION

Young people in industrialized nations have experienced significant changes in the transition to adulthood in past decades. Globalization, via the internationalization and importance of markets, intensified competition, accelerated spread of networks and knowledge via new technologies and the dependence on random shocks, has transformed the transition to adulthood. The purpose of this study is to ask whether these changes have influenced young people's ability to establish themselves as independent adults, to form partnerships, and to become parents. Has globalization produced a fundamental shift in youth behavior as they cope with increasing uncertainty about the future? How are these transformations filtered by different domestic institutions?

To this point, there has been little empirical evidence regarding the consequences of such sweeping social change on the lives of youth. Our central aim is to study the consequences of globalization on the transition to adulthood in a cross-country perspective. We maintain that the impact of globalization will be experienced differently by youth in various countries due to nation-based institutional differences. Institutions such as the education system, employment relations, welfare regimes and family systems serve to buffer the forces of globalization. We examine how changes from national and global forces intersect, how these changes are defined and interpreted, and then how youth react when making pivotal life course decisions. A primary hypothesis is that the increased uncertainty in the early labor market experiences of youth seep into the partnership and parenthood domains of their lives.

Our comparative analysis in this book includes 14 countries from five welfare regimes. Canada, the United States, and Great Britain represent the liberal regimes, with Germany, the Netherlands, and France exemplifying the conservative regimes. Norway and Sweden characterize the social-democratic and Italy, Spain, Mexico, and Ireland are examples of the family-oriented regimes. What we term 'post-socialistic' regimes refers to Estonia and Hungary.

For our purposes, we have defined the transition to adulthood as a stepwise process in which young people adopt specific roles and participate in certain activities. We particularly focus on the age-graded character of labor market entry, the transition to first partnership (cohabitation or marriage), and entry into parenthood. The study of the impact of globalization on this critical and turbulent phase of the early life course is important for several reasons. First, outsiders of the labor market are expected to experience recent shifts towards globalization more directly. Youth entering the labor market, who are unprotected by seniority or experience, are such outsiders. This relates to the second reason: changes that might first appear in the youth labor market indicate tendencies that may soon work their way through the entire age structure (Myles *et al.*, 1993). The findings of this research are thus pertinent to other social groups beyond youth. Finally, repercussions of decisions made at this stage of the life course are likely to have long-term implications. A higher level of volatility during the period of young adulthood has the potential to generate insecurity and conflict at a time when individuals must make long-term binding decisions that shape the remainder of their life course.

After an overview of the research topic, the section 'Globalization and increasing uncertainty' describes the causal mechanisms that relate globalization to the generation of uncertainty in the lives of youth. The section 'Globalization and institutional filters' chronicles the importance of national institutions such as educational systems, employment relations, welfare regimes and family systems in filtering the impact of globalization. A theory of how these processes are experienced at an individual level is introduced in the section 'Micro-level response to increasing uncertainty'. The micro-level response to globalization positions the actor as attempting to make rational decisions in a context of increasing economic, employment relation and temporal uncertainty. The data and methods used in the empirical analyses are then briefly discussed in the section 'Data and methods', followed by a summary of results and concluding remarks.

GLOBALIZATION AND INCREASING UNCERTAINTY

Globalization is an inherently complex concept (Guillén, 2001). Yet in recent years, it has become a central point of reference for media, politicians, academics, and policy-makers to understand social change. Our concept of globalization can be summarized under four interrelated structural shifts which are affecting the life courses in modern societies during the last two decades: (1) the swift internationalization of markets after the breakdown of the East-West-Divide; (2) the rapid intensification of competition based on deregulation, privatization, and liberalization within nation states; (3) the accelerated diffusion of knowledge and the spread of global networks that are connecting all kinds of markets on the globe via new information and communication technologies (ICTs); and, (4) the rising importance of markets and their dependence on random shocks occurring somewhere on the globe. We point to these global mechanisms because together they are generating an unprecedented level of structural uncertainty in modern societies as described below and also illustrated in Figure 1. We then propose a causal connection between these global forces and various kinds of increasing uncertainty that are filtered by domestic institutions and channeled to wards specific social groups. In particular, we create a bridge or middle-range

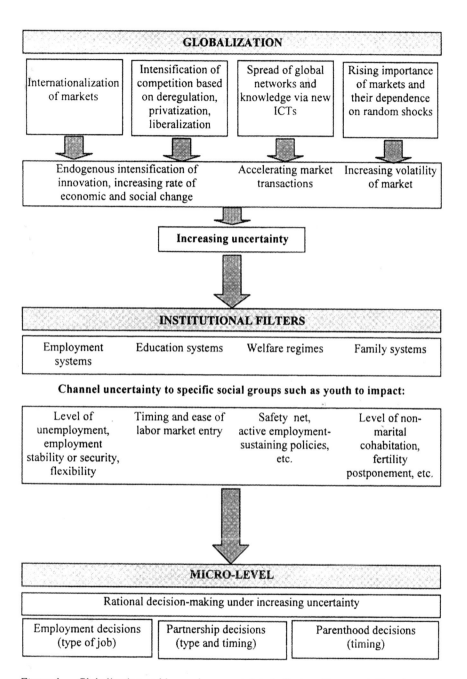

Figure 1   Globalization and increasing uncertainty in the transition to adulthood

theoretical approach that allows testable hypotheses at the individual level of the impact of globalization.

First, globalization refers to the *internationalization of markets and subsequent decline of national borders*. It is connected with changes in laws, institutions, or practices which make various transactions (in terms of commodities, labor, services and capital) easier or less expensive across national boarders. The decline of national borders often relates to the modification of trade regulations and political discourse and treaties. We have witnessed global formal agreements such as the International Labor Organization, World Health Organization, World Trade Organization, International Monetary Fund, United Nations as well as various non-governmental organizations which intensify the interaction among nation states or link social groups from various countries (Verdier and Breen, 1999). As Montanari (2001: 471) argues, many of these organizations: 'operate as pressure groups on governments to enact policies which would enhance and improve the functioning of markets, through measures such as deregulation and privatization.' Tariffs on trade, for instance, have been greatly reduced under the General Agreement on Tariffs and Trade (GATT), and between member states in the European Union (EU) and via the North American Free Trade Agreement (NAFTA). The consequence is that capital flows are facilitated by these types of political agreements, which have also generally liberalized financial markets (Fligstein, 1998). Some have argued that this decline of national borders undermines the authority or even heralds the fall of the nation state (Ohmae, 1990; Beck, 2000). Our position is that the nation state and in particular institutions that shape the lives of youth do not lose their significance, but generate country-specific problems that call for country-specific solutions and transformations (see also Sassen, 1996).

In economic terms, the internationalization of markets is particularly reflected in the rising number of firms conducting business in more than one country, through the presence of multinational corporations (MNCs) and foreign direct investment (FDI). In fact, MNCs are a driving force of the globalization of production and markets since they account for around two-thirds of world trade, 20 percent of world output, and play a primary role in the diffusion of technology (UNCTAD, 1995: 23; Reich, 1991). Internationalization of markets also means the *integration of previously 'isolated' nations into the world economy*. Several areas in our study experienced closure to outside global forces for varying reasons such as a dictatorship (Franco in Spain), communism (East Germany, Estonia, Hungary) or political conservatism tied to the Catholic church (Québec in Canada).

Second, globalization relates to the *intensification of competition*, i.e., the notion that capital and labor is increasingly mobile and forcing firms and national economies to continuously adjust. Within nation states, this is reflected in the increased importance of governments to make their national economies internationally competitive. These policy measures include the improvement of the functioning of markets through the removal or relaxation of government regulation of economic activities (deregulation). It also suggests a shift towards relying on the price mechanism to coordinate economic activities (liberalization), and a transfer to private ownership and control of assets or enterprises that were previously under public ownership (privatization). This neo-liberal shift demands efficiency, productivity and profitability, and often means a push to adjust prices, products, technologies and human resources more rapidly and extensively (Alderson, 1999; Regini, 2000a; Montanari, 2001).

A third feature of globalization is the *spread of global networks of people and firms linked by ICTs* such as microcomputers and the Internet. These ICTs together with modern mass media transmit messages and images instantaneously from the largest city to the smallest village on every continent and allow a faster diffusion of information and knowledge over long distances. They increasingly allow people to share information, to connect and to create an instant common worldwide standard of comparison. Modern ICTs influence communications between individuals, organizations and communities by effectively rendering physical space and distance irrelevant. Thus, although the introduction of technology is not unique in itself, recent ICTs have fundamentally altered the scope (widening reach of networks of social activity and power), intensity (regularized connections), velocity (speeding up of interactions and processes), and impact (local impacts global) of transformations (Held *et al.*, 1999).

Finally, globalization is inherently related to the *rise in the importance of markets*. Globalization not only speeds up the process of exchange and communication across national borders, but due to the intensification of global competition also increases the relevance of markets in the coordination of decisions in all modern societies. These developments inherently strengthen the worldwide interdependence of decision-making.

As a consequence of these structural developments, market prices and their changes increasingly convey information about the global demand for various goods, services and assets, and the worldwide relative costs of producing and offering them. In a globalizing market, individual suppliers and consumers are increasingly exposed to a rising number of traders on each side of the market and become 'price-takers', able to buy and sell any quantity at a price which they generally cannot influence. Thus, prices produced by globalizing markets increasingly set the standards to which individuals, firms and nation states then try to comply.

However, globalization does not only mean that actors are increasingly in the hands of anonymous global markets. What is equally important is that the changes on these markets are becoming more dynamic and less predictable. First, the globalization of markets endogenously intensifies competition between firms, forcing them to be innovative, to use new technological developments or to invent new products. This in turn increases the instability of markets (Streeck, 1987). Second, modern ICTs and deregulation and liberalization measures allow individuals, firms and governments to react faster to observed market changes and simultaneously accelerate market transactions (Castells, 1996). This in turn makes long-term developments of globalizing markets inherently harder to predict. Third, global prices tend to become exogenously more liable to fluctuations because worldwide supply, demand, or both are getting increasingly dependent on *random shocks* caused somewhere on the globe (e.g., major scientific discoveries, technical inventions, new consumer fashions, major political upsets such as wars and revolutions, economic upsets, etc.). The accelerated market dynamics and the rising dependence of prices on random events happening somewhere on the globe produce a higher frequency of surprises and lead to market prices which are different to an important extent from what people reasonably could have expected given the restricted information available to them. In other words, the increasing dynamics and volatility of outcomes of globalizing markets makes it more difficult for individuals, firms and governments to predict the future of the market and to make choices between different alternatives and strategies. Increasing uncertainty about economic and social developments is therefore a definitive feature of globalization in advanced economies.

GLOBALIZATION AND INSTITUTIONAL FILTERS

It is not essentially increasing uncertainty as such that is important if we analyze the consequences of globalization; rather, it is how rising uncertainty is 'institutionally filtered' and channeled towards specific social groups in various countries. Increasing uncertainty does not impact all regions, states, organizations or individuals in the same way. There are institutional settings and social structures, historically grown and country-specific, that determine the degree to which people are affected by rising uncertainty (DiPrete *et al.*, 1997). These institutions have a certain inertial tendency to persist (Nelson, 1995; Esping-Andersen, 1993) and act as a sort of intervening variable between global macro forces and the responses at the micro level (Hurrell and Woods, 1995; Regini, 2000a). Thus, we do not expect that increasing uncertainty leads to a rapid convergence of life courses in all modern societies, as claimed, for example, by neo-institutionalists (see for e.g., Meyer *et al.*, 1992) or the proponents of the modernization hypothesis (see for e.g., Treiman, 1970; Treiman and Yip, 1989). Rather we claim that there are path-dependent developments within countries (Nelson, 1995; Mayer, 2001). The institutions that most impact the life courses of youth are employment relations, educational systems, national welfare state regimes, and the family.

Employment relations systems

Given the specific phase of the life course, we expect that *in all countries* the global increase of uncertainty is experienced more directly by *youth entering the labor market*. They are unprotected by seniority and experience and they do not yet have strong ties to work organizations and work environments. Thus we propose a *life course hypothesis* that youth entering the labor market are more exposed to global uncertainty in all countries. In contrast, we assume that people who are already established in their job career or have already gained several years of labor force experience should be less influenced by global forces.

However, countries also differ significantly with respect to the nature of their employment relations between employers and workers and make it therefore more or less easy for youth to establish themselves in the labor market. These country-specific differences surface in elements such as types of work councils, collective bargaining systems, strength of unions versus employer organizations, labor legislation or administrative regulations. They produce distinct national variations of occupational structures and industries, patterns of labor-capital negotiations, strike frequencies and collective agreements on wages, job security, labor conditions, and work hours (Soskice, 1993; Streeck, 1992). How these systems diverge has been characterized as 'coordinated' and 'uncoordinated' market economies (Soskice, 1998), 'individualist' or 'collective' regimes (DiPrete *et al.*, 1997), or 'open' and 'closed' employment relations (Sørensen, 1983). We first define these systems and position the 14 countries on a continuum according to the degree of open or closed employment relations, followed by a link to the type of labor market flexibility measures introduced within each nation.

The *open employment relationship* reigns in the United States, Canada, Ireland, and Britain (after Margaret Thatcher) and has a severe manifestation in Mexico. It is characterized as decentralized, dualistic and based on free market forces and competition. It is a system where employment relations are open in the sense that protective factors such as labor unions, legislation related to job security and stability are weak. Shielding of workers is at a minimum, market mechanisms are central and individuals' labor market resources or human capital such as social origin, education, labor force experience are crucial (DiPrete *et al.*, 1997). Many European countries, on the other hand, such as Sweden, Norway, Germany, France, the Netherlands, Italy and Spain, are often classified as having labor markets with relatively *closed employment relationships* and centralized procedures for negotiating wages (Regini, 2000a). Sweden and Germany are countries with particularly strong labor unions, while Southern European countries like Spain and Italy are taken as extreme cases of an 'insider-outsider' labor market.

A fascinating evolution of employment relation systems exists in countries which belonged to the eastern side of the Iron Curtain, which in our study includes Estonia (Katus *et al.*, this volume), Hungary (Róbert and Bukodi, this volume) and former East Germany (Kurz *et al.*, this volume). These countries not only experienced a severe political and economic 'shock' from a socialist to a more market driven economy, but also incredible transformations from an agricultural to industrial society, coupled with sudden exposure to the accelerated and volatile global market at the beginning of the 1990s. This meant a rapid shift from closed to open employment systems. Older cohorts grew up in a system where employment was guaranteed, with extraordinarily high job security, even for women, youth and older workers (see Katus *et al.*, this volume). Younger cohorts entered the labor market after this 'shock' during a period of economic depression and tumultuous change.

Based on these systems, we propose an *employment relationship hypothesis* regarding the early labor market experiences of youth in various countries. We expect that the main consequences of the open employment relationship for young people will be: (1) comparatively low economic security (e.g., wages, benefits) for most jobs; (2) an environment that fosters precarious employment and labor market flexibility to the extent that it becomes more widespread among various social groups; (3) importance of individual human capital resources; (4) relatively easy entry into the labor market; (5) unemployment of a shorter duration; and, (6) a relatively high rate of job mobility (i.e., hire-and-fire principle). The central impact of a closed employment relationship is expected to be that: (1) precarious employment forms (e.g., fixed-term contracts, part-time work) are highly concentrated among specific groups seeking access to the labor market (youth, women, unemployed); (2) individual human capital resources are less important; (3) entry in the labor force is problematic, particularly under conditions of high general unemployment; (4) unemployment is usually of a longer duration; and, (5) the rate of job mobility is relatively low. Within these systems most of the already employed workers, the so-called 'insiders', will be relatively shielded against the growing uncertainty and flexibility demands of the world market, which is explored in the second volume of the GLOBALIFE project that examines mid-career men (see Blossfeld, Mills and Bernardi, forthcoming). Globalization in these countries tends to create a new kind of underclass of the socially excluded, while the employed have high levels of job security with relatively high wages, reminiscent of dual and segmented labor market theories (Piore, 1970; Fine, 1998).

The type of employment relation system also shapes the impact of the globalization process, which is witnessed in the level of unemployment, employment stability or security and labor market flexibility of young people (see Figure 1 and Klijzing, this volume). A key discussion is the type and degree of labor market flexibility that each nation institutes (Bernardi, 2000; Regini, 2000b; Standing, 1997). Labor market flexibility can be distinguished into five different types: external numerical (ability to adjust number of employees), externalization (outsourcing, subcontracting), functional (insider employees moved between tasks), wage (adjust labor costs, benefits), and temporal or internal numerical (adjust working time, cyclical or seasonal shifts) (Atkinson, 1984; Bruhnes, 1989; Regini, 2000b).

We propose a *labor market flexibility hypothesis*, which contends that firms implement different types of flexibility depending on the rigidity of the employment relation system. Not only the level or type of flexibility will differ, but also the meaning and function attributed to it. Our anticipation is that in rigid closed labor markets, functional flexibility for labor market insiders is often the primary option for employers. However, for outsiders such as youth, one way to implement flexibility will be a combination of numerical/temporal flexibility in the form of fixed-term or temporary contracts. Furthermore, externalization – related to the growing number of self-employed youth not bound to a contract of employment – may also serve an increasingly important purpose (see Bernardi and Nazio, this volume). Whereas, in more deregulated open labor markets built on the premises of flexibility, market economic relations, and a non-interventionist state (Mayer, 2001), we expect flexibility to pervade in many forms. As new labor market entrants, youth will be party to numerical flexibility as the last hired and first fired, a pattern likely accentuated during periods of economic recession. Externalization will also play a more central role (see Róbert and Bukodi, this volume). Since labor costs are more readily adjusted to the firms' needs in open markets, we likewise expect that this will translate into wage flexibility evident in lower earnings and more implicit economic reductions such as no or fewer benefits (e.g., pension, sickness). Our last expectation is that open systems are able to adjust labor using temporal flexibility in accordance with cyclical or seasonal shifts and to vary the hours worked in a day, week or year (Mills, this volume).

Regini (2000a) argues that the use of temporary contracts in Europe as a form of flexibility was more of a controlled exception or experiment in Italy, Germany, France, Spain and Norway. By contrast, in Britain, Ireland, the Netherlands, and Denmark and to some extent Sweden, flexibility is a general or guiding principle for all employment relationships. In countries that experimented with fixed-term contracts, flexibility was not a permanent solution but was designed to inject flexibility into a certain segment of the labor market (Regini, 2000a). This technique achieves similar objectives without substantially lowering the level of protection enjoyed by the core insider labor market. The sweeping form of flexibility in Britain, Ireland, the Netherlands and North America enables firms to rapidly reduce costs and adjust more quickly to rapid changes in the global market, which in turn affords better competitiveness in the global market and higher employment. However, the long-term prospect of these short-term solutions remains to be seen.

Educational systems

In the globalized, knowledge-based society, education and labor force experience become the most important types of human capital. Since youth are generally lacking the latter they have to focus on the former, which is evident in educational expansion across most of the industrialized world (see Klijzing, this volume). We therefore propose a *human capital hypothesis* that gauges the significance of characteristics required in all knowledge-based economies. Educational attainment and occupational standing measure human capital, which may increase with labor force experience and age. The expectation is that those lacking human capital, such as youth with lower education, weak occupational standing or lacking experience, will feel the impact of globalization more immensely in *all* modern societies. In other words, they are at a higher risk to enter a more precarious, flexible and uncertain employment situation (e.g., fixed-term contract, part-time, irregular hours). Conversely, those with higher education or the 'knowledge workers' will conceivably have more favorable experiences.

However, we expect that white-collar workers are not entirely immune to changes such as the use of temporary short-term contracts. Thus there may be a change also for those in higher occupations or higher education. Yet the main difference is that for them, unstable or inadequate work may serve as a bridge whereas for lower skilled wage-workers, it may become a trap (see Bernardi and Nazio; Layte *et al.*, this volume). Therefore, a second general expectation is that *globalization accentuates or even cultivates inequality* by offering better opportunities to the better educated youth and constraining the chances of the less educated. To test this hypothesis, many of the country chapters that follow examine the transition to employment by educational level, occupational class, age, sex, labor force experience, and in some cases, by migrant status (Estonia, Germany) or visible minority or race (Canada, United States).

There are, however, also great differences among nations in the way they (1) differentiate the maximum number of school years attended by all and tracking (stratification), (2) value certificates or ability-based learning (qualificational versus organizational), (3) standardize the quality of education (standardization), and (3) link education with entry into the labor market. Using Maurice and Sellier's (1979) regimes of school-to-work transitions, we can think of differences in terms of 'qualificational' versus 'organizational' space and, following Allmendinger (1989), the degree of educational 'standardization' or 'stratification' (see also Blossfeld, 1992; Shavit and Müller, 1998). In unstratifed systems, all children have the opportunity to attend school, which may lead to post-secondary education until the age of 18, with the same range of options (theoretically) open to all students. In these countries, a larger proportion of a cohort attains the maximum number of school years provided by the general educational system. Countries with more unstratified systems include the United States, Canada, Great Britain, Sweden, post-1960s Italy, post-1970s Spain and post-1990s Estonia. Whereas in the 'stratified' systems that exist in Germany, the Netherlands, and Hungary, educational opportunities of youth are stratified as they are streamed into specific educational tracks at a younger age.

The manner that countries combine theoretical learning with practical work experience has direct implications for early labor market transitions (Blossfeld, 1992; Blossfeld and Stockmann, 1998/99). In a system of organizational space, education is academic or general in character with specific occupational skills learned on-the-job. These are often the unstandardized systems such as the United States. Whereas in qualificational space, education is closely tied to job requirements in the vocational system with more importance placed on diploma requirements and certificates. In these countries that value qualifications (e.g., Germany), nationwide standardized certificates are easily understood by employers. Here it is important to make a distinction between countries which organize training mainly through (1) 'theoretical' training in vocational schools (France, the Netherlands, Hungary, Ireland, Estonia, Mexico), (2) 'practical' on-the-job training (United States, Great Britain, Canada, Italy, Spain, Sweden, Norway) or (3) the so-called 'dual' system, a pragmatic combination of theoretical learning at school and job experience at the work place (Germany).

Based on these differences, we propose an *educational system hypothesis*, which specifies the impact of the type of educational system on labor market entry in the following way. First, we expect that *theoretical training in vocational schools* promotes a broader understanding of occupational activities, but does not confront youth with real work situations. Since practical experience is shifted to the period after theoretical vocational training, our anticipation is that youth engaged in training from these systems will have a relatively more difficult transition from school to work (see unemployment figures in Klijzing, this volume). Second, in the organizational system of *practical on-the-job training*, (often unstratified, unstandardized) we expect that young workers will be less restricted to narrowly defined occupational fields, have fewer structural barriers in terms of recognized certificates, and have a weaker link between the type of qualification they possess and the type of job they obtain. Due to the heterogeneous quality of on-the-job training, however, we foresee that this lack of shared definitions and standards with respect to skills, income and job requirements will increase the risk of workers to move between firms. Although the transition from school to work will be relatively easy in these systems, we predict intense mobility and a protracted duration for youth to find a suitable and permanent job match. In an analysis of entry into the labor force, Oppenheimer and Kalmijn (1995) demonstrate that young Americans increasingly start their job career in relatively unskilled and temporary jobs but, after a short period, they are able to move to normal career-entry positions. Thus, these unskilled occupational activities at entry into the labor force or 'stop-gap-jobs' have the character of temporary bridges (Myles *et al.*, 1993). The phenomenon and relative mismatch of stop-gap-jobs are particularly important as our study examines entry into first job. Finally, in the *dual-system*, (often qualificational, highly standardized and stratified), we expect youth to have less turbulent early labor market experiences (see Klijzing, this volume). This is due to the fact that the dual-system provides a smooth transition from the general educational school system to the employment system because the vocational training system feeds directly into the job system (Blossfeld and Stockmann, 1998/99). Young people are also effectively 'screened' during their education with exams and certificates expected to show their abilities. The disadvantage of such a system in a global era of rapidly shifting occupational structures is, however, that it leads to a close coupling of vocational certificates and educational opportunities, and thus to a high degree of rigidity and low level of job mobility (Blossfeld, 1992).

A related point is the *degree of educational expansion* in each country. When we examine the cohort-specific attendance rates across various levels of education for the 14 countries in this study, there has been a prolonged extension of school participation over time (see Klijzing, this volume). A longer stay in school proxies the degree to which the transition to economic independence has been postponed across birth cohorts in different countries. This belated timing in reaching economic independence is particularly important for our study of partnership formation and the transition to parenthood. There is a link between educational expansion and increasing youth unemployment, or an *alternative role hypothesis*. This identifies a tendency among young adults to opt – if this is structurally possible in a given educational system – for the role as a student instead of becoming unemployed in the process of transition from youth to adulthood. The educational system then serves as a reservoir for otherwise unemployed youth, which is increasingly strong in Southern European countries like Italy and Spain. There is likely also a relation to the national support systems for young adults who prefer to stay in education. Some countries such as Germany, the Netherlands, Norway and Sweden have a more generous system of education grants or loans, which is limited (e.g., Canada, Great Britain, France, post-1990s Estonia, Ireland), highly insufficient (e.g., United States) or virtually non-existent in others such as Italy, Spain, Hungary and Mexico.

Welfare regimes

The impact of increasing uncertainty on social inequality among young people is strongly dependent on the welfare state. Modern countries have created different welfare regimes implying diverse national ideologies about social solidarity (Flora and Alber, 1981) as well as gender and social equality (Esping-Andersen, 1999; Orloff, 1996). We first outline the main characteristics of the five welfare regime categorizations of liberal, social-democratic, conservative, family-oriented and post-socialistic. Differences between welfare regimes manifest themselves in the priority of: (1) active employment-sustaining labor market policies (i.e., the commitment to full employment); (2) welfare-sustaining employment exit policies (i.e., support for those who are outside of the labor market such as youth, unemployed, ill, poor, family care workers, pensioners); (3) the scope and generosity of family allowances and services (i.e., maternity/paternity leave, childcare) (Gauthier, 1996); and, (4) the share of the public sector in the labor force. Together, these differences form a *welfare regime hypothesis*. The expectations of the impact of each regime on the lives of youth are formulated following the description of each regime.

To varying degrees, the United States, United Kingdom, and Canada in this study are viewed as *liberal* welfare regimes characterized by passive labor market policies, moderate support for the underprivileged, and relatively small public sector employment. As outlined in the previous section, the comparatively high employment performance is likely related to the reduction of rigidities such as union power, restrictive labor legislation, and general flexibility of the labor market. Due to these factors, our expectation is that although there will be an overall higher employment level for youth, it will be at the expense of greater inequality and poverty. This is the result of an environment of passive employment policies, a marginal safety net, such as limited or highly conditional unemployment benefits, and mixed (i.e., generous child allowance and limited parental leave in Ireland) or means-tested family benefits (Canada, United States), and more exposure to the competitive private sector.

Norway and Sweden are in contrast considered as examples of the *social-democratic* welfare regime model. Active labor market and taxation policies in these countries are aimed at full employment, gender equality at the workplace as well as at home, and a 'fair' income distribution with a high degree of wage compression. Achieving full employment is mostly attempted by a combination of Keynesian demand policies and mobility stimulating measures such as retraining, mobility grants, and temporary jobs. The large participation of (married) women in full-time employment in these welfare regimes rests on both: (1) the rapid expansion of job opportunities in the service and public sector, engendered in particular by the demands of social services (kindergartens, schools, hospitals, day care centers and homes for the elderly); and, (2) the highly progressive individual income tax that makes a second household income necessary for most families if they want to enjoy the products of a technologically advanced service society (Blossfeld and Drobnič, 2001). In this welfare regime, the government tries to achieve full-employment through an expanding public service sector with relatively low wages for public employees and a high rate of female employment, in particular. Our expectation is that youth making the transition to adulthood can fall back on a relatively generous safety net, which combined with other factors such as gender equality and full-employment, better enables them to combine work with family formation (i.e., forming partnership, becoming a parent).

Germany and the Netherlands are often cited as examples of *conservative* welfare regimes. Social policies in these countries are not so much designed to promote employment opportunities, job mobility, and full employment by Keynesian demand policy measures but rather to ensure that those workers who leave employment because of job loss, disability, or in some cases as part of an early retirement program, are protected against serious declines in living standards. Of course, this is costly and leads to tax increases, particularly during periods of high unemployment. This type of welfare regime is therefore strongly transfer-oriented, with decommodifying effects for those who are economically inactive. It is also committed to the traditional division of labor in the family that makes wives economically dependent on their husbands, often referred to as the 'male-breadwinner model'. In particular, it supports wives and mothers who give priority to family activities (taking care of children and the elderly) and seek to work part-time. Correspondingly, welfare state provisions (e.g., day care) are far less developed than in the social democratic model and female economic activity rates are considerably lower and mostly restricted to part-time jobs (Blossfeld and Hakim, 1997). Our main prediction is that the increased economic uncertainty combined with the lack of public support will impact the decision to enter parenthood for certain groups of youth, who, due to an inability to combine education or labor force participation with family careers, will increasingly postpone or even forgo parenthood (Blossfeld and Drobnič, 2001). France is hard to classify since it reflects features of various welfare regimes. We place it next to the conservative regimes, but expect that it will exhibit sharp contrasts due to pro-natalistic policies, combined with measures that promote female employment and the combination of work and family careers (see Blossfeld, 1995).

Southern European countries like Italy and Spain, and to some extent Mexico and Ireland, also share common features. They have developed a welfare regime model that might be called *family-oriented* (Jurado Guerrero, 1995). In terms of labor market policy, support for the less privileged, and the importance of public sector employment, this welfare regime is very similar to the liberal one. Unlike the latter, however, it is characterized by a strong ideological and indeed practical involvement of family and kinship networks in protecting its members against economic and social risks. Due to the meager or non-existent safety net (e.g., family support, unemployment benefits), the state shifts the responsibility for the support of the unemployed and other vulnerable 'outsider' groups to families and kinship networks. This model is based on the deeply rooted cultural view that family and kinship represent an important institution of reciprocal help and that family members should thus support each other. Jurado Guerrero (1995) has argued that the long stay of youth in the parental home in Southern Europe is 'closely associated with the high labor market risks and the lukewarm protection that the state provides against them.'

In reality this family support is, however, mostly provided by women, with two important results: (1) their labor force participation (including part-time work) is, by international standards, extremely low (Blossfeld and Hakim, 1997); and, (2) especially if young women want to make a career, there is a particularly severe conflict between family tasks and (mostly full-time) job requirements. This leads to exorbitantly low fertility levels in Spain or Italy, for example. Thus, a paradoxical result in the family-oriented Mediterranean welfare regime appears to be that the extended family is rapidly disappearing.

Finally, we add the *post-socialistic* welfare regime to include countries in the former socialist Eastern Europe, which in this study include Estonia and Hungary. Hungary is perhaps closer to the social democratic regime, characterized by both egalitarianism and de-familialization. There is relatively more generous support for the family, with the dual-earner family model favored by fiscal arrangements, but with a highly conditional to limited degree of support for unemployed youth (Róbert and Bukodi, this volume). Whereas Estonia has taken a more liberal direction with limited next to non-existent unemployment and family benefits for youth (Katus *et al.*, this volume). However, considering the rapid transformations after 1990, the trajectory of these welfare regimes is still in evolution.

Family systems and interdependence of careers

The family system and the interdependence between family, education and employment careers have direct consequences for the transition to adulthood, specifically the transition to first partnership and parenthood. Family systems regulate the degree of pluralization of private living arrangements. Pluralization refers to lifestyles beyond the traditional marital couple or nuclear family to include non-marital cohabitation, remaining single, or postponement or forgoing of fertility (Corijn and Klijzing, 2001).

A north-south divide in the pluralization of private living arrangements emerges due to institutional, but also cultural differences (Blossfeld, 1995). Scandinavian countries like Sweden and Norway seem to have a pioneering role, while countries like Germany, France, the Netherlands, United Kingdom, United States and Canada appear to follow this trend. Familistic countries such as Italy, Spain, Ireland and Mexico are even less affected. The strong institutionalization of marriage in Southern Europe and Mexico, translates into small numbers of non-marital unions and one-person households among youth (Nazio and Blossfeld, 2003), low divorce and extra-marital birth rates as well as into an asymmetrical relationship between the sexes within the family.

There is *interdependence* between educational and employment systems on the one hand, and the family system on the other. Our expectation is that educational expansion impacts entry into first union and parenthood in several ways. First, we anticipate that prolonged education requires that youth maintain the role of an economically dependent student for a longer period of time, which increases their level of economic uncertainty (see next section), and thus leads to postponement of partnership and parenthood across cohorts (Blossfeld, 1995). The growth of qualified women in particular means that women will have their first child later due to extended education, effective contraception and the competing demands of employment and childcare.

Second, we presume that highly educated individuals have different values and preferences such as independence, autonomy and a higher attachment to career building and the labor force (Liefbroer, 1991; Mills, 2000). Those with higher education are thus more willing and able to adopt flexible and innovative behavior that leads to the pluralization of living arrangements (e.g., cohabitation, voluntary childlessness). Others have also argued the contrary. Since educational attainment increases earning propensity and the capacity to marry, in some circumstances, those with less education may be more likely to cohabit (e.g., Rindfuss and Vandenheuvel, 1990; Thornton *et al.*, 1995). This is related to the theory that highly qualified women are more likely to postpone family formation (Becker, 1981). Yet postponement behavior is not only based on educational qualifications, but also on the compatibility of combining a family and a career. We expect that countries with poor maternity or parental leave and particularly childcare arrangements, such as the conservative or familistic welfare regimes, reduce the opportunity for women to have interdependent careers.

Third, based on previous research, we anticipate that educational enrollment status will 'compete' with family formation and will thus reduce both the chances of entering a union (specifically marriage), and having a child (Blossfeld and Huinink, 1991; Liefbroer, 1991; Blossfeld, 1995; Rindfuss and Vandenheuvel, 1990). Students are less likely to enter a union, especially marriage and enter into parenthood for several reasons (Mills, 2000). First, students possess fewer material resources. Second, they often have less leisure time, and finally, 'due to their transient and uncertain position they may be less inclined to commit themselves to a long-term binding decision such as partnership or marriage' (Mills, 2000: 189). Conversely, being a student is more compatible with entering a cohabiting union due to the fact that it is less costly than a marriage, more flexible, has less legal restrictions, is easier to dissolve and has fewer normative expectations.

We therefore propose a *flexible partnership hypothesis*, which maintains that consensual unions represent a 'rational' reply to growing uncertainty that surrounds the transition to adulthood in a globalizing world. To reduce uncertainty, youth are more likely to bind themselves to the more flexible union of cohabitation as it is largely independent of the future (Mills, 2004; Wu, 2000). These living arrangements permit the postponement of long-term commitments and self-binding decisions such as marriage at least for the time being. Reminiscent of Easterlin's (1976) theory of economic deprivation, this applies in particular to historical periods of general economic uncertainty and rising unemployment, when the tendency to marry and have children appears to diminish. Our perspective also clearly relates to Oppenheimer's (1988; 2003; Oppenheimer *et al.*, 1997) work on the impact of uncertainty in social and economic roles on the timing of family transitions. As Oppenheimer (1988: 583) states: 'Cohabitation gets young people out of high-cost search activities during a period of social immaturity but without incurring what are, for many, the penalties of either heterosexual isolation or promiscuity, and it often offers many of the benefits of marriage, including the pooling of resources and the economies of scale that living together provide.' In many ways, the flexibility of cohabitation matches the flexible labor market circumstances that many youth experience during the era of globalization.

MICRO-LEVEL RESPONSE TO INCREASING UNCERTAINTY

Many decisions in the early life course have long-term implications. People have to opt for educational and professional tracks, enter job careers or make long-term binding family and fertility decisions. However, higher levels of uncertainty for youth generate insecurity and potential conflict and make it increasingly difficult to make such choices. Young people respond and adapt to the complex structural shifts brought about by globalization. A central hypothesis of this study is that the uncertainty generated by globalization at the social-structural level reduces or delays the propensity of youth to enter long-term binding commitments such as partnerships and parenthood (see Figure 1). Our attention thus turns to changes in rational decision-making under conditions of increasing uncertainty and descriptions of the schema developed to measure uncertainty at the individual level.

Rational decision-making under increasing uncertainty

We propose the use of a dynamic rational choice model to understand individual decision-making under conditions of increasing uncertainty (Blossfeld and Prein, 1998). We do not advocate a model of individual action as deterministic behavior, but rather as a tool to find regularities among a larger number of actors. A dynamic rational choice model assumes in particular that typical actors try to act rationally. Following Elster (1989), such rational decision makers are characterized by trying to achieve three optimizations: 1) finding the best action that fits with their given beliefs and desires, 2) developing the most appropriate belief given the evidence at hand; and, 3) collecting the correct amount of evidence while taking into account their given desires and prior beliefs. Yet due to the process of globalization described at the onset of this chapter, such as the accelerating pace of change, volatility and unpredictability of social and economic developments, and deluge of information, youth now face three major decision problems.

First, there is *rising uncertainty about the behavioral alternatives themselves*. This issue becomes more important when young actors have to make rational choices among alternatives that become progressively more blurred. For instance, due to the increased uncertainty that has emerged at the macro level it becomes more difficult for young adults to compare and rank the various options for educational, professional or partnership careers, simply because they know less and less about future alternatives. The problem here is not only which alternative to choose but increasingly when to choose it. Second, there is *growing uncertainty about the probability of behavioral outcomes*. This problem is especially acute when actors are less and less able to assign in a reliable manner subjective probabilities to the various outcomes of their future courses of action. In the process of globalization, this uncertainty becomes particularly severe when a decision requires beliefs about choices to be made by other people in the future (e.g., partner, employer). Third, there is *increasing uncertainty about the amount of information to be collected for a particular decision*. Collecting information is necessary, but costly and time-consuming. With the accelerated spread of global networks and knowledge, the question of how much information one should optimally collect before one is ready to form an opinion becomes more serious because the marginal costs and benefits for further information searches are increasingly unclear. One has therefore to assume that actors – whether consciously or not – will set certain threshold limits, which, once satisfied, stop the search for additional information.

As described in the previous section on institutional filters, decision-making and risk calculations to cope with uncertainty are firmly embedded within the social context of the nations in which the perceptions of risk are maintained. As Regini (2000a: 8) states: 'The institutional context, in fact, provides actors with a set of resources and constraints that they must necessarily take into account when choosing among different alternatives and consequently shapes their actions.' Lindenberg (1983) and Esser (1991) use the terms 'habits' and 'frames' as nation- or class-specific ways to interpret decision situations. Heiner (1983) argues that cultural traditions, social institutions or norms serve as rule-mechanisms that restrict the flexibility to choose potential courses of actions, or which produce a selective alertness to information. For instance, a young person in Spain entering into a partnership has not only a restricted amount of choices that more likely leads to marriage than a consensual union, but also reflects cultural traditions that frame her/his decision in a very specific way. Rules and norms that stigmatize certain behavior also limit young people's ability to see a consensual union as a viable partnership option. Country-specific institutions and national norms generate effective decision 'heuristics' (see also Gigerenzer *et al.*, 1999), which are not thoughtlessly repeated (as in the 'homo sociologicus'), but used as problem-solving tools.

Types of uncertainty in the transition to adulthood

Since a main premise of this study was to either find evidence or dispute the impact of globalization on the early life course, we required an empirical research design that offered tangible findings. We therefore devised a measurement design to theoretically and empirically gauge the impact of uncertainty that arises from globalization factors on individual transitions in the early life course.

The schema consists of three types of uncertainty: economic, temporal, and employment relation.

First, *economic uncertainty* is defined as the caliber of economic precariousness of an individuals' employment and educational enrollment circumstances (Bernardi, 2000). We anticipate that labor market positions with high degrees of economic uncertainty will inhibit youth to make long-term binding commitments such as partnerships, and particularly marriage, or parenthood that require a secure economic basis (Oppenheimer, 1988; Oppenheimer *et al.*, 1997). Youth require a necessary minimum or what Rindfuss and Vandenheuvel (1990) refer to as the 'affordability clause' to enter into a binding relationship or have a child. As Oppenheimer (1988), we expect that youth will avoid commitment such as marriage and parenthood, but still desire the rewards of having a relationship (i.e., consensual union).

In this study, economic uncertainty is captured in four central ways. First it is measured by an activity status indicator of education and employment.[2] A second dimension is occupational class, using Erikson and Goldthorpe's (1992) class schema. Our expectation is that compared to the higher level service or routine white collar classes, the lower classes such as unskilled manual workers are more likely to be in economically precarious situations. In other words, skilled occupations (and as we will argue shortly stable employment) can reduce uncertainties (Oppenheimer *et al.*, 1997). Whether individuals receive extra benefits with their jobs (e.g., pension) is a third measure of economic uncertainty used in some of the country chapters. A final measure included in some of the country studies (e.g., France, Hungary) is earnings. Thus, the comparative yardstick to measure uncertainty is against the relative 'certainty' of youth holding certain statuses such as not being enrolled in education, being employed, and if so, in a higher occupational class, or receiving benefits or higher earnings.

Second, according to Breen (1997: 477) 'Temporal uncertainty reduces the attractiveness of long-term commitment and increases that of "contingent asymmetric commitment".' In other words, due to *temporal uncertainty*, youth are less able to make long-term binding commitments which may translate into, for example, opting for cohabitation instead of marriage or forgoing partnership and parenthood until they feel they have obtained adequate certainty for their future life path (see also Kurz *et al.*, this volume). Contingent asymmetric commitment is a useful concept to understand the consequences of labor market flexibility experienced by youth. In relation to temporary contracts, for example, it refers to a relationship where one party of the agreement (employer) retains the option to withdraw from the relationship at any time, while the other party (youth) can only comply to what the first party requests.

Temporal uncertainty and the concept of 'long-term commitment' is reminiscent of Elster's (1979) notion of 'self-binding'. In order to reduce choice complexity of long-term courses of action under uncertainty, individuals tend to constrain or bind their own future actions (i.e., commit themselves to a specific action in the future). Self-binding is an effective technique to make one's promises to significant others (e.g., partners, actors in industrial relations) more credible. This technique makes communication about what one is going to do under still unknown future conditions more reliable. According to Elster (1979), this credibility enhances the *trust* that actors will have in each other and enables them to interact and cooperate more effectively than without such self-binding commitments. Self-binding, however, is also paradoxical, particularly in a life phase in which the transition to adulthood takes place. On the one hand, it is a prerequisite for creating certainty for young people as well as credibility and trust in one's dealings with others. On the other hand, it diminishes the ability to react in a flexible manner during later stages of the life course, which clashes with the rapidly changing demands of a globalizing society.

Third, *employment relationship uncertainty* is characterized as whether youth are a) self-employed (with no employees), or, b) dependent workers (see Bernardi, 2000). We hypothesize that the lone self-employed worker will have a higher degree of uncertainty, due to lower protection measures. Depending on the labor market context, uncertainty for dependent workers is measured by whether workers are in: a) public or private sector employment, and, b) a less precarious relationship such as a permanent versus a temporary contract (in closed employment systems), or by measures such as a regular versus irregular work shift (in open employment systems). Whether an individual is employed in the public or private sector is a key factor in determining how they are sheltered from risk, with those employed in the public sector 'relatively isolated from the operation of market forces' (Esping-Andersen, 1993). Employment in the public sector is much farther removed from the impetus of productivity and profitability of global competition. Here we expect that those with lower levels of relationship security (i.e., self-employed, private sector, temporary contract, irregular shifts) will experience higher levels of uncertainty, which will in turn generate a similar response of postponement or forgoing binding life course commitments. Employment relation uncertainty is closely tied, yet distinct from temporal uncertainty. Although temporal uncertainty can include types of employment relation insecurity, it has a broader scope to capture how different kinds of uncertainty make it more difficult for youth to make long-term binding decisions.

We expect that the effects of uncertainty will, however, differ for men and women, particularly those from conservative welfare regimes. A *gender hypothesis* anticipates that in countries where the male-breadwinner model is predominant, it will be more important for males to establish themselves in a more secure job as opposed to females (Oppenheimer *et al.*, 1997). For this reason, we predict a stronger effect of uncertainty on men than women, which will be particularly evident in the male-breadwinner countries of the conservative and family-oriented welfare regimes.

DATA AND METHODS

Our intention to strive for empirical evidence to either confirm or disconfirm the impact of globalization on the lives of youth led to the use of individual-based event history data and longitudinal analytical methods and techniques (Blossfeld and Rohwer, 2002). The majority of data used in this study came from retrospective or longitudinal panel surveys collected in the 1990s. This included the German Socio-Economic Panel (1984-1998), data pooled from seven retrospective life history surveys and the Panel Study of Social Integration (1987, 1989, 1991, 1995) for the Netherlands, and for France, the Young People and Careers survey (1997). The Swedish analysis draws on the Swedish Level of Living Survey (1991), with Norway using KIRUT (10% sample of public register data, 1989-1996) and the Database of Generations (1950-1990). The Hungarian study employs the Way of Life and Time Use Survey (1999-2000) and the General Youth Survey (2000). Both Estonia and Spain used the Fertility and Family Survey from 1994 and 1995 respectively. The British Household Panel Survey (1991-1999) was used for the United Kingdom, the Survey of Labour and Income Dynamics (1993-1998) for Canada, the National Survey of Family Growth (1995, women only) for the United States and the National Retrospective Demographic Survey (1989, women only) for Mexico. The analysis of Italy was based on the Italian Longitudinal Household Survey (1997) with work for Ireland using both the Irish School Leavers Survey (1987-1993, 1992-1998) and the Follow-up of the School Leavers Survey (1992, 1998).

For our purposes, event history methods were ideal as they allow for 'causal-type' analysis of events that represent changes from one discrete life course state to another. Since we also wanted to examine empirical consequences at the individual level, this general approach was the most desirable. The analyses examined the transition of entry into employment, first union formation, first child and in some cases, entry into unemployment. Statistical applications included piecewise exponential, piecewise constant exponential, logistic, and Cox semi-parametric proportional hazard models. Since technical and mathematical aspects of the models and methods have been specified elsewhere (Blossfeld and Rohwer, 2002), we focus on substantive results instead of explanations of the methods.

As with any secondary data analysis, comparability of analyses is dependent on the various available datasets. All countries explored entry into employment and transition to first partnership and parenthood in a way befitting to their country-specific context. The diverse pathways and impacting factors in the transition to adulthood across the 14 countries is reflected in the choice of dependent and explanatory variables. The analyses for each country differed slightly due to data availability, but also for substantive reasons. For example, non-marital cohabitation has taken over as the choice of first partnership in Sweden, necessitating a model of transition to first union that examines only cohabitation. Conversely, only the transition to marriage is included in the analysis of first partnerships in Italy due to the fact that there are too few individuals reporting a consensual union (Bernardi and Nazio, this volume; Nazio and Blossfeld, 2003).

STRUCTURE OF THE BOOK

Chapter 2 sets the country studies into context by providing a short comparative description of selected economic and demographic trends: educational expansion, youth unemployment, change in the occupational structure, trends in atypical employment and female labor force participation, as well as the pluralization of living arrangements. The country-specific chapters then follow. The book is divided into five sections that partition the countries by welfare state regimes. The first section contains the conservative regimes of Germany (Chapter 3), the Netherlands (Chapter 4) and the related country of France (Chapter 5). This is followed by the social-democratic regimes of Sweden (Chapter 6) and Norway (Chapter 7), the post-socialistic countries of Hungary (Chapter 8) and Estonia (Chapter 9), and the liberal regimes of Britain (Chapter 10), Canada (Chapter 11), the United States (Chapter 12), and finally the family-oriented regimes of Mexico (Chapter 13), Italy (Chapter 14), Spain (Chapter 15), and Ireland (Chapter 16). Chapter 17 synthesizes the results, confronts the expectations from this introductory chapter and discusses the added value of this approach for the field of youth studies and globalization research.

NOTES

1   The authors would like to thank Wout Ultee and members of the GLOBALIFE project for detailed comments on a previous version of this chapter.
2   Measures befit the country context. In some cases it measures combinations of whether the individual is enrolled in education, working, unemployed or out of the labor force (e.g., Bygren *et al.*; Francesconi and Golsch; Kurz *et al.*, this volume), or it gauges their educational and work status including the number of work hours (e.g., Simó *et al.*, this volume). Others include employment status and divide educational enrollment further by whether youth are in full or part-time school or work throughout the year (e.g., King; Mills; Parrado, this volume). While others include activity status in combination with aspects of employment uncertainty (e.g., Kieffer *et al.*; Liefbroer; Róbert and Bukodi, this volume).

BIBLIOGRAPHY

Alderson, A.S. (1999) 'Explaining deindustrialization: Globalization, failure, or success?', *American Sociological Review*, 64: 701-721.
Allmendinger, J. (1989) 'Educational system and labor market outcomes', *European Sociological Review*, 3: 231-250.
Atkinson, J. (1984) 'Manpower strategies for flexible organizations', *Personnel Management*, 15: 28-31.
Beck, U. (1997; 2nd edn 2000) *What is Globalization?*, Cambridge: Polity Press.
Bernardi, F. (2000) 'Employment flexibility, class and risk at entry into the labor market; Patterns of early careers in Italy', GLOBALIFE Working Paper No. 7, Faculty of Sociology, University of Bielefeld.
Blossfeld, H.-P. (1992) 'Is the German dual system a model for a modern vocational training system?', *International Journal of Comparative Sociology*, 33: 168-181.
Blossfeld, H.-P. (ed.) (1995) *The New Role of Women: Family Formation in Modern Societies*, Boulder: Westview Press.

Blossfeld, H.-P. and Hakim, C. (1997) *Between Equalization and Marginalization. Women Working Part-Time in Europe and the United States of America*, Oxford: Oxford University Press.

Blossfeld, H.-P., Mills, M. and Bernardi, F. (forthcoming) *Globalization, Uncertainty and Men in Society*.

Blossfeld, H.-P. and Prein, G. (1998) *Rational Choice Theory and Large-Scale Data Analysis*, Boulder (CO): Westview Press.

Blossfeld, H.-P. and Rohwer, G. (2002) *Techniques of event history modeling. New approaches to causal analysis*, 2nd edn, Hillsdale (NJ): Erlbaum.

Blossfeld, H.-P. and Stockmann, R. (1998/99) *Globalization and Chances in Vocational Training Systems in Developing and Advanced Industrialized Societies*, Volume I-III, Armonk (NY): Sharpe.

Blossfeld, H.-P. and Drobnič, S. (eds) (2001) *Careers of Couples in Contemporary Societies. A Cross-National Comparison of the Transition from Male Breadwinner to Dual Earner Families*, Oxford: Oxford University Press.

Breen, Richard (1997) 'Risk, Recommodification and Stratification', *Sociology*, 31(3): 473-489.

Bruhnes, B. (1989) 'Labor Market Flexibility in Enterprises: A Comparison of Firms in Four European Countries', in *Labor Market Flexibility: Trends in Enterprises*, Paris: OECD.

Castells, Manuel (1996) *The Rise of the Network Society, The Information Age: Economy, Society and Culture*, Volume I, Oxford: Blackwell Publishers.

Corijn, M. and Klijzing, E. (2001) *Transitions to adulthood in Europe*, Dordrecht: Kluwer Academic Publishers.

DiPrete, T., de Graaf, P.M., Luijkx, R., Tåhlin, M. and Blossfeld, H.-P. (1997) 'Collectivist versus Individualist Mobility Regimes? Structural Change and Job Mobility in Four Countries', *American Journal of Sociology*, 103(2): 318-358.

Easterlin, R. (1976) 'The conflict between aspirations and resources', *Population and Development Review*, 2(3): 417-425.

Elster, J. (1979) *Ulysses and the sirens*, Cambridge, MA: Cambridge University Press.

Elster, J. (1989) *Solomonic Judgements – studies in the limitations of rationality*, New York: New York University Press.

Erikson, R. and Goldthorpe, J. H. (1992) *The constant flux: a study of class mobility in industrial societies*, Oxford: Clarendon Press.

Esping-Andersen, G. (1993) 'Post-industrial class structures: An analytical framework', in G. Esping-Andersen (ed.) *Changing Classes*, London: Sage.

Esping-Andersen, G. (1999) *Social Foundations of Postindustrial Economies*, Oxford: Oxford University Press.

Esser, H. (1991) *Alltagshandeln und Verstehen*, Tübingen: Mohr.

Fine, B. (1998) *Labour Market Theory: A Constructive Reassessment*, London: Routledge.

Fligstein, N. (1998) 'Is Globalization the Cause of the Crises of Welfare States?', European University Institute Working Paper SPS No. 98/5, San Domenico, Italy.

Flora, P. and Alber, J. (1981) 'The development of welfare states in Western Europe', in P. Flora and A.J. Heidenheimer (eds) *The development of welfare states in Europe and America*, New Brunswick and New Jersey: Transaction Books.

Gauthier, A.H. (1996) *A Comparative Analysis of Family Policies in Industrialized Countries*, Oxford: Clarendon Press.

Gigerenzer, G., Todd, P.M. and the ABC Research Group (eds) (1999) *Simple Heuristics That Make Us Smart*, Oxford: Oxford University Press.

Guillén, M. (2001) 'Is globalization civilizing, destructive or feeble? A critique of five key debates in the social science literature', *American Review of Sociology*, 27: 235-260.

Heiner, R.A. (1983) 'The origin of predictable behavior', *The American Economic Review*, 73: 560-595.

Held, D., McGrew, A., Goldblatt, D. and Perraton, J. (1999) *Global Transformations. Politics, Economics and Culture*, Oxford: Polity Press.

Hurrell, A. and Woods, N. (1995) 'Globalization and Inequality,' *Millennium. Journal of International Studies*, 24(3): 447-470.

Jurado Guerrero, T. (1995) 'Legitimation durch Sozialpolitik? Die spanische Beschäftigungskrise und die Theorie des Wohlfahrtstaates', *KZfSS*, 47: 727-752.

Liefbroer, A. (1991) 'The choice between a married or unmarried first union by young adults: A competing risks analysis', *European Journal of Population*, 7: 273-298.

Lindenberg, S. (1983) 'Utility and morality', *Kyklos*, 36: 450-468.

Maurice, M. and Sellier, F. (1979) 'A Societal Analysis of Industrial Relations: A Comparison between France and West Germany', *British Journal of Industrial Relations*, 17: 322-336.

Mayer, K.-U. (2001) 'The paradox of global social change and national path dependencies: Life course patterns in advanced societies,' in A. Woodward and M. Kohli (eds) *Inclusions and Exclusions in European Societies*, Routledge: New York.

Meyer, J. W., Ramirez, F. O. and Soysal, Y. (1992) 'World expansion of mass education, 1970-1980', *Sociology of Education*, 65: 128-149.

Mills, M. (2000) *The Transformation of Partnerships. Canada, the Netherlands and the Russian Federation in the Age of Modernity*, Amsterdam: Thela Thesis Population Studies Series.

Mills, M. (2004) 'Stability and Change: The structuration of partnership histories in Canada, the Netherlands, and the Russian Federation', *European Journal of Population*, 20(2): in press.

Montanari, I. (2001) 'Modernization, globalization and the welfare state: A comparative analysis of old and new convergence of social insurance since 1930', *British Journal of Sociology*, 52(3): 469-494.

Myles, J., Picot, G. and Wannell, T. (1993) 'Does Post-Industrialism Matter? The Canadian Experience', in G. Esping-Andersen (ed.) *Changing Classes*, London: Sage.

Nazio, T. and Blossfeld, H.-P. (2003) 'The Diffusion of cohabitation among young women in West Germany, East Germany and Italy', *European Journal of Population*, 19: 47-82.

Nelson, R.R. (1995) 'Recent evolutionary theorizing about economic change', *Journal of Economic Literature*, 33: 48-90.

Ohmae, K. (1990) *The Borderless World*, New York: Harper Business.

Oppenheimer, V.K. (1988) 'A theory of marriage timing', *American Journal of Sociology*, 94: 563-591.

Oppenheimer, V.K. (1990) 'Life cycle jobs and the transition to adulthood', unpublished document, Department of Sociology, UCLA, Los Angeles.

Oppenheimer, V.K. (2003) 'Cohabiting and Marriage During Young Men's Career-Development Process', *Demography*, 40: 127-149.

Oppenheimer, V.K. and Kalmijn, M. (1995) 'Life Cycle Jobs', *Research in Social Stratification and Mobility*, 14: 1-38.

Oppenheimer, V.K., Kalmijn, M. and Lim, N. (1997) 'Men's Career Development and Marriage Timing During a period of Rising Inequality', *Demography*, 3: 311-330.

Orloff, A. (1996) 'Gender and the Welfare State', *Annual Review of Sociology*, 22: 51-78.

Piore, M.J. (1970) 'The Dual Labor Market: Theory and Implications', in S. Beer and R.E. Barringer (eds) *The State and the Poor*, Cambridge, Mass.: Winthrop Publications.

Regini, M. (2000a) 'Between deregulation and social pacts: The responses of European economies to globalization', *Politics and Society*, 28(1): 5-33.

Regini, M. (2000b) 'The dilemmas of labor market regulation', in G. Esping-Andersen and M. Regini (eds) *Why Deregulate Labor Markets?*, Oxford: Oxford University Press.

Reich, R. (1991) *The Work of Nations: Preparing Ourselves for 21st Century Capitalism*, London: Simon and Schuster.

Rindfuss, R. and Vandenheuvel, A. (1990) 'Cohabitation: A precursor to marriage or an alternative to being single?', *Population and Development Review*, 16(4): 703-726.

Sassen, S. (1996) *Losing Control? Sovereignty in an Age of Globalization*, New York: Columbia University Press.

Shavit, Y. and Müller, W. (1998) *From School to Work: A Comparative Study of Educational Qualifications and Occupational Destinations*, Oxford: Clarendon Press.

Sørensen, A. B. (1983) 'The structure of allocation to open and closed positions in social structure', *Zeitschrift für Soziologie*, 12: 203-224.

Soskice, D. (1993) 'The institutional infrastructure for international competitiveness: a comparative analysis of the UK and Germany', in A.B. Atkinson and R. Brunetta (eds) *The Economics of the New Europe*, London: MacMillan.

Soskice, D. (1998) 'Divergent production regimes: Coordinated and uncoordinated market economies in the 1980s and 1990s', in H. Kitschelt, P. Lange, G. Marks, and J. Stephens (eds) *Continuity and Change in Contemporary Capitalism*, Cambridge: Cambridge University Press.

Standing, G. (1997) 'Globalization, labor flexibility and insecurity: The era of market regulation', *European Journal of Industrial Relations*, 1: 7-37.

Streeck, A. (1987) 'The uncertainties of management in the management of uncertainties: employees, labor relations and industrial adjustment in the 1980s', *Work Employment and Society*, 1: 281-308.

Streeck, W. (1992) *Social institutions and economic performance. Studies in industrial relations in advanced capitalist economies*, London: Sage.

Thornton, A., Axinn, W.G. and Teachman, J.D. (1995) 'The influence of school enrollment and accumulation on cohabitation and marriage in early adulthood', *American Sociological Review*, 60(5): 762-774.

Treiman, D. J. (1970) 'Industrialization and social stratification', in E. O. Laumann (ed.) *Social stratification: research and theory for the 1970s*, Indianapolis: Bobbs Merrill.

Treiman, D. J. and Yip, K.-B. (1989) 'Educational and occupational attainment in 21 countries,' in M. L. Kohn (ed.) *Cross-national research in sociology*, Newbury Park (CA): Sage.

UNCTAD (1995) *World Investment Report 1995: Transnational Corporations and Competitiveness*, New York: United Nations.

Verdier, D. and Breen, R. (1999) 'Europeanization and globalization: politics against markets in the European Union', unpublished manuscript, Florence: European University Institute.

2 Globalization and the early life course

A description of selected economic and demographic trends

Erik Klijzing

INTRODUCTION

The purpose of this chapter is to present some graphic materials that illustrate at the aggregate level selected points made by Mills and Blossfeld in the introduction to this volume. It is divided into 2 sections, the first on economic developments related to the globalization process, the second on demographic developments that can be seen as related to changes in economic opportunities and constraints over time. The graphic materials presented in both sections follow a similar design. That is, the 14 countries reported on in this volume are grouped into 5 ideal-typical clusters corresponding to (the expanded version of) Esping-Andersen's (1999) scheme of welfare regimes: conservative (Germany, the Netherlands, France), social-democratic (Sweden, Norway), post-socialist (Hungary, Estonia), liberal (Great Britain, Canada, United States of America), and familistic (Mexico, Italy, Spain, Ireland). Where possible, each cluster is supplemented with data on 1 or 2 additional countries that are not included in this volume but which may make it easier to generalize more broadly. The time series data to be presented for these countries are ordered either by calendar year (covering the last 5 or 2 decades of the 20th century, depending on data availability), or by birth cohort. Sources used vary from several ILO, OECD and EUROSTAT publications to country-specific FFS[1] or other reports, as indicated at the bottom of each graph. Great care has been taken to make all data series as comparable as possible.

ECONOMIC DEVELOPMENTS

As Mills and Blossfeld already stated, over the centuries there have been fundamental changes in the way economies operate. The expansion of the service sector in the latter half of the 20th century has been particularly pronounced. Let us therefore look first at the tertiarization of labor markets during this phase of accelerated globalization (Figures 2.1a and 2.1b).

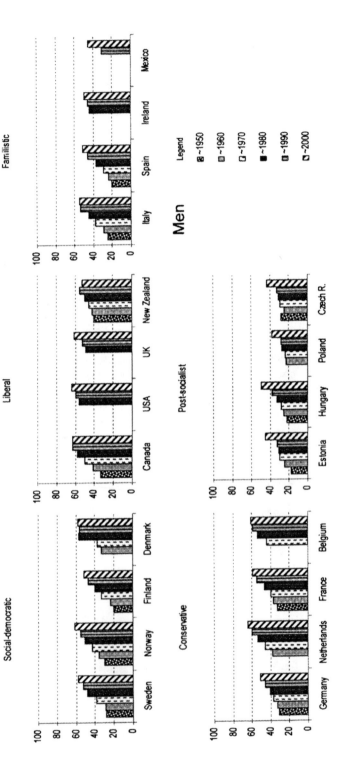

Figure 2.1a Tertiarization of the labor market - percent of employed men working in the service sector, 1950-2000, by country according to welfare regime

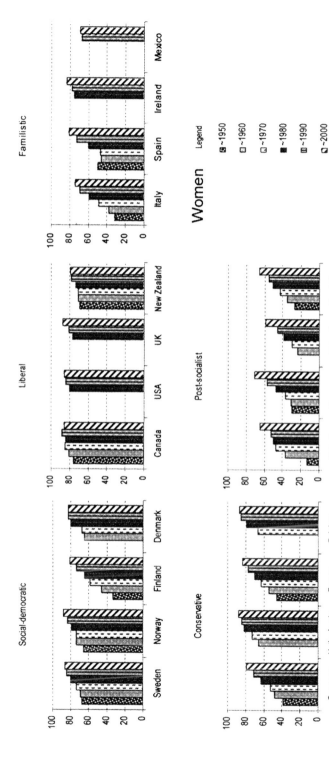

Figure 2.1b Tertiarization of the labor market – percent of employed women working in the service sector, 1950–2000, by country according to welfare regime

Whether one considers changes over time in the relative number of men (Figure 2.1a) or of women (Figure 2.1b) employed in the service sector, the picture is clear and unambiguous. The tertiarization of labor markets has been a pervasive, unidirectional, and uninterrupted process in all countries considered, although the level and pace at which this occurred may differ. For instance, in countries with a post-socialist welfare regime it is not as advanced yet as in others due to the emphasis under socialism on the secondary sector: only around 40 percent of men and 60-70 percent of women in these countries are currently tertiary-sector workers. They are followed by some 50 percent of men and 70-80 percent of women in countries with a familistic welfare regime. The highest percentages are found in countries with a social-democratic, liberal or conservative welfare regime, where nowadays some 60 percent of men and 80-90 percent of women[2] are employed in the service sector. Thus, invariably, women are more likely to be employed in the service sector than men. Their integration into the labor market makes modern economies therewith more service-oriented. But here one should of course take into account that their paid labor force participation - often based on part-time work (Blossfeld and Hakim, 1997) - across all sectors is generally below that of men.

As suggested by Figure 2.2, levels of labor force participation[3] among women 25-54 years old - when most of the family formation, childbearing and rearing take place - used to be highest (close to 100 percent) in the post-socialist countries. This is due to the fact that under socialism it was still the rule rather than the exception that women would work for pay and mostly on a full-time basis, although nowadays this is rapidly changing in the direction of declining female labor force participation. In countries with a social-democratic welfare regime levels of female labor participation seem to have reached their plateau at 80-90 percent from the late-1980s onward, after which they have remained constant. This is probably related to the general promotion of gender equality as well as to the greater need for dual incomes as a result of relatively low wages in much of Scandinavia (Blossfeld and Drobnič, 2001). Female labor force participation rates in all the other country clusters are still on the rise, although from varying starting values and at varying speeds. For instance, in countries with a liberal welfare regime they have increased from about 60 to 80 percent. Equally high levels can currently be observed for countries with a conservative welfare regime, although here starting values were generally much lower. The spectacular rise in female employment in the Netherlands, from below 40 to above 70 percent, is mainly based on part-time work, as will be explained below. Finally, although in countries with a familistic welfare regime female labor force participation rates have risen by comparable magnitudes of about 20-30 percentage points, they did so largely from much lower starting values. As a result, at around 60 percent or less they are presently still the lowest. This is undoubtedly related to the rather women-unfriendly labor market and family policies that these predominantly catholic countries have pursued in the past, although in more recent times there have been various government attempts in some of them to partly remedy this situation (see Bernardi and Nazio; Simó et al., this volume).

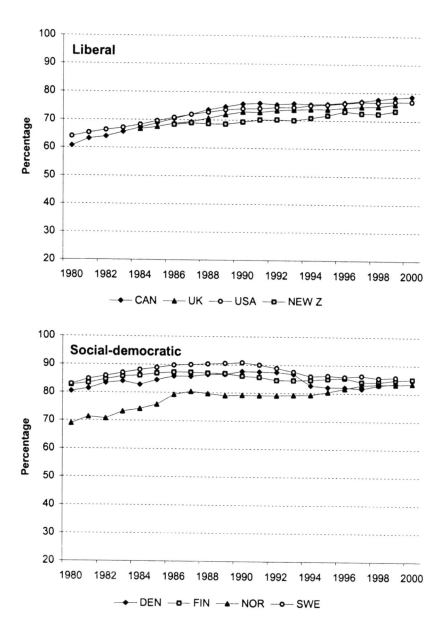

Figure 2.2   Female labor force participation (part-time plus full-time) among women 25-54 years old, 1980-2000, by country according to welfare regime

Source: Key Indicators of the Labour Market (KILM 1), ILO, 2001-2002

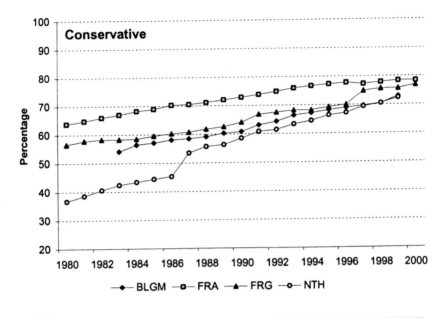

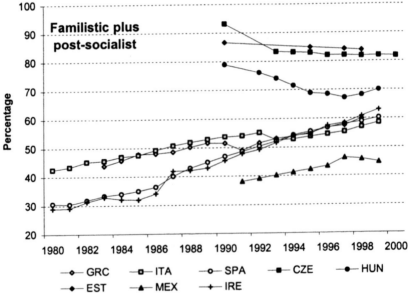

Figure 2.2   Female labor force participation (part-time plus full-time) among women 25-54 years old, 1980-2000, by country according to welfare regime *(continued)*

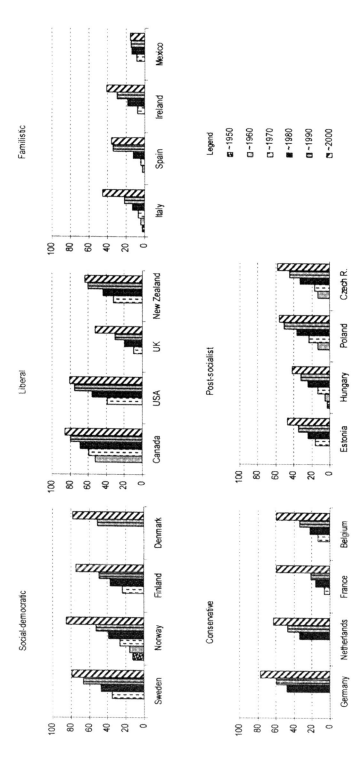

Figure 2.3   Educational expansion: percent of women with medium or higher level qualifications, 1950-2000, by country according to welfare regime

Source: FFS Standard Country Reports, table 1f, except for the USA, Ireland, UK and Mexico (ILO, 2001-2002, gross enrolment ratios in tertiary education).

Female paid labor force participation may appear to be lowest in Mexico, but one should not forget that large numbers of women in this country work in the informal sector (see Parrado, this volume). If included, they would yield female labor force participation rates that are comparable to those of other countries with a familistic welfare regime.

The general increase in labor force participation among women over time is of course closely related to their growing aspirations for professional activity and concomitant investments in human capital as part of the process of educational expansion (Figure 2.3). Here the picture of change over time is as pervasive and ubiquitous as it was in the case of the tertiarization of the labor market. That is, women are nowadays much better trained than they were some 50 years ago, and thus much better equipped to enter the knowledge-based, service-oriented economy. At 60-85 percent the percentage of women with medium or higher level qualifications is highest in countries with a social-democratic, liberal or conservative welfare regime, but in countries with a post-socialist (below 60 percent) or familistic (below 50 percent) welfare regime the upgrading of skills still appears to lag somewhat behind. But chances for women to cash in on their human capital investments depend among other things on employment opportunities as a function of the business cycle. It makes sense, therefore, to briefly examine developments in youth unemployment and to place these against the backdrop of different institutional settings.

Youth unemployment rates among men and women aged 15-24 who have left the educational system during the last two decades under consideration in Figure 2.4 have generally shown 2 cycles, with an upswing during the mid-1980s and one during the mid-1990s. But these cycles were much more pronounced - above 30 percent - in countries with a familistic welfare regime, in particular Spain and Italy, which are characterized by a tight insider-outsider labor market and little government support to ease the transition from school to work. Youth unemployment rates in all other welfare regimes have usually stayed (well) below 30 percent. For instance, due to the dual system of vocational training and apprenticeships in Germany (Kurz *et al.*, this volume), youth employment rates in this country are generally quite low (less than 10 percent). For countries with a post-socialist welfare regime it remains to be seen what the future will bring in terms of levels of youth unemployment. Currently existing systems of unemployment benefits are either very limited as in Estonia or highly conditional as in Hungary (see Róbert and Bukodi; Katus *et al.*, this volume).

But, as Mills and Blossfeld (this volume) make clear, it is not just the difficulties faced by youngsters at entering the labor market that matter, of equal importance are the employment conditions then offered to them. With globalization various forms of "atypical" employment have come to the fore that hardly existed only half a century ago, when an employment contract was usually full-time and life-long, with all guarantees for a good pension after retirement. Nowadays, such guarantees are much harder to obtain. One form of atypical employment, for instance, is employment based on a fixed-term contract. The need for firms to swiftly respond to the ever changing demands imposed by

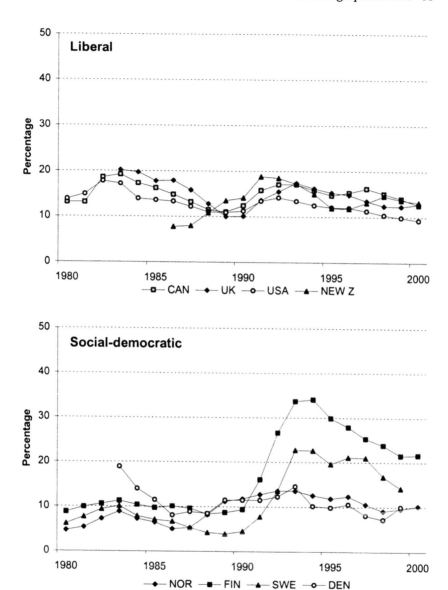

Figure 2.4   Rates of youth unemployment among the 15-24 years old, 1980-2000, by country according to welfare regime

Source: Key Indicators of the Labour Market (KILM 9), ILO, 2001-2002

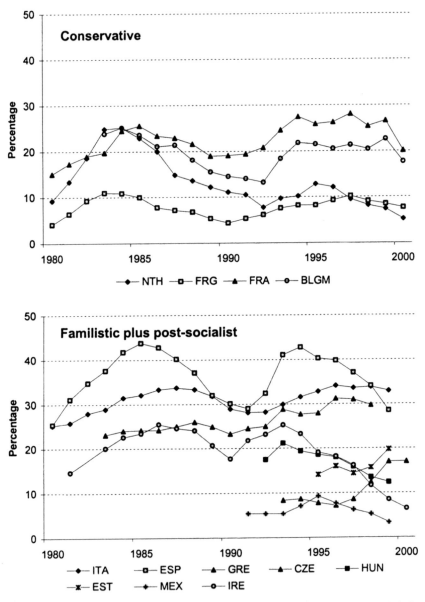

Figure 2.4   Rates of youth unemployment among the 15-24 years old, 1980-2000, by country according to welfare regime *(continued)*

intensified competition in a globalizing context has induced a gradual proliferation of such contracts across Europe (Figure 2.5), although with much variation among countries and across welfare regimes as a result of different labor market (de)regulation policies and approaches. For instance, there appears to have been a modest but continuous growth in this form of atypical employment for men and women in countries with a conservative welfare regime and closed employment relationships (except Luxembourg). In countries with a liberal welfare regime and open employment relationships, on the other hand, temporary contracts have never amounted to much more than 5 percent. In Canada, for instance, they are rather a non-issue compared to the importance of irregular work shifts in this 24-hour economy (see Mills, this volume), whereas in the United States of America most hiring arrangements constitute employment at will (see Berkowitz King, this volume). In other words, the meaning of fixed-term contracts differs across welfare regimes. At the other extreme are countries with a familistic welfare regime, with a particularly high (though nowadays slowly declining) prevalence of fixed-term contracts in Spain. In fact, it is the inclusion of this country in Figure 2.5 that has forced its left-hand scale to twice the size that would other-wise have sufficed.

As Mills and Blossfeld argue, it is in the nature of fixed-term contracts that, if not extended, they may lead to short- or long-term unemployment and thus cre-ate temporal uncertainty. It is important to note, though, that fixed-term contracts are not always and exclusively to the advantage of employers only, giving them greater freedom in terms of personnel management. Temporary employment can also imply a certain degree of flexibility for employees, if that is what they seek. Women considering to have a child, for instance, may even prefer an employ-ment relation of a definite rather than indefinite duration. Indeed, as Schömann *et al.* (1998) have convincingly demonstrated, women are generally much more likely to have fixed-term contract jobs than men.[4] The same can in principle be said of another form of atypical employment, namely, part-time work, which may be easier to combine with motherhood than full-time work (Blossfeld and Hakim, 1997). Following OECD usage, part-time employment in Figure 2.6 is defined as employment involving fewer than 30 working hours per week. At a scale of 0-60 percent, the highest levels of female part-time employment are to be found in the Netherlands (see Liefbroer, this volume), where it has indeed become increasingly fashionable nowadays to speak, not of "male breadwinner", but of "one-and-a-half career" couples (SCP, 2000). It is largely this increase in part-time work among Dutch women that is behind their spectacular increase in labor force participation, as observed in Figure 2.2. Contrary to countries with a conservative welfare regime, in countries with a liberal welfare regime part-time work has essentially remained unaltered, although at various levels (20-40 per-cent), whereas in countries with a social-democratic welfare regime part-time work seems to be on its way out, thus gradually giving way to the true "dual" career pattern (Blossfeld and Hakim, 1997). Again, countries with a familistic welfare regime appear to form a class of their own: fixed-term contracts may be their prevalent form of atypical employment but this is hardly the case for part-time work that has increased only marginally. The only exception is Ireland where part-time work is more general than fixed-term work (see also Layte *et al.*, this volume). As indicated before, part-time employment is by tradition very uncommon in most post-socialist countries (pooled together with the conserva-tives in Figure 2.6 for reasons of readability).

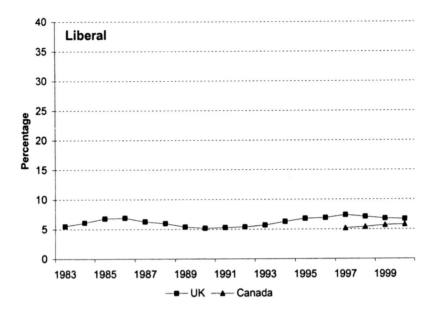

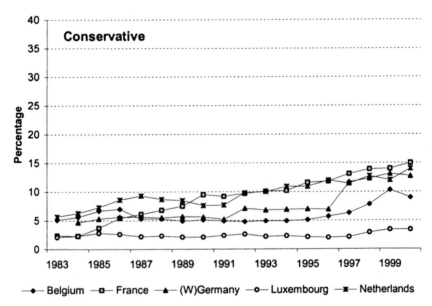

Figure 2.5   Fixed-term employment as a percentage of total dependent employment, 1983-2000, by country according to welfare regime

Source: Schömann *et al.* (1998) for the period 1983-1996, Eurostat (various years) for the period 1997-2000 except Canada (Statistics Canada, 2000)

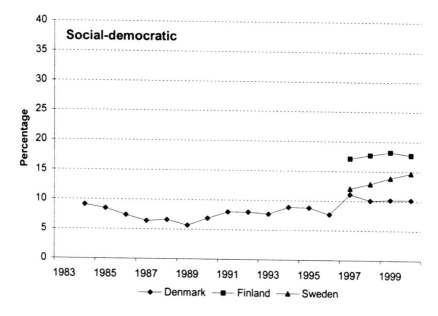

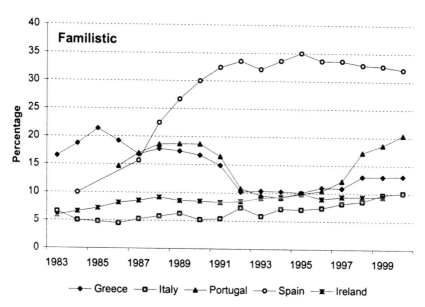

Figure 2.5   Fixed-term employment as a percentage of total dependent employment, 1983-2000, by country according to welfare regime *(continued)*

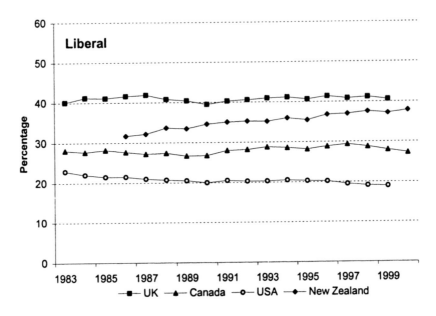

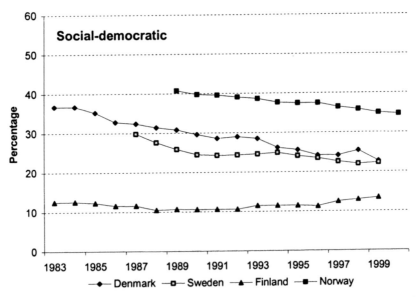

Figure 2.6   Part-time employment among women as a percentage of their total employment, 1983-2000, by country according to welfare regime

Source: Key Indicators of the Labour Market (KILM 5), ILO, 2001-2002

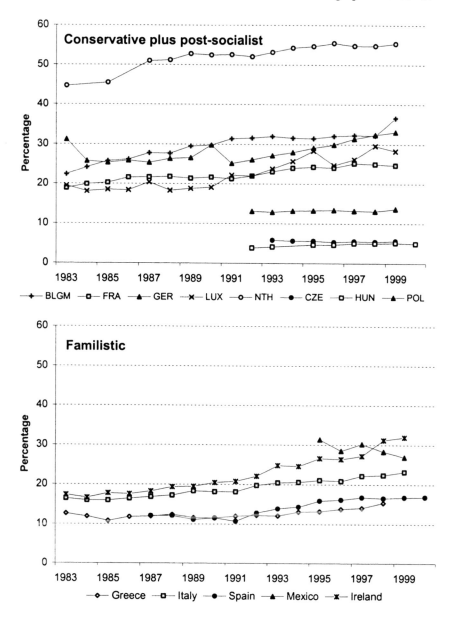

Figure 2.6   Part-time employment among women as a percentage of their total employment, 1983-2000, by country according to welfare regime (*continued*)

In summary, atypical employment forms such as fixed-term or part-time work are not necessarily always to be seen as examples of the negative sides of globalization.[5] Nonetheless, as Mills and Blossfeld argue, they do in principle carry certain risks for the individuals concerned, namely, temporal uncertainty for those on fixed-term contracts while economic uncertainty for those depending on wages from part-time work only. Both forms of uncertainty are in this volume hypothesized to have the potential of postponing decisions in other domains of life that require a high degree of self-binding commitment from individuals on their way to becoming adults, such as in the family domain. Indeed, also here some "atypical" forms of living arrangements have popped up that were rarely found only some 50 years ago.

DEMOGRAPHIC DEVELOPMENTS

In the context of the transition to adulthood, two questions can be posed: (i) at what ages do youngsters leave the parental home; and (ii) what type of household do they then form (Corijn and Klijzing, 2001)? A central tenet of the globalization paradigm developed by Mills and Blossfeld in the introduction to this volume is that as a result of the various forms of flexibility and insecurity brought about by the globalization process, first union formation will be increasingly characterized by either postponement, replacement (of marital by non-marital cohabitation), or both.

As Oppenheimer (1988) has argued, replacement is quite a logical strategy for young couples to follow in uncertain times. As a proxy for the replacement of marital by non-marital cohabitation one could for instance look at changes across birth cohorts in the cumulative percentage up to a certain age, say 23, of women who by that time had entered a consensual union as their first partnership (Figure 2.7). The emerging picture is revealing. On the one side, Sweden stands out for its sustained high proportion of such women, indicative of a long tradition of non-marital cohabitation that now appears to have reached a saturation point (Granström, 1997; see also Bygren *et al.*, this volume). On the other side, Poland, Ireland, Italy and Spain stand out for their sustained low proportions of such women (Holzer and Kowalska, 1997; De Sandre *et al.*, 2000; Delgado and Castro Martín, 1999). Although Poland has so far been treated as a country with a post-socialist welfare regime, what all these four countries have in common of course is a strong familistic ideology that, if coupled with a lack of affordable housing, keeps youngsters at the parental home until late marriage. In most other welfare regimes there has been a rather pronounced increase in non-marital cohabitation[6], and an immediate end to the further diffusion of this alternative living arrangement may not be in sight yet (Nazio and Blossfeld, 2003). Remarkably, among the post-socialist countries Estonia (Katus *et al.*, 2000; this volume) stands out for its rather high prevalence of this union type, at all times and at rates that are currently much closer to those of its neighboring countries in the North like Finland (Nikander, 1998) than in the South like Lithuania (Stankuniene *et al.*, 2000).

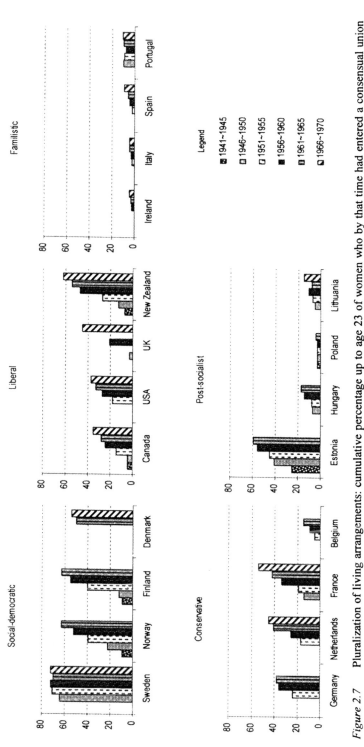

Figure 2.7 Pluralization of living arrangements: cumulative percentage up to age 23 of women who by that time had entered a consensual union as their first partnership, by birth cohort and country according to welfare regime

Source: FFS Standard Country Reports, table 8c, except for Ireland (Kiernan, 2002) and the UK (Ermisch and Francesconi, 2000).

However, women whose first partnership was a consensual union may first have lived through various other types of households - alone or together with other persons unrelated to them - after leaving the parental home.[7] For instance, in a competing risk study on household and union formation after leaving the parental home, Billari *et al.* (2002) have demonstrated that Italian, but in particular Spanish women are most likely to immediately get married when moving out, while Italian women are slightly more likely to first live on their own for a while before marriage. This is also what one observes when examining median ages of women at leaving the parental home and at first partnership formation in these two countries (Figure 2.8). The difference between these two measures gives a crude approximation of the time spent in various forms of non-family households including living alone before any first partnership formation, whether marital or not.

According to this measure, then, non-family household formation is apparently out of the question at all times in some of the post-socialist countries, in particular Poland, Hungary, and the Czech Republic, where housing shortages are known to have often forced newly-wed couples to double up with their parents before suitable accommodation finally became available to them (Holzer and Kowalska, 1997; Kamarás, 1999; Rychtarikova and Kraus, 2001). In other post-socialist countries like the Baltic States non-family household formation prior to first partnering used to be much less seldom, although here the time spent in non-family living arrangements after leaving the parental home and before any first partnership formation appears to be shortening over time. For Latvia one can even observe a reversal in the order of these two events among the two youngest birth cohorts: first couple formation in the parental home, then departure (see also Zvidrins *et al.*, 1998).

Evidence for a shrinking tendency to live on one's own for a while before first partnering appears also to be present for countries with a social-democratic welfare regime, for reasons not quite understood yet or it must be that non-marital cohabitation occurs at increasingly younger ages. But other than that, as one would expect under conditions of educational expansion, the general tendency for youngsters having left their parental home is to increasingly spend some time outside any family household. This appears to be particularly true for countries with either a continental (Germany, Netherlands, France) or liberal welfare regime (Canada, United States of America), a development which of course can not help but to push the mean age at first partnering upwards. Again, for institutional reasons explicated above, the "latest-late" home leaving and first partnership (marriage) patterns remain reserved to countries with a familistic welfare regime.

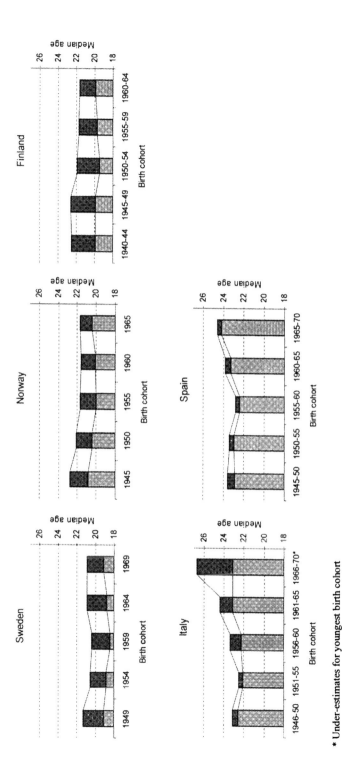

* Under-estimates for youngest birth cohort

Figure 2.8 Pluralization of living arrangements: median ages of women at leaving home (light grey) and first partnering (dark grey), by birth cohort and country

Source: FFS Standard Country Reports, tables 6e and 8a.

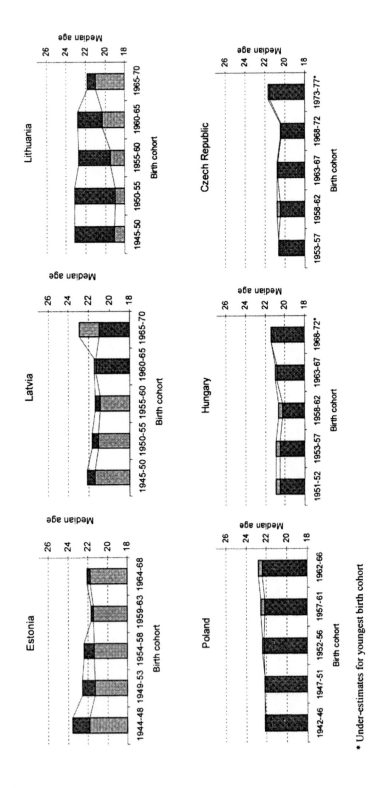

* Under-estimates for youngest birth cohort

Figure 2.8 Pluralization of living arrangements: median ages of women at leaving home (light grey) and first partnering (dark grey), by birth cohort and country *(continued)*

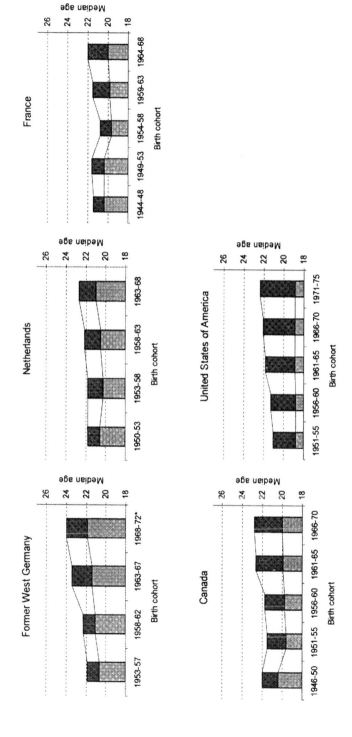

* Under-estimates for youngest birth cohort

Figure 2.8 Pluralization of living arrangements: median ages of women at leaving home (light grey) and first partnering (dark grey), by birth cohort and country *(continued)*

Calot (1998) and Frejka and Calot (2001) have fully documented the changes in the female mean ages at first marriage and childbearing by year of observation (1950-2000) as well as by year of birth (1915-1965), for all the countries considered in this volume, so that there is little reason to duplicate their comprehensive analyses here. They show that postponement of first marriage among the post-war birth cohorts has had rather obvious repercussions for the timing of childbearing, which - Sweden notwithstanding - in the majority of countries still occurs within marriage. Upward trends in the mean age at first motherhood among these post-war birth cohorts are indeed an almost perfect and exact copy of the upward trends in nuptiality. Because there is a biological upper limit to the age at which women conceive easily, postponed childbearing has a direct and brutal effect on total fertility levels. As a result, the majority of countries are nowadays showing total cohort fertility rates that are well below replacement levels.

In the individual country chapters that follow, these particular developments will be examined in more detail using longitudinal data that allow one to separate more clearly globalization factors from their demographic effects. They will show that educational expansion, labor market flexibilization and other globalization factors do have an impact on the partnering and parenting behavior of adolescents on their way to full adulthood. However, this impact is indirect and mediated by the various forms of social and economic insecurity that are engendered by these globalization factors. Country-specific institutional packages determine which forms of global insecurity come to the fore plainest and how they then impinge on decision making processes and, ultimately, behavioral outcomes.

CONCLUDING REMARKS

The graphic materials presented in this chapter convincingly demonstrate that at least for an aggregate-level analysis of the impact of globalization on the transition to adulthood it makes sense to group countries according to their prevalent welfare regime. No matter whether one examines the tertiarization of the labor market, female labor force participation, educational expansion, youth unemployment, fixed-term contracts, part-time employment, first partnering or leaving the parental home, inter-country variability appears smaller within than across welfare regimes. It now remains to be tested whether a classification of countries according to welfare regime is also a useful device to reduce complexity in the case of the 14 individual-level analyses that follow.

NOTES

1   FFS is the acronym for Fertility and Family Surveys, a project carried out during the 1990s in 23 Member States of the United Nations Economic Commission for Europe. The country-specific FFS reports used for this chapter are listed in the bibliography by author name.

2 For Canadian women this appears to be true for quite some time already.
3 Including both part- and full-time work.
4 Apart from gender, they have also documented important differentials by age, education and occupation.
5 Self-employment is left out of consideration here for lack of consistent time series, but is known to be on the rise in some countries, predominantly a male affair, and of decreasing duration.
6 Note that these national proportions may hide important differentials, as between Quebec and the other provinces in the case of Canada (Wu, 1999), or between the Maori and non-Maori populations in the case of New Zealand (Johnstone *et al.*, 2001).
7 Although it is in principle possible to reconstruct the entire household history of FFS respondents, this is not so easily accomplished. The country-specific FFS reports used in this chapter do not provide any information on this, only on (median) ages at leaving the parental home and at partnership formation and dissolution. Nonetheless, this information is already quite useful.

BIBLIOGRAPHY

Billari, F.C., Castiglioni, M., Castro Martín, T., Michielin, F. and Ongaro, F. (2002) 'Household and union formation in a Mediterranean fashion: Italy and Spain', in E. Klijzing and M. Corijn (eds) *Dynamics of fertility and partnership in Europe: insights and lessons from comparative research*, Volume II, Geneva/New York: United Nations.

Blossfeld, H.-P. and Hakim, C. (1997) *Between Equalization and Marginalization. Women Working Part-Time in Europe and the United States of America*, Oxford: Oxford University Press.

Blossfeld, H.-P. and Drobnič, S. (eds) (2001) *Careers of Couples in Contemporary Societies. A Cross-National Comparison of the Transition from Male Breadwinner to Dual Earner Families*, Oxford: Oxford University Press.

Calot, G. (1998) 'Fertility in Europe and North America', paper presented at the Regional Population Meeting, Budapest (Hungary), 7-9 December 1998.

Carneiro, I., and Knudsen, L.B. (2001) 'Fertility and Family Surveys in Countries of the ECE Region, Country Report Denmark', Comparable FFS-data, Economic Studies No. 10t, Geneva: United Nations Economic Commission for Europe.

Carrilho, M. J., and Magalhães, G. (2000) 'Fertility and Family Surveys in Countries of the ECE Region, Standard Country Report Portugal', Economic Studies No. 10p, Geneva: United Nations Economic Commission for Europe.

Corijn, M., and E. Klijzing (eds) (2001) *Transitions to adulthood in Europe*, Dordrecht: Kluwer Academic Publishers.

Delgado, M., and Castro Martín, T. (1999) 'Fertility and Family Surveys in Countries of the ECE Region, Standard Country Report Spain', Economic Studies No. 10i, Geneva: United Nations Economic Commission for Europe.

De Sandre, P., Ongaro, F., Rettaroli, R. and Salvini, S. (2000) 'Fertility and Family Surveys in Countries of the ECE Region, Standard Country Report Italy', Economic Studies No. 10o, Geneva: United Nations Economic Commission for Europe.

Ermisch, J. and Francesconi, M. (2000) 'Cohabitation in Great Britain: Not for Long, but Here to Stay', *Journal of the Royal Statistical Society*, Series A, 163(2): 153-171.

Esping-Andersen, G. (1999) *Social Foundations of Postindustrial Economies*, Oxford: Oxford University Press.

Eurostat (1998) 'Labour Force Survey', Principal Results 1997, Statistics in focus, Theme 3 (Population and Social Conditions), Luxemburg.

Eurostat (1999) 'Labour Force Survey', Principal Results 1998, Statistics in focus, Theme 3 (Population and Social Conditions), Luxemburg.

Eurostat (2000) 'Labour Force Survey', Principal Results 1999, Statistics in focus, Theme 3 (Population and Social Conditions), Luxemburg.

Eurostat (2001) 'Labour Force Survey', Principal Results 2000, Statistics in focus, Theme 3 (Population and Social Conditions), Luxemburg.

Frejka, T. and Calot, G. (2001) 'Contemporary cohort reproductive patterns in low fertility countries', *Population and Development Review*, 27(1): 103-132.

Granström, F. (1997) 'Fertility and Family Surveys in Countries of the ECE Region, Standard Country Report Sweden', Economic Studies No. 10b, Geneva: United Nations Economic Commission for Europe.

Holzer, J., and Kowalska, I. (1997) 'Fertility and Family Surveys in Countries of the ECE Region, Standard Country Report Poland', Economic Studies No. 10d, Geneva: United Nations Economic Commission for Europe.

ILO (2001-2002) *Key Indicators of the Labour Market*, Geneva: International Labour Organisation.

Johnstone, K., Baxendine, S., Dharmalingam, A., Hillcoat-Nallétamby, S., Pool, I. and Paki Paki, N. (2001) 'Fertility and Family Surveys in Countries of the ECE Region, Standard Country Report New Zealand', Economic Studies No. 10s, Geneva: United Nations Economic Commission for Europe.

Kamarás, F. (1999) 'Fertility and Family Surveys in Countries of the ECE Region, Standard Country Report Hungary', Economic Studies No. 10j, Geneva: United Nations Economic Commission for Europe.

Katus, K., Puur, A. and Sakkeus, L. (2000) 'Fertility and Family Surveys in Countries of the ECE Region, Standard Country Report Estonia', Economic Studies No. 10n, Geneva: United Nations Economic Commission for Europe.

Kiernan, K. (2002) 'The state of the European Union: An analysis of FFS data on partnership formation and dissolution', in M. Macura and G. Beets (eds) *The dynamics of fertility and partnership in Europe: insights and lessons from comparative research*, Volume I, Geneva/New York: United Nations.

Latten, J., and de Graaf, A. (1997) 'Fertility and Family Surveys in Countries of the ECE Region, Standard Country Report The Netherlands', Economic Studies No. 10c, Geneva: United Nations Economic Commission for Europe.

Lodewijckx, E. (1999) 'Fertility and Family Surveys in Countries of the ECE Region, Standard Country Report Belgium', Economic Studies No. 10l, Geneva: United Nations Economic Commission for Europe.

Nazio, T., and Blossfeld, H-P. (2003) 'The diffusion of cohabitation among young women in West Germany, East Germany and Italy', *European Journal of Population*, 19(1): 47-82.

Nikander, T. (1998) 'Fertility and Family Surveys in Countries of the ECE Region, Standard Country Report Finland', Economic Studies No. 10g, Geneva: United Nations Economic Commission for Europe.

Noack, T., and Østby, L. (1996) 'Fertility and Family Surveys in Countries of the ECE Region, Standard Country Report Norway', Economic Studies No. 10a, Geneva: United Nations Economic Commission for Europe.

Oppenheimer, V.K. (1988) 'A theory of marriage timing', *American Journal of Sociology*, 94: 563-591.

Rychtarikova, J., and Kraus, J. (2001) 'Fertility and Family Surveys in Countries of the ECE Region, Standard Country Report Czech Republic', Economic Studies No. 10v, Geneva: United Nations Economic Commission for Europe.

Schömann, K., Rogowski, R. and Kruppe, T. (1998) *Labour Market Efficiency in the European Union. Employment protection and fixed-term contracts*, London: Routledge.

SCP (2000) *De kunst van het combineren. Taakverdeling onder partners* [The art of combining. Division of labour between partners], Den Haag: Sociaal Cultureel Planbureau.

Stankuniene, V., Baublyte, M., Kanopiene, V. and Mikulioniene, S. (2000) 'Fertility and Family Surveys in Countries of the ECE Region, Standard Country Report Lithuania, Economic Studies No. 10q', Geneva: United Nations Economic Commission for Europe.

Statistics Canada (2000) 'Labour force historical review', Catalogue 77F0004XCB, Ottawa.

Symeonidou, H. (2002) 'Fertility and Family Surveys in Countries of the ECE Region, Standard Country Report Greece', Economic Studies No. 10w, Geneva: United Nations Economic Commission for Europe.

Toulemon, L., and de Guibert-Lantoine, C. (1998) 'Fertility and Family Surveys in Countries of the ECE Region, Standard Country Report France', Economic Studies No. 10e, Geneva: United Nations Economic Commission for Europe.

Wu, Z. (1999) 'Fertility and Family Surveys in Countries of the ECE Region, Standard Country Report Canada', Economic Studies No. 10k, Geneva: United Nations Economic Commission for Europe.

Zvidrins, P., Ezera, L. and Greitans, A. (1998) 'Fertility and Family Surveys in Countries of the ECE Region, Standard Country Report Latvia', Economic Studies No. 10f, Geneva: United Nations Economic Commission for Europe.

3 Case study Germany

Global competition, uncertainty and the transition to adulthood

Karin Kurz, Nikolei Steinhage and Katrin Golsch

INTRODUCTION

The aim of this chapter is twofold. First, we want to better understand how labor market entrants in Germany in the 1980s and 1990s have been affected by precarious employment and unemployment. Second, we will investigate how being in a precarious position influences first partnership formation and the conception of a first child.

The transition from school to work in Germany has been described as being rather smooth (Müller *et al.*, 1998; Winkelmann, 1996). This has largely been attributed to the specifics of the German vocational training system, in particular to its dual nature. This training system has the effect that even in the 1990s – in contrast to most other OECD countries – almost all potential labor market entrants found jobs in a very short time (OECD, 1998; Bowers *et al.*, 1998). Therefore, we will not concentrate on the transition from school to work as such but, in a first step, on the first (full-time or part-time) employment position after having left the general educational or vocational training system, by asking whether this position is fixed-term or permanent. Whereas fixed-term contracts clearly involve uncertainty about the future employment career, this will normally be much less the case for permanent contracts. In a second step we analyze for those who had a first employment the risk of becoming unemployed according to the type of their first contract. Unemployment implies again uncertainty about the prospective development of one's employment career, but also economic insecurity. Both analyses center around the question of social inequalities, that is, we ask whether the risks of precarious employment or of unemployment are stratified by education, vocational training, occupational class, gender, ethnic origin and region (East vs. West Germany). In other words: are precarious jobs and unemployment "individualized", that is, more or less evenly spread over all labor market entrants, or are certain groups more affected by these risks than others (Bernardi, 2000; Bernardi and Nazio, this volume)? And further: do we observe an accumulation of risks within certain groups?

In the second part of our analyses we scrutinize to what extent inequalities in terms of job security spill over to major life course decisions during early adult life. We start from the hypothesis that long-term commitments such as marriage and parenthood require some stability in life circumstances and a secure economic basis (Oppenheimer, 1988; Blossfeld, 2002). We therefore ask whether positions of insecurity – employed on the basis of a fixed-term contract, unemployed or in further education – make such long-term commitments less likely. Do individuals in such positions postpone first marriage and parenthood? Given the still rather clear-cut gender division of labor in Germany, we expect that positions of insecurity have different meanings and consequences for men and women. All research questions are studied using data from the first fifteen waves (1984 – 1998) of the German Socio-Economic Panel (GSOEP).

We will proceed as follows. In the next section we outline some specifics of the German institutional context, namely, those of the economic system determining the prevalence of certain types of precarious positions and those of existing welfare state provisions affecting the gender division of labor. We then turn to the macro-economic conditions at labor market entry. Next we present our research hypotheses. These are followed by a description of the data and methods and by the empirical results. We conclude with a summary and discussion of our findings.

THE INSTITUTIONAL CONTEXT

Type of economy

Germany's economy has often been classified as flexibly coordinated (Soskice, 1999; Mayer, 1997). At the core of the employment relationships in such economies are long-term cooperative relationships based on trust. Various institutions work as a framework of incentives and constraints that help to create and maintain this kind of relationships (Soskice, 1999). First among them is the vocational training system[1] in which apprentices are intensively trained over 2 to 3 years. Job rotation is part and parcel of this training process (Maurice *et al.*, 1986), and narrow job demarcations like in British and American firms are rare (Jürgens *et al.*, 1993). These features foster functional flexibility as well as employment relationships that are governed by mutual cooperation and trust (Marsden, 1995). Second, workers' councils within firms help to keep up cooperative relationships between employers and employees by their involvement in a wide range of decisions concerning the company. Third, wages are set by collective bargaining agreements between region-specific industrial unions and employers' associations. About 84 percent of all German employees are covered by such collective agreements (Bispinck, 1997). These regional tariff agreements or "Flächentarifverträge" as they are called in German are binding for all employers who are member of a particular association.[2] This collective wage setting mechanism thus keeps conflicts about wages largely away from the company level.

All three institutional features – the apprenticeship system, workers' councils and collective bargaining – help to strengthen a work environment of cooperative exchange and trust. In addition, all workers with permanent full-time or part-time jobs (of about 15 hours or more) are protected by dismissal procedures that require an advanced notice of at least 6 weeks and the spelling out of specific reasons before an employee can be fired. Also, in matters of any lay-off the workers' council has to be heard, a regulation that makes quick firings unlikely.

Deregulation of the labor market since 1980s

In the face of economic problems and continuously high unemployment since the early 1980s, the highly regulated and cooperative institutional setting of Germany's economy has come under attack. Deregulation of the labor market has been a heavily debated issue in German politics for years. Two major arguments against it from the employers' side are, on the one hand, that wages cannot be easily adapted to the specific economic situation of the firm and, on the other, that due to the existing dismissal procedures the size of the work force cannot be easily adjusted to economic fluctuations. The two most important changes introduced so far – the opening clauses ("Öffnungsklauseln") of collective agreements and changes of dismissal procedures – directly address these problems.

Opening clauses mean that certain regional tariff agreements are opened up for exceptions on the firm-level, that is, for firm-specific agreements. The discussion on this key issue resulted from problems of East German firms to pay wages that had been agreed upon in collective negotiations. After conflicts between the union of the metal industry and employers in the East, opening clauses were first introduced in East Germany in 1993. They permit wage reductions for firms that are in serious economic difficulties. Since 1997, opening clauses have also been applied in the West German metal industry (Fuchs and Schettkat, 2000: 225). They contribute to a diversification of wage levels, but do not concern the employment contracts themselves.

The most important step to deregulate employment contracts came with the Employment Promotion Act ("Beschäftigungsförderungsgesetz") introduced in 1985, which made it easier for employers to use fixed-term contracts. As these end at a specific date, they therewith circumvent dismissal protection. Before 1985 such contracts were only possible under specific conditions, but with the Employment Promotion Act employers gained freedom to conclude fixed-term contracts of up to 18 months with new employees and former apprentices.[3] The original legislation was first limited to the year 1990, but was extended several times thereafter. Since January 1996 the law allows for fixed-term contracts of up to two years. As of January 2001 the Employment Promotion Act was substituted by the Part-time and Fixed-term Contract Act which still allows to offer fixed-term contracts of up to two years to newly hired employees without having to give specific reasons. In contrast to the private sector, fixed-term contracts in the public sector can only be provided under specific requirements. Nevertheless, they have a long tradition and are still much more common than in the private sector.

The German microcensus of 1991 reported that 7.5 percent of all employees had fixed-term contracts; this figure rose to 9 percent in 1999. With about 21 percent in 1991, temporary contracts were most prevalent in the age group of employees of 30 years or younger. Due to employment creation measures ("Arbeitsbeschaffungsmaßnahmen") that provide fixed-term positions for formerly unemployed persons, these positions are also more common in East Germany. According to the microcensus data, men are somewhat more likely than women to be on a temporary contract. In contrast, another survey reports that in the case of new hirings, women are more likely to receive a fixed-term contract (Bielenski *et al.*, 1994).

Types of precarious positions

The last section focused on one important form of precarious work in Germany in the 1980s and 1990s: fixed-term contracts. Another form of employment that is often characterized as precarious is part-time work (see, for example, Berkowitz King, this volume). However, in the German context this is less the case than in other countries such as the US: part-time positions of about 15 hours or more enjoy the same fringe benefits as do full-time positions. They are covered by the social security system and, as already mentioned, protected by the same dismissal procedures as full-time jobs. However, most part-time jobs are precarious in the sense that they may not allow for economic independence.[4]

Given the fact that in Germany employees working part-time for 15 hours or more usually enjoy the same rights and benefits as other employees, it is clear that the creation of part-time jobs is not connected to a flexible organization of work in times of global competition. Employers do not gain much in terms of numerical flexibility or reduced labor costs when they hire standard part-timers. This is not true, however, for part-time positions involving less than 15 work hours. These are, on the one hand, financially attractive for employers because – until recently at least – they did not have to pay contributions for health, unemployment and old age insurance and, on the other, they allow for numerical flexibility since dismissals are easier. In general, part-time positions (whatever the number of work hours) are not very common for labor market entrants in Germany, but rather for women with children.

To capture different dimensions of precariousness or insecurity we suggest to distinguish between *temporal* insecurity – or what Bernardi and Nazio (this volume) call *employment* insecurity – and *economic* insecurity (Kurz and Steinhage, 2001). We use the term "temporal insecurity" to describe positions that imply relative uncertainty about future employment developments. With "economic insecurity" we refer to positions that involve comparably low pay which might in some cases not allow for economic independence. Based on this distinction, Table 3.1 classifies several positions as precarious.

Some of these positions can be linked to globalization. That is, global competition should increase the likelihood of firms to create precarious jobs – in Germany, in particular, fixed-term positions – and/or to downsize the work force, thus resulting in an increased risk of unemployment (see the introductory chapter to this volume). As has been mentioned above, only part-time jobs of less than 15 hours can be seen as part of the flexibility strategies of firms. Furthermore, being in education can indirectly be related to globalization in the sense that knowledge (and the permanent updating of it) is supposed to become increasingly important for success in the labor market (Blossfeld, 2002).

Table 3.1   Positions of economic and temporal insecurity

	Economic insecurity (dependence)	Temporal insecurity
Precarious employment:		
Part-time position + fixed-term contract	+	+
Part-time position + permanent contract	+	0
Full-time position + fixed-term contract	0	+
Self-employed (without employees)	+	+
Not employed:		
In education	+	+
Unemployed	+	+
Housekeeping (when married)	+	0
Other not employed (e.g., military service)	+	+

Relating these positions to our later analyses, the following can be stated: Labor market entrants might encounter the risk of finding a job that is only fixed-term (temporal insecurity) and thus of becoming unemployed thereafter (temporal plus economic insecurity).[5] Furthermore, if they do find a position, they might face the risk of low pay (economic insecurity). In a difficult labor market situation new entrants might also follow the strategy of becoming self-employed (without employees), which means in many cases that they are insecure economically as well as in terms of future career prospects (Leicht, 2000).[6]

Gender and the welfare state

Belonging to the so-called 'conservative' cluster of welfare regimes (Esping-Andersen, 1993;1999), the German welfare system is strongly transfer-oriented and its social policies are primarily designed to decommodify economically active individuals. At the same time, in contrast to some Nordic countries such as Sweden (see Bygren *et al.*, this volume), the conservative welfare state supports in various ways the traditional division of labor in the family (Kurz, 1998; Meyers *et al.*, 1999). In particular, the parental leave legislation in Germany allows for an employment interruption (of mother or father) of up to three years[7] with full job guarantees. At the same time, the provision of child care facilities for small infants is very low. Hence, while the successive activity pattern is supported when a mother (or father) interrupts her (or his) employment to take care of a young child, the simultaneous combination of having a baby *and* being employed is left to the creativity of the parents. In almost all cases it is the mother and not the father who takes up the parental leave, which seems rational in economic terms given the usually lower wages of wives. Consequently, women with young children are likely to be housewives or, as the availability of part-time positions is very high, to work on a part-time basis (Blossfeld and Rohwer, 1997). In contrast, diverse social policies in the former GDR such as an extended network of child care facilities eased the combination of labor force participation and family obligations (Geißler, 1996; Huinink and Wagner, 1995; Strohmeier and Kuijsten, 1997). The female employment rate in general, and full-time employment in particular, was therefore considerably higher in East Germany. Since the reunification, however, due to cut-backs in child care facilities and generally dim job prospects it has become increasingly difficult for East German women to realize their labor market and childbearing wishes.

MACRO-ECONOMIC CONDITIONS AT LABOR MARKET ENTRY

Within the time frame given by the GSOEP data used in our empirical analysis, from the mid-1980s to the end of the 1990s, three phases of macro-economic conditions can be distinguished. At the beginning of the 1980s the overall and youth unemployment rates started to rise (see Table 3.2), with youth unemployment reaching a high of 9.1 percent in 1983 after having been as low as 3.2 in 1980. At the same time, the demand for apprenticeship places exceeded the supply of such vacancies (Winkelmann, 1996). In the second half of the 1980s total as well as youth unemployment rates began to fall. Between the end of the 1980s and the beginning of the 1990s West Germany experienced a short economic boom mainly caused by German unification and the opening-up of new markets. Thus in 1991, West German youth unemployment was once again very low at 4.5 percent, and the supply of apprenticeships well exceeded demand. However, from around 1993 total and youth unemployment rates began to rise again, reaching a high of 11.0 and 9.2 percent, respectively, in West Germany in 1997. The total unemployment rates in East Germany were considerably higher than in the Western part of the country in all available years starting with the unification in 1991. In contrast, in the first years after unification the East German youth unemployment rates among those 20 years of age or younger were similar to those in the West. From 1997 onwards, however, they started to exceed the Western rates. When the focus is on unemployment of youngsters 25 years of age or younger, a clearly higher risk of the East Germans becomes obvious for all years of observation. For example, in 1998, 17 percent of the East Germans in this age group were unemployed compared to 10.4 of the West Germans.

Up to 1993, West German women always had higher unemployment rates than men. In the following years, however, their rates were about the same or slightly lower. This is in contrast to the situation in East Germany, where the female unemployment rate has always (since 1991) considerably exceeded the male one. It is only in recent years that the differential has shrunk somewhat.

In sum, we can identify a phase of difficult labor market prospects from the beginning to the end of the 1980s, an upward trend since then until the beginning of the 1990s, and again more difficult prospects during the remainder of the 1990s. Furthermore, we find clear differences between the two parts of the country, with the East German unemployment rate (for the whole population as well as for young people under age 25) being notably higher than the West German one. In addition, while there are practically no gender differences in West

Table 3.2   Unemployment trends in West and East Germany

	West	East	Men West	Women West	Men East	Women East	Foreigners West	< age 20/25[a] West	< age 20/25[a] East
1980	3.8		3.0	5.2			5.0	3.2	
1981	5.5		4.5	6.9			8.2	4.9	
1982	7.5		5.8	8.6			11.9	7.7	
1983	9.1		3.4	10.1			14.7	9.1	
1984	9.1		8.5	10.2			14.0	7.9	
1985	9.3		8.6	10.4			13.9	8.1	
1986	9.0		8.0	10.5			13.7	7.4	
1987	8.9		3.0	10.2			14.3	6.6	
1988	8.7		7.3	10.0			14.4	6.1	
1989	7.9		6.9	9.4			12.2	-	
1990	7.2		5.3	8.4			10.9	5.0	
1991	6.3	10.3	5.8	7.0	2.5	12.3	10.7	4.5	-
1992	6.6	14.8	6.2	7.2	10.5	19.6	12.2	5.0 (5.8)	-
1993	8.2	15.8	8.0	8.4	11.0	21.0	15.1	6.4 (7.5)	7.1 (12.8)
1994	9.2	16.0	9.2	9.2	10.9	21.5	16.2	7.3 (8.6)	6.7 (13.2)
1995	9.3	14.9	9.3	9.2	10.7	19.3	16.6	8.0 (8.8)	7.4 (12.3)
1996	10.1	16.7	10.4	9.9	13.7	19.9	18.9	9.0 (10.3)	9.0 (13.8)
1997	11.0	19.5	11.2	10.7	16.6	22.5	20.4	9.2 (11.1)	10.9 (16.2)
1998	10.5	19.5	10.6	10.3	17.4	21.8	19.6	8.7 (10.4)	10.8 (17.0)
1999	9.9	19.0	9.9	9.8	17.1	20.9	18.4	7.9 (9.1)	10.2 (15.8)
2000	8.7	18.8	8.8	8.5	17.7	19.9	16.4	5.9 (7.7)	10.1 (16.6)

Sources: Statistisches Bundesamt, time series, http://www.statistik-bund.de.

Notes

a   Unemployment rates for persons 25 years or younger in brackets.

Germany, in East Germany the unemployment rate for women is considerably higher than for men.

HYPOTHESES

Fixed-term contracts and unemployment: who is most affected?

As to general labor market prospects, we expect the risk of precarious employment and unemployment to be lowest from the end of the 1980s to the beginning of the 1990s. In our analyses we will therefore distinguish three labor market entry cohorts: 1985 to 1989, 1990 to 1993, and 1994 to 1998. At the same time, we suppose that – given the turbulence of the East German labor market throughout the 1990s – East Germans are generally more likely to face precarious jobs (fixed-term contracts) and unemployment. Furthermore, for all labor market entrants educational qualification and occupational position should matter. As has been pointed out by Breen (1997), employers will try to shift the market uncertainties that they face to their employees, but surely not to all of them alike. The basic distinction is hypothesized to lie between employees with clearly defined tasks which are easily supervised, and those with less specific tasks which cannot be monitored directly. That is, the distinction is between the labor contract prevalent in manual and low-qualified non-manual work, on the one hand, and the service relationship common in high-qualified non-manual work, on the other (see also Erikson and Goldthorpe, 1992). In the latter type of relationship, where exchanges are of a more diffuse character, the employer will have to ensure the employee's motivation and commitment by offering favorable employment conditions like a permanent contract, good fringe benefits and other forms of security. Following Marsden (1995), we extend this thesis from the service class to employees with qualified vocational training (mostly with an apprenticeship), since within the German context of a flexibly coordinated economy also these workers usually work rather autonomously and, therefore, employers are likely to implement measures to ensure their commitment (Kurz and Steinhage, 2001).

Several studies have found a close link between occupational qualification and unemployment. Labor market entrants with an apprenticeship and university graduates are less likely to become unemployed than those without occupational qualification (Winkelmann, 1996; Franz et al., 1997; Brauns et al., 1999). With respect to fixed-term contracts, results from existing studies are not quite in line with our hypotheses. While it has been confirmed that low-qualified employees are clearly more at risk than higher qualified, also university graduates are more often found in fixed-term contracts (Bielenski et al., 1994). This has been attributed to the fact that many university graduates work in the public sector where fixed-term contracts are more common than in private firms.

With respect to the consequences of a fixed-term position, our hypothesis is straightforward: fixed-term contracts should heighten the risk of unemployment since they end per definitionem at a certain point in time. Particularly when a firm finds itself in circumstances of economic insecurity, extensions of fixed-term contracts or their conversion to permanent ones are less probable (Bielensky *et al.*, 1994).

The public sector is usually looked upon as offering high employment protection. However, as just mentioned, fixed-term contracts have always been more widespread in this sector than in the private one. Accordingly, we assume a higher likelihood of receiving a temporary position at employment entry in the public sector. Regarding the risk of unemployment, we therefore also expect *overall* lower employment security for young employees in the public sector. But once the type of contract is controlled for in our models, we do not envision to find a higher risk of unemployment in the public sector anymore.

Given on average the lower educational and vocational qualification of migrants (Alba *et al.*, 1994; Seifert, 1992), we further presume that also these persons are more at risk of fixed-term employment and unemployment than native Germans. But again we suspect a composition effect to be at work here, that is, we expect this differential to disappear once educational and vocational levels have been taken into account. We predict this because the collective bargaining system (with the resulting tariff wages) as well as the activities of workers' councils have probably prevented obvious forms of discrimination (like wage discrimination) within firms on the basis of ethnic origin. Finally, on similar grounds we expect that women do not fare worse than men at labor market entry once educational and vocational qualifications have been controlled for.

Marriage and parenthood: different effects of insecurity for men and women?

According to Oppenheimer (1988), individuals are more likely to make long-term commitments such as entering a marriage if their future career prospects are predictable and if they can rely on a certain economic basis. If this is not the case – e.g., when individuals are in education, have not yet found a stable job or have only a low income – decisions about entering marriage are likely to be postponed. Hence, Oppenheimer (1988) addresses economic as well as temporal insecurity as two major factors that might hinder the transition to marriage.[8] Her argument can easily be extended to the decision of conceiving a first child, since having a child – even more than being married – requires economic resources and long-term commitments between the parents and towards the child.

However, positions of economic and temporal uncertainty are not automatically assumed to lead to a postponement of marriage and parenthood. Rather, gender-specific behavior is to be expected (Oppenheimer, 1988). According to the traditional male bread-winner model still prevailing in Germany, we suspect that it is usually the man who takes up the major responsibility for providing an economic basis, while the woman is likely to take care of the household and child raising activities. If she does contribute to the household income, it is possibly on a part-time basis. Women in part-time positions and those out of the labor force (housewives) have probably already made the decision to pursue a family career (Hakim, 2000). We therefore expect those women to be more likely to get married and pregnant than full-time employed women. Further, being unemployed or having a fixed-term contract should not impede their entry into first marriage and parenthood. Women in such situations might choose to get married and have a child because, on the one hand, being a housewife and mother is a socially recognized role alternative to that of an employee and, on the other, a male-breadwinner marriage offers some measure of security to them. Finally, we expect women working in the public or the private sector to be equally likely to make the transitions to first marriage and childbearing. That is, provided that the male-breadwinner model is still in place for most couples, we assume that positions of more or of less employment security should not matter much for women's family formation. Probably the least likely to make the transition to marriage and motherhood are women still in education. Since we look at individuals who have already entered their first employment, we can presume that these are predominantly career-oriented women who have gone back to school for further education. Following the arguments put forward by Gary Becker (1981), we suppose that these women face high opportunity costs with respect to the transitions to getting married and having children.

With respect to educational level and class position, again Becker's (1981) argument can be applied. Due to their rising economic independence (and the resulting higher opportunity costs), women with high human capital and those in high class positions are less likely to enter marriage and to give birth to a child. However, as the studies in Blossfeld (1995) suggest, there might be a difference in the effects of education on the decision to marry and on the decision to have children: If it is just the transition to parenthood that involves a change towards a traditional sexual division of labor but not the transition to marriage, then Becker's opportunity cost argument should apply to the former transition only. In that case we should observe educational and class effects in the transition to motherhood, but not in the transition to marriage. But even for the transition to motherhood this is not entirely clear. For instance, Blossfeld and Huinink (1991) do not find support for the opportunity cost argument, but only for a timing effect that simply results from women's extended participation in the educational system. According to their analysis, highly educated women postpone family formation; however, if they have left the educational system they will conceive their first child rather soon due to social age norms (Blossfeld and Huinink, 1991).

In contrast to women, for men all positions of insecurity – be they unemployment, part-time or fixed-term employment, being in education or non-employed – should lower the tendency towards entry into marriage and fatherhood. This is so because temporal insecurity involves uncertainty about whether the breadwinner role can be fulfilled in the future, while economic insecurity makes it harder to fulfill this role currently. This also means that overall men working in the public sector should have a lower transition rate (because of the higher proportion of fixed-term positions), but a higher rate when the type of contract has been controlled for.

A security argument can also be put forward with respect to educational level and occupational class. Men with low education and those in low-paid positions (lower non-manual and un- or semi-skilled manual workers) should be less likely to get married and have a child since they can less easily fulfill the breadwinner role and are thus less attractive as marriage partners (Blossfeld and Timm, 1997; Wirth and Lüttinger, 1998). On the other hand, by leaving the educational system and starting to work at a young age they make the first transition to adult roles early in life and they may, therefore, also get married and/or become fathers earlier than others. As these two influences act in opposite directions, they might cancel out each other, in which case we might not observe any effect. A similar argument can be forwarded for highly educated men and those in service class positions. They can on the one hand be expected to be attractive marriage partners but, on the other, they should make the transition to marriage and fatherhood relatively late in life. However, if we assume the existence of relative age homogamy we might, in contrast, expect that these highly educated men – similar to their female partners – make the transitions rather quickly once they have left the educational system and entered the labor market. In short, there are no clear predictions possible on the directions of education and class effects.

In the former GDR there was relative certainty about future developments. The decision to begin a partnership and family was mainly bound to leaving the educational system, and marriage and childbearing took place earlier in life than in West Germany (Sommer *et al.*, 2000). However, since the unification job precariousness has been exceptionally high in East Germany. This should have made long-term commitments increasingly difficult. Therefore, we predict that East Germans today are less likely to make these two long-term commitments during their early adult life than West Germans.

DATA AND METHODS

For all four analyses – on the type of first contract, the risk of becoming unemployed, the transition to first marriage and first parenthood – we use data from the first fifteen waves (1984 - 1998) of the German Socio-Economic Panel (GSOEP).

The GSOEP is a general household panel which started with approximately 6,000 households and about 12,000 individuals in 1984 (Hanefeld, 1987). It provides a rich set of detailed labor market and household related information collected prospectively on a yearly basis as well as retrospective employment and household information on a monthly basis for the time elapsed since the previous panel wave. The GSOEP comprises several samples for different parts of the population. We use the samples for West Germans, foreigners (immigrants from Turkey, Italy, Greece, Spain and Portugal and their offspring), and East Germans. Because foreigners and East Germans have been over-sampled compared to West Germans, we use design weights to adjust the sample sizes to the actual proportions in the German society.

All analyses will be based on labor market entrants identified as those individuals who left general education, vocational training[9] or tertiary education between 1984 and 1997[10], and who report to be full- or part-time employed in at least one later wave. We further restrict our sub-sample to individuals who started employment within 5 years after having left education and who where 35 years of age or younger at the time of finding their first employment position.

A few problems concerning the data need to be mentioned. First, it is very likely but not entirely sure that the labor market entry we observe for a given individual is indeed his or her first entry.[11] The detailed retrospective information we would need for this is not available in the GSOEP. Second, for almost 25 percent of the labor market entrants according to our definition above we do not know whether they started their employment with a fixed-term or permanent contract. This problem is related to the questionnaire and the respondents' understanding of apprenticeship contracts.[12] We had to exclude these missing cases from our analysis on the type of contract. However, for the analyses on the transition to unemployment and on family formation all cases are included, with the missing group being indicated by a dummy variable. Third, less than 5 percent of the individuals who find a job are self-employed; about half of them work without employees. Because of the small number of cases, we removed them from our analysis on the type of contract of the first job.

In Germany youngsters do seem to find a first job quite quickly. When the above definition of labor market entry is used (but without the restriction of entering within a five year period), we find that one year after leaving education already 84 percent of them have a full- or part-time employment position, while after two years the percentage has risen to 96 percent. We therefore do not study the timing of entry but only the type of first job that school leavers find and take. We use binominal logit analyses (Agresti, 1990; Aldrich and Nelson, 1984) to estimate the effects of explanatory variables on the odds of having a fixed-term or a permanent contract.

For the analysis on the transition to unemployment we use the monthly calendar of the GSOEP. We start to observe individuals when they entered their first job and follow up on them until they fall into unemployment for the first time. Individuals who never left employment up to their last interview and those who changed to another status like "back to school" or "on parental leave" are treated as right-censored. For the analysis of the transitions to first marriage and parenthood we restrict our sample to those having had a first job and observe them until they experience the event of interest; if not, we treat them as right-censored. For the transition to the first birth, in order to come closer to the actual timing of the decision to have a child, we do not consider the month of birth per se but the month of birth minus nine. For the analyses on family formation as well as on unemployment we use piecewise constant exponential models to estimate the effects of explanatory variables on the hazard rate (Blossfeld and Rohwer, 1995).

In all analyses we control for labor market entry cohort (1985-1989, 1990-1993, 1994-1997 or 1998), migration status and region (migrant, West Germany, East Germany), sex and educational level.[13] These variables are time-constant. Furthermore, we include class position[14] (Erikson and Goldthorpe, 1992), sector (public vs. private), working hours (part- or full-time) and also the type of contract[15] (permanent contract, fixed-term contract, self-employment, missing information). In the transition rate models these explanatory variables are allowed to vary over time, except for working hours and type of contract in the models on unemployment where they refer to the first employment position.

ANALYSIS

Entry into the labor market

The estimation results for both analyses – the logit models for type of contract at employment entry and the hazard rate models for the risk of unemployment – are reported in Table 3.3. We start with the models on type of contract.

In model A1 the labor market entry period, migration status, region (East/ West), sex, and occupational qualification were included to predict the odds of a fixed-term contract. In model A2 occupational class, working hours and sector (public vs. private) were introduced instead of occupational qualification.[16] In line with the changing macroeconomic situation we observe that individuals entering the labor market between 1990 and 1993 were less likely to receive a temporary position than those who entered between 1985 and 1990 or between 1994 and 1998. Thus, it seems that under favorable labor market circumstances fixed-term jobs are less prevalent. At the same time we find no indication that East Germans and migrants are more likely to work under a temporary contract.[17] Furthermore, for women our model A1 results show that they are as likely as men to receive a fixed-term contract at labor market entry. They seem to be even *less* likely to do so when occupational class and sector have been controlled for (model A2). This suggests that compared to men in the same position, sector or with the same working hours, women receive fixed-term contracts less often.

In accordance with our hypotheses we observe that labor market entrants without an apprenticeship or other qualified occupational training are more likely to start in a fixed-term position than those with an occupational qualification. Furthermore, in line with the results by Bielenski *et al.* (1994), graduates from a technical college or a university are also more likely to have a fixed-term job at the beginning of their career. This contradicts Breen's (1997) hypothesis that due to their qualification and the type of work they perform, employees with a strong bargaining power should receive a secure employment contract. As to working hours we find (model A2) that part-timers are more than twice[18] as likely as full-timers to work on a fixed-term basis, meaning that this group has to face insecurity not only in financial terms but also with respect to the prospective occupational career. It should be mentioned, though, that because part-time employment is not very common for labor market entrants in Germany, this group is numerically quite small (6.8 percent of the sample).

With respect to occupational class, we observe – in line with our hypotheses – that manual un- and semi-skilled workers have a risk of being temporary employed that is considerably (about 2.7 times) higher than among their skilled colleagues. However, there are no indications that fixed-term jobs are also more common for the lower routine non-manual occupations, which mostly comprise work that is rather easily supervised and which therefore – in theory at least –

Table 3.3   Type of contract at labor market entry (logistic regression models) and the transition to unemployment after the first employment (piecewise exponential transition rate models), Germany

	Type of contract		Transition to unemployment		
	Model A1	Model A2	Model B1	Model B2	Model B3
Constant	-1.52**	-1.67**			
Time since start of first job					
Up to 6 months			-6.50**	-6.35**	-6.99**
6 to 12 months			-6.17**	-6.02**	-6.93**
12 to 18 months			-5.55**	-5.40**	-6.46**
18 to 24 months			-6.18**	-6.02**	-6.95**
24 to 36 months			-6.28**	-6.11**	-7.00**
36 to 48 months			-6.45**	-6.28**	-7.09**
48 to 60 months			-6.40**	-6.21**	-6.94**
60 and more months			-6.59**	-6.38**	-7.07**
Employment entry period			-		
Between 1985 and 1989	0.29*	0.35*	-0.23+	-0.28*	-0.14
Between 1990 and 1993 (Ref.)	0.00	0.00	0.00	0.00	0.00
Between 1994 and 1997	0.50**	0.67**	0.06	0.06	0.21
Migration status/region					
German / West (Ref.)	0.00	0.00	0.00	0.00	0.00
Migrant / West	-0.11	-0.34	0.76**	0.41+	0.45*
German / East	-0.00	-0.16	0.59**	0.70**	0.45**
Sex					
Male (Ref.)	0.00	0.00	0.00	0.00	0.00
Female	-0.09	-0.26*	0.28*	0.31**	0.10
Type of contract at LM entry					
Permanent contract (Ref.)			0.00	0.00	0.00
Fixed-term contract			0.85**	0.88**	0.53**
Self-employed			-0.52	-0.45	-0.18
Working hours at LM entry					
Full-time (Ref.)		0.00	0.00	0.00	0.00
Part-time		0.83**	-0.19	-0.12	-0.26
Educational qualification					
Compulsory education without occupational qualification	0.53**			0.58**	
Compulsory educat. + occup. qualification (Ref.)	0.00			0.00	
Middle school / Abitur without occupational qualification	0.70**			-0.56*	
Middle school / Abitur with occupational qualification	-0.21			-0.30*	
Technical college / university degree	0.79**			-0.59**	

Table 3.3 continued

	Type of contract		Transition to unemployment		
	Model A1	Model A2	Model B1	Model B2	Model B3
Class position (EGP)					
Higher service class		0.58**			-0.72+
Lower service class		-0.40**			-0.35
Routine non-manual class		0.14			0.32
Lower routine non-manual cl.		0.07			0.77*
Self-employed		-			0.31
Qualified manual worker / technician (Ref.)		0.00			0.00
Un-/semi-skilled manual worker		1.00**			0.93**
Sector					
Private sector (Ref.)		0.00			0.00
Public sector		1.04**			0.00
Log-likelihood	-1212.09	-1167.52	-2249.25	-2230.47	-1942.27

Sources: Own calculations based on the German Socioeconomic Panel (GSOEP), waves 1984 to 1998; weighted to correct for different selection probabilities of East Germans, West Germans and migrants.

Notes
** Effect significant at $p < 0.01$
* Effect significant at $p < 0.05$
\+ Effect significant at $p < 0.10$

should be more at risk of bad labor contracts. Furthermore, incumbents of the *lower* service class have a lower risk of temporary employment than all others. This fits neatly with the idea that persons in a service employment relationship are better sheltered (Breen, 1997). At the same time, however, members of the *higher* service class start over-proportionally in a fixed-term position. This result holds even though the sector of employment has been controlled for. In this respect we find – as expected – that employees in the public sector have a considerably higher risk (about 2.8 times) of a temporary position than those in the private sector. Thus, the results do not unequivocally support the hypothesis that those in the service class are in general better protected against insecure employment contracts.

But this picture changes when we look at the risk of experiencing unemployment after the first employment spell. We estimated three separate models: in model B1 variables for labor market entry period, migration status, region, sex, type of contract and working hours were included; in model B2 indicators of occupational qualification were added; finally, in model B3 these qualification variables were substituted by occupational class and sector. Somewhat surprisingly, we do not find clear differences between the labor market entry cohorts. We speculate that it is not so much the period of entry, but rather the current calendar time while being in a job that is relevant for the risk of unemployment. Migrants apparently have a higher risk of unemployment than West Germans, a fact that cannot be simply attributed to differences in occupational qualification or class (although the effects do become somewhat weaker when these variables are taken into account in models B2 and B3). The unemployment risk is also higher for East Germans in all models. This suggests that the turbulence of the East German labor market exerts a genuine effect on the unemployment risk which is not due to the specific educational or occupational composition of the work force. Furthermore, according to our estimations, the unemployment risk of women is higher than that of men even if occupational qualification is taken into account. As additional analyses revealed, these differences are – surprisingly – mainly a result of a higher unemployment risk for *West German* women. When occupational class is controlled for the differences between men and women disappear, which means that women are more likely to be employed in class positions with a relatively high unemployment risk. Finally, and in line with our hypothesis, we find that employees with fixed-term contracts indeed face a higher risk of unemployment than those with permanent contracts. This means that those with initial temporal uncertainty are also at risk of suffering economic insecurity.

According to model B2, individuals with only compulsory schooling and no occupational qualification face the highest risk of unemployment. This risk lowers significantly, however, for employees with completed compulsory schooling and an apprenticeship. Individuals with higher general school levels are even better protected, no matter whether they have no occupational qualification at all, an apprenticeship or a university degree. Employees who started in a part-time position have a transition rate to unemployment that is not any higher than for full-time employees. This fits with the fact that part-timers (with more than 15 hours) enjoy the same dismissal protection as full-timers. With respect to occupational class, our analysis suggests a clear pattern (model B3): un- and semi-skilled manual workers as well as lower routine non-manual employees have a clearly higher risk of unemployment than skilled manual workers and technicians. For the secondary sector of the economy this fits with the idea that the low-skilled part of the work force is the first to be laid off when new technologies are introduced. Also, in general, low skilled (manual and non-manual) workers are easiest to substitute since firms make only minor training investments in them. Best shielded against unemployment are the members of the service classes, in particular the higher service class. This is again well in accordance with our hypotheses. Finally, when it comes to the risk of unemployment, working in the public sector does not seem to offer greater security than working in the private sector. Further analyses showed that this is a result of two counteracting effects. Public sector employees with a permanent contract are better shielded against unemployment than their colleagues in the private sector. At the same time, however, public sector employees with a fixed-term contract have a higher risk of unemployment than those in the private sector (Kurz and Stein-hage, 2001).

Transition to first marriage and first birth

We now turn to the analysis of the transition to first marriage and parenthood. As these two transitions are strongly interrelated (Hullen, 2001), we discuss their results simultaneously. We employ piecewise constant exponential models, pursue the analyses for men and women separately, and report results for three different specifications.[19] In each specification we control for migration status, region, labor market entry period, age, employment status, type of contract and working hours. In addition to these, we include in specification 2 educational qualification, while in specification 3 class position and sector instead. Because of the high correlation between education and class position, we do not use both indicators together in one specification. Table 3.4 presents the results on women's entry into first marriage and parenthood, whereas Table 3.5 shows the corresponding findings for men. We will concentrate our discussion on those variables that have been introduced as indicators of temporal and economic uncertainty. Moreover, we investigate whether and to what extent the impact of temporal and economic insecurity differs between men and women, on the one hand, and between the two transitions, on the other.

As can be seen from table 3.4, compared to full-time employed women, those in education[20] seem to be the least likely to enter first marriage. We assume that the latter are investing in their job career and trying to avoid potential conflicts that might arise once they get married. The coefficient for education is even stronger in the model on the transition to the first birth. This is plausible since having a baby makes for even more conflicts with an employment career than being married (Blossfeld, 1995). We had hypothesized that in contrast to more career-oriented women who are in further education or full-time employment, family-oriented women who are not employed (housewives) or employed in a part-time position are more likely to enter marriage or have a first birth. Our hypotheses are only partly confirmed. We observe that part-time employed women are indeed somewhat more likely than full-time employed women to get married (an effect that is statistically significant only when educational level and occupational class are not controlled for), and definitely more likely to have a baby. However, we find no such effects for women who are not employed. This is probably due to the fact that it is very unusual for women in this early phase of their employment career to exit employment (if they do not have children yet). For instance, only 4 percent of the female respondents included in the analyses are at any point in time not employed (and not looking for a job).

Consistent with the thesis that women have the option of taking up the alternative role of a housewife/mother or of trying to acquire more security through marriage, our results show that unemployed women are more likely to get married (effects significant in specifications 1 and 3, but not in 2). The coefficients are also positive but insignificant for the transition to first birth. The fact that the effects for marriage are clearer supports the view that marriage for women in

LIVERPOOL JOHN MOORES UNIVERSITY
LEARNING SERVICES

Table 3.4   Piecewise exponential model of the transition to first marriage and first birth (after having entered first employment), women, Germany

	Marriage			First birth		
	1	*2*	*3*	*1*	*2*	*3*
Periods						
Up to 12 months	-16.01**	-15.96**	-16.24**	-18.20**	-18.75**	-18.22**
12 to 24 montns	-15.52**	-15.46**	-15.84**	-17.47**	-18.03**	-17.58**
24 to 36 months	-15.61**	-15.54**	-15.94**	-17.89**	-18.45**	-18.01**
36 to 48 months	-15.26*	-15.17**	-15.56**	-17.77**	-18.32**	-17.84**
48 to 60 months	-15.41**	-15.31**	-15.71**	-17.64**	-18.18**	-17.72**
60 to 72 months	-15.49**	-15.37**	-15.80**	-17.41**	-17.94**	-17.46**
72 and more months	-15.91**	-15.75**	-16.16**	-17.84**	-18.35**	-17.86**
Migration status/region						
German / West (Ref.)	0.00	0.00	0.00	0.00	0.00	0.00
Migrant / West	0.48*	0.47+	0.43+	0.17	0.06	0.09
German / East	-0.25	-0.24	-0.30	-0.02	0.04	0.04
Start of first job						
1984-88	-0.04	-0.03	-0.06	0.09	0.09	0.10
1989-93 (Ref.)	0.00	0.00	0.00	0.00	0.00	0.00
1994-98	-0.29	-0.28	-0.31+	-0.52*	-0.51*	-0.53*
Age	0.79**	0.79**	0.79**	0.93**	0.98**	0.96**
Age^2	-0.01**	-0.01**	-0.01**	-0.02**	-0.02**	-0.02**

Table 3.4 continued

	Marriage			First birth		
	1	2	3	1	2	3
Employment status						
Employed (Ref.)	0.00	0.00	0.00	0.00	0.00	0.00
In education	-0.81**	-0.77*	-0.64+	-1.32**	-1.28**	-1.58**
Unemployed	0.46+	0.41	0.64+	0.44	0.33	0.18
Not employed	-0.53	-0.55	-0.36	0.30	0.13	0.03
Type of contract						
Permanent contract (Ref.)	0.00	0.00	0.00	0.00	0.00	0.00
Fixed-term contract	-0.11	-0.15	-0.17	-0.27	-0.31	-0.37
Self-employed	0.29	0.27	0.29	-0.45	-0.49	-0.86+
Missing values	0.02	0.03	-0.23	0.06	0.04	-0.31+
Working hours						
Full-time (Ref.)	0.00	0.00	0.00	0.00	0.00	0.00
Part-time	0.42+	0.37	0.27	0.89**	0.84**	0.81**
Educational qualification						
Compulsory education without occupational qualification (Ref.)		0.00		0.00	0.00	0.00
Compulsory educat. + occupat. qualification		-0.20			-0.35+	
Middle sch./Abitur w/out occupat. qualif.		-0.52*			-0.72**	
Middle school/Abitur + occupat. qualif.		-0.18			-0.53**	
Technical college / university degree		0.09			-0.26	

Table 3.4 continued

	Marriage			First birth		
	1	*2*	*3*	*1*	*2*	*3*
Class position (EGP)						
Higher service class			0.06			0.15
Lower service class			-0.03			-0.50*
Routine non-manual class			0.03			-0.56*
Lower routine non-manual class			0.30			-0.36
Qualified manual worker/technician			0.07			-0.16
Un- /semi-skilled manual worker (Ref.)			0.00			0.00
Sector						
Private sector (Ref.)			0.00			0.00
Public sector			0.02			-0.27
Log-likelihood	-2124.95	-2121.03	-2074.81	-1988.16	-1982.52	-1928.95
Number of events	359	359	359	330	330	330
Number of episodes	11263	11263	11263	12858	12858	12858

Sources: Own calculations based on the German Socioeconomic Panel (GSOEP), waves 1984 to 1998; weighted to correct for different selection probabilities of East Germans, West Germans and migrants.

Notes

** Effect significant at p < 0.01
* Effect significant at p < 0.05
+ Effect significant at p < 0.10

such a situation might function as a safety net. In contrast, there seems to be no impact of the type of contract on either the transition to first marriage or to first parenthood. This is still in accordance with our prediction that where a traditional breadwinner model exists, as in Germany, the temporal uncertainty of a fixed-term contract should not impede family formation for women. It is also worth mentioning that self-employed women have a lower transition rate to first motherhood once occupational class is controlled for (specification 3). This is plausible if one assumes that self-employment requires a high input of time, especially in the beginning of a career, which is not be easily compatible with having a baby.

As regards educational qualifications, our results show almost no differences with respect to the likelihood of entering marriage.[21] This is in accordance with the view that marriage for young birth cohorts should not change the sexual division of labor in the household, thereby making opportunity cost arguments less relevant. In contrast, looking at first birth, we find that women with a medium educational level (compulsory education with occupational qualification and middle school/Abitur with or without occupational qualification) are significantly less likely to experience this transition than low-educated women. This result is consistent with Becker's opportunity cost argument. Still, for women with the highest educational level (technical college or university degree) we do not observe any clear differential. Again we speculate that this might be the result of two opposing influences. Women with a university degree face higher opportunity costs if they interrupt their career for having a baby, but at the same time they might – in contrast to women with lower levels of education – conceive a child rather shortly after labor market entry (Blossfeld, 1995; Blossfeld and Huninink, 1991).

With respect to class positions we again find no effects on the transition to first marriage. For the transition to first birth, however, the results indicate that women belonging to the lower service class or to the routine non-manual class are less likely to become mothers than un- or semi-skilled manual workers, but the transition rate for women from the higher service class is not significantly different from the reference group. Finally, for the transitions to marriage and first child it does not matter whether women work in the public or in the private sector.

Regarding the other control variables in our various specifications, the results point to the following. There is no empirical evidence supporting the hypothesis that East German women are less likely than West German women to make either of the two long-term commitments. This is true even if we do not control for positions of insecurity (figures not shown). A possible explanation for this rather unexpected result could be that child-care facilities remain more widespread in East Germany and that women in that part of the country are more job oriented and willing to combine full-time work with childraising than their West German counterparts. While compared to Germans migrant women show a higher rate of entering first marriage, we do not find such differences for entering first parenthood. The former effect might reflect a greater prevalence of the traditional partnership model in the migrant population. Finally, it should be mentioned that the coefficients for age and age squared reveal that the transition rates to first marriage and parenthood rise with age but less and less so at higher ages. With respect to labor market entry cohorts we hardly find any significant impact on entry into first marriage. However, our findings show that women who entered the labor market between 1994 and 1998 are less likely to become a mother. But this might simply result from the fact that these women have been observed for only a rather short time period.

We now turn to the results for men (table 3.5). In our hypotheses we postulated that men who cannot provide a solid economic basis or who are in positions that make future developments uncertain should be less likely to get married and become a father. Our results give some support to this hypothesis. In contrast to women, being unemployed makes it clearly more difficult for men to make the transition to marriage and fatherhood. However, compared to having a full-time, permanent position (the reference group), being in education or not employed does hardly seem to reduce the transition rate to marriage, but more so the one to fatherhood.[22] While the latter finding is in line with our expectations, the former requires further consideration. Men in education are probably into further education, which might increase their career prospects and at the same time their attractiveness as marriage partners. This might thus explain the lack of a clear effect on the transition to marriage. For the results on men who are not employed – mainly due to military service (about 15 percent of our sample) – we have no straightforward interpretation. Furthermore, we cannot sustain our hypothesis on the impact of temporal uncertainty as a result of working on a fixed-term contract. Men in these positions are about equally likely to make the transition to marriage or fatherhood as those in permanent positions. This unexpected finding might result from the fact that employees with fixed-term contracts are very heterogeneous with respect to their human capital, class position and, consequently, their job prospects. Finally, we do not find any differences between part- and full-timers regarding the transitions under study. Men on part-time posts do seem to be less likely to make these long-term commitments but none of the effects is statistically significant. This is probably due to the fact that only a small proportion of men (about 7 percent) worked part-time during the observation period.

Switching to the effects of educational level, we find that men with the lowest level of education (compulsory education and no occupational qualification) have a higher transition rate to first marriage than those with medium levels. This result is consistent with the timing hypothesis, but not with the one on economic insecurity. However, we should keep in mind that timing and education effects cannot be disentangled properly because of the way our models are specified.[23] Furthermore, the coefficient for technical college and university graduates is not significantly different from the reference group, thus giving no support to any of our hypotheses. With respect to the transition to first birth we do not observe any particular pattern for the education effects. When we turn to the effects of occupational class, the results mirror to a large extent those of education. In consonance with the timing hypothesis, un- or semi-skilled manual workers tend to marry earlier than qualified manual workers. But in the case of

Table 3.5   Piecewise exponential model of the transition to first marriage and first birth (after having entered first employment), men, Germany

	Marriage			First birth		
	1	2	3	1	2	3
Periods						
Up to 12 months	-24.03**	-24.07**	-23.32**	-23.59**	-23.89**	-23.61**
12 to 24 months	-24.10**	-24.14**	-23.37**	-23.38**	-23.68**	-23.39**
24 to 36 months	-24.66**	-24.70**	-23.93**	-23.55**	-23.86**	-23.57**
36 to 48 months	-24.42**	-24.46**	-23.68**	-23.62**	-23.93**	-23.63**
48 to 60 months	-24.41**	-24.44**	-23.65**	-23.51**	-23.82**	-23.54**
60 to 72 months	-24.74**	-24.78**	-23.97**	-23.60**	-23.92**	-23.61**
72 and more months	-24.71**	-24.76**	-23.91**	-23.70**	-24.03**	-23.70**
Migration status/region						
German / West (Ref.)	0.00	0.00	0.00	0.00	0.00	0.00
Migrant / West	0.84**	0.72**	0.75**	1.10**	1.03**	1.08**
German / East	-0.14	-0.11	-0.12	-0.01	0.02	-0.02
Start of first job						
1984-88	0.16	0.15	0.16	0.18	0.16	0.16
1989-93 (Ref.)	0.00	0.00	0.00	0.00	0.00	0.00
1994-98	-0.23	-0.25	-0.21	-0.30	-0.31	-0.28
Age	1.26**	1.26**	1.23**	1.18**	1.20**	1.19**
Age²	-0.02**	-0.02**	-0.02**	-0.02**	-0.02**	-0.02**

Table 3.5 continued

	Marriage			First birth		
	1	2	3	1	2	3
Employment status						
Employed (Ref.)	0.00	0.00	0.00	0.00	0.00	0.00
In education	-0.32	-0.28	-0.57*	-0.41+	-0.35	-0.54+
Unemployed	-1.39*	-1.38*	-1.61**	-0.79+	-0.80+	-0.90+
Not employed	-0.75	-0.73	-1.00*	-1.45*	-1.45*	-1.56*
Type of contract						
Permanent contract (Ref.)	0.00	0.00	0.00	0.00	0.00	0.00
Fixed-term contract	0.00	-0.01	-0.13	-0.02	-0.01	-0.13
Self-employed	-0.40	-0.38	-0.57*	-0.34	-0.31	-0.42
Missing values	0.04	0.03	0.07	-0.36+	-0.38+	-0.33+
Working hours						
Full-time (Ref.)	0.00	0.00	0.00	0.00	0.00	0.00
Part-time	-0.90	-0.89	-0.93	-0.15	-0.12	-0.12
Educational qualification						
Compulsory education without occupational qualification (Ref.)		0.00			0.00	
Compulsory educat. + occupat. qualification		-0.43*			-0.23	
Middle sch./Abitur w/out occupat. qualif.		-0.77**			-0.70*	
Middle school/Abitur + occupat. qualif.		-0.37+			-0.30	
Technical college / university degree		-0.27			-0.29	

Table 3.5 continued

	Marriage			First birth		
	1	2	3	1	2	3
Class position (EGP)						
Higher service class			-0.02			-0.01
Lower service class			-0.18			-0.24
Routine non-manual class			-0.48			-0.29
Lower routine non-manual class			-0.56			-0.83
Qualified manual worker/technician			-0.34+			-0.04
Un- /semi-skilled manual worker (Ref.)			0.00			0.00
Sector						
Private sector (Ref.)			0.00			0.00
Public sector			0.30+			0.32+
Log-likelihood	-2062.12	-2057.30	-2057.19	-2124.16	-2121.29	-2119.16
Number of events	341	341	341	370	370	370
Number of episodes	16267	16267	16267	18283	18283	18283

Sources: Own calculations based on the German Socioeconomic Panel (GSOEP), waves 1984 to 1998; weighted to correct for different selection probabilities of East Germans, West Germans and migrants.

Notes

** Effect significant at p < 0.01
* Effect significant at p < 0.05
+ Effect significant at p < 0.10

the transition to fatherhood we do not find any differences between the class positions. Finally, in line with our hypothesis, men working in the public sector show a higher transition rate to first marriage and to first fatherhood, which supports the view that the public sector offers more security and long-term prospects provided one has a permanent contract.

Let us now turn to the results for the other control variables in our model specifications. As for women, our results do not lend support to the hypothesis that East German men are less likely than West German men to make either of the two long-term commitments. On the other hand, male migrants show a higher rate of entering first marriage than Germans and they are also more likely to become fathers or to enter fatherhood earlier than West German men. For both transitions the coefficients for age and age squared imply again an increase with age followed by a flattening out. With respect to labor market entry cohorts we do not find any impact on either first marriage or first birth.

SUMMARY AND CONCLUSIONS

To summarize, our models for the type of contract only partially support the view that employees with comparatively high bargaining power are the best sheltered. University graduates and members of the higher service class are as likely to receive a fixed-term contract as are un- and semi-skilled manual workers. We suspect that the reason lies in the heterogeneity of temporary positions. On the one hand, they are found in occupations where an initial training period is likely or even obligatory. These fixed-term contracts – or rather, training contracts – are quite independent of the bargaining power of the employee in question. For example, physicians have a first obligatory fixed-term employment phase which in fact is a practical training period. Also other university graduates (e.g., those with a diploma in business administration) often receive a temporary training position (as "trainee") in their first employment with a company before they are hired on a permanent basis. On the other hand, there are groups who receive a fixed-term contract because of their bad bargaining position. These might be employees without occupational qualifications but also higher qualified labor market entrants who have been trained in fields with an oversupply of qualified workers. Thus, ideally we should distinguish between these two categories – trainee contracts on the one hand, and regular fixed-term contracts, on the other. But the GSOEP does not allow to distinguish between these two types of non-permanent contracts. Finally, it should be mentioned that employment positions in the German public sector are very often fixed-term, quite independently of their hierarchical position and, thus, bargaining power. However, we controlled for this factor in our analyses.

In contrast to the results on the type of contract, we find a clear stratification of the unemployment risk for the labor market entry cohorts from the mid-1980s to the end of the 1990s. General and occupational qualification, class position, gender as well as region (East-West) and migration status seem all to matter for the risk of experiencing an episode of unemployment. This contradicts any claim of an individualization of labor market risks in German society.

Our basic prediction with respect to the transitions to first marriage and parenthood was that as long as a traditional breadwinner model is still prevailing, positions of insecurity – be it temporal or economic – should matter mostly for men but not for women (Oppenheimer, 1988). At the same time, following Gary Becker (1981), we argued that women with high human capital should be less likely to start a marriage or have a baby. The empirical evidence for both predictions is mixed. Beginning with the latter we find that women in further educational training – thereby investing in their occupational career – are indeed less prone to marry or to have children. Also women with a medium level of education have a lower transition rate to motherhood than lower educated women. But it is worth noting that this does not hold for the transition to first marriage, which thus lends support to the thesis that today marriage does not typically involve a conflict between women's labor market participation and the division of domestic tasks (Blossfeld, 1995). But the human capital argument is not unequivocally supported by our data. For instance, highly educated women with a university degree and also higher service class members do *not* have a lower rate to motherhood. This finding is consistent with Blossfeld and Huinink's (1991) argument that highly educated women might simply postpone family formation, but move quickly to motherhood when they have left the educational system.

In line with our predictions that positions of insecurity should not lead to a lower transition rate to marriage and parenthood for women, we find that part-time working women are indeed more likely to conceive a child than those working full-time. Moreover, women with a fixed-term contract seem to be as inclined as those in a more secure position to make the transition to marriage and motherhood, whereas unemployed women seem to be somewhat more inclined (but statistically not significant). Thus, this is clear empirical evidence that when it comes to family formation, positions of insecurity do not have a negative impact for women. This indicates that the male breadwinner model is still well in place in Germany.

In contrast, our corresponding analysis for men gives some support to the hypothesis that men in insecure positions are less likely to enter marriage and fatherhood. Unemployed and not employed men (mainly those in military service) facing economic as well as temporal insecurity are indeed less likely to become fathers, with the unemployed also less likely to marry. At the same time, however, we do not find empirical evidence for the impact of temporal uncertainty as a result of a fixed-term contract. Neither do men in economically less rewarding positions such as un- or semi-skilled manual workers have a lower transition rate to family formation. If anything, theirs is higher, which points to an earlier timing of partnership and family formation in their life course. Thus, all in all, our findings indicate that it really matters whether a man is employed or not, but *not* what type of employment position he has. Nevertheless, two cautionary notes are in order. First, we are not able to determine whether different educational or class groups have different timing patterns or different probabilities of family formation. Thus, we cannot exclude the possibility that un- or semi-skilled workers have in the end a lower probability of marrying, as studies on marriage patterns suggest (see e.g. Blossfeld and Timm, 1997). Second, as mentioned above, employees with fixed-term contracts are a very heterogeneous group. They are not only found in occupations with low bargaining power, but also – often as a type of training period – in occupations with secure employment perspectives. These latter types of contract do not imply temporal uncertainty and should, therefore, not have a negative effect on long-term commitments such as marriage or parenthood.

NOTES

1   For an overview of the general and vocational education system in Germany, see Kurz and Steinhage (2001).

2   With more than 90 percent, the degree of employer organization in Germany is exceptionally high (Fuchs and Schettkat, 2000: 211).

3   Fixed-term contracts had not been limited to specific conditions already before in firms with up to 5 employees and for contracts of up to 6 months (Bielenski et al., 1994: 2).

4   Of course, this does not preclude that a part-time position (and the resulting economic dependency) has been chosen voluntarily. As in many other countries, part-time work permits German women to balance paid work and their commitments in the family domain more easily than full-time work (Blossfeld and Hakim, 1997).

5   In our analyses, however, we look at this as a stepwise process: the first position in the labor market and the likelihood of becoming unemployed thereafter. For details, see section "Entry into the labor market".

6   We do not investigate self-employment without employees as another form of precarious work in this paper, since the number of such cases among the labor market entrants in the GSOEP is too low to justify an analysis.

7   From 1979 to 1986 the maternal leave legislation allowed for an employment interruption of 6 months after the birth of a child. In 1986 the parental leave legislation was introduced, making it possible also for fathers to take up the leave (or part of it). The maximum duration of the parental leave was 10 months in the beginning; after several extensions it has been 36 months since January 1992 (Kurz, 1998).

8   Oppenheimer's (1988) interest is in the *searching process* for a marriage partner as well as in the subsequent transition to marriage. In the context of our analysis, only the second aspect is relevant.

9   It should be stressed that vocational training (predominantly apprenticeships) is thus considered as part of the education period and not as first employment.

10   East Germans are observed only from 1990 onwards.

11   For the sake of simplicity we will still use the term "first employment".

12   The question on the type of contract – fixed-term vs. permanent – was in most waves asked only if the respondent had started a new employment since the last interview. If apprentices continued to work in the firm where they had received their vocational training and if they considered themselves as having been employed while being apprentices, they did not answer the question on the type of contract.

13   For educational level we distinguish the categories compulsory education without occupational qualification, compulsory education with occupational qualification,

Middle School or Abitur without occupational qualification, Middle School or Abitur with occupational qualification, and technical college or university degree.

14 For occupational class the categories are higher service class, lower service class, routine non-manual class, lower routine non-manual class, qualified manual worker/technician, un- or semi-skilled manual worker, and being self-employed.

15 In the models on the type of first contract this variable is, of course, excluded.

16 We did not include both educational qualification and occupational class because of the rather high correlations between the two groups of variables.

17 As further analyses showed, this is true even if educational qualification or class position is not taken into account.

18 This was calculated from the coefficient for part-time work, taking $\exp(0.83) = 2,29$.

19 We also specified a fourth model where we added information on pregnancy and the presence of children in the analysis of the transition to first marriage, and on marital status in the analysis of the transition to first birth. Since we are primarily interested here in the impact of positions of insecurity and not so much in the well-known effects of children or marital status, we do not present this model here.

20 Since the sample is restricted to respondents who have already entered the labor market, 'being in education' refers to persons who have taken up some kind of education or occupational training thereafter. Short-term education or training of less than six months has not been counted.

21 Women with middle school or Abitur and no further occupational qualification seem to be less likely to make the transition to marriage.

22 The effect of being in education on the transition to fatherhood reaches conventional levels of significance for the first and the last model specification, but not for the second where we control for educational level.

23 We introduced interaction effects between age and education but these were not significant. This might be caused by the low number of cases.

BIBLIOGRAPHY

Agresti, A. (1990) *Categorical Data Analysis*, New York, Chichester, Bisbane: Wiley.

Alba, R. D., Handl, J. and Müller, W. (1994) 'Ethnische Ungleichheit im Bildungssystem', *KZfSS*, 46(2): 209-237.

Aldrich, J. H. and Nelson, F. D. (1984) *Linear Probability, Logit, and Probit Models*, Newbury Park: Sage.

Becker, G. S. (1981) *A treatise on the Family*, Cambridge, Massachusetts, London: Harvard University Press.

Bernardi, F. (2000) 'Globalization, recommodification and social inequality: changing patterns of early careers in Italy', GLOBALIFE Working Paper No. 7, Faculty of Sociology, University of Bielefeld.

Bielenski, H., Kohler, B. and Schreiber-Kittl, M. (1994) *Befristete Beschäftigung und Arbeitsmarkt. Empirische Untersuchung über befristete Arbeitsverträge nach dem Beschäftigungsförderungsgesetz* (BeschFG 1985/90), München: Bundesministerium für Arbeit und Sozialordnung.

Bispinck, R. (1997) 'Deregulierung, Differenzierung und Dezentralisierung des Flächentarifvertrags. Eine Bestandsaufnahme neuer Entwicklungstendenzen der Tarifpolitik', *WSI-Mitteilungen*, 50(8): 551-561.

Blossfeld, H.-P. (2002) 'Globalization, Social Inequality and the Role of Country-Specific Institutions', in P. Conceicao, M. V. Heitor, and B.-A. Lundvall (eds) *Innovation, Competence Building and Social Cohesion in Europe: Towards a Learning Society*, Cheltenham/Lyme: Edward Elgar.

Blossfeld, H.-P. (1995) *The new role of women. Family formation in modern societies*, Boulder: Westview Press.

Blossfeld, H.-P. and Hakim, C. (1997) *Between Equalization and Marginalization: Women Working Part-Time in Europe and the United States of America*, New York: Oxford University Press.

Blossfeld, H.-P. and Huinink, J. (1991) 'Human capital investments or norms of role transition? How women's schooling and career affect the process of family formation', *American Journal of Sociology*, 97(1): 148-163.

Blossfeld, H.-P. and Rohwer, G. (1997) 'Part-time work in West Germany', in H.-P. Blossfeld and C. Hakim (eds) *Between equalization and marginalization. Women working part-time in Europe and the United States of Amerika*, Oxford: Oxford University Press.

Blossfeld, H.-P. and Rohwer, G. (1995) *Techniques of Event History Modeling. New Approaches to Causal Modeling*, New Jersey: Lawrence Erlbaum

Blossfeld, H.-P. and Timm, A. (1997) 'Der Einfluß des Bildungssystems auf den Heiratsmarkt', *KZfSS*, 49: 440-476.

Bowers, N., Sonnet, A. and Bardone, L. (1998) *Background report. Giving young people a good start: the experience of OECD countries*, Paris: OECD.

Brauns, H., Gangl, M. and Scherer, S. (1999) 'Education and Unemployment: Patterns of Labour Market Entry in France, the United Kingdom and West Germany', Arbeitspapiere 6, Mannheimer Zentrum für Europäische Sozialforschung.

Breen, R. (1997) 'Risk, recommodification and stratification', *Sociology*, 31(3): 473-489.

Erikson, R. and Goldthorpe, J. (1992) *The Constant Flux. A Study of Class Mobility in Industrial Societies*, Oxford: Calderon Press.

Esping-Andersen, G. (1993) *Changing classes*, London: Sage.

Esping-Andersen, G. (1999) *Social foundations of postindustrial economies*, Oxford: Oxford University Press.

Franz, W., Inkmann, J., Pohlmeier, W. and Zimmermann, V. (1997) 'Young and out in Germany: on the youths' chances of labour market entry in Germany', Working Paper 6212, National Bureau of Economic Research. Cambridge.

Fuchs, S. and Schettkat, R. (2000) 'Germany: a regulated flexibility', in G. Esping-Andersen and M. Regini (eds) *Why deregulate labour markets?*, Oxford: Oxford University Press: 211-243.

Geißler, R. (1996) *Die Sozialstruktur Deutschlands. Zur gesellschaftlichen Entwicklung mit einer Zwischenbilanz zur Vereinigung*, Opladen: Westdeutscher Verlag.

Hakim, C. (2000) *Work-lifestyle choices in the 21st century. Preference theory*, Oxford: Oxford University Press.

Hanefeld, U. (1987) *Das Sozio-ökonomische Panel - Grundlagen und Konzeption*, Frankfurt/New York: Campus.

Huinink, J. and Wagner, M. (1995) 'Partnerschaft, Ehe und Familie in der DDR', in J. Huinink et al. (eds) *Kollektiv und Eigensinn*, Berlin: Akademie-Verlag.

Hullen, G. (2001) 'Transition to adulthood in Germany', in M. Corijn and E. Klijzing (eds) *Transitions to adulthood in Europe*, Dordrecht: Kluwer Academic Publishers.

Jürgens, U., Malsch, T. and Dohse, K. (1993) *Breaking from Taylorism: changing forms of work in the automobile industry*, Cambridge: Cambridge University Press.

Kurz, K. (1998) *Das Erwerbsverhalten von Frauen in der intensiven Familienphase. Ein Vergleich zwischen Müttern in der Bundesrepublik Deutschland und in den USA*, Opladen: Leske+Budrich.

Kurz, K. and Steinhage, N. (2001) 'Global competition and labour market restructuring: The transition into the labour market in Germany', GLOBALIFE Working Paper No. 15, Faculty of Sociology, University of Bielefeld.

Leicht, R. (2000) 'Die "neuen Selbständigen" arbeiten alleine: Wachstum und Struktur der Solo-Selbständigen in Deutschland', *IGA - Zeitschrift für Klein- und Mittelunternehmen*, 48(2): 75-90.

Marsden, D. (1995) 'Deregulation or cooperation? The future of Europe's labour markets', *Labour* (IIRA), 49: 67-91.

Maurice, M., Sellier, F. and Silvestre, J.-J. (1986) *The social foundations of industrial powers: a comparison of France and Germany*, Cambridge: MIT Pr.

Mayer, K. U. (1997) 'Notes on the comparative political economy of life courses', *Comparative Social Research*, 16: 203-226.

Meyers, M., Gornick, J. and Ross, K. (1999) 'Public childcare, parental leave, and employment', in D. Sainsbury (ed.) *Gender and Welfare State Regimes*, Oxford: University Press.

Müller, W., Steinmann, S. and Ell, R. (1998) 'Education and Labour-Market Entry in Germany', in Y. Shavit and W. Müller (eds) *From School to Work. A Comparative Study of Educational Qualifications and Occupational Destinations*, Oxford: Clarendon Press.

OECD. (1998) *Employment Outlook*, Paris: OECD.

Oppenheimer, V. K. (1988) 'A theory of marriage timing', *American Journal of Sociology*, 94(3): 563-591.

Seifert, W. (1992) 'Die zweite Ausländergeneration in der Bundesrepublik. Längsschnittbeobachtungen in der Berufseinstiegsphase', *KZfSS*, 44: 677-696.

Sommer, T., Klijzing, E. and Mills, M. (2000) 'Partnership formation in a globalizing world: the impact of uncertainty in East and West Germany', GLOBALIFE Working Paper No. 9, Faculty of Sociology, University of Bielefeld.

Soskice, D. (1999) 'Divergent production regimes: Coordinated and uncoordinated market economies in the 1980s and 1990s', in H. Kitschelt, P. Lange, G. Marks and J. D. Stephens (eds) *Continuity and change in contemporary capitalism*, Cambridge: Cambridge University Press.

Strohmeier, K. P. and Kuijsten, A. (1997) 'Family life and family policies in Europe: an introduction', in F.-X. Kaufmann, A. Kuijsten, H.-J. Schulze and K. P. Strohmeier (eds) *Family life and family policies in Europe*, Oxford: Clarendon Press.

Winkelmann, R. (1996) 'Employment prospects and skill acquisition of apprenticeship-trained workers in Germany', *Industrial and Labour Relations Review*, 49(4): 658-672.

Wirth, H. and Lüttinger, P. (1998) 'Klassenspezifische Heiratsbeziehungen im Wandel? Die Klassenzugehörigkeit vor Ehepartner 1970 und 1993', *KZfSS*, 50: 47-77.

4 Transition from youth to adulthood in the Netherlands

Aart C. Liefbroer

INTRODUCTION

Globalization is by no means a new phenomenon to Dutch society. Due to its strategic position in North-Western Europe, international trade relationships formed the backbone of the Dutch economy in past and present. In that respect, the Netherlands have been integrated into the global economic system for more than four centuries (De Vries and Van der Woude, 1997). Four centuries ago, the Netherlands was a country that accumulated its wealth by international trade. Ships brought cargo from all across the world to Amsterdam from where these goods were further distributed across the European continent.

Viewed from this perspective, not much seems to have changed. Nowadays, the Dutch economy still depends to a large degree on international trade relationships, with Rotterdam having replaced Amsterdam as the world's most important port. However, such a view would be too superficial for a number of reasons. First, in their history the Dutch have also experienced the seamy side of their openness to global economic influences. After losing its dominant position in international trade to the English late in the seventeenth century, the Netherlands gradually declined to a nation of marginal importance both politically and economically. Thus, it can be argued that the Netherlands have become familiar with the vicissitudes of globalization at a very early stage. One might even speculate that this experience has contributed to the early development of an elaborated welfare system to protect citizens against the uncertainties of economic life. Second, the current process of globalization is different from the one experienced by the Dutch during their Golden Age. Then, the Dutch controlled much of international trade, whereas nowadays they are much more dependent on the actions of other international players, governments and corporate actors alike. The Dutch do not set the rules of the globalization game any longer, but have to abide by them. In the current era of globalization, the Netherlands' openness to the global economy both holds promises and poses threats.

In this chapter, the impact of globalization on the entry into adulthood of Dutch young adults will be discussed. A first question that needs answering is to what extent Dutch society is touched by globalization. To what extent are the most important features of globalization present in Dutch society? This question will be discussed in the section "Globalizing influences on Dutch society". Next, attention has to be paid to specific features of Dutch society that mediate the impact of globalizing forces. As Mills and Blossfeld ascertain in the introductory chapter of this volume, the impact of globalization is path dependent. It depends on the institutional arrangements, economic conditions and cultural settings that exist in the countries that are faced with the challenges of globalization. The section "The institutional context of the transition to adulthood" deals with the peculiarities of Dutch society that mediate the impact of globalization. After these preliminaries, I turn in the section "The impact of globalization on the transition to adulthood in the Netherlands" to a discussion of the changes that have occurred in the transition to adulthood in the Netherlands (see also Jansen and Liefbroer, 2001) and the extent to which these changes could be related to the process of globalization. In the section "Data" I briefly discuss the data sources and methods I have used to study this relationship. In the section "The educational and labor market positions of young adults", changes in the entry into the 'public' domain of education and employment are dealt with, whereas in the section "The impact of globalization on entry into family roles among young adults" the focus is on changes in the 'private' domain of family life, namely, partnering and parenting. Finally, the section "Discussion" contains a discussion of the results of this study and an interpretation of them in terms of the potential impact of globalization on the transition to adulthood in the Netherlands.

GLOBALIZING INFLUENCES ON DUTCH SOCIETY

In the introductory chapter of this volume, Mills and Blossfeld suggest that globalization includes four different aspects: (i) economic globalization, (ii) network globalization, (iii) globalization as a discourse, and (iv) political globalization. From the Dutch perspective, in particular the first two aspects seem relevant.

Trade flows, foreign investments, the emergence of multinational corporations and international financial flows are important indicators of economic globalization. The increasing impact of globalization on the Dutch economy is clearly visible if one looks at the ownership and behavior of firms with a total balance of more than 25 million guilders (11.4 million euro). In 1983, 6.0 percent of all of these firms had a majority of Dutch shareholders and large investments in foreign companies. In 1997, the percentage of Dutch firms having foreign interests had increased to 7.0 percent. Dutch investment companies are active on a global scale as well. Just about 20 percent of all investments of these companies are made within the Netherlands. The bulk of these investments is made in companies that operate at a global level (CBS, 2001). But not only are Dutch firms increasingly active on a global market, at the same time a growing influence of foreign capital in Dutch firms can be noticed. In 1983, 30.9 percent of all large firms were owned for more than 50 percent by foreign shareholders. By 1998, this percentage had risen to 35.1 as the result of an increase in so-called supranational corporations, i.e., Dutch corporations with a majority of foreign shareholders having large investments in foreign companies as well. At the same time the share of such supranational corporations in all Dutch large corporations had more than doubled, from 6.2 percent in 1983 to 13.7 in 1997. Another way to show the impact of globalization on the Dutch economy is to compare the yearly trade flow of the Netherlands to its national income. The net national income of the Netherlands in 1999 amounted to 322 billion euro. In that same year the import of goods and services amounted to 209 billion euro, whereas the export of goods and services to 227 billion euro. Thus, the international trade flow of the Netherlands is much larger than its national income.

Network globalization is linked to the increase in Information and Communication Technologies (ICT). This has had an impact both on the economy and on personal lives. The impact of ICT on the economy is visible in the behavior of corporations. For instance, corporate investments in computer hardware almost doubled between 1995 and 1998, from 2.1 to 3.9 billion euro (CBS, 2001). The same trend is visible in the total ICT expenditures of corporations, which doubled from 8.1 billion euro in 1995 to 16.2 in 2000 (CBS, 2001). Meanwhile, the proportion of corporations that has access to internet increased from 11 to 56 percent. Of corporations having more than 100 employees, 86 percent has access to internet (CBS, 2001). Another way in which globalization influences Dutch society is by its impact on personal lives. Information from all across the world reaches virtually every household in the Netherlands by way of television and radio. In addition, a growing proportion of the Dutch population has a personal computer at home. In 1995, 21 percent of all Dutch households had a personal computer compared to 55 percent in 1998.

These figures show that Dutch society is highly integrated into the global economy. As a result, one would expect that Dutch society is highly susceptible to the vicissitudes of the global economy and to the uncertainties that surround it. The extent to which globalizing forces impact the lives of Dutch citizens will, however, also depend on the extent to which institutional structures in the Netherlands are able to buffer their impact. In the next section, some main features of Dutch institutional arrangements are therefore discussed. In this discussion, the focus will be on those features that are most relevant to the lives of young adults.

THE INSTITUTIONAL CONTEXT OF THE TRANSITION TO ADULTHOOD

Institutional structures shape the opportunities and constraints that young adults face during their transition to adulthood. Three institutional structures can be viewed as central in this respect (see Blossfeld, 2002). The first one is the educational system, because the way this is organized affects the timing and relative smoothness of the transition into employment. The second one is the structure of the labor market, because labor market arrangements define the opportunities for employers to deal flexibly with shortages and surpluses in labor supply. The third institutional structure is the welfare system. This system defines the level and duration of benefits to the unemployed and disabled, as well as the opportunities for combining paid employment and other activities like caring for children. Each of these aspects will be discussed in turn.

The Dutch educational system has experienced an enormous expansion during the course of the last century (Rupp, 1992). In 1850 mass education - i.e., when more than 75 percent of persons of a particular age group are enrolled in full-time education - extended to the age of 12. The upper age limit of mass education slowly increased to 14 years in 1956, but then accelerated to 17 years in 1982. This increase in actual enrollment in education has more or less paralleled the developments in the legal minimum age of leaving school (Veld, 1987). The educational system itself is characterized by the existence of two parallel tracks, a general and a vocational one. Because of the rather theoretical nature of the Dutch vocational track, shifts from one track to the other are quite common. As Blossfeld (2002) argues, the high theoretical nature of this system has the advantage that young adults who enter the labor market are well-equipped with general skills that allow them to be flexible on the labor market, but the disadvantage of few job-specific skills. A final important characteristic of the Dutch educational system is its relatively generous provision of student loans and grants. It is a mixed system; on top of the grant given by the state, parents are also expected to contribute to the study costs of their children. If necessary, students can apply for additional loans. Although still rather generous from an international perspective, cutbacks in the system during the 1980s and early 90s have increased the financial dependence of students on their parents.

The Dutch labor market can be characterized as offering a high level of employment security (DiPrete *et al.*, 1997). The level of protection of employees is relatively high, making it hard for employers to adjust flexibly to changes in market conditions. The economic recession of the 1980s forced many corporations to downsize; this was mainly done by allowing older employees to leave before the official retirement age (Henkens, 1998). This was a costly operation. At the same time, the number of young people newly hired was severely limited. In addition, those who did enter often did so on temporary, fixed-term contracts and on conditions that were far less favorable than before. The weakened labor market position of young adults was clearly visible in the strong increase in youth unemployment, from 6 percent in 1979 to more than 20 percent at the height of the recession in 1983. After 1983, youth unemployment gradually declined again. However, it took until 1998 for the youth unemployment rate to drop below 10 percent (see also Klijzing, this volume).

Another special feature of Dutch labor relations is the low labor force participation rate of women. This rate has always been extremely low by international standards, mainly because of the fact that most Dutch women used to retreat from the labor market at the birth of their first child or even at marriage. It is only since the 1980s that an increase in female labor force participation is visible. Although the participation rates of women have now reached those of most other Western European countries, the Netherlands still stand out for their very high proportion of part-time jobs (see also Klijzing, this volume). Most of the women who are active on the labor market - and those who have children in particular - hold part-time jobs.

As far as the Dutch welfare system is concerned, Blossfeld (2002) characterizes it as a 'conservative' welfare regime, suggesting that it is mainly committed to protecting people who drop out of the labor market - the unemployed, disabled, pensioners - from serious declines in their standard of living. Indeed, the Dutch system has always been very generous and from an international, comparative perspective it still is, although in reaction to its high costs measures have been put in place from the early 1990s onwards that have made it somewhat less generous. An additional feature of a conservative welfare regime is that it is also committed to the traditional division of labor in the family that makes wives economically dependent on their husbands. As a result, existing fiscal arrangements have always favored one-earner over dual-earner families, and childcare facilities are still few and far between. It is only recently that the Dutch government has begun to redress this situation by increasing the number of publicly funded day care centers and by amending fiscal regulations that used to favor one-earner families.

THE IMPACT OF GLOBALIZATION ON THE TRANSITION TO ADULTHOOD IN THE NETHERLANDS

The ways in which globalization will influence the transition to adulthood in the Netherlands depend on the specific characteristics of Dutch society, as discussed above. In this section some hypotheses will be formulated concerning this influence. First, I will focus on the consequences that globalization might have on the entry into the labor market. Next, I turn to its potential impact on entry into adult family roles.

Kurz *et al.* (this volume) suggest that the process of globalization has an impact on the transition to adulthood mainly by heightening young adults' sense of insecurity. They argue that two aspects of insecurity are particularly crucial, namely, economic and temporal - or, what Bernardi and Nazio (this volume) call, employment relationship - insecurity. Economic insecurity relates to the occupational class, income and number of working hours of the jobs available on the labor market. The lower the occupational class, income or number of hours of a specific job, the more precarious this job will be and the less security it offers to its incumbent. Temporal insecurity, on the other hand, relates to the temporary or permanent character of jobs. Temporary jobs offer their incumbents much less temporal security than permanent ones do.

One of the potential consequences of the process of globalization could be that the supply of jobs that offer a high level of both economic and temporal security will decline. In the case of the Netherlands, it seems particularly likely that the number of temporary jobs will increase. This will mainly influence young adults because they are the new entrants on the labor market, to whom it is much easier to offer temporary contracts than to people who apply from a permanent position. With regard to economic insecurity, the situation is somewhat more complicated. Given the fact that the Dutch economy is very knowledge-based, a general downgrading of positions open to new entrants seems highly unlikely. On the other hand, it might happen that positions offered to new entrants ask for the same high level of qualifications but at lower starting wages. In addition to the change in the type of jobs available to new entrants, overall insecurity may also increase due to a decline in the number of jobs available to young adults. To the extent that the economic recession in the 1980s was induced by globalizing tendencies, the increase in unemployment among young adults can also be viewed as a rise in insecurity resulting from globalization.

It might be expected that a worsening of labor market positions for young adults will also have an impact on their decisions concerning entry into the labor market. If young adults perceive the risk of unemployment upon entry into labor market as high and the chance of obtaining a secure job position as low, they might react by postponing entry into the labor market through upgrading their educational qualifications. Given the relatively generous state support for students that allow them to remain in the educational system at relatively low costs, such a reaction seems particularly likely in the Dutch case. The above considerations thus lead to the first hypothesis:

H1   The proportion of Dutch young adults in precarious positions - unemployed, on fixed-term contracts, at low wages - is expected to increase. At the same time, the proportion of young adults who delay entry into the labor market by staying in the educational system will grow as well.

It is in this way that globalization is expected to cause an increase in economic and temporal insecurity among young adults. This should show up as an increase in the proportion of young adults in precarious labor market positions. The next issue to be addressed is to what extent the actual experience and perception of this insecurity influence the family-life decisions of young adults.

People in most Western societies are expected to leave their parental home when they wish to start a family of their own. In these societies it is generally necessary for young adults to be able to economically support such a family before actually starting one. Therefore, an increase in insecurity will probably lead to a postponement of family formation, as it will take young adults longer before they have firmly established themselves on the labor market (see also Simó et al., this volume). However, this general hypothesis needs qualification on a number of points.

First, the Dutch welfare system offers fairly generous support to people without stable employment. Grants received by students and unemployment benefits by the unemployed may facilitate family formation even if stable employment is lacking. This support could act as a buffer to the delay that globalization would otherwise produce through enhanced insecurity. Whether and to what extent the Dutch welfare system will be able to counteract this delay is still open for research.

Second, young adults may opt for alternative living arrangements that entail less commitment than marriage and parenthood, but which offer some of the same 'rewards'. Oppenheimer (1988) suggests that this is one of the reasons why unmarried cohabitation has become increasingly popular among young adults. Therefore, insecurity may lead to the postponement of marriage and parenthood, but not necessarily to the postponement of union formation in general.

Third, the effects of insecurity might differ for men and women. Although the roles of men and women are slowly being redefined, men are still generally viewed as the main breadwinners. As a result, it might be more important for males than for females to establish themselves in an economically secure job (Oppenheimer *et al.*, 1997). If so, one might expect a stronger effect of economic and temporal insecurity on the timing of family formation among men than among women.

Fourth, among women it is usually the highly educated who - given their orientation towards pursuing a career - are most likely to postpone family formation (Becker, 1981; Blossfeld and Huinink, 1991). In times of insecurity, they will probably be more willing to postpone family formation than women with less educational attainment. Actual postponement behavior will, however, partly depend on the compatibility of combining a career and having a family (Liefbroer and Corijn, 1999). Given the existence of relatively poor childcare arrangements in the Netherlands, the opportunities to combine these two roles are relatively bad. Therefore, it is expected that highly educated women are much more likely to postpone family formation than women with less educational attainment. Among men, such an educational gradient in the effect on family formation is much less likely.

The above considerations lead to the following general hypothesis:

H2 Young adults holding insecure labor market positions - those enrolled in education, the unemployed or the employed on temporary contracts, or those in lower class positions - will postpone entry into family roles such as marriage and parenthood that ask for high levels of commitment from the partners involved. Furthermore, this postponement effect of insecure labor market positions will be stronger for males than for females.

Globalization might influence the behavior of young adults in two distinct ways. So far the discussion has been on its impact on family formation through an increased likelihood of experiencing precarious labor market positions. But globalization can also influence the behavior of young adults by creating perceptions of insecurity. If young adults perceive the economic climate to be insecure, they may become reluctant to enter into family roles that require strong commitments, even if they themselves are not in insecure positions. This leads to the formulation of a third hypothesis:

H3 In times of a heightened sense of insecurity, young adults will postpone entry into family roles such as marriage and parenthood that ask for high levels of commitment from the partners involved.

DATA

Two datasets will be used to study the impact of globalization on the transition to adulthood in the Netherlands. The first dataset contains information on the timing of life course transitions among approximately 26,000 persons born between 1903 and 1970. Liefbroer and Dykstra (2000) compiled this source by pooling data from seven retrospective life history surveys conducted in the Netherlands between 1987 and 1995. Information from this dataset will be used to describe the long-term changes in the timing of entry into adult roles. This serves as a backdrop for the more detailed discussion of the impact of insecurity on the transition to adulthood among cohorts born during the 1960s, for which the second dataset will be used.

This second dataset is the Panel Study of Social Integration in the Netherlands (PSIN). This panel survey was initiated by the Departments of Organizational Psychology and Social Research Methodology of the Free University in Amsterdam, and later continued by the Department of Sociology at Utrecht University. In the first wave of 1987, 1,775 young adults born in 1961, 1965 and 1969 were interviewed. The second wave of data collection was in 1989. This was a short mail questionnaire, the main purpose of which was to update the life course events between 1987 and 1989 of the participants. A third wave of interviews was held in 1991 and a fourth one in 1995. The respondents were approximately 18, 22, and 26 years of age at the time of the first survey wave in 1987, and 26, 30 and 34 years of age in 1995. In 1987, respondents were selected by taking random samples stratified by sex and year of birth from the population registers of 25 municipalities in the Netherlands. These municipalities formed a random sample of all Dutch municipalities, stratified by degree of urbanization and region. The response rate of the initial sample members was 63 percent. Of these respondents, 54 percent (N=962) were re-interviewed in 1995. (Additional information on the methodology of this panel survey can be found in Liefbroer and Kalmijn, 1997).

A valuable feature of the PSIN is that it contains rich information on all aspects of the life course of young adults. It has information on the timing of major life events in the domains of education, employment, union formation and parenthood. In addition, for each employment spell, information is available on the type of job, the number and regularity of working hours, the type of contract and the number of subordinates. This information will be used to describe the educational and employment positions of young adults in the next section, and the impact of these positions on their entry into family roles in the section "The impact of globalization on entry into family roles among young adults".

THE EDUCATIONAL AND LABOR MARKET POSITIONS OF YOUNG ADULTS

First, a brief description will be given of the long-term trends in the ages at which young adults exit from full-time education and enter into employment, and of the prestige of their first occupation. Given that globalization is a relatively new phenomenon, it is expected to have an impact on the transition to adulthood mostly among young adults born from the 1960s onwards. A comparison of their transition experience with that of cohorts born earlier during the twentieth century will provide a first indication of the extent to which globalization might have had an impact on the lives of young adults in the Netherlands. Next, PSIN data will be used to present a more detailed description of the changes that have occurred in the educational and occupational domain among the cohorts born in the 1960s.

Table 4.1 presents information on the long-term trends in entering adult roles among cohorts born between 1900 and 1970. Column 1 shows the age at which half of all men and women from each cohort have exited full-time education. It shows an increase in the median age of about seven years for males and six and a half years for females. The duration of educational enrollment has increased most dramatically among the cohorts born since the 1950s: more than half of the total increase in the median age occurred among the two youngest cohorts. These data also show that women consistently leave the educational system at an earlier age than men, but this does not necessarily imply that they have lower educational credentials. Cohort trends in educational attainment (Liefbroer and Dykstra, 2000: 231) reveal that women have almost completely made up for their arrears in this respect. This thus suggests that females move through the educational system at a somewhat higher speed than men.

Column 2 of Table 4.1 shows the age at which half of all men and women have entered into the labor market.[1] Once again, a remarkable increase can be observed in the median age at which young adults experience this event. And again it is for the cohorts born since the 1950s that the biggest increase is recorded, particularly for the cohort 1961-1970. This suggests that the youngest cohort delays its entry into the labor market more strongly than earlier ones.

It is not only important to know at what age young adults enter the labor market, but also at what level. To get an impression of the developments in this respect, column 3 of Table 4.1 shows the trends in the average occupational prestige of the first job that young adults occupy.[2] It is evident that the occupational prestige of the first job has increased quite strongly for cohorts born since the 1940s. However, this increase seems to have come to a halt among young adults born in the 1960s: the occupational prestige of their first job is lower than that of the cohorts born in the 1950s. One reason for this could be that - although already a majority - not all young adults from the youngest cohort had yet entered the labor market at the time that the various surveys were taken. If so, some increase in the mean occupational prestige score of this cohort could still be expected. However, it seems unlikely that it will ultimately exceed that of the cohort 1951-1960.

The long-term trends presented thus far seem to offer some slight indications of changing behavioral patterns among cohorts born in the 1960s. First, their entry into the labor market has been delayed and the gap between the median age of leaving the educational system and entering the labor market has widened. This suggests that the transition from the educational system into the labor market among them occurs less smoothly than among cohorts born in the 1950s.

Table 4.1   Long-term trends in the timing and outcomes of the transition into adulthood in The Netherlands

	Median age at leaving school (1)	Median age at entry into first job (2)	Occupational prestige of first job (3)	Median age at first union (4)	Percentage entering first union by marriage (5)	Median age at first marriage (6)	Median age at first childbirth (7)
Males							
Cohort 1901-1910	13.4	15.4	37.5	28.7	97	28.7	30.9
Cohort 1911-1920	14.1	15.8	35.7	27.9	97	28.0	30.2
Cohort 1921-1930	15.3	17.0	36.1	27.5	96	27.6	29.8
Cohort 1931-1940	16.1	16.8	37.6	25.4	92	26.4	28.3
Cohort 1941-1950	17.0	17.7	40.8	24.4	81	24.6	28.2
Cohort 1951-1960	19.5	19.3	42.3	24.3	52	26.2	31.3
Cohort 1961-1970	20.6	20.9	40.4	25.1	24	30.1	32.7
Females							
Cohort 1901-1910	12.7	16.3	35.0	26.8	98	26.8	29.5
Cohort 1911-1920	13.7	16.3	34.2	25.9	98	25.9	28.1
Cohort 1921-1930	14.4	16.9	34.9	25.0	96	25.0	27.0
Cohort 1931-1940	15.5	17.2	36.1	24.3	94	24.3	25.9
Cohort 1941-1950	16.1	17.2	39.3	22.5	84	22.7	25.6
Cohort 1951-1960	17.9	18.3	42.0	21.8	61	22.9	27.5
Cohort 1961-1970	19.4	20.1	41.3	22.6	30	26.4	29.5

Source: Liefbroer and Dykstra, 2000.

Second, the rise in the occupational prestige of young adults' first job has come to a halt with the youngest cohort, apparently indicating that the quality of jobs available to new entrants on the labor market is not increasing any longer but may be even slightly decreasing. To get a better understanding of how globalization affects the transition into the labor market, I will now focus in more detail on developments among cohorts born in the 1960s.

In discussing the impact of globalization on the labor market position of Dutch young adults, it was emphasized that one should not only look at changes in the type of first jobs that they occupy and in the percentages of the unemployed, but also at the extension of their stay in the educational system, as this could constitute a rational reaction to the insecurity resulting from globalization. Data on the various positions that young adults hold at ages 20 and 25 in the educational and occupational domain are presented in Table 4.2. Based on whether or not young adults are still enrolled in (part- or full-time) education and/or hold a part-time or full-time job[3], Table 4.2 distinguishes 6 positions (columns 1-6). The top part of this table shows the activity status of males and females in the educational and occupational domain at age 20.

Table 4.2   Positions in the educational and occupational domain at ages 20 and 25 of women and men born between 1961 and 1969 in The Netherlands (in percentages of total)

				Activity status in the educational and occupational domain		
	In school (1)	*Un-employed* (2)	*In school+ full-time job* (3)	*In school+ part-time job* (4)	*Part-time job* (5)	*Full-time job* (6)
Age 20						
Males						
Cohort 1961	30	10	9	1	0	50
Cohort 1965	43	13	8	2	1	32
Cohort 1969	49	5	10	13	1	23
Females						
Cohort 1961	22	15	10	1	5	47
Cohort 1965	32	15	9	2	8	34
Cohort 1969	49	5	10	13	1	23
Age 25						
Males						
Cohort 1961	10	10	7	1	1	71
Cohort 1965	7	3	11	3	1	75
Cohort 1969	18	19	10	5	1	46
Females						
Cohort 1961	6	35	3	1	11	44
Cohort 1965	7	18	8	3	12	53
Cohort 1969	10	17	6	5	13	49

Table 4.2 continued

	Type of contract				Social class		
	Perma-nent (7)	Training (8)	Fixed-term (9)	Free-lance / self-employed (10)	Service class (11)	Non-manual (12)	Manual (13)
Age 20							
Males							
Cohort 1961	66	6	24	4	9	17	74
Cohort 1965	50	9	36	6	4	13	83
Cohort 1969	50	11	29	9	9	21	70
Females							
Cohort 1961	75	12	9	4	8	70	22
Cohort 1965	72	9	14	5	9	68	23
Cohort 1969	59	16	20	5	8	67	25
Age 25							
Males							
Cohort 1961	80	0	8	11	26	19	55
Cohort 1965	83	2	9	6	30	21	49
Cohort 1969	67	0	23	10	24	21	55
Females							
Cohort 1961	85	0	8	8	30	51	19
Cohort 1965	87	3	5	6	30	54	16
Cohort 1969	75	0	21	3	37	47	16

Source: PSIN.

Among males this young, a dramatic decrease in the proportion holding a full-time job is visible. Half of the men born in 1961 already had left the educational system and found a full-time job at age 20, whereas this was the case for less than a quarter of those born in 1969. At the same time, the percentage of men still being enrolled in school increased from 30 percent among those born in 1961 to 49 percent among those in 1969. Another remarkable observation is that the proportion of 20-year-old males without a job decreased from 13 to 5 percent from cohort 1965 to cohort 1969, whereas the proportion combining school and a part-time job increased from 2 to 13 percent during the same period. The patterns among females strongly resemble those among males. These figures thus suggest that young adults try to cope with the growing risk of unemployment by remaining in the educational system for a longer period of time. Combining educational enrollment and part-time employment may be either a way of financing their prolonged stay in the educational system or a means of smoothing their entry into the labor market.

The activity status of successive cohorts of young adults at age 25 in the bottom part of Table 4.2 shows rather divergent trends among males and females. Among males, the percentage of 25-year-olds having a full-time job drops from more than 70 percent among those born in 1961-65 to 46 percent among those in 1969. At the same time, both the proportion of 25-year-old males who are still enrolled in education and the proportion being unemployed increase. This pattern suggests that the strategy to avoid the risk of unemployment by prolonging one's stay in the educational system that was observed at age 20 has only met with partial success. At age 25, many young adults in the 1969 cohort - almost one-fifth - have become unemployed. Among women, the pattern is quite different which mainly results from the specific meaning of the category of the 'non-employed'. This category will include both people who are unemployed involuntarily and people who are so at their free choice. The latter group will be small among males, but among females it will include those who quit a job to take care of a family. Given that the age at which a family is started is increasing (see later in this chapter), fewer women will voluntarily leave the labor market at age 25, thus resulting in a drop (from 35 to 17 percent) in the proportion being non-employed at that age.

Columns 7-10 of Table 4.2 provide information on the type of contract young adults have at ages 20 and 25. Four types of contracts have been distinguished, namely, permanent ones, training contracts that combine work and on-the-job training, temporary (fixed-term) contracts, and free-lancers plus other self-employed (these last two have been combined to overcome problems of small numbers). The results demonstrate that the jobs occupied by young adults have become more precarious for younger cohorts. For instance, both at age 20 and at age 25, the percentage of young adult men and women who have a permanent contract has decreased. At age 20, this has been compensated by an increase in both training and temporary contracts. Probably as a result of the fact that training contracts are mainly used for young adults who have just left school, this type of contract is virtually absent among young adults aged 25. Among them, temporary contracts are increasingly substituting for permanent ones. Free-lance employment and other forms of semi-independent employment (see Bernardi and Nazio, this volume) are clearly not very popular among young Dutch adults; there are no clear signs of an increase in their proportions.

Finally, the last 3 columns (11-13) of Table 4.2 concentrate on the social class positions of young adults who occupy a job at ages 20 and 25. They provide the percentages of young adults being part of the service class, the routine non-manual workers and the manual workers. No clear trends in class positions are visible among males and females, neither at age 20 nor at age 25. Two things stand out, however. First, there is a strong increase between ages 20 and 25 in the percentage of young adult men and women who hold positions in the service class. Second, males predominantly occupy manual jobs, whereas females occupy non-manual ones. Furthermore, women at age 25 seem somewhat more likely to hold positions in the service class than males. However, males are more likely than females to rank among the higher service class (figures not shown).

All in all, these results clearly show that young adults are increasingly confronted with insecurity on the labor market. Compared to young adults born in the early 1960s, those born in the late 1960s are more likely to experience unemployment and they more often hold jobs with temporary or training contracts rather than with permanent ones. In addition, there is evidence that young adults extend their stay in the educational system to update their qualifications and to reduce the risk of unemployment. However, as the data on unemployment among 25-year-old males demonstrate, this strategy is only partially successful.

THE IMPACT OF GLOBALIZATION ON ENTRY INTO FAMILY ROLES AMONG YOUNG ADULTS

The next question to be answered is: to what extent does globalization have an impact on young adults' timing of their entry into family roles? This issue will be studied using the same strategy as in the preceding section. That is, first the long-term trend in the timing of family formation processes will be discussed, followed by a more detailed examination of the factors influencing union formation and parenthood among cohorts born in the 1960s.

Whereas in the past marriage was the 'normal' route to union life, nowadays many young adults opt for unmarried cohabitation. Changes in the age at which males and females from successive birth cohorts start a first union and in the proportion who do so by marriage are presented in Table 4.1. These data show that the age at entry into a first union decreased by about five years between the cohorts born in 1901-10 and those in 1951-60. However, among the cohorts born in the 1960s entry into a union is delayed. Also clear from Table 4.1 is that almost all young adults born between 1901 and 1940 entered their first union by marriage. From cohort 1941-50 onwards this changed dramatically, and among young adults born in the 1960s it is for unmarried cohabitation rather than marriage that the large majority opt.

Table 4.1 also presents the ages at which 50 percent of males and females have entered into marriage and parenthood, respectively (columns 6 and 7). Both processes exhibit the same U-shaped pattern as first union formation. That is, from cohort 1901-10 until cohort 1941-50 the median ages at which young adults entered marriage and parenthood dropped by three to four years, approximately. For the cohorts born since 1950 an increase in the median ages at marriage and parenthood is visible. This increase is particularly large for the cohorts born in the 1960s. Their median age at first marriage increased with more than three years compared to the previous birth cohort, whereas their median age at first childbirth with one and a half to two years.

These long-term trends show that recent cohorts have undergone a dramatic change in the process of family formation. Engagements in long-term commitments like marriage and parenthood are postponed, while unmarried cohabitation has become a 'standard' part of the young adult life course. Postponement of long-term commitments is exactly what one would expect from the 'narrative' of globalization. However, other 'anchored narratives' to explain these shifts in patterns of family formation exist as well (Van de Kaa, 1996).[4] Therefore, a much more convincing test of the extent to which these shifts are caused by processes of globalization could be provided by focussing on the impact of growing insecurity on entry into family roles among young adults born in the 1960s.

This impact is examined by estimating exponential hazard models for entry into a first union - both as a general and as a competing risk process, with marriage and unmarried cohabitation as competing choices - and for entry into parenthood, separately for males and females.[5] These models include controls for cohort, parental level of education and religiosity, as well as parameters to measure the age-dependent nature of these processes.[6] To capture the impact of globalization, I make multiple comparisons. On the one hand, I compare young adults who have a job with young adults who are enrolled in education or without employment. On the other, I compare employed young adults according to different job characteristics. To accomplish this in one analysis, I take young adults holding a permanent, full-time service class job as the reference category and I compare young adults having other characteristics to this group.[7] In addition, I include in the models time-varying measures of the educational attainment of young adults and of the societal level of unemployment. The estimation results are presented in Table 4.3.

Compared to young adults with a permanent, full-time position in the service class, students are likely to delay both first union formation and parenthood. In addition, if they do form a first union, it is through unmarried rather than married cohabitation. These effects are observed for both men and women. Also young adults without employment delay union formation compared to young adults with a permanent, full-time position in the service class. Again this effect is observed among both men and women. But while being without employment has no consequences for entry into fatherhood, it even accelerates entry into motherhood. Two explanations for this finding can be proposed. First, a selection process could be operative in the sense that women with traditional views on family relationships leave the labor market voluntarily in anticipation of motherhood. A second explanation could be that women who have become unemployed involuntarily may opt for motherhood to reduce insecurity or as an alternative mode of giving structure and meaning to their lives (cf. Friedman *et al.*, 1994).

Job characteristics among employed young adults are found to have an impact on the timing of entry into family-related roles as well. Part-time work among women delays union formation but it increases the probability of marriage rather than unmarried cohabitation, and it also leads to earlier motherhood. This could be explained by the same kind of mechanisms as suggested above with regard to the effect of unemployment. On the other hand, having a temporary contract rather than a permanent one delays both union formation and parenthood among women. Among men, its effect is restricted to reducing the chance of direct marriage. Basically the same pattern is observed for those having a training contract, but this effect is weaker and even nonexistent with regard to entry into parenthood. This may result from the fact that most training contracts have ended before the age at which young adults start contemplating the possibility of parenthood. Finally, some differences also exist for young adults whose jobs are classified as routine non-manual or manual labor. Women who have such jobs delay entry into a union and are particularly reluctant to enter a union by unmarried cohabitation, whereas men who have a manual working class position delay parenthood.

As expected, level of education delays entry into a union and parenthood for females. Unexpectedly, though, the same holds for males. This runs contrary to the ideas of the New Home Economics (Becker, 1981). According to that theoretical framework, a higher earning potential of males should lead to earlier - not later - union formation and parenthood.

Table 4.3   Transition rate models for entry into first union (both general and as a competing risk) and entry into first parenthood among women and men born between 1961 and 1969 in The Netherlands[a]

	Women			
	First union	Unmarried cohabitation	Marriage	Motherhood
Constant	-19.77**	-17.32**	-33.69**	-13.77**
Log(Age-15)	2.32**	1.94**	3.97**	2.03**
Log(39-Age)	4.54**	3.72**	8.19**	2.12**
Cohort 1965	-0.11	-0.04	-0.18	-0.08
Cohort 1969	-0.25**	0.07	-1.40**	-0.85**
Educational level father	-0.00	-0.01	0.01	0.02
Educational level mother	0.02	0.04*	-0.02	-0.05*
Level of religiosity parents	-0.12**	-0.24**	0.18**	-0.03
Enrolled in education	-0.91**	-0.92**	-1.58**	-1.59**
Without employment	-0.48**	-0.42**	-0.70**	0.67**
Service class, full-time, permanent	—	—	—	—
Part-time	-0.30**	-0.66**	0.43*	0.85**
Training contract	-0.28	-0.08	-0.79*	0.01
Temporary contract	-0.48**	-0.35*	-0.77**	-0.64**
Non-manual labor	-0.26**	-0.37**	-0.00	-0.16
Manual labor	-0.30**	-0.40**	-0.21	-0.28
Educational level	-0.07**	-0.01	-0.20**	-0.22**
Level of youth unemployment	-0.01	-0.01	-0.06**	-0.03*
Number of subepisodes	10237	10237	10237	14111
Number of events	634	442	192	325

Table 4.3 continued

	Men			
	First union	Unmarried cohabitation	Marriage	Fatherhood
Constant	-23.63**	-24.18**	-24.88**	-3.79
Log(Age-15)	3.51**	3.49**	3.63**	1.49**
Log(39-Age)	4.72**	4.90**	4.27**	-1.26
Cohort 1965	-0.27**	-0.18	-0.45**	-0.40**
Cohort 1969	-0.48**	-0.35**	-1.25**	-0.67*
Educational level father	-0.02	-0.03	0.02	-0.01
Educational level mother	0.03	0.05**	-0.05	-0.01
Level of religiosity parents	-0.05	-0.16**	0.30**	0.03
Enrolled in education	-0.60**	-0.55**	-1.07**	-1.13**
Without employment	-0.47**	-0.32	-0.77**	-0.45
Service class, full-time, permanent	—	—	—	—
Part-time				
Training contract	-0.39*	-0.25	-0.86*	0.33
Temporary contract	-0.17	-0.02	-0.64**	-0.15
Non-manual labor	-0.07	0.03	-0.27	-0.28
Manual labor	-0.23	-0.18	-0.34	-0.44**
Educational level	-0.05**	-0.03	-0.11**	-0.15**
Level of youth unemployment	-0.00	-0.02	0.03	0.01
Number of subepisodes	12223	12223	12223	15136
Number of events	493	365	128	221

Source: PSIN.

Notes
a   Reference category: Cohort 1961, Full-time service class employees having a permanent contract.
* $p < 0.10$
** $p < 0.05$

Two explanations can be offered for this rather surprising finding. First, it could be due to processes of assortative mating, i.e. homogamy (see Blossfeld and Timm, 2003): higher educated males marry higher educated females. What appears then to be an effect for males in a one-sex model, could well turn out to be an effect for females if it were analyzed from a two-sex (partner) perspective. Second, higher educated males could hold individualistic values making it more likely that they will postpone far-reaching commitments in the family domain.

A final finding from Table 4.3 that warrants consideration is the impact of the level of youth unemployment. This macro indicator can be viewed as a proxy for young adults' perceptions of economic insecurity. The expectation was that young adults would postpone family formation if they perceive their economic prospects as insecure. Although no such effects are found for men, a rise in the level of youth unemployment leads among women to delayed motherhood and to a stronger reluctance to enter a first union by marriage.

DISCUSSION

In this chapter the potential impact of globalization on the transition to adulthood in the Netherlands has been studied. Globalization is predicted to result in growing insecurity among young adults. If young adults feel insecure about their economic prospects, they are expected to be reluctant to commit themselves whole-heartedly to the long-term obligations that marriage and parenthood imply. Therefore, in an era of globalization a delay in family formation is anticipated among young adults.

Based on this reasoning, three hypotheses have been tested. The first hypothesis states that, under conditions of globalization, the proportion of young adults in precarious labor market positions is likely to increase. This hypothesis received partial support. Among cohorts born in the 1960s a marked increase both in the incidence of unemployment and in that of temporary employment was observed. This underscores the contention that employers - in times of globalization - will try to enhance their flexibility by reducing the proportion of permanent staff. The easiest way to do so is by offering only temporary contracts to new entrants. Young adults seem to be aware of this situation and try to adjust to their worsening labor market prospects by prolonging their stay in the educational system. By doing so, they at least temporarily avoid unemployment while they can upgrade their educational credentials, in the hope that this will enhance their future chances on the labor market.

The second hypothesis states that young adults in precarious labor market positions - assumed to result from globalizing tendencies - are more likely to postpone family formation than those in secure labor market positions. Again, partial support was found for this hypothesis. The most striking contrast was between young adults in the most secure labor market position - a permanent, full-time position within the service class - and those in other positions. The differences between young adults in other positions were generally much smaller. In general, young adults who hold part-time jobs, temporary jobs and jobs outside the service class postpone family formation. This also holds - generally even stronger - for the unemployed and students. However, some unexpected results were found as well. Most strikingly, unemployed and part-time employed women become mothers sooner than women with secure economic prospects. Likely explanations for this finding are that full-time working women anticipate motherhood by reducing their working hours or quitting altogether, or that they opt for motherhood as an alternative means of gaining security.

Another corollary of the second hypothesis was that higher educated women should be postponing family formation because of the potential conflict between their career and motherhood. Level of education was indeed found to operate in this direction for women. However, the same pattern was observed for men as well. This probably results from processes of assortative mating and/or from the fact that higher educated males and females may value individualization more highly and therefore postpone the far-reaching commitments of family life.

Finally, the third hypothesis states that also young adults' perceptions of insecurity at large will influence their transition to adulthood. Young adults who perceive their economic prospects as unfavorable, will probably postpone family formation. This hypothesis received only limited support. I used the level of youth unemployment in Dutch society as an indicator of the perceived economic climate. It only decreased the likelihood of opting for marriage as the start of the first union and the rate of entry into parenthood among females. Therefore, general perceptions of economic insecurity seem much less influential than actual experiences of economic insecurity in postponing the transition to adulthood, at least among Dutch young male adults.

In sum, these results suggest that even in a rather transfer-oriented, protective welfare state like the Netherlands, economic insecurity influences the transition to adulthood. Its generous social benefits system might be able to partially buffer the impact of globalization, but it seems incapable of eradicating these consequences completely.

NOTES

1   Entry into the labor market has been defined by the first job young adults occupy *after* they have left full-time education.
2   Occupational prestige has been measured by a scale developed by Sixma and Ultee (1983).
3   If part-time courses would be discarded, the percentage of young adults categorized as 'in school, full-time job' would decrease with 5 percent, whereas the proportion classified as 'not in school, full-time job' would increase by the same amount. The effect on other categories would be minimal. Part-time jobs are jobs with contracts of less than 24 hours a week.
4   Van de Kaa (1996) uses the term 'anchored narratives' to describe the competing theories that are used to explain the decline in fertility. Among the competing narratives explaining the change in family patterns in Western countries, those of the New Home Economics (Becker, 1981) and of the Second Demographic Transition (Van de Kaa, 1987) are the most prominent ones.
5   To avoid uncertainties about causal relationships, I focus on the timing of the pregnancy leading up to the first birth rather than the timing of the first birth itself.
6   This has been done by adding two time-varying age covariates that capture the well-known bell-shaped curves of the rate of entry into union life and parenthood (cf. Blossfeld and Huinink, 1991).
7   All these covariates are time-varying. I do not take multiple roles at a time (e.g. in education and having a part-time job) as this would lead to a too large reduction in

the number of respondents per category. Among men, no distinction is made between part- and full-time employment because the number of males holding a part-time position is very small.

BIBLIOGRAPHY

Becker, G.S. (1981) *A treatise on the family*, Cambridge, Mass.: Harvard University Press.

Blossfeld, H.-P. (2002) 'Globalization, Social Inequality and the Role of Country-Specific Institutions', in P. Conceicao, M. V. Heitor and B.-A. Lundvall (eds) *Innovation, Competence Building and Social Cohesion in Europe: Towards a Learning Society*, Cheltenham/Lyme: Edward Elgar.

Blossfeld, H.P. and Huinink, J. (1991) 'Human capital investments or norms of role transition? How women's schooling and career affect the process of family formation', *American Journal of Sociology*, 97: 143-168.

Blossfeld, H.-P. and Timm, A. (eds) (2003) *Educational systems as marriage markets in modern societies. A comparison of thirteen countries*, Oxford: Oxford University Press.

CBS (Central Bureau of Statistics) (2001) *Statistisch Jaarboek 2001*, Voorburg: CBS.

DiPrete, T.A., de Graaf, P.M., Luijkx, R., Tåhlin, M. and Blossfeld, H.-P. (1997) 'Collectivist versus individualist mobility regimes? Structural change and job mobility in four countries', *American Journal of Sociology*, 103: 318-358.

Erikson, R., Goldthorpe, J.H. and Portocarero, L. (1979) 'Intergenerational class mobility in three Western European societies: England, France and Sweden', *British Journal of Sociology*, 30: 415-451.

Friedman, D., Hechter, M. and Kanazawa, S. (1994) 'A theory of the value of children', *Demography*, 31: 375-401.

Henkens, K. (1998) *Older workers in transition. Studies on the early retirement decision in the Netherlands*, The Hague: NIDI.

Jansen, M. and Liefbroer, A.C. (2001) 'Transition to adulthood in the Netherlands', in M. Corijn and E. Klijzing (eds) *Transitions to adulthood in Europe*, Dordrecht: Kluwer Academic Publishers: 209-232.

Liefbroer, A.C. and Corijn, M. (1999) 'Who, what, where and when? Specifying the impact of educational attainment and labour force participation on family formation', *European Journal of Population*, 15: 45-75.

Liefbroer, A.C. and Dykstra, P.A. (2000) *Levenslopen in verandering. Een studie naar ontwikkelingen in de levenslopen van Nederlanders geboren tussen 1900 en 1970*, Den Haag: Sdu Uitgevers (WRR Voorstudies en Achtergronden V107).

Liefbroer, A.C. and Kalmijn, M. (1997) 'Panel study of social integration in the Netherlands 1987-1995 (PSIN8795)', Codebook, ICS Occasional Papers and Documents Series (ICS Code Books-30), Utrecht: Interuniversity Center for Social Science Theory and Methodology.

Oppenheimer, V.K. (1988) 'A theory of marriage timing', *American Journal of Sociology*, 94: 563-591.

Oppenheimer, V.K., Kalmijn, M. and Lim, N. (1997) 'Men's career development and marriage timing during a period of rising inequality', *Demography*, 34: 311-330.

Rupp, J.C.C. (1992) 'Politieke sociologie van onderwijsdeelname en nationale curricula', in P. Dykstra, Kooij, P. and Rupp, J. (eds) *Onderwijs in de tijd: Ontwikkelingen in onderwijsdeelname en nationale curricula*, Houten: Bohn Stafleu Van Loghum.

Sixma, H., and Ultee, W.C. (1983) 'Een beroepsprestigeschaal voor Nederland in de jaren tachtig', *Mens en Maatschappij*, 58: 360-382.

Van de Kaa, D.J. (1987) 'Europe's second demographic transition', *Population Bulletin*, 42(1): whole issue.

Van de Kaa, D.J. (1996) 'Anchored narratives: the story and findings of half a century of research into the determinants of fertility', *Population Studies*, 50: 389-432.

Veld, Th. (1987) *Volksonderwijs en leerplicht. Een historisch sociologisch onderzoek naar het ontstaan van de Nederlandse leerplicht 1860-1900*, Delft: Eburon.

de Vries, J. and van der Woude, A. (1997) *The first modern economy. Success, failure and perseverance of the Dutch economic performance*, Cambridge: Cambridge University Press.

5 The case of France

Family formation in an uncertain labor market

Annick Kieffer, Catherine Marry, Monique Meron and Anne Solaz

INTRODUCTION

Globalization translates in France into an increase in flexibility and uncertainty on the labor market. This degradation gives rise to inequalities of various forms and types. Job scarcity is particularly felt among the young who are much more affected by it than their older peers, especially at the start of their professional career. Notwithstanding measures that the government has more or less put in place on their behalf, those without the least diplomas are hard-hit by unemployment or unstable employment. As far as gender inequalities are concerned, even though they have diminished in school, they persist on the labor market. At equal levels of education, entry into professional life takes longer for women than for men and is also more difficult. For instance, unemployment and precarious jobs are more frequent among them, and gender gaps in professional positions tend to widen during their careers. The question arises, therefore, what the impact is of these inequalities on the various stages of the family life cycle.

Young adolescents of the most recent decades have gone more slowly than their older peers through the various stages that are normally considered as part of the transition to adulthood, such as completing education, departure from the parental home, start of a first partnership, searching for a job, etc. (for France, see e.g. Corijn, 2001). But it should be kept in mind that the rules governing the passage through these stages - in particular partnership formation - have changed fundamentally. The rise and generalization of female labor force participation have replaced the traditional family model of one (male) breadwinner with one that is more symmetric and which consists of two individuals who are financially independent of each other. Such a scheme leaves more room for partners to negotiate but, unfortunately, this room is limited by the bad situation of the labor market. Since the mid-1970s the female age at first childbirth has gone up while unemployment rates - in particular for young women - have steadily risen.

How do the difficult economic conditions in France of the 1990s that are having a direct impact on the start of a professional career, affect the formation of a family by young people? The objective of this chapter is to study the links between increased uncertainty on the labor market and the start of family life. In a first step we will describe the specific features of France with respect to the globalization process from a historical perspective. To this end we will highlight the consequences that this evolution has had for the labor market opportunities of youngsters, as well as the inequalities that have been induced or aggravated by this situation. In the next step we will then seek to demonstrate the interdependence between the most difficult situations (unemployment, precariousness) and the delay in partnering and parenting behavior.

THE FRENCH LABOR MARKET AND EDUCATIONAL SYSTEM

The history of the French labor market: increasing uncertainty over time

As a colonial power oriented towards the Mediterranean region, Africa and Asia, France has seen its political and economic situation weakening considerably in the course of the 20th century. Part of its industry benefited from a protected market and steady export facilities that did little in the way of motivating enterprises to keep up with the pace of modernization (Woronoff, 1994). However, the independence of its former colonies has forced France to implement important political and economic transformations. Big firms have increased their numbers of branch offices abroad but - contrary to the Japanese and Americans, for instance - they have privileged the countries of the former colonial empire as well as the nearest European countries. The French state has intervened in order to accelerate the pace of modernization and concentration of firms, create industrial groups of international dimensions, and enlarge the scale of international exchanges beyond the boundaries of the old empire. Also the construction of a united Europe has played an important role in the prosperity of the post-war period.

Faced with the lasting crisis that hit the world economy after the first oil shock of the 1970s, companies in France as in other industrialized countries have responded with an increased integration in international exchanges and a re-allocation of industrial activities back to the OECD rather than with a further expansion of the number of their branch offices in South-East Asia.[1] Given the increased uncertainty on the French labor market that resulted from this, companies have opted for a more flexible and parsimonious management style. This has translated into a shift of stable job positions towards the most experienced and qualified employees, the installation of early retirement schemes and, for the youngest and least qualified, a growing dependence on precarious, short-term labor contracts.

In order to mitigate the social consequences that this has had for the young and least qualified, the French state multiplied its interventionist policies. Apart from its attempts at the redeployment of laid-offs and promotion of early retirement agreements, it has taken a series of measures to counteract the negative influences of rising youth unemployment, in particular for the least qualified. For instance, certain measures have favored the system of vocational training by alternating theoretical classroom learning with on-the-job training, whereas others were dedicated to alleviating the salary costs of particular firm jobs. The efficiency of these measures, which were aimed at rendering labor contracts for young entrants more flexible at the risk of higher professional precariousness, is still a subject of debate among specialists. Nonetheless, their success in certain cases is beyond any doubt, in particular when their implementation coincided with periods of economic recovery. In any case, the employment by the government and certain big businesses of various tens of thousands of youngsters under specific contracts called "emplois-jeunes" that had a duration of 5 years and which allowed for on-the-job training, has been a decisive element in the reduction of youth unemployment since 1997-98. Similar state interventions in the mid-1980s were aimed at a partial deregulation of the labor market. Apart from the young it was in particular the immigrants and women who were exposed to the tight labor market conditions that resulted from it. At constant prices, the salaries of young men and women under 30 years of age are nowadays lower than what their older peers earned twenty years ago. Also their prospects of making a career within the same firm are often also less bright (Baudelot and Establet, 2000). It is the impact of these changing conditions in the professional, social and family domains of young people on their transition to adulthood that is at the chore of this chapter.

Education: quantitative democratization

The rise in enrollment figures between 1985 and 1995 results from a threefold development. It is partly due to family strategies that - in the face of rising unemployment and precariousness - seek to provide children with diplomas that are more profitable on the labor market. But the rise is equally a response to the growing awareness of the importance of formal knowledge for professional activity, in the sense that it gives children a better general capacity to appreciate how jobs have changed intrinsically. Finally, the rise in enrollment figures has been actively supported by state reforms that are fully in line with those that have favored educational expansion all along the 21st century. Even if it may be still true that there is an upward shift of social disparities, the result of this threefold development has been a democratization - particularly in quantitative terms - of the educational system (Duru-Bellat and Kieffer, 2000). Thus, whereas only 10 in 100 children born in the 1950s to blue-collar workers obtained a high school diploma, this figure rose to 20 for the generations born between 1964 and 1968 and to 46 for those born between 1974 and 1978. Furthermore, between 1984 and 1993 opportunities for higher education have multiplied by a factor of 2.2 on average, and 3.6 times for children from blue-collar families.

At the same time, gender inequalities in enrollment figures have diminished and even reversed, as illustrated by the absolute and relative improvement of female certificates (Table 5.1). Nonetheless, the educational expansion has hardly altered the gendered nature of chosen curricula. Thus, even if women are nowadays professionally better trained and have higher diplomas than men, they still are a minority in industrial training programs and other so-called "hard" curricula (mathematics, physics, engineering, etc.). After high school more women than men (47.3 versus 37.3 percent) enter the university, but fewer of them enroll in the very restrictive and selective tracks of higher technical

Table 5.1   Gender- and cohort-specific changes in educational attainment in France (in percent)[a]

	<1929		1929-38		1939-48		1949-53		1954-58		1959-63		1964-73	
	F	M	F	M	F	M	F	M	F	M	F	M	F	M
1 ab no qualif., diploma, CEP	77.3	69.3	68.0	57.8	49.3	46.4	43	37.7	36.4	33.2	23.4	27.3	18.7	21.3
1 c CAP, EFAA	8.7	13.8	15.4	25.4	14.9	21	14.7	25.4	9.7	20.8	9.5	19.5	11	16.7
II a BEPC	4.4	2.6	4.3	2.1	9.6	7.3	9.5	8	13.9	11.4	14.2	11.1	10.5	11
2 b BEP	2.5	4.3	4.2	5.7	5.7	3.6	9.1	7.1	13.7	11.5	18.3	17.7	13.6	11.5
2 c 1 Bac Academic	4.2	3.7	4.6	2.9	3.9	5.2	4.4	4.3	4.2	4.1	5.9	4.8	15.5	12
2 c 2 Bac Voc., Tech..	0.1	0.8	0.2	1.1	6.6	4.2	7	4.7	7.5	5.6	12.6	9.1	10.5	10.8
III a BTS-DUT	0.8	0.8	0.7	1.2	7.4	8.0	8.6	7.8	9.0	6.9	8.5	5.0	9.5	9.0
III b Upper Tertiary	2.0	4.7	2.6	3.8	2.6	4.3	3.7	5.0	5.6	6.5	7.6	5.5	10.7	7.7
All	100	100	100	100	100	100	100	100	100	100	100	100	100	100

Sources: Duru-Bellat et al., 2001. Own calculations from FQP Surveys (up to 1949), FQP 85 (up to 1964), FQP 93 (afterwards).

Note: The Casmin nomenclature is used here. The CEP is the primary school leaving certificate (7 years' compulsory education). The CAP is a vocational qualification awarded after 2-3 years' study by lower-secondary school completers (end of 5th, 4th and recently end of 3rd years) school-leaving classes. The BEPC is the lower secondary school leaving certificate. The BEP is a vocational qualification awarded after two years' further study by lower secondary school-leavers. The general or technical baccalauréat is the upper secondary school leaving qualification which is also the higher education matriculation certificate. Higher technical education here is both short-course (2-3 years) and longer (engineering qualifications).

education (BTS and DUT)[2] or in the preparatory classes for the "grandes écoles".[3] Still, better educated as they are than their peers in previous times, young French women of today have a higher propensity to enter professional life and to stay there. Given the context of a tighter and more flexible labor market, this raises the question to which extent these characteristics will play a role in the start of their occupational career.

A longer and more difficult entry into the labor force

Although better trained and educated, young people have been increasingly hard-put to find work since the end of the 1970s. They bear the brunt of unemployment and economic insecurity in France, especially in the post-school period (or national service completion for males).[4] Unemployment amongst first-job seekers rose steadily throughout the 1990s before the economic upturn of 1997, affecting 4 in 10 labor force entrants in March 1996 compared with under 3 at the end of the 1980s. The access of school leavers to the labor force is anything but certain, however: in the latter half of the 1990s, 65 percent of a school-leaver cohort experienced at least one spell of unemployment, and half were in a short-term job.[5] Instability and unemployment affect in particular the less qualified and the less skilled young workers. The "Young People and Careers 1997" Survey[6] found that 16 percent of unqualified men and 20 percent of unqualified women born in 1978 were still unemployed 7 years after leaving school, compared to only 4 and 6 percent, respectively, among those with higher education qualifications.

And yet unemployment, insecurity and growing instability are not driving young women away from the world of work. The same survey found that only 6 percent of women aged 30-45 in 1997 had been completely economically inactive since completing their education, compared to 53 percent who had had no spells of inactivity. Furthermore, half or nearly half of those who had never worked were unqualified young women, which is twice the rate for the population as a whole. Thus, notwithstanding an uncertain and insecure labor market situation for young women, including those living in a union, only a very small minority of them choose full-time homemaking after leaving the educational system, and complete non-participation in the labor force is rare.

A steadily rising female labor force participation rate

Since the turn of the 1960s, participation rates among women aged 15-64 have risen steadily from 46.8 percent in 1962 to 61.7 in 2000. But part of this growth in female employment was part-time work (see Table 5.2) that developed from the mid-1970s on hand-in-hand with the employment slump and which hit the retail and service sectors hardest (Kergoat, 1984; Maruani, 1996; Coutrot *et al.*, 1997; Kergoat and Nicole-Drancourt, 1998). Two periods can be distinguished in this respect (Angeloff, 1999). The first concerns the years 1982-86 when the legal framework was put in place to permit and define part-time work.[7] The

Table 5.2   Age- and gender-specific changes in part-time work in France

	1972	*1977*	*1982*	*1987*	*1992*	*1997*	*2000*
No. (000s)	1202.5	1876.8	1996.8	2546.8	2798.6	3726.9	3962.7
Index	100	156	166	212	233	310	330
% among workforce in employment	5.8	8.7	9.2	11.8	12.7	16.7	16.8
% women among part-timers	82.5	79	83.7	82.1	83.7	81.9	82.5
% among women in employment	13.1	16.7	17.9	22.6	24.5	30.8	31.1
% among men in employment	1.6	1.6	1.7	3.0	3.1	4.7	5.4

Sources: French Labor Force Surveys (INSEE), 1972 to 2000. Own calculations.

second period (1992-95) reflects government policy to extend it by cutting the social security costs of part-time workers. This made it more advantageous for employers to hire two part-time workers for one full-time position and so undermined the status of part-time work, which eventually became generally synonymous with job insecurity, non-standard working times, low-skilled jobs, and poverty (Angeloff, 2000; Meurs and Ponthieux, 1999). With the economic upturn in 1998, this type of work pattern leveled-off or even began to decrease, especially among young people (35 percent of women and 13.8 of men aged 15-24 working part-time in 2000). As in all European countries, part-time work in France mainly affects women (81 percent of part-time workers).

But working women with children have a more unbroken and full-time activity status than in other European countries (for a comparison of France with Sweden, see e.g. Corman, 2002). The most spectacular rise is among mothers with two children: their participation rate between ages 25 and 49 rose from 26.1 percent in 1962 to 75.9 in 2000. Of mothers surveyed by INSEE in 1989[8], 30 percent in the 1919-29 cohorts had always worked against 45 percent in the 1945-1959 cohorts (Nétumières, 1994). But the proportion of French women who stop working after their first birth remained constant in all cohorts (at around 20 percent), with childbirth always holding back women's labor force participation, especially among women with children under the age of three. So, in March 2000, the participation rate among women of parity two was 57.6 percent when the youngest child was under 3 years of age, rising to 83.7 percent when it was older than 6. Many observers have jumped to conclusions about the causal relationship in the correlation between labor force participation and family life cycle. The mother's withdrawal from the labor force in connection with the birth of a third child (Desplanques *et al.,* 1991) is a case in point; in fact, this generally happens with the first birth (Nétumières, 1994). The differentials by age at first birth that Battagliola *et al.* (1997) found for economic inactivity illustrate the importance attached to the role of mother and homemaker: 34 percent of the women of parity one who gave birth under the age of 24 are already economically inactive, compared to just 13 percent among those aged between 24 and 29 at first birth. Other female biography findings make it increasingly hard to attribute long-term career suspensions to childbirth alone

(Kempeneers and Lelièvre, 1991). However, most of their spells out of employment are related to family circumstances.[9] Career breaks are temporary for most mothers, who start working again once their child has started school. As a form of labor force participation of mothers in general, part-time work among women with children is less widespread in France (in 1996, 17 percent of mothers aged 20-39 worked part-time and 44 percent full-time in 1991) than it is in Germany (28 and 20 percent, respectively) or Great Britain (35 and 18 percent, respectively).[10] French family and employment policies on creches, day care centers, and "full-time" preschool from the age of two[11] (Jenson and Sineau, 1997; Letablier and Lurol, 2000) are generally more supportive of working mothers than those in many other countries, which may go some way to explain these pro-work behaviors.

Labor force participation by mothers has been sustained by public family policies that since the end of the second world war have always been pro-natalist and pro-active in this respect.[12] The last twenty years of the 21st century have seen a reinforcement of these policies. Apart from creches and kindergartens, it is nowadays also the parental leave system in France that allows mothers as well as fathers to interrupt their professional life and fall back on various forms of state subsidies. On top of all this there are also fiscal benefits for those who have to hire domestic help for baby-sitting, child-minding, etc. Taken all together these measures have certainly served to ease the barriers that used to stand in-between women's aspirations for combining family life with a professional career. What has not changed that much, however, is the traditional labor division at home: domestic tasks are still predominantly performed by women (Kieffer *et al.*, 2000).

In the following we will try to empirically investigate and answer the question whether unemployment delays first union formation, and how it affects the decision to have a first child. Before doing so, however, we will first briefly introduce our data, methods and variables.

DATA, METHODS AND VARIABLES

The survey "Young People and Careers" on which the following analyses are based was carried out by INSEE[13] in 1997. It is based on a sample of some 20,000 individuals aged 19-45 years from the last round of the 1997 national employment survey of around 9,000 households. This sample consists of the following two sub-groups: (1) those younger than 30 who were born in 1968-78 or who have finished their studies less than 7 years ago (N = 8,373); and (2) those older than 30 who were born before 1968 (N = 12,397). The survey "Young People and Careers" was a retrospective survey collecting biographic information on the professional, relational and residential trajectories.

One of the main themes of the survey concerned the occupational history of the respondents. Thus, a first part of the questionnaire was devoted to unravel the various transition paths from school to work (defined as the first employment that lasted more than six months). A second part inquired about the current activity status of the respondent, whether employed or not, as well as about opinions and future intentions. Another main theme concerned family events and other hallmarks of the life course.

The semi-parametric proportional hazard model that we have used in our two substantive analyses has the general form:

$$h\,[t, Z_1, Z_2(t)] = h_0(t) \exp\,[b_1\,Z_1 + b_2\,Z_2(t)]$$

where $h_0(t)$ is the baseline hazard, Z_1 a vector containing time-constant covariates only, and $Z_2(t)$ a vector containing time-varying covariates. Our dependent variables are the time elapsed since school completion for the study of union formation, and since union formation for the study of first motherhood. Our explanatory variables are principally birth cohort, occupational category, level of education, labor market activity status and type of job, as applicable. Certain variables - labor force activity status in particular - change values over time, others like birth cohort do not.

DOES UNEMPLOYMENT DELAY FIRST UNION FORMATION?

Given the integration of women in professional activity as their preferred family model, and given the fact that their human capital is by now at least as good as that of men, one may ask: how are dual-income couples adjusting to the worsening labor market conditions? More specifically, how is first union formation affected by job insecurity and unemployment? If the partner is working, then living in a union can be an insurance against risk for the unemployed, but joblessness may also imply an imbalanced relationship from the outset.

Job insecurity, first job pay and first union formation

As indicated, a semi-parametric proportional hazard analysis (Cox model) was performed over the period between completion of studies and first union formation. Table 5.3 shows that a blue-collar or agricultural background makes for a later first union. Furthermore, both unqualified and highly qualified women are less likely to form a union, while for men the probability rises almost monotonically with educational attainment (see also Ekert-Jaffé and Solaz, 2001).

Using these survey data, the concept of insecurity can be defined in terms of the pay and nature of the first job (permanent contract, agency work, short-term contract, paid training, etc.), its actual duration and cause of severance, if any. The *first secure job* can then be defined as one that lasted for more than six months, was based on a permanent contract, held uninterruptedly either prior to the first union or at the survey date, or "voluntarily" interrupted by resignation, parental leave or resumption of studies. By contrast, *insecure first jobs* would then be all other types of job or those interrupted by severance before the first union for exogenous reasons (dismissal, call for national service, end of short-term contract, etc.). As the results for professional status in Table 5.3 indicate, joblessness and job insecurity thus defined are seriously adverse to first union formation for both men and women, but in particular for men.

As far as wages are concerned, *starting pay* was present-discounted for between-cohort comparability.[14] Classes 1-4 in Table 5.3 are presented in ascending order.[15] Results indicate that a man on very low pay (class 1) has a lower probability of forming a union, while a very low pay has the opposite effect among women. What we are undoubtedly seeing here is the entrenched traditional model, i.e., different career plans for men and women. Presumably it is in this class of low-wage earners that trade-offs between family and working life are felt most sharply, especially among earlier generations of women.[16]

On the one hand, a very low starting pay offers few prospects for career advancement, thus distracting women more readily from the labor market. On the other, these women could also have a weaker relation with work to begin with, finding domestic life more attractive. In this sense, qualitative (Nicole-Drancourt, 1989) and quantitative (Marry *et al.*, 1995) surveys on young women have shown that actually two groups of low-educated women exist. Some of them have a weak attachment to the labor market and begin their first partnership and maternity soon, maybe because of a traditional family model that they inherited from their parents. Others have a strong work attachment and are still working in spite of the difficulties on the labor market, preferring this activity to living as a housewife.

The traditional family model among the youngest cohorts, therefore, seems to be a thing of the past. By contrast, for women in well-paid jobs that enable them to live alone, it is apparently the type of job that counts most. If insecure, it will delay their first union ($e^{-.213} = .808$), because the financial autonomy that their high wages provide them with - at least temporarily - enables them to put it off. For men, the probability of first union formation rises steadily with the level of their starting pay.

Recent birth cohorts: the importance of the work insertion path

From the population in the "Young People and Careers" survey, we can distinguish those under age thirty (born between 1968 and 1978), for whom the information on the annual timing of career and family events since the date of completing their training[17] is more detailed. This eliminates potential cohort effects, at the risk of introducing a possible selectivity bias.[18] However, there are two advantages to be had from restricting the study to young people under age thirty. One is to be able to distinguish unemployment from economic inactivity[19]; the other is to account for the whole career by including different instances of economic insecurity (recurrent unemployment, paid training, subsidized jobs). This allows us for the youngest cohort (Table 5.4) to address the question: which degree of insecurity is the most adverse to first union formation?

Table 5.3 Probability of first union formation in France (survey "Jeunes et Carrières" 1997) - Cox model on the duration between the end of studies and the first partnership (global population)

Covariates	Females			Males		
	Parameter	*Risk ratio*	*Standard deviation*	*Parameter*	*Risk ratio*	*Standard deviation*
Age group						
Under 26	0.043	1.044	0.042	-0.073	1.167	0.053
26 – 32	0.023	1.023	0.030	0.049	0.127	0.032
33 – 39	0 (ref.)	1	-	0 (ref.)	1	-
40 – 46	-0.141**	0.868	0.031	-0.002	0.959	0.033
Age at end of studies						
9 – 16	-0.131**	0.850	0.031	-0.137**	0.872	0.032
17 – 20	0 (ref.)	1	-	0 (ref.)	1	-
21 – 24	-0.007	0.993	0.035	0.339**	1.404	0.042
25 – 35	-0.183*	0.833	0.109	0.400**	1.492	0.095
Wages						
Class 1 (below 30% of the mean)	0.192**	1.212	0.034	-0.111**	0.895	0.039
Class 2 (between 30% below the mean and the mean)	0 (ref.)	1	-	0 (ref.)	1	-
Class 3 (between the mean and 30% above the mean)	0.015	1.015	0.040	0.035	1.036	0.037
Class 4 (30% above the mean)	-0.058	0.944	0.045	0.071*	1.073	0.038
No response	-0.061	0.940	0.073	-0.166**	0.847	0.067

Table 5.3 continued

Covariates	Females			Males		
	Parameter	Risk ratio	Standard deviation	Parameter	Risk ratio	Standard deviation
Professional status						
No employment	-0.327**	0.721	0.049	-0.922**	0.398	0.051
Insecure job	-0.213**	0.808	0.032	-0.169**	0.844	0.028
Secure job	0 (ref.)	1	-	0 (ref.)	1	-
Farmer or manual worker	-0.065**	0.938	0.031	-0.121**	0.886	0.030
Likelihood: -2log L	121869			101937		
Observations	8770			8462		

Notes
* Effect significant at p < 0.10
** Effect significant at p < 0.05

Table 5.4 Probability of first union formation in France among people born after 1968 - Cox model on the duration between the end of training and the first partnership (population less than thirty in 1997)

Covariates	Females			Males		
	Parameter	Risk ratio	Standard deviation	Parameter	Risk ratio	Standard deviation
Age group						
18 – 22	-0.101	0.904	0.080	-0.373**	0.689	0.123
23 – 25	0 (ref)	1	-	0 (ref)	1	-
26 – 30	-0.049	0.952	0.057	0.152**	1.164	0.068
Education						
No qualification	-0.201**	0.818	0.069	-0.148*	0.863	0.081
BEP, CAP, BEPC	0 (ref)	1	-	0 (ref)	1	-
Baccalaureat	-0.106	0.899	0.072	0.051	1.053	0.094
Baccalaureat +2	-0.038	0.962	0.074	0.212**	1.237	0.101
Employment status						
Long-term contract, full time	0 (ref)	1	-	0 (ref)	1	-
Long-term contract, part-time	0.023	1.024	0.110	-0.467	0.627	0.293
Short-term contract	-0.109	0.897	0.073	-0.211**	0.810	0.080
Self-employed	-0.137	0.872	0.186	-0.596**	0.551	0.197

Table 5.4 continued

Covariates	Females			Males		
	Parameter	Risk ratio	Standard deviation	Parameter	Risk ratio	Standard deviation
Unemployment before first job	-0.346**	0.708	0.106	-0.628**	0.505	0.160
Unemployment after first job (wage < half-mean)	-0.360**	0.698	0.115	-1.115**	0.315	0.216
Unemployment after first job (wage > half-mean)	0.515	1.674	0.417	-0.067	0.935	0.364
Integration, contract, training period	-0.285**	0.752	0.115	-0.805**	0.447	0.187
Further training, free training period	-0.406*	0.666	0.205	-0.956**	0.384	0.254
National service	-	-	-	-0.424**	0.654	0.117
Inactive	-0.165*	0.848	0.100	-1.065**	0.345	0.338
Others	-0.389**	0.619	0.111	-0.978**	0.376	0.206
Manual worker or farmer	0.058	1.060	0.078	0.085	1.089	0.945
Likelihood: -2log L	22729			15135		
Observations	2483			2443		

Notes

* Effect significant at p < 0.10
** Effect significant at p < 0.05

We control for cohort effects[20] using qualification level and age at training completion as measures of educational attainment and time spent in education.[21] Generally speaking, a low diploma will diminish one's chances to form a union. But oddly enough, as Table 5.4 demonstrates for women and men alike, qualification level has little impact on the probability of first union formation; it is only the lack of qualifications that is adverse. For this young generation, employment status is much more important and, where this is clearly defined, it eliminates the qualification effect.[22] What is expected of young people, and what they delay their union formation for, is a source of income as recognition from the labor market rather than from the educational system: qualification levels operate through labor market opportunities. However, men's high qualification levels remain statistically significant (e$^{.212}$ = 1.237). Their possibilities for couple formation are defined by both educational attainment and employment status, as opposed to females for whom the career path is the most important factor.

The total number of the unemployed among these younger cohorts was adequate enough to clarify the unemployment effect by distinguishing between unemployment spells before the first job and those thereafter. For the latter it was furthermore possible to differentiate according to the wage level of the first job (below and above half of the mean). As the results in Table 5.4 demonstrate, unemployment for women is equally adverse no matter whether it occurs before or after the first job if that is low-paid, because they will be entitled to only a low or no unemployment benefit at all. For men, however, unemployment is more adverse if it occurs after a first low-paid job (e$^{-1.115}$ = 0.315). This gender disparity clearly bespeaks differences in social perceptions. It is harder for men to deal with unemployment after a first low-paid job because the main benchmark for their worth (including family values) is paid work. The incidence of first union formation among unemployed men is significantly lower than among women. On the other hand, unemployment after a first well-paid job is not adverse for both sexes (but the total numbers are quite low).

Career path was introduced dynamically.[23] Interestingly, there is no significant difference between permanent part- or full-time employment, neither among women nor among men. The adverse effect for young males who are in self-employment is low (e$^{-0.596}$ = 0.551), and nil for young females. Other insecure situations like work experience training (paid placement or subsidized jobs) are also adverse, but their effect on first union formation differs for men and women. For instance, a short-term contract is not adverse for women but strongly so for men. More extreme insecurity (subsidized jobs, training-for-work schemes, unpaid training, etc.) is adverse for both sexes, thus promoting social exclusion.

Large question marks, therefore, now hang over the economic theory of marriage, according to which the male purchases the female's domestic labor. Female labor force participation is always an advantage, even for the pre-1968 birth cohorts (see below). Labor force participation offers opportunities to extend one's network of relationships outside the immediate circle of relatives and friends, thus increasing chance encounters. This network can also profit the career of the prospective partner (Bernasco *et al.*, 1998). Unemployment for women remains more adverse than economic inactivity, but in the latter case it is not known whether union formation is delayed by the woman's own choice (until she finds work) or by a lack of interest from men (with a preference for working women).

Pre-1968 birth cohorts: the role of women's inactivity

A similar study[24] (Table 5.5) was carried out on men and women older than 30 at interview time (born between 1952 and 1967). As was the case in the younger generation, qualification level and employment status are both significant for men, but less so for women. The male but not the female probability of first union formation rises monotonically with educational level. Other gender differentials are also discernible for the variables under study. For instance, unemployment is adverse to males but not to females for whom it is neutral.

Contrary to what we found for the younger generation, inactive women appear advantaged on the marriage market (e $^{.378}$ = 1.459). In combination, these two findings seem to suggest that the traditional family model according to which an inactive woman should be advantaged, is on its way out. Nowadays it is a woman's activity - not inactivity - that is one of the conditions for starting a partnership relation.

To sum up, the two cohorts that we have studied formed their first unions at different times - in the 1990s for the younger one, in the mid-70s for the older one - and in different labor market contexts (10 and 6 percent unemployment, respectively). In a globalization context of rising unemployment, qualification levels - previously an important factor - become less important as a determinant of delayed first union formation in the post-1968 birth cohorts than career path and employment since completion of studies. Naturally, this raises the question whether growing labor market uncertainty will have a similar postponement effect on parenthood.

DOES UNEMPLOYMENT AFFECT THE FIRST CHILD DECISION?

There are many important cohort- and training-specific differentials in women's fertility experience and exposure to the risk of unemployment. Even when one attempts to factor in all these differentials, current statistical analyses do not always permit a clear linkage between fluctuations in unemployment rates and the mother's age at first birth.

Biographic analysis (Courgeau and Lelièvre, 1989) at least enables one to study individual life courses in all their diversity. We applied this method first to the timing of first births to more than 5,500 women aged 31-45 years who were or had been in a conjugal relationship. These were interviewed in 1997 by INSEE as part of the nationally representative survey "Young People and Careers", the same data source that was used for the previous analysis. Thereafter we examined whether the observed trends continued among young people (aged 24-29), in a sample of 1,600 women taken from the same survey (Meron and Widmer, 2001).

Table 5.5 Probability of first union formation in France among people born between 1952 and 1967 - Cox model on the duration between the end of training and the first partnership (population more than thirty in 1997)

Covariates	Females			Males		
	Parameter	*Risk ratio*	*Standard deviation*	*Parameter*	*Risk ratio*	*Standard deviation*
Age group						
30 – 35	0.053*	1.055	0.032	-0.035	0.966	0.035
36 – 39	0 (ref)	1	-	0 (ref)	1	-
40 – 45	-0.092**	0.912	0.033	-0.012	0.988	0.035
Education						
No qualification	-0.188**	0.828	0.038	-0.162**	0.850	0.039
CEP, BEP, CAP	0 (ref)	1	-	0 (ref)	1	-
CAP, BEPC	-0.040	0.961	0.043	0.055	1.057	0.044
Baccalaureat	0.061	1.063	0.043	0.152**	0.164	0.052
Baccalaureat +2	-0.032	0.968	0.042	0.338**	1.403	0.049

Table 5.5 continued

Covariates	Females			Males		
	Parameter	Risk ratio	Standard deviation	Parameter	Risk ratio	Standard deviation
Employment status						
Job (more than 6 months)	0 (ref)	1	-	0 (ref)	1	-
Unemployment	-0.056	0.945	0.066	-0.504**	0.604	0.096
Insecure job	-0.123**	0.884	0.051	-0.361**	0.697	0.059
Studies (after discontinuation), apprenticeship, training	-0.244**	0.783	0.067	-0.745**	0.475	0.104
Homemaker, Inactive	0.378**	1.459	0.043	-0.821**	0.440	0.161
Others	-0.174	0.840	0.117	-0.509**	0.601	0.075
Farmer or manual worker	-0.008	0.992	0.034	-0.055**	0.946	0.036
Likelihood: -2log L	91098			79292		
Number of observations	6212			5764		

Notes
* Effect significant at p < 0.10
** Effect significant at p < 0.05

Women were followed from the starting time of their first union up to a maximum of eight years after the start of that union. Our analysis focuses on the gap between the starting time of the first union and the date of the first birth or the survey date, if earlier. Women whose unions dissolved while they were still childless are treated as "right-censored". As before, changes in economic activity status were identified dynamically from the woman's annual work event schedule (studies, unemployment, continuous employment, intermittent employment, economic inactivity, etc.). Initially, the life courses of 5,506 women born between 1952 and 1966 who were or had been in a union were analyzed. Before we report on these results, we first briefly discuss some relevant literature and/or descriptive statistics.

Rising female labor force participation

In France the mean age of mothers at first birth rose from under 24 years in 1972 through 25 in 1983 to 26 in 1989. The spread of new contraceptive technologies from the 1970s onward brought improved fertility control, which enabled couples to postpone parenthood until later ages. But additional mechanisms are behind the continued increase in the duration of voluntary childlessness during the 1980s and 90s. The weakening of partner relationships and rise in non-marital unions were some of them (Prioux, 1996; Toulemon, 1994).

More education and labor force participation are also often offered as explanations for women's postponement of motherhood. A later age at first birth can be observed amongst a growing number of educated women (Galland, 2000; Galland and Meron, 1996). Finally, there is a clear linkage between parity and female labor force participation rates, which have steadily risen since the turn of the 1970s. But little study has yet been made about the effect of women's employment status.

Risks of exclusion delay family formation

No direct link can be made between unemployment and fertility from a comparison between economic trends and family events. To the contrary, whereas during 1975-89 women with hardly any education delayed the birth of their first child to more or less the same extent - although at much lower ages - as those with (much) more education (Figure 5.1), they were nonetheless the most affected by the general increase in youth employment during this same period (Figure 5.2). Some case studies based on personal life course accounts by young women living in economic insecurity tend to show that those who have difficulties finding work may refocus their lives on the family, hope for the long-term best, and use the opportunity to take a first child decision (Nicole-Drancourt, 1989). These case studies also found that unemployment affects family life in many different ways, depending on the unemployed person's position in the household and the type of unemployment involved. Furthermore, young women's (childbearing) intentions vary with age, social background, partner's employment status, and the duration of the union.

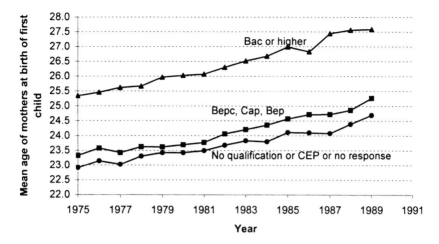

Figure 5.1   Mean age of French mothers at birth of first child, by major diploma
Source: Enquête famille 1990.

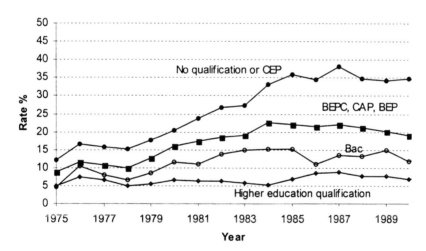

Figure 5.2   Unemployment rate of French women aged 15-29, by major diploma

Younger, better-qualified women remain longest voluntarily childless

One in two women of the 1952-66 cohorts had a first child during the first 3 years of their conjugal life. But the median is only 2.1 years for women with no qualification or only primary school completed, and rises to 3.7 years for secondary school completers and to 4.7 for women with a qualification level higher than 2 years post-secondary education.

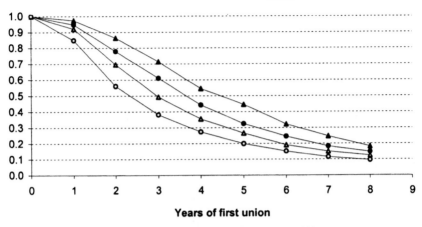

Figure 5.3   Transition to first child for French women aged 31-45; grouped by birth cohort and qualification (survivor function)

Source: Survey "Jeunes et carrières 1997", INSEE.

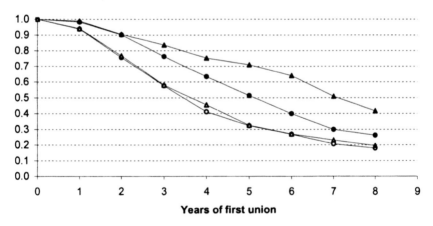

Figure 5.4   Transition to first child for French women aged 24-29; grouped by birth cohort and qualification (survivor function)

Source: Survey "Jeunes et carrières 1997", INSEE.

The median duration of voluntarily childless unions also increases in line with the women's birth date. One in two women born between 1952 and 1954 postponed her first child for at least 2.4 years after the starting time of her first union, whereas among the youngest women in this sample (born between 1961 and 1966) the interval was one and a half times longer: 3.7 years. The survivor functions in Figures 5.3 and 5.4 illustrate the differences in delayed childbearing in the older, respectively, younger samples of women, according to their years of birth and qualification levels.

Table 5.6   Semi-parametric analysis of the duration between the start of the union and the first child according to situations experienced since the start of the union (France, 1952-1966 cohorts)

	Parameter	*Multiplier Effect*
Birth cohort		
1952 – 1954	0.1141**	1.21
1955 – 1960		1
1961 – 1966	-0.1227***	0.884
Qualification		
Higher than bac+2	-0.4991***	0.607
From bac to bac+2	-0.2182***	0.804
BEPC, CAP, BEP		1
No qualification or CEP	0.1861***	1.205
*Activity*****		
Experienced unemployment	-0.4071***	0.665
Not experienced unemployment	.	1
Experienced inactivity	0.1468***	1.158
Not experienced inactivity	.	1

Sources: "Young People and Careers 1997" survey by INSEE.

Notes
    reference category
*   Effect significant at p < 0.05.
**   Effect significant at p < 0.005.
***   Effect significant at p < 0.001.

Interpretation:
A woman with no qualification or only CEP has (all else being equal) an $e^{.1861} = 1.205$ greater probability of birth since the start of the union than a woman in the reference group with a qualification equivalent to the BEPC, CAP or BEP.

Women exposed to unemployment postpone first births

For women of the same cohort and qualification level, those in the labor force delayed their first child for longer after the starting time of their first union. But this increase in the childless period of union duration is longer for women who have experienced spells of intermittent employment than for those who report only periods of continuous employment, while periods of continuous unemployment delay first births longest of all. The latter is illustrated in Figures 5.5 and 5.6 for women at comparable levels of education and birth cohorts.

These results clearly vary with birth cohort and qualification level. Again, in the semi-parametric proportional hazard analysis (Table 5.6), the unemployment effect remained highly significant.

By contrast, women who had experienced spells of inactivity had shorter childless periods in unions than others (Figures 5.7 and 5.8). This confirms that the behavior of unemployed women differs from that of full-time homemakers (Marry *et al.*, 1995).

The under-30s follow in their elder sisters' footsteps

Although the variables are not wholly identical, the impact of employment status on first birth was also tested for women aged 24-29 as interviewed in the same survey of "Young People and Careers". The employment statuses of 1,565 women born between 1968 and 1973 who were or had been in a union were analyzed by the same method.

One in two of these women had postponed their first birth for more than 4.4 years, with persisting differences between the cohorts: women born at the end of the 60s had a first child sooner after the start of their conjugal life (4.1 years) than those born in the early 1970s (4.9 years). Female secondary school completers always remain longer in voluntarily childless unions than unqualified women (5.8 years against 3.5 years), regardless of employment status.

These women under age 30 have borne even more of the brunt of the job shortage than their elder sisters: twice as many of them remain in education after the starting time of their first union. On the other hand, increasingly fewer drop out of the labor market.

Like their elders, women of the younger cohorts who remain in education or are on the labor market have significantly later first births than those who experience spells of economic inactivity. The influence of unemployment is more discernible among young women from failed educational backgrounds. The sample cannot be regarded as complete for the best-qualified, however, because at the ages concerned (24 to 29 years) many are still in education and have not yet formed a first union. The Cox analysis confirms the influence of labor force participation status on the birth of the first child also for these youngest cohorts (Table 5.7).

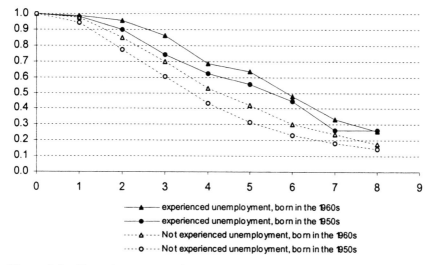

Figure 5.5   Unemployment experience among French women born in 1952-66 with upper-secondary school-leaving certificate born in 1952-66

Source: Survey "Jeunes et carrières 1997", INSEE.

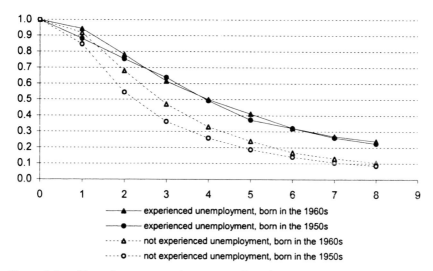

Figure 5.6   Unemployment experience among French women born in 1952-66 without upper-secondary school-leaving certificate

Source: Survey "Jeunes et carrières 1997", INSEE.

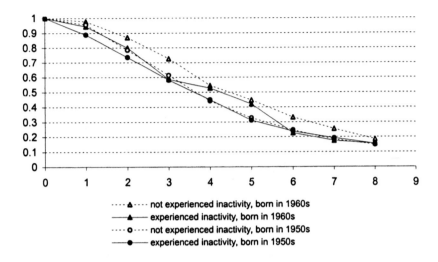

Figure 5.7 Inactivity experience among French women born in 1952-1966 with upper-secondary school-leaving certificate

Source: Survey "Jeunes et carrières 1997", INSEE.

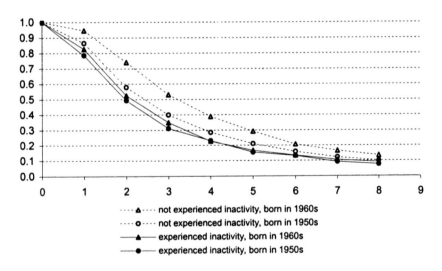

Figure 5.8 Inactivity experience among French women born in 1952-1966 without upper-secondary school-leaving certificate

Source: Survey "Jeunes et carrières 1997", INSEE.

Table 5.7   Semi-parametric analysis of the duration between the start of the union and the first child according to situations experienced since the start of the union (France, 1968-1973 cohorts)

	Parameter	Multiplier Effect
Birth cohort		
1971 – 1973	-0.1910*	0.826
1968 – 1970	.	1
Qualification		
Above bac+2	-1.2983***	0.273
From bac to bac+2	-0.4633***	0.629
BEPC, CAP, BEP	.	1
No qualification or CEP	0.2215*	1.248
Activity		
Experienced unemployment	-0.4537***	0.635
Not experienced unemployment	.	1
Experienced inactivity	0.4644***	1.591
Not experienced inactivity	.	1

Sources: "Young People and Careers 1997" survey by INSEE.

Notes
.   Reference group
*   Effect significant at $p < 0.05$
**   Effect significant at $p < 0.005$
***   Effect significant at $p < 0.001$

Interpretation:
A woman with no qualification or only CEP has (all else being equal) an $e^{.2215} = 1.248$ greater probability of birth since the start of the union than a woman in the reference group with the BEPC, CAP or BEP.

CONCLUSION

The economic context that surrounds the transition to adulthood in France during the 1990s is characterized by continued learning, a labor market that is increasingly difficult to enter, and high youth unemployment. Globalization can explain these tendencies to a large extent. But there are other co-existing phenomena that are specific to France and its societal history and which either mitigate or aggravate these influences, such as the work attachment of women or the prevailing system of social protection.

Globalization - that is to say, a labor market becoming both more open and flexible - is one of the main causes that explains the increasing insecurity in work, the rise in part-time jobs (mainly for women) and unemployment rates, especially for the young people of the 1990s. These phenomena have contributed to exacerbate all sorts of inequalities, such as those between the qualified and unqualified, the employed and unemployed, etc. The access nowadays to higher education for a majority of school-leavers means that those without any diploma are henceforth all the more marginalized: they see themselves excluded from both the labor and marriage market. Unemployment rates among the unqualified are extremely high. True, they are the first to benefit from job creation programs but, paradoxically, such jobs are often precarious and without perspective.It is in this way that the gap between the unemployed and employed widens. Those excluded from the labor market accumulate health and marginalization problems, and they have more difficulties to establish a family.

These growing inequalities notwithstanding, a specific feature of French culture is the resilience of women both in the educational system and on the labor market. They perform better in the former, from which they exit with higher qualifications than men do. In spite of a persisting gender discrimination on the labor market, women continue to wish to work, preferably full-time. Female participation rates remain quite high, including those among mother of two children. Although the number of part-time jobs has expanded considerably, they are not always chosen and they are less of a norm than in many other countries (see e.g. Liefbroer on the Netherlands, or Bygren *et al.* on Sweden, this volume).

Thus, high unemployment does not keep women away from the labor market in France. They have integrated their labor force participation into their family model. Hence, unemployment and insecurity that delay the entry into a first stable job also tend to postpone the various stages of the family life cycle.

The spread of the dual-income couple model has brought men and women's first union formation behaviors more closely into line. Unemployment for females is now almost as adverse to union formation as it is for males but other than that, the impact of significant job insecurity still differs by gender. For instance, short-term contracts are equivalent to a secure job for women of the younger cohorts, while an insecure job delays couple formation among men. That being said, there remain a few inconsistencies which are probably a hangover from the traditional model. For example, a high qualification level encourages earlier first union formation among men but later among women, whereas very low-paid entry jobs have a positive effect for women but negative for men. The career pathways after completion of training become a key explanatory factor of first union formation for women and men alike, in the younger cohorts even more so than education. Recurrent spells of unemployment combined with increasing job insecurity delay the first union decision.

Unemployment also delays the arrival of the first child to young women born between 1952 and 1973. This trend is even more discernible amongst the least qualified in the youngest cohorts. By contrast, full-time homemakers tend to have their first child earlier, which presumably reflects precipitated decisions. This finding confirms that a spell of unemployment is not the same as a period of economic inactivity.

The rather protective welfare framework of French society, which aims to compensate for the handicaps of less-educated and unemployed young people, does not manage to erase the main effects of globalization. Economic insecurity and unemployment negatively influence the transition to adulthood.

NOTES

1   In 1992 exports represented 35.7 percent of the national product and the penetration rate of the internal market was 36.7 percent. France is the second largest industrial investor after the USA (Woronoff, op. cit.).

2   Brevet de Technicien Supérieur and Diplôme Universitaire de Technologie, obtained after two years of preparatory courses.

3   These classes last two years and give access to the competition for entering the "grandes écoles", which specialize mainly in scientific but also in economic and literary subjects.

4   The 10-month duty of national service has been abolished for males born in or since 1979.

5   Source: Cereq "Génération 92" survey.

6   Supplementing the 1997 Employment Survey, which tracks the careers and life courses of people aged 30-45 at survey date.

7   A provision of the Labour Code (L.212.4.2) defines part-time work as working hours that are at least one-fifth below the statutory number of working hours or those fixed by agreement for the workplace or industry segment.

8   In the "Carrières" survey supplementing the 1989 Employment Survey.

9   Three in ten young women stopped work at least once between 1979 and 1992, three-quarters of them for family reasons: 53 percent to look after their children, 8 percent to be closer to or move with their spouse, and 15 percent for some other family reason.

10 Source: Women and Employment in the European Union, Newsletter No. 6, April 1995.

11 The preschool enrolment ratio in 1998-1999 was 35.2 percent from age 2 and 99.9 from age 3, rising to 100 thereafter (source: Ministry of Education, 2000, Repères et références statistiques, p. 22).

12 First the reconstruction, then the modernization of the French productive machinery necessitated lots of labor. During this period there was therefore a massive recourse to foreign labor (from Poland, Italy, Spain, Portugal, North and later sub-Saharan Africa) for the industry and construction sectors, followed by an influx of women in the service sector and public domain.

13 In collaboration with INED, CEREQ, CNRS, CEE and various ministerial departments.

14 An indicator was developed to compare first-job pay between different cohorts. We compared the individual starting pay with the average private sector pay for young people (either in the 18-20 or 21-25 age group) in the year of their first job. These data result from continuous pay series (1998 edition) and give thus relative rather than fully present-discounted pay figures.

15 Class 1 represents a starting pay below 30 percent of the then-current average, class 2 is from 30 percent below average to the average itself, class 3 runs from average up to 30 percent above it, while class 4 contains the very top.

16 This is confirmed if the cohorts are split into two populations. The positive coefficient of the first pay class is more significant for women aged thirty and above (at 2 percent) than for those of lesser age (at more than 10 percent).

17 By this we mean the latest date at which education was interrupted or at which education, training or national service was completed. The actual date can then be factored in, which is more relevant to the study of first union formation than the date

of completing education itself, especially for unqualified populations undergoing a protracted job transition period.

18 The sample may then be biased because the better-educated young people will be more easily excluded, as they are less likely to have completed their education at the survey date or to have been in a union before completion. Nevertheless, they are also the least affected by unemployment and exclusion from work.

19 The measurement of life course events was more detailed for those under age 30.

20 The rising coefficients of age group parameters for both men and women may be due to an under-representation of members of collective households in the survey, but more probably to the selectivity effect mentioned above. Because the highest-qualified individuals were more often excluded from our sample, the cohort variable corrects this effect but it is not interpretable.

21 Qualification level was preferred here to age at education completion: the steadily rising age at education completion within a fairly narrow age group is increasingly less discriminatory.

22 In a regression analysis performed only on age, social background and qualification level, qualification level came out statistically significant for women. This clearly confirms that including the career path eliminates the education effect, except for those without qualifications who are also more excluded from the labor market.

23 Thus, in each year after training completion the employment status variable can change. Employment, unemployment, economic inactivity, work experience and training can all be differentiated from each other. If a person has a job, its type can be identified: fixed-term contract, permanent part-time or full-time contract, self-employed. The main employment status in a given year is defined as that economic activity that lasted more than six months. If there was no economic activity lasting that long, an ancillary activity lasting more than three months was used. Thus defined, 20 percent of the women had no main employment status, and fewer than 10 percent no ancillary activity.

24 The measurement of employment status does not follow exactly the same path as for the younger cohorts. Two situations may be reported in the same year. In such a case, we have prioritized employment (necessarily over six months), then unemployment, insecurity (defined by the survey as alternating spells of unemployment and short periods of employment), training and resumption of studies.

BIBLIOGRAPHY

Angeloff, T. (1999) 'Des miettes d'emploi: temps partiel et pauvreté', *Travail, Genre et Sociétés*, 1: 43-69.

Angeloff, T. (2000) *Le temps partiel, un marché de dupes?*, Paris: Syros, La Découverte.

Battagliola, F., Brown, E., and Jaspard, M. (1997) 'Être parent jeune: quels liens avec les itinéraires professionnels?', *Economie et Statistique*, 304-305: 191-207.

Baudelot, Ch. and Establet, R. (2000) *Avoir 30 ans en 1968 et en 1998*, Paris: Éditions du Seuil.

Bernasco, W., de Graaf, P. M., and Ultee, W. C. (1998) 'Couple Careers, Effect of Spouse's Resources on Occupational Attainment in the Netherlands', *European Sociological Review*, 14(1): 15-31.

Corijn, M. (2001) 'Transition to adulthood in France', in M. Corijn and E. Klijzing (eds) *Transitions to Adulthood in Europe*, Dordrecht: Kluwer Academic Publishers.

Corman, D. (2002) 'Family policies, work arrangements and the third child in France and Sweden', in E. Klijzing and M. Corijn (eds) *The dynamics of fertility and partnership in Europe: lessons and insights from comparative research*, Volume II, Geneva/New York: United Nations.

Courgeau, D. and Lelièvre, E. (1989) *Analyse démographique des biographies*, Paris: INED.

Coutrot, L., Fournier-Mearelli, I., Kieffer, A., and Lelièvre, E. (1997) 'The Family Cycle and the Growth of Part-Time Employment in France, Boon or Doom?', in H.-P. Blossfeld and C. Hakim (eds) *Between Equalization and Marginalization: Part-Time Women in Europe and the United State of America*, Oxford: Oxford University Press.

Desplanques, G., Raton, I., and Thave, S. (1991) 'L'activité féminine. Résultats de l'enquête familles de 1990', INSEE Résultats, 118.

Duru-Bellat, M., Kieffer, A., and Marry, C. (2001) 'La dynamique des scolarités des filles : le double handicap questionné', *Revue Française de Sociologie*, 42(2): 251-280.

Duru-Bellat, M., and Kieffer, A. (2000) 'La démocratisation de l'enseignement en France : Polémique autour d'une question d'actualité', *Population*, 55(1): 51-80.

Ekert-Jaffé, O. and Solaz, A. (2001) 'Unemployment, Marriage and Cohabitation in France', *Journal of Socio-Economics*, 30: 75-98.

Galland, O. (2000)'Entrer dans la vie adulte: des étapes toujours plus tardives mais resserrées', *Economie et Statistique*, 337-338: 13-36.

Galland, O. and Meron, M. (1996) 'Les frontières de la jeunesse', *Données sociales*, 1996: 324-327.

Jenson, J. and Sineau, M. (1997) *Qui doit garder le jeune enfant? Mode d'accueil et travail des mères dans l'Europe en crise*, Paris: Librairie générale de Droit et de Jurisprudence.

Kempeneers, M. and Lelièvre, E. (1991) 'Analyse biographique du travail féminin', *European Journal of Population*, 7: 377-400.

Kergoat, D. (1984) *Les femmes et le travail à temps partiel*, Paris: La Documentation Française.

Kergoat, D. and Nicole-Drancourt, C. (1998) 'Temps partiel et trajectoires. Itinéraires de salarié(e)s à temps partiel', Report Dares/Gedisst/Grass: Paris.

Kieffer, A., Marry, C. and Selz, M. (2000) 'Les débuts de carrière des couples, Communication au colloque du réseau européen Transition in Youth', Anvers, 7-10 septembre 2000.

Letablier, M.T., and Lurol, M. (2000) 'Les femmes entre travail et famille dans les pays de l'Union Européenne', La Lettre du Centre d'Etudes de l'Emploi, no.63, juillet.

Marry, C., Fournier-Mearelli, I. and Kieffer, A. (1995) 'Activité des jeunes femmes : héritages et transmissions', *Economie et Statistique*, 283-284 (3/4): 67-79.

Maruani, M. (1996) 'L'emploi féminin à l'ombre du chômage', *Actes de la Recherche en Sciences Sociales*, 115 (décembre): 48-57.

Meron M. and Widmer I. (2002) 'Unemployment leads women to postpone the birth of their first child', *Population - E*, 2: 301-330.

Meurs, D. and Ponthieux, S. (1999) 'Emploi et salaires, les inégalités entre femmes et hommes en mars 1998', Premières Synthèses, Paris Ministère du travail DARES, 99.08 (32.2).

Nétumières, (Hay des) F. (1994) *L'arrêt de travail des femmes. Mariage et maternité*, Paris-Sorbonne: Mémoire de DEA se sociologie, Université René Descartes.

Nicole-Drancourt, C. (1989) *Le labyrinthe de l'insertion*, Paris: La Documentation Française.

Prioux, F. (1996) 'Le premier enfant: de plus en plus tard', in *Population, l'état des connaissances: la France, l'Europe, le Monde'*, Paris: INED/La Découverte.

Toulemon, L. (1994) 'La place des enfants dans l'histoire des couples', *Population*, 49 (6): 1321-1346.

Woronoff, D. (1994) *1998. Histoire de l'industrie en France du XVIème siècle à nos jours*, Paris: Le Seuil, col. Points Histoire.

6 Elements of uncertainty in life courses

Transitions to adulthood in Sweden

Magnus Bygren, Ann-Zofie Duvander and Mia Hultin

INTRODUCTION

According to the idea of a globalizing world, modern society is characterized by intensified demands on productivity, competition, and flexibility, whereby individuals have come to face increased uncertainty about future outcomes of their choices and investments. However, globalization neither takes identical routes nor has the same consequences in all modern societies. Nation-specific structures, institutions, and traditions condition the impact of globalization on societal development (see Mills and Blossfeld, this volume). The current study takes the Swedish case as a starting point for analyzing instances and consequences of uncertainty in people's major life transitions. Have processes of globalization implied a gradual postponement of transitions into adulthood also in a welfare state like Sweden?

Sweden is a welfare state of a "social democratic" kind (Esping-Andersen, 1999), with comprehensive societal programs stretching out to a number of life spheres. From a political perspective, Sweden shows a strong tradition of homogeneity and stability. From 1932 onwards save for nine years, the social democratic party has been in office. One important function of the welfare state that developed during this time has been to mitigate major life transitions, mainly through redistribution between individuals and between individuals' various life stages. Sweden's high degree of unionization, collective bargaining system, active employment policies, and job protection legislation have arguably given to Swedish workers a sense of security about their labor market prospects (van den Berg *et al.*, 1997). However, there are reasons to believe that this sense of security prevails mainly among those who have a reasonably stable attachment to the labor market. The generosity of the unemployment insurance and parental leave programs is heavily dependent on previous labor market activity. Thus, individuals with no, or only a loose attachment to the labor market (e.g. the young) may during certain periods experience a high degree of uncertainty about their future prospects.

In this chapter, we examine in what ways growing general uncertainty about future prospects may manifest itself in three major and interrelated life transitions in Sweden, namely, from education to work, to living in a co-residential union, and to first parenthood. We begin by describing the Swedish institutional framework related to the educational system, the labor market, and the family sphere. Thereafter, we discuss and examine empirically patterns of transitions to adulthood for different Swedish cohorts. Finally, we summarize and discuss the main findings.

MODERN BEHAVIORAL AND INSTITUTIONAL CHANGES IN SWEDEN

The educational system

Since the early 1960s, the Swedish educational system is made up of four major elements, namely, compulsory primary school, voluntary secondary school, university or university college education, and adult education. During the last 50 years, enrollment in higher education has expanded tremendously in Sweden. The number of newly enrolled students at undergraduate levels has increased from about 4,000 in 1950 to almost 67,000 in 1998 (Öckert, 2001). The expansion was most accentuated in the 1960s, a period during which the number of students in higher education increased around three times (National Agency for Higher Education, 1999). From the end of the 1970s and during most of the 1980s, the number of students remained relatively constant. Towards the end of the 1980s, a new expansion started that continued throughout the 1990s.

In Sweden, university studies are free of charge and the state offers fairly generous student assistance in the form of allowances and loans. Loans are only means-tested on the basis of the individual student's own income, thus disregarding partners' or parents' economic resources (Aronsson and Walker, 1997). Hence, young students' dependence upon their parents in terms of economic support and housing is relatively limited. Traditionally, admission to higher education in Sweden was formally unrestricted, but since the late 1970s – *pari passu* with increasing cohort sizes and periods of higher unemployment – potential students must fulfill certain eligibility requirements.

Another specific feature of the Swedish school system is its relative lack of educational dead-ends (Erikson and Jonsson, 1998). Students finishing a vocational training are in principle eligible for studies at higher levels, although additional qualifications must sometimes be taken, for instance, within the encompassing Swedish system of adult education. Adult education has a strong tradition in Sweden, expanding markedly from the end of the 1960s onwards. It is also important to note that a fairly large fraction of all university students does not enter directly from secondary school, but has first worked for some time before enrolling in higher education. One important distinction is to what extent educational systems emphasize general and transferable qualifications, on the one hand, versus specific vocational education, on the other. In Sweden, educational institutions are to a high degree subject to state intervention and standardization, and employers have not been directly involved in curricula development (Erikson and Jonsson, 1998). This has implied that the element of specialized vocational training is relatively modest, and firm-specific training has been almost entirely left to the employing organizations (cf. Jonsson, 1994).

The labor market

The Swedish model of industrial relations has often been internationally applauded for conveying economic growth as well as a high degree of equality and low unemployment. From the mid-1950s to the beginning of the 1980s, wages were to a large extent determined through centralized collective bargaining at the national level. Partly as a result of an egalitarian bargaining strategy on behalf of the blue-collar unions, wage inequality decreased markedly from the mid-1960s throughout the 1970s (Hibbs, 1991). By 1980, Sweden showed the lowest level of income inequality and one of the highest living standards in the whole Western world (Edin and Topel, 1997).

This favorable picture of the Swedish economy and labor market has become continuously less unequivocal, however (e.g. Freeman *et al.*, 1997). After a period of overheating in the 1980s, the Swedish economy got into a severe recession in the beginning of the 1990s. From 1990 to 1993, GDP dropped every single year for a total of about 5 percent, while unemployment rose from less than 2 to 8 percent. Young people were especially hard-hit by the employment crisis. The downturn of the economy in Sweden was more accentuated than in most other Western economies. Since the mid-1990s, the national economy and the labor market situation have gradually improved again.

The focus on full employment has been an important element in Swedish labor market policies. Figure 6.1 gives a picture of men's and women's labor force participation during the period 1963-2000. We can safely conclude that the total employment growth since the 1960s is entirely attributable to women's intensified labor market participation (cf. Edin and Topel, 1997). From the late 1960s, the demand for labor in traditionally female occupations in the public sector grew considerably, and women of all ages – single or married, mothers or childless – flocked into the labor market (Axelsson, 1992). In terms of labor force participation, men's and women's rates have clearly come to approach each other.

The Swedish labor market is, however, markedly segregated by gender in that men and women to a great extent work in different occupations and sectors (Jacobs and Lim, 1992; Nermo, 1996). Although Sweden is often put forward as the guiding nation with regard to women's labor market situation, women still face inferior opportunities for promotion and for reaching supervisory positions. A gendered wage inequality is a consequence of this (e.g., Hultin, 2001).

As shown in Figure 6.2, unemployment has been quite low in Sweden up to the beginning of the 1990s (ranging from 1.5 percent in 1970 to 3.5 in 1983). Hence, even during the 1970s and 1980s when large parts of the industrialized world experienced the adverse effects of oil shocks and rising unemployment, Swedish unemployment remained fairly low.

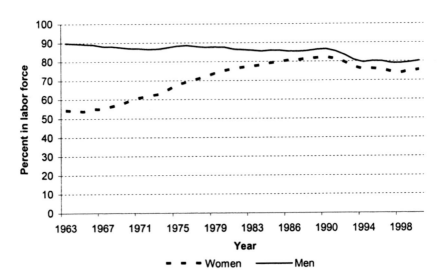

Figure 6.1   Percentages in the labor force of men and women (aged 16-64) in Sweden, 1963-2000

Source: Statistics Sweden

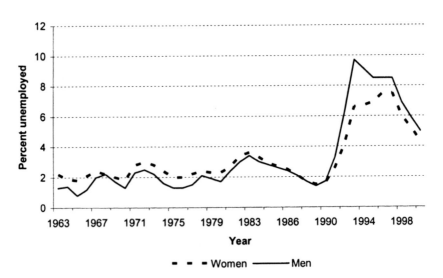

Figure 6.2   Percentages unemployed among men and women (aged 16-64) in Sweden, 1963-2000

Source: Statistics Sweden

It is a well-known fact that young people are especially vulnerable to unemployment (e.g. Lundborg, 2000). Young people often end up with the shortest stick, not least because the principle of "last in, first out" is widely institutionalized and adopted in the Swedish labor market. In 1994, for instance, almost 35 percent of those aged 16-23 had experienced unemployment sometime during the year. Corresponding figures for people aged 24-55 and 56-65 were 15 and 9 percent, respectively.

The young population not only has problems *keeping* a position during hard times, they also face problems *entering* the labor market to begin with. And their labor market problems are not particularly softened by the design of the Swedish unemployment insurance. It may be true that the trade unions administer unemployment benefit funds that at present (2001) compensate for 80 percent of prior earnings, up to a certain ceiling. But the coverage of this insurance is conditioned upon fund membership and earlier labor market experience. This makes it difficult for first-time labor market entrants such as young people and immigrants to qualify for compensation from this schema. For those who are not covered by this insurance, an alternative compensation system exists, but this is nowhere as generous as the fund schema.

Family policies and patterns of union formation and childbirth

One aspect of the transition to adulthood is the establishment of more or less enduring partnerships. Sweden is a clear-cut example of the development towards pluralization of private living arrangements. Since the 1960s, non-marital cohabitation has become highly widespread in Sweden, whereas marriage rates have declined. Over time, consensual unions have come to start at earlier ages (Etzler, 1984; Hörnqvist, 1994), to last longer (Hoem and Rennermalm, 1985), and to include childbearing. More than half of all first-born children are born out-of-wedlock (Statistics Sweden, 1999), with the overwhelming majority of them being born in consensual unions. One of the more important factors behind this development is the fact that since the end of the 1980s the legal status of non-marital and marital unions has become very similar in Sweden, with inheritance rights as an important exception. Also the moral status of non-marital unions is rarely questioned (Duvander, 1998).

Another step on the road to adulthood, normally taken after union formation, is that of becoming a parent. Swedish fertility shows strong fluctuations over time and has even been characterized as a "roller-coaster fertility" (Hoem and Hoem, 1999). In the mid-1960s, the total fertility rate was around 2.4, a figure comparable to those in other European countries at the time. Thereafter, fertility steadily decreased to around 1.6 at the end of the 1970s and the beginning of the 1980s. But the subsequent dramatic increase from the mid-1980s was unique both for Sweden and in comparison with other countries (Hoem and Hoem, 1999). For instance, in 1990, the total fertility rate had reached 2.1, one of the highest figures in Europe at that time. It is important to note that this "baby boom" around 1990 occurred at the same time that Swedish society showed a flourishing economy with close to full employment among both men and women. During the

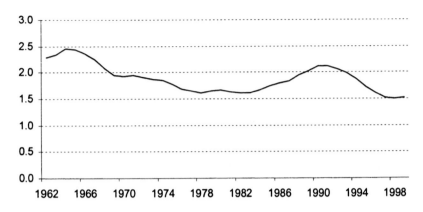

Figure 6.3   Total fertility rates in Sweden, 1962-1999

Source: Andersson (1999)

1990s, however, fertility plummeted again to record low levels. These trends in the Swedish fertility pattern are illustrated in Figure 6.3.

Women in Sweden have continuously come to postpone first birth to older ages (Hoem, 1998). The proportion of women at the age of 25 who are childless increased from 43 percent in 1975 to 62 in 1985 (Hoem, 1998). Despite the postponement of childbearing to older ages, the proportion of women who are still childless at ages above their reproductive years has not increased substantially over time (Duvander, 2000).

The Swedish case is interesting not only because family-related welfare institutions are more extended than in most other countries, but also because welfare policies in general are intimately connected to recipients' labor market activity. The system's generosity heavily hinges upon the extent to which parents have been active in the labor market before childbirth. Thus, the fertility pattern in Sweden is comparatively sensitive to general opportunities in the labor market. Hence, the discussion of the connection between fertility trends and women's labor market participation has been especially vivid in Sweden (e.g. Hoem, 1998; Andersson, 2000; Santow and Bracher, 2000).

One of the most important institutional factors enabling and even stimulating the combination of work with parenthood was the introduction of the parental leave program in 1974 which granted both mothers and fathers the right to temporary retreat from the labor market after the birth of a child. Originally, this program included six months of leave with a wage replacement level of 90 percent of prior earnings, up to a certain ceiling. The length of the leave period was gradually extended to 15 months in 1989. Parents without earnings prior to childbirth are compensated according to a low flat rate (note the similarity with the unemployment benefit policy). Hence, the design of the parental leave system implies a strong incentive to work before childbirth until a sufficiently high earnings level has been reached. This pertains especially to mothers, who use the overwhelming part of all leave days (cf. Sundström and Stafford, 1992; Sundström, 1996). Taken together, these various features of the Swedish parental leave program reduce the costs of having children by encouraging the combination of paid labor with childbearing (Sundström and Stafford, 1992).

It is common to see postponement of family formation as an effect of prolonged education and increased labor force participation among women (Blossfeld and Huinink, 1991). In the case of Sweden, however, education has not been extended by nearly as much as childbirth has been postponed. From the 1970s onwards the "postponing effect" of being a student on union formation has become less and less important (Hoem, 1995).

TRANSITIONS TO ADULTHOOD IN SWEDEN

From education to work

Leaving the educational system and entering the job market is one of the most crucial transitions that people make during their lives. In industrialized societies, although they differ in the ways in which education is organized and in how transitions between education and work are made (Müller and Shavit, 1998), education is one of the key determinants of an individual's labor market career. Especially for young people, the institutional connection between the educational system and the labor market is of paramount significance (cf. Rosenbaum *et al.*, 1990). Sweden has a long tradition of strong labor movements whose influence on negotiations has implied a marked prevalence of "closed" employment relationships, at least when compared with the US or Great Britain (cf. Sørensen and Kalleberg, 1981). This means that competition has revolved a great deal around vacancies and that seniority has been of huge importance for allocation processes, with "insiders" being advantaged in comparison to "outsiders". Although the extent of job mobility has increased over time in Sweden (see Bygren, 2001), there may be more obstacles to young people's entry into the labor market than in societies with stronger elements of "open" employment relationships.

There are reasons to believe that the transition between school and work has become more problematic over time, in Sweden just as in many other Western countries. The enormous expansion of higher education over the last decades has brought about a general postponement of young people's entry into the labor market. This development has occurred alongside with rising educational requirements in the labor market. During recent decades, the proportion of jobs with low demands on education has declined in Sweden (Åberg, 2001). Interestingly, however, the *number of people* with low educational attainment appears to have decreased more than the *number of jobs* with low educational demands, with the result of rising over-education in unskilled jobs. It appears as if the share of people in unskilled jobs who have more education than normally required has increased from the mid-1970s to the late 1990s (ibid.).[1]

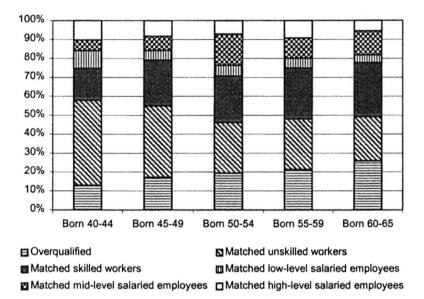

☐ Overqualified   ⊠ Matched unskilled workers
▨ Matched skilled workers   ▥ Matched low-level salaried employees
▨ Matched mid-level salaried employees   ☐ Matched high-level salaried employees

Individuals classified as "matched" have jobs that correspond to or pose higher educational demands than incumbents' educational credentials

Figure 6.4   Percentages of qualified and over-qualified among Swedish employees, by birth cohort

Consistent with these results, it can be observed in Figure 6.4 that the proportion of overqualified employees is substantially higher in younger than in older Swedish cohorts.[2]

The proportion of overqualified among those born in 1940-45 is 13 percent, and this figure rises gradually for each younger cohort to around 26 percent among those born in 1960-65. It can also be seen that the group of unskilled workers with only basic education has become smaller over time, whereas the group of all salaried employees with matching education taken together remained fairly constant.[3]

The continuous expansion of education has raised the question whether modern societies are experiencing an "educational inflation". If people in fact become more educated than "needed" – considering the structure of available jobs in the labor market – then increasing proportions of the educated will have difficulties finding a job that matches their qualifications. During times of unemployment, competition for existing jobs becomes intensified because the better educated are induced to take jobs below their formal credentials, at least until prospects get better (Åberg, 2001). In whatever ways this process of over-education is brought about, it is reasonable to assume that over time the well educated have come to face more difficulties in finding a "good job".

There are also reasons to believe that the matching mechanisms behind young people's transitions from education to work are a bit different for men and women. To the extent that women are disadvantaged in those recruitment processes in which selection is primarily based on *informal* qualifications, women are restricted to make use of their formal credentials only, whereas men can rely on alternative career routes. If men more easily reach good jobs by means other than formal education, the matching quality between education and occupational attainment should be greater for women than for men. This assumption is supported by Erikson and Jonsson's (1998) analyses showing that (i) the connection between education and class position is stronger for women than for men, and (ii) labor market experience pays off more for men's than for women's occupational attainment.

Table 6.1 shows the rate at which people with various social characteristics have obtained a job commensurate with their highest level of education.[4] Compared to those in the older birth cohorts, people in younger cohorts tend to need more time to find a job matching their educational level, as indicated by the negative coefficients for the cohorts born from 1950 to 1965. However, it seems as if this cohort effect is mostly accounted for by heterogeneity in educational attainment between different cohorts. The educational expansion has implied that people in general are more highly educated in younger than in older birth cohorts. *Ceteris paribus*, having an education above compulsory schooling is associated with lower chances for attaining a job with qualifications matching the education. Since the reference category is constituted by those with compulsory education who by definition cannot be overqualified, the sign of the effect is hardly surprising. Nevertheless, judging by the size of the effects, it is primarily those with secondary and tertiary education who run risks of being overqualified, whereas those with vocational education differ only slightly from the reference group. Men tend to need more time than women to attain a job that is commensurate with their education.

To see whether the chances of finding a job that matches the educational level have deteriorated over time for those with higher education, we estimated interaction terms between education and cohort affiliation. Indeed, there is a trend indicating that difficulties with finding a good job match have increased for later cohorts (see Table 6.1, columns 3 and 6). Those with secondary education appear to have seen their chances substantially worsening over the cohorts, whereas no such trend can be revealed for those with tertiary education. Hence, the former group appears to have suffered the most from a general educational inflation in Swedish society. As expected, the matching quality for women is higher than for men: their proportion of events as well as their baseline rates are in general higher.[5]

To sum up, later cohorts (i.e., those born in the 1950s and 1960s) seem to be disadvantaged compared with those born in the 1940s when it comes to finding a job that matches their education. Larger shares of individuals in the younger birth cohorts experience a delay in the job-matching process. This is primarily a result of them being more educated than earlier cohorts, which *per se* heightens their risk of being overqualified. For those with an intermediate level of education, however, there also seems to be an educational inflation effect present.

Table 6.1 Piecewise constant exponential hazard rate estimates for transitions to first job matching highest education attained in Sweden (episodes pertaining to women and men aged 15-35 separately)

	Men				Women	
Baseline rate						
1-12 months	-2.955**	-2.608**	-2.726**	-3.051**	-2.786**	-2.883**
13-24 months	-3.718**	-3.271**	-3.375**	-3.672**	-3.330**	-3.418**
25-36 months	-4.501**	-4.009**	-4.109**	-4.103**	-3.718**	-3.806**
37-48 months	-4.649**	-4.127**	-4.222**	-4.411**	-3.999**	-4.088**
49-59 months	-5.173**	-4.628**	-4.721**	-4.809**	-4.381**	-4.469**
60- months	-5.373**	-4.832**	-4.925**	-4.967**	-4.492**	-4.581**
Birth cohort						
1940-49 (ref.)	0.000	0.000	0.000	0.000	0.000	0.000
1950-59	-0.279**	-0.136	0.024	-0.275**	-0.091	0.075
1960-65	-0.396**	-0.215*	0.195	-0.112	-0.020	0.238
Education						
Compulsory educ. (1) (ref.)		0.000	0.000		0.000	0.000
Vocational educ. (2)		-0.266**	-0.047		-0.170*	-0.068
Secondary educ. (3-4)		-1.141**	-0.793**		-1.444**	-0.849**
Lower tertiary educ. (5)		-1.167**	-0.947**		-0.894**	-0.811**
Higher tertiary educ. (6)		-1.278**	-1.045**		-0.632**	-0.412**

Table 6.1 continued

	Men			Women		
Birth cohort * education						
(B-coh. 1950-59)*Educ. 2			-0.195			-0.115
(B-coh. 1950-59)*Educ. 3-4			-0.564*			-1.047**
(B-coh. 1950-59)*Educ. 5			-0.315			-0.158
(B-coh. 1950-59)*Educ. 6			-0.543			-0.376
(B-coh. 1960-65)*Educ. 2			-0.758**			-0.342
(B-coh. 1960-65)*Educ. 3-4			-0.893*			-0.861*
(B-coh. 1960-65)*Educ. 5			-0.557			-0.241
(B-coh. 1960-65)*Educ. 6			-0.204			-0.534
Number of events	792	792	792	960	960	960
Number of episodes	1077	1077	1077	1189	1189	1189
Likelihood ratio	795.72	999.92	1019.32	600.52	781.16	796.78
Df	2	6	14	2	6	14

Notes

** $p \leq 0.01$ for the estimate to be 0,

* $p \leq 0.05$ for the estimate to be 0.

Entering the first co-residential union

In the last decades, non-marital cohabitation has taken over as the starting state of union formation in Sweden, even though a majority of couples eventually get married. As many as 92 percent of the women born in 1964 started their first union in this manner (Statistics Sweden, 1995), and this proportion is likely to be even higher for younger cohorts. Cohabitation is seen as a more gradual, and less definite, transition than marriage (Hoem, 1995). The separation risk is higher for unmarried than for married couples (Hoem and Hoem, 1992), implying that cohabitation may involve less commitment.

Non-marital unions can in a sense be seen as a "rational" reply to growing uncertainty. They permit the postponement of long-term commitments, but they still include most of the advantages of co-residential living. The trend towards cohabitation at younger ages together with the use of effective family planning devices have made the link between union formation and childbirth weaker over time (Finnäs, 1995). Nevertheless, completed studies and economic independence still often act as prerequisites of union formation (Hoem, 1986). Traditionally, men's economic self-sufficiency has been recognized as a factor that increases rates of union formation, and analyses based on Swedish data reveal the same pattern for women (Bracher and Santow, 1998). The Swedish pattern of a gradual entry into union life may, however, dampen the effect of uncertainty and insufficient economic resources that otherwise would act to postpone union formation.

Our analysis indicates a trend towards *earlier* union formation in younger cohorts (see Table 6.2).[6] We also find that both educational level and labor market activity are important predictors for union formation. Both women and men have higher propensities to start a union if they have more than compulsory education. More specifically, those with lower secondary education have the highest propensities, which then decrease slightly for those with educational levels above that. Once current activity status is accounted for, men with higher tertiary education have similar entry rates as those with only compulsory education, whereas women with a relatively high education have lower transition rates than women with lower education.

Those without attachment to the labor market (students, and those in-between education and their first job) have dramatically lower propensities for starting a first union. Specifically, the period intervening studies and work appears to be connected to a high degree of uncertainty that prevents individuals from engaging in union formation until more certainty can be reached. It should be noted that being unemployed appears to have no effect on union formation. Unemployment spells often occur after labor market entry, and may be regarded as reflecting only temporary uncertainty.

It could be argued that people outside the labor force lack the economic resources required to start a new household. However, as the normative climate and policy developments in Sweden have made it easier to start co-residential unions, also in life stages during which people lack a stable income from work, such a connection may have grown less salient over time. This expectation, however, is only weakly supported by our analyses of the interaction effects between

Table 6.2   Piecewise constant exponential hazard rate estimates for transitions to first cohabitation in Sweden (episodes pertaining to women and men aged 15–45 separately)

	Men			Women		
Baseline rate						
1-12 months	-5.348**	-5.736**	-5.216**	-5.293**	-5.620**	-5.200**
13-24 months	-5.363**	-5.726**	-5.222**	-5.341**	-5.638**	-5.211**
25-36 months	-5.543**	-5.877**	-5.341**	-5.539**	-5.797**	-5.344**
37-48 months	-5.655**	-5.971**	-5.413**	-5.604**	-5.842**	-5.361**
49-59 months	-5.826**	-6.115**	-5.523**	-5.856**	-6.079**	-5.563**
60- months	-7.268**	-7.441**	-6.545**	-7.387**	-7.494**	-6.572**
Birth cohort						
1940-49 (ref.)	0.000	0.000	0.000	0.000	0.000	0.000
1950-59	-0.022	0.003	0.064	0.128	0.119	0.126
1960-65	0.062	0.198*	0.296**	0.263**	0.203	0.299*
Education						
Compulsory educ. (1) (ref.)		0.000	0.000		0.000	0.000
Vocational educ. (2)		1.009**	0.475**		0.836**	0.385**
Lower secondary educ. (3)		1.012**	0.575**		0.968**	0.565**
Higher secondary educ. (4)		0.764**	0.267		0.865**	0.457**
Lower tertiary educ. (5)		0.745**	0.279*		0.813**	0.487**
Higher tertiary educ. (6)		0.480**	-0.103		0.109	-0.352*

Table 6.2 continued

	Men			Women		
Employment status						
Employed (ref.)			0.000			0.000
Unemployed			0.715			0.425
Student			-1.779**			-2.142**
Between education and work			-1.238**			-0.577**
*B-coh. * employment status*						
(B-coh. 1950-59)*unemployed			-0.804			-0.260
(B-coh. 1950-59)*student			0.166			0.518
(B-coh. 1950-59)*between			0.333			0.064
(B-coh. 1960-65)* unemployed			-0.695			-0.564
(B-coh. 1960-65)* student			0.371			0.898*
(B-coh. 1960-65)* between			-0.772			-0.185
Number of events	811	811	811	774	774	774
Number of episodes	6360	6360	6360	5701	5701	5701
Likelihood ratio	442.86	577.82	840.28	472.46	599.69	785.04
Df	2	7	16	2	7	16

Notes

** p ≤ 0.01 for the estimate to be 0,
* p ≤ 0.05 for the estimate to be 0.

activity status and cohort membership (Table 6.2, columns 3 and 6). In fact, the only statistically significant difference between cohorts is that female students in the youngest cohort start their first cohabitation earlier than women in the oldest cohort.

In sum, even though union formation has come to take place at earlier ages for younger cohorts, economic uncertainty – more prevalent among men and women with only compulsory education and among those who have not yet entered the labor market – still acts to postpone union formation. Also those with the highest education tend to do so, either because they require relatively more certainty in their life course before taking the step to form a first union, or because they can make use of or prioritize other ways of reaching stability in life.

Entering into first parenthood

A general trend in Europe since the 1960s is that more and more women have come to combine childbearing with labor market activity. Sweden is perhaps the most clear-cut example of this development. Today, over 80 percent of women with children under the age of seven are active in the Swedish labor force, although many of them work part-time.

The issue of (un)certainty in decision processes related to entry into parenthood has been lively discussed in the fertility literature. One important question is whether individuals prefer to achieve a certain amount of certainty and stability in their lives before deciding to have their first child or, conversely, whether a child can rather be seen as a compensation for a lack of certainty and stability experienced in other spheres of life. The first assumption implies a positive relationship between stability in, say, career terms and first-birth fertility, whereas the second assumption implies a negative one.

Having children, being in a stable job career, and being married are examples of global strategies for reducing uncertainty (cf. Friedman *et al.*, 1994). Such commitments place actors in recurrent social relations that in turn augment predictability in people's lives. Friedman and her colleagues argue that the propensity to enter the parenthood status should be strongest among people who have limited or blocked alternatives to reduce uncertainty in their lives. Since a stable and successful career is an important source of certainty, people with good prospects for a career should therefore have relatively low propensities to enter this status. However, Friedman and her collaborators' reasoning has met with considerable criticism from other researchers in the field (e.g. Lehrer *et al.*, 1996; Myers, 1997). Also the Swedish fertility pattern appears to contrast with the main predictions generated by Friedman and colleagues. Swedes with a strong labor market attachment and successful in career terms, it seems, show relatively *high* fertility rates, notwithstanding the fact that over time people have come to postpone entry into parenthood. For instance, Swedish research findings indicate that first-birth rates are *positively* affected by income level (Andersson, 2000; Hoem, 1998) and work experience (Santow and Bracher, 2000). This would thus imply that in Sweden there is a positive relationship between various aspects of labor market resources and first-birth fertility, which is quite the opposite of what Friedman and her collaborators' general uncertainty reduction theory suggests. The Swedish parental leave policy may have enforced this positive relationship between labor market status and first-birth rates over time. As indicated before, payment during parental leave is based on prior earnings and couples are therefore likely to wait with children until earnings are sufficiently high.

Our empirical analyses indicate that certainty is indeed an important incentive for childbearing in Sweden (see Table 6.3).[7] As regards education, we expected that relatively high levels would bring certainty to people's lives in the form of enhanced chances for job attainment, more stable positions, and sufficient economic resources to support a child. Indeed, those who have attained high educational levels have relatively high childbearing propensities.

As was the case for union formation, this education effect is partly accounted for by current activity status. People outside the labor market – students and those in-between education and their first job – have dramatically lower propensities for entering into parenthood than the employed. This finding is entirely consistent with a rational adaptation to the economic incentives offered by the Swedish parental leave system. The effects are, as expected, stronger for women because they use the larger part of the parental leave days. Interestingly, the unemployed do not differ significantly from the employed as regards first-birth rates. However, under the assumption that those who are unemployed will generally have gathered at least some work experience with which to qualify for a reasonable replacement level during parental leave, this pattern is not entirely unexpected.

The general postponement of childbearing across birth cohorts is most evident when we consider men's first-birth rates: those in the youngest cohort (1960-1965) have especially low rates of transition to parenthood. For women this cohort pattern cannot be confirmed, presumably due to large period variations in Swedish fertility rates and due to the fact that current activity status is more important for women than for men.

To sum up, the analysis does neither reveal any general patterns of postponement of childbirth across cohorts, nor does it indicate that activity status has become a more important predictor over time (cf. Table 6.3, columns 3 and 6). What stands out, however, is that economic certainty – in part reflected by employment and higher education – is a very important prerequisite for entering first parenthood in Sweden.

SUMMARY AND CONCLUSIONS

In this chapter we have studied how aspects of (un)certainty influence major transitions to adulthood in Sweden. We have performed longitudinal analyses of processes behind: (i) matching one's educational qualifications to the occupational requirements of a first job; (ii) entering a first co-residential union; and (iii) choosing to become a parent for the first time. The underlying assumption behind these analyses was that over time young people have come to experience more uncertainty regarding major choices and their outcomes during the life course.

Table 6.3 Piecewise constant exponential hazard rate estimates for transitions to parenthood in Sweden (episodes pertaining to women and men aged 15–45 separately)

	Men			Women		
Baseline rate						
1-12 months	-5.659**	-6.152**	-5.507**	-5.577**	-6.070**	-5.299**
13-24 months	-5.581**	-6.047**	-5.422**	-5.339**	-5.793**	-4.996**
25-36 months	-5.687**	-6.128**	-5.480**	-5.468**	-5.875**	-5.047**
37-48 months	-5.515**	-5.941**	-5.277**	-5.591**	-5.977**	-5.129**
49-59 months	-5.851**	-6.244**	-5.549**	-5.447**	-5.816**	-4.954**
60- months	-6.965**	-7.200**	-6.209**	-6.884**	-7.096**	-5.866**
Birth cohort						
1940-49 (ref.)	0.000	0.000	0.000	0.000	0.000	0.000
1950-59	-0.107	-0.103	0.052	0.026	-0.036	0.040
1960-65	-0.507**	-0.359**	-0.352**	-0.189	-0.305**	-0.068
Education						
Compulsory educ. (1) (ref.)		0.000	0.000		0.000	0.000
Vocational educ. (2)		1.034**	0.333**		1.192**	0.266*
Lower secondary educ. (3)		1.088**	0.474**		1.050**	0.237*
Higher secondary educ. (4)		0.623**	-0.064		0.967**	0.093
Lower tertiary educ. (5)		1.079**	0.457**		0.858**	0.096
Higher tertiary educ. (6)		1.138**	0.404**		1.258**	0.368**

Table 6.3 continued

	Men			Women		
Employment status						
Employed (ref.)			0.000			0.000
Unemployed			0.757			0.496
Student			-2.158**			-3.066**
Between education and work			-1.330**			-1.750**
B-coh. * employment status						
(B-coh. 1950-59)*unemployed			-7.593			0.085
(B-coh. 1950-59)*student			-0.487			0.337
(B-coh. 1950-59)*between			-0.384			-0.191
(B-coh. 1960-65)* unemployed			-0.072			0.168
(B-coh. 1960-65)* student			-0.624			0.055
(B-coh. 1960-65)* between			-0.687			-0.651
Number of events	748	748	748	817	817	817
Number of episodes	7493	7493	7493	6597	6597	6597
Likelihood ratio	241.14	432.81	789.49	270.38	505.21	1011.53
Df	2	7	16	2	7	16

Notes

** $p \leq 0.01$ for the estimate to be 0,
* $p \leq 0.05$ for the estimate to be 0.

Although the Swedish welfare state is known for its capacity to mitigate major life transitions, young people in Sweden seem to have responded to the growing general uncertainty through delaying their entry into adulthood roles, both in the public and private sphere. Our analyses indicate that their transition between education and work has become more problematic. The time that it takes them to find a job matching their attained education has been prolonged, meaning that the proportion of overqualified employees has grown larger. This pattern should partly be seen in the light of the general educational expansion in Sweden during recent decades. Quite naturally, the general risk for "over-education" in the population increases as more and more people attain higher educational levels. But apart from this, we also found that nowadays having an intermediate level of education is more strongly associated with lower chances to find a good job than before. Not unlikely, educational inflation has implied that jobs previously attained by people with intermediate qualifications now require tertiary education.

The second life transition under study in this chapter was the entry into the first co-residential union. Sweden is a clear-cut example of the pluralization of living arrangements, and it is at the same time a country where non-marital unions are in principal and in practice equal to marriages. In many other countries where marriage is still the only feasible alternative for people who want to live together (see Simó *et al.*; Bernardi and Nazio, this volume), growing uncertainty as a result of globalization has implied a gradual postponement over time of union formation in general. In Sweden, however, the relative simplicity with which consensual unions can be started (and ended) has rather brought about a trend towards earlier union formation, at least among the youngest cohorts. In a sense, this development can be seen as a rational reply to growing uncertainty. That is to say, young people can reap the advantages that living together implies both economically and socially, while at the same time it allows them to postpone long-term commitments such as marriage and parenthood, attaining these goals more gradually. It should be mentioned, however, that also in Sweden the entry into co-residential unions involves command over resources. This is illustrated by the fact that those with relatively high education and active in the labor market have greater propensities than others to enter a co-residential union. Being outside of the labor market is evidently a condition of high uncertainty, which prevents people from partnering until a higher degree of stability is reached.

Finally, becoming a parent is no doubt one of the most important single events in many people's lives. Over time, Swedish policy has created and reinforced incentives for people to combine paid work with childbearing. Our analyses show that certainty in terms of labor market attachment and educational level indeed affects both men's and women's first-birth rates positively. Interestingly, however, this effect is absent among men and women with higher secondary education. This result should be seen in light of the fact that people with this level of education face the greatest difficulties in finding a job that matches their diploma. This instance of uncertainty *vis-à-vis* the labor market apparently acts as to delay childbearing, too. In other words, a smooth entry into the labor market seems to be a prerequisite for entry into parenthood.

Also interestingly, men and women with the highest levels of education have relatively low propensities to enter a first union, while at the same time they show comparatively high first-birth rates once they have done so. One interpretation of this finding thus is that for them union life and parenthood are more closely connected than for other educational groups. Those with high education are likely to postpone union formation but once they start to cohabit, they tend to have their first child quite soon. Earlier studies have found that highly educated people who cohabit non-maritally are also the ones most likely to get married (Duvander, 1998), which may indicate a relatively accentuated stability in their unions.

In some respects, these patterns of entry into adulthood in Sweden differ considerably from those often found outside Scandinavia. For instance, the processes of the transition to adulthood in Sweden are very similar for men and women. We found no dramatic gender differences as regards the impact of (un)certainty on young people's job attainment, their entry into cohabitation, or their transition to parenthood. Higher education and good economic resources increase both men's and women's propensities of entering parenthood.

To conclude, young people in Sweden have come to postpone some salient transitions into adulthood. People in younger cohorts need more time to find a job that matches their educational attainment, and they become parents at older ages. This pattern of postponing adulthood can be seen as part of a more general trend pertaining to a large part of the Western world. When it comes to young Swedes' entry into first co-residential unions, however, the pattern is rather the opposite: they have started to cohabit at continuously lower ages. Presumably, this finding reflects nation-specific institutional and normative changes that have conveyed a certain redefinition of private living arrangements.

ACKNOWLEDGEMENT

We gratefully acknowledge comments from participants at a seminar at the Department of Sociology in Stockholm, June 5th, 2001. Especially, we wish to thank Göran Ahrne and Eero Carroll for constructive suggestions.

NOTES

1   However, the "overeducated" leave unskilled jobs quicker than those who have lower education (ibid.).
2   If a person has a job below that of its commensurate education, over-qualification is at hand. Commensurate is:
     a   Compulsory education   Unskilled workers
     b   Vocational education   Skilled workers

c   Secondary education (2-4 year theoretical gymnasium)   Low-level   salaried
    employees
d   Lower tertiary education (short university education)   Mid-level   salaried
    employees
e   Higher tertiary education (long university education)   High-level   salaried
    employees

3   Of course, these results may be an effect of the older cohorts having had more time
    to attain jobs commensurate with their education. Whether this is true or not is
    examined in the multivariate hazard rate analysis reported below. Older cohorts have
    also had more time to attain necessary educational credentials for higher-level jobs,
    which may account for the stable proportion of matched salaried employees over
    birth cohorts.

4   We have conducted multivariate hazard regressions estimating the time elapsing
    from the point in time at which the highest level of education is attained up until a
    match is realized, implying that the individual attains a job with qualifications com-
    mensurate with his or her education. Selected for the analysis are those who were
    born between 1940 and 1965 and who were not in education at the time of the inter-
    view. The episode duration starts once the highest level of education is reached, and
    censoring occurs when the first "matching" job is attained, or when the age of 35 is
    reached. If not otherwise stated, all empirical analyses in this chapter use data from
    the 1991 Swedish Level of Living Survey's retrospective economic activity histories
    (for details on the data set, see Jonsson and Mills, 2001). For more details on the
    piecewise constant exponential model estimated here, see Blossfeld and Rohwer
    (1995).

5   When the effect of sex is estimated without other controls (results not shown), this
    assertion is also confirmed: women have significantly higher transition rates than
    men.

6   For these analyses we have selected those individuals who are born between 1940
    and 1965. The episode duration starts at the age of 15, and censoring occurs when
    the respondent starts his or her first cohabitation, or when age 45 is reached.

7   For these analyses we have likewise selected those who are born between 1940 and
    1965. The episode duration starts at the age of 15, and censoring occurs when the age
    of 45 is reached or at respondent's first childbirth. In order to come closer to the time
    of the decision to have a child, we have subtracted 9 months from the child's birth
    month.

BIBLIOGRAPHY

Åberg, R. (2001) 'Skill-Education Mismatch and Employment Possibilities for the Less
    Educated', paper presented at the Euresco Conference Labour Market Change and Citi-
    zenship in Europe, Helsinki, April 20-25, 2001.
Andersson, G. (2000) 'The Impact of Labor Force Participation on Childbearing Behav-
    ior: Pro-Cyclical Fertility in Sweden During the 1980s and the 1990s', *European Jour-
    nal of Population*, 16: 293-333.
Aronsson, T. and Walker, J. R. (1997) 'The Effects of Sweden's Welfare State on Labor
    Supply Incentives', in R.B. Freeman, R. Topel and B. Swedenborg (eds) *The Welfare*

State in Transition. Reforming the Swedish Model, Chicago: University of Chicago Press and National Bureau of Economic Research.

Axelsson, C. (1992) 'Hemmafrun som försvann' [The Housewife that Disappeared], doctoral dissertation, Stockholm: Swedish Institute for Social Research, Stockholm University.

Blossfeld, H-P. and Huinink, J. (1991) 'Human Capital Investments or Norms of Role Transition? How Women's Schooling and Career Affect the Process of Family Formation', *American Journal of Sociology*, 97: 143-168.

Blossfeld, H-P. and Rohwer, G. (1995) *Techniques of Event-History Modeling: New Approaches to Causal Analysis*, Mahwah, N.J.: Erlbaum.

Bracher, M. and Santow, G. (1998) 'Economic Independence and Union Formation in Sweden', *Population Studies*, 52: 275-294.

Bygren, M. (2001) 'Career Outcomes in the Swedish Labor Market: Three Contextual Studies', Doctoral dissertation, Stockholm: Swedish Institute for Social Research, Stockholm University.

Duvander, A-Z. (1998) *Why Do Swedish Cohabitants Marry?*, Stockholm: Demography Unit.

Duvander, A-Z. (2000) 'Couples in Sweden. Studies on Family and Work', Doctoral dissertation, Stockholm: Swedish Institute for Social Research, Stockholm University.

Edin, P. A. and Topel, R. (1997) 'Wage Policy and Restructuring: The Swedish Labor Market since 1960', in R. B. Freeman, R. Topel and B. Swedenborg (eds) *The Welfare State in Transition. Reforming the Swedish Model*, Chicago: University of Chicago Press and National Bureau of Economic Research.

Erikson, R. and Jonsson, J. O. (1998) 'Qualifications and the Allocation Process of Young Men and Women in the Swedish Labour Market', in W. Müller and Y. Shavit (eds) *From School to Work: A Comparative Study of Educational Qualifications and Occupational Destinations*, Oxford: Clarendon Press.

Esping-Andersen, G. (1999) *Social Foundations of Postindustrial Societies*, Oxford: Oxford University Press.

Etzler, C. (1984) 'Första steget i familjebildningen' [The First Step in Family Formation], Stockholm Research Reports in Demography, 21, Stockholm: The Demography Unit.

Finnäs, F. (1995) 'Entry into Consensual Unions and Marriages among Finnish Women Born between 1938 and 1967', *Population Studies*, 49: 57-70.

Freeman, R. B., Topel, R., and Swedenborg, B. (1997) 'Introduction', in R. B. Freeman, R. Topel and B. Swedenborg (eds) *The Welfare State in Transition. Reforming the Swedish Model*, Chicago: University of Chicago Press and National Bureau of Economic Research.

Friedman, D., Hechter, M., and Kanazawa, S. (1994) 'A Theory of the Value of Children', *Demography*, 31: 375-401.

Hibbs, D. A. Jr. (1991) 'Market Forces, Trade Union Ideology and Trends in Swedish Wage Dispersion', *Acta Sociologica*, 34: 89-102.

Hoem, B. (1995) 'Sweden', in Blossfeld, H-P. (ed.) *The New Role of Women. Family Formation in Modern Societies*, Boulder, Colorado: Westview Press.

Hoem, B. (1998) 'Barnafödande och sysselsättning' [Childbirth and Employment], Demografiska Rapporter 1998: 1, Örebro: Statistiska Centralbyrån.

Hoem, B. and Hoem, J. M. (1992) 'The Disruption of Marital and Non-Marital Unions in Contemporary Sweden', in J. Trussel, R. Hankinson and J. Tilton (eds) *Demographic Applications of Event-History Analysis*, Oxford: Clarendon Press.

Hoem, B. and Hoem, J. M. (1999) Fertility Trends in Sweden up to 1996', *Population Bulletin*, 40/41: 318-333.

Hoem, J. M. (1986) 'The Impact of Education on Modern Family-Union Initiation', *European Journal of Population*, 2: 113-133.

Hoem, J. M. and Rennermalm, B. (1985) 'Modern Family in Sweden: Experience of Women Born Between 1936 and 1969', *European Journal of Population*, 1: 81-112.

Hörnqvist, M. (1994) 'Att bli vuxen i olika generationer' [Becoming Adult in Different Generations], in J. Fritzell and O. Lundberg (eds) *Vardagens villkor* [The Conditions of Everyday Life], Stockholm: Brombergs.

Hultin, M. (2001) 'Consider Her Adversity: Four Essays on Gender Inequality in the Labor Market', Doctoral dissertation, Stockholm: Swedish Institute for Social Research, Stockholm University.

Jacobs, J. and Lim, S. (1992) 'Trends in Occupational and Industrial Sex Segregation in 56 Countries 1960-1980', *Work and Occupations*, 19: 450-486.

Jonsson, J. O. (1994) 'Utbildning och social reproduktion: Sverige ur ett internationellt perspektiv' [Education and Social Reproduction: Sweden from an International Perspective], in R. Erikson and O. Jonsson (eds) *Sorteringen i skolan* [Sorting in School], Stockholm: Carlssons.

Jonsson, J. O. and Mills, C. (eds) (2001) *Cradle to Grave: Life-Course Change in Modern Sweden*, Durham: Sociologypress.

Lehrer, E. L., Grossbard-Shechtman, S., and Leasure, W. J. (1996) 'Comment on A Theory of the Value of Children', *Demography*, 33: 133-136.

Lundborg, P. (2000) 'Vilka förlorade jobben under 1990-talet?' [Who Lost their Jobs during the 1990s?], in J. Fritzell (ed.) *Välfärdens förutsättningar. Arbetsmarknad, demografi och segregation* [The Conditions for Welfare. Labor Market, Demography, and Segregation], Stockholm: Fritzes.

Müller, W. and Shavit, Y. (1998) 'The Institutional Embeddedness of the Stratification Process', in W. Müller and Y. Shavit (eds) *From School to Work: A Comparative Study of Educational Qualifications and Occupational Destinations*, Oxford: Clarendon Press.

Myers, S. M. (1997) 'Marital Uncertainty and Childbearing', *Social Forces*, 75: 1271-1280.

National Agency for Higher Education (1999) 'Swedish Universities and University Colleges 1999', Annual Report, Stockholm: National Agency for Higher Education.

Nermo, M. (1996) 'Occupational Sex Segregation in Sweden 1968-1991', *Work and Occupations*, 23: 319-332.

Öckert, B. (2001) 'Effects of Higher Education and the Role of Admission Selection', Doctoral dissertation, Stockholm: Swedish Institute for Social Research, Stockholm University.

Rosenbaum, J. E., Settersten, R., and Maier, T. (1990) 'Market and Network Theories of the Transition from High School to Work: Their Application to Industrialized Societies', *Annual Review of Sociology*, 16: 263-299.

Santow, G., and Bracher, M. (2000) 'Deferment of the First Birth and Fluctuating Fertility in Sweden', Stockholm Research Reports in Demography no. 141, Stockholm: The Demography Unit, Stockholm University.

Sørensen, A. B. and Kalleberg, A. (1981) 'An Outline of a Theory of the Matching of Persons to Jobs', in I. Berg (ed.) *Sociological Perspectives on Labour Markets*, New York: Academic Press.

Statistics Sweden (1995) *Kvinnors och mäns liv* [Women's and Men's Lives], part 2, Stockholm: Statistics Sweden.

Statistics Sweden (1999) *Statistisk årsbok 1999* [Statistical Yearbook of Sweden 1999], Stockholm: SCB Förlag.

Sundström, M. (1996) 'Determinants of the Use of Parental Leave Benefits by Women in Sweden in the 1980s', *Scandinavian Journal of Social Welfare*, 5: 76-82.

Sundström, M. and Stafford, F. P. (1992) 'Female Labour Force Participation, Fertility and Public Policy in Sweden', *European Journal of Population*, 8: 199-215.

Van den Berg, A., Furåker, B., and Johansson, L. (1997) *Labour Market Regimes and Patterns of Flexibility. A Sweden-Canada Comparison*, Lund: Arkiv Förlag.

7   Transitions to adulthood in Norway

Øivind Anti Nilsen

INTRODUCTION

During their early lives, adolescents encounter major changes in their lives such as completing education, getting a first job, going through frequent job turnovers, building a family and becoming parents. Furthermore, increased globalization is likely to make the future of an adolescent today less secure relative to what older cohorts experienced. This is due to several reasons. First, when it comes to deciding which type of education to follow, students can choose among a wide range of options that vary in length and quality. This may make choices less secure with regard to the returns to education. At the same time, the reduced barriers for citizens of different nationalities to take a job in a foreign country, at least within Europe, may increase competition in the labor market. This again makes the returns to education today less secure than some decades ago. However, the openness of the contemporary labor market gives eager individuals a lot of new choices, and thus may increase their labor market success. "Success" in this context includes the returns to human capital investment (wages), and also the time spent in and (involuntarily) out of employment.

From the perspective of firms, globalization increases competition between countries (see Mills and Blossfeld, this volume). Thus, only the best, the most productive, flexible and competitive firms will survive. This increased competition induces the need for a more educated work force, since increased education will improve each employee's productivity and flexibility. Firms' survival is also dependent on being able to attract the more qualified workers. The least qualified will lose in the competition for jobs and, thus, education becomes a more and more important factor for both the individual worker and the economy as a whole.

In several European countries an increasing amount of resources have been invested in the educational system in order to improve its quality and to keep the young longer at school. The early histories of new entrants into the labor market may turn out as important for their early as for their prime-aged labor market behavior. This may be particularly relevant for the lowly educated. As several empirical studies have shown, these young lowly educated persons with little work experience have higher risks of unemployment and particular problems in finding a permanent job. Authorities, however, also invest in the educational system to correct for potential market inefficiencies. If the returns to education do devolve less on the individuals receiving education than on the society at large, individuals may take too little education relative to what is found to be optimal for the economy as a whole. To counteract such market failures, the authorities will find it necessary to finance and encourage young individuals to take more education.

In this chapter we summarize empirical findings from a number of studies about Norwegian youth and their early labor market career, and discuss these findings in the light of increased globalization. From these studies we learn about a number of issues that are related to education. Bratberg and Nilsen (2000), for instance, analyze how searching for a job after completing education is connected to the accepted wage level and the subsequent employment period. Nilsen and Risa (1999) focus on the early employment history of school-leavers and pay particular attention to the duration of employment in order to examine whether there is duration dependency. Nilsen *et al.* (2000) focus more on the early labor market career, not only for school-leavers but also for young individuals with some years of work experience. In this latter study, particular attention is paid to the importance of education for the transition from employment into various states, such as unemployment, education, and "other", a residual category. It has been documented that young individuals are over-represented among the unemployed, not because of long unemployment spells but because of high inflow rates (see Layard *et al.*, 1991: 297). An open question, therefore, is whether unemployment leaves a "scar" in the form of an increased probability of future unemployment. Grasdal (2001) investigates this issue by looking at the short- and long-term relationship between past and current unemployment for young graduates.

Just as a higher educational level will positively affect the labor market success of young individuals, so it may also lead to changes in the fertility pattern. Therefore, we also give a brief description of fertility in Norway and pay particular attention to the importance of education for the postponement of maternity. The descriptive statistics reported by Lappegård (1998; 1999) and the results of a more thorough econometric analysis by Naz (2000) indicate that an increased level of education leads to a postponement of the first birth. However, in order to overcome some of the limitations in these studies, we present a supplementary empirical analysis using data drawn from the so-called Database of Generations (Generasjonsdatabasen). These unique and previously unutilized Norwegian data are collected from public registers and include information about every individual born in every fifth year during the period from 1950 to 1990. The data also contain information about parents and grandparents. For this study we have sampled women from the 1955, 1960 and 1965 cohorts. As we will see, the empirical findings confirm that there is indeed a negative effect of the time spent in education on the time until the first childbirth. Furthermore, this negative effect seems to become more important over time.

This chapter is organized as follows. First, we give a brief survey of the institutional features of the Norwegian education system and labor market together with a description of the fertility patterns in Norway over the last decades. Second, the Norwegian data sources are described. In the remainder we discuss each of the studies in more detail. Here we focus on the importance of education, but also try to look upon the empirical results in the light of increased globalization. Finally, we summarize and conclude in the last section.

INSTITUTIONAL BACKGROUND

The educational system and labor market features

Norwegian children attend primary school for six years from the age of seven, and continue with three years in comprehensive (lower-secondary) school. There is very little specializing at this level. Upon completion of these nine years of compulsory education, pupils typically go on to upper-secondary school. In 1995, 96.7 percent of all pupils went from lower-secondary to upper-secondary school (Statistics Norway, 1999). In October 1977 there were approximately 157 000 pupils in upper-secondary school (secondary general schools and vocational schools); the corresponding figure for 1995 was 210 000. There are several areas of study in the upper-secondary school, the most important distinction being between vocational and general orientations. The most general education lasts for three years and prepares the students for further studies at universities or other institutions of higher education.[1] Most university studies take between four and seven years. College educations, such as nursing, primary school teaching, and engineering, last three years. In 1997 there were roughly 172 000 students at universities and other institutions of higher education.

In 1995 the number of males and females in the secondary school is almost the same. However, at the graduate schools and the universities (below the Ph.D. level) the fraction of females attending is higher. We should also note that females are underrepresented in apprenticeships and vocational training.

Figure 7.1 shows the labor force participation rates from 1980 to 1995 (percentages of the total number of persons in each age group). The participation rate for young people aged 16-19 peaked in the economic boom years of 1987-1988. We see a similar pattern for individuals aged 20-24 as well as for those of all ages (16-74), however, the fluctuations are most pronounced for the youngest group. The development of the unemployment rates is shown in Figure 7.2. After the boom period, the unemployment rate for the youngest group increases sharply to stay relatively constant at a high level thereafter. For individuals aged 20-24, we also see a significant growth in the unemployment rate, at least when compared to the total unemployment rate (age 16-74).

Most of the studies discussed in this survey are from the late eighties and early nineties. This was a time of a cyclical downturn in Norway's economy. For instance, aggregate employment in the construction industry was reduced by as much as 25 percent from 1988 to 1993, while manufacturing industries shrunk by 10 percent. On the other hand, employment in public and private services increased by 10 percent. From 1994 to 1998 the Norwegian economy has been booming again, and seen a sharp increase in manufacturing and construction employment. The differences in occupational and educational choices among males and females persisted in the nineties, and it is to be expected that the increased education levels of females will have a lasting impact. A survey of the Norwegian labor market situation in the period from the late 80s to 1995 is given in Torp (1996).

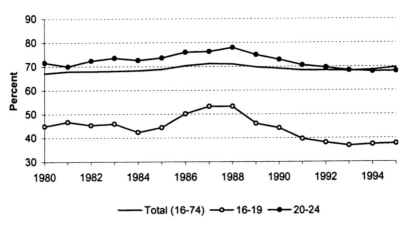

Figure 7.1   Labour force participation rates in Norway, 1980-1995

Source: Statistics Norway.

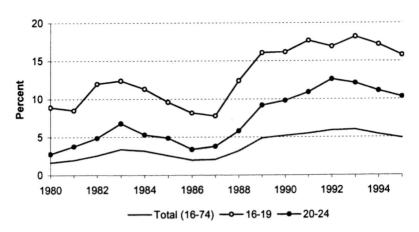

Figure 7.2   Unemployment rates in Norway, 1980-1995 (LFS)

Source: Statistics Norway.

Fertility in Norway[2]

Figure 7.3 gives the development in the period total fertility rate for Norway since 1960. The figure indicates that fertility has slightly increased since 1983. Note, however, that this pattern hides the fact that women seem to postpone their childbirths. For instance, the fertility among young females - 25 years and younger - has dropped significantly from the early 70s, while the fertility for older cohorts has increased since 1977.

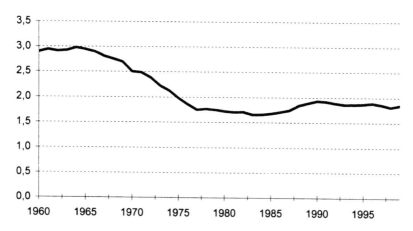

Figure 7.3   Total fertility rate in Norway, 1960-1999

Source: Statistics Norway.

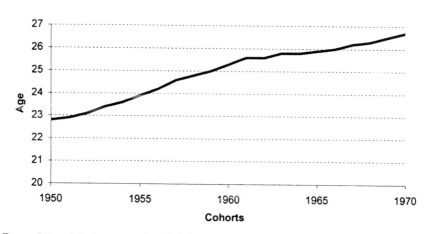

Figure 7.4   Median age at first birth in Norway, cohorts 1950-1970

Source: Statistics Norway.

If we look at the median age at first birth (Figure 7.4), i.e. the age at which 50 percent of a cohort has got their first child, we find that this age has increased from 22.8 years for the 1950 cohort to 26.7 for the 1970 cohort. The postponement of first births can also be seen from Figure 7.5. In addition, we find that cohort fertility has dropped: completed fertility for younger generations seems to be small relative to older generations.

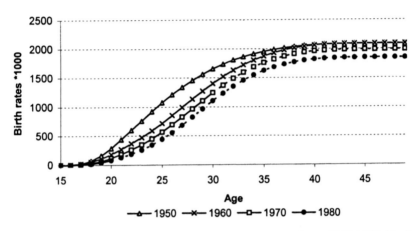

Figure 7.5   Accumulated birth rates *1000 in Norway, cohorts 1950-1980 (the last years are extrapolated)

Source: Statistics Norway.

The level of governmental transfers to parents has improved over time. For instance, the current Norwegian maternity leave system is quite generous, compensating for 100 percent of work income for 42 weeks or 80 percent for 52 weeks (in addition to universal child benefits).[3]

DATA SOURCES

Most of the studies discussed in this paper are based on data from the "KIRUT" (a Norwegian acronym) database, which contains detailed individual information from public registers for a random 10 percent sample of the Norwegian population aged 16-67. This information is merged from several different public registers, with the consent and under the supervision of the Norwegian Data Protection Agency. Currently, data for the period 1989-1996 are available and the total sample includes more than 300 000 individuals. The data provide information on socio-economic background, labor market participation by industrial branch as well as working hours, and social insurance payments.

The data used for the supplementary study of the postponement of first births, presented towards the end of this chapter, are drawn from the so-called Database of Generations (Generasjonsdatabasen). These unique and previously unutilized data are collected from Norwegian public registers and include information about every individual born in every fifth year in the period from 1950 to 1990. In this database there is information about family characteristics, education and labor market attachment of the individuals, together with information about their income and wealth. All this information is given for the sampled individuals and their parents and grandparents. Thus, information across three generations can be linked. Not all of the variables in the database are collected with the same frequency, however. For instance, family status, the length and type of education, wealth and variables describing the labor market attachment are given in every tenth year, while income and childbearing are recorded annually.

TRANSITIONS FROM SCHOOL TO WORK

Bratberg and Nilsen (2000) consider the transitions from school to work together with early market experiences. An individual who has finished school is assumed to search for jobs and, if s/he eventually gets a job offer, it is accepted if the associated wage exceeds his/her reservation wage. The probability of leaving unemployment any day is thus the product of the probability of getting a job offer that day and the probability that the wage offer is above the reservation wage. The three measures of educational outcomes are unemployment, wage, and job duration. These are treated as interrelated in the analysis. The length of the unemployment period and the duration of the first job may supplement the information in a wage equation. In addition, the accepted wage is related to the reservation wage and, hence, the employment hazard rate. Therefore, a wage equation must be estimated in such a way that the dependence between wages, unemployment, and job duration are taken into account, and the duration of post-school unemployment, accepted wage, and job duration are estimated simultaneously.

The individuals considered finish their education and begin to work if they get a job. They are followed until they part from their jobs or are censored. The sampled individuals are all school-leavers in the period from 1989-1991. In the study, 11 239 school-leavers aged 16-33 were extracted from the KIRUT database.

The average time from school completion to the first job is 30 weeks for the individuals with 12 years of education (sample means for the uncensored observations). This seems to be quite a long period of non-employment. However, the education coefficients are negative, implying that the time taken to find a job is shorter for those with higher levels of schooling. For instance, those with 15 years of education (except for nurses and teachers) have a 16 weeks shorter search time. The unemployment spell is even shorter for nurses and teachers. The difference in search times between the ones with 15 years of education and those with the longest educations is marginal and statistically insignificant.

There is a non-monotonic relationship between education and job duration. Those with relatively low education levels (less than 12 years) and those with high education (15 or more) keep their job somewhat longer than those with an intermediate length of education. Teachers and nurses are among those with 12-15 years of education, and it seems reasonable that the probability of a good match in the first job is higher for such specialized educations. Note, however, that this positive effect of education on job duration is partly due to industry attachment. Individuals with highly occupation-specific education are over-represented in the governmental sector. Thus, returns to education may be biased in that it is not a pure effect but may also reflect industry attachment and the degree of specializing. Another finding worth mentioning is that apprentices get a job at a rate that is 20 percent faster compared to individuals with other types of education at the same educational level, i.e. 12 years. Apprentices also tend to stay 10 percent longer in their first job. There are several possible reasons for this. First, uncertainty and information asymmetries are lower for apprentices if they start to work in the firm where they received their training. In addition, if an apprentice leaves the firm where he received his training, a portion of the acquired human capital and firm-specific skills is lost. Thus, apprentices have incentives to stay in the firms where they were trained.

Turning to gender differences, females have shorter search periods, lower wages and longer job durations than males. These findings are consistent with the notion that female labor force entrants have a lower reservation wage than men. In part, this may be explained by the Norwegian maternity leave system that - as said before - is quite generous, but it requires a minimum of 10 months' paid work previous to giving birth for eligibility. Females who plan to have a child may therefore accept lower paid jobs. The fact that the first job lasts longer for women than for men is consistent with a lower degree of on-the-job search, but this may also in part be explained by the strong protection against dismissals during maternity leave. Another explanation for these gender differences is the gender segregation in the Norwegian labor market. Women are over-represented in the governmental sector, where wages are relatively low but where job pro-tection and flexibility are better than in private industry. Thus, working in the governmental sector makes it easier to combine a job and taking care of children. Such job characteristics may be more important for women than for men.

TRANSITIONS FROM EMPLOYMENT

Nilsen *et al.* (2000) analyze the importance of education for the transitions from employment early in the career to unemployment, education and other exits. In their study they also use data from the KIRUT database. They analyze 32 202 workers aged 18 to 29 who are followed from January 1989 to December 1990. This was a period of a cyclical downturn in Norway, such that quite a few youngsters lost their jobs due to layoffs. The authors analyze the gross exits to unemployment, education, and "others" by means of a reduced form multinomial logit model. This captures the competing risk aspect of the inflow into youth unemployment from employment.

All effects relating to education are statistically significant for both males and females. Education is a good insurance for staying employed and, at the same time, it decreases the probability of becoming unemployed.[4] For instance, one additional year of education reduces the probability of becoming unemployed by 1.5 percentage points. Thus, with the average probability of becoming unemployed equal to 5.8 percent (sample mean), one extra year of education reduces the probability of becoming unemployed to 4.3 percent, which is 25.9 percent lower.

There are some important gender differences. Having children is not affecting males' behavior, only females'. It is found that for married women the number of children increases the probability of staying employed, while it decreases the probability of transiting to the residual group, "other". This result may be partly due to non-random self-selection. For instance, labor force participation by mothers with several children is probably an indication of a high endowment of personal human resources. Non-participating mothers with many children may on average not be as fortunate. Thus, if such self-selection effects are present, we may find that children have the described positive effect on labor market attachment.

The early labor market experience of adolescents is also analyzed by Nilsen and Risa (1999), who focus on the job duration of school-leavers completing their education between October 1989 and October 1990. Out of the 4 723 sampled school-leavers, 2 172 have a full-time job (defined as more than 20 hours worked per week) in the beginning of 1991. These full-time workers are followed until the end of 1993 and are defined as either "working", "unemployed" or "other" during the sample period. Note that the sampled individuals in this study are a highly selected group where unobserved characteristics may affect the job duration positively. Thus, care should be taken when generalizing the findings to the total population of school-leavers. The model used is a reduced form Weibull duration regression. With this model the authors are able to address questions regarding duration dependence in the work experience of the school-leavers. Properties of duration models are interesting for public policies aiming to facilitate the integration of school-leavers into the labor market. It is sometimes argued that gaining some initial experience supports the integration process. A process where the gain of some initial experience improves later labor market attachment corresponds to a negative duration dependence in models of unemployment duration. That is to say that the hazard rate out of employment decreases over time. Negative duration dependence indicates that labor market attachment increases with job duration. If this is the case, a public policy aimed at providing labor market training to youngsters may be an effective remedy against youth unemployment. With their duration model the authors are also able to estimate differences in exit routes to unemployment and the residual end-state, "other", which most often are exits to part-time work or out of the labor force. The summary statistics reveal that during the three-years period from 1991 to 1993 there are 505 exits to unemployment and 786 exits to "other".

Nilsen and Risa find that the introduction of various covariates leads to the elimination of duration dependence, i.e. they end up with a constant hazard. This finding suggests that the strong negative duration dependence found in the (mis-specified) parsimonious model only reflects sampling effects. Hence, one may conjecture that a policy of labor market training in the sense of providing work experience will have scant effects on the youth labor market. However, one may keep in mind that the sample contains only individuals who managed to enter full-time work by the end of 1990. It may well be that labor market policies are directed primarily towards school-leavers that fail to secure a job at an early stage. Therefore, results may differ for those who did not manage to get a job.

Compared to those with the highest level of education, the hazard rate to unemployment increases for both females (165 percent) and males (114 percent) that leave school with only 9-11 years of education. For females leaving with 12-14 years of education the increase in the hazard rate is even greater.

Nilsen and Risa (1999) also find other gender differences. Females experience fewer exits to unemployment than males. The fraction of females remaining in full-time work across the total observation period is 41.3 percent against 39.6 percent for males. Nilsen and Risa conclude that the descriptive statistics suggest that females have a higher entry rate to employment after school and a higher probability of staying in work. Furthermore, it is the type of education that plays a significant role for females, while it is the industry of occupation that is most important for males.

UNEMPLOYMENT PERSISTENCE

In general young individuals demonstrate a high turnover in the labor market, which in turn exposes them to a higher risk of experiencing unemployment. If state dependence creates unemployment persistence among labor market entrants, policies reducing short-term unemployment are important to prevent negative demand shocks to have negative long-term consequences on young workers.

Grasdal (2001) investigates how much of the observed persistence in unemployment is attributed to previous experience of unemployment. The sample used covers school-leavers with 10 years of education or more who were aged 16-29 in 1989 and left the educational system in the fall of 1989 or spring of 1990, and who are observed for at least the six months from July 1990 to December 1990. For each month during this observation period the final sample of 4 521 individuals is observed to determine whether or not they are registered as unemployed. These individuals are followed until they leave the labor force due to either childbirth, education, emigration or death. It is assumed that they are working as long as they are not registered as unemployed or temporarily out of the work force.

Different from the studies discussed above, Grasdal does her analysis separately for various educational groups, conditioning on the years of schooling for each individual. Summary statistics show that those with higher education on average experience fewer and shorter spells of unemployment than school-leavers with less education. On average, 60 percent of school-leavers from the secondary education level (10-12 years of education) and about 26 percent of school-leavers with higher education (13 or more years of education) have at least one spell of unemployment during their sample periods. These results indicate that education is an insurance against unemployment.

Grasdal analyses both short- and long-term state dependence by comparing work states, first, in two subsequent quarters and, then, in the 4th quarter with the state one year back. The results show that state dependence accounts for a substantial part of the observed persistence in unemployment at all educational levels. However, state dependence becomes less important for higher educated individuals. The short-term state dependence for individuals with lower and secondary education (9-12 years) is 0.5. This means that compared to someone who was employed in the previous month, an individual who was not so has a 50 percent higher probability of being still unemployed in the present month. Short-term state dependence for those with higher education (13 or more years of education) is 0.4, but this decreases over time. Although Grasdal concludes that the types of educational qualifications are important in this respect, this may actually be due to a mixture of sectoral and educational effects. For instance, she finds that secondary school graduates (10-12 years of education) with an industry- and craft education have a significantly higher probability of experiencing unemployment than secondary school graduates with health related studies.

As expected, ranging from 0.111 to 0.146, the long-term state dependence is lower than the short-term. However, the average long-term state dependence is very similar for the various educational levels (with the exception of those with 17 years or more). This latter finding indicates that once an individual has entered the labor market, its education level is not very important for subsequent labor market behavior. This result is consistent with the ones in Nilsen and Risa (1999), who found that the state dependence disappears once covariates are taken into account.

POSTPONEMENT OF FIRST BIRTH

As stated in the introductory section of this chapter, education becomes increasingly important in a more globalized world (see also Mills and Blossfeld, this volume). From a policy point of view it is also important to know what the effect is of increasing educational levels on fertility rates. This is so because extra years of schooling are likely to induce significant changes in the fertility patterns of modern females. For instance, their increased educational level may affect the average age at first birth. For Norway this pattern has been described by Lappegård (1999).

When we look at the median age at first birth by educational length for various cohorts (Figure 7.6), we see that the age at first birth is higher for the more educated groups, and also that it has increased over time for all educational groups. Furthermore, the older the mother is at first birth, the more likely it is that subsequent births will be closely spaced in-between, unless of course her total demand for children is small to begin with. As is well known, changes in the timing of childbearing can lead to strong annual fluctuations in overall fertility rates.

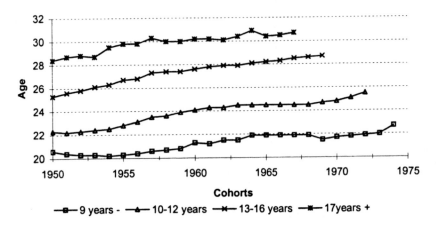

Figure 7.6   Median age at first birth, by educational groups in Norway

Source: Statistics Norway.

From a theoretical point of view, education affects fertility in several ways. First, and perhaps the most direct, is the effect of education related to time use: most women postpone childbearing until after their education is finished, leaving them less (of their fertile) time for having children. Obviously, this suggests a negative relation between fertility and education.[5] Second, higher education most likely affects fertility positively through higher wages (the income effect), but negatively through cost of time.[6]

Various sociological studies have shown a remarkable pattern of "assortative mating", in the sense of a strong positive correlation between the levels of education of partners living as couples.[7] This correlation gives rise to another effect of education on fertility: if a highly educated woman expects her future husband to be of similar level, then this would amount to a free-free income that should have a positive effect on fertility. Moreover, the higher the husband's wage is, the lower the wife's free market participation will tend to be and, therefore, the lower the opportunity cost of bearing children.[8] This substitution effect clearly increases fertility. Still, we believe that the income effect is more important for total fertility than for the timing of the first birth.[9]

Naz (2000) investigates the relationship of education and the timing of first births in Norway based on data from the KIRUT database. Using a hazard rate model (a Cox proportional hazard specification), she finds a strong negative effect of educational level on the timing of first births for young women aged 20-24 years, and a positive effect for women aged 35-39 years. The explanation is that women in education postpone first birth. Another interesting finding in the study is that there is a strong negative relationship between local unemployment rates and the probability of a first birth. Interpreting (high) unemployment as an effect of globalization and a cause of increased uncertainty, this latest finding suggests that globalization may induce further postponement of the first birth. Note, however, that in a generous welfare state like Norway, with substantial public funded childcare and other forms of family support, having a child may be seen as a way of reducing financial uncertainty.

A limitation of the study by Naz is that it includes only married women. Aggregate statistics from Norway reveal that the average age at first marriage in the period 1990-1995 was approximately 26.9 years. Furthermore, higher educated individuals tend to get married later than those with lower education. Using a highly selected sample of married women may give biased estimates, since those with higher education are more likely to be excluded from the sample.

Due to this limitation of the study by Naz (2000), we analyze the correlation between education and age at first birth using another sample, where also unmarried and previously married women are included. (The latter category includes the separated, divorced, and widowed.) To test which of the competing hypotheses about the correlation between education and age at first birth dominates, we estimate a duration model where we use educational length as one of the explanatory variables.

DATA

In the empirical analysis of the postponement of maternity we use data from the Database of Generations. Due to data limitations, we are only able to analyze the duration of time since the woman turned 18 years. We have sampled women from the 1955, 1960 and 1965 birth cohorts. These individuals we follow until their first child is born, or until 1991. Thus, the right censoring varies for the three cohorts from ages 36 through 31 to 26. In the data there is information on the educational level in 1970, 1980, and 1990. Based on this information, we have constructed a variable that measures years of schooling when the first child was born (assuming that women go to school without any interruptions). The educational level of the women's fathers is based on their highest level of education as reported in 1970, 1980 or 1990. Changes in marital status are also known from the data, with both the new state and the year of the transition given. From this information we have defined the marital status of the women as either unmarried, married, or previously married, measured at the time of the first birth.

The final sample consists of 90 870 individuals, of whom 30 066 were born in 1955, 29 598 in 1960, and 31 206 in 1965. The mean educational lengths for the 1955, 1960 and 1965 cohorts are, respectively, 11.5, 12.0, and 12.1 years. Note, however, that the sample from the 1965 cohort is censored at age 26, i.e. before those women with the longest educations have completed their education. Thus, the average reported educational length for the 1965 cohort is smaller than the true one.

EMPIRICAL RESULTS

We estimate a Weibull model to analyze the duration of time until the first birth. The estimation results are reported as hazard ratios in Table 7.1. This ratio tells us the relative effect on the hazard rate, i.e. the effect of one unit increase in the explanatory variables. A hazard ratio equal to 1 indicates that the covariate has no impact on the probability of getting a child, a hazard ratio larger than 1 implies a positive effect of the covariate, while less than 1 indicates a negative effect.

We see that there is a negative effect of the educational length on the time until the first childbirth. This finding supports the hypothesis that higher educated women postpone their entry into motherhood, which is in line with other studies on Norway (see e.g. Noack, 2001; Kravdal, 1994; Naz, 2000) or other countries (see e.g. Blossfeld and Jeanichen, 1992; Gustafsson *et al.*, 2001). Compared to the results by Naz (2000), however, we find a much stronger negative effect for the level of education. This might be due to the fact that we included unmarried women in our study. It seems likely that marriage gives access to more financial resources. This increased access to funding may reduce the importance of women's own education. Furthermore, the time constraint that childcare will have on time spent on education (and *vice versa*) may be less binding for married women.

Another interesting finding is that the negative effect of education seems to become more important over time. As expected, marriage has a positive effect of the probability of becoming a mother. That previously married women in the two oldest cohorts have a lower probability of becoming a mother relative to unmarried individuals is somewhat surprising. One explanation might be that marital dissolution is such a dramatic experience that forming a family and becoming a mother is not on the agenda anymore. If we interpret the length of father's education as a proxy for social status, we see that females of high social status postpone their first birth longer than women of lower classes. The cohort dummies in the last column of Table 7.1 are greater than unity, which is consistent with the pattern described in Figure 7.4: more recent cohorts have their first birth later.

SUMMARY AND CONCLUDING REMARKS

The accelerated speed of change in modern societies, including economical, social and political changes, may be seen as effects of increasing globalization. At the same time, authorities have interests in increasing the average educational level, namely, in order to have a more productive and flexible labor force. It is likely that in the long run a better-educated labor force will be an advantage in the intensified competition among nations. From an individual's point of view, education may be seen as an insurance against unemployment and declining income, effects that could be the consequences of intensified globalization. The Norwegian empirical studies discussed in this chapter show that education plays an important role in getting youth established in stable jobs and prevents them

Table 7.1   Duration of time since age 18 until first birth in Norway (hazard ratios)

	1955 cohort		1960 cohort		1965 cohort		All cohorts	
	Hazard ratio	z-values	Hazard ratio	z-values	Hazard ratio	z-values	Hazard ratio	z-values
Education at birth	0.891	-31.60	0.888	-39.88	0.812	-48.13	0.876	-54.23
Married	2.914	50.53	2.437	55.71	3.274	3.27	2.840	97.90
Previously married	0.837	-4.02	0.837	-3.84	1.520	7.24	0.934	-2.44
Father's education	0.977	-7.22	0.969	-10.02	0.947	-14.20	0.966	-17.93
1960 cohort							1.327	29.28
1965 cohort							2.286	70.93
Log L	-31233.84		-25254.129		-19973.527		-78366.974	
Nr. of observations	30066		29598		31206		90870	
Nr. of censored obs.	4525		7391		15350		27266	

from experiencing long unemployment spells. Thus, the evidence is in accordance with policies adopted in most European countries, to increase resources put into the educational sector to fight youth unemployment (see also Layte *et al.*, this volume).

There are also clear indications of the changing role of gender both in the educational system and in the free market. Change becomes evident from the fact, for example, that presently a majority of Norwegian university students are females. In addition, compared to many other countries (see Klijzing, this volume), the female labor force participation rate in Norway is high. Finally, Norwegian family policy is aimed at bolstering female labor force participation through generous regulations for maternity leave and ample provisions for subsidized childcare. Norway may therefore be an interesting case to study when it comes to changing gender roles and differences, and this for several reasons.

Even though these results support the policy of the free market authorities of increasing the educational level, it is not clear that the importance of education will be the same in a youth population where everyone is highly educated. To be able to shed light on the long-term effect of an increased educational level, and thus to determine whether potential job competition will reduce the aggregate effect of increased education, one would need longer individual data series. However, until the most recent years, such data have been hard to get hold of. Thus, the results of the utilization of such datasets in the near future will be interesting. Note that with such long individual time series one may also be able to analyze whether individuals are "scarred" by unemployment spells early on in their careers.

Other empirical findings discussed in this study indicate that the educational expansion during the most recent decades will postpone the arrival of the first birth. It also seems evident that increased uncertainty, as approximated by rising unemployment, induces postponement of first births, which may reduce cohort fertility and thus total fertility. Globalization is, therefore, likely to have important effects on the transition to adulthood.

One final comment should be given. With an increased degree of globalization, the importance of education and early market experience may change. One conceivable scenario would be that education becomes more and more important to secure a stable and well-paid job. However, if increased globalization causes higher levels of turbulence in the free market, it may also have the effect that early free market experiences are wiped out in the long run due to high depreciation of human capital. Which one of these two competing hypotheses dominates empirically is still an open question.

NOTES

1   Compared to other countries, the number of apprenticeship positions in Norway is quite small. A reform of the system of upper-secondary education and training came into effect in 1994 (Reform-94). Among the most important aims of the new law

were improving the quality of the vocational training and increasing the number of pupils taking vocational education, up to a third of their cohort size.

2   Most of the information in this sub-section stems from NOU (1996: 13) and Lappegård (1998; 1999).

3   This compensation requires for eligibility a minimum of 10 months' paid work previous to giving birth.

4   The material reveals that 70 percent of those that occupied a job in the end state had held that same job during the two years, while 80 percent of the unemployed became unemployed within the last six months before our time of final observation. These figures indicate that round tripping is not a very significant problem in the sample used.

5   Note that unless one has rich enough data it is difficult to empirically distinguish this effect from the reverse effect of fertility on education: some women drop out of education because they become pregnant. This also suggests a negative correlation, but the causality is reversed.

6   Although intuitively perhaps reasonable, theoretically it is actually not at all clear that, even if children are a normal good, the income effect is necessarily positive, as pointed out by Becker and Lewis (1973). If children are a normal good, normality only requires the family to spend more money on their children as income rises. However, this increase can be taken out in other directions than an increase in the number of children, depending on the income elasticities of the number of children vs. the "quality" of the children (i.e., the money spent on each child). See also Willis (1973).

7   Cf. e.g. Blossfeld *et al.* (2000). Economic explanations of this observed pattern come in three categories. First, if education is regarded as a sufficiently important good for everybody, then all women will want men with high education as will all men want women with high education, with the result that those with the most education will tend to form a couple, and so will those with the second most education, etc. This kind of sorting is referred to as "assortative mating" (cf. e.g. Becker (1991, Ch. 4)). Second, joint consumption of family public goods is one of the economic important determinants of who marries whom, and similarity of tastes is necessary to exploit the gains from sharing public goods. If persons with similar educational backgrounds have similar tastes, they will tend to marry each other for this reason. (Weiss (1997), among others, develops the family public goods argument in some detail.) Third, search models predict that the probability of ending up with a specific partner is related to the probability of meeting that specific partner, and similarity of education increases the probability of such encounters. (Weiss (1997) also surveys this strand of the literature.)

8   Some degree of specialization according to comparative advantages is predicted by practically any kind of model of intra-family decision-making, cf. e.g. Weiss (1997).

9   From an econometric point of view, it is also hard to fully take into account the endogeneity problem of income and fertility, i.e. in what direction the causality goes.

BIBLIOGRAPHY

Becker, G. (1991) *A treatise on the family*, Cambridge: Harvard University Press.

Becker, G. and Lewis, H.G. (1973) 'On the interaction between quantity and quality of children', *Journal of Political Economy*, 81: 279-288.

Blossfeld, H.-P. and Jeanichen, U. (1992) 'Educational Expansion and Changes in Women's Entry into Marriage and Motherhood in the Federal Republic of Germany', *Journal of Marriage and the Family*, 54: 302-315.

Blossfeld, H.-P., Timm, A. and Dasko, F. (2000) *The educational system as a marriage market: A longitudinal analysis of marriage decisions in the life course*, Mimeo: Bremen University.

Bratberg, E. and Nilsen, Ø. A. (2000) 'Transitions from School to Work and the Early Labour Market Experience', *Oxford Bulletin of Economics and Statistics*, 62(1): 909-929.

Grasdal, A. (2001) *Unemployment Persistence among young Norwegian labour market entrants*, Mimeo: Department of Economics, University of Bergen.

Gustafsson, S., Kenjoh, E. and Wetzels, C. (2001) *The Role of Education in Postponement of Maternity in Britain, Germany, The Netherlands and Sweden*, Mimeo: Department of Economics, University of Amsterdam.

Kravdal, Ø. (1994) 'The importance of economic activity, economic potential and economic resources for the timing of first birth in Norway', *Population Studies*, 48: 249-267.

Lappegård, T. (1998) 'Større ulikhet i barnetallet' [Greater variation in the number of children], *Samfunnsspeilet 5/1998*, Statistics Norway.

Lappegård, T. (1999) 'Akademikerne får også barn, bare senere' [Academics also get children, only later], *Samfunnsspeilet 5/1999*, Statistics Norway.

Layard R., Nickell, S. and Jackman, R. (1991) *Unemployment*, Oxford: Oxford University Press.

Naz, G. (2000) 'Determinants of fertility in Norway', Working Paper no. 1400, Department of Economics, University of Bergen.

Nilsen, T. S, and Risa, A. E. (1999) 'Duration in work after leaving school', STT-TSER Working Paper 02-99, University of Bergen.

Nilsen, Ø. A., Risa, A. E. and Torstensen, A. (2000) 'Transitions from Employment among Young Norwegian Workers', *Journal of Population Economics*, 13(1): 21-34.

Noack, T. (2001) 'Transition to adulthood in Norway', in M. Corijn and E. Klijzing (eds) *Transitions to Adulthood in Europe*, Dordrecht: Kluwer Academic Publishers.

NOU (1996) *Offentlige overføringer til barnefamilier*, Oslo: Statens Trykning.

Statistics Norway (1999) *Statistical Yearbook 1995*, Oslo: Statistics Norway.

Torp, H. (1996) 'Unemployment in Norway', in E. Wadensjö (ed.) *The Nordic labour markets in the 1990's*, Amsterdam: Elsevier Science B.V.

Weiss, Y. (1997) 'The formation and dissolution of families: Why marry? Who marries whom? And what happens upon divorce?', in M.R. Rosenzweig and O. Stark (eds) *Handbook of population and family economics*, North-Holland: Elsevier Science.

Willis, R. (1973) 'A new approach to the economic theory of fertility behaviour', *Journal of Political Economy*, 81: 14-64.

8 The effects of the globalization process on the transition to adulthood in Hungary

Péter Róbert and Erzsébet Bukodi

INTRODUCTION

In modern societies, there is a growing uncertainty concerning the outcome of different individual choices including educational decisions, those pertaining to the (first) job, partner selection, or the timing of parenthood. In a "runaway world" (Giddens, 1999), structural conditions and social norms provide less and less support or guidelines for taking decisions. As a result of this, individuals face increasing uncertainties, particularly during the process of the transition to adulthood. This analysis investigates the impact of globalization on this complex process in a post-communist country, Hungary.

The transition to adulthood involves several interrelated changes in social and individual states like labor market entry, partnership formation, or first parenthood, which influence each other reciprocally (Marini, 1985). In a regular sequence of the life course, completion of education and beginning of an occupational career are generally the first major steps in the transition to adulthood, followed by establishing stable family relations including partner selection and childbearing. As far as the transition from dependent "child" to independent "earner" is concerned, this process has become much longer and more flexible during the last decades. As it is increasingly difficult to consider a large variety of options, educational choices have become much harder to make. More and more information needs to be processed for an optimal selection among the many alternatives nowadays offered by the educational market as well as by the labor market. Since individuals have serious doubts about the necessary amount of information to be collected before making a good decision, they feel that their educational choices as well as the selection of their first job become more and more risky. In such a "risk society" (Beck, 1992), it is ever more difficult to calculate the different possible outcomes of any decision concerning type of school, educational track, subject of study, sort of occupation, kind of employer, etc.

Increasing uncertainty on entry into the labor force, flexible forms of employment as well as their financial consequences such as unfavorable or doubtful material prospects have all a strong influence on family formation. These economic factors go hand-in-hand with a decline in norms about legal marriage being the only stable form of a partnership. Thus, establishing a traditional family relationship is frequently postponed because individuals prefer more flexible forms like non-marital cohabitation for their first partnership. Partner selection is also a matching process where individuals evaluate and consider various types of attractiveness of the other, including physical characteristics as well as economic prospects. But under conditions of increasing global risks, youngsters of both sexes are less and less able to show firm signals to each other. Choosing less stable family relationships then seems to be the most rational thing to do. Child-bearing requires even more responsibility from both partners, which they can hardly afford if their economic position is unstable. This in turn leads to more and more postponement of the first birth and therewith to a general decline in fertility in modern societies.

Without going deeper into the description of these phenomena and their conceptual background as summarized by Klijzing and by Mills and Blossfeld (this volume), we now turn to the present Hungarian context surrounding the transition to adulthood. Then we portray research questions and hypotheses. The descriptive results and the findings from the causal analysis are presented in the section "The main characteristics of the transition to adulthood as process" and "The causal determinants of the transition to adulthood as process", respectively. The chapter ends with a concluding discussion of the transition to adulthood in Hungary.

THE HUNGARIAN CONTEXT OF THE TRANSITION TO ADULTHOOD

Institutional changes in the educational system and in the labor market

Both the institutions of the educational system and those of the labor market in Hungary have undergone significant changes during the 1990s. These institutional changes were embedded in an economic depression. In fact, economic difficulties started already in the 1980s but the collapse of communism has brought about a further significant fall in the economic performance of the country. The economic problems resulted in a decline in labor force participation (especially for women), an increase in unemployment (especially among young adults), and a drop in GDP with obvious consequences for the state budget and welfare spending.

With respect to the educational system, tracking was already a typical feature under communism, and this has only increased during the 1990s. Emerging types of private and religious education have made the system more complex. Nevertheless, the two main tracks of secondary schooling continued to exist: the vocational secondary and the academic secondary (grammar) schools. The curriculum of the former is more practical and provides more job-related skills, which enhances the labor market value of this type of education. The academic secondary school has much more the function of preparing students for further learning than of meeting the requirements for labor market entry. Tertiary education consists of two levels as well. The colleges with a 6-semester curriculum are more practical oriented; engineers, primary and secondary school teachers are some of the typical diploma holders from this sort of tertiary education, but the increasingly fashionable business schools also belong to this type. The universities with an 8-10-semester curriculum have a stronger emphasis on professional training in arts, science, law, or medicine.

The 1990s saw an educational expansion at both the secondary and tertiary level, but especially at the latter. There is a danger that increasing participation in education may result in an inflation of certificates and diplomas and that such a "credential inflation" may have negative consequences for the transition to work (Shavit and Müller, 1998). Indeed, the variation in the labor market value of different diplomas has already started to widen in Hungary. Thus, there is a rising uncertainty about the exact educational investments that will provide good returns, and this makes educational decisions more risky. On the other hand, the system has grown more flexible. Compared to secondary vocational or grammar schools, paths leading to a "dead-end street" like apprenticeships (which provided no route to tertiary education) have become much less of a typical choice for youngsters. For those in post-secondary training it is nowadays also much easier than in earlier times to correct wrong decisions but, obviously, at the cost of losing time.

Abolishing the planned economic system was one of the most important institutional modifications after the collapse of communism. The former routine solutions for the planned pathways from school to work hardly exist anymore. The Hungarian system used to be meritocratic in the sense that the educational prerequisites of the different jobs were well described, there was a strong link between education and occupation, and mobility space was typically *qualificational* in nature (cf. Maurice and Sellier, 1979). This feature of the system, however, started to change slowly in the direction of an *organizational* mobility space, where the curriculum of the educational institutions is more general and where the match between the type of qualification and the type of job is not so strong anymore. This means that for one and the same job employers can select from people with different qualifications, but also that one and the same qualification can entitle people to different jobs. This may make the transition from school to work more flexible but at the same time, young job seekers who entered the labor market after 1990 faced an increasing risk of a mismatch between their type of qualifications and their type of first jobs.

Structural changes in the Hungarian economy over the last decades have strongly influenced the demand side of the labor market. Agricultural employment decreased continuously and, on the whole, the country moved in the direction of an industrial society. Whereas these processes took place mostly during the 1960s and 1970s, employment in the service sector only started to increase in the 1980s and 1990s when more and more jobs became available in the tertiary sector compared to the traditional secondary (or even primary) sector. This process sped up in the 1990s when especially the demand for unskilled service jobs rose (class IIIb of Erikson and Goldthorpe, 1992).

As mentioned above, due to the economic depression there was a strong decline in employment possibilities in Hungary in the first part of the 1990s. Under socialism unemployment had been completely unknown, and it is no wonder then that the society was shocked by two-digit unemployment rates which reached their highest level (13 per cent) in 1992. During the second half of the 1990s, however, the unemployment rate dropped to one-digit figures (around 7-8 per cent). Economic circumstances combined with the political inclination to support private initiatives have led to a rapid increase of self-employment, which can be seen as just another form of flexible employment (see Bernardi and Nazio, this volume). After the nationalization program in the 1950s, the proportion of the self-employed had been as low as about 3 per cent of the total labor force. This percentage rose to 10-11 per cent in the 1990s[1], whereas other forms of flexible employment remained relatively low. For instance, the proportion of fixed-term employment was just about 6 per cent in 1999. Occasional and seasonal work is characteristic of certain branches only, like the food industry or trade. Like in the other post-communist countries, part-time employment hardly exists in Hungary (cf. Drobnič, 1997).

The emerging cleavage between the growing private and shrinking public sector is another new development of the post-communist era. Trends of employment in these two spheres have moved in opposite directions, with employment in the public sector down to 36 per cent while that in the private sector up to 58 per cent by the year 2000 (6 per cent of employment cannot be entirely classified according to this scheme). The private sector dominates in manufacturing, construction and a large part of services, whereas typical public employers can be found in administration, education and health. Although the private sector is more selective, in public employment there are strong budget constraints, new job openings are scarce and, consequently, fixed-term employment is more frequent.

Globalization evidently leads in all modern societies to a decline of the national character of the economy, and this process was especially rapid in Hungary during the 1990s. Starting from nothing (considering the socialist period before 1990 as a baseline), the share of partially or totally foreign-owned enterprises was already 43 per cent in 1995, and 65 per cent in 1997 (Árva, 1999). This means that young job seekers are entering a labor market where both local and foreign multinational employers exist with different expectations and wage compensation offers. Learning to meet the requirements of this new type of global labor market in the 1990s increases the risk and uncertainty for members of the globalization cohort.

Institutional context of family formation and related welfare policies

One of the most important demographic trends in Hungary during the last two decades was the decline and delay of first marriage and first birth. In fact, the marriage rate had already been decreasing since the beginning of the 1970s (Csernák, 1992). The age at first marriage is traditionally lower in Hungary than in Western European countries, but in the last decades there has been a tendency to postpone marriages until ever higher ages. Vital statistics show, for instance, that the female mean age at first marriage rose from 21.4 in 1989 to 25.7 in 2002. This increase is partly due to the increase in women's educational attainment and, consequently, their longer time spent in education.

During the socialist period when favorable opportunities for labor force participation and high governmental support for childcare co-existed together with traditional cultural values, the propensity to enter into non-marital cohabitation was relatively low. Not only the rates but also the nature of non-marital partnerships were completely different from those in other countries. As Carlson and Klinger (1987) have shown, cohabitation was most widespread among poor-educated individuals and only a small part of cohabiting unions involved persons who were never-married; in other countries the size of this group was much larger. In short, cohabitation in Hungary was chosen to a large extent by persons who could not get married for socioeconomic reasons.

Similarly to the age at first marriage in the socialist period, the age at entry into motherhood was also relatively low, with little difference between the two. However, in the last two decades there have been a significant rise in the age at first birth and a substantial decline in the birth rate. In 1975 the total fertility rate[2] stood still at 2.3 children per woman, the "second peak" according to this measure since World War II. Thereafter it has decreased almost continuously to only 1.31 in 2002. This tendency is confirmed by the number of live-births per 1,000 females: 160 among the 21 years-old in 1980 as opposed to 65 in 1999. Remarkable changes are detectable in women's mean age at first childbirth as well, increasing from 22.8 in the mid-1970s to 25.7 in 2002.

In terms of family support, Esping-Andersen (1990) distinguished originally three types of welfare regimes: conservative, liberal and social-democratic. With its socialist tradition of state-dominated welfare during the first four decades after the World War II, Hungary is perhaps closest to the social-democratic regime. More recently, Esping-Andersen (1999) re-examined his classification and discussed the possibility of a fourth – Mediterranean or East-Asian – regime. However, Blossfeld and Drobnic (2001) extended this typology even further and introduced the "former state socialist" welfare regime. It is characterized by a strong egalitarianism as well as by a de-emphasis of the family, with the state playing a dominant role in the entire system.

The developments in the era of globalization and system transformation in Hungary after 1990 did not bring about fundamental changes to this regime, though a definite move towards familialism and a decreasing role of the state could be observed.[3] In the dual-breadwinner family system under socialism, public childcare was an important welfare institution. Many of these nurseries and kindergartens were operated by local municipalities, others by firms where working parents could bring their pre-school children for day care. This system has largely collapsed in the 1990s. The budget of the local municipalities has been cut so that nowadays they can spend much less for such purposes. Furthermore, many firms were privatized and, consequently, more profit-oriented so that they hardly finance such childcare facilities anymore.

But despite the decline in employment in the 1990s (especially for women), the dual-breadwinner family system in Hungary has largely survived the collapse of communism. The most important changes in the welfare system were caused by the decrease in GDP and the economic difficulties that the country had to face in the 1990s. These developments have strongly influenced the safety net in general, but particularly those who came from disadvantaged families had difficulties with starting their own life. Changes in the originally quite generous Hungarian welfare system were relatively minor in the first half of 1990s. In fact, new measures like unemployment benefits were introduced, and families with children were granted special tax exemptions as from 1992 onwards. Later on, between 1995 and 1997 when the country was governed by a social-liberal coalition, a small "shock therapy" was applied. That is, the tax exemption for families with children was abolished and childcare benefits were reduced or partly withdrawn. But when a conservative coalition came to power again in 1998, the new government re-installed several elements of the previous welfare system, such as a universal allowance and tax exemptions for families with children.

RESEARCH QUESTIONS AND HYPOTHESES

How does the globalization process influence the transition from school to work?

As demonstrated by Becker (1975), human capital investments have a strong influence on labor market success. Although his strict economic approach mainly focuses on the returns to education in terms of earnings, the latter is also determined by the type of job and contract that one is able to obtain in the labor market. The first decision to be made in this respect relates to finishing school, continuing studies or entering the labor force. A relevant part of the recent literature on this question puts the problem into a rational choice framework (cf. Goldthorpe, 1996; Breen and Goldthorpe, 1997). However, a critical argument in this reasoning is that increasing uncertainty under conditions of globalization may undermine the rationality of any calculation. The essence of a risk society is that one cannot predict the outcomes of decisions.

Nonetheless, the main argument of human capital investment theory, namely, that young people have better chances to find a good job with an appropriate contract and promising financial arrangements if they are higher educated, still holds. In fact, tertiary school and especially university diplomas signal an individual's abilities and efforts, which in most societies where meritocratic principles dominate are highly appreciated by employers. On the other hand, a typical feature of modern employers (especially multinational companies) is that education is just one of the prerequisites to be considered. They are similarly interested in the motivation, ambition, and other personal characteristics of the job seekers.

Indeed, the skills and knowledge that many jobs require nowadays can mostly be gathered through on-the-job training. Therefore, employers do not look so much for employees who know everything but for employees who are willing and able to learn what the job requires. But even a very careful selection process, in-depth interviews with the job seekers, and full familiarity with what a company can get from a person with certain qualifications cannot guarantee that the employer will choose the best candidate for a given position. Under such conditions, when both the employer and the employee need time to get to know each other better, fixed-term employment is probably a good solution.

General conditions on the labor market have a strong impact on individuals' chances of finding a good job. Post-industrial labor markets are segmented in the sense that – in addition to highly specialized jobs with special requirements – there is also a strong need for less qualified labor, especially in the service sector. Young job seekers searching for first employment with a fresh school qualification but without any experience or "good record" from previous employment have frequently to be satisfied with precarious jobs at the beginning of their occupational career.

In order to find a better job, members of the globalization generation seem to follow different strategies. One of the possibilities is to stay in the educational system as long as possible. Another is to postpone final decisions, which makes the transition from school to work only longer. During this search period young adults are in a state of "not in education, not in the labor force". A third possibility is when youngsters start to work already during their years of (higher) education, thus combining the role of a full- or part-time student with that of a labor force participant. The whole process of the transition from school to work becomes in this way more flexible and, with emerging forms of flexible employment (fixed-term contracts, part-time work, self-employment), so does the labor market.

On a descriptive level, it is therefore expected that participation in education has expanded in particular for the globalization cohort. We also assume that more students start to work during their studies. On the other hand, finding a proper job takes longer, especially for those who search for their first employment in the 1990s.

Several analytical research questions with respect to transition from school to work could be derived at this point but the availability of information in our data allows us to focus on only three. First, we consider the probability of entering the labor market within a ten-year period after completing day-time education. We assume that chances of finding a job within this period are worst for members of the globalization cohort. We further assume that those with higher levels of schooling have better chances. Applying a cohort perspective, we will test the hypothesis of credential inflation as well. We allow for the possibility that somebody returns to education, which will obviously decrease the odds of entering the labor force. Supposing that a long search period will have a negative impact on the success of finding a job, we also consider the length of the job search.

Second, we turn to investigating the entry class of youngsters' first job. In this case we predict the probability on entering into various class positions after the completion of daytime education. This analysis thus focuses on selected class positions. It is expected that the odds of labor market entry in the upper service class is smaller for the globalization cohort. However, young job seekers have higher chances of becoming self-employed in their first job. They are also more likely to start their occupational career in precarious jobs in the unskilled service or worker class. Educational attainment is again assumed to influence first class positions. Higher (tertiary) levels of education provides for higher odds of ending up in an upper service class position, while the probability of getting a precarious job in the unskilled service or worker class is higher for the lower educated.

Third, the probability of fixed-term employment is investigated as a competing risk of permanent employment among employees (not considering the self-employed). We assume that the odds of entering into a fixed-term job have grown larger for the globalization cohort. Distinguishing between private and public sector will allow us to test the hypothesis that fixed-term jobs are more frequent in the public sphere, where job openings are very limited due to funding problems. It is also presumed that fixed-term employment is more typical in low status, precarious jobs.

For the analysis of the transition from school to work two data sets are being used, both taken from the Hungarian Central Statistical Office. The Way of Life and Time Use Survey, carried out in 1999-2000, is based on a random sample of about 10,000 respondents aged 15-85 years. The General Youth Survey, fielded in 2000, is based on a random sample of about 8,000 respondents aged 15-29 years. These two data sets have been pooled together resulting in a file of exactly 18,476 cases. This design is particularly appropriate for the research purpose at hand because the globalization cohort (respondents born between 1971 and 1985) is over-represented, while a sufficient number of respondents remain to serve as reference group.

How does the transition from school to work as a process influence first partnership formation?

The consequences of the fundamental changes that have taken place since 1990 – increasing uncertainties about career entry, quite high unemployment as well as the collapse of the "old" family system – together with the effects of the "globalization shock" may result in a substantial increase in non-marital cohabitation. It is to be expected that not only the rate but also the underlying causal factors of union formation are influenced by these recent socioeconomic and cultural changes.

In line with the results of many other studies, the most recent analysis of marriage in Hungary (Róbert and Blossfeld, 1995) found that school enrolment had a tendency to postpone union formation, thus confirming the hypothesis that school completion is a key marker of the transition to adulthood. Their predictions concerning the effect of school participation on marriage may apply to non-marital cohabitation as well. The two types of unions resemble each other in many ways: they both involve a time-intensive relationship between the partners, a shared living arrangement, etc. It is reasonable to expect, therefore, that they carry similar implications of economic independence. Thus, we anticipate that school attendance has a negative influence on the rate of non-marital as well as of marital cohabitation. However, because cohabitation is better compatible with full-time education than marriage, it may be predicted that the magnitude of this influence is smaller for a non-marital partnership than for legal marriage (Hoem, 1986; Thornton *et al.*, 1995; Liefbroer and Corijn, 1999; Berrington and Diamond, 2000). Non-marital unions do not necessarily involve the same commitments and investments as those associated with marital unions. This means that the opportunity costs of cohabitation may be lower than those of marriage, so that students may be more willing to enter into a consensual union than to get married.

It may be expected that cohabitation is also the best choice for students who combine school attendance with employment. Individuals who are in full-time education are hardly able to support themselves. In addition, the demands of school participation may limit their amount of time available for other roles such as those implied by marriage or parenthood. Thus, we hypothesize that the negative effect of school enrollment on the cohabitation rate is smaller for individuals attending school and working than for students not being employed.

The activity status "not in school, not working" deserves particular attention. Because of the career uncertainties attached to this status, we expect that young individuals who are not in school and not working tend to postpone first partnership formation – particularly marriage – until they manage to establish a steady job career. For those who have left school and are currently working, however, the story is different. Difficulties to enter the labor force as a result of the substantial changes in economic conditions as well as of the insecurity arising from the globalization process may lead to the emergence of various atypical forms of employment such as low-paid routine service jobs, fixed-term contracts, occasional work, etc. The impact of employment on first partnership formation is therefore supposed to depend on the kind of job, i.e., individuals in precarious employment may be inclined to choose consensual unions, whereas persons with a steady job may rather prefer marriage.

The economic theory of marriage predicts a gender-specific effect of economic resources – educational qualifications, earnings – on the propensity of family formation (Becker, 1981). Men with higher educational attainment and good labor market prospects would have a greater attractiveness on the marriage market. For women, however, labor force participation and increased earnings reduce the gains they could have from marriage, since the division of labor within the family would become less advantageous to them. Previous studies on couples' employment careers in Hungary (Róbert *et al.*, 2001; Róbert and Bukodi, 2002), however, have questioned the validity of this argument of a "traditional" sexual division of labor. In the framework of employment patterns based on a family model with *two* earners, strong evidence was found for the positive effects of the spouse's resources on the labor force success of both the husband and the wife. In addition, no negative effect was found for women's level of education on their odds of getting married – as would be predicted from Becker's theory (Róbert and Blossfeld, 1995). Taking these results into account, we therefore expect an event-specific – instead of a gender-specific – impact of economic resources on partnership formation. That is, educational attainment and earning potentials have only a delaying effect on entry into marriage: better educated individuals tend to postpone it until they finish their education and establish a steady employment career.

How does the process of the transition from school to work influence first parenthood?

As far as the impact of different activity statuses on the propensity of becoming a parent is concerned, we expect similar effects as those on the transition rate of first marriage. The only exception is the influence of not working among women. The theory on the traditional division of labor in the household yields two hypotheses concerning fertility behavior (Becker, 1981). On the one hand, men who do not work are supposedly unable to support their families and are thus expected to postpone fatherhood. Females' non-employment, on the other hand, would encourage couples to have children because it decreases the time costs of childbearing. This would make it reasonable for women who are neither in school nor in the labor force to give birth.

However, this neoclassic framework does not involve fertility decisions in the context of females' careers. According to the human capital approach, women (with children) show a resource investment behavior that is different from men's (Mincer and Ofek, 1982). The life cycle of women with children can be divided into several stages which differ in the degree of labor force versus home involvement. Generally, there is continuous participation in the labor force up to the birth of the first child. The second phase in the life cycle is a period of non-participation in the labor force due to childbearing. This is followed by a third period in which there is a permanent return to the labor market. In contrast to this, the "conventional" type of employment pattern is one in which women leave the labor market before their first childbirth and they never return thereafter. But this pattern applies less and less in modern societies, where mothers tend to go back to the labor force. Today also in Hungary a large majority of wives return to work, either before their last childbirth or after it, and only 12 per cent of married women remain homemaker after a break for childbearing (Róbert et al., 2001). These facts imply that if a woman decides to have a child while not employed, she may experience a substantial deterioration in her acquired knowledge and skills. This would seriously reduce her chances of returning to the labor market, let alone of experiencing upward career mobility.

These arguments concern only well educated women who have enough human capital "to deteriorate". However, in a society where starting a professional career becomes more and more difficult for larger numbers of individuals, women may increasingly face a choice between two alternatives: an employment career or a motherhood career. Females with poor employment prospects may tend to choose the latter because it offers a predictable and secure future instead of unpredictable and unsuccessful labor market participation. Thus, we hypothesize that the impact of non-employment is mediated by economic resources. For females with good education and attractive earnings this impact may be negative, while for women without career resources unemployment may have an accelerating effect on childbirth.

As for the impact of economic resources, we expect similar effects as those found in another recent study (Róbert and Blossfeld, 1995). Namely, higher qualified women 1) have their first child later, and 2) are more likely to remain childless – at least until their thirties – because of the competing demands of a job career and childbearing.

For the analysis of family formation – entry into first partnership and parenthood – data of the General Youth Survey are being used. In this case we selected persons born between 1971 and 1980 (N=5,847).

THE MAIN CHARACTERISTICS OF THE TRANSITION TO ADULTHOOD AS PROCESS

Transition from school to work

We start our analysis by providing a descriptive view of the different phases of the school-to-work relationship. We follow a life course approach and display the different combinations of states between being in or out of school and in or out of work, at the ages of 19 and 23, for both men and women. Figure 8.1 shows the proportion of individuals who attend school and who are not in labor force, according to their year of birth. In line with the expectations about the educational expansion, the percentages of these individuals when 19 increase slightly for the cohorts born between 1931 and 1970 but steeper for the globalization cohort born thereafter. The proportion of the same individuals at the age of 23 indicates more stability between 1931 and 1970, and the increase is less steep for the globalization cohort. Indeed, expansion of tertiary education under socialism was not as much as that of secondary education; it only sped up in the 1990s.

Figure 8.2 exhibits the proportion of individuals who neither attended school nor worked at those ages. These percentages are falling, and steeper so for women. This proves that school enrolment and labor force participation increased to a higher degree for women, and that differences in levels of schooling between men and women diminished. This whole process was more pronounced during the first part of the socialist era, becoming less pronounced later. Data for the globalization cohort indicate a slight upswing in the proportion of these individuals, which demonstrates that this cohort faces growing difficulties with finding a job.

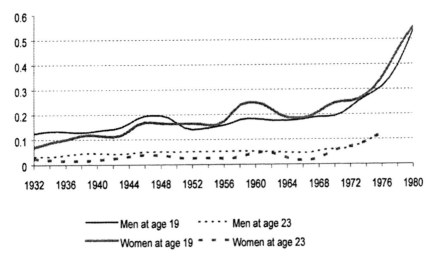

Figure 8.1   Proportion of individuals enrolled in school and not working at different
ages (persons born in 1931-1980)

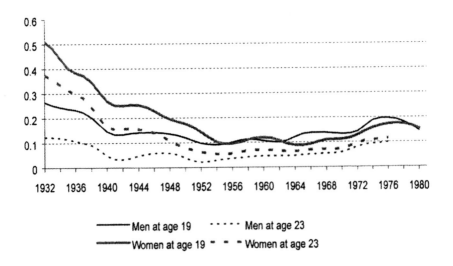

Figure 8.2   Proportion of individuals not enrolled in school and not working at
different ages (persons born in 1931-1980)

Individuals not attending school and being at work, as presented in Figure 8.3, represent an inverse pattern compared to individuals in Figure 8.1. That is, the trend is upward first, especially for women, but downward for the globalization cohort born after 1970, although this is more marked at the age of 19.

Next we investigate the proportion of individuals attending school and being in the labor force at the same time (Figure 8.4). At less than 7 per cent, this is a rather small group, even for the globalization cohort. The increase in this state is steeper at the age of 23, which reflects a normal aging effect: the combination of learning and working occurs mostly at older ages, namely, during tertiary education.

Figures 8.5 and 8.6 outline the changes over time in the type of first employment for those members of the globalization cohort who do not attend school but who are in the labor force. Data indicate a steep and steady decline of permanent employment, especially at the age of 19. This result is the outcome of three developments: educational expansion, rising unemployment and increased flexibility in the job market. There is not much change over time in fixed-term employment for individuals aged 19. However, it increases for those aged 23, especially men. This is also an indication of growing uncertainty surrounding first employment.

Finally, Figure 8.7 displays the change in the length of time devoted to searching for a first job. This length of time, measured in years, first decreased for those who left the educational system between 1950 and 1985 but it increased again thereafter. This reversal started earlier for men, and theirs was also more pronounced than for women.

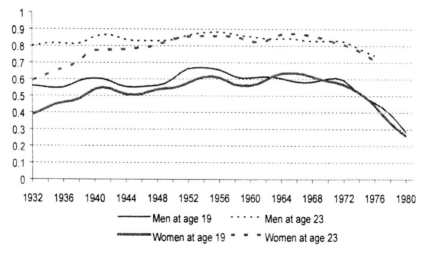

Figure 8.3   Proportion of individuals not enrolled in school and working at different ages (persons born in 1931-1980)

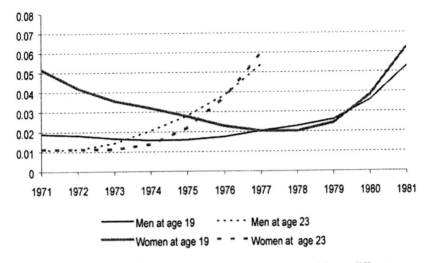

Figure 8.4   Proportion of individuals enrolled in school and working at different ages (persons born in 1971-1980)

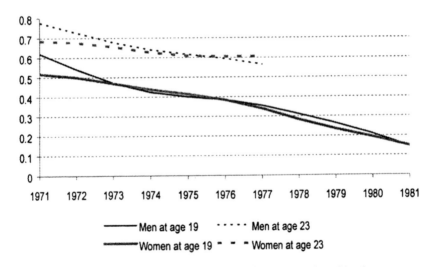

Figure 8.5   Proportion of individuals not enrolled in school and working in permanent contract job at different ages (persons born in 1971-1980)

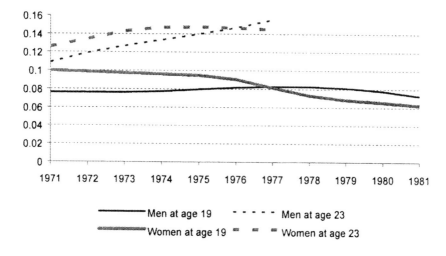

Figure 8.6   Proportion of individuals not enrolled in school and working in fixed-term contract job at different ages (persons born in 1971-1980)

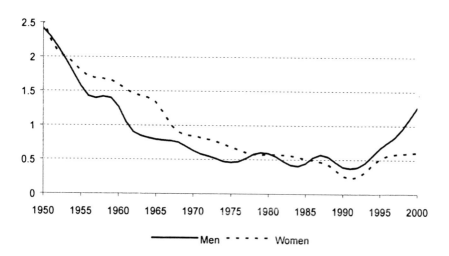

Figure 8.7   Time elapsed between the first exit from day-course education and the entry into labour force (in years)

LIVERPOOL JOHN MOORES UNIVERSITY
LEARNING SERVICES

Family formation

The intensity and timing of first marriage is radically different for persons born before and after 1970: the proportion of people married by the age of 25 is much lower in the latter cohort. For instance, only some 50 per cent of all women born in the first half of the 1970s had married by their mid-twenties, whereas this percentage was still 75 to 80 per cent for those born in the 1960s. This means that members of the youngest cohorts postpone marriage to later ages.

For young individuals, the lower intensity of marriage is compensated by a higher incidence of non-marital cohabitation, which increases over time. For instance, only 7 per cent of single women born in 1955-59 had cohabited before the age of 29, but this figure rises to 25 per cent for women born in the early seventies.

Figures 8.8.1 and 8.8.2 show the observed rates of entry into first cohabitation and first marriage for women and men born in the 1970s who had remained single until a certain age. Marriage rates peak at age 22 for females and at age 24 for males, whereas cohabitation rates at later ages but lower levels. Early partnership formation – particularly non-marital cohabitation – is more common among individuals in less advantageous social positions. The population remaining single in their mid-twenties constitutes a rather heterogeneous group consisting of people with attractive economic potentials as well as of unemployed persons with poor educational capital. The propensity to enter into cohabitation may be relatively high in both groups, but for different reasons. Individuals with good labor market prospects tend to choose this type of union as a temporary living arrangement in order to establish their occupational career. Persons in less advantageous positions, on the other hand, are forced to choose this form of partnership due to the lack of any sign of future labor market success.

In terms of the possible outcomes of non-marital unions, 18 per cent of all cohabiting males born in 1971-80 had converted their partnership into marriage by the age of 29, whereas another 33 per cent had seen their partnership dissolved by that age. Corresponding figures for cohabiting females are 28 and 54 per cent, respectively. This means that half of males' first non-marital unions had survived at least until their late 20s, while for females the corresponding figure did not even reach 20 per cent. As far as the duration of non-marital unions is concerned, they are usually short-lived: their mean duration is only 3.5 years.

Similarly to marriage, first parenthood occurs much earlier among individuals born before 1970 than among those thereafter (Figures 8.9.1 and 8.9.2). Among women born in 1961-65, around 70 per cent had become mothers by age 25 whereas this was only the case for some 45 per cent of females born ten years later. For males the general pattern is similar, only the percentages are lower.

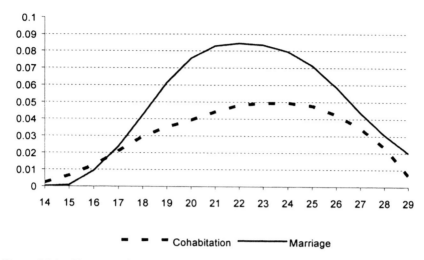

Figure 8.8.1   The rates of entry into first cohabitation and first marriage, women born in 1971-1980

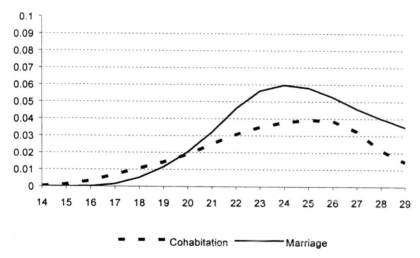

Figure 8.8.2   The rates of entry into first cohabitation and marriage, men born 1971-1980

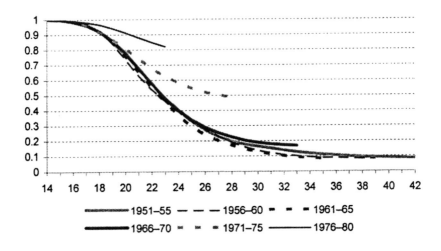

Figure 8.9.1   Proportion of women who never had a child, according to birth cohort

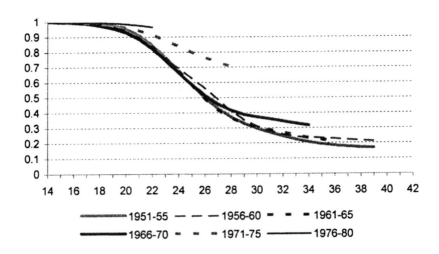

Figure 8.9.2   Proportion of men who never had a child, according to birth cohort

THE CAUSAL DETERMINANTS OF THE TRANSITION TO ADULTHOOD AS PROCESS

Entry into labor force

The first multivariate model refers to the probability of entering the labor market within a ten-year period after completing daytime education. Results for men and women are displayed in the first columns of Tables 8.1.1 and 8.1.2, respectively. In order to estimate the period effects of changes over time, the year of completing daytime education is grouped into five cohorts of 10 years each. Compared to the 1950s which is the reference category, the economic reforms apparently offered better opportunities for young men in the 1970s but not so in the 1980s, whereas the globalization cohort leaving school during 1990-2000 clearly had significantly worse chances for entering the labor market. In line with the increasing labor force participation of women, their chances for entering the labor market have gradually improved under the socialist era. However, also for them this favorable trend stopped with the arrival of the globalization cohort.

Generally speaking, the higher the level of education that young job seekers have, the better their chances of finding a first job. Some gender differences appear in the effect of educational credentials: for men a university degree provides for the best odds, for women a college degree. But for both it is the grammar school with its academic curriculum that decreases the probability of labor force entry relative to apprenticeships, which constitute the reference category, while those with only primary education have the worst chances. The cohort analyses in the last three columns of Tables 8.1.1 and 8.1.2 do not support the assumption of credential inflation. In fact, a degree from tertiary education seems to improve the odds for entering the labor market over time. As more and more women complete university nowadays, gender differences in this respect tend to decline.

If one returns to education after having left the school system, the odds for labor market entry will obviously deteriorate. This pattern seems to be particularly strong among the globalization cohort. Finally, the longer the time spent on a job search, the lower the chances of finding any work. The cohort analyses indicate that also this pattern is more pronounced for the globalization cohort than for those job seekers who completed daytime education under socialism.

Entry class at first employment

The second multivariate model investigates the probability of finding a first job in selected classes as compared to remaining out of the labor market. Estimates are shown in Tables 8.2.1 (men) and 8.2.2 (women). As far as changes over time are concerned, the chances of beginning a career immediately in the upper service class have significantly decreased for the globalization cohort, especially among men. However, the odds of self-employment in a first job have increased

Table 8.1.1 Probability of entry into the labor market within a ten-year period after completing daytime education, Hungarian men

	All	*Completion of education*		
		1950-69	*1970-89*	*1990-2000*
Year of completion of daytime education				
1990-2000	-0.163*	-	-	-
1980-1989	0.115	-	-	-
1970-1979	0.182*	-	-	-
1960-1969	0.115	-	-	-
1950-1959 (ref.)	0			
Highest level of education				
University	0.539***	0.254	0.399*	0.839***
College	0.504***	-0.128	-0.180	1.083***
Academic secondary (grammar school)	-0.698***	-0.782***	-0.994***	-0.459***
Vocational secondary	0.043	0.392*	0.094	-0.025
Apprenticeship (ref.)	0	0	0	0
Primary education	-1.588***	-1.384***	-1.708***	-1.684***
In education	-3.194***	-2.690***	-3.238***	-3.409***
Time elapsed since completion of daytime education				
9-10 years	-1.903***	-1.133***	-2.036***	-2.752***
7-8 years	-1.370***	-0.796***	-1.406***	-1.614***
5-6 years	-0.730***	-0.130	-0.859***	-0.931***
3-4 years	-0.429***	0.011	-0.201*	-0.820***
0-2 years (ref.)	0	0	0	0
Intercept	0.394***	0.116	0.603***	0.304***
-2 Log Likelihood (model)	16362.98	3374.29	5450.31	7404.53
-2 Log Likelihood (initial)	21701.16	4019.31	7397.73	10255.46
Number of events	4941	856	1731	2354
Number of subepisodes	18875	3739	6282	8854

Results from discrete-time event history analysis; reference: not entering into the labor market

Notes
*** p < 0.001
** p < 0.01
* p < 0.05

Table 8.1.2   Probability of entry into the labor market within a ten-year period after completing daytime education, Hungarian women

	All	Completion of education		
		1950-69	*1970-89*	*1990-2000*
Year of completion of daytime education				
1990-2000	0.113	-	-	-
1980-1989	0.432***	-	-	-
1970-1979	0.353***	-	-	-
1960-1969	0.294***	-	-	-
1950-1959 (ref.)	0			
Highest level of education				
University	0.755***	0.546+	0.113	1.386***
College	1.159***	0.664*	0.811***	1.502***
Academic secondary (grammar school)	-0.266***	-0.425**	-0.075	-0.315***
Vocational secondary	0.151*	0.152	0.237*	0.110
Apprenticeship (ref.)	0	0	0	0
Primary education	-1.562***	-1.493***	-1.443***	-1.924***
In education	-3.161***	-2.548***	-3.154***	-3.486***
Time elapsed since completion of daytime education				
9-10 years	-2.278***	-1.410***	-2.746***	-3.625***
7-8 years	-1.854***	-1.050***	-2.142***	-2.560***
5-6 years	-1.305***	-0.599***	-1.782***	-1.525***
3-4 years	-0.731***	-0.243*	-0.779***	-1.041***
0-2 years (ref.)	0	0	0	0
Intercept	0.192*	0.041	0.596***	0.453***
-2 Log Likelihood (model)	22343.58	4499.62	5120.19	6672.98
-2 Log Likelihood (initial)	16458.55	5249.08	7015.78	9873.23
Number of events	4828	978	1594	2256
Number of subepisodes	20432	5758	6113	8561

Results from discrete-time event history analysis; reference: not entering into the labor market

Notes
*** $p < 0.001$
** $p < 0.01$
* $p < 0.05$

Table 8.2.1   Probability of entry into the labor market within a ten-year period: effects on selected[a] entry classes, Hungarian men

	Upper service	Self-employed	Unskilled service	Unskilled manual
Year of completion of daytime education				
1990-2000	-0.966***	2.818**	0.499	0.190
1980-1989	-0.516+	2.711*	0.453	0.170
1970-1979	-0.077	2.191*	-0.689+	0.346*
1960-1969	0.130	1.210	-0.381	0.114
1950-1959 (ref.)	0	0	0	0
Highest level of education				
University	5.680***	0.127	-2.820	-1.372***
College	5.053***	0.372	0.623*	-1.557***
Academic secondary (grammar school)	2.139***	-0.411	0.250	-0.831***
Vocational secondary	2.815***	0.292	0.920***	-0.078
Apprenticeship (ref.)	0	0	0	0
Primary education	-0.730	-1.877***	-1.897***	-0.625***
In education	-3.222***	-3.491***	-3.128***	-3.338***
Time elapsed since completion of daytime education				
9-10 years	-2.664***	-0.974	-1.614*	-1.387***
7-8 years	-1.111**	-0.655	-1.265**	-0.894***
5-6 years	-0.613*	-0.612+	-1.143***	-0.252*
3-4 years	-0.541*	-0.010	-0.745***	-0.060
0-2 years (ref.)	0	0	0	0
Intercept	-4.790***	-5.658***	-3.041***	-1.544***
-2 Log Likelihood (model)	4063.79	4063.79	4063.79	4063.79
-2 Log Likelihood (initial)	12741.16	12741.16	12741.16	12741.16
Number of events	288	174	284	1143
Number of subepisodes	18836	18836	18836	18836

Results from discrete-time event history analysis; reference: not entering into the labor market

Notes
a   Other class positions estimated but not reported.
*** $p < 0.001$
** $p < 0.01$
* $p < 0.05$
+ $p < 0.1$

Table 8.2.2   Probability of entry into the labor market within a ten-year period: effects on selected[a] entry classes, Hungarian women

	Upper service	Self-employed	Unskilled service	Unskilled manual
Year of completion of daytime education				
1990-2000	-0.634+	2.724*	0.958***	0.384***
1980-1989	-0.136	2.897**	0.815***	0.570***
1970-1979	0.372	1.855	0.693**	0.539***
1960-1969	0.270	1.980+	0.322	0.343**
1950-1959 (ref.)	0	0	0	0
Highest level of education				
University	4.929***	-0.815	-1.390**	-20.592
College	4.264***	-0.238	-0.509*	-2.243***
Academic secondary (grammar school)	0.744+	-0.204	-0.833***	-1.202***
Vocational secondary	1.391***	-0.183	-0.304**	-0.831***
Apprenticeship (ref.)	0	0	0	0
Primary education	-2.225***	-2.201***	-2.532***	-0.858***
In education	-3.993***	-2.898***	-3.084***	-3.518***
Time elapsed since completion of daytime education				
9-10 years	-1.967***	-15.022	-2.097***	-2.161***
7-8 years	-2.127***	-0.748+	-1.923***	-1.646***
5-6 years	-1.517***	-1.128*	-1.955***	-1.089***
3-4 years	-0.987***	-0.887**	-0.591***	-0.567***
0-2 years (ref.)	0	0	0	0
Intercept	-4.246***	-5.680***	-1.727***	-1.389***
-2 Log Likelihood (model)	4278.65	4278.65	4278.65	4278.65
-2 Log Likelihood (initial)	13769.77	13769.77	13769.77	13769.77
Number of events	175	106	760	1012
Number of subepisodes	20394	20394	20394	20394

Results from discrete-time event history analysis; reference: not entering into the labor market

Notes
a   Other class positions estimated but not reported.
***   p < 0.001
**   p < 0.01
*   p < 0.05
+   p < 0.1

over time, gradually for men but sharply for women. A straightforward interpretation of this finding is not immediately obvious. It may partly reflect the impact of growing uncertainty and flexibility on the labor market as a result of globalization, but it may also be a consequence of the gradual liberalization of the Hungarian economy, in which private initiatives were already better tolerated during later phases of communism. Finally, the hypothesis about the rise of unskilled service jobs at the beginning of the occupational career is confirmed for women but not for men.

Entry into upper service class positions clearly requires high levels of schooling, in particular university degrees. Compared to finding employment as unskilled manual worker, more education is also needed for entering into unskilled service jobs. But educational attainment is insignificant as predictor for self-employment in a first job.

The negative effect of returning to school is present in this case, too: it reduces the odds of entering into any class position. The same is true for extending search periods, except when self-employment ensues.

Permanent versus fixed-term contract at first employment

Finally, in Table 8.3, the process of the transition from school to work is operationalized by means of the type of first employment. Models 1 and 2 predict, for men and women separately, the probability of fixed-term employment (including occasional work) as compared to permanent employment. Only employees are investigated, the self-employed are excluded, and the analysis focuses on the experience of the globalization cohort. In line with the expectations set out above and the descriptive results presented in Figures 8.5 and 8.6, positive estimates for the members of the globalization cohort reveal that they have significantly higher chances to find fixed-term employment at labor market entry during the 1990s than the previous cohort that had completed their education in the 1980s. The effects are stronger for men.

Also men with primary education only have significantly higher odds than those with an apprenticeship of ending up in fixed-term employment. But, contrary to expectations, education higher than that does not lower the probability of fixed-term employment. On the contrary, college education slightly raises it. The effect of the public vs. private sector is moderate (especially for men), but it suggests that fixed-term employment is somewhat more probable in the public sector. With respect to entry class, it is clear that fixed-term jobs are more likely – for both men and women – in the unskilled worker and service class. In addition, for women, they are also more likely in the lower service and non-manual class.

Table 8.3   Probability of entry into fixed-term employment, Hungarian men and women

	Men		Women	
	Model 1	*Model 2*	*Model 1*	*Model 2*
Year of completion of daytime education				
1990-2000	0.632***	0.619***	0.361*	0.425*
1980-1989 (ref.)	0	0	0	0
Highest level of education				
University	-0.602	0.186	0.162	-0.088
College	0.443+	0.497+	0.591**	0.046
Academic secondary[1]	0.055	-0.082	0.202	-0.116
Vocational secondary	0.006	-0.074	-0.242	-0.620***
Apprenticeship (ref.)	0	0	0	0
Primary education	0.945***	0.697***	0.349+	0.286
Employment in private sector		-0.227+		-0.396**
Entry class				
Upper service (I)		-0.619		-0.389
Lower service (II)		0.193		0.812**
Non-manual (clerical) (IIIa)		0.231		0.635**
Skilled worker (ref.) (V+VI)		0		0
Unskilled service (IIIb)		0.519*		0.411*
Unskilled worker (VIIa)		0.525***		0.433*
Agricultural worker (VIIb)		0.476+		0.741
Intercept	-2.098***	-2.096***	-1.733***	-1.790***
-2 Log Likelihood (model)	1951.19	1928.52	1952.34	1916.66
-2 Log Likelihood (initial)	1993.33		1978.21	
Number of cases	2000		1929	

Results from logistic regression analysis, performed on individual level. Reference: permanent employment, self-employed excluded

Notes
1   Grammar school
*** $p < 0.001$
** $p < 0.01$
* $p < 0.05$
+ $p < 0.1$

Entry into first partnership

Table 8.4 shows the effects of different explanatory variables on the rates of transition to non-marital and marital cohabitation, treated as competing risks. With respect to the impact of the transition from school to work on the propensity of first partnership formation, strong support for our hypotheses is found.

Firstly, full-time school enrolment – without labor force participation – significantly reduces the hazard of forming any type of partnership, both among men and among women. A comparison of the effects of this particular status on non-marital versus marital cohabitation, however, confirms our hypothesis that full-time school enrolment reduces the odds of marriage much more than those of a consensual union. In other words, role incompatibility between school enrolment and marriage is larger than between school enrolment and cohabitation.

Secondly, if full-time school enrolment is combined with labor force participation, then the reduction in partnership rates is less than it was for school participation without any labor force experience. As far as non-marital cohabitation is concerned, the status "in school/working" has even no significant effect at all. These results are consistent with the idea that role incompatibilities between school enrolment and union formation are smaller for students who participate in the labor force than for those who do not. The majority of students belonging to the former attend tertiary education, and their labor market experience makes it easier for them to establish a union, especially a consensual one.

Thirdly, for individuals who are neither in school nor in the labor force it is fairly difficult to form a union regardless of its type. For women not studying and not working the odds of getting married are ($e^{-2.301} - 1=$) 90 per cent lower than for females having a permanent job. For males not studying and not working the reduction in the marriage rate is smaller, only 25 per cent. In the case of non-marital unions the pattern is similar, but the magnitudes of the effects are lower.

Finally, the dummy variable capturing the effect of fixed-contract employment on the propensity of partnership formation reveals a particularly interesting pattern of results. Working in a job with a fixed-term contract show opposite effects on marital (-) and non-marital (+) cohabitation (even though the former ones are insignificant). Women working under a fixed-contract are ($e^{+.181} - 1 =$) 20 per cent more likely to move into non-marital cohabitation than women in permanent employment; the corresponding figure for men is 6 per cent. These findings thus suggest that people with greater temporal uncertainty about their own economic prospects tend to choose non-marital cohabitation. A possible explanation for this could be that they need to spend some time in such a trial union in order to allow their career uncertainties to diminish.

To capture the effect of economic resources on the entry into a first partnership we include two variables in our models: (1) educational accumulation, and (2) monthly earnings. Each additional year of schooling decreases for both sexes the

Table 8.4   Hazard of entry into first partnership up to the age of 29, Hungarian men and women born in 1971-80

	Men		Women	
	Cohabitation	*Marriage*	*Cohabitation*	*Marriage*
Age				
Log(age-14)	1.809***	3.352***	1.227***	2.270***
Log(29-age)	0.803***	1.249***	0.923***	2.214***
Transition from school to work				
In school/not working	-1.651***	-2.082***	-1.214**	-3.876***
In school/working	-0.893	-1.298**	-0.840	-0.799**
Not in school/not working	-0.270*	-0.293*	-0.178*	-2.301***
Not in school/working/ fixed-term job	0.060*	-0.178	0.181*	-0.074
Not in school/working/ permanent job (ref.)	0	0	0	0
Economic resources				
Educational accumulation[a]	-0.085**	-0.043**	-0.062**	-0.041*
Earnings[b]	-0.106*	0.053	-0.044*	-0.211***
Social origin				
Religious affiliation[c]	-0.010	0.552***	0.020	0.378***
Non-intact family[d]	0.150	-0.262	0.591***	-0.119
Intercept	-7.262***	-12.998***	-6.774***	-8.976***
-2 Log Likelihood (model)	3761.49	4159.67	4833.14	6443.67
-2 Log Likelihood (initial)	(4169.80)	(5159.70)	(5295.30)	(7734.80)
Number of events	398	514	564	917
Number of subepisodes	27915	28031	22970	23323

Results from discrete-time event-history analysis

Notes:
a   Number of completed classes after completion of primary school.
b   Natural log of mean monthly earnings.
c   Dummy variable which sets 1 if respondent belongs to any religion, otherwise it is 0.
d   Dummy variable which sets 1 if respondent was brought up in a non-intact family, otherwise it is 0.
*** $p < 0.001$
** $p < 0.01$
* $p < 0.05$

odds of marriage by 4 per cent, i.e., after controlling for age, temporal uncertainty and social origin. Educational accumulation has a negative effect on the rate of non-marital cohabitation as well. These results thus suggest that, regardless of the type of first union, partnership formation is more likely among young people with less education than among well-educated individuals.

Table 8.5   The effect of educational accumulation and earnings on the hazard of entry into first partnership according to age groups, Hungarian men and women born in 1971-80

Age intervals	Men		Women	
	Cohabitation	*Marriage*	*Cohabitation*	*Marriage*
Educational accumulation				
14-19 years old	-0.124**	-0.123*	-0.113**	-0.143***
20-24 years old	-0.053*	-0.048*	-0.046*	-0.035
25-29 years old	-0.042*	0.014	-0.047*	0.024
Earnings				
14-19 years old	-0.011*	0.187	-0.023*	-0.078*
20-24 years old	-0.105*	0.033	-0.068*	-0.323***
25-29 years old	-0.206*	0.089	-0.875**	0.054

Results from discrete-time event-history analysis

Note:
a   The estimates are controlled for the variables on the transition from school to work and social origin.
*** $p < 0.001$
** $p < 0.01$
* $p < 0.05$

To investigate this pattern in more detail, we run separate models for several age intervals (Table 8.5). The impact of educational capital according to these estimates appears to be stronger at early ages than later on during the period of young adulthood. Educational attainment has a negative effect on first marriage for both men and women in their teens, but this effect lessens or disappears when they are in their (late) twenties. As for non-marital cohabitation, the pattern is a bit different: educational accumulation exerts a negative effect at each age interval.

The gender specialization hypothesis implies that economic resources in terms of earnings have a negative effect on the rate of family formation among women but a positive one among men. Comparing the results on earnings in Table 8.4 shows that this hypothesis is only supported to a limited extent. Monthly earnings have indeed a negative effect on the rate of entry into first marriage for females, but the positive one for males is not significant. Furthermore, in the case of non-marital cohabitation, the parameter estimates for earnings reveal no gender inequalities: they are negative for both sexes.

As before, we rerun our models for the three age intervals separately (Table 8.5). According to the parameter estimates obtained, the older the individual is, the more negative is the impact of earnings on the odds of entering into non-marital cohabitation. In the case of women getting married, this trend is to some extent reversed: the negative earnings effect is the most salient at the age of 20-24 but it turns positive (although insignificant) by the age of 25-29. These results suggest that individuals with moderate earning power may be forced to choose non-marital cohabitation, while persons with higher earning power appear to have more options including marriage – at least in their late twenties.

From premarital to marital cohabitation

In addition to the type of first partnership, another important question concerns whether and when young people convert their consensual union – if still intact - into marriage. Table 8.6 presents information on these two competing risks, although we will mostly restrict our attention to union conversion rather than dissolution.

Educational accumulation increases the odds of converting a consensual union into marriage for both sexes. With respect to characteristics of the transition from school to work, the outcomes of non-marital unions are generally more dependent on the man's than on the woman's employment status. For instance, cohabiting couples in which the male is a full-time student not participating in the labor force are 100 per cent less likely to get married than couples in which the man has a permanent job. This negative effect of the status "in school/not working" for women is only 77 per cent lower. If the male does not work and he currently does not attend school either, the probability of union conversion is 99 per cent lower. Also a fixed-contract employment reduces men's chances of getting married. These findings thus support our prediction that developments in the economic situation of male rather than female partners – such as accumulating educational capital and establishing a labor market career – accelerate marriage.

Entry into parenthood

As a third step in the family formation process we now analyze the propensity of becoming a parent. As far as activity status is concerned, the expectation of a strong negative effect of participation in education is confirmed. The rate of conceiving the first child is lowest when individuals are enrolled in full-time education without labor force participation, and it remains fairly low when they have some employment experience while still in school. Not studying and not working has opposite impacts on the first birth risk for men and women (Table 8.7, model 1).

The negative impact for men (-0.354*) confirms the prediction of a traditional approach to the division of labor in the household. Namely, males' non-employment should have a postponing effect on childbirth because in this status they are unable to support their families. In this same framework, however, females' non-employment should promote childbirth because this situation reduces the time costs of having children. Our result of a positive effect coefficient (+0.271**) supports this expectation.

Table 8.6   The outcomes of cohabitation: the hazard of marriage and dissolution up to the age of 29 among Hungarian men and women born in 1971-80

	Men		Women	
	Dissolution	*Marriage*	*Dissolution*	*Marriage*
Age at cohabitation	-0.008	-0.095	-0.075	-0.073
Transition from school to work				
In school/not working	-1.017*	-5.627*	-1.144*	-1.451*
In school/working	0.667	-4.568	0.351	-1.189
Not in school/not working	0.230	-4.900*	0.673	-0.438
Not in school/working/ fixed-term job	0.307	-0.903*	0.439	0.190
Not in school/working/ permanent job (ref.)	0	0	0	0
Economic resources				
Educational accumulation[a]	0.128	0.111*	0.133	0.155***
Earnings[b]	0.033	-0.443	0.113	-0.051
Social origin				
Religious affiliation[c]	0.049	0.085	-0.235	0.317
Non-intact family[d]	0.097	-0.598	0.374	-0.666*
Intercept	-3.055*	-3.248*	-2.675**	-1.455*
-2 Log Likelihood (model)	902.34	574.15	1109.68	1154.02
-2 Log Likelihood (initial)	(920.00)	(592.80)	(1157.50)	(1181.90)
Number of events	133	74	307	159
Number of subepisodes	1669	1608	2504	2518

Results from discrete-time event-history analysis

Notes:
a   Number of completed classes after completion of primary school.
b   Natural log of mean monthly earnings.
c   Dummy variable which sets 1 if respondent belongs to any religion, otherwise it is 0.
d   Dummy variable which sets 1 if respondent was brought up in a non-intact family, otherwise it is 0.
*** $p < 0.001$
** $p < 0.01$
* $p < 0.05$

According to our hypothesis, the impact of non-employment is largely mediated through economic resources. Adding these economic characteristics, the impact of non-employment becomes negative for women as well (Table 8.7, model 2). We interpret this change of sign as an indication that non-employment has a positive impact of the risk of the first birth for women without qualifications and reasonable earnings. This means that females with uncertain employment prospects respond to their unfavorable situation by choosing the predictable and secure "career" of a mother or housewife.

Regarding the effect of economic resources, educational accumulation decreases the hazard of entry into parenthood by age 29 for both sexes. This result suggests that young individuals with higher education tend to postpone first parenthood, at least until their thirties. The impact of earnings on the propensity of becoming a parent is similar to the pattern revealed for the transition to marriage. Namely, a one-point increase in monthly earnings leads to a reduction of 16 per cent in the odds of entry into motherhood; for men this effect is positive but statistically insignificant. This pattern is in line with our finding concerning the effect of non-employment: women with less human capital and with an uncertain labor force future are forced to choose motherhood instead of an employment career.

Not surprisingly, union status improves the model fit enormously (Table 8.7, model 3). That is so because individuals are considerably less likely to become parent while they are living as cohabiting instead of married partners, and certainly if they are single. However, introducing union status into the model does not result in any considerable changes in the effects of our key variables. This thus indicates that the process of the transition from school to work and the accumulation of economic resources influence the propensity and the timing of the first childbirth independently of union status.

DISCUSSION AND CONCLUSION

Contrary to the general view that the collapse of communism did not bring about significant changes in Hungary and that ongoing economic and social processes of the 1980s simply continued or at best accelerated during the 1990s, our analysis has demonstrated that the circumstances surrounding the transition from youth to adulthood have substantially altered. We know that period effects like the rapid economic transformation of the country have their strongest impact on the younger cohorts. This happened in Hungary after 1949 when the young generation was favorably influenced by the political changes of those times, which for a short period diminished the importance of social origin for individuals' career developments. The globalization cohort born between 1971 and 1981 has had similar experiences as a consequence of rapid and major changes in the society at large, but these changes have probably affected them less positively.

Growing uncertainty can be considered a consequence of globalization, i.e., the process of how societies are getting more and more risky. One may add here

Table 8.7   Hazard of the entry into parenthood up to the age of 29, Hungarian men and women born in 1971-80

	Men			Women		
	Model 1	*Model 2*	*Model 3*	*Model 1*	*Model 2*	*Model 3*
Age						
log(age-14)	1.340***	1.609***	0.118	0.844***	1.341***	0.509***
log(29-age)	0.025	0.077	0.288	0.453***	0.511***	0.447***
Transition from school to work						
In school/not working	-2.543***	-2.032***	-1.489**	-4.615***	-4.054***	-2.702***
In school/working	-1.807*	-1.274*	-0.344	-2.703***	-2.164***	-1.447*
Not in school/not working	-0.354*	-0.234*	0.190	0.271**	-1.458***	-0.731*
Not in school/working/fixed-term job	0.089	0.094	0.441	-0.055	-0.088	-0.030
Not in school/working/permanent job	0	0	0	0	0	0
Economic resources						
Educational accumulation[a]	–	-0.124***	-0.088*	–	-0.161***	-0.119***
Earnings[b]	–	0.021	0.023	–	-0.178***	-0.134***
Social origin						
Religious affiliation[c]	0.313**	0.381**	0.107	0.230**	0.223*	-0.024
Non-intact family[d]	-0.183	-0.219	-0.209	-0.064	-0.171	-0.093

Table 8.7 continued

	Men			Women		
	Model 1	*Model 2*	*Model 3*	*Model 1*	*Model 2*	*Model 3*
Union status						
Single	–	–	-4.606***	–	–	-3.329***
Marriage (ref.)			0			0
Cohabitation			-1.654***			-1.345***
Intercept	-6.454***	-6.942***	-1.957*	-5.122***	-3.793***	-1.076*
-2 Log Likelihood (model)	4438.71	4105.23	2827.78	7665.70	7232.45	5681.10
-2 Log Likelihood (initial)	(4832.70)	(4832.70)	(4832.70)	(8721.30)	(8721.30)	(8721.30)
Number of events	468	468	468	1029	1029	1029
Number of subepisodes	30405	30405	30405	26755	26755	26755

Results from discrete-time event-history analysis

Notes

a   Number of completed classes after completion of primary school.
b   Natural log of mean monthly earnings.
c   Dummy variable which sets 1 if respondent belongs to any religion, otherwise it is 0.
d   Dummy variable which sets 1 if respondent was brought up in a non-intact family, otherwise it is 0.
*** $p < 0.001$
** $p < 0.01$
* $p < 0.05$

that political and economic changes in a society always result in an increase in uncertainty, because people have to adapt to new circumstances. As they change their behavior in order to overcome the new difficulties that they face, old solutions for old problems lose their relevance. The main feature of the Hungarian case is that the planned economic system dominated by state ownership collapsed, and that subsequently a market economy emerged that was dominated by private ownership. A specialty of this development has been that the Western market economies, which could in principle provide an example and a sense of direction as to where the new democracies might wish to go, had to undergo significant changes in the last decades as well. This meant that if a post-communist country like Hungary after decades of delay caused by the communist system tried to catch up with the modern world of developed democracies, this catching-up modernization process had in actual fact to follow a moving target. This is a highly "reflexive" (Beck, 1994) form of modernization in which people have to continuously re-evaluate their positions, possibilities as well as the consequences of their decisions. This holds especially for young people who have to make crucial decisions about continuing school, entering the labor market, establishing a partner relationship or becoming a parent.

Our analysis has revealed that the behavior of youngsters was strongly influenced by the developments summarized above. With regard to entering the labor force, young people tried to remain in the school system as long as possible, an endeavor that was supported by the educational policy of the different governments in the 1990s concerning the expansion of tertiary education. Our data has supported the assumption that higher education increases the odds of finding a better first job. Although the globalization cohort has a higher educational level than all previous cohorts, in particular women still had more chances to find a precarious job in the unskilled service or worker class at the beginning of their occupational career. Flexibilization of the labor market increased in the 1990s, with the result that more and more young job seekers could enter the labor force only through self-employment. In the light of the privatization of the market, this phenomenon is sometimes evaluated positively. However, it is also the case that young people – and not just the lower educated among them – have higher odds of finding only fixed-term or other precarious jobs. In order to reduce such a risky labor market entry, more and more young people start to work already while still attending school. Data clearly show that if they start to search for a job only after completing school, and if they fail to find one, then their longer search period decreases the probability of ever entering the labor force.

Extended participation in education as well as the character of the first job have a strong impact on the behavior of the globalization cohort with respect to family formation and parenthood. Compared to previous cohorts, more men and women remain single even at older ages. And if they do form a first partnership, the probability of that being a non-marital cohabitation is much larger. Our findings thus lead to several insights in the effect of temporal and economic insecurity on family formation. Consistently with our hypotheses, we found that partnership initiation requires from both potential partners some kind of economic independence. However, school enrolment affects less the hazard of entering into cohabitation than that of getting married, indicating that educational participation – accompanied by greater financial uncertainties – is more compatible with consensual unions. A strong event-specific effect was found for the type of employment contract. Individuals in fixed-term jobs are more likely to choose cohabitation rather than marriage because they need time to reduce their career uncertainties. Our results also provide interesting insights in the influence of economic resources. Youngsters with less education and earnings tend to substitute cohabitation for marriage, particularly at later ages. In order to get married it is important to minimize these different kinds of uncertainties which is supported by our additional result indicating that the establishment of a steady employment career and the accumulation of educational capital accelerate the conversion of pre-marital to marital cohabitation. Findings concerning the entry into parenthood neatly fit into the picture outlined above. Namely, women with poor economic resources and uncertain employment prospects tend to choose the more secure motherhood instead of labor market career, while better educated women tend to postpone motherhood or remain childless.

In sum, this analysis on Hungary has proven that the 1990s have brought a new era for the young generation by making their transition from youth to adulthood significantly different from the experiences of foregoing cohorts in many respects. Globalization in Hungary as in other countries means a combination of local and international processes. But, without doubts, both types of developments have led to increasing uncertainty for young Hungarians in the 1990s.

NOTES

1 For further details on the transition to self-employment, see Róbert and Bukodi, 2000; 2004).
2 Based on the birth frequency in the respective year, it expresses how many children a female would give birth to during her life.
3 On this latter issue, see e.g. Ferge (1995).

BIBLIOGRAPHY

Árva, L. (1999) 'Hungary in the Whirlwind of Globalization: An Economic and Social Analysis', in Cs. Makó and C. Warhurst (eds) *The Management and Organisation of Firm in the Global Context*, Gödöllő - Budapest: University of Gödöllő and University of Budapest.
Beck, U. (1992) *Risk Society. Towards A New Modernity*, London: Sage Publications.
Beck, U. (1994) 'The Reinvention of Politics: Towards a Theory of Reflexive Modernization', in U. Beck, A. Giddens and S. Lash (eds) *Reflexive Modernization. Politics, Tradition and Aesthetics in Modern Social Order*, Stanford: Stanford University Press.

Becker, G. (1975) *Human Capital. A Theoretical and Empirical Analysis with Special Reference to Education*, Chicago: University of Chicago Press.

Becker, G. (1981) *A Treatise on the Family*, Cambridge, MA: Harvard University Press.

Berrington, A. and Diamond, I. (2000) 'Marriage or cohabitation: a competing risks analysis of first-partnership formation among the 1958 British birth cohort', *Journal of Royal Statistical Society*, 163: 127-151.

Blossfeld, H-P. and Drobnic, S. (2001) 'Theoretical Perspectives on Couples' Careers', in H.-P. Blossfeld and S. Drobnic (eds) *Careers of Couples in Contemporary Societies. A Cross-National Comparison of the Transition from Male Breadwinner to Dual Earner Families*, Oxford: Oxford University Press.

Breen, R. and Goldthorpe, J. (1997) 'Explaining Educational Differentials. Towards a Formal Rational Action Theory', *Rationality and Society*, 9: 275-305.

Carlson, E., and Klinger, A. (1987) 'Partners in life: Unmarried couples in Hungary', *European Journal of Population*, 3: 85-99.

Csernák, Józsefné (1992) 'Házasság és család: a demográfiai változások újabb irányvonalai és összefüggései' [Marriage and Family: Recent Trends and Connections in Changes in Demography], *Demográfia*, 35: 87-112.

Drobnic, S. (1997) 'Part-time Work in Central and Eastern European Countries', in H.-P. Blossfeld and C. Hakim (eds) *Between Equalization and Marginalization. Women Working Part-time in Europe and the United States of America*, Oxford: Oxford University Press.

Erikson, R. and Goldthorpe, J. H. (1992) *The Constant Flux*, Oxford: Clarendon Press.

Esping-Andersen, G. (1990) *The Three Worlds of Welfare Capitalism*, Cambridge: Polity Press.

Esping-Andersen, G. (1999) *Social Foundations of Post-Industrial Economies*, Oxford: Oxford University Press.

Ferge, Zs. (1995) 'Is the World Falling Apart? – A View from East of Europe', *Review of Sociology of the Hungarian Sociological Association*, Special Issue: 27-45.

Giddens, A. (1999) *Runaway World. How Globalisation is Reshaping our Live'*, London: Profile Books, Ltd.

Goldthorpe, John (1996) 'Class analysis and the reorientation of class theory: the case of persisting differentials in educational attainment', *British Journal of Sociology*, 47: 481-505.

Hoem, J. (1986) 'The impact of education on modern family-union initiation,' *European Journal of Population*, 2: 113-133.

Liefbroer, A., and Corijn, M. (1999) 'Who, what, where, and when? Specifying the impact of educational attainment and labour force participation on family formation', *European Journal of Population*, 15: 45-75.

Marini, M. M. (1985) 'Determinants of the Timing of adult Role Entry', *Social Science Research*, 14: 309-350.

Maurice, M and Sellier, F. (1979) 'A Societal Analysis of Industrial Relations: A Comparison between France and West Germany', *British Journal of Industrial Relations*, 17: 322-336.

Mincer, J., and Ofek, H. (1982) 'Interrupted Work Careers: Depreciation and Restoration of Human Capital', *Journal of Human Resources*, 17: 1–23.

Róbert, P., and Blossfeld, H.-P. (1995) 'Hungary', in H.-P. Blossfeld (ed.) *The New Role of Women: Family Formation in Modern Societies*, Boulder: Westview Press.

Róbert, P. and Bukodi, E. (2000) 'Who are the Entrepreneurs and Where Do They Come From? Transition to Self-employment Before, Under and After Communism in Hungary', *International Review of Sociology*, 10 (1): 147-171.

Róbert, P., and Bukodi, E. (2002) 'Dual career pathways: The occupational attainment of married couples in Hungary', *European Sociological Review*, 18 (2): 217-232.

Róbert, P. and Bukodi, E. (2004) 'Winners or Losers? Entry into and exit from self-employment in Hungary: 1980s and 1990s', in R. Arum and W. Müller (eds) *The Reemergence of Self-Employment: A Cross-National Study of Self-Employment Dynamics and Social Inequality,* Princeton: Princeton University Press.

Róbert, P., Bukodi, E. and Luijkx, R. (2001) 'Employment Patterns in Hungarian Couples', in H.-P. Blossfeld and S. Drobnic (eds) *Careers of Couples in Contemporary Societies. A Cross-National Comparison of the Transition from Male Breadwinner to Dual Earner Families,* Oxford: Oxford University Press.

Shavit, Y. and Müller, W. (1998) From School To Work, Oxford: Clarendon Press.

Thornton, A., Axinn, W. and Teachman, J. (1995) 'The influence of school enrolment and accumulation on cohabitation and marriage in early adulthood', *American Sociological Review*, 60: 762-774.

9 Transition to adulthood in Estonia

Evidence from the FFS[1]

Kalev Katus, Allan Puur and Luule Sakkeus

INTRODUCTION

The aim of the present chapter is to provide an insight into the processes by which young people in Estonia become adults. Following the general analytical framework provided in the introductory chapter (Mills and Blossfeld, this volume), the chapter covers three specific events or transitions that represent central steps in the progression from adolescence to adulthood: completion of schooling and entry into labor force (Bernardi, 2001); formation of first partnership (Sommer *et al.*, 2000); and entry into parenthood (Simó *et al.*, 2000).

To cast light on the embeddedness of these processes in the societal context, including the varying degrees of uncertainty faced by young individuals, the present chapter applies two complementary perspectives. Firstly, the transition to adulthood is examined from a dynamic perspective by comparing the experience of successive birth cohorts. Variation between them could point, among other things, to the changing role of societal institutions in structuring the life courses of generations. Secondly, the chapter addresses these inter-cohort differences by comparing the transition experience across various subgroups of the population. This intra-cohort heterogeneity could provide further indications about the range of choices and constraints involved in the attainment of adult status.

The data for the analysis come from the Estonian Family and Fertility Survey, which was carried out in the framework of the European FFS as coordinated by United Nations Economic Commission for Europe. In this context, two aspects of the Estonian FFS should be underlined. Firstly, the Estonian FFS extended the cohort range of the target population twenty years beyond the fertile age, to the 1924 birth cohort. Secondly, the target population of the Estonian FFS also included the foreign-origin population. The high proportion of first and second generation immigrants in the total population (36 percent) together with their distinct behavioral patterns led to the decision to perform separate analyses of the native and foreign-origin populations. This methodological approach has been applied systematically in previous analyses of the Estonian FFS, and will also be followed in the present chapter. Detailed descriptions of survey methodology, procedures and results are available from a set of publications, including methodological reports, standard tabulations and country reports (EKDK, 1995a; 1995b; 1999; 2002; Katus *et al.*, 2000a; Katus *et al.*, 2002).

The chapter is structured in three main sections, the first of which (section "Societal context of the transition to adulthood") outlines the main features of the societal context in which the progression of FFS cohorts from adolescence to adulthood has occurred in Estonia. The section "Cohort trends in the entry into adulthood" then focuses on changes across cohorts in the transitions referred to above, treating each of them separately as well as jointly, by means of survivorship functions. The section "Modeling the transition to adulthood" explores the intra-cohort heterogeneity in the transition to adulthood by means of multivariate event history models, paying special attention to the modifications in the effects of covariates across cohorts. Finally, the concluding section "Discussion of results" summarizes the findings from the perspective of the globalization process.

SOCIETAL CONTEXT OF THE TRANSITION TO ADULTHOOD

The Estonian FFS birth cohorts range from 1924 to 1973, which implies a fifty-years time span between the experiences of the oldest and the youngest. The oldest has undergone the passage to adulthood already in the 1940s and early 1950s, while for the youngest cohort the corresponding transition has occurred mostly in the 1990s. Such a prolonged time period already covers a considerable alteration of societal conditions by itself, however, in the case of Estonia the turbulence has been further enhanced by repeated systemic changes. The first of these dates back to the aftermath of WW-II, when existing geopolitical arrangements and principles of societal organization were declared obsolete and replaced. The Molotov-Ribbentrop Pact by the Soviet Union and Germany divided Eastern Europe into their own spheres of interest, as a result of which, in 1940, the Soviet Union occupied and annexed Estonia. From 1941 to 1944 Estonia was under German occupation; thereafter the second Soviet occupation began which lasted for almost 50 years. Unlike in Central Europe, this period not only involved the absence of self-determination but also the dismantling of national institutions; the position of Estonia under Soviet rule has been shortly defined as a state of dependence (Misiunas and Taagepera, 1983; 1993).

During the first decade or so that the new regime was in power, it introduced forceful and rapid rearrangements of the entire societal organization by means of political terror, arrests and mass deportations. To escape their fate, about 7 percent of the population fled the country to form the basis of the Estonian diaspora to the West. The impact of these violent changes is revealed by the combined population losses from war and repression: discounting post-war immigration flows originating mostly from the Soviet Union (see below), Estonia is one of the very few European countries where the pre-war number of the native population has never been fully restored (Katus, 1990). From the viewpoint of social structure, the activities of the new regime were deliberately targeted against the higher social and professional strata, which suffered particularly heavy losses. Although the official propaganda attempted to demonstrate a general improvement in living standards, the period has been marked by a significant deterioration in most welfare indicators ranging from the infant mortality rate to dwelling density or crime rate (Eesti saatuseaastad, 1963-1972).

Following the extreme turbulence of this first post-war decade, the period from the mid-1950s to the 1980s was characterized by relative stabilization: societal conditions became generally less harsh, as reflected by a gradual recovery in economic and social development. During the 1960s the agricultural sector began to recuperate from the impact of forced collectivization and, within the confines of the Soviet Union, Estonia gained importance as a supplier of food products. This meant, however, that in contrast to established market economies the share of employment in the agricultural sector during the referred period stood rather high (close to one fifth of the total labor force), while even rising during the 1980s. Regarding the development of other sectors, Soviet policies dealing with economic development favored heavy industries also in Estonia. This of course implied a vast expansion in industrial production, and already by the end of the 1950s the secondary sector dominated the entire structure of the labor force.

Also characteristic of centrally planned economies, demand for labor by far exceeded supply, thus securing full employment for all who were able and willing to take up a job. Aside from offering extraordinarily high degrees of job security, employment policies resulted in noticeably high levels of labor force participation among women and older workers (Puur, 1995). Moreover, in the case of Estonia, the strategy of economic development required a sizable input of labor, which was unavailable locally. The demand for labor, therefore, gave an important extra impetus to immigration into Estonia, which during the immediate post-war decade had already been strengthened by considerations of a more geopolitical nature. Immigration flows into Estonia originated mostly from the European part of Russia which by that time had entered a stage of mobility transition featuring considerable migration potential (Sakkeus, 1991; 1996).

The maintenance of high immigration volumes throughout the 1970s and 1980s implied an enlargement of the migration "hinterland" from the neighboring regions of Russia to more distant ones. These latter regions had entered the demographic transition later and, hence, were still characterized by rapid population growth. Immigrants from these new regions came from socially and culturally diverse environments with few, if any, historical ties to Estonia, thus introducing considerable heterogeneity into the immigrant population itself. It is important to note, however, that the distinction between native and foreign-origin populations should not be mixed with the ethnic dimension. The 1989 census, for example, revealed the presence of more than 120 ethnic backgrounds in the foreign-origin population, but the native population includes - besides Estonians - many ethnic minorities that have settled long ago (Viikberg, 1999; Katus *et al.*, 2000b).

Turning to education, high literacy rates (94.3 percent of the total population aged 14+ able to read or write) were already reported by the 1881 census. This level of literacy was typical of the entire Baltoscandian region and exceeded that of several Western European countries (Reiman, 1937). The expansion of school enrollment continued in Estonia until the late 1960s, with each next cohort reaching a higher attainment of secondary and tertiary education. In terms of the FFS cohort range, primary and incomplete secondary education was still most common among cohorts born in the late 1920s and early 1930s. Starting with the birth cohorts of the late 1930s, completed secondary education had become the prevailing standard. Regarding tertiary education, however, the upward trend came virtually to a halt at the end of the 1960s, with the 1970s and 80s witnessing a stagnation in the proportion of graduates from university or equivalent programs. Taking into account the continued expansion of secondary education, which reached a peak in the 1980s, continuation ratios to tertiary level studies even fell after 1970 (Helemäe *et al.*, 2000). Nevertheless, the excessive demand for labor referred to above secured a smooth transition from school to work.

As elsewhere in Central and Eastern Europe, the period of relative stability in societal conditions in Estonia came to an abrupt end at the beginning of the 1990s. Compared to the systemic changes of the 1940s and 1950s, this recent transition has received considerable attention from various disciplinary perspectives. One unwillingly notices several similarities between the direction of these recent transformations in Central and Eastern Europe, on the one hand, and some of the major social and economic changes in the established market economies which have often been conceptualized as part of the globalization process, on the other.

The recent transition has implied a departure from previous economic isolation, adjustment to world prices, diversification and re-orientation of trade flows, substantial influx of foreign investments, etc. As a result of all this, formerly closed economies have become more integrated and, at the same time, dependent on developments at the global scene. From the viewpoint of the national economies, the adjustment to these new realities has necessitated an extensive restructuring that involved substantial declines in previously favored economic sectors, on the one hand, and the emergence and expansion of new and other sectors, on the other. Alongside these sectoral shifts, there has been a significant change in the demand for particular skills, a re-allocation of jobs from large to medium and small enterprises, a re-emergence of self-employment, diversification of work patterns, etc.

From the viewpoint of individuals, the recent transition has first and foremost implied the loss of previously lifetime job security. This sudden decrease in certainty is most vividly manifested in the decline of employment opportunities and the upsurge of unemployment. In most countries of Central and Eastern Europe, unemployment rates nowadays are close to or in the double digits (EC, 2000a). Similar to the experience of established market economies, the recent transition has increased the significance of knowledge and information, as reflected for instance by the growth in educational enrollment. However, compared to the former, social safety net and welfare policies in Central and Eastern European countries have offered much less to those who have failed to keep up with the pace of these changes (UNECE, 1995-1999).

With regard to the transition experience of Estonia against the general background of Central and Eastern European countries, several features are worth mentioning. On the one hand, as belonging to the former Soviet Union, the country's starting conditions were significantly less favorable than in, say, the Czech Republic, Hungary, Poland or Slovenia. Following the dissolution of the Soviet Union, Estonia together with the two other Baltic States chose to remain outside the Commonwealth of Independent States, which due to their former close intergration caused an even greater transition shock. Additionally, the transition needed to be accomplished in parallel with the re-establishment of national institutions. On the other hand, right from the beginning of the 1990s Estonia opted for a rather radical path of economic reform by placing few obstacles in the way of price adjustment, international trade, privatization and foreign investment (Lugus and Hatchey, 1995). Liberal economic policies went hand-in-hand with the introduction of remarkably low payroll taxes, minimum wages, unemployment benefits as well as pensions.

This particular combination of a relatively disadvantaged starting position and the absence of attempts to slow down inevitable changes has resulted in relatively quick structural adjustments in Estonia. As measured by the gross sectoral shift, for example, only Hungary had greater reallocations of employment between sectors. According to the share of the tertiary sector, which is often being used as an indicator of modernization, Estonia together with Hungary has already reached the levels observed in certain EU countries (EC, 2000b). Recent statistics on educational enrollment indicate that the progression rate towards higher education has risen sharply during the 1990s. For example, at the end of that decade students represented close to 40 percent of the age group 20-24 (ESA, 2000). The progression towards a knowledge-based society has been remarkably rapid in the field of communication infrastructure and Internet access.

Unfortunately, the Estonian FFS does not cover the two societal transitions discussed in this section in an equal manner. While the experience of the first transition is fully captured by the life courses of the oldest cohorts of women born in the late 1920s and early 1930s, the timing of data collection in early 1994[2] allows the most recent transformation to be reflected to only a limited extent, at least for quantitative analysis. Attempts to make generalizations about emerging and new behavioral patterns from severely censored life histories can easily lead to methodological difficulties (Sommer *et al.*, 2000). Therefore, this chapter puts its main emphasis on the societal transition of the 1940s–50s rather than on the recent transformation. In the context of globalization research, however, this still allows for an interesting possibility to test the hypothesis of uncertainty, although in a different context. It is the extended cohort range of the Estonian FFS that provides the opportunity to explore this avenue, to an extent that is not quite possible in other countries of Central and Eastern Europe.

COHORT TRENDS IN THE ENTRY INTO ADULTHOOD

This section provides a description of the changes that have occurred in major life events defining the entry into adulthood: completion of education and entry into the labor force, first partnership, and first parenthood. The alteration in the timing of these events among the native and foreign-origin populations is high-lighted by means of survivorship functions for five-year birth cohorts. For all events concerned, the presentation of these survivorship functions starts at age 15; the upper limit depends on the age at which each process approaches its ceiling. The calculation of survivorship functions was performed using the TDA software package (Blossfeld and Rohwer, 1995).

It is important to note that, as at the time of the interview the FFS cohorts had reached different points in their respective life courses, the duration of their exposure to the risk of experiencing different events on the road to adulthood varies a great deal. Particularly the two youngest cohorts have not yet had suffi-cient time to go through all the events. Although survival analysis takes this censoring into account, the patterns of transition for these cohorts cannot be explored to the same extent as for the older cohorts.

Timing of the school-to-work transition

The change in the timing of school completion has been mostly driven by the extension of school enrollment and the increased progression to higher levels of education. In Estonia as well as in most other European countries, a remarkable rise in educational attainment has taken place across the FFS cohorts. The proportion of the female population having at least secondary education increased from roughly a third in the 1924-28 cohort to over 90 percent among women born in the 1950s and 60s. While in the two older cohorts the most prevailing educational attainment was still primary education, starting with the 1934-38 cohort it is (upper) secondary education that has become the most usual standard. As noted earlier, the share of women with higher education expanded up to the birth cohorts of the early 1940s, who completed their schooling in the 1960s: nearly one in five graduated from a higher educational establishment. In later cohorts, however, the proportion of university graduates remained virtually unchanged at slightly above 20 percent.

These trends in educational attainment are characteristic of both the native and foreign-origin population, although there are also certain differences. For instance, a longer tradition of comprehensive education among the native popu-lation has resulted in virtually negligible proportions of illiterates or persons without primary education already in the oldest cohort. In corresponding cohorts of the foreign-origin population, however, these two categories still exist. On the other extreme of the attainment scale, the data suggest a slightly higher propor-tion of university graduates among the native population. Although the issue of gender differences will not be addressed in this chapter, it is interesting to note that - with the exception of some of the oldest cohorts - native women have gen-erally exceeded men in terms of the proportions having secondary or tertiary education. Among the foreign-origin population the gender difference in educa-tion is mostly in the opposite direction: men feature higher attainment in tertiary education.

Figure 9.1 presents information on the shift in the timing of school completion by means of survivorship functions. Half of the oldest cohort in the native population had already completed their full-time studies by age 16.3. The following four five-year birth cohorts (of which for clarity's sake only two are shown in Figure 9.1) demonstrate a relatively rapid postponement of school completion.

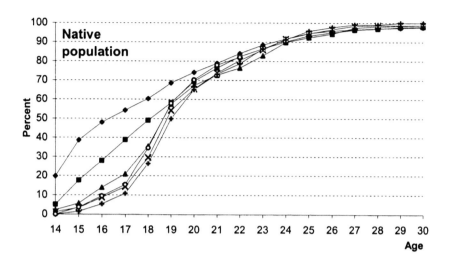

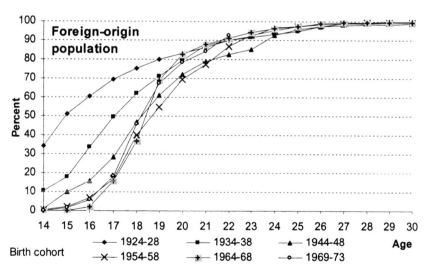

Figure 9.1   School completion among the native- and foreign-origin populations of Estonia

For instance, in the 1939-43 cohort the median age at school completion already reached 18.7 years. Reflecting the stagnation in tertiary education referred to above, this trend towards ever more schooling then largely ceased. The median age at completion of full-time studies peaks at 19 years in the 1964-68 cohort. Conclusions about school completion in the youngest cohort of 1969-73 should be regarded with caution because a substantial proportion of its members had not yet completed their studies by the time the data were collected.

The foreign-origin population has largely shared these developments, albeit with some specific features of its own. In general, this population has completed education earlier. On average the difference between the two subpopulations in the median age at completion of full-time studies is 0.8 years, being greatest among the older cohorts and diminishing towards the younger. At least partly, this reflects differences in educational systems in the countries of origin. A one-year shorter duration of general secondary education in the school curricula adopted from the Russian Federation implies that foreign-origin women have on average spent less time in the educational system, compared to native women at the same level of education.

Survivorship functions for entry into the labor force are presented on Figure 9.2. As the proportion of women who never worked during their lifetime had virtually dropped to nil already in the last pre-FFS cohorts, observed differences between successive FFS cohorts refer to true changes in the timing of this event. Judging from the relatively rapid prolongation of studies and postponement of school completion as discussed above, one would assume a shift towards later entry into employment. However, moving from the oldest to the younger cohorts the opposite development can be observed, particularly among the native population. The 1924-28 cohort members started their first job at a median age of 20.9 years, which dropped to 18.3 for the 1934-38 cohort. It is interesting to note that across the entire range of FFS cohorts, the oldest is simultaneously characterized by the earliest completion of schooling as well as by the latest entry into the labor force.

This large interval between their last school and first job could be explained by several factors. First of all, the youth of these women coincided with WW-II and its societal rearrangements, which may have introduced various irregularities and thus delayed their transition to working life. The behavior of this oldest cohort could also reflect the characteristic features of a farm-based agriculture driven to an important degree by unpaid family work, which was later eliminated during the sovietization. Another possibility is that this large interval between school completion and work is linked to the disappearance of the breadwinner-home-maker model (Davis, 1984). Data on the mothers of FFS respondents suggest that in the case of Estonia this model was most prevalent in the cohorts born around the 1890s. In following generations it gradually weakened, leading finally to its disappearance. The relatively late entry into the labor force of the 1924-28 birth cohort could thus be regarded as a concluding stage in this development, which was subsequently sharply accelerated by the sovietization.

Starting with the 1934-38 cohort there has been relatively little change in the timing of the first job. The median age at first job increased only slightly from

18.3 to 18.9 years for the 1964-68 birth cohort. The foreign-origin population has followed basically the same trend but with smaller differences between cohorts, particularly between the oldest and next oldest. The difference in the median ages between the two subpopulations amounted to 2.7 years in the oldest cohort but later this decreased to less than 1 year.

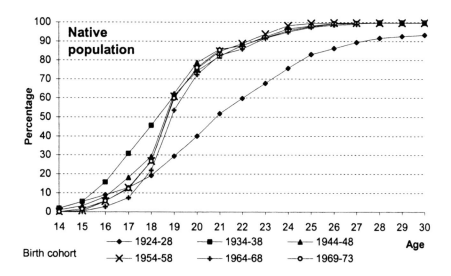

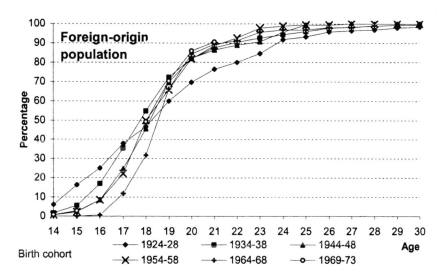

Figure 9.2   Entry into the labor force among the native- and foreign-origin populations of Estonia

Timing of first partnership

Historically, Estonia has belonged to the region of the "European" marriage pattern (Hajnal, 1965). This pattern of relatively late marriage and high proportions never marrying had already established itself in Estonia at least by the 18th century, clearly distinguishing the country from its eastern neighbors which never experienced such a pattern (Palli, 1988; Vishnevski and Volkov, 1983). An examination of vital and census statistics for the 1920s and 30s indicates that between the two World Wars this European marriage pattern in Estonia still prevailed. The mean age at first marriage in the late 1930s was above 26 years among females and above 29 years among males (RSKB, 1937-1940).

Figure 9.3 presents the survivorship functions for first partnership formation, i.e. the transition from singlehood to conjugal life, whether through marriage or non-marital cohabitation. The FFS data reveal a strong and systematic shift towards *younger* union formation in Estonia, which evidently got started already in the pre-FFS cohorts. In the three oldest FFS cohorts of the native population, born in 1924-38, the juvenation of partnership formation was still concentrated at the later end of the age spectrum: the biggest increase in the cumulative percentage of women who had formed a first partnership occurred beyond age 25. In subsequent birth cohorts, however, the changes in the timing of first partnership shifted towards the younger end of the age spectrum. For example, from the 1939-43 to the 1964-68 cohort the percentage of women who started their first partnership before age 20 more than doubled. Women born in the youngest cohort of 1969-73 started their first partnerships very early indeed: almost one-fifth of them were already in a partnership at the age of 18.

The trend towards earlier entry into first partnerships is also reflected in the development of the median age, which dropped from 23.5 years in the oldest cohort to 20.0 in the youngest. This decline in the median age at first union formation has been the most rapid among women born in the 1940s, but in general the trend continued until the very end of the FFS cohort range. In comparative perspective it is particularly this aspect of a *continuing* juvenation of first partnership formation that distinguishes Estonia from other countries that experienced the demise of the European marriage pattern after WW II.

The trend towards younger entry into first partnership can also be observed for the foreign-origin population, but there are some noticeable differences. A comparison of the survivorship functions reveals that across all cohorts foreign-origin women started their first partnership on average earlier - depending on the cohort, up to one year earlier - than native women. It should also be noted that this earlier start of unions does not reflect a higher frequency of very early partnerships but rather a lower frequency of late partnerships.

The start of a first union in a person's life may be either through marital or non-marital cohabitation, which may or may not be converted into marriage in a later stage. Compared to a registered marriage, non-marital cohabitation has usually been regarded as a more flexible form of conjugal life entailing less social and legal obligations for the partners involved. Based on this distinction between direct marriage and non-marital cohabitation, Figure 9.4 decomposes the transition to the first partnership according to the type of union. Even a short glance is enough to notice a much greater inter-cohort change in the proportion of consensual unions and thus of its complement (marital unions) than in the timing of all first partnerships combined (Figure 9.3).

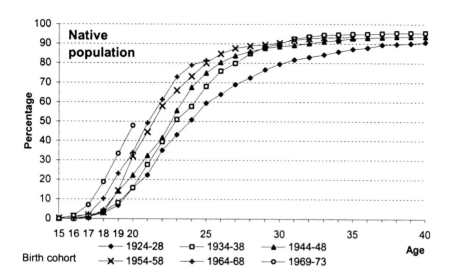

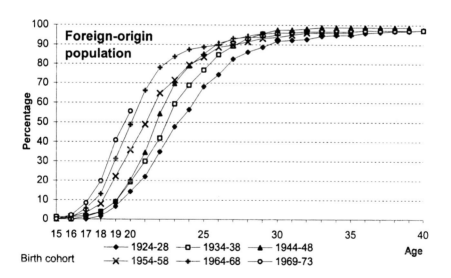

Figure 9.3   Entry into first partnership among the native- and foreign-origin populations of Estonia

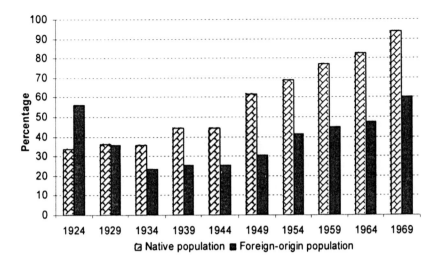

Figure 9.4   Proportion of first partnerships that started as consensual unions, native-
and foreign-origin populations of Estonia

Direct marriage accounted for close to two-thirds of all first unions in the oldest cohorts of the native population, a proportion that remained fairly stable until
the 1939-43 cohort. Starting with the 1949-53 cohort, however, proportions were
reversed and consensual unions replaced direct marriage as the mainstream route
to family building. In the youngest cohort of the native-born population, no less
than 94 percent of all first partnerships began as consensual unions. Although
this percentage is likely to be somewhat affected by censoring, such a frequency
of consensual unions resembles that observed for Scandinavian countries
(Manting, 1994; Trost, 1988). In this context it should be noted that the definition of consensual unions as applied in the Estonian FFS was even rather conservative: "fully shared family life except for the fact of formal registration as marriage" (EKDK, 1995a).

Similarly to the timing of first partnerships, the foreign-origin population
shows considerable difference in the way in which they begin. Despite the same
societal environment, foreign-origin persons have overall been much less prone
to start their first partnership as a consensual union. While in the 1924-28 cohort
the proportion of direct marriages and consensual unions appears still quite
similar, in the 1929-43 cohorts of the foreign-origin population direct marriage
increases in importance, accounting for 75 percent of all first unions. The next
transformation in the proportions of first partnership types among the foreign-
origin population has proceeded with a substantial time lag: consensual unions
outnumber direct marriage only in the 1964-68 cohort. In the 1969-73 cohort,
consensual unions account for 63 percent of all first partnerships.

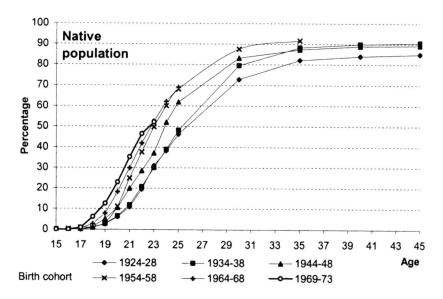

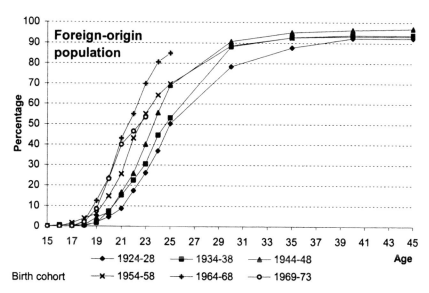

Figure 9.5   Entry into parenthood among the native- and foreign-origin populations of Estonia

Timing of entry into parenthood

The birth of a first child is another important family-related event that marks the progression to adulthood. In the process of family formation, parenthood typically follows the entry into partnership with a certain time lag. Partnering could from that perspective be regarded as a first step towards "readiness" for procreation (see also Simó *et al.*, this volume). Survivorship functions for first births are presented in Figure 9.5. These data reveal among other things a gradual decrease in the proportion of women remaining childless up to the end of their reproductive years. For instance, among the native-born cohorts who have (almost) completed their childbearing career the percentage of childless women has decreased from 15 to 7-8 percent. It is worth noting that this proportion has been as high as 25 percent in the older pre-FFS cohorts. Thus, Estonia has witnessed a lengthy process of decreasing childlessness, the closing stage of which has been captured by the FFS. This decline in ultimate childlessness is closely related to the disappearance of the European marriage pattern discussed above.

There has been a noticeable shift in the timing of first births towards younger ages, however, this shift is not evenly distributed across cohorts. In the four oldest five-year cohorts, 1924-43, relatively small but systematic and unidirectional changes occurred in the timing of first births in the age span beyond 25 years, which were likely a reflection of the decrease in ultimate childlessness. The median age at first birth in these cohorts fluctuated around 24.5 years, without any sign of a secular trend. The fifth birth cohort born in 1944-48, however, introduced the largest shift in the timing of first births, which concerned the entire reproductive age span. This trend towards earlier parenthood, although gradually decelerating, continued well into the following cohorts including the youngest. For instance, 35 percent of the women born in 1969-73 gave birth to their first child by age 20. Quite likely, this cohort has experienced the youngest entry ever into parenthood since the formation of the European marriage pattern in Estonia in the 18th century.

A similar trend can be observed among the foreign origin population. Nevertheless, the starting point of their fertility pattern was characterized by somewhat earlier childbearing and a significantly lower proportion of ultimate childlessness. Also the change over the course of fifty years has been somewhat greater. As a result, the younger cohorts of the foreign-origin population demonstrate a remarkably early start in childbearing. Half of its 1964-68 cohort members had their first child by age 22, and only one-fifth (compared to two-fifths among the native population) had not yet entered parenthood by age 24. Still, the difference in the timing of first births between the native and foreign-origin populations does not stem from the higher proportion of very young mothers among the latter but from the lower proportion of women who enter motherhood at later ages.

Because of its important implications for the careers of Estonian women in other domains of life, this continued trend towards early motherhood needs an explanation. One possible candidate could be the Soviet housing policy, according to which a person or family could not buy a dwelling but was given a flat or house upon fulfilling several preconditions. For instance, the arrival of a child enlarged the number of family members and thus the occupancy density, which according to the prevailing procedures contributed to the chances of a couple to qualify for a new dwelling. As voluntary childlessness was rarely an option, these pragmatic considerations may have had a certain effect on the timing of first births.

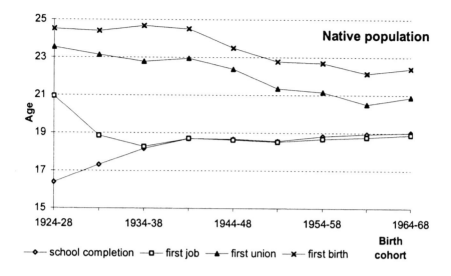

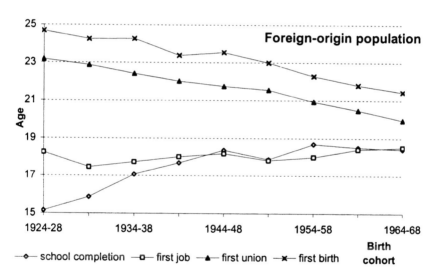

Figure 9.6   Median age at the transition to adulthood, native- and foreign-origin populations of Estonia

An integrated biographical perspective

In the previous subsections the completion of schooling and the entry into the labor force, first partnership and parenthood were discussed one by one. The purpose now is to bring these individual strands in the transition to adulthood together and to synthesize them into some general pattern. To this end it is important to note that the events may be thought as being at the core of the transition to adulthood, in the sense that they all mark important steps towards adult status and that they are all expected to be experienced by an overwhelming majority of cohort members. To summarize the trends in the timing of events across cohorts, Figure 9.6 presents them by way of median ages.

The data reveal quite dissimilar developments for different types of events. On the one hand, the prevailing tendency in family-related transitions has been juvenation: the declines in the median age at first partnership and at first parenthood have followed markedly parallel trajectories. On the other hand, the timing of non-family transitions has featured much greater heterogeneity. In the three oldest cohorts the entry into the labor force underwent a remarkably rapid shift towards younger ages, particularly for the native population. As noted above, however, this shift reflected not just a change in the timing of the event but much more a general transformation in the pattern of female labor force participation. However, starting with the 1939-43 cohort, the timing of labor force entry remained virtually unaltered. The only event that has never featured any shift towards younger ages is the completion of full-time education: it has been postponed for 2.7 years among the native population and for even a longer period among the foreign-origin population. Similarly to labor force entry, major changes in the timing of school completion occurred only in the three oldest cohorts. Also, it should be noted how closely the completion of full-time studies and entry into the labor force coincide from the cohort 1934-38 on.

The observed trends in the timing of familial and non-familial events can be summarized in terms of two major changes in the transition from adolescence to adulthood. First, despite the increase in the duration of schooling, the transition to adulthood if judged from the entry into parenthood appearing last in the series of events has been accomplished at progressively younger ages. While in the older FFS cohorts this was on average completed between ages 24 and 25, in the younger cohorts the attainment of full adult status had dropped noticeably below age 23. The largest shift in this direction among the native population was introduced by the birth cohorts of the 1940s, among the foreign-origin population the juvenation has been more linear. Despite the fact that subsequent cohorts display some signs of cessation, the shift towards an earlier attainment of adult status has continued until the youngest cohort.

Another major change has been the concentration of the transition from adolescence to adulthood into a much shorter age span. This development can be observed at two complementary levels. From the viewpoint of cohort experiences, the compression of events into shorter intervals across all individual processes implies a decrease in the heterogeneity among cohort members. Among the native population, the interval between the medians of the earliest event - completion of full-time studies - and the latest - entry into parenthood - has shortened from 8.2 to 3.4 years. Among the foreign-origin population the compression of the transition has been even greater.

From a life course perspective the concentration of the transition to adulthood into a shorter age span has implied a closer spacing of individual events. In other words, in younger cohorts the transition to adult status has been accomplished in steps that are more simultaneous, for the importance of intermediate steps - some already taken and others not yet - has been significantly reduced. This closer spacing between individual events has also intensified the overlap between the attainment of adult status in different spheres. Although on average family transitions have continued to occur prior to non-family transitions in all cohorts, there has also been an increase over time in the proportion of individuals who have experienced a reverse ordering of events (figures not shown). Available information from period statistics suggests that several of these and other features discussed above may have undergone further modifications during the second half of the 1990s (ESA, 2000). However, these new features of the transition to adulthood can only be captured once new FFS-type life course data are collected in Estonia.

MODELING THE TRANSITION TO ADULTHOOD

In the following sections the transition to adulthood is examined by means of piecewise constant transition rate models (Blossfeld *et al.*, 1989; Blossfeld and Rohwer, 1995). In building these models, the time axis has been split into sixteen intervals, which are based on the age of an individual. Between ages 15 and 24 the time axis has been split into single-year intervals, beyond that range into five-year intervals. This procedure has been followed for all three processes under consideration. The observation ends either with an event (first partnership, parenthood or entry into the labor force), or with the date of the interview for right-censored cases.

Regarding the covariates, it was decided to use exactly the same set of covariates in the analyses of all three processes. Although this set may not be optimal from the viewpoint of each particular transition, priority was given to the comparability between models and to the possibility to compare the impact of selected characteristics across events. In other words, the aim of the models to be presented is not so much to study the determinants of the three events in detail but to provide an account of the existing inter-cohort heterogeneity. In addition to the time axis (age), the models include six time-constant categorical covariates: birth cohort, type of settlement, educational attainment, religion, social origin and locus of control.

From the viewpoint of globalization, particular attention should be paid to the locus of control, which reflects the level of personal independence as manifesting itself in all major life decisions. The concept, which was first introduced by Julian Rotter, distinguishes between two opposite poles: internal and external locus of control (Laird and Thomson, 1991). Individuals who feature an internal locus of control ("internals") tend to be self-contained and convinced of their ability to control their own life course. On the other hand, individuals with an external locus of control ("externals") are characterized by a lack of confidence: they are inclined to think that external forces determine their destiny. Based on such individual psychological characteristics, the difference between internals

Table 9.1   Number of observations, Estonian FFS, female survey

	1924 -1928	1929 -1933	1934 -1938	1939 -1943	1944 -1948	1949 -1953	1954 -1958	1959 -1963	1964 -1968	1969 -1973	Total
Type of settlement											
Urban	190	202	231	247	191	188	201	201	206	225	2082
Rural	123	133	126	137	124	114	120	120	127	101	1225
Educational level											
Primary	196	196	144	114	64	56	35	21	15	35	876
Secondary	93	87	155	190	180	184	217	229	246	273	1854
Tertiary	24	52	58	80	71	62	69	71	72	18	577
Religion											
Religious	54	52	29	25	18	15	24	21	23	27	288
Following customs	56	71	101	129	111	110	136	130	164	174	1182
Indifferent	203	212	227	230	186	177	161	170	146	125	1837
Social origin											
Self-employed	203	201	216	215	173	164	173	170	168	150	1833
White-collar	19	25	28	35	29	29	32	37	48	33	315
Blue collar	91	109	113	134	113	109	116	114	117	143	1159
Locus of control											
Internal	60	66	67	91	85	75	83	93	91	89	800
Neutral	211	231	238	239	438	200	212	203	214	216	2156
External	42	38	52	54	38	27	26	25	28	21	351
Total	313	335	357	384	315	302	321	321	333	326	3307

Note: Table 9.1 includes respondents from the native population only.

and externals may be said to capture the effect of increased uncertainty and lower control over the social environment in the context of globalization. Information about the operationalization of the variables related to the locus of control can be found in the relevant publications (EKDK, 1995a; 1995b). Table 9.1 provides information on the number of observations included in the transition rate models by birth cohort and covariates.

For each transition - entry into labor force, first partnership and first parenthood - three sets of models were estimated. The purpose of the first was to produce non-adjusted estimates for each of the covariates by including them one at a time in addition to age (duration) and birth cohort. The purpose of the second set of models was to produce estimates that were adjusted for the effects of all other covariates. Correspondingly, this set included age (duration), birth cohort and all the covariates discussed above. Estimates for the first and second set of models are presented systematically in all the tables that follow. Additionally, a third set of models was run for each of the successive birth cohorts so as to check for potential changes in the transition to adulthood over time and to test for relevant interactions. This third set of models included all the covariates except birth cohort, which was used as a case selection criterion. Results of this last set will be discussed where relevant, but they are not systematically presented.

In addition to these transition rate models, logistic regression analysis was used to study the type of first partnership. The dependent variable was set to 1 if the respondent had started the first partnership through a consensual union, and 0 if through direct marriage. The set of covariates as well as the basic strategy were the same as in the case of the transition rate models. The fitting of the latter was done using TDA software package, whereas the logistic regression models were estimated using SPSS.

Timing of entry into the labor force

Model estimates for entry into the labor force are presented in Table 9.2. Compared to the reference cohort of 1924-28, the model reflects a shift towards a younger start of working life in all of the cohorts that follow. Consistent with the evidence presented in Figure 9.6, however, this shift was most pronounced over the first few cohorts only; thereafter there has been little change in the timing of the event. A comparison of the non-adjusted with the adjusted model estimates indicates that the shift towards earlier entry into the labor force observed for the older cohorts has to a noticeable extent been attenuated by the simultaneous expansion in educational enrollment.

According to the non-adjusted model, rural residence appears to be related to a slightly earlier entry into the labor force. The relative risk is 14 percent higher than for the reference category, a difference that is statistically significant. The introduction of controls for other covariates, however, leads to the complete disappearance of this effect, which now comes out negative. Examination of the effect of rural residence across cohorts provides some support to the hypothesis that the dismantling of the farm-based agriculture in the late 1940s and early 50s may indeed have contributed to the decline in the age at entry into the labor force

Table 9.2   Transition rate model of entry into labor force, Estonian women (relative risks)

	Non-adjusted	Adjusted
Birth cohort		
1924-1928	1.00	1.00
1929-1933	1.77**	2.16**
1934-1938	2.44**	3.48**
1939-1943	2.16**	3.07**
1944-1948	2.36**	3.69**
1949-1953	2.41**	3.82**
1954-1958	2.36**	3.71**
1959-1963	2.25**	3.64**
1964-1968	2.02**	3.28**
1969-1973	(2.35**)	(3.13**)
Type of settlement		
Urban	1.00	1.00
Rural	1.14**	0.98*
Educational level		
Primary	1.52**	1.53**
Secondary	1.00	1.00
Tertiary	0.45**	0.45**
Religion		
Religious	1.09*	0.88
Following customs	1.02	0.96
Indifferent	1.00	1.00
Social origin		
Self-employed	0.86**	0.87**
White-collar	0.75**	0.94
Blue collar	1.00	1.00
Locus of control		
Internal	0.85**	0.94
Neutral	1.00	1.00
External	0.97	0.90

Notes
** $p < 0.01$.
* $p < 0.05$.

as observed for the older cohorts but, evidently, other factors have played a more important role in this development.

Educational attainment makes as expected a strong distinction in the timing of entry into the labor force. Because of the difference in the duration of schooling the relative risk of this event for respondents with primary education appears more than 50 percent higher than in the reference category. Respondents with tertiary education feature accordingly a relative risk that is more than 50 percent lower. Although the direction of these gradients was maintained across all birth cohorts, the models ran separately for each of them revealed a relatively strong interaction between educational attainment and cohort. For instance, the relative risks for both primary and tertiary education increased steadily when moving from the older to the younger cohorts. Reflecting the well-established connection between school completion and the start of working life as well as a subsequent decline in the role of part-time studies, the contrast in relative risks between the respondents with primary and tertiary education increased from 1.6 times to more than 7.5 times.

The effect of religion on the timing of entry into the labor force is quite similar to that observed for partnership formation and entry into parenthood. In the adjusted model, being religious is related to a somewhat later start of working life (the 12 percent difference in relative risks is close to statistical significance). An examination of the cohort-specific models revealed a negative gradient of religiosity in the older cohorts, which disappears, in the intermediate cohorts to reappear again in the youngest, where it reaches statistical significance.

Having self-employed or white-collar (grand)parents tends to postpone the start of working life for the respondent. The effect of having white-collar parents is reduced after introducing controls for other covariates, primarily through the intergenerational transfer of educational attainment, while the effect of having self-employed parents remains statistically significant. Interactions of social origin with birth cohort reveal no clear pattern. The gradient of the relative risks of internal versus external locus of control runs in similar directions but it remains below the level of statistical significance, at least in the adjusted model.

Timing of first partnership

The model for starting a first partnership reveals a steady and statistically significant increase in the relative risks of this event across birth cohorts up to the youngest (Table 9.3). It should be noted, however, that the estimates for the youngest cohort should be treated with caution (hence the parentheses). Judging from available evidence based on vital statistics, the 1969-73 cohort has been affected by a sharp shift towards *later* partnership formation and particularly parenthood, but this trend reversal is not yet visible in the FFS data. In other words, had the data collection occurred a few years later, one would likely have found a different gradient for the youngest cohort. Comparing adjusted and non-adjusted model estimates it is interesting to note that after introducing controls for the other covariates the effect of birth cohort even strengthens. This implies that the observed shift towards earlier partnership formation would have been greater, if other factors - primarily the rise in educational attainment - had not exerted a certain influence in the opposite direction.

Residence in rural area contributes to a slightly earlier entry into first partnership. A comparison of adjusted and non-adjusted coefficients indicates that about half of the observed effect can probably be attributed to lower education attainment of the rural population. Still, even after controlling for this and other characteristics, a statistically significant 10 percent excess in relative risk persists. Examination of the set of models run separately for each birth cohort shows that the earlier partnership formation among rural residents starts with the 1934-38 birth cohort. With only slight deviations in a couple of intermediate generations, this timing difference reaches its highest level among the youngest cohort, where rural residents have a relative risk that is 30 percent higher than for their urban counterparts.

Educational attainment makes for a systematic and statistically significant difference in the timing of partnership formation. Compared to the reference category with secondary education, respondents with primary education feature a 30 percent higher probability of union formation[3], whereas graduates from tertiary education a 35 percent lower risk. Differently from birth cohort and place of residence, controlling for other characteristics has neither an effect on the direction nor on the strength of this gradient. The observed pattern appears also relatively stable across cohorts, except that the difference between primary and secondary education increases for the three to four youngest cohorts.

Table 9.3   Transition rate model of entry into first partnership, Estonian women (relative risks)

	Non-adjusted	Adjusted
Birth cohort		
1924-1928	1.00	1.00
1929-1933	1.14	1.18*
1934-1938	1.27**	1.39**
1939-1943	1.23**	1.41**
1944-1948	1.34**	1.59**
1949-1953	1.69**	1.98**
1954-1958	1.61**	1.91**
1959-1963	1.87**	2.26**
1964-1968	1.86**	2.25**
1969-1973	(2.79**)	(3.08**)
Type of settlement		
Urban	1.00	1.00
Rural	1.20**	1.10*
Educational level		
Primary	1.31**	1.30**
Secondary	1.00	1.00
Tertiary	0.65**	0.64**
Religion		
Religious	0.91	0.90
Following customs	1.02	0.98
Indifferent	1.00	1.00
Social origin		
Self-employed	0.91*	0.92*
White-collar	0.90	1.04
Blue collar	1.00	1.00
Locus of control		
Internal	1.05	1.11*
Neutral	1.00	1.00
External	0.89*	0.85**

Notes
** $p < 0.01$.
* $p < 0.05$.

Being religious is related to a somewhat later start of first partnership formation, although the difference from the reference category (indifferent) does not
attain statistical significance. The behavior of respondents who follow (some)
religious customs but do not consider themselves religious proves closely similar
to the reference category. The introduction of controls for other covariates did
not imply any noticeable change in the model estimates, which should be
regarded as an indication of the relative independence of religiosity and its
related value patterns. An examination of the religiosity differential across
cohorts reveals an interestingly curvilinear pattern. A negative gradient which at
first appears quite stable for the older cohorts weakens and vanishes in the intermediate cohorts of 1944–58, only to resurface thereafter. What is more, in the
two youngest cohorts it becomes statistically significant, exceeding for example
the magnitude of the urban-rural differential.

Having self-employed (grand)parents slows down the entry into a first partnership; the effect is not particularly strong in general but sufficient to reach statistical significance. It is interesting to note that this is the case starting with the
cohort born in 1944–48, i.e. for generations completing their socialization during
or after the social discontinuities introduced by the sovietization. Having white-
collar (grand)parents exerts a weak but statistically insignificant effect in the
opposite direction, at least according to the adjusted model. Models run for all
birth cohorts separately demonstrate that this results from significant interaction
effects. Being born to white-collar parents in 1924–48 implied a noticeably earlier partnership formation, whereas in most of the following cohorts the direction
of this gradient was reversed.

Finally, an internal locus of control seems to be related to earlier entry into
first partnership while an external locus to a later start of it. In other words, the
lack of self-confidence and a lower perceived ability to control the external
forces which shape the life course are associated with a postponement of union
formation. In the adjusted model the difference of both categories from the reference (neutral) reaches statistical significance. In the broader context of globalization this finding gives support to the hypothesis that increasing uncertainty is
a likely determinant of the change in the timing of family formation. Despite
some irregular variations across cohorts, these gradients maintain their direction
and display no major change, as can be expected from a characteristic representing a psychological personality orientation.

Type of first union

In order to study the way in which first partnerships are started while at the same
time controlling for the differences in overall union formation probabilities,
logistic regression models were applied. Table 9.4 presents the likelihood estimates of starting the first partnership as a consensual union against the odds of a
direct marriage. Consistent with the findings of Figure 9.4, the data reveal a
remarkably strong shift away from direct marriage in favor of consensual unions.
The increase in the likelihood of consensual unions started to accelerate with the
1949–53 birth cohort, and this trend continued until the very end of the FFS

Table 9.4   Logistic regression model of the type of first partnership[a], Estonian women (relative risks)

	Non-adjusted	Adjusted
Birth cohort		
1924-1928	1.00	1.00
1929-1933	1.12	1.11
1934-1938	1.10	1.15**
1939-1943	1.56**	1.68**
1944-1948	1.55**	1.70**
1949-1953	3.18**	3.43**
1954-1958	4.30**	4.74**
1959-1963	6.61**	7.41**
1964-1968	9.53**	10.58**
1969-1973	(31.10**)	(33.63**)
Type of settlement		
Urban	1.00	1.00
Rural	1.14	1.08
Educational level		
Primary	1.34**	1.32**
Secondary	1.00	1.00
Tertiary	0.96	0.94
Religion		
Religious	0.76*	0.75*
Following customs	0.91	0.90
Indifferent	1.00	1.00
Social origin		
Self-employed	0.99	0.99
White-collar	1.04	1.11
Blue collar	1.00	1.00
Locus of control		
Internal	0.92	0.94
Neutral	1.00	1.00
External	0.53**	0.54**

Notes
a   Dependent variable coding: consensual union=1, direct marriage=2
** $p < 0.01$.
* $p < 0.05$.

cohort range. Due to selection bias, however, the change in the relative risk for the 1969-73 appears overestimated. As consensual unions tend to be formed at younger ages, part of this upsurge in relative risks likely reflects the change in the timing of first unions.

Rural residence is related to a somewhat greater likelihood of entering a first partnership through a consensual union. Similarly to the timing of first partnerships, the comparison of adjusted and non-adjusted model estimates suggests that this effect can be partly attributed to structural differences between rural and urban populations, particularly the lower educational attainment of rural residents. Fitting the model to each of the birth cohorts separately reveals an interesting interaction pattern. A higher likelihood of consensual unions among rural residents is characteristic of the cohorts up to 1954-58, but in the three youngest cohorts this pattern is reversed, with now urban residents having become more prone to start their first partnership through non-marital cohabitation.

The likelihood of consensual unions versus direct marriages was also found to vary by educational attainment. Respondents with lower than secondary education had a more than 30 percent higher probability of a non-marital start of their first partnership than their counterparts with secondary education. Evidently, the observed effect reflects to an important extent earlier partnership formation among less educated women. Higher education implies a somewhat lower probability of starting the first partnership as a consensual union, however, the difference is statistically insignificant. An examination of the models fitted separately for each of the birth cohorts indicates that the effect of educational attainment has undergone certain modifications over time. For primary education, the gradient changes direction in some of the youngest cohorts, suggesting a lower likelihood of consensual unions among those who have not completed secondary education. For higher education the distinction from the reference category disappears in the middle cohort range but it re-emerges again among younger cohorts.

Adherence to religion made also a visible difference in the mode of entry into first partnerships. Being religious reduced the likelihood of starting a first partnership as a consensual union by 25 percent, an effect that is statistically significant. The direction of the gradient is consistent across all cohorts, displaying a tendency towards greater strength in the youngest cohorts. In the cohorts of 1959-73, for example, the respondents who defined themselves as religious featured a chance of entering partnership life through a consensual union that was approximately 50 percent lower than for the reference group. This difference could reflect a stronger commitment to prevailing norms and expectations from parents and kin, however, at the same time a greater propensity of externals to marry directly evidently stems from their later entry into first union, as discussed in the previous section. Similarly to the timing of first partnership, following religious customs did not make any significant difference in the pattern of union formation.

Compared to the other covariates, however, social origin of the respondent displayed a relatively weak relationship to the mode of union formation. Respondents with white-collar (grand)parents had about 11 percent more chances to start their first partnership in a consensual union, however, the difference from the reference category proved statistically insignificant. The effect of having self-employed (grand)parents proved likewise negligible. Regarding the locus of control, if this was external then the probability of starting through non-marital cohabitation was close to 50 percent lower. This strong and statistically significant distinction from the reference category did not display major change across cohorts.

Table 9.5   Transition rate model of entry into parenthood, Estonian women (relative risks)

	Non-adjusted	Adjusted
Birth cohort		
1924-1928	1.00	1.00
1929-1933	1.07	1.11
1934-1938	1.19*	1.32**
1939-1943	1.15	1.32**
1944-1948	1.37**	1.64**
1949-1953	1.78**	2.14**
1954-1958	1.68**	2.05**
1959-1963	1.94**	2.42**
1964-1968	1.81**	2.27**
1969-1973	(2.64**)	(3.07**)
Type of settlement		
Urban	1.00	1.00
Rural	1.41**	1.28**
Educational level		
Primary	1.41**	1.35**
Secondary	1.00	1.00
Tertiary	0.63**	0.64**
Religion		
Religious	0.91	0.90**
Following customs	1.07	1.01
Indifferent	1.00	1.00
Social origin		
Self-employed	0.92*	0.94
White-collar	0.78**	0.94
Blue collar	1.00	1.00
Locus of control		
Internal	1.05	1.13**
Neutral	1.00	1.00
External	0.95	0.92

Notes
** $p < 0.01$.
* $p < 0.05$.

Timing of entry into parenthood

Model estimates in Table 9.5 for the timing of first births appear closely similar to those of first partnerships. That is, the data reveal a continuous increase in the likelihood of this event across birth cohorts, however, again a word of caution with respect to the youngest cohort of 1969-73 is in order. The effect of birth cohort grows stronger after the introduction of controls for other covariates, which means that the shift towards earlier entry into parenthood would have been even greater if other factors had not withheld it. The latter mainly refer to the rise in educational attainment of the population.

Rural residence is clearly related to an earlier timing of first parenthood, even more so than to an earlier timing of first partnership. According to the non-adjusted model rural residents feature a 41 percent higher risk of a first birth than their urban counterparts. After controlling for the effects of the other covariates, the excess in relative risk is reduced to 28 percent but remains statistically significant. Models fitted for each of the birth cohorts separately indicate the consistency in the direction of this observed gradient across the entire FFS cohort range. Moving from older to younger cohorts, relative risks show a tendency towards a gradual increase: rural residents of the youngest cohort of 1969-73 have more than 50 percent excess over their urban counterparts.

The timing of first birth appears linearly related to the educational attainment of the respondent. After controlling for the effects of the other covariates, it is still the case that respondents with primary education have a 35 percent higher relative risk of entering parenthood than those with completed secondary education. Graduates from tertiary education, on the other hand, are characterized by 36 percent lower risk of becoming a parent. Consistent with the findings for first partnership, the observed pattern remains basically unchanged across birth cohorts. (The only exception worth mentioning perhaps is the difference between primary and secondary education, which widens in a couple of the youngest cohorts.)

Respondents who had defined themselves as religious are characterized by - surprisingly - somewhat later entry into parenthood, although this only holds in the adjusted model. Across cohorts this negative gradient proved relatively stable in the four older cohorts, then disappeared and reversed itself in the intermediate cohorts of 1944-58, and re-appeared again in the following cohorts. Introduction of controls for other covariates implied no noticeable change in either the direction or strength of the gradient. The behavior of respondents who follow (some) religious customs but do not consider themselves religious proves closely similar to the reference category.

Having self-employed or white-collar (grand)parents slightly delays entry into parenthood, but these effects loose their statistical insignificance in the adjusted model. Examination of the models across cohorts, however, reveals that the absence of a clear-cut differential on the aggregate level stems from the interaction between social origin and birth cohort. For instance, respondents of the four older cohorts with self-employed or white-collar (grand)parents display relative risks of becoming a parent that are above the reference category. In the 1944-48 cohort, however, the direction of the gradient switches so that respondents with self-employed or white-collar (grand)parents in the following cohorts feature an increasingly slower entry into parenthood compared to the reference category.

As was the case with first partnership formation, an internal locus of control seems to be related to a somewhat earlier entry into parenthood whereas an external locus to later childbearing, even though the latter effect is not significantly different from the reference category. Similarly to partnership formation, later entry into parenthood among externals could be interpreted as a possible manifestation of perceived uncertainty and lower ability to control one's social environment. To this end it is interesting to note that externals stayed in school for a somewhat shorter period, thus starting their working careers earlier. In the globalization framework, however, postponement of family formation is generally linked to a prolongation of school enrolment and a later start of economic activity (Simó *et al.*, 2000; Sommer *et al.*, 2000). But there are of course also other possible explanations for the observed differential by locus of control. For example, a complementary explanation could be derived from a stronger commitment to prevailing norms and expectations about the proper timing of major life course events. In such a perspective, externals could represent a more traditional behavior, lagging behind the internals who tend to follow more innovative patterns. In the case of Estonia this hypothesis also fits the empirical findings, as the trend towards juvenation of first parenthood and partnership formation has prevailed throughout the entire FFS cohort range. However, even if the latter assertion appears true, one would probably still observe a reversal of the gradient in later birth cohorts, as the age at first parenthood turned to increase in the 1990s. The test of this hypothesis can be undertaken after a new FFS-like survey is undertaken in the country.

DISCUSSION OF RESULTS

We will now summarize the main findings on the transition to adulthood in Estonia from the perspective of the globalization process. During the period covered by the experience of FFS cohorts the prevailing regime imposed a relatively strong isolation of the country from the rest of the world. However, one can identify several developments and features that have direct or indirect parallels in the globalization framework (see Mills and Blossfeld, this volume). The growth in educational enrollment, for example, progressed rather rapidly in Estonia until the 1970s. Indirect parallels evidently include the rise in uncertainty about future developments and the disruption of the entire spectrum of social relations, as introduced by the violent societal rearrangements of the 1940s and 1950s. Although the origin and nature of the uncertainty experienced by Estonians during much of the second half of the twentieth century differ greatly from those in contemporary OECD-type societies, its disruptive impact on the lives of individuals and the nation as a whole can hardly be overestimated.

These parallels beg the question whether and to what extent such developments may have influenced the transition to adulthood in Estonia. In particular, the globalization framework attempts to link modern societal developments to changes in family formation and childbearing through the mechanism of uncertainty. According to this theoretical framework, if uncertainty is rising, then changes in partnership and reproductive behavior are to be anticipated. These include not only a postponement of partnering and parenting but also a growing preference for consensual union because these leave room for greater flexibility and require less long-term commitment from the individuals involved. The Estonian case may be interesting for it allows to test these hypotheses about the mechanisms of uncertainty in a different societal context. Additionally, Estonia shares close similarity with OECD-type countries in terms of several long-term population developments. For instance, it has long shared the European marriage pattern and it also belongs to the pioneering countries of the second demographic transition, reaching below-replacement fertility already by the 1920s (Katus, 1994).

The analyses revealed a shift towards *earlier* formation of partnerships and entry into parenthood over the entire cohort range of the Estonia FFS. This implies that neither the societal transformation of the 1940s-50s nor that of the 1990s has been accompanied by a postponement of these events. In the light of recent statistics, however, this statement may likely need to be revised for the most recent societal transformation, which has been covered by the FFS to only a limited extent. Nevertheless, the absence of postponement behavior surely holds for the societal transformation of the 1940s-50s. Besides the evidence from the FFS, this has also been verified on the basis of other national surveys, particularly the Estonian Health Survey, which allows to go back to the cohorts born during the First World War (Leinsalu *et al.*, 1998). While it is hardly possible to cast doubt on the hardship and disruption experienced by the Estonian population during the soviet period, why did these conditions *not* translate in later partnership formation and entry into parenthood?

A possible explanation for the contradiction between the loss of security and the shift towards earlier partnership formation and parenthood could be sought in the regularities of long-term population developments. The shift towards earlier partnership formation and childbirth has been a common feature of most, if not all, nations historically characterized by the European marriage pattern. Evidently, in the case of Estonia the disappearance of the European marriage pattern and ensuing developments have overridden the effects of extremely harsh societal conditions. Although the latter thus proved insufficient to alter the course of long-term population trends, their impact can still be found in specific features of partnership and fertility behavior. Most importantly, Estonia - together with Latvia - is the only nation with an early demographic transition that did not experience a post-war baby-boom (Katus, 1997; Zvidrins *et al.*, 1998). However, a closer examination of this phenomenon is beyond the scope of the present study.

Another feature of earlier partnership formation and entry into parenthood in Estonia requiring explanation is the *continuation* of this trend until the youngest cohorts covered by the FFS. This feature distinguishes Estonia - again, together with Latvia - from other countries with comparable patterns of an early demographic transition. One possible reason for this deviation as put forward in this chapter with regard to parenthood could be the housing policy that prevailed under the previous regime. As dwellings were distributed by the authorities, a true housing market did not exist; persons could only apply for a dwelling upon fulfilling certain preconditions. Since the birth of a child enlarged the family and thus the number of household members per square meter, it enhanced one's chances to qualify for a new dwelling. For couples planning to have a child anyway, this kind of pragmatic considerations could have influenced the timing of their decision to actually do so.

Aside from the juvenation of partnership formation and parenthood, another finding from the Estonian case study that deserves attention is the change in the way in which first partnerships are started. Across the FFS cohort range there has been a switch from direct marriage to a consensual union as the dominant mode of first partnership formation. It is noteworthy that this switch was accomplished *prior* to the most recent societal transformation. Hence, it cannot be attributed to rising uncertainty about future developments or youth unemployment among successive cohorts. Nor can it be explained by any institutional factor as operational in Estonia during the 1970s and 80s because if the switch would have been supported by particular Soviet economic and/or social policies, one would have likely observed similar responses among native and foreign-origin populations. In reality, however, the native population accomplished the switch towards non-marital cohabitation about two decades earlier than the foreign-origin population (see Figure 9.4).

Evidently, then, the explanation for this particular pattern should also be sought in long-term population developments that date back to the beginning of the second demographic transition. Seen this way, partnership formation in Estonia displays considerable similarity with Scandinavian countries like Sweden, Denmark and Norway, with Latvia, and to a somewhat lesser extent with Finland. The role of consensual unions versus registered marriage can be clearly seen in the patterns of non-marital fertility, in terms of which Estonia has followed the examples of Sweden, Denmark and Norway throughout the whole post-transitional period (Katus, 1992). Already in the early 1990s the number of non-marital births exceeded by 50 percent the total number of births. Based on the evidence from FFS, the proportion of women in registered marriage at the moment of their first birth has been continuously declining ever since the cohort born in 1934-38. Among the youngest FFS cohort only half of first children were born in legal marriage, and the developments in the 1990s have considerably diminished this proportion.

At the same time it should be noted that compared to the Western countries of the Baltoscandian region, the prevailing societal conditions in Estonia made its pattern of consensual unions rather special. Most importantly, non-marital cohabitation in Estonia has until very recently been a relatively short stage at the beginning of a partnership career rather than a long-lasting status. To a considerable extent this shorter duration of non-marital cohabitation has been mediated by a shorter interval between the start of the union and ensuing pregnancy. FFS data on family planning behavior and contraception suggest that poor knowledge and limited availability of efficient contraceptives have been primarily responsible for this. Consensual unions were usually converted to marriage upon the arrival of the child.

The need to consider long-term population developments is also supported by our results from event history modeling. They showed that certain population groups can be regarded as forerunners with regard to innovative partnership and parenting behavior, while other groups switch to these new patterns with some delay. For instance, the observed time lag between native and foreign-origin populations in switching from direct marriage to consensual unions can be interpreted in this light. This view seems to also hold for the observed differentials by urban-rural residence and social origin in the timing of partnership formation and parenthood. In the oldest cohorts, in which the juvenation of partnership formation gained momentum, rural residents and those from a blue-collar background featured somewhat later entry into first partnership. In younger cohorts, however, in which the juvenation trend started to approach its end, this gradient reversed so that now a later timing of the event in question became characteristic of urban residents and of those with white-collar or self-employed (grand)parents.

In the context of globalization, particular attention should be paid to the findings concerning the differential timing of life course events according to the locus of control. The analysis revealed that in the case of Estonia, an external locus is related to postponed first union formation as well as delayed first parenthood. In other words, persons with lower ability to control their lives and social environment experienced these events later. Without ruling out alternative explanations, this could be regarded as an indication that there is a link between perceived societal uncertainty and the timing of major life course events.

In short, the main findings from the analysis of the transition to adulthood in Estonia can be summarized in the following main points. First, certain developments - in particular the shift from marriage to cohabitation - that are often related to the globalization process could in some cases also present themselves under relatively stable and secure societal conditions. Second, in the case of the societal transformation of the 1940s-50s, the loss of security, high uncertainty about future developments and disruption of social relations have not necessarily translated into a postponement of partnership formation and parenthood. This seeming contradiction could be explained by the fact that aside from the mediating role of institutional factors, the outcomes of globalization may be also influenced - strengthened or moderated - by the path dependence of long-term *population* developments.

NOTES

1   This case study has been carried out in the framework of research project 0501463s00. The authors gratefully acknowledge support from ETF grant No. 5982.
2   Men were interviewed with a three-year time lag in 1997 (EKDK, 1999, 2002), and will not be considered here.
3   Earlier analyses on the timing of partnership formation in Estonia that were based on a relatively small sample of the capital city population did not reveal any significant differences between those with completed secondary education and those with less.

BIBLIOGRAPHY

Bernardi, F. (2001) 'Globalisation, Recommodification and Social Inequality: Changing Patterns of Early Careers in Italy', GLOBALIFE Working Paper No. 7, Faculty of Sociology, University of Bielefeld.

Blossfeld, H.-P., Hamerle, A. and Mayer, K. U. (1989) *Event History Analysis. Statistical Theory and Application in the Social Sciences*, Hillsdale, New Jersey: Lawrence Erblaum Associates Publishers.

Blossfeld, H.-P. and Rohwer, G. (1995) *Techniques of Event History Modeling. New Approaches to Causal Analysis*, New Jersey: Lawrence Erblaum Associates Publishers.

Davis, K. (1984) 'Wives and Work: the Sex-Role Revolution and its Consequences', *Population and Development Review*, 10(3): 397-417.

European Commission (EC) (2000a) 'Employment in Europe 1999', Eesti saatusaastad 1945-1960 (1963-1972), kd.1-6, Stockholm: Kirjastus EMP.

European Commission (EC) (2000b) 'Labor Market Bulletin of Central and East European Countries', Eesti saatusaastad 1945-1960 (1963-1972), kd.1-6, Stockholm: Kirjastus EMP.

EKDK (1995a) 'Estonian Family and Fertility Survey', Methodological Report, RU Series A (39), Tallinn: EKDK.

EKDK (1995b) 'Estonian Family and Fertility Survey': Standard Tabulations. RU Series C, No.6. Tallinn, EKDK.

EKDK (1999) 'Estonian Family and Fertility Survey', Methodological Report of Male Survey, RU Series A, No.40, Tallinn: EKDK.

EKDK (2002) 'Estonian Family and Fertility Survey': Standard Tabulations of Male survey', RU Series C, Tallinn: EKDK.

ESA (2000) *Statistika aastaraamat*, Tallinn: Eesti Statistikaamet.

Hajnal, J. (1965) 'European marriage patterns in perspective', in D. Glass and D. Eversley (eds) *Population in History*, Chicago: Aldine Publishing Company.

Helemäe, J., Saar, E. and Vöörmann, R. (2000) *Kas haridusse tasus investeerida?*, Tallinn: Teaduste Akadeemia Kirjastus.

Katus, K. (1990) 'Demographic Trends in Estonia Throughout the Centuries', in *Yearbook of Population Research in Finland*, Helsinki: Population Research Institute.

Katus, K. (1992) Trends in Non-Marital Fertility in the Baltic Region, EAPS/BIB Seminar on Demographic.

Katus, K. (1994) 'Fertility Transition in Estonia, Latvia and Lithuania', in W. Lutz, S. Scherbov and A. Volkov (eds) *Demographic Trends and Patterns in the Soviet Union Before 1991*, London-New York: Routledge.

Katus, K. (1997) 'Long-term Fertility Development in Baltoscandia', *Yearbook of Population Research in Finland*, Vol.XXXIV, 18-34.

Katus, K., Puur, A. and Sakkeus, L. (2000a) Fertility and Familiy Surveys in the Countries of the ECE Region, Standard Country Report Estonia, *Economic Studies* No. 10n, New York and Geneva: United Nations.

Katus, K., Puur, A. and Sakkeus, L. (2000b) 'Development of National Minorities in Estonia', in W. Haug, P. Compton and Y. Courbage (eds) *Demographic Characteristics of National Minorities in Certain European States*, Strasbourg: Council of Europe.

Katus, K., Puur, A. and Põldma, A. (2002) 'Eesti põlvkondlik rahvastikuareng', RU Series D, No.2, Tallinn: EKDK.

Laird, J. and Thomson, N. (1991) *Psychology*, Boston-Toronto: Houghton Mifflin Company.

Leinsalu, M., Grintshak, M., Noorkõiv, R. and Silver, B. (1998) *Estonian Health Survey. Methodological Report*, Tallinn: EKMI.

Lugus, O. and Hatchey, G. (eds) (1995) *Transforming the Estonian Economy*, Tallinn: Institute of Economics.

Manting, D. (1994) *Dynamics in Marriage and Cohabitation. An Intertemporal Life Course Analysis of First Union Formation and Dissolution*, Amsterdam: Thesis Publishers.

Misiunas, R. and Taagepera, R. (1983) *The Baltic States. Years of Dependence 1940-1980*, Berkeley: University of California Press.

Misiunas, R. and Taagepera, R. (1993) *The Baltic States. Years of Dependence 1940-1990*, Berkeley: University of California Press.

Palli, H. (1988) *Otepää rahvastik aastail 1716-1799*, Tallinn: Eesti Raamat.

Puur, A. (1995) 'Labor Force Participation Trends in the Baltic States 1959-1989', in C. Lundh (ed.) *Demography, Economy, Welfare*, Lund: Lund University Press.

Reiman, H. (1937) 'Kirjaoskus ja haridus Eestis', *Eesti Statistika Kuukiri*, 183(2): 49-57.

RSKB (1937-1940) *Eesti Statistika Kuukiri*, Tallinn: Riigi Statistika Keskbüroo.

Sakkeus, L. (1991) 'Post-war Migration Trends in Estonia', RU Series B, No.15, Tallinn: EKDK.

Sakkeus, L. (1996) 'Trends of International Migration in Estonia', in T.Freijka (ed.) *International Migration in Central and Eastern Europe and the Commonwealth of Independent States*, New York and Geneva: United Nations.

Simó, C., Golsch, K. and Steinhage, N. (2000) 'Entry into First Parenthood in Spain and the Process of Globalisation', GLOBALIFE Working Paper No. 8, Faculty of Sociology, University of Bielefeld.

Sommer, T., Klijzing, E. and Mills, M. (2000) 'Partnership Formation in a Globalizing World: The Impact of Uncertainty in East and West Germany', GLOBALIFE Working Paper No. 9, Faculty of Sociology, University of Bielefeld.

Trost, J. (1988) 'Cohabitation and Marriage. Transitional Pattern, Different Lifestyle or Just Another Legal Form', in H.Moors and J.Schoorl (eds) *Lifestyles, Contraception and Parenthood*, The Hague/Brussels: NIDI.

UNECE (1995-1999) *Economic Survey for Europe*, New York and Geneva: United Nations.

Viikberg, J. (ed.) (1999) *Eesti rahvuste raamat*, Tallinn: Eesti Entsüklopeediakirjastus.

Vishnevski, A. and Volkov, A. (eds) (1983) *Vosproizvodstvo naselenia SSSR*, Moscow: Finansi i Statistika.

Zvidrins, P., Ezera, L. and Greitans, A. (1998) Fertility and Family Surveys in the Countries of the ECE Region, Standard Country Report Latvia, *Economic Studies* No. 10f., New York and Geneva: United Nations.

10 The process of globalization and transitions to adulthood in Britain

Marco Francesconi and Katrin Golsch

INTRODUCTION[1]

This chapter investigates the impact of the globalization process on entry into the labor market, partnership formation, and transition to parenthood in Britain during the 1990s. We use the term "globalization process" to refer to the complex interactions between the increased volatility of the labor, capital and product markets, the higher interdependence of regional and national economies around the world and the pronounced uncertainty in individual, family, social and political life, described, among others, by Blossfeld (2002) and Mills and Blossfeld (this volume). It has been argued that this globalization process is inherently unstable and leads people to experience different types of uncertainty, which in turn may affect people's life chances, including some of the salient transitions from youth to adulthood (e.g., Blossfeld, 2002).

Prior research analyzing young people's transitions to the adult life course in Britain has focused on the effects of such factors as parents' education and socio-economic status, parental income, childhood family structure and divorce, house prices and local labor market conditions (Berrington, 2001; Cherlin *et al.*, 1995; Kiernan, 1992 and 1997a; Ermisch and Di Salvo, 1997; Ermisch, 1999; Ermisch and Francesconi, 2000a, 2001a and 2001b). But these studies have not taken into account the role played by the globalization process and its various types of uncertainty on early life transitions.

Using data from the first nine waves of the British Household Panel Survey (1991-1999), this chapter tries to fill this gap up by addressing the following three questions: (1) To what extent are young people faced with labor market uncertainty which may affect their first entry into the labor market? (2) Are temporary employment and part-time employment systematically related to men's and women's early living arrangements and partnership formation? (3) How does the globalization process affect young people's decision to have their first child? Labor market uncertainty, which is likely to surround young people's socio-economic position and employment relationships and is a potential result of the process of globalization, is operationalized by two features of the labor supply, namely, temporary employment and number of hours of work. These two aspects of the labor supply are important because one of them - temporary employment - is meant to affect the "extensive margin" of the labor supply (through the number of people who are in temporary jobs), whereas the other - hours of work - practically defines the "intensive margin" (Heckman, 1993). Thus, by looking at these two aspects together we are likely to improve our understanding of how both shifts and slope changes in the labor supply and, therefore, the presence of economic and employment relationship uncertainties will affect young people's transitions to adulthood. This is clearly relevant to policy, as policy makers in Britain as well as in other industrialized countries have increasingly used temporary and part-time employment to achieve higher levels of labor market flexibility.[2]

The case of Britain may be relevant not only in its own right but also for purposes of cross-national comparison. In fact, we begin to accumulate some knowledge of the effect of the globalization process on youth transitions into adulthood for Germany (Sommer *et al.*, 2000; Kurz *et al.*, this volume), Spain (Simó *et al.*, 2002; Simó *et al.*, this volume) and Italy (Bernardi, 2001; Bernardi and Nazio, this volume). At present, however, our knowledge of the relationships between temporary and part-time employment and transitions to adulthood for Britain is scant and merely based on anecdotal evidence. Yet Britain is an example of a 'liberal' welfare regime (Esping-Andersen, 1993 and 1999) and has, as such, already experienced some effects of the globalization process in terms of increased levels of deregulation and liberalization of the labor market (Deakin and Reed, 2000), a secular decline of traditional unionism (Machin, 2000; Booth and Francesconi, 2001), a concentration of long-term unemployment on a minority of households and individuals with certain characteristics (Gregg and Wadsworth, 1996; Arulampalam, 2000), a rather limited upward mobility (Dearden *et al.*, 1997), an increased wage and income inequality (Machin, 1999; Jenkins, 2000), and increased poverty rates (Dickens and Ellwood, 2001; Jenkins and Rigg, 2001). Britain, therefore, is likely to be an extraordinary social laboratory, which allows us not only to gauge how globalization affects British youth in their transitions to the adult life course but also to anticipate (at least part of) future early life transitions in other countries. The difference between what one would predict from our analysis and the eventual observed responses will probably capture the functioning of country-specific institutions, which either mitigate or reinforce the impact of the globalization process on individuals, families and other social groups. Measuring and explaining such differences or similarities will be an ambitious task for future research.

The remainder of this chapter is structured as follows. In the section "Research Questions" we present the three research questions that are pursued in our empirical analysis. This enables us, first, to outline the background against which we motivate our study and, second, to provide an overview of the social, economic and institutional contexts in Britain by describing the salient characteristics of labor market entry, partnership formation and transition into motherhood. The section "Data and Methods" presents the data and the statistical methods used in the analysis, whereas the section "Results" discusses our main findings. The final section summarizes our principal conclusions.

RESEARCH QUESTIONS

This chapter addresses three main interdependent questions. The first is:

1   To what extent are young people in Britain faced with labor market uncertainty that may affect their first entry into the primary labor market?

Blossfeld (2002) argues that the globalization process is accompanied by an increasing importance of higher educational attainments. Indeed, there is evidence of a rapid growth in participation rates in full-time further education following compulsory schooling over the last three decades and, particularly, after 1988 when the General Certificate of Secondary Education (GCSE) was introduced (Steinmann, 1998/1999; McVicar and Rice, 2001). This may reflect not only the need for constantly upgrading workers' skills but also fluctuations in the labor market, with a substantial rise in youth unemployment in the 1980s and early 1990s (Golsch, 2001) and an increasing demand for labor market flexibility (Dex and McCullogh, 1995). Taylor (2000) emphasizes the increased prevalence of unemployment, part-time work and inactivity (relative to full-time employment) among new labor market entrants during the 1990s. Taken together, all these patterns point to a postponement of the first entry into the primary labor market and a more uncertain transition from education to employment for more recent cohorts of individuals. On the other hand, some commentators have described the stepwise nature of the early labor market careers of young adults in Britain and the strong presence of 'informal' channels (Lindley, 1996; Heath and Cheung, 1998; Scherer, 2001). These two last characteristics are likely to amplify the problems faced by young people while entering the labor market, because they have to rely on less well-defined (probably more uncertain) procedures to start their careers in the primary labor market.

The school-to-work transition is obviously important to individuals' subsequent life opportunities. Decisions on whether or not to stay on at school at age 16 (the mandatory minimum school-leaving age) will have substantial effects of their accumulation of human capital and skills. For example, low educational attainment is one mechanism through which childhood disadvantage is translated into poor social and economic opportunities. Similarly, the increased prevalence of unemployment among men and women leaving full-time education could have a serious impact on their future labor market career if a causal link exists between current unemployment and future labor market performance. For instance, it is possible that previous unemployment experience increases the probability of future unemployment (Arulampalam, 2000).[3]

The increasing prevalence of non-standard work forms such as temporary and part-time employment (particularly for women) and self-employment (particularly for men) is an indication of the changing structure of the British labor market, with the decline in the availability of full-time regular employment. Having entered work, individuals experience different patterns of labor market mobility and success. These depend on factors such as their education, gender, personal ambition and motivation, family background and macroeconomic conditions

(Taylor, 2000). However, we do not know yet whether or not the globalization process or its observed outcomes in terms of temporary and part-time employment has any disadvantageous effect on subsequent transitions in the labor market. In particular, we do not know whether it has an impact on the transition to unemployment. This is what we will analyze below.

The globalization process is likely to affect not only young people's labor market behavior but also their psychological well-being, perceptions and expectations about their role as workers, parents and citizens. In the last thirty years, two major changes have occurred in the patterns of family formation. Marriage and childbearing are occurring increasingly later in people's lives, and there has been a dramatic increase in childbearing outside formal marriage (Ermisch and Francesconi, 2000a). The next two research questions ask whether or not the globalization process has a direct effect on such patterns. The second question, therefore, is:

2   Is temporary and part-time employment systematically related to men's and women's early living arrangements and partnership formation?

Many Western societies have recently observed trends of declining marriage rates, higher divorce rates, and the rise of alternative living arrangements such as single-mother families, non-marital cohabitation and single-person households. These changes have been related to the increased labor market participation of women (Michael, 1988), changes in government intervention in the form of taxes and subsidies and in the laws regulating marriage and divorce (Peters, 1986; Friedberg, 1998), changes in the technology of producing and rearing children, in particular, lower mortality rates and more effective birth control (Lesthaeghe, 1983; Kohler, 1997; Thomson, 1997; Goldin and Katz, 2000), the erosion of religious and political authority and the rise of individual freedom (Bumpass, 1990; Goldscheider and Waite, 1991). It can be argued that an inherently uncertain globalization process would lead young adults to be less committed to long-term durable relationships, particularly during the early stages of their working career (Mills and Blossfeld, this volume). Ermisch and Francesconi (2000a) find that although a minority of British young people in the 1990s move directly from their parental home into their first partnership, the large majority will enter a partnership while living independently from their parents. Regardless of the family situation before a partnership is formed, however, three-quarters of first partnerships in Britain are consensual unions rather than legal marriages. In fact, it is the dramatic shift to non-marital cohabitation as the mode of first live-in partnership that is primarily responsible for the major changes in family formation patterns mentioned above (Ermisch and Francesconi, 2000b). This is the reason why in our empirical analysis we shall specifically focus on the transition to consensual unions.

We do have some understanding of how the prevalence of consensual unions is correlated with circumstances of the family of origin and individual demographic characteristics in Britain. For example, there is evidence that while the upper-middle classes were pioneers in non-marital cohabitation in the 1960s and

1970s, social class differences in the odds of cohabiting relative to marrying no longer exist in the 1990s. There is also evidence that cohabitation continues to increase among more recent cohorts, although these young people delay first partnership formation all together (Haskey and Kiernan, 1989; Kiernan, 1999; Ermisch and Francesconi, 2000a and 2000b). However, there has not been any investigation on the relationship of the globalization process and its various forms of uncertainty with the formation of consensual unions. Similarly, we do not know how the globalization process affects the eventual transition from cohabitation to marriage. Therefore, we will analyze this relationship, thus adding to our current understanding of whether and when young people convert their cohabitation into marriage (Berrington and Diamond, 1995 and 2000; Lillard *et al.*, 1995; Ermisch and Francesconi, 2000b).

3 How does the globalization process affect young people's decision to have their first child?

The postponement of marriage discussed above and the fact that at least three in five first births are still within marriage immediately suggest that the shift to cohabitation as the dominant form of first partnership is also associated with the postponement of parenthood. In the last three decades there has also been a dramatic rise in the percentage of births in Britain that occur outside marriage, a trend that steepened after 1980. It appears that about three-fifths of all recent out-of-wedlock births occur within cohabiting partnerships (Ermisch and Francesconi, 2000a and 2000b).[4] In addition, other research indicates that nearly 40 percent of mothers in Britain spend some time as a lone parent, with a median duration of lone motherhood of about 4 years (Ermisch and Francesconi, 2000c). This evidence clearly points to an increasing complexity of family relationships as well as to an increasingly uncertain definition of parental roles, parenting styles and attitudes to careers and children.

Although researchers have related fertility to a wide range of observable and unobservable characteristics (see Hotz *et al.*, 1997 for a survey of recent contributions), there is no evidence about the effect of temporary and part-time employment on the transition to motherhood for Britain. Blossfeld and Drobnič (2001) and Simó *et al.* (2002) have argued that through its effects on the labor market and particularly the availability of part-time and flexible jobs, the globalization process may modify people's attitudes to work, affect their work and family identities, and make it easier for some women to combine careers and children. On the other hand, the widespread uncertainty that is inherent in the globalization process may discourage other women to either start a career or become mothers in the first place. How exactly the globalization process affects the transition to motherhood is, therefore, at this point an empirical matter that will be analyzed in the rest of this study.

DATA AND METHODS

The data analyzed for this research come from a sample selected using the first nine annual waves of the British Household Panel Survey (BHPS). In autumn 1991, the BHPS interviewed a representative sample of about 5,500 households containing approximately 10,000 people randomly selected south of the Caledonian Canal.[5] Since then, the same individuals have been re-interviewed each successive year. However, if they leave their original households to form new households, then all the adult members of the new households are also interviewed as part of the study. Children in the original households are also interviewed once they reach the age of 16. Some 88 percent of the original BHPS sample members were re-interviewed for the second wave, and from the third wave onwards the response rates have been consistently higher than 95 percent. The BHPS data are, therefore, unlikely to suffer from any serious bias resulting from attrition. This means that the sample remained broadly representative of the population of Britain as it changed during the 1990s.

Our analysis is based on a sample of young men and women who were born after 1960 (thus aged at most 38 in 1999, the last available survey year), who are not disabled and who reported complete information on all the variables of interest.[6] We have herewith an unbalanced longitudinal sample of 6,409 individuals with 29,468 person-wave observations.

Proxy variables for the globalization process

Most of the discussion above has emphasized the centrality of flexible forms of employment as an indicator of the globalization process. We primarily focus on two measures. The first is an interaction term between being employed and working part-time (working in a full-time job is the base in the multivariate analysis).[7] The second measure refers to the interaction term between being employed and working in temporary employment. The BHPS data allow us to distinguish two types of temporary employment: seasonal/casual jobs and jobs done under contract for a fixed period of time (employment in a permanent contract is the base).

It is important to study the effects of part-time and temporary employment in the context of other labor market influences on the transitions to adulthood. One of these, which has already been taken into account in the previous measures, is the respondent's employment status. Unarguably, all the transitions under study - to non-marital cohabitation, from cohabitation to marriage, and to parenthood[8] - are linked to the individual's employment situation. For instance, it is likely that having a job makes it easier to start up a partnership, simply because the financial burden associated with such a choice is reduced when a person works compared to the case in which he or she does not. We distinguish between four labor market states, that is, being (i) in education, (ii) unemployed, (iii) out of the labor force, and (iii) employed, which is the base. Another important aspect of the individual's labor market position that is potentially relevant for all the transitions to adulthood studied here is his or her occupation. The degree of uncertainty faced by professionals is expected to differ from that faced by unskilled workers or by the self-employed. These differential degrees of uncertainty are then likely to have a differential impact on each of the transitions to the adult life course. We distinguish six occupational categories (Erikson and Goldthorpe, 1992): (i) self-employed, (ii) manager, (iii) professional, (iv) non-manual, (v) manual occupations, and (vi) semi-skilled and unskilled occupations (our base category in the multivariate analysis).

Other variables

There are other variables that are legitimately believed to influence the transitions to adulthood and that we control for in our analysis. These are:

1 Gender (one dummy variable for men). We use this variable only in the study of the transition to unemployment. In the analysis of the other transitions, we distinguish our sample between men and women.
2 Birth cohort (three dummy variables for 1960-64, 1965-69, 1970-74, base = 1975-83), which is meant to reflect secular variations across age groups.
3 Age and age squared. As explained in the next section, the age variables capture the duration effects on the hazard functions.
4 Time trend (eight dummy variables from 1992 to 1998, base = 1999). These variables are included to capture variations in the business cycle and macro-economic conditions.
5 Highest educational level achieved (five dummies for: higher and first university degree, higher vocational qualification, A level or equivalent, GCSE/O level or equivalent, less than O level, base = no qualification). The educational qualification of individuals may identify differences in ability and cultural attitudes that influence the transitions to adulthood and cannot be explained by differences in occupation.
6 Marital status ((i) in the case of entry into unemployment, two dummies for: cohabiting/being married, separated/divorced/widowed, base = never married; (ii) in the case of entry into parenthood, three dummies for: never married, cohabiting, other, base = married). Some of the transitions of interest (e.g., entry into parenthood) may dramatically differ depending on, say, whether people have never been married or already experienced a divorce.
7 Living with parents (dummy variable).
8 Children ((i) in the case of the transition from cohabitation to marriage, one dummy for having a child; (ii) in the case of entry into unemployment, number of own children in the household).
9 Labor force experience (measured in years). This variable is meant to reduce heterogeneity between individuals that is driven by different patterns in the labor market.
10 Attendance at religious services (three dummy variables for: once a week, once a month, once a year, base = never).[9] Differences in religiosity are likely to be correlated to different paths of entry into cohabitation and marriage.

We gauged the impact of the proxy variables for the globalization process as presented in the previous section on the three transitions to the adult life course in a sequential manner. We initially estimated each model (using the method described in the section "Methods") through a parsimonious specification that included the globalization variables only. We then gradually included the other potential explanatory variables and assessed the residual power of the globalization variables. However, because of space limitations, in the section "Results" we only report the results obtained from our full specifications.

Methods

Using the sample described above, all these variables are considered in a multivariate analysis of the three transitions of interest. The models that we estimate are discrete-time competing risks transition models. Of course, the risks and the groups of individuals exposed to such risks are different vis-à-vis the transition under analysis. In particular, (a) in the sub-sample of employed individuals the two risks are entry into unemployment and exit out of the labor market; (b) in the sub-sample of un-partnered individuals the two risks are entry into cohabitation and entry into marriage directly, while in the sub-sample of cohabiting people the two risks are marriage and dissolution of the union; and (c) in the sub-sample of childless individuals the only risk is that of having a child and, therefore, there are no competing risks. Under the conventional independence assumptions, the log-likelihood function factors into a sum of terms, each of which is a function of the parameters of a single transition rate only. As a consequence, we can estimate each of the competing risk transition rates by treating the alternative outcome as censoring at that point (Narandranathan and Stewart, 1993). Furthermore, the resulting log-likelihood function is identical with that of a binary logit model for each type of transition (see Allison, 1982).

The outcome-specific rate for each of the transitions of interest in year t for the jth individual (or couple), p_{ijt}, is assumed to take the form

$$\ln[\, p_{ijt} \,/(1 - p_{ijt}\,)] = \alpha_i \ln(dur_{jt-1}) + \beta_i X_{jt-1} + \gamma_j Z_{jt-1}$$
$$i = 1,2,$$

where dur_{jt-1} is the length of time in which the individual (or couple) has been employed (case (a) above), un-partnered or in a cohabiting union (case (b)) at year t-1;[10] X_{jt-1} is the vector of the proxy variables for the globalization process measured at year t-1; and Z_{jt-1} is the vector containing all the other variables.

The variables in X are always the same for each of the transitions under analysis.[11] But the vector Z differs slightly depending on the type of transition. Specifically, in estimating the transition to unemployment, we control for gender, a quadratic polynomial in age, time trend, education, labor force experience, marital status, and number of children. In estimating the entry into cohabitation, the variables in Z are birth cohort, age and age squared, education, living with parents, and religious attendance, while in estimating the outcome of cohabiting unions (entry into marriage) we control for the same variables as for the previous transition except that living with parents is excluded and having a child is included. Finally, in estimating the transition to parenthood the variables in Z are birth cohort, age and age squared, education, living with parents, and marital status.

In the case of transition (a) above, the data used to estimate model (1) are annual observations on employed individuals at risk either to become unemployed or exit the labor market in the following year (i.e., employed at year t-1). Some of these observations come from individuals who are employed at the beginning of the panel study (1991). The contribution to the likelihood function of such individuals must, therefore, condition on surviving in employment up to the time of the start of the panel. Jenkins (1995) showed that owing to a 'canceling of terms' in the conditional survivor probability their likelihood contribution depends only on the transition rates and data for years since the beginning of the panel study, provided that the total elapsed duration of employment (dur_{jt-1}) is used for the transition rates in model (1). Notice, however, that this convenient canceling result does not carry over to models in which there is unmeasured individual-specific heterogeneity, nor to analogous continuous-time transition models (see Lancaster, 1990).[12]

RESULTS

A description of the transition into employment

Before focusing on the results obtained from the regression analyses, we first offer a useful description of the transition to employment. This information provides us with the background against which to interpret the regression estimates. Table 10.1 shows the distribution of different types of contract (permanent, fixed-term, seasonal, self-employed) at labor market entry by gender and previous status. Almost two-thirds of the transitions for men - either from school or from out of the labor force (OLF) - are to a permanent job. A relatively large proportion of inactive men (11 percent) enter into self-employment, and almost 30 percent of those leaving school start their working career in a seasonal/casual job or in a job with a fixed-term contract. Compared to men, the transition rate into a permanent job for young women is higher: 71 and 77 percent of them gain a permanent job if they come from school and from out of the labor force, respectively. Only a handful of women move into self-employment, particularly after having left school (less than 2 percent). More than one in four women start their career in temporary employment after having left school, while nearly one in six do so if they have been previously inactive.

Table 10.2 reports the same type of information but distinguishes between part-time and full-time employment (because of small cell sizes, the transitions of men and women are pooled). The differences between part-time and full-time workers across contract type and self-employment are stronger among those who have left school than among those who come from out of the labor force. For example, in the latter case, 57 percent of those who gain a permanent job move

Table 10.1   Type of contract at labor market entry and gender in Britain

	Men	Women
Transition School to Work		
Permanent	65.9%	71.1%
Seasonal	15.9%	16.8%
Fixed-term	14.0%	10.4%
Self-employed	4.1%	1.7%
Total	100%	100%
	(364)	(405)
Transition OLF to Work		
Permanent	65.1%	77.0%
Seasonal	14.3%	12.4%
Fixed-term	9.6%	3.9%
Self-employed	11.0%	6.7%
Total	100%	100%
	(519)	(805)

Note: Column percentages for type of contract achieved at labor market entry in the 1990s by gender and previous labor force status (school / being out of the labor force). Number of wave-to-wave transitions in parentheses.

into a full-time position whereas 43 percent into a part-time position. Corresponding figures for those who were previously at school, however, are 78 and 22 percent. Among temporary workers and the self-employed, seasonal/casual workers are systematically more likely to be in part-time jobs than people who start on fixed-term contracts or become self-employed. In the case of the school-to-work transitions, these percentages are 41 versus 16 and 23 percent, respectively.

Table 10.3 shows the distribution of permanent and temporary employment by occupation and previous labor force status. The table clearly documents that young people who enter employment from inactivity (out of the labor force) are more likely to be in semi-skilled or unskilled jobs than people who enter employment from school. Interestingly, this is true regardless of the type of contract. For instance, among those in a permanent job, 23 percent start their career in semi-skilled or unskilled occupations if they leave inactivity, while only 12 percent start in such occupations if they leave school. Another interesting feature of the first transition into the labor market refers to the difference between seasonal/casual workers and those who are on fixed-term contracts. In fact, the former ones are more often in non-manual occupations, while the latter are more concentrated in professional occupations.

These three cross-tabulations reveal two important pieces of information. First, in the 1990s there has been a sizeable group of young men and women in Britain who started their working careers in non-standard temporary jobs or in self-employment. Second, there is a fair amount of heterogeneity across workers in

Table 10.2   Type of contract at labor market entry and working hours in Britain

	Full-time	Part-time	Total	
Transition School to Work				
Permanent	77.5%	22.5%	100%	*(528)*
Seasonal	58.7%	41.3%	100%	*(126)*
Fixed-term	83.9%	16.1%	100%	*(93)*
Self-employed	77.3%	22.7%	100%	*(22)*
Transition OLF to Work				
Permanent	57.2%	42.8%	100%	*(958)*
Seasonal	52.3%	47.7%	100%	*(174)*
Fixed-term	74.1%	25.9%	100%	*(81)*
Self-employed	66.7%	33.3%	100%	*(111)*

Note: Percentages for type of contract achieved at labor market entry in the 1990s by working hours and previous labor force status (school / being out of the labor force). Number of wave-to-wave transitions in parentheses.

Table 10.3   Type of contract at labor market entry and occupation in Britain

	Permanent	Seasonal	Fixed-term
Transition School to Work			
Managerial	3.0%	0.0%	3.2%
Professional	23.3%	9.5%	36.6%
Non-manual	54.6%	56.4%	47.3%
Manual	7.4%	4.0%	6.5%
Semiskilled / unskilled	11.7%	30.2%	6.5%
Total	100%	100%	100%
	(528)	*(126)*	*(93)*
Transition OLF to Work			
Managerial	5.1%	1.7%	3.7%
Professional	11.8%	4.0%	29.6%
Non-manual	50.1%	47.1%	27.2%
Manual	10.2%	5.2%	14.8%
Semiskilled / unskilled	22.8%	42.0%	24.7%
Total	100%	100%	100%
	(958)	*(174)*	*(81)*

Note: Percentages for type of contract achieved at labor market entry in the 1990s by occupation and previous labor force status (school / being out of the labor force). Self-employed excluded. Number of wave-to-wave transitions in parentheses.

different types of non-standard employment. For instance, seasonal/casual workers are the ones most likely to be found in part-time jobs and in low-level occupations, while people on fixed-term contracts are more concentrated in full-time jobs and professional occupations. This means that young workers in such jobs are probably facing different career trajectories with different types of uncertainties. They may also be exposed to differential degrees of risk in their subsequent transitions to the adult life course. Three of these transitions are what we turn to analyze next.

The entry into unemployment

Table 10.4 shows the estimates obtained from a discrete-time competing risk transition model for entry into unemployment. We report the results from two specifications. Specification [2] differs from specification [1] for having included marital status and number of children in the household. Regardless of the specification, the risk of experiencing unemployment is substantially greater for workers in temporary employment than for workers in permanent employment. A seasonal/casual (fixed-term contract) worker is more than 3 times (2.5 times) more likely than a permanent worker to become unemployed. Although a higher labor market turnover is inherently related to such types of jobs and fully expected, these estimates document that workers in such jobs are also exposed to a higher hazard of unemployment experiences. Being in part-time employment does not have any significant impact on the probability of entering unemployment according to the estimates of specification [1]. The estimates from specification [2] are, instead, more accurately measured. They reveal that part-time workers are about 28 percent less likely to enter unemployment, but part-time working men are 67 percent *more* likely to do so. Although only 5 percent of working men are in part-time employment versus 40 percent of working women, this result suggests that men in part-time jobs are likely to be in a particularly precarious labor market position.

The table further shows that occupation is clearly another powerful predictor of the transition to unemployment. Individuals in semi-skilled and unskilled occupations (our base category) are more likely to enter unemployment than individuals in any other occupational group. For example, those in managerial and professional occupations are, respectively, 74 and 70 percent less likely to become unemployed than are those in the base category.

Finally, the results from the other covariates are in line with previous research. For instance, entry into unemployment is more likely to occur in bad economic times, that is, during a downturn of the business cycle as in 1992-1993 compared to 1999. We find that men are 34 percent (39 in specification [1]) more likely to enter into unemployment than women, who are more likely to exit the labor force. There is no significant impact of age, nor is there any effect of the number of children. But married or cohabiting people are almost 44 percent less likely to experience a transition to unemployment, reflecting perhaps a stronger labor market attachment than individuals without a partner. There is also a clear human capital effect: both education and labor market experience are negatively

Table 10.4   Entry into unemployment in Britain – logit regressions

	Specification	
	[1]	*[2]*
Working hours[a]		
Part-time	.753	.721*
Men * Part-time	1.626	1.671*
Full-time (base)		
Type of contract[a]		
Permanent (base)		
Fixed-term	2.588***	2.498***
Seasonal	3.346***	3.177***
Own occupation[a]		
Self-employed	.636**	.640**
Managerial	.263***	.278***
Professional	.301***	.308***
Non-manual skilled	.714**	.714**
Manual skilled	1.091	1.110
Semi/unskilled (base)		
Time trend		
1992	1.889***	1.883***
1993	1.778***	1.766***
1994	1.320	1.299
1995	1.074	1.048
1996	.779	.775
1997	.710*	.699*
1998	.872	.869
1999 (base)		
Age[a]	.971	1.067
Age squared[a]	1.000	.998
Sex		
Men	1.393**	1.339**
Women (base)		
Educational Qualification[a]		
Higher and first degree	.223***	.220***
Vocational degree	.389***	.390***
A Level (or equivalent)	.268***	.270***
GCSE/O Level (or equiv.)	.334***	.339***
Less than O Level	.450***	.459***
No Qualification (base)		
Labor Force Experience[a]	.845***	.841***

Table 10.4 continued

	Specification	
	[1]	[2]
Own marital status[a]		
Single (base)		
Living as a couple		.565***
Separated, Divorced, Widowed		1.016
Number of own children in household[a]		1.127
Log Likelihood	-1640	-1630
Number of person wave observations	11852	11851
Number of events	440	440

Obtained from discrete-time competing risk transition model for leaving a job position that has started in the 1990s. The figures are odd ratios from logit regressions.

Notes
a   Variable is lagged by one period.
*** $p < 0.01$
** $p < 0.05$
* $p < 0.10$

correlated with entry into unemployment. Regardless of the model specification, the probability of experiencing such a transition for individuals with university or higher degrees is almost 80 percent lower than for individuals without any qualification. Similarly, one extra year of labor market experience reduces the hazard of unemployment by some 15 percent, suggesting a substantial state dependence.

In sum, individuals who are better educated, more experienced, married and employed in any occupation except for an unskilled manual one are less likely to enter into unemployment. These results are consistent with those reviewed by Taylor (2000). But over and above these effects, the labor market characteristics that are posited to signal the globalization process - part-time and particularly temporary employment - are positively associated with the risk of becoming unemployed. This is so for men in part-time jobs, and for both men and women in any form of non-permanent contract. Labor market flexibility is thus likely to come at the cost of greater instability in the early stages of young people's careers.

The transition to non-marital cohabitation and its evolution

Table 10.5 presents the estimates of discrete-time competing risk transition models for the entry into first cohabitation for men and women separately. We report the results from two different specifications, one that excludes attendance at religious services and one that includes it.[13] The estimates document that the

Table 10.5　　Entry into cohabitation in Britain – logit regressions

	Men		Women	
	[1]	[2]	[1]	[2]
Working hours[a]				
Full-time (base)				
Part-time	.655	.637	.616**	.535**
Type of contract[a]				
Permanent (base)				
Seasonal	.733	.811	.902	.916
Fixed-term	.680	.737	.435*	.397*
Employment status[a]				
Employed (base)				
In education	.281***	.268***	.355***	.368***
Unemployed	.946	.972	.768	.742
OLF	.181**	.343	.944	.978
Own occupation[a]				
Self-employed	.755	.855	.476	.321
Managerial	1.595*	1.980**	.995	.958
Professional	.782	.853	.756	.685
Non-manual skilled	.616**	.656	1.020	1.093
Manual skilled	1.539**	1.884***	.652	.703
Semi/unskilled (base)				
Age[a]				
Age	2.730***	2.293***	2.266***	2.963***
Age squared	.981***	.984***	.984***	.978***
Birth Cohort				
1960-64	.789	.782	.292***	.257***
1965-69	.787	1.014	.498**	.339***
1970-74	1.010	1.170	.692**	.494***
1975-83 (base)				
Educational Qualification[a]				
Higher and first degree	.810	.803	1.226	1.475
Vocational degree	.810	.794	1.182	1.487
A Level (or equivalent)	.698*	.729	1.064	1.207
GCSE/O Level (or equiv.)	.878	1.037	1.047	1.251
Less than O Level (base)				
No Qualification	.811	.650	1.051	1.132
Living with parents	.510***	.429***	.577***	.582***

Table 10.5 continued

	Men		Women	
	[1]	[2]	[1]	[2]
Attendance at religious service[a]				
Once a week		.155***		.439**
Once a month		.460		.473**
Once a year		.571**		.730*
Never (base)				
Log Likelihood	-1196	-755	-1297	-806
Number of person wave observations	5454	3424	4749	2954
Number of events	365	239	406	259

Obtained from discrete-time competing risk transition model. The figures are odd ratios from logit regressions.

Notes
a   Variable is lagged by one period.
*** $p < 0.01$
** $p < 0.05$
* $p < 0.10$

globalization process - as approximated by working hours and type of contract - has no impact on the transition to cohabitation for men. Although men in part-time and temporary employment are always less likely to enter a cohabiting union than men in either full-time or permanent employment, this difference is never statistically significant. This may suggest that men do not perceive their 'instability' in the labor market as an element that deters union formation and partnership life. But the story appears to be different for women. In fact, women in part-time jobs are between 38 and 47 percent less likely to enter into cohabitation than their full-time counterparts (specifications [1] and [2], respectively). Similarly, women on fixed-term contracts are 56 to 60 percent less likely to cohabit than women in permanent jobs. Furthermore, being in education substantially reduces the chance of cohabiting for both men and women. But we cannot detect any differential risk among people in the other labor force states (except for inactive men who, according to specification [1], are 82 percent less likely to be in a cohabiting union than employed men). Occupation does not play any significant role for women, suggesting that there are no social class differences in the odds of cohabiting relative to marrying (this is in line with the findings presented in Ermisch and Francesconi, 2000a). However, some differences do emerge in the case of men, with individuals in managerial and skilled manual occupations being more likely to cohabit than those in unskilled occupations.

In addition, Table 10.5 shows that - in line with the literature discussed in section "Research Questions"- both men and women are more likely to form a cohabiting union while living independently from their parents. There is a strong positive age effect, and women born after 1975 are considerably more likely to cohabit than women born earlier. This clearly reveals that cohabitation has increasingly become an important route for them into first partnership formation. For men, however, there is no evidence of a cohort effect. We also do not find any educational gradient, suggesting that cohabitation is a common form of partnership among all educational groups. Finally, religious activity is a powerful predictor of this transition, with men and women who attend religious services once a week being, respectively, 86 and 56 percent less likely to cohabit than those who never attend. Even those going to church only once a year still have a lower likelihood (but if they do start to cohabit, they will get married soon; see further below).

There is a conspicuous body of research examining the role of different socio-economic and demographic characteristics in accounting for variations among persons in partnership dissolution patterns (Berrington and Diamond, 2000; Ermisch and Francesconi, 2000a and 2000b; Böheim and Ermisch, 2001). But, once such characteristics are controlled for, is there any room left for the impact of the globalization process? Table 10.6 reports the results obtained from discrete-time competing risk transition models for the outcome of cohabiting unions for men and women separately. The table shows the estimates of the effects on the odds of marrying the partner relative to remaining in the cohabiting union, with the other risk being that of dissolving the union. There is a clear 'deterrent' effect for men in temporary employment. In fact, compared to those in permanent jobs, men in seasonal and casual jobs are 88 percent less likely to convert their cohabitation into marriage, and those on fixed-term contracts are 44 percent less likely to do so (specification [1]). Once we control for religious activity, however, the latter effect disappears, but the former remains large and significant. The effect of part-time employment shows a similar pattern to that of fixed-term employment, that is, negative and significant under specification [1] and again negative but insignificant under specification [2]. We also find lower odds of converting their cohabitation into marriage for men who are unemployed or still in education. But there is no real difference in behavior across the different occupational groups; only the self-employed are 1.8 times more likely to marry their partner. The estimates for women show that none of the globalization process variables has any impact on the odds that they will convert their cohabiting unions into marriages. Actually, there are very few significant predictors of the outcomes of cohabiting unions for women. In specification [1], the single most important predictor is having a child. Being a mother reduces the odds of converting the union into marriage by 55 percent.[14] This holds true also in specification [2], with an estimated lower impact of 51 percent. Interestingly, this effect does not emerge at all in the case of men. But the estimates in specification [2] identify religious attendance as the most powerful predictor of the transition from cohabitation to marriage among both sexes. Even an annual attendance at religious services still increases the odds of converting the union into a marriage by about 80 percent. Those who attend once a week are even some 4 times more likely to marry.

Table 10.6 The transition from cohabitation to marriage in Britain – logit regressions

	Men		Women	
	[1]	*[2]*	*[1]*	*[2]*
Working hours[a]				
Full-time (base)				
Part-time	.340*	.289	1.321	1.522
Type of contract[a]				
Permanent (base)				
Seasonal	.119**	.155*	.645	.414
Fixed-term	.559*	.544	1.009	1.214
Employment status[a]				
Employed (base)				
In education	.203**	.114**	.363*	.474
Unemployed	.585*	.494*	.434*	.746
OLF	.374	.284	1.105	.978
Own occupation[a]				
Self-employed	1.507	1.831*	.748	.498
Managerial	.812	.743	.733	.446
Professional	.950	.909	1.382	1.725
Non-manual skilled	1.056	1.082	1.047	1.095
Manual skilled	.977	1.331	1.324	1.287
Semi/unskilled (base)				
Age[a]				
Age	1.361	2.224**	1.296	1.295
Age squared	.994	.985**	.995	.995
Birth Cohort				
1960-64	2.333*	1.993	2.036*	1.541
1965-69	1.618	1.282	1.821*	1.780
1970-74	1.399	1.632	1.512	1.741
1975-83 (base)				
Educational Qualification[a]				
Higher and first degree	1.303	1.383	.708	.591
Vocational degree	1.167	1.159	.871	.968
A Level (or equivalent)	.973	1.028	.902	.956
GCSE/O Level (or equiv.)	1.029	1.069	1.144	1.329
Less than O Level (base)				
No Qualification	.609	.773	.859	1.343
Has a child[a]	.840	.934	.453***	.486***

Table 10.6 continued

	Men		Women	
	[1]	*[2]*	*[1]*	*[2]*
Attendance at religious service[a]				
Once a week		4.225**		3.730***
Once a month		5.547***		4.047***
Once a year		1.783**		1.801***
Never (base)				
Log Likelihood	-789	-470	-912	-522
Number of person wave observations	1826	1063	2244	1302
Number of events	301	197	335	202

Obtained from discrete-time competing risk transition model. The figures are odd ratios from logit regressions.

Notes
a   Variable is lagged by one period.
***   p < 0.01
**   p < 0.05
*   p < 0.10

In sum, the globalization process and its increased uncertainty seem to delay the entry into cohabitation for women, but they have no impact on such type of partnership formation for men. On the other hand, once cohabiting, women in part-time or temporary employment convert their unions into marriages at the same rate as women in full-time or permanent jobs do. But cohabiting men who are employed in non-standard and part-time jobs are less likely to marry their partners, a result that suggests that if the labor market position of men is characterized by instability, then this is at least partially transferred to their family life.

The transition to parenthood

Table 10.7 presents the results for a discrete-time transition model for entry into parenthood.[15] Again we compare the results from two specifications. In addition to the variables used in specification [1], specification [2] controls for marital status. Regardless of the specification, entry into fatherhood is clearly uncorrelated to the globalization process variables. But female part-timers are more likely to become mothers than full-timers are, suggesting the diffusion of part-time jobs among women and perhaps reflecting a labor supply adjustment of full-time working women who anticipate having a child (see also Liefbroer as well as Kurz *et al.*, this volume). The transition to motherhood is also heavily influenced by the woman's employment status before birth. According to the estimates of specification [2], women who are out of the labor force are about 2.1 times more likely to have their first child than women who are in employment. For those who are unemployed, the odds increase to 3.1. Conversely, women who are still in full-time education have a 72 percent lower probability of becoming mothers one year later. This may in part reflect an age effect, which disappears once we control for marital status. But it may also suggest that human capital investments are, to some degree, incompatible with motherhood. For men we do find the same negative relationship between the probability of becoming a father while being in full-time education but we cannot detect any significant effect of the other labor force states.

Table 10.7　　Entry into parenthood in Britain – logit regressions

	Men		Women	
	[1]	*[2]*	*[1]*	*[2]*
Working hours[a]				
Full-time (base)				
Part-time	.470	.563	1.961***	1.439**
Type of contract[a]				
Permanent (base)				
Seasonal	.702	.987	.466*	.657
Fixed-term	.815	.905	.823	.952
Employment status[a]				
Employed (base)				
In education	.152***	.190***	.166***	.278***
Unemployed	.685	1.281	3.109***	3.116***
OLF	.716	1.514	3.133***	2.135***
Own occupational class[a]				
Self-employed	1.088	1.035	.603	.567
Manager	1.084	.919	1.334	1.208
Professional	.761	.672*	1.809**	1.576*
Non-manual	.863	.845	1.411*	1.243
Manual	.859	.787	2.002*	1.687
Semi/unskilled (base)				
Age[a]				
Age	2.662***	1.208	1.869***	.884
Age squared	.984***	.996	.989***	1.002
Birth Cohort				
1960-64	.614	.484*	.798	.823
1965-69	.531*	.383*	.694	.816
1970-74	.602*	.483*	.739	.830
1975-83 (base)				

Table 10.7 continued

	Men		Women	
	[1]	*[2]*	*[1]*	*[2]*
Educational Qualification[a]				
Higher and first degree	.671	.595*	.527***	.508***
Vocational degree	.801	.679*	.814	.650**
A Level (or equivalent)	.768	.674	.634**	.506***
GCSE/O Level (or equiv.)	.909	.797	1.158	1.038
Less than O Level (base)				
No Qualification	.712	.571*	.978	.887
Living with parents		.011***		.002***
Own marital status[a]				
Never married		.100***		.171***
Married (base)				
Cohabiting		.264***		.345***
Other		.090***		.223***
Log Likelihood	-1179	-1022	-1393	-1229
Number of person wave observations	7095	7094	7783	7781
Number of events	311	311	383	383

Obtained from discrete-time transition model. The figures are odd ratios from logit regressions.

Notes
a   Variable is lagged by one period.
*** $p < 0.01$
** $p < 0.05$
* $p < 0.10$

For both men and women there is no substantial occupational gradient, with just professional men being less likely to become fathers and professional women being more likely to become mothers than their unskilled counterparts. These effects are significant at the 10 percent level only. But a social class effect does emerge through education, particularly for women. For example, women (men) with a university or higher degree are almost 50 (40) percent less likely to have a child than those with some qualification short of O level or GCSE. As already mentioned, the strong age effect found in specification [1] vanishes when marital status is included in the regressions, while birth cohort has an impact only for men but it is not precisely measured. For both men and women, entry into parenthood is most likely if they are married. Even those who are in cohabiting unions have 65 and 74 percent lower odds of becoming mothers and fathers, respectively.

In sum, the globalization process affects the transition to parenthood only for female part-timers who are more likely than full-timers to become mothers. But the indirect effect of the globalization process is potentially large. Indeed, as the analysis of partnership formation presented in the section "The transition to non-marital cohabitation and its evolution" revealed, young people in temporary and part-time employment stay single longer (particularly women) and tend to remain cohabiting instead of marrying (particularly men). At the same time, having the first child is still strongly related to marriage. A further postponement of parenthood through the impact of the globalization process is therefore likely to be observed.

CONCLUSIONS

In this study we investigated the impact of the globalization process on young people's transitions to the adult life course in Britain during the 1990s. Using longitudinal data from the first nine waves of the British Household Panel Survey, covering the period between 1991 and 1999, we analyzed three major transitions, that is, entry into the labor market (and entry into unemployment in particular), partnership formation (entry into cohabitation) along with the transition from cohabitation to marriage, and the transition to parenthood. We operationalized the notion of 'globalization process' by using temporary employment and number of hours of work, two crucial features of the labor supply in a flexible labor market. In addition, we analyzed the impact of such forms of employment in the context of other labor market influences on the transitions to adulthood, namely, employment status and occupation. *A priori* it might be expected that the globalization process adversely affect all of these transitions by generating an environment characterized by increasing uncertainty in the capital, labor and product markets and in social relations (see Mills and Blossfeld, this volume). But, on one hand, Britain has already experienced some of the (negative) effects of the globalization process in terms of increased levels of deregulation of the labor market, a rather limited upward mobility and increasing income inequality and poverty rates. On the other hand, the economic, social and institutional mechanisms enacted by a liberal welfare state - such as Britain - might have reinforced or compensated for the negative effects of the globalization process. Although several previous studies (e.g. Berrington, 2001; Cherlin *et al.*, 1995; Kiernan, 1992 and 1997a; Ermisch and Di Salvo, 1997; Ermisch, 1999; Ermisch and Francesconi, 2000a, 2001a and 2001b) had already analyzed transitions to adulthood from different demographic and socio-economic perspectives, none has yet revealed how the globalization process has affected these transitions. Our research therefore aimed at filling this gap.

Our principal findings are as follows. First, starting a career in a non-standard temporary job or as a self-employed person has become increasingly common in Britain of the 1990s. The workers in such forms of employment are however extremely heterogeneous, with some being more concentrated in part-time jobs and low-level occupations and others more in full-time jobs and professional occupations. Nonetheless, there is evidence that the early stages of young people's careers are marked by instability and high labor market turnover. We find, in fact, that young people in part-time jobs (particularly men) and in temporary employment are more likely to enter unemployment than their full-time permanent counterparts.

Second, the globalization process and its inherent uncertainty tend to delay the entry into cohabitation for women, but to have no impact on early partnership formation for men. However, once cohabiting, women in part-time or temporary jobs convert their unions into marriages at more or less the same rate as women in full-time or permanent jobs do. But cohabiting men who are employed in non-standard and part-time jobs are less likely to marry their partners, a result which suggests that the instability characterizing the position of men in the labor market is partially transferred to their family life. This may also be related to a male-breadwinner view of the relationship between career and family formation, whereby men are more likely to marry when they are steadily attached to the primary labor market.

Third, the globalization process directly and positively affects the transition to parenthood only for women in part-time employment. But the indirect effect of the globalization process is potentially large, because it works through its effects on the early stages of young people's career and family formation patterns. We find that having the first child is still critically related to marriage for both men and women. Now, because young people in temporary and part-time employment stay single longer and tend to live in cohabiting unions instead of marrying, the globalization process is likely to provide an additional source of postponement of parenthood.

NOTES

1   Acknowledgements: The data used in this paper were made available through the ESRC Data Archive. The data were originally collected by the ESRC Research Centre on Micro-social Change (now incorporated within the Institute for Social and Economic Research) at the University of Essex. Neither the original collectors of the data nor the Archive bear any responsibility for the analyses or interpretations presented here.

2   It is worth noticing that part-time employment in Britain is not a new phenomenon, particularly for women (see, among others, Blossfeld and Hakim, 1997; Burchell *et al.*, 1997). However, as suggested by Hakim (1998), part-time employment comprises a highly heterogeneous set of jobs, such as half-time and marginal jobs.

3   Böheim and Taylor (2000) find some evidence that unemployment has a severe penalty on subsequent job tenure. Individuals who enter a job from unemployment are three times more likely to be in temporary employment when re-entering the labor market. Moreover, about 20 percent of men and women who find a job after a spell of unemployment re-enter unemployment within twelve months. Gregg and Wadsworth (1999) show that only one-third of the job positions taken up by individuals after a spell out of work are full-time and permanent compared with nearly three-quarters of all jobs. One in three jobs involve a temporary contract, compared with just 7 percent of all positions, and entry wages are substantially below the average for all workers with a rising wage gap over time.

4   Using data from the BHPS, Ermisch (1997) estimates that a similar proportion of
    extra-marital first births is born within cohabiting unions. For a discussion of the
    factors associated with teenage fertility, see Kiernan (1997b).
5   Thus the north of Scotland is excluded.
6   Individuals who did not provide the relevant information to construct either the
    transition variables or the globalization variables or the other variables, and
    individuals who were proxy respondents are excluded from our analysis.
7   Part-time employment is defined as working less than 30 hours per week.
8   Of course, the exception is the transition to unemployment, because this analysis is
    performed on a sample of individuals who are in employment.
9   Information on attendance at religious services is only available in wave 1,3-5, 7, and
    9. The inclusion of this set of dummy variables leads to a large loss in sample size.
    We therefore report results for two different specifications, one that excludes and one
    that includes this set of dummy variables.
10 Naturally, the entry into parenthood is modeled using simple binomial logit
    regressions, that is, without any competing risk. Notice also that after having
    controlled for birth cohort in all regressions, we will be using age rather than
    duration.
11 As mentioned in the data and methods section, we do not include the employment
    status variables in estimating the transition into unemployment because we condition
    the sample on those who are in employment.
12 A similar observation applies to the case of the two transitions considered under (b).
13 Religious attendance may capture characteristics that are potentially correlated with
    personal moral values and habits and that would otherwise be unobserved. Ermisch
    and Francesconi (2000a and 2000b) find some impact of religious activity on
    partnership formation.
14 This finding is consistent with Ermisch and Francesconi's (2000a) results (their
    Table 2.6, p. 37) based on BHPS data. It is also consistent with Lelièvre's (1993)
    results (her Figure 7.7, p. 120) based on data from the 1989 General Household
    Survey.
15 As explained in the methods section, these estimates are not obtained from a
    competing risk model, because the only risk is that of having a child.

BIBLIOGRAPHY

Allison, P.D. (1982) 'Discrete-time Methods for the Analysis of Event Histories', in S.
    Leinhardt (ed.) *Sociological Methodology*, San Francisco: Jossey-Bass.
Arulampalam, W. (2000) *Is Unemployment Really Scarring?*, Mimeo: University of
    Warwick.
Bernardi, F. (2001) 'Globalization, recommodification and social inequality: changing
    patterns of early careers in Italy', GLOBALIFE Working Paper No. 7, Faculty of
    Sociology, University of Bielefeld.
Berrington, A. (2001) 'Transition to adulthood in Britain', in M. Corijn and E. Klijzing
    (eds) *Transitions to Adulthood in Europe*, Dordrecht: Kluwer Academic Publishers.
Berrington, A. and Diamond, I. (1995) 'First Partnership Formation Amongst the 1958
    British Birth Cohort: A Discrete Time Competing Risks Analysis', paper presented at
    the European Population Conference, Milan, September.

Berrington, A. and Diamond, I. (2000) 'Marriage or Cohabitation: A Competing Risks Analysis of First Partnership Formation Among the 1958 British Birth Cohort', *Journal of the Royal Statistical Society*, Series A, 163(2): 127-151.

Blossfeld, H.-P. (2002) 'Globalization, Social Inequality and the Role of Country-Specific Institutions', in P. Conceicao, M.V. Heitor and B.-A. Lundvall (eds) *Innovation, Competence Building and Social Cohesion in Europe: Towards a Learning Society*, Cheltenham/Lyme: Edward Elgar.

Blossfeld, H.-P. and Drobnič, S. (2001) *Careers of couples in contemporary societies*, Oxford: Oxford University Press.

Blossfeld, H.-P. and Hakim, C. (eds) (1997) *Between Equalization and Marginalization. Women Working Part-Time in Europe an the United States of America*, Oxford: Oxford University Press.

Böheim, R. and Ermisch, J. (2001) 'Partnership Dissolution in the UK – the Role of Economic Circumstances', *Oxford Bulletin of Economics and Statistics*, 63(2): 197-208.

Böheim, R. and Taylor, M. (2000) 'Unemployment duration and exit states in Britain', working paper 2000 –1, Institute for Social and Economic Research, University of Essex.

Booth, A.L. and Francesconi, M. (2001) 'Union Coverage for Non-standard Workers in Britain', unpublished paper, University of Essex.

Bumpass, L. (1990) 'What's Happening to the Family? Interactions between Demographic and Institutional Change', *Demography*, 27: 483-498.

Burchell, B., Dale, A. and Joshi, H. (1997) 'Part-time work among British women', in H.-P. Blossfeld and C. Hakim (eds) *Between Equalization and Marginalization. Women Working Part-Time in Europe an the United States of America*, Oxford: Oxford University Press.

Cherlin, A.J., Kiernan, K.E. and Chase-Lansdale, P.L. (1995) 'Parental Divorce in Childhood and Demographic Outcomes in Young Adulthood', *Demography*, 32(3): 299-318.

Deakin, S. and Reed, H. (2000) 'River Crossing or Cold Bath? Deregulation and Employment in Britain in the 1980s and 1990s', in G. Esping-Andersen and M. Regini (eds) *Why Deregulate Labor Markets?*, Oxford: Oxford University Press.

Dearden, L., Machin, S. and Reed, H. (1997) 'Intergenerational Mobility in Britain', *Economic Journal*, 107: 47-64.

Dex, S. and McCullogh, A. (1995) 'Flexible Employment in Britain: A Statistical Analysis', Research Discussion Series No. 15, Manchester: Equal Opportunity Commission.

Dickens, R. and Ellwood, D. (2001) 'Whither Poverty in Great Britain and the United States? The Determinants of Changing Poverty and Whether Work Will Work', Working Paper No. 8253, Cambridge MA: National Bureau of Economic Research.

Erikson, R. and Goldthorpe, J. H. (1992) *The constant flux: a study of class mobility in industrial societies*, Oxford: Clarendon Press.

Ermisch, J. (1997) 'Pre-marital Cohabitation, Childbearing and the Creation of One-parent Families', in C. Jonung and I. Persson (eds) *Economics of the Family*, London: Routledge.

Ermisch, J. (1999) 'Cohabitation and Childbearing Outside Marriage in Britain', paper presented at the Institute for Research on Poverty Conference on Non-marital Fertility, University of Wisconsin-Madison.

Ermisch, J. and Salvo, P. Di. (1997) 'The Economic Determinants of Young People's Household Formation', *Economica*, 64: 627-644.

Ermisch, J. and Francesconi, M. (2000a) 'Patterns of household and family formation', in R. Berthoud and J. Gershuny (eds) *Seven Years in the Lives of British Families. Evidence on the dynamics of social change from the British Household Panel Survey*, Bristol: Policy Press.

Ermisch, J. and Francesconi, M. (2000b) 'Cohabitation in Great Britain: Not for Long, but Here to Stay', *Journal of the Royal Statistical Society*, Series A, 163(2): 153-171.

Ermisch, J. and Francesconi, M. (2000c) 'The Increasing Complexity of Family Relationships: Lifetime Experience of Lone Motherhood and Stepfamilies in Great Britain', *European Journal of Population*, 16: 235-249.

Ermisch, J. and Francesconi, M. (2001a) *The Effects of Parents' Employment on Children's Lives*, London: Family Policy Study Centre for the Joseph Rowntree Foundation.

Ermisch, J. and Francesconi, M. (2001b) 'Family Matters: Impacts of Family Background on Educational Attainments', *Economica*, 68: 137-156.

Esping-Andersen, G. (1993) *Changing classes. Stratification and mobility in post-industrial societies*, London: Sage.

Esping-Andersen, G. (1999) *Social Foundations of Postindustrial Societies*, Oxford: Oxford University Press.

Friedberg, L. (1998) 'Did Unilateral Divorce Raise Divorce Rates? Evidence from Panel Data', *American Economic Review*, 88(3): 608-627.

Goldin, C. and Katz, L.F. (2000) 'The Power of the Pill: Oral Contraceptives and Women's Career and Marriage Decisions', Working Paper No. 7527, Cambridge MA: National Bureau of Economic Research.

Goldscheider, F. and Waite, L.J. (1991) *New Families, No Families?*, Berkeley: University of California Press.

Golsch, K. (2001) 'Transition to adulthood in Great Britain and the process of globalization', GLOBALIFE Working Paper No. 17, Faculty of Sociology, University of Bielefeld.

Gregg, P. and Wadsworth, J. (1996) 'More Work in Fewer Households', in J. Hills (ed.) *Income and Wealth: New Inequalities*, Cambridge: Cambridge University Press.

Gregg, P. and Wadsworth, J. (1999) 'Mind the Gap, Please: The Changing Nature of Entry Jobs in Britain', *Economica*, 67: 499-524.

Hakim, C. (1998) *Social Change and Innovation in the Labor Market*, Oxford: Oxford University Press.

Haskey, J. and Kiernan, K.E. (1989) 'Cohabitation in Great Britain: Characteristics and Estimated Numbers of Cohabiting Partners', *Population Trends*, 58: 23-32.

Heath, A. and Cheung, S. Y. (1998) 'Education and Occupation in Britain', in Y. Shavit and W. Müller (eds) *From School to Work: A Comparative Study of Educational Qualifications and Occupational Destinations*, Oxford: Clarendon Press.

Heckman, J.J. (1993) 'What Has Been Learned About Labor Supply in the Past Twenty Years?', *American Economic Review Papers and Proceedings*, 83(2), 116-121.

Hotz, V.J., Klerman, J.A. and Willis, R.J. (1997) 'The Economics of Fertility in Developed Countries', in M.R. Rosenzweig and O.Stark (eds) *Handbook of Population and Family Economics*, Amsterdam: Elsevier Science.

Jenkins, S.P. (1995) 'Easy Estimation Methods for Discrete Time Duration Models', *Oxford Bulletin of Economics and Statistics*, 57: 129-138.

Jenkins, S.P. (2000) 'Trends in the UK income distribution', in R. Hauser and I. Becker (eds) *The Personal Distribution of Income in an International Perspective*, Berlin: Springer Verlag.

Jenkins, S.P. and Rigg, J.A. (2001) 'The Dynamics of Poverty in Britain: Routes In and Out of Poverty', unpublished paper, University of Essex.

Kiernan, K. E. (1992) 'The Impact of Family Disruption in Childhood on Transitions Made in Young Adult Life', *Population Studies*, 46: 213-234.

Kiernan, K.E. (1997a) 'Becoming a young parent: a longitudinal study of associated factors', *British Journal of Sociology*, 48(3): 406-428.

Kiernan, K.E. (1997b) 'The Legacy of Parental Divorce: Social, Economic and Demographic Experiences in Adulthood', CASEpaper 1, London School of Economics.

Kiernan, K.E. (1999) 'Cohabitation in Western Europe', *Population Trends*, 96: 25-32.

Kohler, H.-P. (1997) 'Learning in Social Networks and Contraceptive Use', *Demography*, 34(3): 369-383.

Lancaster, T. (1990) *The Econometric Analysis of Transition Data*, Cambridge: Cambridge University Press.

Lelièvre, E. (1993) 'Extra-marital Births Occurring in Cohabiting Unions', in M. Ní Bhrolcháin (ed.) *New Perspective on Fertility in Britain*, London: The Stationery Office.

Lesthaeghe, R. (1983) 'A Century of Demographic and Cultural Change in Western Europe: An Exploration of Underlying Dimensions', *Population and Development Review*, 9: 411-435.

Lillard, L.A., Brien, M.J. and Waite, L.J. (1995) 'Pre-marital Cohabitation and Subsequent Marital Dissolution: A Matter of Self-Selection?', *Demography*, 32: 437-458.

Lindley, R. (1996) 'The School-to-Work Transition in the United Kingdom', *International Labor Review*, 135(2): 159-180.

Machin, S. (1999) 'Wage Inequality in the 70s, 80s and 90s', in P. Gregg and J. Wadsworth (eds) *The State of Working Britain*, Manchester, UK: Manchester University Press.

Machin, S. (2000) 'Union Decline in Britain', *British Journal of Industrial Relations*, 38(4): 631-645.

McVicar, D. and Rice, P. (2001) 'Participation in further education in England and Wales: an analysis of post-war trends', *Oxford Economic Papers*, 53(1): 67-93.

Michael, R.T. (1988) 'Why Did the U.S. Divorce Rate Double Within a Decade?', *Research in Population Economics*, 6: 367-399.

Narendranathan, W. and Stewart, M. (1993) 'Modelling the Probability of Leaving Unemployment: Competing Risks Models with Flexible Baseline Hazards', *Applied Statistics*, 42: 63-83.

Peters, E.H. (1986) 'Marriage and Divorce: Informational Constraints and Private Conrtacting', *American Economic Review*, 76(3): 437-454.

Scherer, S. (2001) 'Early Career Patterns: A Comparison of Great Britain and West Germany', *European Sociological Review*, 17 (2): 119-144.

Simó, C., Golsch, K. and Steinhage, N. (2002) 'Increasing uncertainty in the Spanish labor market and entry into parenthood', *GENUS*, LVIII: 77-119.

Sommer, T., Klijzing, E. and Mills, M. (2000) 'Partnership Formation in a Globalizing World: The Impact of Uncertainty in East and West Germany', GLOBALIFE Working Paper No. 9, Faculty of Sociology, University of Bielefeld.

Steinmann, S. (1998/1999) 'The vocational Education and Training System in England and Wales', *International Journal of Sociology*, 28(4): 29-56.

Taylor, M.P. (2000) 'Work, non-work, jobs and job mobility', in R. Berthoud and J. Gershuny (eds) *Seven Years in the Lives of British Families. Evidence on the dynamics of social change from the British Household Panel Survey*, Bristol: Policy Press.

Thomson, E. (1997) 'Couple Childbearing Desires, Intentions, and Births', *Demography*, 34(3): 343-354.

11 The transition to adulthood in Canada

The impact of irregular work shifts in a 24-hour economy[1]

Melinda Mills

INTRODUCTION

In the last two decades, the rhetoric of globalization has emerged, a process characterized by shifts in competition, deregulation and technological change (Mills and Blossfeld, this volume). The underlying assumption is that the globalization process generates the mobility of capital which in turn necessitates increased international competition for nations, industries and firms. Competition means increasingly looking to cost advantages that incorporate not only local, regional and national, but also global concerns. For workers, the result is often flexible or uncertain employment relations (Standing, 1997). Firms react by implementing various measures of labor market flexibility (e.g., numerical, outsourcing, functional, wage, temporal) which vary depending on the institutional context.

Other contributions to this volume (e.g., Bernardi and Nazio; Kurz *et al.*) examine flexibility in the form of temporary versus permanent contracts, a response characteristic of the more rigid and regulated European labor markets. The emphasis on job security and permanence in many European countries is virtually extraneous to the deregulated North American environment which is built on the premises of flexibility, market economic relations and a non-interventionist state (Mayer, 2001). Here the elasticity of the labor market often takes the form of 'temporal' (Regini, 2000) or 'internal numerical' flexibility (Bruhnes, 1989). This is the ability to adjust the amount of hours and 'when' labor is required in accordance to cyclical or seasonal demands, rather than the number of people employed or the degree of stability of their employment (Regini, 2000). Since it is this type of flexibility that is pertinent to the Canadian case, the impact of irregular work shifts on the transition to adulthood is examined.

To ignore the rise in this type of flexibility would be to exclude one of the fastest growing groups of workers in North America. Between 1985 and 1997, the number of workers in the United States holding irregular schedules doubled (Beers, 2000). In fact, in the early 1990s, only 31.5 percent of employed Americans worked a 'standard' schedule, defined as employed during the daytime, 5 days a week, Monday to Friday, 35-40 hours a week (Presser, 1995). Canada has witnessed a similar transformation with a 17 percent increase in workers with irregular work schedules from 1991 to 1995, which in 1995 represented 33 percent of the Canadian labor force (Johnson, 1997). The large proportion of workers engaged in irregular work schedules has led researchers to contemplate the consequences for other domains of the life course. Previous research concerning the impact of irregular work schedules on family life has focused on dual-earners, split-shift couples, child care (e.g., Presser, 1986; 1998; Marshall, 1998), and marital stability, generally within the context of the United States (e.g., Weiss and Liss, 1988; White and Keith, 1990). Less is known, however, about how irregular shifts impact partnership formation and family-building during the transition to adulthood, whether irregular shifts are taken for voluntary or involuntary reasons, and patterns in countries beyond the United States.

The primary goal of this chapter, therefore, is to examine who works irregular work shifts, why they do so and if these shifts have impacted the transition to partnership and parenthood in Canada in the 1990s. The transition to adulthood is thus defined by labor market entry, and transition to first partnership and parenthood. For several reasons, only youth (broadly defined as those aged 16 to 35) were chosen. First, previous research has focused exclusively on the impact of irregular work schedules at the phase of post-family formation, leaving little known about youth, singles or family formation itself. Second, recent shifts in society are experienced more directly by new labor market entrants, such as young adults, who are unprotected by seniority or experience. Furthermore, changes that first appear in the youth labor market may indicate tendencies that will soon work their way through the entire age structure (Myles *et al.*, 1993). Finally, turbulence at a formative life course phase where individuals must make long-term binding decisions for the future may produce uncertainty and postponement, having ramifications for the entire life course and thus demographic trends in general.

This chapter introduces a type of flexibility more unique to the North American context and contributes to several understudied areas in this topic by asking the following research questions. First, why the inundation of irregular work schedules in Canada? Second, what are the implications of this type of work for inequality? In other words, are certain groups such as students, women, lower-skilled or educated workers, members of visible minorities or those in the private sector more prone to this type of work? Third, how do irregular schedules impact youth who are in the midst of making long-term binding life course decisions? The answer to this question depends to a major extent on *why* youth work in these jobs. Hence, a fourth question asks, do youth demand these jobs to combine labor market careers with other activities such as education, or are they forced to take them for involuntary reasons? In other words, do these shifts meet a need for individual-level flexibility or generate uncertainty in the early life course? Although the particular type of flexibility that is studied differs from others within this volume for contextual reasons, the impact of flexibility and uncertainty on the transition to adulthood is unquestionably comparable.

Irregular work shifts are defined first, followed in the section 'Theoretical Perspectives' by a theoretical exploration of the underlying macro-level mechanisms for the upsurge in this type of work and the importance of the Canadian context. This is complemented by an individual-level theory that focuses not only on how irregular shifts may generate uncertainty, but asks if they may also answer demands for flexibility. This is followed in the section 'Data and Methods' by a description of the data, methods and models. Analyses presented in the section 'Results' show the odds of engaging in different types of work shifts at labor market entry, whether they are voluntary, and their impact on entry into first partnership (cohabitation or marriage) and parenthood, while controlling for relevant explanatory factors. The chapter concludes with a critical discussion of the repercussions of this general trend toward irregular work.

IRREGULAR WORK SHIFTS

Following Presser and Cox (1997), Table 11.1 provides a description of the work shift measures used in this study. A regular work schedule is defined as a fixed daytime shift, with the remaining shifts being irregular.[2] Irregular work shifts differ from flextime, which refers to workers who personally set the time they begin and end within a few hours of their core schedule. The vital distinction is that irregular work schedules are often employer defined and not individually regulated. As Presser (1998: 40) asserts: 'non-standard work schedules are set by employers to meet their needs, not those of their employees.'

Table 11.1   Work shift measures

Type of work schedule	Detailed definition
Fixed daytime shift	Roughly 9am to 5pm
Fixed afternoon / evening shift	3-4pm for a few hours or until midnight
Graveyard shift	Midnight to roughly 8am
Rotating shift	Combination of two or more of the above shifts
Split shift, on call, irregular	Split, precarious or irregular combination of shifts, as determined by the employer

THEORETICAL PERSPECTIVES

The emergence of irregular shifts: macro-level mechanisms

A satisfying theoretical framework to understand the emergence of irregular work shifts and how they impact the early life course is one that accounts for macro-level changes, the institutional context, and micro-level responses in behavior. Although inferring direct causation is difficult, potential mechanisms that have contributed to the upsurge in irregular work shifts can be summarized under several themes: entry of women into the labor market, increased demand for leisure and personal services, population aging, and, under the umbrella of globalization, new technologies, competition and subsequent deregulation and restructuring (Mills and Blossfeld, this volume).

First, the growth of irregular shifts is strongly related to changes in labor supply via the influx of women into the labor market. Whereas men are considered as the breadwinners and women as primary caregivers and part-time workers in some countries (e.g., Spain, the Netherlands), Canadian women are perceived primarily as workers and experience a greater degree of gender sameness (O'Connor *et al.*, 1999). Since the dual-earner family is the prominent family form in Canada, the implication for work schedules is clear – as more and more women are employed during the day, the demand for evening and weekend services increases. The shopping and household maintenance that was formerly the domain of housewives becomes the second work day for women and their partners. This is associated with an overall increased consumer demand for leisure and personal services which produces a 'self-servicing' economy where material household commodities are increasingly purchased. For instance, families outsource household duties which translates into more jobs in personal services such as dining, shopping and entertainment, all of which largely consist of irregular work hours. However, women do not only use these services, they are also more likely to be employed within them since they bestow flexibility to combine work and family careers. Most individuals need to share household and child care responsibilities with their partner or other family members, with women taking alternative work schedules to accommodate others (Presser, 1986; 1995). Previous studies have found that women, and specifically mothers, are more likely to hold irregular shifts such as night schedules (Hamermesh, 1996). This theory leads to the first research hypothesis, a *gender hypothesis* arguing that women will be over-represented in irregular work shifts. Since this study focuses only on youth where the majority are single, it is interesting to test whether women are more likely to work irregular shifts before they enter partnerships and parenthood or whether this pattern arises only after family formation.

The second impetus for the growth in irregular schedules is the rise of the service sector, which brings 'bad' types of unskilled service jobs (Tilly, 1996). By 1991, services accounted for almost 65 percent of Canadian business sector employment, with the fastest increases taking place in the hotel and restaurant industry, community and personal services, real estate, business, finance and insurance (Gera and Massé, 1996: 3). Although the following results are shown by occupation and not industry for reasons of brevity, analysis by industry supported previous findings (e.g., Beers, 2000; Marshall, 1998; Presser, 1998) that irregular shifts are more concentrated in sectors that provide round-the-clock services and lower in those which dictate a fixed begin and end time (e.g., teachers, construction workers) or have rigid safety regulations (e.g., manufacturing, mining). These 24-hour sectors include emergency and protective services but also workers employed in eating and drinking establishments, entertainment, convenience services (e.g., banks, gas stations, retail outlets), transportation and hospitals.

Within the service sector there is a polarization between 'good' and 'bad' jobs (Lowe and Krahn, 2000; Tilly, 1996), with the bad jobs often concentrated in the two lower-tier service industries of retail trade and other consumer services (Krahn, 1991). Relatively 'good' service jobs ask for higher skills, provide higher wages and employer-sponsored benefits (e.g., pension, health and dental plans, leave) and better hours, whereas the bad 'McJobs' have lower skill demands and equally low wages, prestige, benefits and future prospects (Akyeampong, 1997). In Canada, the service industry has the lowest level of unionization or protection from collective agreements, is largely part-time and relies on student labor (Krahn, 1991). For this reason, a large number of irregular shifts are likely to be these 'bad' jobs that require semi- or unskilled workers (Beers, 2000; Presser and Cox, 1997). Conversely, with the aging population's necessity for round-the-clock medical services, health or social service workers are also required. These jobs are relatively 'good' service jobs frequently offering a 'rotating shift' and – since many are in the public sector – more protection for the worker. Although a rotating shift differs from consistent regular daytime work, it combines different types of shifts and is often scheduled in advance providing the worker with more certainty in daily planning. In other words, not all service jobs and irregular shifts are necessarily 'bad' jobs.

This leads to two hypotheses. First, the *type of shift hypothesis* argues that due to their concentration in the 'good' service sectors, workers with rotating shifts will have relatively 'good' jobs and therefore fare better than those in other types of irregular shifts. Second, the *occupational class hypothesis* proposes that since the majority of service jobs with irregular shifts require low levels of skill, there will be a higher probability that workers in irregular shifts are in semi- and unskilled occupations, particularly manual ones. A compounding factor is that at this 'stop-gap' stage in their labor market career, young adults are already more likely to work in unskilled entry-level occupations within the service industry (Myles *et al.*, 1993). The reason for this shift to a service society has been extensively studied in the post-industrial society literature (e.g., Esping-Andersen, 1993). The adverse impact of technological changes on low-skilled workers is a leading theme within this field, with the central argument that technological advances have transformed the nature and organization of production, hence the shift from an industrial to post-industrial society. Here, technology contributes to the transfer in entry level jobs away from the traditional sectors of primary, manufacturing and construction towards the service sector.

However, new technologies unique to the globalization process may impact different types of workers in distinct ways. Information communication technologies (ICT) such as computers, faxes and the internet, have likewise radically altered the organization of work. For irregular work shifts, ICT means that the worker is able to be on call or reachable 24 hours a day. This, combined with multinational corporations, increases the demand that branch offices operate at the same time as corporate headquarters (Presser, 1998). The technology characteristic of globalization thus adds a twist to the post-industrial society thesis which assumes that technology impacts lower skilled workers only. Although the previous *occupational class hypothesis* is expected to hold, an additional sub-hypothesis is in order. This is the notion that the ICT characteristic of globalization begins to influence classes that were previously shielded. This leads to the expectation that higher-level clerical and managerial staff are increasingly prone to work irregular shifts, albeit for different reasons than their lower-skilled counterparts, a finding already confirmed in the United States (Hamermesh, 1999).

A final reason for the rise in irregular shifts can be attributed to the globalization of markets and intensification of international market competition which has resulted in the sentiment that economies must grasp the ideologies of liberalization, privatization, and deregulation (Cole, 1998). At the core of this discourse is the threat of capital mobility and subsequent focus on efficiency to increase competitiveness (Smith, 1994). As O'Connor *et al.* (1999: 220) summarize:

> 'Fiscally restrictive policies are often justified by reference to globalization, in particular the threat posed to employment by the increasing competitiveness of the globalized economy and globalized financial markets. The former was linked to the importance of attracting foreign direct investment as well as competing in international markets. There was political and business pressure to 'harmonize' programs with other countries and to increase labor market flexibility, for example in Canada vis-à-vis the United States.'

In Canada, as in many other industrialized nations, the focus is on the notion that the government should operate as a private business and introduce labor market flexibility measures following its southern neighbor (e.g., Rugmann, 2001). As the Canadian state withdraws from its traditional function in the marketplace due to mounting pressure to decrease the provision of public services and be more competitive in the global market, the result is increased labor market flexibility, wage inequality and a decline in working conditions, in which irregular schedules play a major part (Baker and Tippin, 1999). This change in rhetoric to deregulation and shifting public services to the private sector results in the effective sanctioning of these types of non-standard or flexible jobs. The consequence is that the entrepreneurial state shifts the risk or onus of security and responsibility to the shoulders of the individual worker.

The Canadian context

It is not macro-level change in itself that is important when examining the impacts of globalization on the transition to adulthood, rather how they are 'institutionally filtered' (Esping-Andersen, 1993). Pertinent filters consist of the education system, structure of the labor market and economy, welfare regime and related family policies.

The education system is central to understanding labor market entry processes. The Canadian system falls under 'organizational space', where education is general in character with specific occupational skills learned on-the-job (Shavit and Müller, 1998). As opposed to countries with a dual vocational system such as Germany, education in Canada is not as closely tied to job requirements. Furthermore, it is an unstratified system (Allmendinger, 1989) giving all children the opportunity to attend school which may lead to post-secondary education, not tracking them into a certain academic or vocational stream at a young age. However, students in the tracked system who are enrolled in vocational and apprenticeship programs early are much better prepared to enter the work force and less likely to go through the intense mobility and protracted transition to find a suitable and permanent job often characteristic of early Canadian labor market experiences (Myles *et al.*, 1993). The longer search process at the beginning of the labor market career due to the general, unstratified education system leaves youth more likely to take less favorable positions, such as those with irregular hours as a stop-gap job until they find a better job match.

In the 1990s, due to the government's response to the globalization rhetoric discussed previously, Canadian educational institutions experienced a cut in transfer payments, spurring an extraordinary rise in post-secondary tuition fees. In fact, between 1989-90 and 1998-99 tuition fees doubled (Zhao, 2000). Canadian parents, and in many cases, students themselves must pay for their own post-secondary education. The result is that students often take out personal student loans to finance their studies, which in 1990 for instance was the case for around 50 percent of University students. These students later shouldered high debt burdens (Zhao, 2000). Canadian youth are thus left in the paradoxical situation of needing to obtain more skills in order to secure a good job in the globalized knowledge-based economy, but being unable to pay for these skills. To avoid excessive loans, an increasingly common option is to combine school and work. As Akyeampong (1997: 49) argues for the Canadian case: 'the need to balance work and school plays a crucial role in the decisions of young students'. The labor force participation rate for full-time students rose from 29 percent in 1976 to around 40 percent in the 1990s (Statistics Canada, 2001). The result is a supply of young students into the labor market who must work and require flexible hours that can be combined with their studies. For this reason, it is necessary to examine labor market entry separately for students and non-students.

Educational enrollment may also be a reaction to a poor economic cycle and avoidance of unemployment. Labor market conditions for youth deteriorated during the early to mid-1990s when there was an economic recession similar to the one that occurred in the early 1980s. In 1994, strong job growth began, followed by a tough labor market year in 1995 and better conditions from 1996 on. During both recessions, the unemployment rate for 15-24 year olds rose to around 20 percent (Lowe and Krahn, 2000: 2; see also Klijzing, this volume). The response of many young adults to high unemployment was opting for more education, which meant that by the end of the 1980s Canada had the largest proportion of young adults attending University of any major OECD nation (Lowe and Krahn, 2000). In 1995, 46.4 percent of men and 48.4 percent of women in the labor force had a post-secondary certificate, diploma or university degree (OECD, 1998). This leads to an *economic cycle hypothesis* where it is the expectation that more youth will be working irregular shifts for involuntary reasons during the difficult economic years when the labor market is tight.

The distinct history and character of industrial relations, collective bargaining, and protective legislation are also vital to understanding youth's ability to choose the type of work at labor market entry. Labor market policies in Canada have tended to have a history of being passive, with measures such as unemployment insurance, as opposed to more active labor market training programs (Van den Berg *et al.*, 1997). Compared to many of the European countries examined in this volume, labor legislation in Canada has resulted in lower conditions of job security, easier hiring and firing and higher overall flexibility of the labor market. Canadian unions have a weak and long-standing history of disunity and were often American dominated (Van den Berg *et al.*, 1997). A comparatively deregulated labor market means the ability to lay-off workers, demand irregular schedules, give lower levels of compensation and less protection or recourse to workers than the more regulated European labor markets. This has resulted in a surge in various forms of non-standard work, including not only irregular schedules but also part-time and temporary jobs (Krahn, 1991).

Another ingredient in the ability to make a smooth transition to adulthood is the safety-net provided by the welfare state. The Canadian welfare state is similar to the United States in that it is a comparatively low spender relying on means-tested (residual) forms of welfare and private insurance (Myles, 1996). However, what differentiates it from the United States is its history of universal citizenship programs, family allowances, old-age pensions, guaranteed income supplements and health insurance (Myles, 1996). The duration and levels of unemployment insurance have been well above the United States since 1971 and also cover sickness, parental and maternity benefits. In fact, the 'liberal' welfare state of Canada actually spends a larger share of GDP (2.46 percent) on unemployment compensation than the average of all of the 18 OECD countries (2.37), and is clearly above American levels (0.76) (Myles, 1996: 126). However, the 1990s brought large changes to the eligibility requirements, level and vision of unemployment insurance, which was recently renamed 'Employment' as opposed to 'Unemployment' Insurance (Guest, 1997). The program provides short-term protection for workers who have recently held a job and are available for work. For unemployed youth without any insurance coverage (i.e., never held a job), there are various forms of social assistance. From 1966 to 1995, the Canadian Assistance Plan provided a guaranteed safety net for all persons. In 1995, this was replaced by the Canadian Health and Social Transfer program, which provided a (substantially reduced) grant to provinces to run their own welfare programs. Towards the end of the 1990s, the move to provincially-run programs led nearly all provinces, most run by conservative administrations, to significantly reduce benefits and turn to American-style 'workfare' programs and a negative income tax-style income-tested benefit system (O'Connor *et al.*, 1999). Although entitlements have weakened in the late 1990s, Canadian youth still have a relatively higher safety net than their American or even some European counterparts.

The ability to make the transition to parenthood in a dual-earner environment is also influenced by welfare state policies. Although the Canadian system offers more public support for child care than the United States, there are no citizenship entitlements to income support for caregivers. Rather, it was in the form of Employment Insurance for workers who get a short paid maternity and parental leave. Except for this, care giving remains largely unpaid and forces individuals to rely on private arrangements (O'Connor *et al.*, 1999).

The province is an important welfare, legislative and cultural unit in Canada, with provinces often developing along different paths. Quebec has a particularly unique historical trajectory which delayed industrialization and urbanization. This was principally due to political conservatism and the power of the Catholic church in government affairs and the education system. After the 1960 election of a liberal government, however, Quebec began to experience what has been become known as the 'Quiet Revolution'. The province was radically transformed from a rural-Catholic to modern urban industrial state, with the most significant effects in the area of values. There was a massive catching-up towards individualism and a backlash against the church accompanied by a resistance against marriage and religion (McRoberts, 1993). For this reason, the *shock hypothesis* is introduced. Due to radical political transformations in Quebec, it is the expectation there will be a rejection of traditional institutions (e.g., marriage, religion) accompanied by a distinct change in life course behavior. In the transition to adulthood, this includes high-rates of cohabitation compared to the other regions. This backlash against harsh institutional constraints is comparable to the sharp rise cohabitation and non-marital births experienced in Eastern European countries after the fall of the iron curtain (see Katus *et al.*, this volume).

Micro-level behavioral responses

Irregular work schedules are not an impetuous macro-level force merely imposed upon individuals. Youth are able to purposively select and shape their own biographies, depending on their facility or power to act, constraints within a finite range of outcomes, and bounded knowledge. They make decisions in response to institutional rules and norms that delimit action that is appropriate to their context and within external constraints which attach distinct consequences to particular courses of action. Yet in the age of globalization, youth are forced to make long-term binding life course decisions under conditions of uncertainty unique to their generation.

Friedman *et al.*'s (1994) 'uncertainty reduction theory' can aid us to understand the mechanisms of decision-making under conditions of uncertainty. Whereas an individual can attach probabilities to alternative consequences and knows (or believes to know) the odds of failure in risk calculation, this is not the case in decision-making under conditions of uncertainty. Since less uncertain states are still preferred to uncertain ones, actors search for ways to reduce uncertainty. This may be done by: 1) gathering information that transfers the problem of uncertainty to one of risk by turning it into a local choice problem, or, 2) pursing 'global strategies' to reduce uncertainty in entire paths of future courses of action. The desire to reduce uncertainty 'impels actors to bind themselves to courses of action that are largely independent of future states of the world' (Friedman *et al.*, 1994: 382). From this we can construct a *flexible partnership hypothesis* which supposes that to reduce uncertainty, youth are more likely to bind themselves to a more flexible union of cohabitation that is largely independent of the future, as opposed to marriage (Mills, 2000; Wu, 2000). Moreover, if they work an irregular schedule with flexible hours, they will require an equally flexible relationship.

Youth make divergent life course decisions depending on their facility to act and constraining or enabling attributes. Friedman *et al.* (1994) argue that the principal global strategies in the life course are stable careers, marriage and children. Those with better prospects for a stable and successful labor market career often use this strategy to reduce uncertainty. This calls for a *human capital hypothesis*, with human capital measured by education, occupational standing, labor force experience, age, sex and visible minority status. The expectation is that youth with higher education and occupational prospects will focus on these life course options, thereby postponing entry into parenthood and any type of partnership, particularly marriage. Conversely, those with lower prospects in the labor market may use entry into a partnership, particularly the more binding relationship of marriage, and parenthood as an effective means to reduce uncertainty. Since higher human capital translates into more bargaining power in the labor market, an added anticipation is that those with higher education and occupational standing have a lower risk of working an irregular schedule. In a comparison of evening and weekend work in the United States and Germany, Hamermesh (1996) showed that those with little human capital, such as minorities in the U.S. and foreign-born Germans, were disproportionately represented in these shifts. Minority status is particularly important in the Canadian context, considering that the proportion of visible minorities in the population rose to 17.7 percent in 2001 and that there is little known about their work schedules (Jamal and Badawi, 1995).

For the purpose of this study, uncertainty is characterized both theoretically and empirically in three ways: economic, employment relation, and social integration. First, adapting the work of Bernardi (2000), economic uncertainty is operationalized by the caliber of precariousness of an individual's: a) employment and educational enrollment status (e.g., annual labor force status, student status), and, among the employed, b) occupational class; with the addition of, c) whether they receive pension benefits, and, d) their work hours (full-time or part-time).[3] A further economic indicator for entry into parenthood is whether they have support from a partner, with higher certainty represented by a marital union followed by common-law, separated/divorced/widowed to never in a union respectively. The *economic uncertainty hypothesis* supposes that youth are in a more uncertain position if they are students, not employed year-round, working in an economically precarious position (part-time, no pension benefits, lower occupational class) and, for entry into parenthood, are single.[4] The first expectation is that irregular shifts are concentrated in positions that have high economic uncertainty. Higher uncertainty then translates into the inability to make definitive life course decisions, with the consequence of a lower risk of entry into long-term binding partnerships such as marriage and entry into parenthood.

A second dimension is employment relationship uncertainty, measured here by whether dependent workers are in public or private sector employment (Bernardi, 2000). The sector of employment is a key factor in determining how individuals are sheltered from risk, with those employed in the public sector 'relatively isolated from the operation of market forces' (Esping-Andersen, 1993). Employment in the public sector is farther removed from the impetus of productivity and profitability of global competition. The *employment relation uncertainty hypothesis* presumes that private sector workers have less secure employment conditions than public workers. Although employment in the public sector is no longer the bastion of security in the 1990s as it had been previously, due to higher worker protection (e.g., unionization, collective agreements), it is a relatively secure employment option in Canada. Hence, we can expect that the introduction of labor market flexibility measures in the form of irregular work shifts will impact the private sector to a larger extent resulting in a higher probability of irregular work shifts.

A final measure is social integration uncertainty (Hamermesh, 1999), defined here as the mismatch with structured and unstructured social relations that arise as a result of irregular schedules. Schedules are measured by comparing 1) split/irregular/on call, 2) rotating shift, and 3) graveyard/evening against the more certain schedule of 4) regular daytime shift. A plethora of studies have shown substantial social consequences of irregular work schedules for the individual and family (e.g., Weiss and Liss, 1988). When working irregular shifts, the individual is at risk of becoming out of sync with the rhythms of society. It is difficult to join or use structured associations such as day care, clubs, community groups and schools that require either fixed time commitments or are available only during regular day shifts (Presser, 1995). When people engage in work at different times of the day, the opportunities for social interaction are also greatly reduced. Unstructured social relations may become strained as it becomes more difficult to maintain relationships with friends, relatives and partners (Jamal and Badawi, 1995; Johnson, 1997). At the individual level, persons may experience biological (sleep disturbance, digestion) or psychological (stress, fatigue, depression, irascibility) problems.

The *social integration hypothesis* proposes that compared to those working regular day shifts, irregular shift workers will experience more problems in entering partnerships and parenthood due to their mismatch with structured and unstructured associations. First, due to the conflict with structured associations that they create, such as with child care, it is the expectation that these shifts inhibit the transition to parenthood. Child care and domestic duties play a persistent role in scheduling choices, particularly for women, making unpredictable work schedules unattractive to combine with motherhood. Child care is rarely available during irregular hours (by virtue of the name 'daycare') or on an ad hoc, last-minute basis. Since there are no previous studies of the impact of irregular schedules on entry into parenthood and fertility in general, this study enters theoretically open ground. As Presser (1998: 46) recently noted: 'As for the issue of work schedules and fertility behavior, there have been no studies to date on this, in the United States or elsewhere.' Second, since irregular shifts inhibit unstructured social interaction, they will hinder the capacity to find a partner and maintain a relationship, thus resulting in a lower probability of partnerships. As hypothesized previously, if individuals do enter a union, it is more likely to be a cohabiting one due to its more flexible nature in comparison to marriage (Mills, 2000).

The focus on the generation of uncertainty (a term laden with negative connotations) partially ignores the fact that we are dealing with purposive or rational actors, some of whom may have chosen to work irregular work shifts. A more balanced argument, therefore, does not take the growth of uncertainty for granted. Individuals are not only pawns of labor market flexibility, but purposive actors that may demand it. This is particularly the case for certain groups such as youth, students and women, who are forced to combine employment with other life course careers. Although the exploration of who holds irregular shifts is an important topic in itself, perhaps a more discerning question is whether individuals are voluntarily or involuntarily in these positions. In this study, reasons for working involuntary shifts are: 'requirement of the job', 'no choice' and 'could only find this type of work'. Voluntary reasons are: 'own illness or disability', 'caring for own children', 'caring for elder relative(s)', 'other personal or family responsibilities', 'going to school' and 'to earn more money'. The *involuntary worker hypothesis* asserts that certain groups – older individuals, men, part-time workers and for students, those who are enrolled full-time – are more likely to work irregular shifts for involuntary reasons. Hence, certain younger individuals, women, part-time workers and part-time students are assumed to have different motivations for holding irregular schedules, such as using them to combine life course careers. If workers report that they are involuntarily forced into these irregular shifts, we can indeed hypothesize that uncertainty may be generated in their lives. However, if they voluntarily desire an irregular work shift to fit their own flexible goals such as combining education or fertility with employment, we must rethink irregular schedules and flexibility as solely in negative terms.

DATA AND METHODS

The analysis uses the first panel of the Survey of Labour and Income Dynamics (SLID), which covers the six-year period from 1993 to 1998. The survey includes men and women aged 16 and over living in the ten provinces, excluding those who are residents of institutions, living on Native Reserves or full-time members of the Canadian Armed Forces living in barracks. The entire sample contains approximately 15,000 households with 31,000 individuals (Statistics Canada, 1997). The sample size was further reduced to include only youth aged 16 to 35 and due to missing values and variable constraints.

Using event history techniques (Blossfeld and Rohwer, 1995), several models are estimated. To accommodate time-varying covariates, the sample includes those who entered their first job, partnership or parenthood from 1993 to 1998. Although temporal information on retrospective job histories is available, only current job characteristics from 1993 to 1998 were collected. With the exception of the analysis of entry into the labor market, lagged endogenous variables are used to explicitly analyze changes over time. Youth had to have had at least one job that lasted 3 months or longer, where the primary work was nonagricultural. If there is more than one work schedule in the reference year, the information pertains to the most recent schedule. A job is defined as the period during which a worker is continuously attached to an employer (i.e., may be either working or absent, but expects to resume work).

The analysis is divided into three distinct aspects of the transition to adulthood, namely, entry into: the labor market, first partnership and parenthood. The first multinomial logistic regression model contains the type of work shift at labor market entry as the dependent variable, testing selected hypotheses discussed previously. Due to the fact that it is customary for students to combine school and work, whether the individual is a student or non-student is controlled for by estimating the models separately for each group, and for students, by whether they were attending full- or part-time. The second binary logistic model estimates whether highly precarious shifts are taken on an involuntary or voluntary (as control) basis, once again run separately for students and non-students and controlling for pertinent variables.[5] The third model is a competing risk logistic regression of entry into first partnership by cohabitation, marriage or right-censoring by the interview date. The fourth logistic model charts the impact of selected variables, including irregular work shifts, on entry into first parenthood or right-censoring by the interview date.[6] Although a series of stepwise models were estimated for each analysis, only final models are shown for ease of comparison and space.

RESULTS

The results for the final models of entry into the labor market are shown in Table 11.2. The first six columns contain findings by type of work shift, using regular day shifts as the control category and divided by student status. The remaining two columns indicate which groups of youth are more likely to work precarious shifts for involuntary reasons. Table 11.3 presents findings by sex for entry into parenthood and first union by whether it is a marriage or consensual union.

Referring to Table 11.2, we see that gender differences indeed emerge with female non-students significantly more likely to work split, on call, irregular and evening or graveyard shifts, a finding that supports the *gender hypothesis*. Since this effect is significant only for non-students, we must redefine this hypothesis into a dynamic one. That is, gender inequalities appear to exist to a lesser extent between male and female students and are enhanced only after youth have left education. In support of the *type of shift hypothesis*, an interesting division by type of irregular work shift emerges when we examine the estimates by pension benefits and age. Although split, on call, irregular and evening or graveyard shift workers are less likely to receive pension benefits than those who work regular day shifts, it is clear that this is not the case for rotating shifts. Furthermore, the

Table 11.2 Logistic regression of type of work shift, first job and voluntary nature of irregular shift, youth, ages 16-35, by student status: Canada, 1993-1998

Variables	Exp(B): Odds Ratio of Type of work shift						Exp(B): Odds Ratio of (In)voluntary shift work	
	Split, on call, irregular		Rotating shift		Evening, Graveyard			
	Student Status		Student Status		Student Status		Student Status	
	Non-student	Student	Non-student	Student	Non-student	Student	Non-student	Student
Age	0.918	1.164*	1.132*	1.232**	1.002	1.104	1.298**	0.951
Age squared	1.001	0.997	0.998**	0.996**	1.000	0.998	0.995**	1.001
Labor force experience	0.991***	0.984***	0.991***	0.982***	0.981***	0.979***	-	-
Work hours								
Full-time	0.184***	0.142***	0.708***	0.517***	0.265***	0.225***	6.887***	7.775***
Part-time	1	1	1	1	1	1	1	1
Occupational class								
Service Class	0.401***	0.405***	0.094***	0.070***	0.146***	0.129***	1.101	1.140
Routine non-manual	0.794**	0.636***	0.451***	0.321***	0.528***	0.446***	0.893	1.206
Skilled	0.580***	0.620***	0.573***	0.624***	0.397***	0.598***	0.806	0.973
Semi / unskilled manual	1.277***	1.319**	1.100	0.978	1.504***	1.465***	0.955	0.832
Semi / unskilled non-manual	1	1	1	1	1	1	1	1
Pension benefits								
Yes	0.677***	0.683***	2.310***	2.744***	0.928	0.915	-	-
No	1	1	1	1	1	1	-	-

Table 11.2 continued

Variables	Exp(B): Odds Ratio of Type of work shift						Exp(B): Odds Ratio of (In)voluntary shift work	
	Split, on call, irregular		Rotating shift		Evening, Graveyard			
	Student Status		Student Status		Student Status		Student Status	
	Non-student	Student	Non-student	Student	Non-student	Student	Non-student	Student
Sector								
Public	0.751***	0.824*	0.698***	0.705***	0.578***	0.837	-	-
Private sector	1	1	1	1	1	1	-	-
Highest education								
<High school	0.756**	1.363*	1.037	1.549**	1.035	1.051	1.204	1.091
Graduated high school	0.733***	1.205	0.941	1.402**	1.035	0.885	1.196	1.109
Non-University certificate	0.781***	1.049	1.003	1.249	0.983	0.916	0.996	1.653***
University certificate, diploma	1	1	1	1	1	1	1	1
Educational enrollment								
Full-time student	-	0.941	-	1.016	-	1.105	-	1.772***
Part-time student	-	1	-	1	-	1	-	1
Time period								
1993	0.912	0.788*	0.954	0.915	0.827	0.810	0.774	1.137
1994	0.787**	0.804	0.967	1.040	1.069	0.736*	1.352	1.443**
1995	0.747**	0.957	0.959	0.928	0.894	0.804	1.333	1.718***
1996	0.963	0.992	0.925	0.917	0.973	0.925	1.058	1.166
1997	0.953	1.042	0.996	0.815	0.979	0.879	0.964	1.265**
1998	1	1	1	1	1	1	1	1

Table 11.2 continued

Variables	Exp(B): Odds Ratio of Type of work shift						Exp(B): Odds Ratio of (In)voluntary shift work	
	Split, on call, irregular		Rotating shift		Evening, Graveyard			
	Student Status		Student Status		Student Status		Student Status	
	Non-student	Student	Non-student	Student	Non-student	Student	Non-student	Student
Visible minority								
Yes	1.001	1.009	0.882	0.865	1.411**	1.674***	0.571**	0.523***
No	1	1	1	1	1	1	1	1
Sex								
Men	0.778***	0.979	0.972	1.015	0.827**	0.980	0.990	1.050
Women	1	1	1	1	1	1	1	1
Constant	5.882*	0.260	0.063***	0.034***	0.634*	0.215	0.970	0.685
-2 Log-Likelihood (null)	35301.37	20508.14	35301.37	20508.14	35301.37	20508.14	4276.05	6178.03
-2 Log-Likelihood (final)	31718.96	17430.14	31718.96	17430.14	31718.96	17430.14	4233.33	6011.62
Chi-Square	3,582	3,078	3,582	3,078	3,582	3,078	561	944
Number of episodes	2,215	1,578	2,477	1,323	1,180	831	5,679	5,293

Notes: Final models only. Reference category for type of work schedule is regular daytime shift (n=13,455 for non-students and n=6,843 for students). Reference category for working shift for involuntary reasons are voluntary reasons. Question asked only for irregular and on-call shifts.

Source: Survey of Labour and Income Dynamics, 1993-98.

***   p < 0.001.
**   p < 0.01.
*   p < 0.05.

probability of having a rotating shift also increases significantly with age. Thus, both results show a hierarchy within irregular schedules themselves. Rotating shifts emerge as a unique and more stable type of irregular work. Further investigation (not shown here) established that these jobs are concentrated in areas such as the health services, which have higher economic and employment relation security.

The descriptive results in Figure 11.1 provide preliminary support for the *occupational class hypothesis*. Irregular shifts, particularly split, on call or irregular, are highly concentrated in the semi- and unskilled occupations, with around 50 percent of these workers engaged in irregular shifts. The results of the regression analysis in Table 11.2 confirm that they are indeed significantly more likely to be employed in irregular shifts, supporting the expectation that these shifts are generally concentrated in the 'bad' unskilled jobs in the service sector. A further sub-hypothesis contended that with the new globalization of ICTs, labor market flexibility begins to also impact the previously shielded higher level classes. The results remain tentative, yet inconclusive. Figure 11.1 shows that certain workers in higher level occupations do have jobs with irregular shifts (e.g., in total around 30 percent of routine non-manual workers). However, these workers still hold irregular shifts to a lesser extent than semi- and unskilled workers.

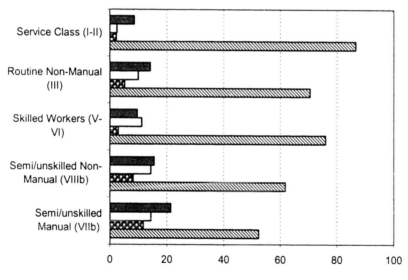

☒ Fixed day ☒ Fixed evening/graveyard ☐ Rotating shift ☒ Split shift, on call, Irregular

Figure 11.1   Percent distribution in occupational groups by employment schedule, age group 15-35, 1993, Canada

Source: Survey of Labor and Income Dynamics Public Use Microdata File, 1993-94.

The *human capital hypothesis* proposed several sub-hypotheses. First, the general hypothesis that those with lower human capital have a higher chance of working an irregular shift is confirmed. Youth with less labor force experience are significantly more likely to work irregular schedules, which was also found by Marshall (1998). As Presser and Cox (1997) also demonstrated for the United States, those with lower education are in general more likely to hold irregular shifts. One exception, however, are non-students who are working split, on call and irregular shifts; they are significantly more likely to be University graduates. After further investigation, it appears that this group consists of those working 'on call' in medical or veterinary professions or are workers in the relatively 'good' service jobs in addition to more routine non-manual workers. Although visible minorities are less likely to work rotating shifts, they are significantly more likely to be employed in evening or graveyard shifts, regardless of educational enrollment. A second sub-hypothesis was that those with higher occupational prospects would focus on their careers to reduce uncertainty and thus show a negative entry into partnerships and parenthood. Conversely, those with lower labor market prospects would use partnerships, and particularly marriage, and parenthood as a means to reduce uncertainty. Using education level as an indicator, this expectation is generally supported in Table 11.3. Although not significantly different, both men and women with University education are less likely to enter marriage. The only group to have a significantly higher likelihood of entry into parenthood are those with a non-university certificate. These are those who opted for a school-based vocational or apprenticeship route. Due to the strong tie of their educational skills to the labor market and the shorter study period to obtain such a certificate, these individuals can enter the labor market sooner, sustaining a faster transition to adulthood. During the early life course, age is also valuable human capital as it reflects the accumulation of experience and resources. For both sexes, the trend to enter unions and parenthood predictably increases with age, particularly for marriage.

Recall that the *economic uncertainty hypothesis* maintained that irregular shifts had a higher probability to cause economic uncertainty which would in turn lower the preparedness of youth to make long-term binding life-course decisions such as entry into marriage and parenthood. To examine the impact of this uncertainty on these other life course events, we turn to Table 11.3 where it is measured by work hours, student and annual labor force status. Men who work part-time and are students are less likely to enter fatherhood and any type of union, with part-time work significantly reducing entry into marriage. This is what Rindfuss and Vandenheuvel (1990) coined as the necessary 'affordability clause' which is an economic certainty required before individuals enter a more long-term binding union such as marriage. The effects of part-time work and student status on women's partnering decisions are negligible, yet both significantly reduce women's likelihood to have a first child. This effect reaffirms the importance of Canadian women's strong attachment to the labor force and educational attainment. Compared to those who are employed year-round, it appears that the most precarious position of the combination of being employed,

Table 11.3 Logistic regression of entry into first partnership and parenthood, youth, ages 16-35, by sex: Canada, 1993-1998, (final model only)

Variables	Exp(B): Odds Ratio of transition to first partnership by type and first birth					
	Women			*Men*		
	Type first partnership			*Type first partnership*		
	Marriage	*Cohab.*	*First birth*	*Marriage*	*Cohab.*	*First birth*
Age	2.824***	2.576***	1.641***	4.596***	2.766***	2.060***
Age squared	0.979***	0.980***	0.989***	0.971***	0.979***	0.986***
Region of residence						
Atlantic provinces	2.946***	0.353***	-	2.070*	0.466***	-
Quebec	1	1	-	1	1	-
Ontario	3.759***	0.268***	-	2.384**	0.261***	-
Prairie provinces	3.950***	0.282***	-	3.468***	0.511***	-
British Columbia	4.640***	0.549**	-	3.212***	0.381***	-
Highest education						
<High school	1.240	0.866	0.933	1.975*	0.939	0.991
Graduated high school	1.531	0.913	1.115	1.849*	1.266	1.083
Non-University certificate	1.988*	0.781	1.420**	3.733***	1.032	1.394**
University certificate	1	1	1	1	1	1
Work hours						
Full-time	1	1	1	1	1	1
Part-time	1.105	1.052	0.746***	0.446***	0.786	0.977

Table 11.3 continued

Variables	Women			Men		
	Type first partnership			Type first partnership		
	Marriage	Cohab.	First birth	Marriage	Cohab.	First birth
Student status						
Student	1.108	1.191	0.644***	0.948	0.746	0.866
Non-student	1	1	1	1	1	1
Annual labor-force status						
Employed all-year	1	1	-	1	1	-
Employed part-year and unemployed or olf part-year	0.867	0.983	-	0.837	1.043	-
Employed, unemployed and olf	0.840	1.383	-	0.748	1.227	-
Regular shift						
Regular day shift	1	1	1	1	1	1
Irregular shift	0.804	1.191	-	0.769	0.746	-
Split, on call, irregular	-	-	1.004	-	-	1.003
Rotating shift	-	-	0.999	-	-	1.007
Evening, graveyard	-	-	1.125	-	-	1.007
Partnership status						
Never married	-	-	1	-	-	1
Married	-	-	9.009***	-	-	23.323***
Common-law	-	-	4.767***	-	-	11.809***
Separated/divorced/widowed	-	-	2.328***	-	-	5.258***

Table 11.3 continued

Variables	Women						Men					
	Exp(B): Odds Ratio of transition to first partnership by type and first birth											
	Type first partnership						*Type first partnership*					
	Marriage	*Cohab.*	*First birth*				*Marriage*	*Cohab.*	*First birth*			
Constant	0.001***	0.054***	0.000***				0.002***	0.042***	0.000***			
-2 Log-Likelihood (Null)	2041.92	2719.52	7673.54				1803.73	2414.86	7379.07			
-2 Log-Likelihood (Final)	2000.63	2626.88	7100.10				1745.13	2351.91	6375.79			
Number of events	198	283	1,027				172	240	1,095			

Notes First birth results for men should be judged with caution due to the fact that related questions were only asked in later waves. Olf = out of labor force. With the exception of sex, all variables are lagged by one year. Includes only events that occurred between 1993 and 1998.

Source: Survey of Labour and Income Dynamics, 1993-1998.

*** $p < 0.001$.
** $p < 0.01$.
* $p < 0.05$.

unemployed and not in the labor force during the year inhibits marriage, but not cohabitation, for both men and women. However, due to model specification, this finding should be examined in perspective.[7] Finally, as expected, those who are not in a union face higher uncertainty to enter parenthood alone and are therefore significantly less likely to do so compared to those who live in partnerships, particularly marital ones.

The *employment relation uncertainty hypothesis* is also upheld: those in the public sector are significantly less likely to work irregular shifts (Table 11.2). This affirms at least in some part that private sector workers are less protected from globalizing forces and deterioration of employment security. Using the Canadian Survey of Work Arrangements (SWA), Marshall (1998) also showed a low incidence of shift work among public employees. Whether irregular shifts produce *social integration uncertainty* and deter entry into binding partnerships and parenthood remains tentative. Although not significant, it appears that having an irregular work shift decreases entry into any type of first union, with the exception of increased entry into cohabitation for women (Table 11.3). This finding only weakly supports the *flexible partnership hypothesis* that those who work in flexible shifts will seek flexible relationships such as cohabitation. For men, working such a shift appears to be a stronger deterrent for entering a union than it is for women. This is conceivably linked to the economic and employment relation uncertainty that comes with these jobs. Finally, there appears to be no significant difference of entry into first parenthood for those who have any kind of irregular shift compared to those working a regular day shift, a finding we will return to in the final discussion.

As expected, whether the respondent is a resident of the province of Quebec is a strong indicator of cohabitation as first-ever union compared to other regions, thus sustaining the *shock hypothesis*. The highest odds of marriage are found in British Columbia, the Prairies, and to a lesser extent Ontario and the Atlantic region. In general, there is no distinct pattern in the type of work schedule over time, with workers in 1996 to 1998 having a slightly higher probability to be employed in these irregular shifts (Table 11.2). For such a short period of time it is difficult to sustain the *economic cycle hypothesis*, which maintained that more youth would work irregular shifts for involuntary reasons when the labor market was tight, which in this case is 1993 and 1995. However, we see that compared to 1998, students were significantly more likely to work these shifts for involuntary reasons in 1994-95 and 1997.

The *involuntary worker hypothesis* maintained that certain groups are more likely to work irregular shifts for involuntary reasons, which had the potential to generate uncertainty. However, if workers voluntarily chose these types of shifts to combine life course careers, the contrary may be the case. Initial descriptive results show that the majority of individuals who are working these irregular shifts do so against their own will. For example, in 1993, for those aged 16 to 35, 64 percent were working irregular hours for involuntary reasons (requirement of job/no choice, could only find this type of work) and 36 percent doing so voluntarily, with the majority of these voluntary workers (30 percent) stating that the reason for working these shifts was to combine school and work (i.e., going to school) (SLID Microdata). These findings coincide with Akyeampong (1997), who using Canadian SWA data found that between 1991 to 1995, the percentage of those who worked irregular shifts for involuntary reasons rose from 69 to 78 percent, with 71 percent of students working these shifts to accommodate educational demands. The classification of combining work and school as 'voluntary' is, however, highly debatable considering the previous discussion of high tuition fees and large student loans. It seems more likely that many may have been forced to work in order to finance their education to obtain the necessary skills to secure a good job, rather than as a preference. We can conclude that the majority of Canadian youth appear to view nonstandard employment schedules as a constraint imposed by the employer and labor market demands, rather than as a strategic choice for flexibility. For the majority, this type of work is not a personal preference, but for one-third of students combining school and work it appears to be adaptive strategic behavior to meet a future labor market goal.

It is evident that in comparison to part-time workers, those who work full-time and are engaged in irregular shifts are clearly and significantly doing so against their will. Full-time students are almost 80 percent more likely to work an irregular shift against their will, reinforcing the expectation that Canadian youth are compelled to combine school and work. This relates to the significantly higher probability of working irregular schedules in the mid-1990s for students, reflecting the climate of rising tuition fees and burgeoning student loans. Although those in the higher occupational classes who work highly precarious shifts are more likely to do so for involuntary reasons, the finding is not significant. The fact that visible minorities are significantly less likely to work highly irregular shifts for involuntary reasons is in need of further exploration. This may be related to a selection effect due to the fact that this question includes only those in highly irregular shifts or to differences in reporting, or it may indeed be the case that visible minorities are more likely to take these precarious shifts for voluntary reasons.

CONCLUSION

This chapter offers an examination of the transition to adulthood that is unique to the North American context. The investigation of who works irregular shifts coupled with whether they voluntarily choose to do so permits deeper theoretical speculation of the consequences of this for the overall transition to adulthood.

A central finding is that youth who hold irregular work schedules have higher economic and employment relation uncertainty. Irregular shifts are concentrated in lower occupational classes, part-time work, the private sector and jobs without pension benefits. These economic factors inhibit transitions to marriage and parenthood, particularly for men as they cannot fulfill the 'affordability clause' which would permit them to make binding decisions to the future. Although higher social integration uncertainty was expected to produce out-of-sync clashes with structured and unstructured social relations, thereby inhibiting the transition to adulthood, findings remain inconclusive. One explanation is the dynamic nature of the impact of irregular schedules throughout the life course. For example, gender inequalities in the sense of an over-representation of women in irregular shifts appear only after youth leave the educational system and are non-students. Johnson (1997) also found that single Canadian men and women are likely to work these irregular types of shifts, however, once a family is formed women become over-represented. Although irregular shifts in themselves do not appear as a clear deterrent to partnership formation and parenthood, the higher economic and employment relation uncertainty that accompany these jobs does appear to play a role.

It is clear that the majority of Canadian youth view irregular work schedules as a constraint imposed upon them by the employer. This provides evidence to support one of the central consequences of globalization, which is a shift of risk from the state or firm to the individual. Irregular shifts are not only a strategic choice made by youth to obtain flexibility. The ability to make life course decisions and adopt a particular work shift is associated with an individual's human capital, something which is lacking for the very young, women, full-time students, and those with less labor force experience or of a visible minority status.

Irregular work in general appears to be the future for Canadian youth. This prompts us to ask: What are the consequences of this type of work? On the one hand, Myles *et al.* (1993) argue that this period of 'apprenticeship' in the low-wage services until young people can enter better occupations lengthens as service employment rises. A longer period of economic, employment relation and social integration uncertainty is certainly linked to the postponement or forgoing of family formation and other events in the transition to adulthood such as buying a home. But does it create an attenuated 'new service proletariat' or post-industrial underclass with inferior life chances? Myles *et al.* (1993: 174) argue that for Canada, this is clearly not the case, rather: "low-wage, low-skill jobs in services and sales are 'stop-gap-jobs' that mainly serve as 'ports of entry' or 'launching pads' for new labor force entrants." In other words, the original port of entry of an irregular shift is most likely a launching pad to a better career or flexible means to work while obtaining more education, that may postpone, but does not permanently damage one's future labor market prospects or entirely block family formation in the Canadian context. In future research, it would therefore be interesting to extend this analysis to examine who remains entrapped in irregular work schedules in the turbulent early labor market careers of young Canadians. Further extensions could also include considering the shifts of both partners once a union is formed, higher birth order parities and, pending data availability, a longer time period.

NOTES

1   Acknowledgements: This analysis is based on Statistics Canada's Survey of Labour and Income Dynamics Public Use Microdata, 1994, which contains anonymized data collected in the Survey of Labour and Income Dynamics, in addition to an extended remote analysis up to 1998 submitted internally using SLIDRET. All computations

on the microdata were prepared by the author and the responsibility for the use and interpretation of these data is entirely that of the author. Thanks to Louise Desjardins of Statistics Canada for invaluable help during remote data analysis.

2   Irregular work schedules include not only the times of work but also the days (e.g., weekends, holidays), not addressed in the confines of this study.

3   Occupational class is defined by using the Erikson and Goldthorpe (1992) schema: 1) Service class (I-II), 2) Routine Non-Manual (III), 3) Skilled Workers (V-VI), 4) Unskilled Manual (VIIb), and, 5) Unskilled Non-Manual (VIIIb). Following Bernardi (2000), unskilled workers are divided into manual and non-manual categories to capture the disparate early labor market experiences of these groups. Due to the fact that only dependent workers were asked information on work schedules, self-employed workers were omitted from the analysis; with their numbers in this age group already small. Using Statistics Canada's standard classification, part-time work is defined as less than 20 hours a week, with full-time work consisting of 30 or more hours per week.

4   A more direct indicator not examined here would be earnings. This is difficult to measure as those working in the most precarious shifts have hours and earnings that often shift from week to week or month to month, necessitating a complicated measure to capture and compare.

5   The reason for working a shift was asked only for those in the most precarious schedules, which includes workers who are on call or report an irregular schedule (not evening, graveyard, rotating or split shifts).

6   Due to the fact that questions on fatherhood were only introduced in later phases of the wave, these results should be examined with caution.

7   This specification of the annual labor force variable reflects Canadian youth's checkered employment history throughout the year. More importantly, since the focus of this examination was on the impact of irregular work shifts, it was necessary for individuals in the sample to have had at least one job. Thus those who are unemployed and not in the labor force for the entire year or a combination of unemployed and out of the labor force part-year were not included in the annual labor force status variable. If the focus of the study was more general, the inclusion of these two categories would inevitably bring slightly different results, particularly by sex.

BIBLIOGRAPHY

Akyeampong, E.B. (1997) 'Work arrangements:1995 overview', *Perspectives*, Spring: 48-52.

Allmendinger, J. (1989) 'Educational system and labour market outcomes', *European Sociological Review*, 3: 231-250.

Baker, M. and Tippin, D. (1999) *Poverty, Social Assistance, and the Employability of Mothers. Restructuring Welfare States*, Toronto: University of Toronto Press.

Beers, T.M. (2000) 'Flexible schedules and shift work: Replacing the "9-to-5" workday?', *Monthly Labor Review*, June: 33-40.

Bernardi, F. (2000) 'Globalization, recommodification and social inequality: changing patterns of early careers in Italy,' GLOBALIFE Working Paper No. 7, Faculty of Sociology, University of Bielefeld.

Blossfeld, H.-P. and Rohwer, G. (1995) *Techniques of Event History Modeling*, Mahwah, NJ: Lawrence Erlbaum Associates.

Bruhnes, B. (1989) 'Labour Market Flexibility in Enterprises: A Comparison of Firms in Four European Countries', *Labour Market Flexibility: Trends in Enterprises*, Paris: OECD.

Cole, M. (1998) 'Globalization, Modernization and Competitiveness: A critique of the New Labour project in Education', *International Studies in Sociology of Education*, 8(3): 315-333.

Erikson, R. and Goldthorpe, J. (1992) *The Constant Flux. A Study of Class Mobility in Industrial Societies*, Oxford: Clarendon Press.

Esping-Andersen, G. (1993) 'Post-industrial class structures: An analytical framework,' in G. Esping-Andersen (ed.) *Changing Classes*, London: Sage.

Friedman, D., Hechter, M. and Kanazawa, S. (1994) 'A theory of the value of children', *Demography*, 31(3): 375-401.

Gera, S. and Massé, P. (1996) 'Employment Performance in the Knowledge-Based Economy', Industry Canada Working Paper No. 14, Ottawa, Canada.

Guest, D. (1997) *The Emergence of Social Security in Canada*, Vancouver: University of British Columbia Press.

Hamermesh, D.S. (1996) 'The time of work time: Evidence from the U.S. and Germany', *Konjunkturpolitik*, 42 (1): 1-22.

Hamermesh, D.S. (1999) 'The timing of work over time', *The Economic Journal*, 109: 37-66.

Jamal, M. and Badawi, J.A. (1995) 'Nonstandard Work Schedules and Work and Nonwork Experiences of Muslim Immigrants: A Study of a Minority in the Majority', *Journal of Social Behavior and Personality*, 10(2): 395-408.

Johnson, K.L. (1997) 'Shiftwork from a work and family perspective', applied Research Branch Strategic Policy, Human Resources Development Canada Research Paper Series, R-98-2E, Ottawa: HRDC.

Krahn, H. (1991) 'Non-standard working arrangements', *Perspectives on Labour and Income*, 2(4): 36-45.

Lowe, G. and Krahn, H. (2000) 'Work aspirations in an era of labor market restructuring: A comparison of two Canadian cohorts', *Work, Employment and Society*, 14(1): 1-22.

Marshall, K. (1998) 'Couples Working Shift', *Perspectives on Labour and Income*, Aut: 9-14.

Mayer, K.-U. (2001) 'The paradox of global social change and national path dependencies: Life course patterns in advanced societies', in A. Woodward and M. Kohli (eds) *Inclusions and Exclusions in European Societies*, New York: Routledge.

McRoberts, K. (1993) *Quebec: Social Change and Political Crisis*, Toronto: McClelland & Stewart.

Mills, M. (2000) *The Transformation of Partnerships. Canada, the Netherlands and the Russian Federation in the Age of Modernity*, Amsterdam: Thela Thesis Population Studies Series.

Myles, J. (1996) 'When Markets Fail: Social Welfare in Canada and the United States', in G. Esping-Andersen (ed.) *Welfare States in Transition. National Adaptations in Global Economies*, London: Sage.

Myles, J., Picot, G. and Wannell, T. (1993) 'Does Post-Industrialism Matter? The Canadian Experience', in G. Esping-Andersen (ed.) *Changing Classes*, London: Sage.

O'Connor, J., Orloff, A. S. and Shaver, S. (1999) *States, Markets, Families. Gender, Liberalism and Social Policy in Australia, Canada, Great Britain and the United States*, Cambridge: Cambridge University Press.

Organization for Economic Co-operation and Development (OECD) (1998) *OECD Employment Outlook, 1996*, Paris: OECD.

Presser, H.B. (1986) 'Shift Work among American Women and Child Care', *Journal of Marriage and the Family*, 48: 551-563.

Presser, H.B. (1995) 'Are the Interests of Women Inherently at Odds with the Interests of Children or the Family? A Viewpoint', in Oppenheim Mason and A.-M. Jensen (eds) *Gender and Family in Industrialized Countries*, Oxford: Oxford University Press.

Presser, H.B. (1998) 'Toward a 24 Hour Economy: The U.S. Experience and Implications for the Family', in D. Vannoy and P.J. Dubeck (eds) *Challenges for Work and Family in the Twenty-First Century*, New York: Aldine De Gruyter.

Presser, H.B. and Cox, A.G. (1997) 'The work schedules of low-educated American women and welfare reform', *Monthly Labor Review*, April: 25-34.

Regini, M. (2000) 'The dilemmas of labour market regulation', in G. Esping-Andersen. and M. Regini (eds) *Why Deregulate Labour Markets?*, Oxford: Oxford University Press.

Rindfuss, R. and Vandenheuvel, A. (1990) 'Cohabitation: A precursor to marriage or an alternative to being single?', *Population and Development Review*, 16(4): 703-726.

Rugmann, A.J. (2001) 'The impact of globalization on Canadian competition policy', paper presented at the conference 'Canadian Competition Policy: Preparing for the Future,' Toronto.

Shavit, Y. and Müller, W. (1998) *From School to Work: A Comparative Study of Educational Qualifications and Occupational Destinations*, Oxford: Clarendon Press.

Smith, B.S. (1994) 'Global Competition Challenges the Socio-Economic Structure of Europe and North America', *Journal of Social, Political and Economic Studies*, 19(4): 447-479.

Standing, G. (1997) 'Globalization, labour flexibility and insecurity: The era of market regulation', *European Journal of Industrial Relations*, 1: 7-37.

Statistics Canada (1997) *Survey of Labour and Income Dynamics Microdata User's Guide*, Ottawa: Minister of Industry.

Statistics Canada (2001) *Labour Force Historical Survey*, Ottawa: Minister of Industry.

Tilly, C. (1996) *Half a Job. Bad and Good Part-time Jobs in a Changing Labor Market*, Philadelphia: Temple University Press.

Van den Berg, A., Furaker, B. and Johansson, L. (1997) *Labour Market Regimes and Patterns of Flexibility. A Sweden – Canada Comparison*, Lund: Arkiv forlag.

Weiss, M.G. and Liss, M.B. (1988) 'Night Shift Work: Job and Family Concerns', *Journal of Social Behavior and Personality*, 3(4): 279-286.

White, L. and Keith, B. (1990) 'The effect of shift work on the quality and stability of marital relations', *Journal of Marriage and the Family*, 52: 453-462.

Wu, Z. (2000) *Cohabitation: An alternative form of living*, Toronto: Oxford University Press.

Zhao, J. (2000) 'University education: Recent trends in participation, accessibility and returns', *Education Quarterly Review*, 6(4): 24-32.

12 The case of American women[1]

Globalization and the transition to adulthood in an individualistic regime

Rosalind Berkowitz King

INTRODUCTION

This chapter explores the impact of globalization on the transition to adulthood among American women in the 1970s and 80s. The transition to adulthood is conceptualized as a process subsuming three underlying transitions: first birth, first union, and first full-time employment. Blossfeld (2002) has argued that globalization in the modern period induces increasing uncertainty which affects life chances in social and economic arenas of the transition to adulthood. The United States economy has been tied to international trade for most of its history. But recent changes such as increasing numbers of immigrants, trade agreements enforced by supranational organizations, the establishment of transnational corporations, increasing flows of foreign direct investment, and shifts in the types of goods that are imported and exported have led to a feeling of intensity that makes the contemporary period unique (Brady and Wallace, 2000; Laws, 1997).

Globalization occurs as a macro-level process of change that affects the structural constraints that individuals face within nation states (see Mills and Blossfeld, this volume). In the context of the United States, structural constraints also include social sources of stratification. The United States has been noted as an individualistic regime, one where individual-level resources play a major role in differentiating the fates of workers in terms of labor market transitions (DiPrete *et al.*, 1997). Since labor market transitions are theorized to be intimately connected to family formation transitions (see Mills and Blossfeld, this volume), entry into unions and parenthood should also fall under the influence of individual-level resources. Thus, research on the effects of globalization within the United States must take into account the pre-existing influence of stratification on birth, union formation, and employment transitions.

This chapter addresses the question of whether structural effects of globalization affect the transition to adulthood in a particularly individualistic regime. I emphasize racial or ethnic categorization and family background as forms of stratification which distinctively shape the life chances of American women. The three events are analyzed using largely the same variables to create consistency across the processes and to generate a synthesis of the transition to adulthood across multiple domains.

GLOBALIZATION IN THE UNITED STATES

Trade agreements enforced by supranational organizations, the establishment of transnational corporations, and increasing flows of foreign direct investment have particularly affected the American manufacturing sector, where the job base shrank over the 1970s and 80s. Foreign competition induced domestic manufacturers to try to lower their labor costs (i.e., wages) by moving production facilities from Northeastern and Midwestern states to either the South and West of the United States or to offshore sites (Grant and Wallace, 1994). An especially popular destination for production facilities has been just across the United States border into Mexico (see Parrado, this volume). Moving production to this area exempts manufacturers from American standards for wages and working conditions while minimizing increases in transportation costs for finished goods.

Lower availability of these jobs and lower wages in this sector are a particular cause for concern. "Manufacturing jobs are critical to a dynamic economy because they provide workers with solid incomes that can support a middle-class lifestyle and because they have a high capacity to fuel secondary growth by generating jobs in other sectors" (Grant and Wallace, 1994: 56). Manufacturing wages are viewed as the backbone of the economic stability of the 1950s and 60s, and their erosion is associated with economic uncertainty, especially for Americans without the college education that provides entrance into professional fields.

But changes in manufacturing jobs and wages have not been uniform over the past few decades because of bifurcation in the manufacturing labor market. Manufacturing jobs require varying levels of skill and producers have disproportionately shifted lower-skilled manufacturing jobs to areas with cheaper labor. Thus, wages in more skilled manufacturing jobs have remained high while those in lower skilled jobs have gone down due to competitive pressures and weakened unions (Davis, 1999). As shown in Figure 12.1, real changes in manufacturing wages have fluctuated considerably on a yearly basis since 1960. In general, increases became smaller over time and some years even saw decreases.

Manufacturing is dominated by male employees, so these fluctuations primarily represent uncertainty about the economic prospects of women's partners in marriage, parenthood, and supporting a household. For insight into women's uncertainty about their own economic prospects, Figure 12.1 also provides trends during this period in the unemployment rate for the female civilian labor force aged 16 years and older. This unemployment rate fluctuated between four and ten percent, peaking in the inflationary and recessionary late 1970s and early 80s.

As described in the conceptual framework (see Mills and Blossfeld, this volume), economic globalization in developed countries generates decreased employment stability within nations, as well as uncertainty about individual employment prospects. Employment instability manifests as fluctuations in the unemployment rate. Decreased employment opportunities directly influence the transition to work by affecting the chances of securing a position, and may also

Figure 12.1 Globalization and the U.S., 1960 to 1995

Source: U.S. Bureau of Labor Statistics, 2001a, 2001b.

have an indirect effect if they change family formation behaviors. Increased unemployment may slow the progression to marriage as women become more wary of commitments to men with uncertain employment prospects (Oppenheimer, 1988), although some women may seek husbands as an economic safety net in case their own employment prospects diminish. Unemployment may accelerate the entry into motherhood if women view working as too uncertain a role, or may slow it if women conform to the American norm that individuals should not become parents if they cannot do so and remain economically self-reliant (Jencks and Edin, 1995).

Globalization may also affect the structure of employment among those who secure a position. The United States differs from Western European nations in the nature of the conditions of employment. Most hiring arrangements constitute employment at will; only selected professionals enter into long-term contracts. In very simplified form, the employee has the right to quit at any time and the employer has the right to fire the employee at any time on any grounds (except gender, race, ethnicity, religion, national origin, age or disability). The three major kinds of work arrangements are full-time, part-time, and temporary. Full- and part-time employees differ only in the number of hours per week worked (35 or more versus less than 35) but both are considered permanent; the expectation is that employment will continue indefinitely. Temporary employees are legally employed by an agency while performing their work under the supervision of an agency client. To avoid being considered an employer, the client erects buffers to distinguish permanent and temporary employees. The largest buffer is the specification that the temporary employee will leave after a specified period (Smith, forthcoming). In most cases the government does not regulate the use of temporary employees.

As in Britain (see Francesconi and Golsch, this volume), American employers are increasingly turning to non-standard employment forms such as temporary contracts to increase their flexibility in competitive globalized markets. "Although employment in the THS [temporary help supply] industry represented only about 2 percent of total non-farm employment in 1997, it accounted for 10 percent of the net increase between 1991 and 1997" (Estevao and Lach, 1999: 1). However, tracking temporary workers is difficult because they are not regularly distinguished in industry and government employment reports or in nationally representative social science surveys.

In contrast, data on part-time workers are widely available. "The proportion of part-timers in the United States increased gradually from 13 % in 1957 to 19 % in 1993, with most of the growth coming before 1980" (Tilly, 1996, as cited in Kalleberg, 2000: 343). The increase in part-time work since 1979 is attributed more to the expansion of such sectors as the service sector that rely heavily on part-timers than to the substitution of part-timers for full-time employees (Kalleberg, 2000). Thus, the growth in part-time employment is also connected to the erosion of manufacturing jobs. Since the mid-1990s, however, part-time employment has slightly decreased (Kalleberg, 2000).

About one-quarter of part-timers would prefer full-time work (Tilly, 1996). Additionally, part-time work encompasses bad jobs with low wages and few benefits as well as good jobs with special arrangements to retain professionals desiring fewer hours (Kalleberg, 2000). Thus, in the United States it is less clear than in Western European nations whether part-time status indicates a greater level of uncertainty than full-time status. If part-time status has the same influence on transitions in the United States as in Europe, it can be inferred that the association with uncertainty is similar.

The impact of globalization on the transition from school to work is also more difficult to assess in the United States than in Western Europe, because that transition is not as structured in the United States (e.g., Mortimer and Kruger, 2000). As Rindfuss (1991) noted, "Some of the diversity in the work/school sphere in the contemporary United States reflects different patterns in the timing of schooling, which in turn reflect our ideology that everyone should have as many chances as possible to achieve his or her maximum potential. For example, our educational system allows and encourages dropouts to return. The formal educational systems in England and Germany, in contrast, are far less fluid or forgiving" (p. 502).

Part-time and delayed enrollments in higher education are widespread in the United States (U.S. Department of Education, 1988) and the combination of part-time schooling with full-time employment is quite acceptable. At the same time, many Americans experience their first part-time employment while enrolled in school full-time. Thus, work status does not necessarily indicate that schooling has been completed, so that delays in family formation among working women may indicate uncertainty due to globalization or simply plans to return for a higher degree.

In the analyses that follow, I use real yearly changes in manufacturing wages, the yearly female unemployment rate, and the respondent's schooling and work status as measures of globalization. Changes in wages and unemployment rates may have direct effects on transition patterns or only indirect effects, through their influence on other individual-level variables. The mechanisms through which globalization affects individual behavior are still in question.

TRENDS IN THE TRANSITION TO ADULTHOOD IN THE UNITED STATES

Entry into the roles of worker, spouse, and parent are among the most significant role changes marking the transition to adulthood in the United States as well as elsewhere (Marini, 1985). Both the timing and ordering of these events have changed over historical time. Entrances into work and family roles are age-normed (e.g., Elder, 1975; Neugarten *et al.*, 1965), and some researchers have posited that the shifting contours of modernization have paradoxically resulted in transitions that are increasingly standardized by age (e.g., Shanahan, 2000; for an opposite view, see Corijn and Klijzing, 2001). Some limits to changes in timing exist because these transitions are regulated by law; American states legislate minimum ages for consenting to sex and marriage, leaving school, and working full-time.

Figure 12.2 indicates changes from 1950 to 1998 in the median age at first marriage and first birth for women in the United States. Both have slowly risen over the past few decades, but the median age at first marriage has increased more quickly and surpassed the median age at first birth in the late 1980s. This crossover reflects the increasing prevalence of consensual unions and childbearing within such unions as well as the rise in the non-marital fertility ratio (Bumpass *et al.*, 1991; Manning and Landale, 1996; Smith *et al.*, 1996).

The degree of flexibility for the order of transitional events has varied over the past century. Flexibility in the first half of the twentieth century was largely generated by external events, such as the world wars and the global economic depression. Hogan's (1978) study of men born from 1907 to 1952 examined adherence to the normative ordering: school completion → first job → marriage → fatherhood. Military service in World War II played a significant disruptive role in the sequencing patterns of birth cohorts from the 1920s. For example, the government-sponsored G.I. Bill for veterans attracted thousands of married men to attend college. Modell *et al.* (1976) demonstrated that transition schedules became tighter and more integrated around the 1940s and 50s; the post-World War II period is noted for stability in economic growth.

Buchmann (1989) in turn found increased variability in the timing of adulthood transitions between the high school graduating classes of 1960 and 1980. The latter of these two cohorts experienced a greater likelihood of moving

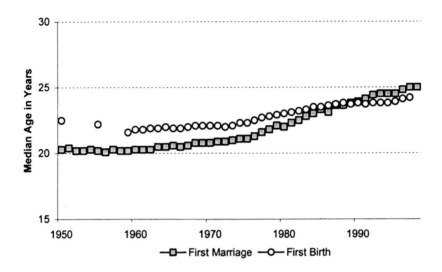

Figure 12.2   Median ages at entries into marriage and parenthood in the U.S., 1950 to 1998

Source: U.S. National Center for Health Statistics 2000b, U.S. Bureau of Census 1999.

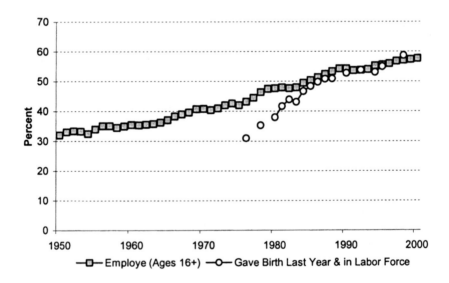

Figure 12.3   Percent of American women employed, 1950 to 2000

Source: U.S. Bureau of the Census 2000, U.S. Bureau of Labor Statistics 2001c.

between school and the labor force. In that group, women's employment status was less directly associated with schooling and marital status. Figure 12.3 shows a steady rise over the second half of the twentieth century in the percentage of all women aged 16 and older who were employed. The partial trend for the percentage of women in the labor force among those aged 15 to 44 who had given birth in the past year shows that new mothers are now as likely to work as other adult women. In addition to the continued influences of the Vietnam War and repeated recessions, Rindfuss (1991) related the increased diversity in sequencing patterns during the second half of the twentieth century to a divergence in expectations and norms among population subgroups and increasing individualism.

STRATIFICATION IN THE TRANSITION TO ADULTHOOD

These national figures include American women from all backgrounds, but documented patterns of differences exist along major lines of social stratification. The most thoroughly researched differences are along racial or ethnic lines (e.g., Ahituv *et al.*, 1994; Geronimus *et al.*, 1999; Stier and Tienda, 1997). Minority and poor women tend to exit formal education and enter motherhood earlier than white and middle-class women. Conversely, the former have fewer opportunities to enter the full-time labor market, are less likely to ever marry, and have higher average completed family sizes. For all these typifications, race and social status produce interactive effects.

Religion currently plays a more important role in the United States than in Europe, as Americans are more likely than Europeans to participate in formal religious activities, such as worship services (Stark and Finke, 2000). Demographers have documented differences in family-related behaviors along religious lines. For example, fertility was especially high during the baby boom among Catholics, while recently members of certain Protestant denominations have produced higher-than-average numbers of children (Mosher *et al.*, 1992). Religious Americans also differ in general from those without an affiliation. Greater involvement in religion directs American women toward family and away from employment (Hertel, 1988). The association between orientation toward the home and religiosity is consistent within such diverse faiths as Judaism and Mormonism (Chadwick and Garrett, 1995; Hartman and Hartman, 1996; see also review in Morgan and Scanzoni, 1987).

Patterns of change in marriage and fertility have also differed by level of education, which is generally used to represent socioeconomic status. The transition to marriage has been delayed and increasingly foregone in the United States, which researchers connect to the rise in non-marital cohabitation. By the 1980s, entrance rates into cohabitation were similar to those into marriage (Thornton, 1988). Bumpass *et al.* (1991) suggested that cohabitation was replacing early marriage primarily for the least educated segment of the population. They characterized cohabitation as differing qualitatively from marriage in the level of uncertainty surrounding the relationship.

The connection between marriage and fertility has loosened somewhat in the United States. Tolerance of out-of-wedlock childbearing has increased (Pagnini and Rindfuss, 1993), and out-of-wedlock childbearing has become more prevalent among both white and black women. Correspondingly, marital status has become less predictive of fertility behavior and its influence varies considerably by race, education, and parity (Rindfuss and Parnell, 1989). The other prominent trend in American fertility is delayed entry into motherhood: first birth rates at ages 15 to 24 have declined while those at ages 25 to 44 have risen (National Center for Health Statistics, 2000a). "Schooling, establishing a career, and financial exigencies are three normatively accepted reasons for postponing the first birth" (Morgan, 1996: 37). Women who postpone their first birth into their thirties or forties are generally highly educated (Rindfuss *et al.*, 1996). If globalization increases the importance of higher education credentials, as Blossfeld (2002) argues, then delayed fertility should spread to increasingly larger proportions of the United States population.

The school-to-work transition has also differed along the lines of socioeconomic background. Low-income women in the United States have always worked for pay in some manner. The growth of formally employed women in recent decades is largely the story of the working and middle classes. Whereas the 1950s and 60s were characterized by smooth economic expansion, the next two decades saw recessions, inflationary periods, and stagnant wages. Edwards (2001) tied the increasing presence of white mothers of infants and toddlers in the workplace to contemporary uncertainty about the ability to maintain middle- or working-class standards on the basis of the husband's income alone. He suggested that the important factor was not the actual income of the family, but the economic misfortunes of others around them.

In summary, the timing of the transition to adulthood in all three domains has changed considerably in the latter half of the twentieth century. As typically occurs in the United States, the degree of change differs by racial or ethnic categorization, religion, and socioeconomic status, but patterns across all women have been similar: delayed entry into parenthood and marriage and more prevalent entry into the labor force. In the next section, I outline the measurement and modeling of these patterns.

DATA AND METHODS

The data analyzed here come from the 1995 National Survey of Family Growth (NSFG), a nationally representative sample of 10,847 American women aged 15 to 44. This retrospective study is designed to elicit information on women's fertility and reproductive histories. The data include over-samples of Blacks and Hispanics, along with appropriate sampling weights. The NSFG researchers drew this sample from respondents to the 1993 National Health Interview Survey. The NSFG sub-sample was stratified for age, race and ethnicity, marital status, and parity (National Center for Health Statistics, 1997).

I limited the sample on three characteristics. Because of the salience of race and ethnicity to family formation behaviors, I only included respondents who characterized themselves as non-Hispanic White, non-Hispanic Black, or Hispanic. I removed respondents who did not provide valid information on the date at which they last attended high school, since this was necessary to model the school-to-work transition. These restrictions left 9,537 respondents.

Proxy variables for globalization

These variables, the rational for which has been given above, are:

1　Yearly real change in manufacturing wages (lagged; see section "Endogeneity in school, employment, union, and parity statuses");
2　Yearly female unemployment rate (lagged);
3　School and work status (five dummy variables for full-time schooling, part-time schooling, combining work and schooling, part-time work, and at home [participating in neither work nor schooling], base = full-time work; lagged); and,
4　Accumulated years of part-time work (time-varying; lagged).

Other variables

Other theoretically important variables are:

1　Age and age squared. Since these transitions are all age-normed, it is necessary to control for duration effects on the hazard functions for these transitions. The squared term for age is required because of the curvilinear pattern of the hazards, a common feature to the United States and Western Europe (e.g., Blossfeld and Huinink, 1991).
2　Racial/ethnic categorization (two dummy variables for non-Hispanic Black and Hispanic of any race, base = non-Hispanic White).
3　Birth cohort (four dummy variables for 1950-54, 1955-59, 1965-69, 1970-79, base = 1960-64). Women born into different birth cohorts experience effects of globalization at different points in their life courses. The interaction between personal time and historical time generates cohort-specific patterns of entry into adulthood (Elder, 1975).
4　Parents' education (three dummy variables for high school graduate, some college, and college graduate, base = less than high school; I also include dummies to control for whether a respondent failed to report a parent's education [not shown in tables]). Parents' education reflects access to economic resources and cultural capital during childhood and adolescence that may affect the ability to complete different levels of education. Greater educational attainment is linked to delays in the transitions to employment and family formation. Also, Boyd (1994) found direct effects of parents' education on women's fertility.

5   Immigrant status (one dummy variable for those born outside the United States), and

6   Religion in which the respondent was raised (four dummy variables for no religion, Catholicism, Judaism, and other religion, base = Protestant). Both of these characteristics are associated with the level of traditionalism in the respondent's childhood socialization. Respondents raised in more traditional households may be more tightly connected to traditional norms and less swayed by uncertainty in any given time period (Johansson, 1987; Lesthaeghe and Surkyn, 1988).

7   Educational attainment (four time-varying dummy variables for earning a high school diploma, a General Equivalency Degree (GED), a Bachelor's degree, and dropping out of high school, base = attending primary or secondary school; lagged).

8   Union status (three time-varying dummy variables for being in a non-marital union, a marital union, divorced and not in either type of union, base = never married and not cohabiting; lagged).

9   Parity (time-varying variable taking on values of zero, one, two, and three plus; lagged).

Endogeneity in school, employment, union, and parity statuses

Including a variable on the right-hand side of the equation implies unidirectional causality, but it is widely acknowledged that school, employment, union, and parity statuses are endogenous to each other. Research using methods that combine simultaneous equations and event history modeling has recently been published (O'Brien *et al.*, 1999), but these methods have not yet been incorporated into commercially available software. Marini (1984; 1985; 1987) used simultaneous equations methods and noted that results obtained by estimating the effects of variables on the timing of entry into marriage and parenthood through a (static) linear structural equations model closely parallel those obtained from a (dynamic) discrete-space continuous-time Markov model. For the purposes of this study, I accept her confidence in the similarity of results from these two methods and use dynamic modeling, asking the reader to take full notice of caveats about reciprocity. The resulting associations can be interpreted as the likelihoods of engaging in multiple roles.

I attempt to somewhat control for reciprocity by lagging the time-varying variables. Each of them represents the macro-level situation or the respondent's activities in the year prior to the one currently being modeled for the event's occurrence. Because decisions about conceiving a child, allowing an unplanned conception to continue, or marrying generally occur at least several months before the birth or marriage, statuses in the prior year are more likely to be contemporaneous with the decision-making process.

Methods

I created three person-year files for each respondent starting with age 11. One file has the transition to parenthood as the event, defined as the first live birth. The second is for the school-to-work transition, defined as the beginning of the first six months of full-time employment (Marini, 1987). The third has the transition to first union, defined as the first marital or non-marital cohabitation; these two events are treated as competing risks. I run discrete-time event history models in Stata (StataCorp, 1999) using a robust cluster estimator, an indicator for stratification, and sampling weights to control for the complex survey design. I use logistic regression for birth and job events and multinomial regression for union events (Allison, 1995).

RESULTS

Table 12.1 presents the distributions of the fixed characteristics for the whole sample and then limited to those who experienced each type of transition. Overall, the women look similar in each column; differences primarily exist between those whose first relationship was a non-marital cohabitation versus those for whom it was a marriage. Women may be distributed disproportionately between cohabitation and marriage for two reasons: a preference for cohabitation versus marriage or a preference to stay single rather than engage in any type of union. In the former case, cohabitation and marriage substitute for each other, while in the latter, women avoid the commitment of marriage or the illegitimacy of cohabitation.

Whites are underrepresented among mothers and over-represented among wives, while blacks are underrepresented among wives and Hispanics underrepresented among cohabiting women. The latter tend to come from younger birth cohorts while the distribution of mothers and wives skews toward the older ones. Immigrants and women whose parents had less education are over-represented among mothers and wives while women whose parents were college-educated are underrepresented in those categories. Women raised without a religion or within Judaism are over-represented among those cohabiting and underrepresented among wives, while those raised as Protestants show the reverse pattern. Women raised in Catholicism are slightly underrepresented among those cohabiting but proportionally represented among wives.

Tabulations (not shown) reveal that the transition most likely to occur first is entrance into full-time employment, followed by a marital union, and then a non-marital union. Cohabitation plays some role as a trial for a more permanent union, as women who enter this union first are then most likely to proceed to marriage. Interestingly, marriage most often leads to motherhood, but women who enter motherhood first are more likely to become single working mothers next rather than enter a union.

Table 12.1   Sample characteristics (percents), American women

	All Women	Women who have a first ... *			
		Birth	Cohabi-tation	Marriage	Work
N	9,537	6,593	3,636	4,067	7,791
Race					
Non-Hispanic White	74.9	72.3	75.7	78.4	77.4
Non-Hispanic Black	14.0	15.1	14.6	9.4	12.8
Hispanic	11.2	12.6	9.7	12.3	9.8
Birth Cohort					
1950 to 1954	17.6	22.6	12.1	28.2	19.9
1955 to 1959	21.0	26.5	20.7	27.6	23.6
1960 to 1964	20.2	23.3	23.6	21.8	22.2
1965 to 1969	17.9	16.3	22.4	14.3	18.9
1970 to 1979	23.3	11.4	21.3	8.1	15.4
Highest Parental Education					
Less than High School	20.2	24.8	18.9	24.2	19.5
High School	40.2	43.7	41.5	42.6	41.7
Some College	15.2	13.7	15.7	13.8	15.0
College or More	24.4	17.8	23.9	19.4	23.9
Immigrant	7.8	9.1	6.6	9.6	7.0
Religion					
Protestant	56.2	57.8	53.9	59.0	56.4
None	6.5	5.6	8.9	3.9	6.0
Catholic	35.1	34.8	34.7	35.3	35.6
Jewish	1.5	1.3	2.1	1.0	1.5
Other	0.6	0.5	0.3	0.8	0.6

Note: *As defined here, women have either a first cohabitation or a first marriage; entering one type of union removes them from the pool eligible for entering the other type.

Table 12.2 shows results from the full multivariate models for each transition (results from nested models available upon request). This section focuses on common patterns across transitions. The existence of numerous similarities is unsurprising given the interrelated nature of the processes.

All transitions are strongly age-patterned. The effects of stratification are powerful as well. The racial and ethnic patterns documented in prior research are statistically significant. Effects of birth cohort are most evident for the transitions to cohabitation and marriage. The decreasing odds from oldest to youngest cohort that a first union is a marriage are mirrored by the increasing odds over time that the first union is non-marital. Immigrants are significantly more likely than natives to delay their entry into the labor force, but they show no differences in the progression to first marriage. Higher levels of parental education have a delaying effect on all transitions. Respondents with the greatest resources from their parents may spend the most time accumulating their own human capital before entering adulthood; thus, stratification continues across generations. Finally, relative to Protestants, respondents raised without religion appear to

Table 12.2 Odds ratios for total effects on the transition to adult roles, American women

	First Birth	First Union		First Work
		Cohabitation	Marriage	
Time				
Current Age	1.8879***	3.3585***	3.6862***	8.1560***
Current Age Squared	0.9866***	0.9754***	0.9725***	0.9571***
Individual Fixed Characteristics				
Race				
Non-Hispanic White	1.0000	1.0000	1.0000	1.0000
Non-Hispanic Black	2.1438***	0.6062***	0.3967***	0.6431***
Hispanic	1.5760***	0.7876**	1.0468	0.6891***
Birth Cohort				
1950 to 1954	0.9193	0.6746***	1.4289***	0.9277
1955 to 1959	1.0013	0.8672*	1.2251**	1.0048
1960 to 1964	1.0000	1.0000	1.0000	1.0000
1965 to 1969	0.9666	1.1268+	0.6951***	0.9000+
1970 to 1979	1.1652*	1.5225***	0.5340***	0.7029***
Immigrant	0.8604*	0.8446+	1.1059	0.6837***
Highest Parental Education				
Less than High School	1.0000	1.0000	1.0000	1.0000
High School	0.9409	1.0236	0.8370**	1.2343***
Some College	0.7687***	0.9496	0.6583***	1.0884
College or More	0.6495***	0.7195***	0.4665***	0.8247**
Religion				
Protestant	1.0000	1.0000	1.0000	1.0000
None	0.9884	1.6320***	0.7756*	0.9579
Catholic	0.9581	0.8821*	0.6553***	1.1670***
Jewish	0.8461	1.0830	0.3499***	0.4681***
Other	0.6964*	0.3430**	0.7401+	0.5889*

Table 12.2 continued

	First Birth	First Union		First Work
		Cohabitation	Marriage	
Globalization				
Macro-Level Indicators				
Yearly Female Unemployment Rate	0.9418***	1.0167	0.9255***	0.9902
Yearly Change in Manufacturing Wages	1.0273+	1.0236	1.0116	1.0178
School and Work Status				
Full-Time Work	1.0000	1.0000	1.0000	-----
Full-Time Schooling	0.3960***	0.4764***	0.5479***	-----
Part-Time Schooling	1.0063	1.4453	0.3500*	-----
Combining School and Work	0.6320***	0.8067*	0.6519***	-----
Part-Time Work	1.2660***	0.9255	1.1239	-----
Home	1.6904***	1.0513	1.2074**	-----
Accumulated Years of Part-Time Work	0.9865	0.9681+	0.9751	0.7152***
Individual Time-Varying Characteristics				
Education				
In Primary or Secondary School	1.0000	1.0000	1.0000	1.0000
High School Diploma	0.3717***	0.7260*	0.8744	1.4523***
High School GED	0.2820***	1.3939	0.7435	1.4474**
High School Dropout	0.8297	1.3742+	1.0750	0.7625**
Bachelor's Degree	0.9295	0.8988	1.2894***	1.4341***
Union Status				
Never Married	1.0000	-----	-----	1.0000
Cohabiting	2.6343***	-----	-----	1.3156**
Married	10.5701***	-----	-----	0.5537***
Divorced	1.4911**	-----	-----	0.5970**
Parity	-----	0.9803	0.7566***	0.6429***
Number of person-years	132,939	112,185		100,786
F-test	237.26***	106.80***		153.38***
Degrees of freedom	33,154	62,125		29,158

Notes
+   statistically significant at the 0.10 level
*   statistically significant at the 0.05 level
** statistically significant at the 0.01 level
*** statistically significant at the 0.001 level

substitute cohabitation for marriage, while respondents raised in other religions show evidence of greater delay in entry into unions overall. The macro-level indicators of globalization are strongly associated with all transitions when stratification and other life events are not included in the models (results not shown).

Increases in female unemployment are associated with slower progression to first birth (p = 0.000) and first marriage (p = 0.000). Increases in manufacturing wages are associated with accelerated progression to first birth (p = 0.001), first marriage (p = 0.000), and first job (p = 0.004) and slower progression to first cohabitation (p = 0.082). Table 12.2 shows that the two effects of female unemployment remain in the full model. Uncertainty about economic conditions may lead women to postpone (normatively) permanent entrance into such consuming roles as wife and mother. Oddly, the female unemployment rate does not influence the transition into full-time employment. These results also show that positive changes in manufacturing wages are marginally associated with accelerating the transition to first birth, which seems logical since better economic prospects for partners would give women added certainty and security about becoming mothers.

The individual-level measures of schooling and work status must be discussed in the context of other on-going life events. The significant results for schooling and work status, union status, and parity emphasize the interdependencies between these three domains of adulthood, as well as between these domains and education. Completing high school is associated with delayed progression to first birth, which fits with previous research on the highly disruptive effects of teen motherhood on educational attainment. Earning a bachelor's degree is associated with an increased hazard of entering marriage, which fits with the increasing concentration of marriage among those with higher socioeconomic status. The results from the model predicting entry into the full-time labor market indicate the importance of educational credentials for obtaining a real job.

Normative prescriptions for exiting full-time schooling before forming a family are reflected in the negative associations between full-time schooling or combining work with schooling and entering motherhood, a cohabiting union, or marriage. The negative association between schooling and first birth may also reflect the difficulty of pursuing motherhood and human capital investments simultaneously, as Francesconi and Golsch (this volume) suggest. The greater likelihood of union formation among women in full-time employment may stem from greater certainty about their future characteristics than can be observed among those still in schooling (Oppenheimer, 1988). The odds of first birth and first marriage are highest among women who are at home, meaning that they are not involved in school or work and thus most likely to have few competing demands on their time. These women may be involuntarily unemployed or may be out of the labor force deliberately in order to focus on family life.

Accumulated years of part-time work have a negative association with the transition to full-time employment. Mortimer and Kruger (2000) reported findings from several studies, which indicated that early employment experiences during high school lead to later positive labor market outcomes. They suggested that high school employment provided an alternative method of human capital accumulation for youth, especially minorities, who anticipate lower returns from formal schooling. When I add interaction terms for race/ethnicity and accumulated years of part-time work, I find a positive interaction with part-time work for black women that reduces the negative effect (0.709 [odds ratio on part-time work] * 1.091 [odds ratio on black] = 0.774; p = 0.005). I also find significant interactions for part-time work with dropping out of high school, marrying, divorcing, and parity (results not shown). Thus, part-time work outside high school years may have different implications. These results are consistent with Blank's (1989) finding that women tend to remain in their particular labor market status over time.

The substantial positive association between union formation and a subsequent first birth transition shows the continuing strength of norms about marital childbearing. However, giving birth first is associated with lower odds of subsequently getting married. Presumably, those who are going to legitimate a birth do so before it happens, and, if not, and the relationship breaks up, it is difficult to find a man willing to raise another man's child. The negative associations between family-related events and entering work suggest that norms about the separation of work and family activities remain influential. Women who cohabited in the previous year have higher odds of entering full-time employment in the current year, but women who got married, divorced, or had children have lower odds of doing so. The inclusion of interaction terms may illuminate the extent to which the effects of marriage and divorce are due to the burden of single parenthood.

The results presented in Table 12.2 show statistically significant positive associations along the normative pathway to adulthood. Completing high school has a significant positive association only with employment, while completing college has significant positive associations with employment and marriage. Employed women have higher odds of family formation than women who are still involved in schooling, and marriage and cohabitation both have significant positive associations with first birth. On the other hand, women whose first transition is the first birth face a statistically significant negative association with making any of the other transitions, especially to marriage or full-time employment. Women who first marry cut their odds of entering full-time employment nearly in half.

DISCUSSION

In the theoretical framework for this volume, Mills and Blossfeld summarize the work of the economist Heiner: uncertainty requires actions to be governed by simple mechanisms that restrict the flexibility to choose from potential courses of action. Heiner interprets cultural traditions, social institutions or norms as such rule mechanisms. My analyses demonstrate the continued importance of mechanisms of racial/ethnic and class stratification, which restrict individual opportunities. They also demonstrate the continued importance of such norms as refraining from family formation activities while still in school (as also found for Germany in Blossfeld and Huinink, 1991).

The results give mixed support to the contention that macro-level indicators of globalization are linked to the timing of the transition to adulthood in the United States. Many other indicators exist and may prove more useful than the ones included here. I focused on manufacturing because of its importance in the popular and academic literatures, but negative developments in this sector have primarily affected only a segment of the population, mainly women and their partners with low skills and levels of education.

Many potentially interesting interaction effects remain to be explored from these analyses. Interactions may explain some of the more puzzling findings here. For example, we can interpret the lack of effect of the female unemployment rate on the transition to first job as a shortcoming of the measure. Perhaps a female unemployment rate limited to a smaller age range or to local metropolitan areas would have a greater effect. But another hypothesis is that since unemployment may disproportionately affect some sectors of the economy, we should interact the unemployment rate with information on types of job seekers. Preliminary analyses show that when the unemployment rate is interacted with the education statuses, the effect of unemployment on women with a bachelor's degree is statistically significant and positive while the effects associated with earning a high school diploma, a GED, and dropping out of high school are significant and negative. This divergence may reflect the increasing bifurcation of labor market prospects among highly skilled and lesser skilled workers in the United States.

As noted earlier, it may also prove informative to tease apart the effects of accumulated part-time work at different stages of the life course. As in Britain (see Francesconi and Golsch, this volume), part-time employment among adults is not especially helpful in transitioning to full-time employment. Accumulating experience in part-time jobs may actually hinder women's transition into the full-time labor market because it is not the right experience, reflecting the bifurcation of the market into good and bad jobs. In this instance, part-time work would be connected to economic changes from globalization. However, among women who engage in part-time work because they prefer it, such as mothers of young children, part-time status is a solution to the work/family dilemma (Bianchi, 2000) rather than a consequence of economic restructuring. These data do not include motivations for particular jobs or work statuses, but some of this information may be inferred by interacting accumulated part-time work with marital status, union duration, and ages of children. Blank (1989) found mixed evidence for the hypothesis that changes in household and family induced women to change their labor market status.

The significant effects of macro-level variables in these models represent potential direct effects of those indicators on individual behavior. The possibility of direct effects leads to the question of reference groups. Does hearing about a national or global economic crisis influence individual decision-making processes, or do women limit their vision of uncertainty to their own and their partner's current work statuses (see for example Edwards, 2001)? The results presented here include each of these two factors, but perhaps adding interactions between macro- and micro-level processes or between macro-level processes and lines of stratification would yield a clearer picture.

NOTE

1   Acknowledgments: This research was supported by a postdoctoral fellowship awarded through the Carolina Population Center, University of North Carolina at Chapel Hill, from the National Institutes of Health, National Research Service Award (T32 HD07168-22) from the National Institute of Child Health and Human Development.

BIBLIOGRAPHY

Ahituv, A., Tienda, M., Xu, L. and Hotz, V.J. (1994) 'Initial Labor Market Experiences of Minority and Nonminority Men', *Industrial Relations Research Association 46th Annual Proceedings*: 256-265.

Allison, P.D. (1995) *Survival Analysis Using the SAS System: A Practical Guide*, Cary, NC: SAS Institute.

Bianchi, S.M. (2000) 'Maternal Employment and Time with Children: Dramatic Change or Surprising Continuity?', *Demography*, 37: 401-414.

Blank, R.M. (1989) 'The Role of Part-Time Work in Women's Labor Market Choices Over Time', *The American Economic Review*, 79: 295-299.

Blossfeld, H.-P. (2002) 'Globalization, Social Inequality and the Role of Country-Specific Institutions', in P. Conceicao, M. V. Heitor, and B.-A. Lundvall (eds) *Innovation, Competence Building and Social Cohesion in Europe: Towards a Learning Society*, Cheltenham/Lyme: Edward Elgar.

Blossfeld, H.-P. and Huinink, J. (1991) 'Human Capital Investments or Norms of Role Transition? How Women's Schooling and Career Affect the Process of Family Formation', *American Journal of Sociology*, 97: 143-168.

Boyd, R.L. (1994) 'Educational Mobility and the Fertility of Black and White Women', *Population Research and Policy Review*, 13: 275-281.

Brady, D. and Wallace, M. (2000) 'Spatialization, Foreign Direct Investment, and Labor Outcomes in the American States 1978-1996', *Social Forces*, 79: 67-99.

Buchmann, M. (1989) *The Script of Life in Modern Society*, Chicago: University of Chicago Press.

Bumpass, L.L., Sweet, J.A. and Cherlin, A. (1991) 'The Role of Cohabitation in Declining Rates of Marriage', *Journal of Marriage and the Family*, 53: 913-927.

Chadwick, B.A. and Garrett, H.D. (1995) 'Women's Religiosity and Employment: The LDS Experience', *Review of Religious Research*, 36: 277-293.

Corijn, M. and Klijzing, E. (eds) (2001) *Transitions to adulthood in Europe*, Dordrecht/Boston: Kluwer Academic Publishers.

Davis, J.B. (1999) 'Is Trade Liberalization an Important Cause of Increasing U.S. Wage Inequality?', *Review of Social Economy*, 57: 88-506.

DiPrete, T.A., de Graaf, P.M., Luijkx, R., Tahlin, M. and Blossfeld, H.-P. (1997) 'Collectivist versus individualist mobility regimes? Structural change and job mobility in four countries', *American Journal of Sociology*, 103: 318-358.

Edwards, M.E. (2001) 'Uncertainty and the Rise of the Work-Family Dilemma', *Journal of Marriage and the Family*, 63: 183-196.

Elder, G.H. Jr. (1975) 'Age Differentiation and the Life Course', *Annual Review of Sociology*, 1: 165-190.

Estevao, M. and Lach, S. (1999) 'The Evolution of the Demand for Temporary Help Supply Employment in the United States', National Bureau of Economic Research Working Paper No. 7427, Cambridge, MA: National Bureau of Economic Research.

Geronimus, A.T., Bound, J. and Waidmann, T.A. (1999) 'Health Inequality and Population Variation in Fertility Timing', *Social Science and Medicine*, 49: 1623-1636.

Grant II, D.S. and Wallace, M. (1994) 'The Political Economy of Manufacturing Growth and Decline across the American States, 1970-1985', *Social Forces*, 73(1): 33-63.

Hartman, H. and Hartman, M. (1996) 'More Jewish, Less Jewish: Implications for Education and Labor Force Characteristics', *Sociology of Religion*, 57: 175-193.

Hertel, B.R. (1988) 'Gender, Religious Identity and Work Force Participation', *Journal for the Scientific Study of Religion*, 27: 574-592.

Hogan, D.P. (1978) 'The Variable Order of Events in the Life Course', *American Sociological Review*, 43: 573-586.

Jencks, C. and Edin, K. (1995) 'Do Poor Women Have a Right to Bear Children?', *The American Prospect*, 20: 43-52.

Johansson, S.R. (1987) 'Status Anxiety and Demographic Contraction of Privileged Populations', *Population and Development Review*, 13: 439-470.

Kalleberg, A.L. (2000) 'Nonstandard Employment Relations: Part-time, Temporary and Contract Work', *Annual Review of Sociology*, 26: 341-365.

Laws, G. (1997) 'Globalization, Immigration, and Changing Social Relations in U.S. Cities', *Annals of the American Academy of Political and Social Science*, 551: 89-104.

Lesthaeghe, R. and Surkyn, J. (1988) 'Cultural Dynamics and Economic Theories of Fertility Change', *Population and Development Review*,14: 1-45.

Manning, W.D. and Landale, N.S. (1996) 'Racial and Ethnic Differences in the Role of Cohabitation in Premarital Childbearing', *Journal of Marriage and the Family*, 58: 63-77.

Marini, M.M. (1984) 'Women's Educational Attainment and the Timing of Entry Into Parenthood', *American Sociological Review*, 49: 491-511.

Marini, M.M. (1985) 'Determinants of the Timing of Adult Role Entry', *Social Science Research*, 14: 309-350.

Marini, M.M. (1987) 'Measuring the Process of Role Change during the Transition to Adulthood', *Social Science Research*, 16: 1-38.

Modell, J., Furstenberg, F.F. Jr., and Hershberg, T. (1976) 'Social Change and Transitions to Adulthood in Historical Perspective', *Journal of Family History*, 1: 7-32.

Morgan, M.Y. and Scanzoni, J. (1987) 'Religious Orientations and Women's Expected Continuity in the Labor Force', *Journal of Marriage and the Family*, 49: 367-379.

Morgan, S.P. (1996) 'Characteristic Features of Modern American Fertility: A Description of Late Twentieth-Century U.S. Fertility Trends and Differentials', *Population and Development Review*, 22 (Supplement): 19-63.

Mortimer, J.T. and Kruger, H. (2000) 'Transition from School to Work in the United States and Germany: Formal Pathways Matter', in M. Hallinan (ed.) *Handbook of the Sociology of Education*, New York: Plenum.

Mosher, W.D., Williams, L.B. and Johnson, D.P. (1992) 'Religion and Fertility in the United States: New Patterns', *Demography*, 29: 199-214.

National Center for Health Statistics (1997) 'Public Use Data File Documentation: National Survey of Family Growth, Cycle 5: 1995', User's Guide, Hyattsville, MD: National Center for Health Statistics, Centers for Disease Control and Prevention, Public Health Service, U.S. Department of Health and Human Services.

National Center for Health Statistics (2000a) Table 1-2. First Birth Rates by Age of Mother, According to Race and Hispanic Origin: United States, Selected Years, 1940-97. Available HTTP: <http://www.cdc.gov/nchs/data/tab1x02p.pdf. >

National Center for Health Statistics (2000b) Table 1-5. Median Age of Mother by Live Birth Order, According to Race and Hispanic Origin: United States, Selected Years, 1940-97. Available HTTP: <http://www.cdc.gov/nchs/data/tab1x05p.pdf.>

Neugarten, B.L., Moore, J.W. and Lowe, J.C. (1965) 'Age Norms, Age Constraints, and Adult Socialization', *American Journal of Sociology*, 70: 710-717.

O'Brien, M.J., Lillard, L.A. and Waite, L.J. (1999) 'Interrelated Family-Building Behaviors: Cohabitation, Marriage, and Nonmarital Conception', *Demography*, 36: 535-551.

Oppenheimer, V.K. (1988) 'A Theory of Marriage Timing', *American Journal of Sociology*, 94: 563-591.

Pagnini, D.L. and Rindfuss, R.R. (1993) 'The Divorce of Marriage and Childbearing: Changing Attitudes and Behavior in the United States', *Population and Development Review*, 19: 331-347.

Rindfuss, R.R. (1991) 'The Young Adult Years: Diversity, Structural Change, and Fertility', *Demography*, 28: 493-511.

Rindfuss, R.R., Morgan, S.P. and Offut, K. (1996) 'Education and the Changing Age Pattern of American Fertility: 1963-1989', *Demography*, 33: 277-290.

Rindfuss, R.R. and Parnell, A.M. (1989) 'The Varying Connection Between Marital Status and Childbearing in the United States', *Population and Development Review*, 15: 447-470.

Shanahan, M.J. (2000) 'Pathways to Adulthood in Changing Societies: Variability and Mechanisms in Life Course Perspective', *Annual Review of Sociology*, 26: 667-692.

Smith, H.L., Morgan, S.P. and Koropeckyj-Cox, T. (1996) 'A Decomposition of Trends in the Nonmarital Fertility Ratios of Blacks and Whites in the United States, 1960-1992', *Demography*, 33: 141-151.

Smith, V.A. (forthcoming) 'Teamwork vs. tempwork: managers and the dualisms of workplace restructuring', in K. Campbell, D. Cornfield, and H. McCammon (eds) *Working in Restructured Workplaces: New Directions for the Sociology of Work*, Thousand Oaks, CA: Sage Publications.

Stark, R. and Finke, R. (2000) *Acts of Faith: Explaining the Human Side of Religion*, Berkeley, CA: University of California Press.

StataCorp (1999) *Stata Statistical Software: Release 6.0*, College Station, TX: Stata Corporation.

Stier, H. and Tienda, M. (1997) 'Spouses or Babies? Race, Poverty, and Pathways to Family Formation in Urban America', *Ethnic and Racial Studies*, 20: 91-122.

Thornton, A. (1988) 'Cohabitation and Marriage in the 1980s', *Demography*, 25: 497-508.

Tilly, C. (1996) *Half a Job: Bad and Good Part-Time Jobs in a Changing Labor Market*, Philadelphia: Temple University Press.

U.S. Bureau of the Census (1999) Table MS-2. Estimated Median Age at First Marriage, by Sex: 1890 to the Present. Available HTTP: <http//:www.census.gov/population/socdemo/ms-la/tabms-2.txt.>

U.S. Bureau of the Census (2000) Table H5. Women 15 to 44 Years Old Who Have Had a Child in the Last Year and Their Percentage in the Labor Force: Selected Years, June 1976 to Present. Available HTTP: <http//:www.census.gov/population/socdemo/fertility/tabH5.txt.>

U.S. Bureau of Labor Statistics (2001a) Major Sector Productivity and Costs Index. Available HTTP: <http://146.142.4.24/cgi-bin/surveymost?pr.>

U.S. Bureau of Labor Statistics (2001b) Unemployment Rate - Civilian Labor Force Female. Available HTTP: <http://www.bls.gov/webapps/legacy/cpsatab1.html>

U.S. Bureau of Labor Statistics (2001c) Civilian Employment-Population Ratio Female. Available HTTP: <http://146.142.4.24/cgi-bin/surveymost?pr.>

U.S. Department of Education (1998) Digest of Educational Statistics, Washington, D.C.: Government Printing Office.

13 Globalization and the transition to adulthood in Mexico

Emilio A. Parrado

INTRODUCTION

The demise of import substitution industrialization in the early 1980s marked the abrupt end of a relatively steady period of economic expansion in Mexico. Since then, the country has been increasingly vulnerable to the forces of globalization, changes in international economic conditions, and financial crises. The rapid deterioration of economic progress in Mexico motivated a series of policy measures intended to incorporate the country into the global economy. Fiscal reforms, privatization of state firms, labor market flexibilization, and export orientation were introduced to shift Mexico from an inward looking to a neoliberal model of development (Dussell Peters, 1998). The success of such policies has recently been called into question, as economic stagnation, political unrest, high rates of migration to the United States, and increased inequality appear to be the defining characteristics of the Mexican economy and society during the 1990s (Castañeda, 1996).

It is difficult to overstate the impact of recent macro-economic changes on the lives of Mexican men and women. Increased levels of unemployment and under-employment, rapid deterioration of real wages, and lack of institutional channels of social support have left an indelible imprint on employment behavior, family life, and economic well-being (Dussell Peters, 1997). Rapidly changing macro-economic conditions motivated micro-level adaptations to cope with globalization and economic restructuring (Gonzalez de la Rocha, 1994). Central to these transformations have been changes in women's roles and behavior patterns. The diversification of survival strategies in the context of economic uncertainty directly affected women's transition to adulthood, as self-binding decisions such as employment, marriage, and childbearing responded to financial crises and instability.

This chapter examines the effect of globalization on women's transition to adult social and economic roles in Mexico. My analytic strategy is to compare employment and family behavior at three points in time by drawing on data from the 1998 National Retrospective Demographic Survey, which collected retro-spective information on three cohorts of Mexican women representative of different periods of Mexican economic and social development. I take advantage of the retrospective information to formulate dynamic models of labor market entry, first occupation, union formation, and first parenthood that relate women's transition to adulthood to changes in other life course domains and macro-economic conditions.

GLOBALIZATION AND MEXICO

Mexico represents an intriguing case study for understanding individual responses to globalization because its population has experienced growing uncertainty both on a macro and micro level. During the past several decades the country has become increasingly susceptible to financial crises and dependent on foreign capital investments, both of which are central for understanding women's transition to adulthood.[1] At the same time, significant improvements in women's socioeconomic characteristics have rapidly altered gender roles, enhanced micro-level uncertainty and deeply affected established patterns of behavior. A central question motivating this research, therefore, is whether secular changes in women's employment and family behavior derive principally from women's changing socioeconomic characteristics or whether the unique effect of macro-level financial crises can also be identified.

In the early 1980s Mexico's per capita GDP was one half of the per capita GDP for other high-income OECD countries. By the 1990s it had declined to a mere one third (Ros, 2000). In fact, per capita income in Mexico today is almost the same as it was in 1980 in constant dollars and the country has not achieved a five percent growth rate for two consecutive years since 1981. This tremendous deterioration of economic conditions and living standards has been directly connected to the process of globalization and the accompanying economic restructuring policies (Castañeda, 1996).

Moreover, the decline in per capita income has been accompanied by recurrent financial shocks that reflect the Mexican economy's increasing dependence on foreign capital and financial institutions. While financial crises are not a new phenomenon in capitalist societies, during the past several decades Mexico has experienced financial shocks with alarming frequency. The financial crises of 1982 and 1987-88, associated with the debacle of import substitution industrialization, were followed by the more recent crisis of 1994 when the Mexican peso collapsed and the country nearly defaulted on its external debt.

The economic crisis of 1994 is of particular significance, as it was the first time that an economic contraction in Mexico generated large-scale layoffs (Cooney, 2001). During 1995 around one million Mexicans lost their jobs, a precarious situation that was exacerbated by the absence of unemployment insurance. In addition, between 1994 and 1996 real wages declined by 27 percent, thus leading to a significant increase in poverty that peaked at an astonishing 75 percent (Barkin and Rosen, 1997). During this period, income inequality also increased substantially. Between 1984 and 1994 the share of national income received by the top decile of the Mexican population increased from 32 to 41 percent, while the fraction received by the poorest half of the population shrank from 21 to 16 percent (Castañeda, 1996). While this crisis had many causes, it certainly reflects the dependence of the Mexican economy on foreign capital that is increasingly dissociated from productive activities. A complete collapse of the Mexican economy was averted in part because of the unprecedented 50 billion dollar aid package put together by the United States and the International Monetary Fund (Cooney, 2001).

The tremendous impact of these recurrent crises on everyday uncertainty is obvious. Unstable employment conditions, rapid declines in personal and family incomes, depletion of accumulated savings, and sudden increases in the cost of living rapidly trigger new survival strategies. The urgency of adapting to these financial shocks is likely to both reinforce the protective resource pooling function of the family and alter well-established patterns of female labor force participation to protect against economic instability and uncertainty.

The second dimension of economic globalization expected to affect women's transition to adulthood is the increasing importance of direct foreign capital investments. During the late 1980s the Salinas administration implemented numerous policies to incorporate Mexico into the global economy and promote an export orientation (Dussel Peters, 1998). In 1985 the country joined the General Agreement on Tariffs and Trade (GATT) and in 1994 signed the North American Free Trade Agreement (NAFTA) with Canada and the United States (Gereffi and Martinez, 2000). This development strategy continued under President Zedillo and is likely to be reinforced during Fox's presidency (Reinhardt, 2000).

A central component in this strategy has been the maquiladora industry. Maquiladoras were introduced in Mexico in 1965 when the government initiated the Border Industrialization Program (BIP) to attract foreign investment and provide cheap Mexican labor to U.S. firms, similar to the *bracero* program.[2] Under the BIP, foreign-owned assembly plants were established along the Mexico-U.S. border. They were granted duty-free importation of machinery, raw materials, parts, and components, primarily from the U.S. After being assembled in Mexico, the final or semi-final product is exported back to the U.S. with import duties paid only on the value added by the Mexican workers, that is, the cost of wages and related costs in Mexico (Kamel and Hoffman, 1999).

Since the establishment of the maquiladora system the number of participating industries has grown steadily, especially after the introduction of economic restructuring policies and the signing of NAFTA. Between 1980 and 1994 the number of maquiladoras factories grew from less than 1,000 to 2,200 and since then it has increased to close to 3,500. Currently, the maquiladora industry employs well over 1 million Mexican workers. Moreover, exports from the maquiladora industry are the largest source of foreign revenue for the Mexican government, surpassing oil in 1999. This has reinforced the export orientation of the Mexican economy; between 1990 and 1997 exports grew by 13.8 percent and currently they represent 48 percent of all exports from Latin American countries (INEGI, 2001; Cooney, 2001).

The main implication of foreign capital investments for changes in women's transition to adulthood lies in the tendency of the maquiladora industry to favor female employees. When it was first introduced in the 1970s, close to 80 percent of all maquiladora workers were women. Even though this percentage has declined in recent years, women still constitute over 60 percent of the maquiladora labor force. The typical maquiladora worker is a young single woman who lives with her parents and contributes her income to the family economy (Kamel and Hoffman, 1999). The prevalence of unattached female workers reflects transnational corporations' preference for what is considered a more docile and pliable labor force. Accordingly, the rapid growth of the maquiladora industry is not only likely to have facilitated the incorporation of women into the labor market but also to have altered the occupational characteristics of the female labor force in favor of blue-collar and other assembly factory occupations (Fernandez Kelly, 1982; Tiano, 1994; Buitelaar and Padilla Perez, 2000).

FINANCIAL SHOCKS, FOREIGN CAPITAL, AND WOMEN'S TRANSITION TO ADULTHOOD

The effect of globalization on individual transitions to adulthood is filtered by country-specific institutions, established patterns of behavior, and defined social and economic roles (Mills and Blossfeld, this volume). In Mexico, prevailing family arrangements and the associated gendered division of labor constitute important mechanisms that mediate women's responses to economic instability and uncertainty. The dramatic deterioration of economic conditions and the flow of foreign capital throughout the period are likely to have altered the established gender specialization of activities, with important implications for women's work and family life.

The transition to employment

Both individual- and macro-level forces affect women's labor market entry. At the individual level, female employment is a function of women's human capital and family characteristics. Higher levels of education raise the opportunity costs of non-work and encourage labor market entry. Family responsibilities, on the other hand, tend to conflict with market work and married women and those with children are less likely to enter the labor market than their single and childless counterparts (Becker, 1991). The constraints imposed by family life on women's employment, however, may vary according to their socioeconomic position. While the prevailing sexual division of labor in Mexico generally confines women to household activities, well-educated women may be able to hire domestic workers and reduce the conflict between home and market production (Garcia and Oliveira, 1994). Thus, we can expect family constraints to interact with education in determining female labor market entry.

Macro-level forces also have an impact on women's transition to employment, although different theories offer competing views of how globalization alters women's labor market entry (Rubery, 1988; ILO, 1993). The "discouraged worker" hypothesis posits that economic crises deter women from seeking employment since "good" jobs tend to be reserved for men, and women's lower educational endowments and skills vis-à-vis men reduce the incentives for firms to employ them. Economic recessions are thus expected to reduce the returns from paid employment and discourage women's labor market entry, particularly among married women (ILO, 1993).

The "job segregation" hypothesis, on the other hand, predicts no effect of financial shocks or other macro-economic conditions on female labor market entry. This perspective links female employment to the extension of menial, low paying, and low-skills service jobs specifically tailored for women. The rigid sex-typing of occupations resulting from this highly segmented labor market implies that women's labor force incorporation will be directly affected by changes in the demand for female-dominated jobs, such as those in the maquiladora industry, while larger cycles of boom and bust will have little effects (Tiano, 1994).

Finally, the "added worker" hypothesis predicts that during financial crises families tend to diversify their sources of income by pushing additional members into the labor market. The deterioration of male employment conditions after the demise of import substitution industrialization made a rigid gender specialization of market and household activities within the family a risky survival strategy (Gonzalez de la Rocha, 1994). A more rational alternative is to incorporate other household members into the labor force, especially married women, so as to protect against breadwinner unemployment or wage deterioration (Rubery, 1988; Cerrutti, 2000). As a result, financial crises are expected to increase female employment by pushing more women into the labor market for the first time.

Recurrent economic crises and period conditions can also affect women's employment opportunities. The expansions of self-employment, home production and other domestic activities associated with economic globalization facilitate women's labor market entry into more flexible (although less protected) forms of employment, since these activities do not necessarily conflict with family responsibilities (Standing, 1989). Moreover, the expansion of multinational corporations and the maquiladora industry can increase women's representation in blue-collar manufacturing occupations, since these industries largely rely on female workers. Overall, as a result of the expansion of unprotected forms of employment and the introduction of direct foreign investments, globalization is expected to alter the occupational distribution of the female labor force.

The transition to marriage and childbearing

The impact of globalization is also likely to be felt in women's transition to marriage and childbearing. Relative to other OECD and more developed countries, Mexico is at a different stage of demographic transformation. The country has only recently completed its first demographic transition and fertility rates are still well above replacement level. Between 1960 and 2000 the Mexican total fertility rate declined dramatically from over 6 to 2.8 children per woman. As in other Latin American countries, the main contributor to this decline has been the extension of stopping behavior after a certain number of children has been achieved, with only modest delays in the timing of marriage or childbearing.

Unlike the more developed countries discussed in this volume, Mexico as yet shows no signs of undergoing a second demographic transition (Van de Kaa, 1987).

Similar to the "family-oriented" welfare regime prevalent in Southern Europe (see Simó *et al.*; Bernardi and Nazio, this volume), the family has long been a central institution for economic survival in Mexico. In precarious socioeconomic contexts that lack institutional and public structures of social support, the family often represents a central organizing principle to protect individuals against economic instability and poverty. Ethnographic studies have documented that the negative effects of financial crises are significantly mitigated among individuals of tightly knit families due to the ability of such families to pool resources among immediate and extended family members (Selby *et al.*, 1990). Even across generations, family structures, networks, and social support are central to employment opportunities, social mobility, unemployment insurance, and childcare support (Balan *et al.*, 1973; Guttman, 1996). In fact, in Mexico family formation is viewed as a highly desirable objective in and of itself (Selby *et al.*, 1990).

Overall, Mexico exhibits remarkable stability in the timing of union formation and first childbearing across generations (Parrado and Zenteno, 2002; Quilodrán, 1995). Nevertheless, there is considerable individual variation in ages at marriage and childbearing that is closely associated with socioeconomic opportunities and macro-economic conditions. Oppenheimer (1988; 1997) has provided a model for understanding differences in the timing of family transitions that links first union formation and parenthood to the uncertainties surrounding individuals' transition to adult social and economic roles (see also Blossfeld, 1995). Given the expectation of economic independence for newly formed unions, a major source of uncertainty lies in the nature and timing of the transition to stable work careers.

Depending on the nature of roles that women fulfill, uncertainties about long-term future prospects are particularly important for them. In contexts where women tend to specialize in home production and childrearing, most of the abilities required are passed from mothers to daughters during adolescence so that knowledge about women's long-term prospects is readily available at an early age. However, when women's roles begin to converge with those of men, there is increased uncertainty about their long-term prospects. In this situation, factors directly associated with changing gender roles - such as educational attainment or employment - can delay union formation, not because they reduce the gains to marriage but because they prolong women's transition to adult economic roles. At the same time, factors that reduce uncertainties - such as very high levels of education, stable employment in professional or skilled occupations, or strong attachment to the labor market - should facilitate marriage.

Moreover, convergence in gender roles implies a significant change in men and women's contributions to the household economy. Achieving economic independence and forming a union in a context of rigid gender specialization is almost completely dependent on men's income. In Mexico, however, unstable economic conditions - such as high levels of unemployment or frequent financial crises - can make rigid specialization of activities a risky strategy. In such an environment, women's labor force participation can actually facilitate marriage.

Also macro-economic uncertainty holds the potential of affecting women's family behavior. Economic crises and growing insecurity could delay marriage and childbearing if they hinder couples' ability to afford an independent household. If, on the other hand, couple formation is sufficiently valued as a personal objective and the family is perceived as a central institution for social support, couples could engage in other strategies to enact their family preferences. Female labor force participation could then be one such strategy for achieving an independent household, even in the face of growing macro-economic uncertainty.

DATA AND METHODS

My analysis assesses the role of economic globalization in women's employment and family behavior by comparing life course transitions across three cohorts of Mexican women. The data come from the 1998 National Retrospective Demographic Survey, known by its Spanish acronym EDER (Encuesta Demográfica Retrospectiva Nacional). The EDER collected retrospective information on family, fertility, and employment behavior[3] for a mature, intermediate, and young cohort of Mexican women. As depicted in Figure 13.1, these three cohorts represent very different periods in Mexican economic development in terms of GNP per capita. The mature cohort born between 1936 and 1938 was 20 years old in the late 1950s and represents the early period of Mexican economic development. The intermediate cohort born between 1951 and 1953 was 20 years old in the early 1970s and represents a period of rapid economic growth when import substitution industrialization in Mexico was at its zenith. Finally, the young cohort born between 1966 and 1968 was in its twenties in the late 1980s when economic restructuring and labor flexibilization policies were implemented, marking a period of prolonged income stagnation. To make the three cohorts perfectly comparable I restrict the analysis to events occurring between ages 12 and 30.

The analysis estimates discrete-time event history models predicting first employment, first union formation, and first child. In addition, since globalization is expected to have an impact on the occupational opportunities available to women, I also estimate discrete-time competing risks models (Blossfeld *et al.*, 1989) that predict labor market entry through particular types of occupation.

Table 13.1 reports changes in the dependent variables across cohorts. The proportion of women working before age 30 increased from 45 to 66 percent across cohorts and the occupational distribution of the female labor force also changed considerably. Even though women remain highly concentrated in only a handful of occupations,[4] over time their representation in professional/clerical[5]

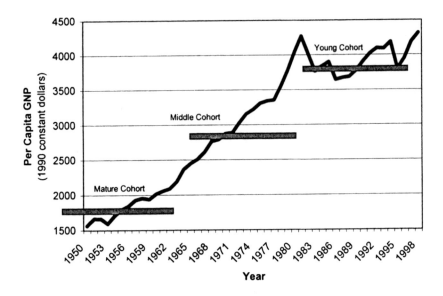

Figure 13.1   Trends in Mexico's per capita GNP and cohorts in the analysis

and retail occupations rose relative to domestic employment. In addition, the proportion of agricultural workers declined, while the proportion in blue-collar/manufacturing occupations rose across generations, although not monotonically.

Family behavior also shows some signs of change across cohorts. Table 13.1 evidences a slight delay in the timing of first union.[6] While about 85 percent of the women in the mature and intermediate generations were married by age 30, the corresponding figure for the younger cohort was only 73 percent. The same delay applies to the proportion of women with children: a much larger share of young women had no children yet by age 30 compared to either mature or intermediate generations of women.

The models to be estimated vary across life course transitions and include as predictors time-varying indicators of women's individual socioeconomic characteristics such as school enrollment, educational attainment, marital status, and labor force participation.[7] In addition, two sets of variables capture changes in period conditions. Dummy variables indicating membership in the mature, intermediate, or young cohort are expected to reflect the different economic and social environments in which each generation grew up. Dummy variables indicating years of boom, bust, or stable economic conditions were constructed using data on GNP per capita from the World Bank (2001). Boom and crises years are years in which GNP per capita grew by more than 3 percent and declined by more than 1 percent, respectively (see Figure 13.1 above). These indicators are intended to capture the direct effect of economic cycles on women's transition to adulthood.

Table 13.1   Changes in life course transitions across cohorts in Mexico

Cohort (birth-year)	Mature 36-38	Middle 51-53	Young 66-68
Employment outcomes			
Ever worked	44.7	52.4	66.3
Type of first occupation[a]			
Agriculture	14.1	7.5	5.9
Blue Collar / manufacturing	11.2	16.7	15.8
Sales / retail	16.5	21.6	23.1
Professional / clerical	20.0	29.1	36.6
Domestic	38.2	25.1	18.7
Marital status			
Ever married	85.7	84.5	72.7
Presence of children			
No children	9.7	12.1	19.5
1-2 children	17.8	25.1	36.4
3 children	72.5	62.8	44.1
N	380	433	412

Note
a   Among ever working women.

RESULTS

Labor market entry

Changes in labor market entry reflect important transformations in women's transition to adulthood. The key question in this analysis is whether rising female employment is a function of evolving human capital and family characteristics over time, or whether unique effects for cohort and economic instability can be identified. Results reported in Table 13.2 indicate that the rapid increase in female labor force participation across cohorts is closely associated with compositional changes in women's socioeconomic characteristics. Model 1 shows that after controlling for women's education and family situation, period conditions including cohort effects and cycles of boom and recessions have no significant effect on labor market entry.

However, we would expect the effect of period conditions to be more pronounced among married women, since they are more directly affected by changes in family income and deteriorating living standards. Model 3 adds an interaction term between marriage and cohort membership and shows that intermediate and young married women, representative of periods of economic

LIVERPOOL JOHN MOORES UNIVERSITY
LEARNING SERVICES

Table 13.2 Estimates from discrete-time models predicting labor market entry in Mexico

	Model 1		Model 2		Model 3		Model 4		Model 5	
	Coef.	(s.e.)	Coef.	(s.e.)	Coef.	(s.e.)	Coef.	(s.e.)	Coef.	(s.e.)
Constant	-5.883**	(0.505)	-6.324**	(0.517)	-5.915**	(0.506)	-6.029**	(0.508)	-6.381**	(0.520)
Baseline										
Age	0.320**	(0.056)	0.382**	(0.058)	0.334**	(0.057)	0.344**	(0.057)	0.398**	(0.059)
Age-squared	-0.008**	(0.001)	-0.009**	(0.002)	-0.008**	(0.001)	-0.008**	(0.001)	-0.010**	(0.002)
Rural community	-0.797**	(0.089)	-0.805**	(0.089)	-0.803**	(0.089)	-0.800**	(0.089)	-0.809**	(0.089)
Cohort (reference: mature)										
Middle	-0.047	(0.112)	-0.034	(0.112)	-0.181	(0.122)	-0.071	(0.112)	-0.135	(0.123)
Young	0.077	(0.117)	0.060	(0.117)	-0.069	(0.125)	0.078	(0.117)	0.027	(0.126)
Economic conditions										
Boom year	-0.109	(0.094)	-0.121	(0.094)	-0.101	(0.094)	-0.159	(0.102)	-0.154	(0.102)
Crisis year	0.012	(0.127)	0.012	(0.127)	0.004	(0.128)	-0.169	(0.142)	-0.148	(0.143)
Educational characteristics										
In school	-1.360**	(0.124)	-1.252**	(0.127)	-1.320**	(0.125)	-1.346**	(0.124)	-1.247**	(0.127)
Years of education	0.130**	(0.014)	0.103**	(0.015)	0.128**	(0.014)	0.129**	(0.014)	0.105**	(0.015)
Marital status (reference: not married)										
Married	-1.370**	(0.163)	-2.191**	(0.266)	-2.016**	(0.274)	-1.781**	(0.252)	-2.728**	(0.355)

Table 13.2 continued

	Model 1		Model 2		Model 3		Model 4		Model 5	
	Coef.	(s.e.)	Coef.	(s.e.)	Coef.	(s.e.)	Coef.	(s.e.)	Coef.	(s.e.)
Presence of children (reference: no children)										
1-2 children	-0.239	(0.181)	-0.240	(0.180)	-0.268	(0.182)	-0.228	(0.181)	-0.238	(0.181)
3+ children	0.003	(0.222)	0.180	(0.224)	0.035	(0.223)	0.015	(0.223)	0.167	(0.226)
Interaction terms										
Married*years of education			0.113**	(0.027)					0.102**	(0.031)
Middle*married					0.787**	(0.299)			0.510*	(0.311)
Young* married					0.882**	(0.292)			0.285	(0.333)
Married*boom year							0.419*	(0.262)	0.331	(0.272)
Married*crisis year							1.010**	(0.323)	0.810**	(0.335)
Chi-squared	728.09		745.10		739.00		737.77		755.61	
Df	12		13		14		14		17	
Person-years	20043									

Notes
* $p < 0.10$
** $p < 0.05$

growth and recession, respectively, are both significantly more likely to enter paid employment than mature married women.

Model 4 tests for the more immediate effect of economic fluctuations on married women's employment entry by adding an interaction term between marriage and boom or crisis year. Results confirm that married women's labor market incorporation is very responsive to rapid economic changes, particularly economic crises. Crisis years almost triple (exp(1.010)=2.746) married women's likelihood of labor market entry. Boom years, in contrast, increase married women's labor market entry by only 50 percent (exp(.419)=1.520). These outcomes would thus seem to speak in favor of the "added worker" hypothesis (see section "The transition to employment").

Model 5, which includes all interaction terms, shows that the effects of generational membership and economic cycles are closely associated. However, the fact that significant positive effects persist only for the interaction between marriage and intermediate cohort membership and for the interaction between marriage and crisis year suggests a different time-span for the effects of growth and recessions on female employment. While economic crises have an immediate effect pushing married women into the labor market, periods of economic growth have the more long-term effect of changing the attractiveness of married women's employment.

Individual characteristics also predict employment decisions in the expected direction. For instance, school enrollment conflicts with labor market activities, thereby significantly reducing the likelihood of labor market entry. Women with higher levels of completed education, on the other hand, are significantly more likely to work than their less educated counterparts. The negative effect of marriage reflects the constraints imposed by family life on market work, with a significant interaction between marital status and socioeconomic conditions. Model 2 confirms that the constraints imposed by marriage on labor market entry decline with higher levels of education. The presence of children however, has no additional effect on first employment once marital status is controlled.

It is important for our purposes to stress that economic crises motivate married women's incorporation into the labor market *for the first time*. The lack of previous labor force experience or employment skills of these new workers and the fact that they often enter the labor market under adverse economic conditions is likely to have a negative impact on their wages and occupational opportunities. It is important, therefore, to consider the impact of globalization on women's employment opportunities in addition to its impact on employment rates.

Type of first occupation

I therefore estimate competing risk models predicting labor market entry into particular types of occupations. Table 13.1 above documented important improvements in women's occupational distribution across cohorts. However, once we control for women's education, family, and period characteristics, the effects of cohort membership on the likelihood of entering employment via

Table 13.3 Estimates from discrete-time multinomial logit model predicting first occupation in Mexico (reference: not working)

	Agriculture		Blue Collar / Manufacturing		Sales / Retail		Professional / Clerical		Domestic	
	Coef.	(s.e.)	Coef.	(s.e.)	Coef.	(s.e.)	Coef.	(s.e.)	Coef.	(s.e.)
Constant	-5.790**	(1.372)	-6.588**	(1.205)	-9.054**	(1.197)	-16.499**	(1.898)	-5.928**	(0.829)
Baseline										
Age	0.092	(0.172)	0.163	(0.133)	0.477**	(0.128)	1.099**	(0.193)	0.351**	(0.100)
Age-squared	-0.005	(0.005)	-0.004	(0.003)	-0.011**	(0.003)	-0.027**	(0.005)	-0.010**	(0.003)
Rural community	0.776**	(0.357)	-0.885**	(0.222)	-1.272**	(0.200)	-0.726**	(0.193)	-0.974**	(0.159)
Cohort (reference: mature)										
Middle	-0.203	(0.339)	0.413*	(0.276)	0.316	(0.251)	-0.512**	(0.238)	-0.061	(0.196)
Young	0.368	(0.379)	0.509*	(0.312)	0.507**	(0.258)	-0.734**	(0.242)	0.346*	(0.215)
Economic conditions										
Boom year	-0.158	(0.306)	-0.049	(0.243)	-0.204	(0.204)	-0.104	(0.188)	0.131	(0.180)
Crisis year	-0.439	(0.528)	0.364	(0.302)	0.198	(0.249)	0.092	(0.224)	-0.003	(0.285)
Educational characteristics										
In school	-2.786**	(0.759)	-1.666**	(0.335)	-1.413**	(0.283)	-1.150**	(0.198)	-1.373**	(0.289)
Years of education	-0.023	(0.056)	0.111**	(0.034)	0.076**	(0.028)	0.402**	(0.031)	-0.148**	(0.031)
Marital status (reference: not married)										
Married	0.520	(0.443)	-1.831**	(0.385)	-1.605**	(0.324)	-1.051**	(0.275)	-1.817**	(0.337)

Table 13.3 continued

	Agriculture		Blue Collar / Manufacturing		Sales / Retail		Professional / Clerical		Domestic	
	Coef.	(s.e.)	Coef.	(s.e.)	Coef.	(s.e.)	Coef.	(s.e.)	Coef.	(s.e.)
Presence of children (reference: no children)										
1-2 children	-2.027**	(0.803)	0.564	(0.400)	0.019	(0.340)	-0.713**	(0.324)	0.291	(0.365)
3+ children	-0.672	(0.697)	0.911*	(0.499)	-0.019	(0.442)	-0.843	(0.562)	0.895**	(0.433)
Chi-squared	1314.5									
Df	60									
Person-years	20043									

Notes
* $p < 0.10$
** $p < 0.05$

higher status occupations are actually reversed. In fact, results suggest that professional, teaching, and clerical opportunities for women in Mexico did not expand at the same pace as education. Table 13.3 reports that intermediate and younger women are actually *less* likely to enter the labor market through professional or clerical occupations than mature women. The insufficient expansion of high status employment opportunities was in part compensated by an increase in entry-level employment through sales and retail occupations across cohorts.

Results from Table 13.3 highlight two main findings. First, cohort effects confirm changes in the occupational distribution of the female labor force associated with globalization and the expansion of the maquiladora industry. Both intermediate and younger women are significantly more likely than mature women to enter employment via blue-collar and manufacturing occupations. Second, young women enter the labor market through domestic occupations at a *higher* rate than mature or even intermediate women. In fact, women in the intermediate cohort were not at all more likely to enter paid employment through domestic work than mature women: their effect was slightly negative (-0.061).

Several processes contribute to the over-representation of younger women in domestic work (Chaney and Garcia Castro, 1989). One of them is the expansion of skilled occupations among women with higher social status, which increases their demand for domestic workers since career-oriented women may try to reduce family obligations by delegating family responsibilities. This process is facilitated by the growing economic inequality that reduces the relative costs of domestic workers (Milkman *et al.*, 1998). Another process is that deteriorating family incomes may force younger women to accept even more flexible forms of employment that do not necessarily conflict with household responsibilities.

As in models of labor market entry (Table 13.2), economic cycles do not exert an independent effect on first occupation. However, it is married women who are hypothesized to be the most strongly affected by macro-economic conditions. Therefore, I tested for an interaction between marriage and economic cycles. Results (not reported) showed that crisis years clearly accelerated the labor market entry of married women through agricultural, domestic, and professional occupations. The push into agricultural and domestic occupations reflects the fact that female employment has become an important household strategy among low-income families to compensate for the deterioration of family income: again, this could be seen as supporting evidence for the "added worker" hypothesis (cf. section "The transition to employment"). The fact that economic crises also push married women into the labor market through professional occupations suggests that in many cases the middle classes were equally threatened by economic recessions. Together, these results confirm the radical change in married women's labor supply conditions under periods of economic uncertainty and financial crises.

Lastly, individual-level characteristics show that better educated women are more likely to enter the labor market through professional, retail, and even blue-collar and manufacturing occupations, but less so through domestic employment. Marriage significantly constrains employment in all but agricultural occupations, while the presence of 3 or more children is a significant trigger of women's employment in both blue-collar and domestic occupations, suggesting that for large families from low socioeconomic origins female employment is an important source of additional household income.

First union formation and parenthood

The other two life course events reflecting important changes in women's transition to adulthood are union formation and first childbearing. Aggregate-level information (Table 13.1) showed relatively little change in the timing of marriage and parenthood over time. Nevertheless, there is considerable individual variation in the timing of these events that is expected to be closely associated with difficulties in the transition to adult social and economic roles.

Table 13.4 reports results from event history models predicting the likelihood of first union formation and parenthood. Given the endogeneity of marriage to the transition to parenthood, I estimated models predicting childbearing without (1) and with (2) marriage as covariate. After controlling for women's socioeconomic characteristics, neither cohort membership nor crisis and boom years have a negative effect on family formation. One period effect appears to actually exert a positive influence: the rate of union formation increases in years subsequent to a crisis, therewith suggesting that the relatively stable economic conditions following a crisis encourage union formation.

The overall lack of clear cohort and crisis effects on family formation supports descriptions given in earlier sections of the centrality of the family in Mexican society. Family formation and childbearing are highly valued in Mexico, and they also provide a vital source of stability in the face of economic insecurity. Seen from this perspective, one could say that macro-economic conditions motivate changes in other realms of behavior - such as female labor force participation - that still allow Mexicans to act on their strong preference to form and build families at more or less prescribed ages.

Micro-economic characteristics related to uncertainly affect family formation in a way that is consistent with expectations from life course models. For instance, school enrollment conflicts with family responsibilities and significantly reduces the likelihood of both marriage and childbearing. Higher levels of education are also associated with later ages at marriage. However, this effect is non-linear and weakens again as years of education increase, reflecting variation across educational groups in the uncertainties surrounding long-term attributes. Unlike poorly and highly educated women, who have more readily discernable economic prospects, women with intermediate levels of education face the greatest uncertainties about their economic potential and average the latest ages at marriage. The effect of education on first childbirth, on the other hand, is nearly linear, which is consistent with the assumption that the costs of childbearing increase with higher levels of education (although these effects are largely mediated through marriage, see model 2).

Table 13.4 Estimates from discrete-time models predicting family transitions in Mexico

	Union formation	First parenthood	
		Model 1	Model 2
Constant	-14.902**	-18.348**	-13.040**
	(0.752)	(0.864)	(0.989)
Age	1.266**	1.533**	0.822**
	(0.076)	(0.083)	(0.095)
Age-squared	-0.029**	-0.034**	-0.019**
	(0.002)	(0.002)	(0.002)
Rural community	-0.041	-0.151**	-0.126
	(0.073)	(0.075)	(0.084)
Cohort (reference: mature)			
Middle	0.093	0.190**	0.230**
	(0.086)	(0.086)	(0.096)
Young	-0.006	0.092	0.158
	(0.094)	(0.096)	(0.113)
Economic conditions			
Boom year	0.075	-0.099	-0.102
	(0.075)	(0.076)	(0.086)
Crisis year	0.002	-0.039	-0.105
	(0.075)	(0.077)	(0.087)
Year after boom year	0.090	0.108	0.142
	(0.093)	(0.093)	(0.107)
Year after crisis year	0.164*	0.093	0.058
	(0.092)	(0.094)	(0.107)
Educational characteristics			
In school	-1.645**	-1.887**	-0.901**
	(0.183)	(0.238)	(0.258)
Years of completed education (reference= no education)			
1-5	-0.266**	-0.198**	0.048
	(0.087)	(0.088)	(0.103)
6-9	-0.516**	-0.497**	-0.080
	(0.117)	(0.118)	(0.136)
10+	-0.299**	-0.413**	-0.119
	(0.140)	(0.139)	(0.168)

Table 13.4 continued

| | Union formation | First parenthood | |
		Model 1	Model 2
Employment (reference=			
not working)			
Agricultural worker	-0.805**	-0.990**	-0.062
	(0.224)	(0.223)	(0.248)
Manufacturing worker	-0.546**	-1.302**	-0.500**
	(0.176)	(0.197)	(0.218)
Professional/clerical	0.301	-0.776**	-0.150
	(0.185)	(0.144)	(0.169)
Sales worker	-0.277	-1.097**	-0.598**
	(0.184)	(0.194)	(0.214)
Domestic worker	-0.155	-1.016**	-0.455**
	(0.138)	(0.159)	(0.171)
Years of work			
experience	0.060**	0.094**	0.034**
	(0.016)	(0.014)	(0.015)
Married			3.964**
			(0.132)
Chi-squared	811.51**	1050.73**	3000.81**
Person-years	11937	13470	

Notes
* $p < 0.10$
** $p < 0.05$

The relationship between labor force participation and women's marriage timing is more complex. Only women employed in agriculture and manufacturing show later ages at marriage than non-employed women, suggesting the importance of family background for the relationship between occupation and marriage (Parish and Willis, 1995). Women's income is an important resource not only for forming an independent household but also for their families of origin. Many households in agricultural areas are dependent on the incomes generated by sons and daughters. Under these conditions there are strong pressures on women to remain with their families of origin, because losing their economic contribution would be very costly for other family members.

Women employed in manufacturing face a different kind of constraint. As mentioned before, various studies have shown that maquiladoras tend to recruit young, single childless women (Fernandez Kelly, 1982; Tiano, 1994). The demand for such a flexible labor force without much family attachments makes manufacturing employment an obstacle to marriage. The fact that women employed in commercial or professional activities do not delay union formation relative to non-working women contradicts female independence theories and suggests that the gains to marriage are not any lower among highly-qualified women.

The importance of economic stability for marriage is evident from the effect of previous work experience, which significantly increases the likelihood of women forming a union. Thus, instead of delaying union formation, work experience reduces uncertainties about women's potential economic contribution and accelerates their transition to other adult social roles.

The effect of employment characteristics on first parenthood indicates a stronger conflict between labor force participation and childbearing, since all types of employment reduce the likelihood of having a child (model 1). Some of these effects, however, disappear once we control for marital status (model 2). The fact that years of work experience actually accelerate having a child confirms the importance of the uncertainties surrounding women's economic roles and the potential financial contribution of women for understanding family life in Mexico.

DISCUSSION

Globalization has significantly altered the Mexican model of development, with direct implications for women's transition to adulthood. Using data from three generations of Mexican women, my analysis compared patterns of labor market entry, type of first occupation, union formation, and first childbearing under different periods of Mexican socioeconomic development. Results show that recurrent financial shocks and the expansion of foreign capital investments have significantly altered women's labor market entry opportunities, with indirect effects on the timing of marriage and childbearing.

Increased economic uncertainty and declining family incomes directly pushed married Mexican women into the labor market. The fact that this effect was present among married women only confirms the importance of income diversification as a household survival strategy to combat the growing insecurity accompanying the expanding global economy. Adding more family members to the labor market appears to be a rational household strategy among Mexican families in order to reduce the negative impact of breadwinner unemployment or rapid declines in household income that result from recurrent financial shocks.

In addition, the occupational composition of the female labor force was affected by changes in the international division of labor. The growth of manufacturing employment associated with the expansion of the maquiladora industry and foreign capital investments has expanded blue-collar employment among younger cohorts of women. At the same time, increasing female labor force participation came at a cost, as members of the younger cohorts required higher levels of education to achieve the same occupational status as earlier cohorts of Mexican women. Particularly important has been the increased representation of younger women in domestic work. This result reflects deteriorating employment opportunities for women after the demise of import substitution industrialization and corroborates the expansion of more flexible and unprotected forms of labor force participation that accompany economic restructuring.

The effect of globalization on first union formation and childbearing, on the other hand, was far more modest and mostly mediated by changes in female labor force participation. This result contradicts the experience of more developed societies, especially those in Southern Europe. The deeply rooted cultural value placed on family formation in Mexico and the importance of kinship networks as institutions of reciprocal support were not affected by macro-level uncertainties. Instead, Mexican women's transitions into marriage and childbearing are explained by micro-level uncertainties regarding the transition to adult economic roles and long-term work careers. In fact, the analysis suggests that Mexican women adapted their employment behavior in order to achieve their family goals. This is a far cry from the situation in, say, Italy and Spain (see Simó *et al.*; Bernardi and Nazio, this volume). Thus, although Mexico is often - and perhaps rightly so - placed on a par with clearly "familistic" welfare regimes, this pooling runs the risk of missing an important finesse (see also Mills, Blossfeld and Klijzing, this volume).

Overall, these results indicate the importance of *household* or couple survival strategies for understanding individual responses to the forces of globalization and uncertainty in Mexico. Financial shocks and foreign capital investments have both altered women's life course transitions and reinforced well-established principles of social organization. The need to protect rapidly deteriorating household incomes by diversifying their sources has significantly altered women's roles and contributions to the family economy, as well as intensified the reliance on mutual structures of social support that revolve around the family.

NOTES

1   The impact of globalization on Mexico is also evident in the large flow of labor migration to the United States, the emergence of new forms of social resistance (such as the Zapatista movement), and democratic reforms. However, these forces are beyond the scope of this chapter.

2   The *bracero* program was a temporary workers program initiated after the Second World War that allowed the U.S. government to contract Mexican agricultural laborers and hire them out to private farmers.

3   It is important to note that the questionnaire did not distinguish between part- and full-time or between public and private sector employment.

4   A mere 20 occupations encapsulate over 80 percent of women's entry-level employment in Mexico, with domestic work comprising the main source of employment, followed by sales, secretarial, and agricultural work.

5   Teachers and secretaries are the most common type of professional workers among women, followed by nurses.

6   Consensual unions among young couples are relatively uncommon in Mexico and my analysis does not distinguish between consensual and formal unions.

7   To mitigate problems of causal direction, time-varying variables were measured in the year prior to the occurrence of an event.

BIBLIOGRAPHY

Balán, J., Browning, H. L. and Jelin, E. (1973) *Men in a Developing Society. Geographic and Social Mobility in Monterrey,* Mexico: Austin and London: University of Texas Press.

Barkin, D. and Rosen, F. (1997) 'Why the recovery is not a recovery?' *NACLA report on the Americas,* 30: 24-25.

Becker, G. (1991) *A Treatise on the Family,* Cambridge: Harvard University Press.

Blossfeld, H.-P., Hamerle, A. and Mayer, K. U. (1989) *Event history analysis: statistical theory and application in the social sciences,* Hillsdale, N.J.: L. Erlbaum Associates.

Blossfeld, H.-P. (ed.) (1995) *The New Role of Women,* Boulder: Westview Press.

Buitelaar, R. M. and Padilla Perez, R. (2000) 'Maquila, economic reform and corporate strategies', *World Development,* 28: 1627-1642.

Castañeda, J. G. (1996) 'Mexico's circle of misery', *Foreign Affairs,* 75: 92-105.

Cerrutti, M. (2000) 'Economic reform, structural adjustment, and female labor force participation in Buenos Aires, Argentina', *World Development,* 28: 879-891.

Chaney, E. M and Garcia Castro, M. (eds) (1989) *Muchachas No More: Household Workers in Latin America and the Caribbean,* Philadelphia: Temple University Press.

Cooney, P. (2001) 'The Mexican crises and the maquiladora boom. A paradox of development or the logic of neoliberalism?', *Latin American Perspectives,* 28: 55-83.

Dussel Peters, E. (1997) *La Economía de la Polarización: Teoría y Evolución del Cambio Estructural de las Manufacturas Mexicanas (1988-1996),* Mexico: UNAM.

Dussel Peters, E. (1998) 'Mexico's liberalization strategy, 10 years on: Results and alternatives', *Journal of Economic Issues,* 32(2): 351-363.

Fernández Kelly, P. (1982) 'Las maquiladoras y las mujeres de Ciudad Juárez, México: paradojas de la industrialización bajo el capitalismo integral', in M. León (ed.) *Sociedad, Subordinación y Feminismo,* Bogotá: Asociación Colombiana para el Estudio de la Población.

Garcia, B and de Oliveira, O. (1994) *Trabajo Femenino y Vida Familiar en Mexico,* Mexico: El Colegio de Mexico.

Gereffi, G. and Martinez, M. (2000) 'Torreón's Blue: Exploring La Laguna's Full Package Solution', *Bobbin,* April: 13-24.

Gonzalez de la Rocha, M. (1994) *The Resources of Poverty. Women and Survival in a Mexican City,* Oxford: Blackwell.

Guttmann, M. C. (1996) *The Meanings of Macho: Being a Man in Mexico City,* Berkeley: University of California Press.

ILO (1993) *Repercusiones de la Reconversion Productiva y del Cambio Tecnológico sobre el Empleo y las Condiciones de Trabajo de la Mujer,* Chile: ILO.

INEGI (2001) *Industria Maquiladora de Exportación en Mexico,* Mexico: INEGI.

Kamel, R. and Hoffman, A. (1999) *The Maquiladora Reader. Cross-border Organizing since NAFTA,* Philadelphia: American Friends Service Committee.

Milkman, R., Reese, E. and Roth, B. (1998) 'The macrosociology of paid domestic labor', *Work and Occupations,* 25(4): 483-510.

Oppenheimer, V. K. (1988) 'A theory of marriage timing', *American Journal of Sociology,* 94: 563-591.

Oppenheimer, V. K. (1997) 'Women's employment and the gain to marriage. The specialization and trading model', *Annual Review of Sociology*, 23: 431-453.

Parish, W. L. and Willis, R. J. (1995) 'Daughters, education, and family budgets: Taiwan experiences', in T. Paul Schults (ed.) *Investment in Women's Human Capital*, Chicago: University of Chicago Press.

Parrado, E.A. and Zenteno, R. (2001) 'Gender differences in union formation in Mexico: Evidence from marital search models', *Journal of Marriage and the Family*, 64: 756-773.

Quilodrán, J. (1995) 'El matrimonio y sus transformaciones', in Paz López, María (ed.) *Hogares y familias: Desigualdad, conflicto, redes solidarias y parentales*, México, D.F.: Sociedad Mexicana de Demografía.

Reinhardt, N. (2000) 'Latin America's new economic model: Micro responses and economic restructuring', *World Development*, 28: 1543-1566.

Ros, J. (2000) 'Employment, structural adjustment, and sustainable growth in Mexico', *Journal of Development Studies*, 36: 100-119.

Rubery, J. (ed.) (1988) *Women and Recession*, London and New York: Routledge and Kegan Paul.

Selby, H. A., Murphy, A. D. and Lorenzen, S. A. (1990) *The Mexican Urban Household. Organizing for Self Defense*, Austin: University of Texas Press.

Standing, G. (1989) 'Global feminization through flexible labor', *World Development*, 17(7): 1077-1095.

Tiano, S. (1994) *Patriarchy on the Line: Labor, Gender and Ideology in the Mexican Maquila Industry*, Philadelphia: Temple University Press.

Van de Kaa, D.J. (1987) 'Europe's second demographic transition', *Population Bulletin*, 42 (1).

World Bank (2001) *World Development Indicators*: CD-Rom, Washington, D.C.: The World Bank.

14 Globalization and the transition to adulthood in Italy

Fabrizio Bernardi and Tiziana Nazio

INTRODUCTION

The aim of this chapter is to study the transition to adulthood in Italy from the perspective of the globalization process. The impact of globalization on individual life courses is studied as an indirect effect that is mediated by the structural changes in production systems and labor markets of OECD-type countries over the last 20-25 years. On the one hand, the diffusion of new information technologies has entailed fundamental transformations in the production processes of goods and services. Automation and the introduction of re-programmable computer machinery in the 1980s and 90s have set the conditions for a shift from large-scale production of standardized goods to flexible specialization and differentiated quality production (Soskice, 1999). This transformation in production processes has also meant a shift away from big to smaller firms and from the hierarchical structure of internal labor markets *within* firms to new forms of network associations *across* firms (Piore and Sabel, 1984; Sabel, 1991). Parallel developments in communication technology have made the transmission of information between separate and even remote locations increasingly faster and cheaper. Thus, telecommunications and computer-based transportation have provided the technological infrastructure for organizational restructuring such as downsizing, outsourcing to satellite firms and subcontracting (Castells, 1996).

On the other hand, the increase in economic interdependence in capital as well as in goods and services markets has prompted managers to search for more flexibility in employment relationships in order to cope more expeditiously with international competition and adapt more speedily to volatile and turbulent markets (Treu, 1992). In addition, the changes in the production and organizational structure of firms described above have contributed to a fragmentation of workers and a weakening of the bargaining power of unions. As a consequence, unions have been less able to oppose managerial claims for more flexibility (Leisink, 1999).

The focus of the empirical analysis presented in this chapter is on the *consequences* of the structural changes in the productive and employment structure for individual life courses. The central idea is that these macro changes have brought about an increase in insecurity at the individual level (Standing, 1999). We focus on two forms of insecurity.[1] At first we consider *economic insecurity*, which is referred to as the insecurity regarding the financial means available to an individual. An example of an economically insecure condition is that of being unemployed, or employed but in an occupation that involves a comparatively low level of pay and offers fewer saving opportunities (see also Kurz *et al.*, this volume). Secondly, we study *employment insecurity*, which is referred to as the insecurity that an employee faces with regard to the future development of his or her current employment position. Crucial in this respect is the reduction in permanent employment and the diffusion of fixed-term contracts, training contracts and semi-independent forms of employment (such as collaborators, consultants) that have taken place in most of the OECD countries in the last decades.

A previous study by one of the authors (Bernardi, 2000a) has focused on the consequences of the rise of these forms of insecurity for the early careers of new entrants in the Italian labor markets. This focus was similar to a series of other studies that have analyzed the process of entry into the Italian labor market (Schizzerotto and Cobalti, 1998; Bernardi *et al.*, 2000; Bernardi, 2000b). In the present chapter we aim to summarize the results of these previous studies on early employment careers and to link them to the analysis of first partnership formation and first childbirth. To this end, the transition to adulthood is studied as the outcome of three interrelated processes: entry in the labor market and early careers, formation of a first union and the transition to parenthood (see also Ongaro, 2001). The main questions that we address are: a) to what extent are economic and employment insecurity on the rise for the youngest cohorts of entrants in the Italian labor market? b) who is more affected by it? Or, in other words, are there some social groups that are more exposed to the rise of economic and employment insecurity than others? c) how does the rise in insecurity during early careers affect the likelihood of forming a first partnership and to have a first child? Needless to say, in trying to answer these questions there is inevitably a trade-off between a broad and synthetic approach and one that considers and discusses at great length all the possible facets of each of the single processes making up the transition to adulthood. In opting for the first approach, we will - when necessary - refer the reader to more specific analyses where early careers, union formation and first parenthood have been studied in more detail.

The main hypothesis put forward by Mills and Blossfeld in the first introductory chapter of this volume and which is also at the core of the analyses presented in the current chapter is that insecurity in early careers spills over into other dimensions of the life course. In other words, increasing difficulties in entering and settling into the labor market faced by younger generations are expected to translate in a delay of the decision to form a union and to have a child. Therefore, it might be argued that economic and employment insecurity should reduce the likelihood of forming a first union and to have a child (Clarkberg, 1999; Oppenheimer, 1988; Oppenheimer *et al.*, 1997). The underlying idea is that both decisions but particularly the one of having a child imply accepting long-term responsibilities with the other individuals involved: the partner and - certainly - the baby. When one of the partners' employment perspective is unclear, for instance in terms of opportunities and/or obligations to move to another city, it should be less likely that long-term commitments are taken. Moreover, both in the case of union formation and of childbearing there are financial costs involved that have to be met: the costs of adequate accommodation for the couple and, eventually, the additional costs incurred by having a child. This is not to suggest that only economic and/or strategic considerations dominate the decision to form a union and have a child. Rather, having achieved a minimal level of economic independence and security with regard to one's future employment situation may be regarded as a sort of "necessary but insufficient" condition to be fulfilled before any union formation and childbearing can take place.

However, the general hypothesis that economic and employment insecurity reduce the likelihood of union formation and childbearing has to be embedded in the specific context of Italy's institutions. National institutional contexts as defined by their different types of educational and training systems, labor market regulations and welfare state provisions play a crucial role in filtering and channeling the pressures brought about by the globalization process towards given social groups (Blossfeld, 2000). In other words, the *level* and *type* of insecurity as well as *who* is more affected by it will ultimately depend on the characteristics of the national institutional context, and thus vary across countries. For instance, in countries with strong institutional links between the educational system and the labor market the school-to-work transition is smoother and, therefore, the search period for a first job shorter (Bowers *et al.*, 1999). Moreover, the existence of generous unemployment benefits might compensate for the economic insecurity involved in a first job search or, more generally, being unemployed. In the same line of reasoning, a large provision of public services for families - for instance, child-care services and housing facilities - might reduce the insecurity related to being employed under a fixed-term contract. Independently from what may happen to such a job, the individual can at least rely on a set of public services that will help in case of need.

As will be discussed at greater length in the next section, neither of these three examples of institutional mechanisms that might reduce insecurity seem to apply to the Italian case. Overall, when compared with their peers in other nations - possibly with the exception of Spain - Italian youngsters seem to be particularly exposed to the new forms of insecurity brought about by the globalization process. Exploring the consequences of this for their transition to adulthood is our aim in the remaining pages.

The structure of the chapter is as follows. In the next section, some institutional features of the Italian labor market are sketched. Then, the data and methods used in the empirical analysis are presented. Finally, in the last two sections the results of the analysis are discussed and some tentative conclusions are drawn.

THE INSTITUTIONAL REGULATION OF THE TRANSITION TO ADULTHOOD IN ITALY

We will only discuss here the main characteristics of the Italian educational and vocational training systems (section "The Italian educational and vocational training systems: weak institutional linkages with the labor market"), labor market regulations (section "Labor market regulations") and public services to families (section "The welfare state and the family").[2] In doing so we will selectively focus on those aspects that seem particularly important for the transition to adulthood.[3]

The Italian educational and vocational training systems: weak institutional linkages with the labor market

In Italy as in other developed countries an impressive increase in educational attainment has occurred since the end of the Second World War. Among school leavers in the period 1950-65, only 15 percent had achieved a diploma of secondary education and 4 percent a university degree. For school leavers after 1984 these proportions have risen to 46 and 13 percent, respectively. The educational expansion has been paralleled by changes in the organization of the educational system. Before the reforms of the 1960s, the Italian educational system was characterized by a high degree of stratification and tracking. Lower-secondary education was divided into two tracks: one academic (*Scuola media unica*) and one vocational (*Scuola complementare* and, since 1930, *Scuola di avviamento professionale*), with the latter offering very limited opportunities to access higher education. The same division between academic and vocational education was present at the upper-secondary level of education: only those who had attended the general education school (*Licei*) had the right to enroll at a university, a privilege mostly restricted to the elite. In 1962 compulsory school age was raised to 14 years, various tracks at lower-secondary education were abolished, and a unified *Scuola media inferiore* was created. Some years later, in 1969, under the pressure of students' mobilization, access to university was also opened to graduates from secondary technical and vocational schools. In this way the already limited practical vocational training provided by these schools has been further reduced.

The greater access to universities, however, has been counter-balanced by an increase in the number of dropouts and in the duration of studies (Schizzerotto and Cobalti, 1998). In order to tackle these problems, new types of courses lasting only 2-3 years (*Lauree brevi*) were created at the beginning of the 1990s. However, given their low level of specialization and their uncertain value in the labor market, only few students have opted for these types of courses. Finally, at the end of the 1990s, a radical reform of the university system was introduced which is currently still being implemented and which divides academic studies into 3 basic years plus 2 optional ones to specialize.

After a reform in 1978, vocational training outside the educational system is run by regional administrations and - in principle - it should provide specific skills that are necessary to enter the work force. However, it has progressively developed into an inferior "B-rate", semi-scholastic system which is mainly attended by dropouts from secondary education. Thus, practical and specific work skills and experience are mainly achieved through on-the-job-training (Regini, 1997).

In brief, the main changes in the Italian educational and training system that are important for the transition to adulthood seem to be twofold. First, a steep rise in educational attainment has taken place across cohorts. This means that nowadays young individuals are spending more and more time within the educational system. There are also hints that the incidence of prolonged university careers has increased (Bernardi, 2000b). Second, in the Italian case the institutional links between the educational and vocational training system, on one side, and the labor market, on the other, are very weak (Hannan *et al.*, 1996). Students exiting from secondary or tertiary education lack specific knowledge that would be directly valuable for entering the labor market. Vocational training programs outside the education system do little to fill this gap. This means that in general employers will have little incentive to hire school leavers when applicants with work experience are readily available. This de-coupling of the educational and vocational system from the labor market makes the school-to-work transition problematic and very long: in 1998, 33.5 percent of all youngsters aged 15-24 years were unemployed (ISTAT, 1999). Moreover, a large fraction (60 percent) of the long-term unemployed consists of young people searching for their first occupation.

Labor market regulations[4]

Following the post-war years of reconstruction and the economic boom of the 50s, which were accompanied by a fast decline in agriculture and a parallel growth in industrial employment, a trend emerged towards more regulation and protection of labor. This trend achieved its peak between the mid-1960s and -70s, a period also known as the era of 'collective action', with high levels of labor unrest and social conflict (Ginsborg, 1989). For instance, in 1966 a law was passed that limited the right to firing in large firms. In 1970 the Workers Statute (*Statuto dei Lavoratori*) further strengthened employment protection (Samek Lodovici, 2000). These reforms came at a time, however, when economic growth was already coming to an end (Wolleb, 1988). The two oil crises in the 1970s and the concomitant rise in unemployment and inflation led at the beginning of the 1980s to one of the deepest economic crises since the end of the Second World War.

It is against this background of high employment protection gained by workers' mobilization, enduring power of unions and serious economic crisis that the pressures of the globalization process as discussed in the introduction have to be framed. Thus, the organizational restructuring and management claims for more employment flexibility so as to adapt to a more volatile market and to face international competition were supported by the Government finding it increasingly difficult to use traditional Keynesian measures to boost the economy. Moreover, the high level of unemployment put the unions in an increasingly defensive position of preserving rights already achieved and protecting workers already employed. Given the unions' resistance to any radical deregulation of the labor market, the measures that favored employment flexibility have been directed mainly towards new entrants into the labor market.

The progressive erosion of employment protection for new entrants and the persistently high rate of unemployment have contributed to the emergence of an insider/outsider labor market that, to a certain extent, follows the division lines between successive labor force entry cohorts. That is, members of the older cohorts enjoy the strong employment protection guaranteed by the regulatory measures of the 1960s-70s, while members of the younger cohorts are more likely to be either unemployed or employed under non-permanent, precarious contracts. Two aspects thus seem important for understanding the situation of young entrants into the labor market: the system of unemployment benefits and the regulation of employment relationships.

With respect to the first, it must be pointed out that people who are looking for their first job as well as the self-employed are not eligible for any unemployment benefits (Dell'Aringa and Samek Ludovici, 1996). Among those who have been employed, the amount and duration of benefits varies greatly, depending on the kind and period of the previous job held, the sector of employment and, above all, the size of the firm.[5] In 1995 the proportion of unemployed workers who obtained some form of economic support was under 10 percent (Gallie and Paugam, 2000).

With respect to the regulation of employment relationships, incentives for training contracts for young people were introduced by means of two reforms, one in 1977 and one in 1984 (Gualmini, 1998). These contracts have a maximum duration of two years, they can be used to hire young people aged 15-29 years[6], they are non-renewable, and work experience should in principle be matched by general courses of vocational training (even if in practice this rarely seems to be the case). Later, incentives for the transformation of training contracts into permanent ones were introduced. As a result, employers could create new training contracts only if at least 50 percent of previous training contracts in their firms had been transformed into permanent ones (Adam and Canziani, 1999). Apart from these training contracts, limitations on using fixed-term contracts were relaxed in 1987, while agency work was liberalized in 1997.

Besides these training and fixed-term contracts for employees, Italy - together with other Southern European countries - may be said to be characterized by one of the highest incidences of irregular employment and self-employment (Mingione, 1995).[7] Moreover, self-employment has become more diversified and new forms of semi-independent employment are on the rise (Reyneri, 1996). Thus, new forms of employment now include the self-employed without employees as well as consultant/collaborators who, while being formally independent - they do not enjoy any protection and security regarding the continuity of their activity - *de facto* work in a dependent, subordinate position. The emergence of these new employment forms can be seen as part of the organizational restructuring induced by the globalization process. On the one hand, they can be interpreted as a way to off-set strict employment regulation and thus to achieve more employment flexibility for the individual; on the other, they can be read as an indicator of the resurgence of an entrepreneur spirit that is fostered by new technologies making it possible for small businesses to find their market niches (Castells, 1996: 221).

The welfare state and the family

The Italian welfare state together with other Southern European ones is well-known for its pronounced *familistic* character (Saraceno, 1994; Esping-Andersen, 1999). At the core of this overall welfare system is its "subsidiarity" principle: the State assumes the family (and women within it in particular) to be the main provider of welfare and limits its intervention to cases where the capacity of the family to cater to the needs of its own members is exhausted. For the impact of the Italian welfare state on the transition to adulthood and in particular to parenthood, three areas of public intervention can be distinguished: housing policies, the system of services and transfers provided for families, and the regulation of maternity and parental leave.

Currently more than 70 percent of all Italian families are home-owners. However, results of a research reported by Saraceno (1998) suggest that achieving home-ownership has become increasingly difficult: if in the 1960s buying a house required 2-3 times the annual income, in the 1990s this ratio has risen to 5-6 times (Tosi, 1994, as quoted by Saraceno, 1998). The situation is not much better if one considers housing rents. In 1978 a law was issued (*Equo canone*) that aimed at regulating them. This law has mainly benefited families who already had a renting contract and who were able to reduce their rent via this new law. Indeed, an unintended effect of the law has been that of reducing the supply of houses in the official renting market and promoting a black market for them. This means that newly-formed families searching for a house were particularly penalized. Public housing has declined in the last decades as well, and is extremely limited now. Since families that have been evicted have priority access to public housing, newly-formed families are *de facto* largely excluded also from this sector.

Moving to services and transfers provided for families, in Italy there is a highly developed public system of kindergartens for pre-school children (3-5 years old), with more than 95 percent of them being covered by this service. However, the supply of day-care facilities for children aged 0-2 years is very limited and mainly delegated to the private market. The public service is a non-compulsory, local responsibility (with selection at entry due to exceeding demand) which is being paid for by the users, at high and in recent years growing costs. As a result, only 6 percent of all children aged 0-2 years have had access to this service (ISTAT, 1995). Moreover, in contrast to other European countries such as France and Germany, child allowances and fiscal deductions available to families are also very scant (Saraceno, 1998).

With regard to maternal and parental leave, Italy seems to have one of the best laws in Europe in terms of length of leave, pay, and guarantees of job conservation. However, access to these rights has long been - and to a certain extent still is - segmented by occupation and type of contract (Saraceno, 1994; 1998). At one extreme, women employed in the public sector can fully enjoy the rights provided by the law; at the other, those employed in the black market do not have any protection. For women employed in the private sector, punishments at re-entry after maternity leave - whether in the form of job downgrading or transfers to another factory or city - are in actual practice by no means rare. Moreover, for people employed under training or other fixed-term contracts, there is no guarantee of job conservation at the end of the leave. That is, once their contract has expired, chances of having it renovated if leave was taken seem small. Finally, autonomous workers (self-employed professionals, consultants, etc.) have long been discriminated in terms of pay received during their maternal leave. It is only at the end of the 1980s that their right to get an amount of money similar to the one received by dependent workers was recognized.

As a consequence of the lack of an adequate child-care system and the segmentation of maternity leave regulations, coupled with the rise in non-standard employment as described in the previous section, the trade-off that women nowadays face between pursuing a career in the labor market and having a child has exacerbated. In fact, as a previous study has shown (Bernardi, 2001), women exit the labor market to become housewives at the time of (or just before) getting married or having a child. As a result, in 1995, one in two married women aged 20-50 was housewife. Thus, the traditional male breadwinner model is still widespread among Italian households.

The institutional context: summary and hypotheses

As comes out clearly from the above discussion, Italian youngsters should be particularly exposed to the rise in economic and employment insecurity brought about by the globalization process. Overall, it would seem that the Italian case can be considered as a "worst-case" scenario with regard to institutional mechanisms that might mitigate the rise in insecurity during early careers in the labor market. The following consequences for the transition to adulthood can, therefore, be expected.

First of all, the very long search period for a first job and the lack of any benefits during this time should reduce the likelihood of assuming any long-term commitment. In the same line of reasoning, the lack of an adequate system of public services or economic support for families should exacerbate the impact of economic differences on the likelihood of marriage and childbearing. Following the segmentation of maternal and parental leave regulations, with some occupational groups enjoying more protection (public sector) than others (non-permanent contracts, new forms of self-employment), further differences can be anticipated in the likelihood of childbearing. Finally, given the persistence of the traditional male breadwinner model, it can be expected that economic and employment insecurity will have a different impact on men than on women. That is, if men are still supposed to provide the financial means of the family, one can surmise that economic and employment insecurity for them will be particularly detrimental to family formation and childbearing. On the other hand, since many women are at best supplementary income earners within the family and since they have the option or perspective of becoming housewife, early career insecurity for them should be less important in explaining their union formation and childbearing behavior.

DATA, VARIABLES AND METHODS

The empirical analysis is based on data from the *Indagine Longitudinale sulle Famiglie Italiane* (ILFI), the Italian Longitudinal Household Survey carried out in 1997 by a consortium of the University of Trento, Istituto Trentino di Cultura and ISTAT (Statistics Italy). The nationally representative sample consisted of 9,770 individuals belonging to 4,457 households throughout Italy.

In order to study the transition to adulthood we consider three separated but interconnected processes: entry and early careers in the labor market, formation of the first union and transition to the first child. For each of these steps we are interested in analyzing the consequences of rising insecurity brought about by the labor market restructuring. As pointed out in the introduction, we focus on two forms of insecurity: economic insecurity and employment insecurity.

As an indicator of economic insecurity we consider the employment status of the respondent and distinguish among the following 7 positions: being (i) in the educational system; (ii) outside the educational system but not yet searching for a first job; (iii) in search of a first job; (iv) unemployed; (v) inactive (housemaker); (vi) outside the labor market for other reasons (disabled, retired, etc.); and (vii) employed. Given the lack of unemployment benefits, individuals in search of a first occupation or the unemployed are particularly exposed to economic insecurity. Among the employed - in the absence of retrospective information on income - we distinguish different occupational classes using Erikson and Goldthorpe's (1992) class scheme. Since people employed in unskilled occupations earn lower incomes and have fewer saving opportunities than those employed in the service class or in skilled occupations, they can be considered to be more economically insecure.[8]

With regard to employment insecurity, among the dependent workers a five-fold distinction was considered: those working (i) with a permanent contract; (ii) with a fixed-term training contract; (iii) with other forms of fixed-term contracts; (iv) as consultants/collaborators; and (v) without a contract.[9] Ideally, this classification provides a hierarchy in terms of employment security, going from a maximum for those with a permanent contract to a minimum for those with no contract at all. The category of consultants/collaborators expresses a grey area between dependent and independent employment: formally they are independent but *de facto* they share the lack of autonomy and the hierarchical relationships that are so typical of dependent employment. Among the dependent workers we further distinguish between employment in the public and in the private sector. This distinction is particularly important in the analysis of parenthood. As we have argued in the previous section, women in the public sector - besides having working hours that allow them an easier reconciliation with family responsibilities - enjoy more protection and they can fully benefit from the rights of maternal and parental leave.

The logic behind the specification of variables used to operationalize the two forms of insecurity is described in Table 14.1.

The three processes that make up the transition to adulthood have been studied using an event history approach. With regard to early careers in the labor market, we summarize the findings presented in more detail by Bernardi (2000a). We focus on two transitions: entry into unemployment for all those who have entered the labor market, and exit out of insecure forms of employment for those who have achieved an insecure contract at entry into the labor market. The key question here is: are the risks of unemployment (economic insecurity) and entrapment in a precarious job (employment insecurity) evenly distributed, or are people employed in given occupational classes more exposed to them?

In the analysis of union formation we only study entry into marriage. Given the limited number of couples starting a non-marital cohabitation in Italy, a substantive analysis of this latter process was not possible. However, entry into cohabitation was defined as a competing risk in the study of entry into marriage. The time axis of the event history analysis for each individual begins at age 14 and is censored at age 35 for those who by that time had not yet experienced the event in question. The same window of observation was used in the analysis of the transition to the first child. The key question here is: to what extent do economic and employment insecurity, as defined above, lower the likelihood of the transition to marriage and first child?

All the analyses have been stratified by cohort of entry into the labor market and, in the case of marriage and parenthood, also by gender. Given our interest in the recent and ongoing changes in the labor market induced by the globalization process, most of the attention will be focused on the experience of the youngest cohorts of entrants in the labor market (after 1977), as these have been more exposed to those changes. Two differences in the analyses of early careers and first marriage/child should be mentioned. First, in the analysis of early careers only those who have ever worked are considered, and their cohort of entry in the labor market is defined according to the starting date of their first job. In the analysis of the transition to marriage and childbearing, also those who have never worked are considered. For these respondents the cohort of entry into the labor market actually refers to their date of exit from the educational system. Second, in the analysis of early careers, when focusing on the experience of the younger cohort we have considered entrants in the labor market after 1984. In the analyses of first marriage and childbirth, however, in order to have more events and robust results we have used a broader definition and considered entrants after 1977.[10] Finally, in addition to the indicators of economic and employment relationship insecurity, other variables have been included in the analyses as well but mostly for control reasons. (The full lists of independent variables with corresponding definitions can be found in Appendix Table 14.1). In the next pages we will present and discuss only the results that refer to the consequences of economic and employment insecurity.[11]

Table 14.1 Variables used to operationalize economic and temporal (employment) insecurity in Italy

Economic/temporal insecurity			Economic insecurity		Temporal insecurity
School enrolment	Employment/non-employment condition	Employment position	Occupational class (Erikson-Goldthorpe's scheme)		Type of contract
Being in school					
	Out of school not yet looking 1st job				
	Looking 1st job				
	Unemployed				
	Inactive (homemaker)		Liberal professions (I)		
			Self-employed with employees (I-IVab)		
			Self-employed with no empl. (IVab)		
			Farmers (IVc+VIIa)		
	Other cond. out of labor market				
		Agriculture			
	Employed (ref.)	Dependent workers	Service class (I-II)		Permanent (ref.)
			Routine non manual (IIIa)		Fixed-term: training contract
			Skilled workers (V-VI)		Other fixed-term contract
		Self-employed	Unskilled manual (VIIb) (ref.)		No-contract
			Unskilled consumer service (IIIb)		Consultant
			Unskilled non manual (IIIb)		
Being out of school (ref.)					

RESULTS

Table 14.2 offers a synthetic overview of various aspects of the transition to adulthood for different cohorts of entrants in the Italian labor market. Thus, for the youngest cohorts of entrants (after 1977), the chances of finding a permanent job at entry in the labor market have declined and the risk of experiencing unemployment in the subsequent 5 years has increased. There is also a rise in the median age at first marriage and childbearing.[12]

In the following section ("Early careers") we investigate in more detail - i.e., at the individual level - the processes related to the rise in economic and employment insecurity as described in the upper panel of Table 14.2. Thereafter we study the consequences of these processes for changes in marriage (section "First marriage") and first parenthood (section "First child").

Early careers

Table 14.3 presents the results of piecewise exponential models for the exit out of insecure forms of employment and for the entry into unemployment. Models 1 and 3 refer to all the cohorts of entrants in the labor market, whereas Models 2 and 4 include only those who have entered the labor market after 1984. The main findings of these analyses can be summarized as follows.

First of all, the results point to a worsening of the employment perspectives for the younger entrants in the labor market. Compared to the reference cohort of entrants in the period of high labor market regulation (between 1966 and 1977), younger entrants have lower chances to transform an insecure contract into a permanent one (Model 1) and they run a higher risk to fall into unemployment (Model 3). Second, if one focuses only on the younger cohort, people in unskilled occupations are more likely to remain entrapped in insecure forms of employment (Model 2) and to experience unemployment (Model 4), when compared to the service class, the white collars and skilled workers. In other words, for the cohort that has been most exposed to the changes induced by the globalization process, there is evidence that economic and employment insecurity tend to accumulate at the bottom of the occupational structure. Moreover, a comparison with the older cohort of entrants in the labor market, as discussed in Bernardi (2000a), suggests that class differences have become more accentuated for the younger cohorts. This clearly contradicts the popular thesis of an individualization of inequality as put forward by some globalization theorists (Beck, 1992).

First marriage

Table 14.4 presents the results of piecewise exponential models for the transition to first marriage, separately for men and women, of the two younger cohorts of entrants in the labor market (in this case, after 1977).

Table 14.2   Early careers, marriage and first child for different cohorts of entry in the Italian labor market: summary prospect

	Men				
	1900-1949	1950-1965	1966-1976	1977-1983	1984-1997
Probability 1st job:					
Permanent	33.9	54.7	58.6	51.9	41.1
Fixed-term training contract	1.7	2.4	4.2	5.2	10.4
Other fixed-term contract	3.6	4.7	5.8	9.4	10.5
No contract	16.6	17.2	14.8	12.3	13.4
Consultant	0.7	1.3	1.3	1.7	2.5
Self-emp. with emp.	5.1	5.5	6.4	8.2	10.2
Self-emp. no emp.	3.6	2.4	2.6	2.7	3.9
Liberal professionals	0.3	0.3	1	2.1	3.7
Missing type of contract	2.2	1.8	1.5	1.9	1.7
Agriculture	32.4	9.7	3.9	4.6	2.6
Percent who have experienced unemployment at least once in the first 5 years of employment	4.1	6.0	8.3	11.5	14.9
Median age at marriage	27.8	27.1	26.7	28.3	31.1
Median age at first child	29	28.5	28.2	31.3	a

Table 14.2 continued

	Women				
	1900-1949	1950-1965	1966-1976	1977-1983	1984-1997
Probability 1st job:					
Permanent	35.0	54.2	55.3	49	41
Fixed-term training contract	1.0	2.8	5.7	3	9.5
Other fixed-term contract	2.9	6.5	11.5	14.6	15.7
No contract	17.8	16.2	16.3	18.3	14.8
Consultant	1.9	1.5	1.1	2.5	5.4
Self-emp. with emp.	3.5	4.2	3.6	5.2	4.2
Self-emp. no emp.	4.6	3.6	1.3	1.5	2.5
Liberal professionals	-	0.1	-	0.7	2.9
Missing type of contract	2.2	2.3	1.8	2.7	2
Agriculture	31.0	8.5	3.6	2.5	1.9
Percent who have experienced unemployment at least once in the first 5 years of employment	2.9	7.3	10.5	14.0	19.4
Median age at marriage	24.3	23.3	22.9	24.8	29.3
Median age at first child	25.4	24.5	24.2	27.3	33.8

Note
a   50% of the members of this entry cohort in the labor market have not had the first child at age 35.

Table 14.3   Transition from insecure to permanent contract (Models 1 and 2) and from employment to unemployment (Models 3 and 4) in Italy

	Exit from insecure contract		Entry into unemployment	
	Model 1	Model 2	Model 3	Model 4
	All entrants	Younger entrants	All entrants	Younger entrants
Entry in the labor market				
Before 1950	-0.66**		-0.47**	
Between 1950-1965	-0.08		-0.24*	
Between 1966-1976 (Ref.)	0.00		0.00	
Between 1977-1983	-0.25*		0.11	
Between 1984-1997	-0.38**		0.58**	
Type of contract [a]				
Fixed-term training contract	0.24*	0.41*	1.40**	1.57**
Other forms of fixed-term contract	0.02	0.12	1.93**	2.20**
Consultant	-1.30**	-1.17*	-0.63	-0.10
No contract (Ref.)	0.00	0.00	1.33**	1.67**
Permanent contract (Ref.)			0.00	0.00
Occupational class				
Service class	-0.20	0.71**	-0.49**	-0.66**
Routine white collar	0.00	0.89**	-0.18	-0.37*
Skilled workers	-0.12	0.44	-0.30**	-0.37*
Unskilled non manual	-0.01	0.38	0.09	-0.31
Unskilled consumer service	-0.01	0.22	0.08	0.07
Unskilled manual (Ref.) [b]	0.00	0.00	0.00	0.00
Self-employed no employees	-1.64**	-0.69	-1.33**	-0.71
Self-employed with employees[c]	-2.21**	-1.21**	-1.52**	-1.54**
Liberal professions	-1.63**	c	-2.03**	c
Number of events	518	140	666	296

Selected effects of piecewise exponential models (controlling also for episode duration, sex, age, education, vocational training, region, previous spells of unemployment, and sector).

Notes
a   Specified only for the dependent workers.
b   With the introduction of the variable "type of contract" for the dependent workers, the reference categories for the self-employed is *unskilled manual worker with no contract* (in models 1 and 2) and *with permanent contract* (in models 3 and 4).
c   Liberal professions are aggregated with the self-employed with employees.
** $p < 0.05$, * $p < 0.10$

Table 14.4   Transition to first marriage in Italy

Younger entrants in the labor market (1977-97)	Model 1 Men	Model 2 Women	Model 3 Men	Model 4 Women
Employment / non employment				
Out of school, not yet looking 1st job	-1.74**	-1.41**	-1.40**	-1.17
Looking 1st job	-1.41**	-0.69**	-1.09**	-0.45*
Unemployed	-0.70**	0.11	-0.41	0.34
Inactive (homemaker)	-	1.24**	-	1.46**
Out of LM	-	-0.25*	-	-0.02
Missing LM	-0.07	-0.05	0.23	0.17
Employed (ref.)	0.00	0.00	0.00	0.00
Type of contract [a]				
Fixed-term training contract	-0.65**	-0.38	-0.65**	-0.37
Other forms of fixed-term contract	0.10	-0.06	0.09	-0.07
Consultant	-0.34	-0.35	-0.27	-0.39
No contract	-0.04	-0.60**	-0.00	-0.60**
Permanent contract (Ref.)	0.00	0.00	0.00	0.00
Occupational class				
Service class			0.42**	0.36
Routine white collar			0.55**	0.24
Skilled workers			0.39**	0.17
Unskilled service workers			0.12	0.24
Unskilled manual (Ref.) [b]	0.00	0.00	0.00	0.00
Self-employed with employees [c]	-0.12	0.19	0.19	0.41
Self-employed no employees	-0.09	-0.54**	0.24	-0.29
Agriculture	-0.03	0.35	0.25	0.56
Number of events	622	832	622	832

Selected effects of piecewise exponential models (controlling also for episode duration, sex, age, educational level, educational enrolment, region)

Notes
a   Specified only for the dependent workers.
b   With the introduction of the variable type of contract for the dependent workers, the reference category for the self-employed is *unskilled manual with permanent contract.*
c   Liberal professions are aggregated with the self-employed with employees.
** $p < 0.05$
* $p < 0.10$

Model 1 shows that both economic and employment insecurity reduce the rate of first marriage: men who are unemployed and in particular those in search of a first occupation are less likely to marry. The same is true for those employed under a fixed-term training contract. It is important to remember (see Table 14.2) that both the duration of the first job search and the probability of having a training contract at entry into the labor market have been progressively increasing over the last years. In Model 3 where we add occupational class, it can be seen that men employed in unskilled manual occupations and thus more economically insecure given their lower salary, are also less likely to make the transition to marriage.

For women the results are remarkably different. In general it seems that economic insecurity is much less a deterrent to marriage for them than for men. Unemployed women do not have a lower first marriage rate, while being inactive strongly increases it (Model 2). Women who - like men - are in search of their first job are less likely to marry, but this effect is much smaller. Moreover, occupational class for employed women does not seem to imply substantial differences in their likelihood to marry (Model 4). On the other hand, employment insecurity is important also for women: those who are employed without a contract or who are self-employed without employees are less likely to marry.

First child

Table 14.5 presents the results of our analysis of the transition to the first child, separately for men and women, for the two younger cohorts of entrants in the labor market (after 1977). The results of Model 1 for men resemble the findings of the analysis of the transition to first marriage. Thus, in general, economic and employment insecurity reduce the rate of first fatherhood: being in search of a first occupation and, among those employed, having a fixed-term training contract make having the first child less likely. On the other hand, a positive effect is found for men who are employed in the service class, a hint that access to greater economic resources facilitates the decision to have a first child.

As was the case in the analysis of first marriage, gender differences become evident when results for women are considered (Model 2). Being a housewife strongly increases the chances of having the first child, while no such effect appears for those in the other categories. Occupational class does again not make a difference among employed women. Thus, overall, the divide seems to run between women who are housewives and those who are part of the labor force.

In Models 3 and 4 for the employed the distinction between public and private sector is introduced. This distinction is important because public employees are fully able to benefit from the existing legislation on maternal and parental leave. As expected, the results show that being employed in the public sector has indeed a positive effect on the rate of first parenthood, particularly among women. This finding supports the idea that the higher employment security enjoyed by women in the public sector increases their likelihood of having a first child.

Table 14.5 Transition to first child in Italy

Younger entrants in the labor market (1977-97)	Model 1 Men	Model 2 Women	Model 3 Men	Model 4 Women	Model 5 Men	Model 6 Women
Employment / non employment						
Out of school, not yet looking 1st job	-1.41**	-1.78**	-1.36**	-1.76**	-0.87**	-0.39
Looking 1st job	-1.61**	-0.39	-1.57**	-0.37	-1.06**	-0.31
Unemployed	-0.30	0.04	-0.27	0.05	-0.14	-0.36
Inactive (homemaker)		1.22**		1.23**		0.23
Out of LM		-0.07		-0.06		-0.11
Missing LM	0.32	0.43	0.35	0.44	0.27	0.23
Employed (ref.)	0.00	0.00	0.00	0.00	0.00	0.00
Type of contract [a]						
Fixed-term training contract	-0.83*	-0.06	-0.82*	-0.04	-0.64	0.37
Other forms of fixed-term contract	0.15	0.21	0.15	0.13	0.27	0.30
Consultant	-0.44	-0.48	-0.34	-0.37	-0.43	-0.25
No contract	0.13	-0.42*	0.20	-0.37	0.58**	0.31
Permanent contract (Ref.)	0.00	0.00	0.00	0.00	0.00	0.00
Occupational class						
Service class	0.37*	0.26	0.34	0.16	-0.02	-0.19
Routine white collar	0.24	0.01	0.18	-0.10	-0.19	-0.20

Table 14.5 continued

Younger entrants in the labor market (1977-97)	Model 1 Men	Model 2 Women	Model 3 Men	Model 4 Women	Model 5 Men	Model 6 Women
Skilled workers	0.31	0.40	0.27	0.36	-0.12	0.20
Unskilled service workers	0.04	0.14	-0.02	0.09	-0.08	-0.09
Unskilled manual (Ref.) [b]	0.00	0.00	0.00	0.00	0.00	0.00
Self-employed with employees [c]	0.13	0.35	0.17	0.36	-0.16	-0.14
Self-employed no employees	0.22	-0.39	0.27	-0.36	0.03	-0.63*
Agriculture	0.45	1.03**	0.48*	1.03**	0.39	0.29
Sector						
Public			0.14*	0.29**	0.15	0.13
Private (ref.)			0.00	0.00	0.00	0.00
Marital status						
Married					3.03**	3.07**
Cohabiting					1.75**	2.43**
Single (ref.)					0.00	0.00
Number of events	471	675	471	675	471	675

Selected effects of piecewise exponential models (controlling also for episode duration, sex, age, education level, educational enrolment, region).

Notes

a Specified only for the dependent workers.
b With the introduction of the variable type of contract for the dependent workers, the reference category for the self-employed is *unskilled manual with permanent contract*.
c Liberal professions are aggregated with the self-employed with employees.
** $p < 0.05$
* $p < 0.10$

Finally, in the Models 5 and 6 a time-varying variable controlling for marital status is added. This overrules most of the effects as commented upon so far. This suggests that getting married is the key intervening variable in explaining the transition to the first child in Italy. Substantively, it points to the fact that the decision to enter a marriage and to have a first child are closely interconnected. Finally, cohabiting couples are also more likely to have a first child than single persons but this differential is much less pronounced than among married couples.

CONCLUSIONS

In this chapter we have studied the impact of globalization on the transition to adulthood. We have argued that one of the consequences of the extensive restructuring of firms and organizations as fostered by the globalization process has been the rise of insecurity at the individual level. We have, then, addressed three questions: a) to what extent are economic and employment insecurity on the rise for the youngest cohorts of entrants in the labor market? b) who are more affected by it? c) how does the rise in insecurity in early careers affect the likelihood of forming a first partnership and of having the first child?

The results presented in the previous sections show that insecurity in early employment careers has indeed increased for the youngest cohort of entrants in the labor market. They need more time to find a first job, they have fewer chances to get a first job with a permanent contract and to transform an insecure contract into a permanent one. Moreover, they run a higher risk of falling into unemployment in the first years of their employment career.

Furthermore, those employed in unskilled occupations among the youngest cohort are particularly at risk of experiencing unemployment and remaining entrapped in a precarious contract situation. Thus, the empirical evidence points to an accumulation of disadvantages at the bottom of the occupational structure. In other words, if early careers for young generations are in general already more insecure, this is particularly true for those employed in unskilled occupations.

Finally, the worsening of employment opportunities for the youngest cohort of entrants in the labor market has a clear impact on both family formation and childbearing. Therefore, our results support the general hypothesis that economic and employment insecurity make the long-term decision to marry and to have children less likely.

However, there are clear gender differences in this respect. These differences reflect the persistence of the traditional male breadwinner model among Italian families. In fact, it is especially economic and employment insecurity among men that influences family formation and childbearing. Thus, for them it is the condition of being unemployed, in search of a first occupation or employed under a precarious contract or in a low paid job that reduces their likelihood of getting married or having the first child. For women these effects are less pronounced, and the main distinction seems to be between inactive women (who are more likely to marry and have their first child) and those who are employed.

However, if one considers the transition to first motherhood only, being employed in the public sector increases the likelihood of childbearing, whereas being employed in the black market (without formal contract) reduces it.

The transitions to marriage and the birth of the first child appear very closely connected. In fact, being married is the single most important predictor for the arrival of the first child. Thus, given the low level of extramarital births in Italy, union formation seems to be the central step in the transition to adulthood. Even if we have not directly explored this in our analysis, one might argue that difficulties in finding suitable accommodation are at the core of the delay in marriage and thus childbearing. The fact that housing rents and prices have strongly risen in the last decades might also explain the strengthening of the economic differences that we found for the youngest cohort of men.

Overall, these result have to be interpreted in the light of the specific characteristics of the Italian institutional context. As we have argued with regard to various institutional features that may help making the transition to adulthood smoother, Italy's can be considered a "worst-all" case. First of all, the pressure of labor market restructuring that was induced by a set of processes collectively referred to as globalization has been largely directed towards young generations. Thus, new entrants in the labor market carry the dual burden of high unemployment and flexible employment. At the same time, there are no institutional mechanisms at work in Italy that might otherwise off-set or partially counterbalance the rise in insecurity in the labor market. As we have pointed out, there are no unemployment benefits for those who are in search of first-time employment, the provision of child-care services is modest, financial support to families scanty, and there are almost no housing policies for new families. Our findings suggest that in the absence of adequate institutional support, rising insecurity in employment careers for the youngest cohorts of Italians contributes to a progressive delay in their transition to adulthood.

Appendix Table 14.1   *Definitions of the independent variables*[a]

In school-out of school

Being out of school — Dummy = 1 if the person has finished education and exited school system

Level of education achieved

Elementary or less — Dummy = 1 if the person has acquired up to a primary educational level
Compulsory (Ref.) — Dummy = 1 if a compulsory educ. level has been acquired (Dipl. Inferiore)
Professional (2-3 years) — Dummy = 1 if professional educ. level has been acquired (Dipl. Profession.)
Technical (5 years) — Dummy = 1 if secondary educ. level has been acquired (Dipl. Superiore)
Liceum (5 years) — Dummy = 1 if a secondary educ. level has been acquired (Dipl. Superiore)
University — Dummy = 1 if a tertiary educ. level has been acquired (Laurea)

Geographical area

North — Dummy = 1 if the person resides in Northern Italy
Third Italy (Centre) — Dummy = 1 if the person resides in Central Italy
South (Ref.) — Dummy = 1 if the person resides in Southern Italy
Being abroad — Dummy = 1 if the person resides abroad

Cohort of entry into the labor market

1900-1959 — Dummy = 1 if the person has entered the labor market between 1900-1949
1950-1965 — Dummy = 1 if the person has entered the labor market between 1950-1965
1966-1976 (Ref.) — Dummy = 1 if the person has entered the labor market between 1966-1976
1977-1983 — Dummy = 1 if the person has entered the labor market between 1977-1983
1984-1997 — Dummy = 1 if the person has entered the labor market between 1984-1997

Employment / non employment

Out of school, not yet looking 1st job — Dummy = 1 if exited the school system but not actively looked for 1st job yet
Looking 1st job — Dummy = 1 if looking for 1st job
Unemployed — Dummy = 1 if unemployed after having worked
Inactive (homemaker) — Dummy = 1 if housewife
Out of the labor market — Dummy = 1 if out of the labor market (renter, military service, and others)
Employed (Ref.) — Dummy = 1 if working

Appendix Table 14.1 continued

Type of contract (only for dependent workers)[b]

Fixed-term training contract	Dummy = 1 if employed with a training contract
Other forms of fixed-term contract	Dummy = 1 if employed with a fixed-term contract other than training
Consultant	Dummy = 1 if employed as a consultant
No contract	Dummy = 1 if the job is without a formal contract
Permanent contract (Ref.)	Dummy = 1 if employed with a permanent contract

Occupational class[b]

Service class	Dummy = 1 if service class (I-II)
Routine white collar	Dummy = 1 if routine non manual worker (IIIa)
Skilled workers	Dummy = 1 if skilled worker (V-VI)
Unskilled service workers	Dummy = 1 if unskilled non manual worker (IIIa)
Unskilled manual (Ref.)	Dummy = 1 if unskilled manual worker (VIIb)
Self-employed with employees	Dummy = 1 if self-employed with employees (I-IVab)
Self-employed no employees[c]	Dummy = 1 if self-employed without employees or liberal prof. (I-IVab)
Agriculture	Dummy = 1 if the job is in the agricultural sector (Ivc+VIIa)

Sector[b]

Public	Dummy = 1 if the job is in the public sector
Private (ref.)	Dummy = 1 if is in the private sector

Marital status

Married	Dummy = 1 if married
Cohabiting	Dummy = 1 if cohabiting
Single (ref.)	Dummy = 1 if not yet in marriage or cohabitation

Notes

a   All variables with the exclusion of the cohort of entry in the labor market are time-varying.

b   Only for those who are employed.

c   Liberal professions are aggregated with the self-employed without employees.

NOTES

1   For a more in-depth discussion on various forms of insecurity in the labour market, see Standing (1999).
2   Another important feature of the Italian case is the geographical segmentation of its labor market (Reyneri, 1996). For this reason we have taken geographical differences into account in our empirical analysis (see Nazio and Bernardi, 2002, for more details). However, given the trade-off between synthesis and comprehensiveness, we will not discuss the implications of geographical cleavages for the transition to adulthood.
3   For a more exhaustive description of the functioning of the educational system, the changes in labour market regulations and characteristics of the Italian welfare state, see e.g. Bernardi (2000b); Samek Lodovici (2000); Saraceno (1994; 1998).
4   This section draws on Bernardi (2000a).
5   For a more detailed discussion of the types of income support for the unemployed in Italy and the criteria of qualification, see Dell'Aringa and Samek Lodovici (1996).
6   The maximum age was raised to 32 in 1994.
7   In the mid-1990s irregular employment was estimated to be around 15 percent of the overall labor force, while the self-employed accounted for more than 25 percent of the employed (ISTAT, 1999).
8   One might argue quite aptly that using social class as an indicator of economic insecurity is not correct. In fact, the concept of class points to a stability and persistence in a given position in the structure of inequality (Erikson and Goldthorpe, 1992). In this respect, people employed in the unskilled classes are *secure* rather than *insecure* of having a low income. But while the income is sure, changes in the environments and in the costs of making a living are not. In particular, one has always to face unforeseeable and unpredictable financial expenses: for instance, car repairing, house maintenance, dentist bill, etc. Thus, working in an unskilled position (however certain the low income and little possibility of saving associated to this position might be) can be considered an economically insecure position because one can not be fully sure of disposing of the financial means needed to make a living.
9   One should be cautious in interpreting the effects for the category "other forms of fixed-term contracts". This is a quite heterogeneous group that includes, for instance, temporary teachers, seasonal workers in the tourist or food industry, occasional workers in construction, etc. Moreover, its composition has changed across cohort and by gender. See Nazio and Bernardi (2002) for more details.
10 Since, as we will show, insecurity in early careers has increased over time, one might speculate that effects found for entrants after 1977 actually underestimate the impact of the worsening employment conditions on the transition to first marriage/childbearing. In this regards, our results can be considered as conservative. In order to assess the full impact of the worsening employment opportunities on the transition to first marriage and child, one would have to wait until the complete marriage and childbearing histories of those who entered the labor market in the second half of the 1980s become available.
11 The entire set of results and the descriptive statistics for the independent variables are reported in Nazio and Bernardi (2002).
12 The results in Table 14.2 regarding first marriage and childbirth for entrants in the labor market after 1984 are at best indicative because the processes under study can only be partially observed.

BIBLIOGRAPHY

Adam, P. and Canziani, P. (1999) 'Partial De-Regulation: Fixed Term Contracts in Italy and Spain', no. 386, Centre for Economic Performance, London School of Economics.

Beck, U. (1992) *Risk Society, Towards a New Modernity*, London: Sage.

Bernardi, F. (2000a) 'Globalization and social inequality: changing patterns of early careers in Italy', GLOBALIFE Working Paper No. 07, Faculty of Sociology, University of Bielefeld.

Bernardi, F. (2000b) 'Educational performance and educational returns at entry into the Italian labor market', GLOBALIFE Working Paper No. 10, Faculty of Sociology, University of Bielefeld.

Bernardi, F. (2001) 'The employment behavior of married women in Italy', in H.-P. Blossfeld and S. Drobnič (eds) *Careers of couples in contemporary societies*, Oxford: Oxford University Press.

Bernardi, F., Layte, R., Jacobs, S. and Schizzerotto, A. (2000) 'Who exits unemployment? Institutional features, individual characteristics and chances of getting a job. A comparison of Britain and Italy', in D. Gallie and S. Paugam (eds) *Welfare Regimes and the Experience of Unemployment*, Oxford: Oxford University Press.

Blossfeld, H.-P. (2000) 'Globalization, Social Inequality and the Role of Country-specific Institutions: Open Research Questions in a Learning Society', GLOBALIFE Working Paper No. 11, Faculty of Sociology, University of Bielefeld.

Bowers, N., Sonnet, A. and Bardone, L. (1999) 'Giving Young People a Good Start: the Experience of OECD Countries', in OECD (ed.) *Preparing Youth for the 21st Century: The Transition from Education to the Labour Market*, Paris: OECD.

Castells, M. (1996) *The Rise of the Network Society*, Oxford: Blackweel Publishers Ltd.

Clarkberg, M. (1999) 'The Price of Partnering: The Role of Economic Well-Being in Young Adults's First Union Experiences', *Social Forces*, 3: 945-968.

Dell'Aringa, C. and Samek Lodovici, M. (1996) 'Policies for the Unemployed and Social Shock Absorbers: The Italian Experience', *South European Society and Politics*, 1: 172-197.

Erikson, R. and Goldthorpe, J. (1992) *The Constant Flux. A Study of Class Mobility in Industrial Societies*, Oxford: Clarendon Press.

Esping-Andersen, G. (1999) *Social Foundations of Postindustrial Economies*, Oxford: Oxford University Press.

Gallie, D. and Paugam, S. (eds) (2000) *Welfare Regimes and the Experience of Unemployment in Europe*, Oxford: Oxford University Press.

Ginsborg, P. (1989) *L'Italia Contemporanea*, Torino: Einaudi.

Gualmini, E. (1998) *La Politica del Lavoro*, Bologna: Il Mulino.

Hannan, D., Raffe, D. and Smyth, E. (1996) *Cross-National Research on School to Work Transitions: An Analytical Framework*, Paris: OECD.

ISTAT (1995) *Rapporto Annuale. La Situazione del Paese nel 1994* [Annual report. The country situation in 1994], Roma: ISTAT.

ISTAT (1999) *Rapporto Annuale 1998*, Roma: ISTAT.

Leisink, P. (1999) 'Introduction', in P. Leisink (ed.) *Globalization and Labour Relations*, Cheltenham: Edward Elgar.

Mingione, E. (1995) 'Labour Market Segmentation and Informal Work in Southern Italy', *European Urban and Regional Studies*, 2: 121-143.

Nazio, T. and Bernardi, F. (2002) 'Globalization and the transition to adulthood: a methodological note and the entire set of results', GLOBALIFE Working Paper No. 29, Faculty of Sociology, University of Bielefeld.

Ongaro, F. (2001) 'Transition to adulthood in Italy', in M. Corijn and E. Klijzing (eds) *Transitions to Adulthood in Europe*, Dordrecht: Kluwer Academic Publishers.

Oppenheimer, V. K. (1988) 'A Theory of Marriage Timing', *American Journal of Sociology*, 3: 563-591.

Oppenheimer, V. K., Kalmijn, M. and Lim, N. (1997) 'Men's Career Development and Marriage Timing During a Period of Rising Inequality', *Demography*, 3: 311-330.

Piore, M. and Sabel, C. (1984) *The Second Industrial Divide*, New York: Basic Book.

Regini, M. (1997) 'Different Responses to Common Demands: Firms, Institutions, and Training in Europe', *European Sociological Review*, 13, 267-282.

Reyneri, E. (1996) *Sociologia del Mercato del Lavoro*, Bologna: Il Mulino.

Sabel, C. (1991) 'Moebius-Strip Organizations and Open Labour Markets: Some Consequences of the Reintegration of Conception and Execution in a Volatile Economy', in P. Bourdieu and J. Coleman (eds) *Social Theory for a Changing Society*, Boulder: Westview Press.

Samek Lodovici, M. (2000) 'Italy: The Long Times of Consensual Re-regulation', in G. Esping-Andersen and M. Regini (eds) *Why Deregulate Labour Markets?*, Oxford: Oxford University Press.

Saraceno, C. (1994) 'The Ambivalent Familism of the Italian Welfare State', *Social Politics*, Spring: 60-82.

Saraceno, C. (1998) *Mutamenti della Famiglia e Politiche Sociali in Italia*, Bologna: Il Mulino.

Schizzerotto, A. and Cobalti, A. (1998) 'Occupational Returns to Education in Contemporary Italy', in W. Müller and Y. Shavit (eds) *From School to Work. A Comparative Study of Qualification and Occupations in Thirteen Countries*, Oxford: Oxford University Press.

Soskice, D. (1999) 'Coordinated and Uncoordinated Market Economies in the 1980s and 1990s', in H. Kiltschelt, P. Lange, G. Marks and J. Stephens (eds) *Continuity and Change in Contemporary Capitalism*, Cambridge: Cambridge University Press.

Standing, G. (1999) *Global Labour Flexibility. Seeking Distributive Justice*, London: MacMillan Press.

Tosi, A. (1994) *La Casa: il Rischio e l'Esclusione - Rapporto IRS sul Disagio Abitativo in Italia*, Milano: Franco Angeli.

Treu, T. (1992) 'Labour flexibility in Europe', *International Labour Review*, 131: 497-512.

Wolleb, E. (1988) 'Belated Industrialization: The Case of Italy', in R. Boyer (ed.) *The Search for Labour Market Flexibility. The European Economies in Transition*, Oxford: Clarendon.

15 The Spanish case

The effects of the globalization process on the transition to adulthood

Carles Simó Noguera, Teresa Castro Martín and Asunción Soro Bonmatí

INTRODUCTION

The global division of labor derived from an increasingly integrated world economy, and the pressing need to adjust to accelerating changes in the international environment have deeply transformed the context of work in most countries (see Blossfeld, this volume). In the process of adapting their productive structures to new demands and increasing competition from other countries with lower labor costs, most post-industrial societies have experienced a sharp increase in unemployment as well as a rise in job precariousness and temporality, as a sort of accommodating strategy to pressures for increasing flexibility, which basically transfers the risks of the employer in a rapidly changing market to the employee (McKay, 1988). Spain is no exception to these developments. In fact, a combination of historical, structural, and institutional factors have converged to exacerbate some of the adverse implications of globalization, such as unemployment and job precariousness, for which Spain holds the highest record in the European Union. This situation at the macro level carries important consequences at the individual level for the transition to adulthood.

The economic system during the Franco regime was extremely rigid, based on secure employment in exchange of modest salaries and absence of workers rights, very low unemployment at the expense of pervasive underemployment, exclusion of women from the labor force, massive migration and a weak welfare system with scarce social services built on the assumption that it would be complemented by women's unpaid work as caretakers. The end of the dictatorship in the mid-1970s marked the onset of a period of intensive political, economic, social and cultural modernization. The democratization of the country and its opening-up to the international arena intensified the influences of the globalization process. In the economy, this process brought about a dramatic decline of the agrarian sector, a deep restructuring of the manufacturing sector (mostly in the metal and textile industries), and a steep rise of the service sector, mainly in administration and tourism (Tamames, 1995). These important economic transformations coincided in time with a substantial rise of the economically active population, due to the entry into the labor market of larger birth cohorts and to the increase in women's labor force participation. The latter is linked to the remarkable expansion of women's education, as well as to their rising aspirations to a work career (Garrido Medina, 1992). This educational expansion is partly in response to the increasing need of knowledge and information that a globalizing world requires (see Blossfeld, this volume).

For a long time the Spanish labor market has been characterized by a strong rigidity. As a consequence, compared to other Western European countries, unemployment rates have increased enormously, broadening the gap between labor market "insiders", mainly adult males, and "outsiders", mainly youngsters and women trying to find or improve their job positions (OECD, 1994; Garrido Medina, 1992). As we will see, several labor market reforms and changes in the educational system have been initially directed to these outsider groups in order to facilitate their entry into the labor market. However, most recent labor policies have only succeeded in introducing deregulation and flexibility in work relations (Moran, 1991). Although these reforms have facilitated the access to the first job, they have primarily brought about an increasing instability and precariousness in working relations for people entering the labor force. In addition to longer waiting times between leaving school and first employment, young men and women are increasingly confronted with unstable labor conditions, such as temporary work and time-limited contracts. Moreover, those developments have not been accompanied by policy attempts to build a social protection system especially addressed to those vulnerable groups. Consequently, the family remains the main institution responsible for providing the necessary support to young adults until they achieve economic emancipation.

We will see that in the Spanish context, characterized by difficult access to the first job and by an increased exposure to unemployment, individuals postpone partnership formation and the family building process. In our reasoning, individuals are assumed to adapt their partnership and childbearing preferences to the new constraints and sources of uncertainty that they are faced with when trying to establish themselves in the labor market. This chapter focuses on how these changes affect the transition to adulthood. It is organized as follows. The first section provides a description of the most relevant developments in those institutions which play a significant role in the transition to adulthood in Spain: the educational system, the labor market and the welfare protection system. Then we present the theoretical framework used as a guideline for the empirical analysis and formulate the hypotheses in the light of this framework. It follows a description of the data set and the methodology. Next we discuss the main results of our analyses and, finally, summarize our major findings and conclusions.

THE ROLE OF THE INSTITUTIONS

The Spanish educational system

As pointed out by Iannelli and Soro-Bonmatí (2000), the Spanish educational system is in many respects similar to that of other European countries such as Italy. According to them, the Spanish system can be classified as one with a high degree of standardization and medium degree of stratification, in which "a common system of curricula, certifications and examinations is decided at the central national level and uniformly applied at the local level, while the upper secondary level is differentiated into tracks (academic and vocational), although the content of vocational education is quite general, so that the degree of stratification is medium" (Iannelli and Soro-Bonmatí, 2000, p. 4).

The peculiarities of the contemporary Spanish educational system reflect the outcomes of the reforms introduced since 1970. The 1970 Education Law (*Ley de Ordenación de Educación Básica*) introduced among other things the following changes in the previous educational system. First, it fixed the end of compulsory education at two years before the legal age of entering the labor market (age 14 for mandatory schooling against 16 for legal labor market entrance). Second, with its application, the Law of 1970 eroded the image of vocational training, which became the *poor brother* of general education programs (Albert *et al.*, 1999, p.28). In order to overcome these problems, a new reform of the Spanish educational system was introduced in the 1990s, known as LOGSE (*Ley de Ordenación General del Sistema Educativo*), which increased the compulsory education up to age 16 and which included basic technical training within this period of compulsory education. Nevertheless, the effects of this recent reform are not yet visible since it has been only gradually implemented, so that the academic year of 1999-2000 was the first in which the entire system was working under the new setting.

Furthermore, the 1983 Law for the Reform of the University System (known as LRU, *Ley de Reforma Universitaria*) played a major role in the rapid expansion of education at the tertiary level. The LRU granted autonomy to Spanish universities which from the mid-1980s onwards have been experiencing a rapid growth, both in number and in the amount of curricula offered. The greatest expansion has been in the supply of short-term degrees (two- or three-years university degrees). As a result, Spain has experienced the fastest development of the higher education system in Europe. As outlined by Iannelli and Soro-Bonmatí (2000), the annual series of the Spanish Labor Force Survey show that the proportion of 25-34 year-olds with a university level of education (including short- and long-term degrees) is three times higher in the 1990s than in the 1970s. Their study also offers a preliminary assessment of the relative weight of short-term degrees in Spain compared to other European countries. According to their figures, in Spain 40 percent of higher education degrees correspond to short-term degrees, while in Italy the equivalent proportion is only 9 percent.

Finally, it is worth remarking that the large educational expansion has significantly narrowed the gender gap in education. In fact, in the 1990s this gap has disappeared, and young men and women now reach analogous levels of educational attainment. As we shall highlight later on, this increase in the educational attainment of Spanish women underlies the notable rise in female labor force participation rates.

The Spanish labor market

As we noted in the introduction, Spain has experienced in the last three decades an intense process of economic modernization and a fast integration into the world economy. These transformations have been accompanied by a sharp increase in the rate of unemployment (see Figure 15.1), which in the 1980s and first half of the 1990s averaged 20 percent, a rate more than twice the Western European average and far exceeding that of any other industrial society (Maravall and Fraile, 1998).

This high level of unemployment has made the Spanish case a central topic of specialized literature (Bentolila and Blanchard, 1991). One of the peculiarities of the Spanish labor market is the uneven distribution of unemployment, which is concentrated among women and youth. In 1995, for instance, the rate of unemployment for women was 30.6 percent compared to 18.2 for men, and among those aged under 25, unemployment rates reached 36.4 percent among men but 48.1 among women. Another characteristic of Spanish unemployment is its persistence. Despite the reforms intended to reduce the long-term unemployment problem, the percentage of Spaniards unemployed for more than twelve months is still very high, especially among those aged 16-24 (around 45 percent in 1995).

However, neither the uneven distribution of unemployment nor its persistence are exclusively Spanish; they are also distinctive features of the labor market in other Southern European countries such as Italy (see for example Bernardi and Nazio, this volume). After recent labor market reforms, the Spanish unemployment problem seems to have been somewhat alleviated in the sense that the percentage of people who are long-term unemployed and looking for a first job has decreased, although at the cost of increased levels of job instability (Iannelli and Soro-Bonmatí, 2000).

The high levels of unemployment in Spain and the increasing need of upgraded skills to ensure a successful job career have probably reinforced the expansion of education, particularly at the post-compulsory level. In contrast to the past, however, the decision to remain longer in education is often no longer based on the prospects of future higher wages (the recent period is characterized by declining returns to education), but on the lack of an alternative occupation or merely on the hope to enhance the chances to avoid unemployment. This has produced a displacement (or *crowding-out*) of young workers with at most compulsory education from their traditional entry jobs - for example, clerical and administrative occupations (Dolado *et al.*, 2000) - by workers with higher levels of educational attainment.

A series of labor market reforms initiated in Spain, as in other European countries, in the mid-1980s in order to introduce flexibility and increase competitiveness have transformed the Spanish labor market structure (Iannelli and Soro-Bonmatí, 2000). Since 1984, when new modalities of fixed-term contracts were introduced, Spain has gone through a series of reforms aimed at reducing hiring and firing constraints (Bentolila and Dolado, 1994). The 1984 reform of the Workers' Statute[1] introduced three new modalities of fixed-term contracts, namely, training contracts, practice contracts and contracts to promote hiring

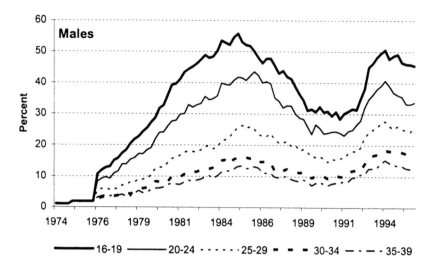

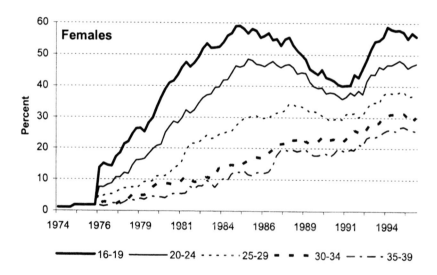

Figure 15.1 Age- and sex-specific unemployment rates, Spain, 1974-1995

Source: ILO, Year Book of Labor Statistics, Genf, 1993; ILO, Year Book of Labour Statistics, 1945-1990; and Spanish Survey of Active Population (EPA). Madrid, National Institute for Statistics (INE). Enquête "Jeunes et carrières 1997", INSEE.

(*contrato de aprendizaje, contrato en prácticas, contratos de promoción de empleo*), which by suppressing the high firing costs of traditional indefinite contracts were assumed to promote hiring. Employers quickly embraced these flexible work arrangements, particularly temporary employment, which then expanded from 10 percent of the salaried labor force in 1984 to about one-third in 1995, by far exceeding the average in the European Union (see also Klijzing, this volume). The expansion has been more marked among those under age 25, for whom the percentage of employees with fixed-term contracts in 1995 was over 70 percent.

The process of flexibilization and deregulation of temporary employment has not affected all age groups homogeneously. Temporary contracts are mainly offered to new entrants in the labor force, leaving unchanged the protection enjoyed by permanent workers. As a result, the Spanish labor market has become a clear example of a dual labor market segmented into two categories of workers (Lindbeck and Snower, 1989): the "insiders" or those enjoying indefinite contracts (predominantly adult males) and coverage by high firing constraints against the risk of being laid off, and the "outsiders" or those with short-term contracts (predominantly the young and women), who endure poor working conditions, instability and few opportunities for advancement. Hence, the risks and uncertainties associated with globalization are not equally spread across all workers but have been channeled towards those age groups which are precisely at the life cycle stage of family formation.

The effects of recent labor market reforms on job stability have often been addressed in the literature (Bentolila and Dolado, 1994; Amuedo-Dorantes, 2000). Although temporary contracts do provide first-entry labor market opportunities, they deepen the insider-outsider divide since long-term jobs are rarely available to new entrants. Furthermore, as several studies have revealed (Amuedo-Dorantes, 2000), temporary work is more likely to become a trap than a bridge to permanent employment and, therefore, the efficacy of temporary employment as a vehicle of job mobility towards a more stable position is dubious.

Hence, young cohorts - despite being the highest educated in Spanish history and the best qualified to meet the challenges of the information society - can not count on stable employment to develop their project of life in other spheres. As we will discuss later on, uncertainty in the work domain is likely to pervade the private domain, reducing their ability and/or willingness to engage in long-term commitments that partnership formation requires. Young adults not only have difficulties entering the labor market but once inside it, they face a pessimistic outlook on their chances of stability and upward mobility. Since education alone is no longer a guarantee of success in a highly competitive environment, they may be also compelled to concentrate all their efforts on building their career at the expense of their private life.

The family-oriented Spanish welfare system

The difficulties of young Spaniards to enter and remain in the labor market are just barely mitigated by the prevailing welfare system. Since social entitlements derive principally from employment rather than citizenship (as is the case in the Nordic welfare model) or proven need, they do not apply to most young job searchers. Furthermore, even those who succeed in entering the labor force do not have their unemployment coverage insured unless they accumulate 12 months of contributions, a requirement difficult to fulfil when individuals work under fixed-term contracts. In the absence of state transfers or supporting policies, young (and adult) aspirants and recent entrants in the labor market typically rely on family support and kinship networks, a pattern that reflects the institutionalized familism embedded in the Spanish welfare system (Esping-Andersen, 1999). In a context where the family plays a central role in sheltering young adults from the hardships of the market forces (Reher, 1998), individuals may be less willing to form a partnership and set up a new household, when that transition implies a relative deterioration of their standard of living with respect to the one they enjoy in the parental household. In Spain, as in other Southern European societies, the family rather than the welfare state plays the major role in decommodifying[2] or reducing uncertainty during difficult periods in the life course: the phase of education, entry into the labor market, building an occupational career, family formation and family dissolution. The role of the family as a safety net has become even more important in the last decades, because when social policies concerning maternity leave, family allowances and free nurseries are lacking or not generous enough, as in Spain (Baizán, 1998), reaching adulthood does not necessarily mark the end of the support period from the family of origin.

It has to be underlined that the labor market career has traditionally played a different role in men's than in women's life courses. In Spain, the predominant family model in the recent past has been that of the male breadwinner and female homemaker (see Blossfeld and Drobnič, 2001). However, with the rise in women's education and labor force participation over the last two decades, dual-earner partnerships have become increasingly common in Spanish society. Yet, the Spanish welfare state has not been able to respond satisfactorily to the growing need for social policies that ease the combination of work and family obligations. This has become especially worrisome since the mid-1980s because labor market deregulation, as previously discussed, has mainly affected young people and women. Spanish females who join the labor force are often confronted with short and unstable contracts. Labor flexibility and the associated increase in rapid job changes (including changes in timetables, positions and responsibilities in the workplace), while reducing the relative importance of the private life sphere, have heightened the relative importance of individuals' commitment to their labor career.

THE RATIONAL ACTOR AND THE SPANISH TRANSITION TO ADULTHOOD

We refer to globalization as the macro process in which most nation states are involved and that is characterized by: (1) the increasing dominance of a single, worldwide market with growing flows of capital, goods, services, labor and information across national borders; (2) the expanding global division of labor that makes national economies, nation states, and multiple cultural settings increasingly interdependent on each other; (3) the rising tendency to set up supranational organizations and the weakening of national ones in the economy and the political sphere; and, (4) the increased pressure on the national economy and the nation state to internally adjust to accelerating changes in the international environment. At the societal level, globalization entails the following developments (see also Blossfeld, this volume): (1) the increasing significance of knowledge and information; (2) the extraordinary rise in productivity; (3) the growing need of flexibility; (4) the increasing uncertainty of future developments and the instability of social relations; and, (5) the intensified competition among nation states and the spread of supranationally ungovernable economic forces that play a prominent role in giving increasing responsibility to the market (Breen, 1997). At the individual level, these dramatic changes in the societal context bear substantial consequences that are particularly important in the transition to adulthood. Since they can be seen as sources of constraints and uncertainty about future developments, they have an important impact on individuals' achievement of autonomy characterizing adulthood. They not only affect decisions that imply a substantial economic effort, like buying a house which in the Spanish context is still one of the markers of the transition to adulthood, but also decision processes implying long-term commitments, like establishing a first union or having a first child.

In order to relate recent changes in the transition to adulthood in Spain to the major social and economic transformations resulting from the globalization process, we use the rational actor approach (Dawes, 1988). In this theoretical framework, individuals may be seen as typical actors who act rationally in typical situations (see also Blossfeld, this volume), i.e., as decision makers attempting to optimize the decision process itself and the output they can obtain from it. In particular, in our analysis of the transition to adulthood in Spain, individuals are seen as rational actors who adapt their decisions on partnership and parenthood to the new sources of uncertainty that they face when entering the labor market.

With the globalization process not only temporal uncertainty increases, but also uncertainty about the behavioral alternatives themselves - which alternative to choose and when - and their outcome probabilities, as well as uncertainty about the amount of information to be collected for a particular decision process (see also Blossfeld, this volume). The position that an individual occupies in the labor market determines his or her degree of economic independence. Economic and residential emancipation from the family of origin are usually regarded as prerequisites for taking long-term commitments, like the decision to establish a first union or to have a first child. This is especially the case in Spain where, as already stated, the degree of welfare assistance is still weak. In analytical terms, we will therefore first examine the impact of globalization on the entrance into the first job and on the risks of subsequent unemployment. Then, the decision process of entering first partnership and parenthood will be analyzed by means of an explanatory choice model based on a dynamic categorization of the level of precariousness of the individual's position in the labor market.

Two major developments have already been highlighted when describing the changing context of the transition to adulthood in Spain: the increased time invested in education and women's remarkable advancement both in educational attainment and labor force participation. Recently, union formation has also undergone significant transformations in Spain. A steady trend towards a progressively later entry into marriage has been manifest since the early 1980s (Miret-Gamundi, 1997; Castro Martín, 1993; Delgado and Castro Martín, 1999). Vital statistics show, for instance, that the mean age at first marriage increased from 23.5 in 1980 to 27.1 in 1996 among females, and from 25.9 to 29.2 among males. Although this upward trend started a decade later than in Northern Europe (Blossfeld, 1995), it proceeded at a faster pace. As a result, the pattern of late marriage currently observed in Spain closely resembles that in most other European countries. This apparent convergence in the timing of family formation is, however, somewhat deceptive. Whereas in many European countries first marriage is often preceded by cohabitation and, consequently, partnership formation occurs significantly earlier than is reflected by marriage statistics (Kiernan, 1999), in Spain the prevalence of non-marital cohabitation is still relatively low. Hence, the documented late pattern of entry into marriage implies also a late pattern of entry into partnership.

Besides the role of legal marriage as the prevailing form of entry into partnership, other distinct features that characterize the transition to adulthood in Spain are the prolonged stay at the parental home and the strong interconnection between leaving it and getting married (Baizán, 2001; see also Klijzing, this volume), the relatively low prevalence therefore of independent living before union formation (Billari *et al.*, 2000), and the relatively low frequency of childbearing outside the context of a marital union (Muñoz Pérez, 1991). The persistence of these "traditional" features which partly challenge the convergence in family patterns initially envisaged under the paradigm of the Second Demographic Transition (Van de Kaa, 1987), has made it increasingly common nowadays to talk about a "Mediterranean" pattern of the transition to adulthood (Billari *et al.*, 2000), thus highlighting the persisting heterogeneity in the various paths to family formation within Europe (Kuijsten, 1996). As a consequence, young Spanish people have been remaining in the parental home longer, waiting for a better moment to leave and/or marry. As has been noted elsewhere (Miret-Gamundi, 1997; Cabré, 1997), 62 percent of young single people living within the parental home do work and could therefore be considered as economically independent, but most of them do not enjoy the work stability that would allow them to marry and leave the parental home.

In such a context, the transition to parenthood has also been delayed. Compared to the traditional pattern in which childbearing started right after marriage, recently married couples have increasingly delayed the conception of their first child (Castro Martín, 1992). Women's labor force participation is regarded as an important factor in this delay. Both working women who anticipate difficulties in combining work and family responsibilities, and unemployed women who aspire to get a stable job before initiating childbearing, have important reasons to delay the arrival of their first child.

In a previous study, Simó *et al.* (2001) reported on the steadily low percentage of women and men having left the parental home before establishing their first union. This pattern suggests the persistency of barriers to young men's and women's residential emancipation. These same researchers also found that among those who had already experienced entry in the labor market, partnership formation and parenthood, a large majority had done so in exactly that order. There were, however, significant gender and generation differentials reflecting the fact that more women than men enter the labor market after partnering, and that the traditional sequence - although still predominant among young cohorts - is becoming less frequent.

HYPOTHESES

In this section we present four hypotheses regarding the impact that the macro process of globalization has on the transition to adulthood. The first hypothesis is related to the precariousness that the young are faced with when entering the labor market for the first time; the second refers to the effects of the globalization process on the mismatch between educational skills and the first job obtained; the third concerns the uncertainty about medium- and long-term commitments; and, finally, the fourth refers to the impact of globalization on gender differentials in work and family role identities.

Globalization increases precariousness in the process of labor market entry

In the section "The role of the institutions" on Spanish institutions, we distinguished three different phases in Spain's recent history of economic and social change. Given the predictions provided by our rational choice model about how the globalization affects the timing and sequencing of life course transitions, we expect the following. First, we anticipate that labor market entry will be delayed for the youngest cohorts. If the individual leaves the educational system in periods of high unemployment, the chances of getting a first job will diminish. Therefore, men and women entering the labor force in 1975-84 or 1985-95 will be less likely to find a job soon than those joining the labor force in 1965-74. Second, this period adversity effect will not only decrease the likelihood of getting a first job, but it will also increase the likelihood of losing it, especially among those who found their first job during 1985-1995, the period when major labor market reforms towards greater flexibility took place. To summarize, our first hypothesis states that the globalization process in Spain augments precariousness in the process of labor market entry: the transition to first jobs is delayed and the early stages of work careers are increasingly characterized by alternating spells of employment and unemployment, until a stable job is found.

Globalization changes the returns to human capital investments

According to Becker (1971), individuals will invest in human capital in order to maximize their future stream of income. This means that the higher the level of education is, the greater are the chances of obtaining better jobs and avoiding unemployment. Thurow (1975) adds another dimension to Becker's human capital theory. He argues that in a labor market context where good jobs are scarce, there will be a queue in which individuals are ordered according to their qualifications, in such a way that highly educated individuals will have more chances to become employed and occupy better positions than individuals with low educational skills, who will be the most affected by the inflation of credentials. The rapid Spanish educational expansion, which can be considered as another effect of globalization (in that it increases the demand for high-level skills), has coincided in time with the worsening of labor market prospects for young people due to high unemployment and increasing job instability during early work careers. Therefore, the following patterns can be expected. First, in periods of high unemployment, individuals with low educational skills will be less likely to enter the labor market than individuals with high skills. Furthermore, we also predict that if educational skills in the first job are low, the likelihood of becoming unemployed will be high since fixed-term contracts are rather frequent in low-skilled occupations. To conclude, our second hypothesis states that in Spain the globalization process has altered the returns to human capital investments: low-skilled people will have higher unemployment risks in the youngest than in the oldest cohorts.

Globalization brings about uncertainty about medium- and long-term commitments

We view economic uncertainty as the outcome of two major changes related to the rapid globalization process to which Spain has assisted in the last two decades: the growing precariousness that individuals face in their labor market entry and the increasing inflation of credentials. This has resulted in a crowding-out of the low-skilled whose job positions are being taken by the high-skilled, who thus tend to occupy jobs for which they are overqualified. According to our rational choice model, we expect to see the impact of this increasing uncertainty on the timing and sequencing of long-term decisions. More concretely, we predict the following. First, long-term decisions such as partnership formation and first parenthood will be delayed among the youngest generations. Second, within each particular cohort, those individuals with a more precarious labor market situation will be less likely to form a couple or have a child (see Sommer *et al.*, 2000; Simó *et al.*, 2000 for further details). Thus, our third hypothesis states that globalization brings about uncertainty for medium- and long-term commitments so that partnership formation and parenthood decisions are more and more delayed. The sequence of these decisions and the emergence of more "flexible" family forms seem also to be affected by globalization. For example, cohabitation before marriage seems to be an increasingly accepted behavior pattern. However, its prevalence is still low in Spain and, therefore, it is too early to evaluate whether in a context discouraging long-term commitments it might serve as an alternative living arrangement.

Gender differences have not disappeared within the process of globalization

In the section "The role of the institutions" we discussed how the role of women in Spain has changed substantially in the last two decades: they have much higher educational levels, their labor force participation has risen dramatically, and they are slightly better protected by the welfare state than thirty years ago. Nevertheless, Spanish men and women still have very different work and family role identities, so that their 'readiness' associated with the decision of partnering and parenting also differs.

In the traditional single-earner model, which in the Spanish context has been mainly the male breadwinner model, work and family role identities differ substantially among women and men, with the result that there is a sharp gender specialization with respect to domestic tasks and those of providing economic resources for the family (Blossfeld and Drobnič, 2001). We argue that for men the distribution of work and family roles has not changed significantly over time, and that a stable position in the labor market still is a key prerequisite for taking the decision of establishing the first union and having the first child. Consequently, economic uncertainty affects the medium or long-term security required for taking such long-term decisions.

At the same time, the lack of adequate social policies makes it difficult for women to combine a labor market career with family responsibilities. For most women belonging to older birth cohorts, being a housewife was the prevailing option and basis to accomplish readiness for family formation. However, because of their investments in higher education, women of the younger cohorts are expected to opt more often for a satisfying job before they accomplish readiness to establish a partnership and fulfil their childbearing plans.

DATA AND METHODS

For the analysis we use longitudinal data from the Spanish Fertility and Family Survey (FFS).[3] The Spanish FFS, carried out in 1995, is based on a nationally representative sample of households. Interviews were conducted with 4,021 women and 1,991 men between the ages of 18 and 49 years (Delgado and Castro Martín, 1999). Some limitations of these data for our analysis have to be noted. First, FFS data do not provide information on the type of contract (fixed-term versus permanent). This information would have been highly valuable, since we argue that one of the key mechanisms through which globalization influences decisions on union formation is job precariousness. However, we have used the distinction between part- and full-time work instead because, given the fact that in Spain part-time employment does not typically provide a viable career prospect, it captures some degree of instability in labor force attachment. A second data limitation is that we can not distinguish between voluntary and involuntary unemployment. This represents a particularly important shortcoming in the case of women, since it is conceivable that voluntary and involuntary unemployment for them have opposing effects on union formation and childbearing. A third shortcoming derives from the lack of retrospective information on the work careers of partners. The decision to form a union and to have a child is usually taken on the basis of *both* partners' resources, but data restrictions oblige us to analyze the transitions to marriage and parenthood from the perspective of the individual respondent rather than the couple, as would have been desirable. A fourth limitation is that no information is available about the region of residence, impeding to outline the important plurality that characterizes the Spanish nation state. Finally, it is worth mentioning that FFS information about the type of work comes in only two of the four digits of the conventional ISCO scheme. This restriction enabled us to construct the 5 categories of the OECD occupational classification, but it did not allow us to use more complex divisions of occupational classes.

For the analysis of the entry into the labor market our window of observation starts at age 10, since an important number of individuals belonging to the oldest generation had their first job at very early ages.[4] Respondents who have not experienced the event in question are censored at age 35 or at the time of the interview, whichever comes first. With regard to the transition to unemployment, our window of observation starts when individuals get their first job and finishes when they fall into unemployment, with other destination states being censored.[5] The analysis of this particular transition is restricted to dependent workers only; the category of the self-employed refers to a very complex mix including own-account workers and employers, and is thus excluded. Finally, in the analysis of the transitions to partnership and parenthood our window of observation starts at age 16. Respondents who have not experienced those events are censored at age 49 (45 in the case of first motherhood) or at the time of interview, whichever comes first. In the analysis of partnership formation, first unions encompass only partnerships that started as a marriage which, even though consensual unions are becoming increasingly popular among the youngest cohorts, is still the majority rule.[6] In the analysis of parenthood we subtract 9 months from the date of birth of the first child so as to come closer to the actual timing of the decision to have it.

We use event history analysis to model the entry into adulthood which is assumed to encompass the above mentioned four interdependent transitions. We use piecewise constant models (Blossfeld and Rohwer, 1995) by defining several intervals in months in order to capture possible changes in transition rates across them. For the analysis of partnership formation and parenthood we have defined a set of time-varying covariates that, based on the information provided by the educational and employment histories, measure activity status on a monthly basis. Following Sommer *et al.* (2000), we distinguish six activity states which are assumed to capture different degrees of relative uncertainty: (1) in school, not working; (2) not in school, not working; (3) in school, working full-time; (4) in school, working part-time; (5) not in school, working part-time; and (6) not in school, working full-time (used as the reference group). We also include a macro indicator, namely, the age- and sex-specific unemployment rate at the time the respondent completes his or her studies. This indicator is intended to reflect not only the actual difficulties of first accessing the labor market but also the individual's (optimistic or pessimistic) perception of the economic climate regardless of his/her own situation. Other variables included are age as an indicator of the life cycle stage, and highest level of education. Respondents with secondary school, vocational training, and unclassified educational certificates are grouped in one category (2), while those with tertiary education diplomas in an other (3). Respondents with only compulsory education as well as those without any diploma belong to the reference group (1). In the transition model of parenthood we have also included a covariate indicating whether marriage has already taken place. To capture changes over time in the various dependent processes we have included 3 birth cohorts in the models, except for the transition from first job to unemployment where we use labor market entry cohorts. In that particular case we have also included 5 categories of occupational class. Because we expect to find significant gender differentials, women and men are analyzed separately.

RESULTS

The survival functions in Figure 15.2 for the transition to the first job show that the youngest cohorts enter the labor market considerably later than the oldest cohorts. At the age of 18, 60 percent of men born during 1965-1977 against 40 percent of those born during 1944-1964 are still in the risk set of individuals who have not yet found a first-time job. The survival functions for women show even greater differences across cohorts: by age 18, around 80 percent of those born during 1965-1977 against 65 percent of those during 1955-1964 and 55 percent of those during 1944-1954 have not yet exited the pool of first-time job seekers. These figures can be interpreted as a reflection not only of the adverse labor market conditions in the last two decades which have delayed the labor market entry of youngsters (especially of women), but also as a consequence of the remarkable educational expansion which has taken place in Spain during the same period. In a previous study (see Simó *et al.*, 2001) examining the transition rates throughout the entire age range, the authors found large gender differentials for all birth cohorts, especially for the oldest ones. As expected, men were more likely to find a first job than women, and the gender gap widened after the age of 18, mainly among those who had entered the labor market before 1975, a period with low male unemployment and very low female employment rates.

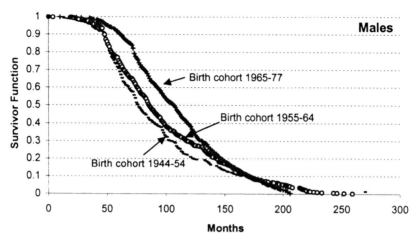

Birth cohort 1944-54 o Birth cohort 1955-64 + Birth cohort 1965-77

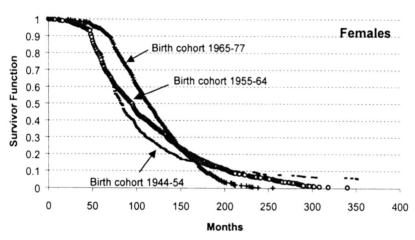

" Birth cohort 1944-54 o Birth cohort 1955-64 + Birth cohort 1965-77

Figure 15.2 Product-limit estimation. Males' and females' transition to the first job from 10 years old

Source: 1995 Spanish FFS.

Table 15.1 Piecewise constant exponential models: main steps of the transition into adulthood in Spain

	From age 10 to first job		First job to unemployment		Partnership formation		Parenthood	
	Men	Women	Men	Women	Men	Women	Men	Women
Periods from age 16								
16-19					-6.9050***	-5.8638***	-7.0507***	-6.4361***
20-24					-4.8374***	-4.5041***	-5.6157***	-5.6950***
25-29					-4.0446***	-4.2225***	-5.0300***	-5.7877***
30-34					-4.4954***	-4.9287***	-5.2762***	-6.4144***
35+					-6.0560***	-6.4273***	-6.7999*	-7.9709***
Periods from age 10								
10-11	-6.8941***	-7.7294***						
12-13	-4.7961***	-6.1573***						
14-15	-3.0811***	-4.3839***						
16-17	-2.7931***	-4.0317***						
18-19	-2.8973***	-3.8670***						
20-21	-2.8986***	-3.8613***						
22-23	-2.7681***	-3.9022***						
24-25	-2.7719***	-3.8923***						
26-27	-2.6798***	-4.1809***						
28+	-3.4511***	-4.4529***						

Table 15.1 continued

	From age 10 to first job		First job to unemployment		Partnership formation		Parenthood	
	Men	Women	Men	Women	Men	Women	Men	Women
Months after having obtained a the first job								
0-5			-5.6704***	-5.0833***				
6-11			-5.4206***	-5.1310***				
12-17			-5.8060***	-5.4541***				
18-23			-6.5646***	-5.8514***				
24-35			-6.1394***	-6.2743***				
36-47			-6.5925***	-6.1135***				
48-59			-6.7462***	-6.6170***				
60+			-7.2984***	-6.9589***				
Education status								
(Out of education)	Ref. Group	Ref. Group						
In the educational system	-0.9575***	-0.8878***						
Birth cohort								
(1945-1954)	Ref. Group	Ref. Group			Ref. Group	Ref. Group	Ref. Group	Ref. Group
1955-1964	-0.1923***	-0.1250**			-0.0656	0.2461***	-0.3005***	0.1605***
1965-1977	-0.3879***	-0.2628***			-0.6043***	-0.1394*	-1.2632***	-0.6715***
Labour market cohort								
(1955-1974)			Ref. Group	Ref. Group				
1975-1984			1.0132***	0.5911***				
1985-1995			1.9667***	1.3555***				

Table 15.1 continued

	From age 10 to first job		First job to unemployment		Partnership formation		Parenthood	
	Men	Women	Men	Women	Men	Women	Men	Women
Educational Level								
(Primary)	Ref. Group	Ref. Group			Ref. Group	Ref. Group	Ref. Group	Ref. Group
Secondary	-0.3786***	-0.3580***	-0.4001***	0.0111	-0.0261	-0.1368***	-0.1397*	-0.2568***
Tertiary	-0.0194	0.1771**	-0.2914	0.323*	-0.0414	-0.2922***	-0.3151**	-0.4069***
Occupational Class								
High skilled and non manual			-0.8298***	-0.7052***				
Medium skilled and non manual			-0.5829*	-0.6022***				
Low skilled and non manual			-0.5713**	-0.5145***				
Skilled and manual worker			-0.5295***	-0.5611***				
(Unskilled manual worker)			Ref. Group	Ref. Group				
Activity status								
In school, not working					-2.9957***	-1.5186***	-2.2615***	-1.1818***
Not in school, not working					-1.1029***	-0.7282***	-1.2499***	0.9002***
In school, working>25 hr. week					-0.6235***	-0.6186***	-0.4140**	-0.9770***
In school, working<24 hr. week					-1.3427**	-2.7832***	-0.6933	-1.9421***
Not in school, working<25 hr. week					-0.3505**	0.0497	-0.2686*	0.0976
(Not in school, working<25 hr. week)					Ref. Group	Ref. Group	Ref. Group	Ref. Group

Table 15.1 continued

	From age 10 to first job		First job to unemployment		Partnership formation		Parenthood	
	Men	Women	Men	Women	Men	Women	Men	Women
Age-specific unemployment rate (macro)					0.0061	-0.0063***	0.0141	-0.0128***
Had first marriage			-0.3659**	-0.1133			1.3893***	1.8900***
Number of cases	1599	2960	220	513	857	2343	858	2301
Number of episodes	3493	6956	3959	5978	210905	330950	225177	371794
Log likelihood (starting values)	-9123.1748	-17313.6462	-1595.0351	-3577.5771	-5575.4065	-13942.1038	-5637.0926	-14001.5761

Source: Spanish FFS, 1995.

Notes
* $p < 0.10$
** $p < 0.05$
*** $p < 0.01$

Table 15.1 presents the coefficients of the piecewise constant models esti-mated to investigate the four interdependent processes of the transition to adult-hood. Columns 1 and 2 correspond to the models for men and women on the entry into a first job. The results confirm the preliminary evidence outlined above by the survival functions of this transition. That is, both men and women born during 1965-1977 and, to a lesser degree during 1955-1964, are significantly less likely to enter a first-time job than those born during 1944-1954. The effect of education is worth highlighting: women with high levels of education are significantly more likely to enter a first-time job than those with low education, whereas women as well as men with medium-level skills are significantly less likely to do so. The latter finding may be related to the fact that fixed-term contracts are being widely used to hire workers in low-skilled occupations (Iannelli and Soro-Bonmatí, 2001). Low-educated individuals may therefore be more likely to find a first-time - probably fixed-term - job than individuals with a medium level of qualifications.

The degree of job stability is examined through the analysis of the transition from first job into unemployment (see columns 3 and 4 of Table 15.1). As expected, the more recent the entry is into the labor market, the more likely it is to move into unemployment. In a previous study the authors have shown that this pattern remains even after controlling for the position in the educational system, the occupational class of the first-time job, and the individual's marital status (Simó *et al.*, 2001). They also found that those who are combining education with a first-time job are significantly less likely to lose that job. This may be the case for instance of students who need the money in order to pay for their living expenses. Concerning the role of education, our results in Table 15.1 show that the likelihood of falling into unemployment lowers for men with secondary edu-cational levels, whereas it increases for women with tertiary education. Regard-ing interaction effects between educational levels and cohorts, the authors found in their previous study that the returns to education are worsening over time. Relative to the members of the oldest labor market entry cohort with primary education only, the likelihood of falling into unemployment increases enor-mously at all educational levels, in the middle as well as in the youngest labor market entry cohort (Simó *et al.*, 2001).

The contrasts according to Table 15.1 are largest between, on the one hand, those entering the labor force in 1985-1995 who were the most affected by the deregularization of the Spanish labor market, and those entering in 1955-1974, on the other, when unemployment rates were low and fixed-term contracts did not yet exist. These results confirm that the degree of instability in early job careers has significantly increased in the last two decades. Unfortunately, as already stated, we do not have information on the type of contract of the first-time job. However, the occupational class in the first-time job could be taken as a proxy for having a fixed-term or permanent contract. As discussed above, after the labor market reforms in the 1980s, most low-skilled workers were offered a fixed-term contract, so that those working in unskilled occupations were also the ones most likely to lose their first-time job. This is precisely the result emerging from the models in Table 15.1: unskilled manual workers are significantly more likely to move into unemployment than workers in any other occupational class. The effect of marital status also deserves attention since it shows that globalization notwithstanding, gender differences in young people's life courses remain: being married significantly reduces the likelihood of losing one's first job for men, but not so for women.[7]

To summarize, our findings for the transition to first jobs and from first jobs to unemployment suggest that for recent cohorts there is a longer waiting time until a first-time job is found and that there is a greater instability associated with this first-time job. Taken together, these results offer support to hypothesis 1 stating that globalization increases the precariousness of youngsters' labor market entry, as well as to hypothesis 2 stating that globalization changes the returns to human capital investments.

Columns 5 and 6 of Table 15.1 present the results of the piecewise constant exponential models of entry into first partnership for men and women. They illustrate the recent trend of delayed entry into first union. As visualized by life table curves in Figure 15.3, the youngest cohort - those born in 1965-1977 - exhibits a far lower rate of transition to first union than previous cohorts, thus reflecting a marked tendency to postpone and/or forgo partnership formation. In order to assess whether this tendency can be partly attributed to the different activity status composition of the youngest cohort with respect to the preceding ones at the time of exposure to union formation (as we have hypothesized when discussing the impact of globalization on recent work patterns), we added to the birth cohort variable in Table 15.1 the time-varying indicator of individuals' activity status and a macro indicator of unemployment rates, both of which reflect the degree of uncertainty. Although the coefficient for the youngest cohort remained sizable and statistically significant, its magnitude lessened when these two variables capturing the degree of attachment to the labor force and the contextual level of unemployment were controlled for, particularly among women. Although this is no conclusive evidence, it still suggests that the changing context of work does indeed play a role in the recent trend of delayed union formation.

As far as educational level is concerned, this variable has been traditionally regarded as having a negative impact on the propensity to marry, at least for women, although recent studies have revealed that this effect is not so much related to human capital accumulation but rather to the incompatibility of educational and marital roles (Blossfeld and Huinink, 1989). Although we expected to find a weak effect of education level once school enrollment status was taken into account, our models show that this is only the case for men. Among women, the negative effect of educational level on union formation remains statistically significant even after controlling for current enrollment, suggesting that the more advanced the educational level is that women have completed, the lower will be their transition rate to partnership. Nevertheless, when separate models were run for each birth cohort (Simó et al., 2001), the results were that educational level inhibits union formation only for the youngest female cohort. This is precisely the cohort that has largely benefited from the remarkable expansion of education

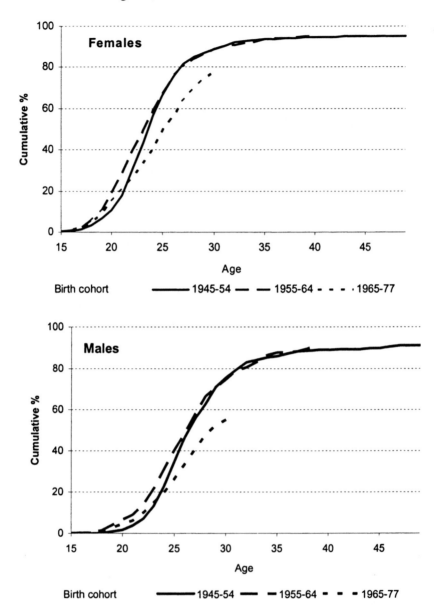

Figure 15.3   Survivor function for the transition to first partnership in Spain – Life table estimates of the cumulative proportion of men and women entering first partnership, by birth cohort

Source: 1995 Spanish FFS.

but which faces more difficulties to get good returns to their educational investment in the labor market.

With regard to the impact of activity status on union formation, our models confirm some of the expected patterns. Being enrolled in school and not working lowers substantially the rate of transition to first partnership for both women and men compared to the reference category (not in school, working full-time), which supposedly represents the lowest degree of uncertainty in socioeconomic terms. Delayed partnering also occurs when school and paid work are being combined, suggesting that the role of student is largely regarded as incompatible with the role of spouse, even when there is already an attachment to the labor force.

The effect of being out of school and not working on union formation, however, differs greatly by gender: while it has a strong negative effect on the marital transition for men, it has a positive effect for women. The results for men confirm the hypothesized association between uncertainty in the work domain and deferment of partnership formation. The results for women, on the contrary, suggest that this status - as we have noted earlier, one of the caveats of the analysis is that we cannot discern between voluntary and involuntary reasons for not working - enhances their transition to first union. Although these results fully agree with the traditional breadwinner-homemaker family model, we expected to find a different pattern for younger cohorts. When we looked at separate models for each birth cohort (see Simó *et al.*, 2001), we found indeed that although the sign of the coefficient for this particular activity status remained positive across all female cohorts, its effect became progressively smaller as we moved from the older to the youngest cohort. In fact, the coefficient for the 1965-1977 cohort - although still positive - was no longer statistically significant. We had also expected that the inhibiting impact of (being out of school and) not working on first union formation would become stronger for males of the younger cohorts, for whom unemployment is less and less a transitory and more and more a long-term stage. However, the results of the cohort-specific models showed that although the negative coefficient associated with this particular status remains sizable also for the most recent cohort, it is no longer statistically significant (Simó *et al.*, 2001), a result that could be related to small sample sizes. Finally, regarding the difference between part- and full-time work, our cohort-specific models show that men who are out of school and working on a part-time basis have a lower transition rate to first union than similar men working full-time, as one would expect given the higher degree of uncertainty associated with part-time positions. The results for women, however, show no such differences in the union transition rates of part- and full-time workers.

In sum, our findings on partnership formation suggest that: (i) the worsening of labor market conditions does delay union formation; (ii) the higher the women's educational level, the lower their transition to partnership; (iii) an uncertain position in the labor market lowers the transition to partnership for both women and men; and (iv) the effect of being unemployed on union formation differs greatly by gender. These results support hypotheses 3 and 4 stating, respectively, that uncertainty hinders medium- and long-term commitments and that gender differences - even if currently being transformed - have not disappeared in the process of globalization.

Lastly, we analyze the transition to parenthood.[8] The results on the proportions of childless men and women by birth cohorts in Figure 15.4 illustrate the remarkable delay that younger generations experience in the onset of childbearing. In columns 7 and 8 of Table 15.1 we can observe that the likelihood of entry into parenthood diminishes considerably for the youngest cohort compared to the cohort born in 1945-1954. (The likelihood of first motherhood for the middle cohort appears to be higher than for the oldest cohort, but it decreases markedly for the youngest cohort.) Concerning education, the results for both men and women show that the higher their level of education, the lower their likelihood of becoming first-time parents. On the other hand, unemployment rates do again not play the same role for men and women. While for women their impact is significant and negative (the higher the female age-specific unemployment rate is when they enter the labor market, the lower is the rate of first motherhood), for men it does not seem to affect significantly the transition to first fatherhood.

Finally, we examine the results of the impact of the various uncertainty categories (built around the dimensions of in/out of school, working/not working, and hours worked) on women's and men's transition rate to parenthood. Both women and men who are still in education and not working have very low odds of entering parenthood. But, as was the case in the models of the transition to first partnership, the effect of being out of education and not working differs greatly by gender. It displays the highest propensity to have a first child among women, while for men this is low. Another clear gender differential is that part-time work decreases the likelihood of parenthood compared to full-time work among men, but not among women.

We summarize our findings on the transition to parenthood as follows. First, as found in the transition to partnership, the worsening of labor market conditions does inhibit and delay parenthood. Second, the higher women's and men's educational level is, the lower becomes their transition to a first child. Third, an uncertain position in the labor market lowers the transition to parenthood, particularly for men. Fourth, being unemployed has a gender-specific impact: while it is negative for men, it is positive for women. Finally, aggregate unemployment rates lower the transition to first births, but only among women. Also these results lend support to hypotheses 3 and 4.

CONCLUSIONS

We have seen that in Spain globalization has increased uncertainty by, on the one hand, a growing liberalization and deregulation of the labor market which has accentuated the fracture between insiders and outsiders and, on the other, a growing need to update skills through continued education, with both macro processes making the entry into the labor market more and more difficult. The

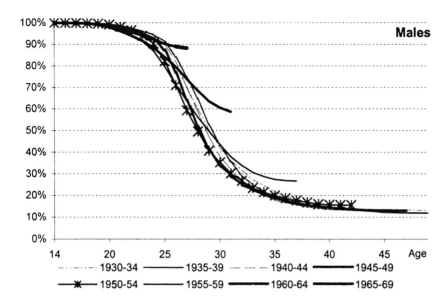

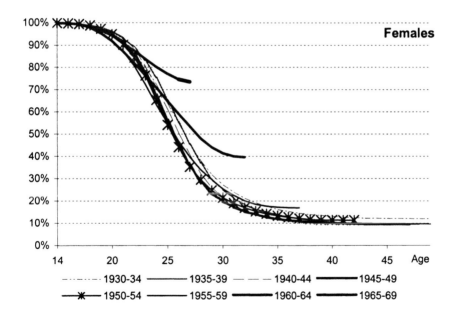

Figure 15.4   Proportion of childless men and women in Spain by age and birth cohort

Source: Own elaboration using 1991 Spanish Sociodemographic Survey. Madrid, National Institute for Statistics (INE).

former has introduced a high degree of precariousness in work relations, affecting particularly low-skilled people in their transitions into partnership and parenthood, since instability in the labor market and uncertainty about future prospects make it difficult for men and women to make such medium- to long-term commitments. Furthermore, even if gender differentials may nowadays be transforming, they have not disappeared. The lack of social policies and welfare support as well as the slow movement towards a more egalitarian family system simply make it very difficult for Spanish women to combine a job career with childbearing. They have increased their investment in education and their participation in the labor market. Due to the growing need for skill upgrading and continuous learning that the globalization process implies, high levels of educational attainment have become almost a necessity for those who want to pursue a job career. While in former times of the single-earner family model men's stable position in the labor market provided a solid basis for the decision of becoming partners and parents, currently young men face increased difficulties to attain such a stable position. Moreover, there is currently a growing awareness that dual-earner families may fare better in the uncertain context of globalization than provider-only families. As Oppenheimer (1994) argues, gendered specialization is a risky strategy for a nuclear family in today's world, because diversifying household income sources could provide economic flexibility and other backup mechanisms. However, in Spain, women face even more barriers than men when trying to find a job, and the lack of supporting social policies makes it difficult for them to combine work and family responsibilities.

NOTES

1   The 1980 Workers' Statute (*Ley de Estatuto de los Trabajadores*, known as LET) was the first law protecting worker rights after the dictatorship.

2   This term is used by Esping-Andersen (1999) to describe how the welfare state in European societies makes the effects of uncertainty more bearable.

3   The authors wish to thank the Advisory Group of the FFS research program of comparative research for its permission, granted under identification number 61, to use the FFS data on which this study is based.

4   1995 Spanish FFS only provides information about the time leaving education when individuals remain in it till the age of 15.

5   As a destination state we use the "unemployed" category appearing as a main activity between job spells. For those having only one job spell we use the main activity at the time of the interview.

6   According to the 1995 Spanish FFS, 7 percent of women and 9 percent of men belonging to the birth cohort 1966-77 started their first partnership before marrying. For women, 15 percent of those partnerships do not end in a marriage, while for men this proportion reaches 24 percent.

7   The sign of their coefficient even switches to positive when the level of education is excluded from the model (see Simó *et al.*, 2001).

8   Most of the results referring to this transition are based on Simó *et al.* (2000).

BIBLIOGRAPHY

Albert, C., Davia, M.A, Hernanz, V, Toharia, L. (1999) 'The General Education System and Further Training in Spain', WZB Working Paper, Berlin.

Amuedo-Dorantes, C. (2000) 'Work transitions into and out of involuntary temporary employment in a segmented market: evidence from Spain', *Industrial and Labor Relations Review*, 53 (2): 309-325.

Baizán, P. (1998) 'Transitions vers l'âge adulte des générations espagnoles nées en 1940, 1950 et 1960', *Genus*, 54(3-4): 233-263.

Baizán, P. (2001) 'Transition to adulthood in Spain', in M. Corijn and E. Klijzing (eds) *Transitions to Adulthood in Europe*, Dordrecht: Kluwer Academic Publishers.

Becker, G. (1971) *The Economics of Discrimination*, Chicago: University of Chicago Press.

Bentolila, S. and Blanchard O. J. (1991) 'El paro en España', in S. Bentolila and L. Toharia (eds) *Estudios de economia del trabajo en Espana. III: El problema del paro*, Madrid: Ministro de Trabajo y Seguridad Social.

Bentolila, S. and Dolado, J. J. (1994) 'Spanish labour markets: labour flexibility and wages: lessons from Spain', *Economic Policy*, 9 (18): 53-99.

Billari, F., Castiglioni, M., Castro Martín, T. and Michielin, F. (2000) 'Transitions to adulthood in a period of deep societal changes: A study of Spanish post-war cohorts', paper presented at the Annual Meeting of the Population Association of America, Los Angeles.

Blossfeld, H.-P., and Huinink, J. (1989) 'Die Verbesserung der Bildungs- und Berufschancen von Frauen und ihr Einfluß auf den Prozeß der Familienbildung', *Zeitschrift für Bevölkerungswissenschaft*, 15(4): 383-404.

Blossfeld, H.-P. (1995) 'Changes in the process of family formation and women's growing economic independence: A comparison of nine countries', in H.-P. Blossfeld (ed.) *The new role of women. Family formation in modern societies*, Boulder: Westview Press.

Blossfeld, H.-P., and Rohwer, G. (1995) *Techniques of event history modeling. New approaches to causal analysis*, Hillsdale, NJ: Lawrence Erlbaum Associates.

Blossfeld, H.-P., and Drobnič, S. (eds) (2001) *Careers of Couples in Contemporary Society. From Male Breadwinner to Dual-Earner Families*, Oxford: Oxford University Press.

Breen, R. (1997) 'Risk, recommodification and stratification', *Sociology*, 31: 473-489.

Cabré, A. (1997) 'Emancipación de los jóvenes y transición familiar. Entrevista con Anna Cabré', in R. Vergés Escuín (ed.) *La edad de emancipación de los jóvenes*, Barcelona: Centre de Cultura Contemporània de Barcelona.

Castro Martín, T. (1992) 'Delayed childbearing in contemporary Spain: trends and differentials', *European Journal of Population*, 8: 217-246.

Castro Martín, T. (1993) 'Changing nuptiality patterns in contemporary Spain', *Genus*, 49 (1-2): 79-95.

Dawes, R. M. (1988) *Rational Choice in an Uncertain World*, Orlando: Harcourt Brace Jovanovich, Publishers.

Delgado Pérez, M., and Castro Martín, T. (1999) *FFS Standard Country Report, Spain*, Geneva: United Nations.

Dolado, J. J., Felgueroso, F. and. Jimeno, J.F. (2000) 'Explaining Youth Labor Market Problems in Spain: Crowding –Out, Institutions or Technology shifts?', Working Paper 2000-09, FEDA: Madrid.

Esping-Anderson, G. (1999) *Social foundations of postindustrial economies*, Oxford: Oxford University Press.

Garrido Medina, L. (1992) *Las dos biografías de la mujer en España*, Madrid: Instituto de la Mujer, Ministerio de Trabajo y Asuntos Sociales.

Iannelli, C. and Soro-Bonmatí, A. (2000) 'The transition from school-to-work in Southern Europe: the cases of Italy and Spain', paper prepared for the CATEWE project.

Kiernan, K. (1999) 'Cohabitation in western Europe', *Population Trends*, 96 (Summer): 25-32.

Kuijsten, A. (1996) 'Changing family patterns in Europe: A case of divergence?', *European Journal of Population*, 12 (2): 115-143.

Lindbeck, A. and Snower, D.J. (1989) *The Insider-Outsider Theory of Unemployment*, Cambridge, Mass: MIT Press.

McKay, R. (1988) 'International competition: its impact on employment', in *Flexible Workstyles: A Look at Contingent Labor*, Washington DC: Women's Bureau, US Department of Labor.

Maravall, J.M. and Fraile, M. (1998) 'The politics of unemployment: the Spanish experience in a comparative perspective', Working Paper 1998/14, Instituto Juan March, Centro de Estudios Avanzados en Ciencias Sociales.

Miret Gamundi, P. (1997) 'Pasado y presente de las pautas de emancipación juvenil en España', in R. Vergés Escuín (ed.) *La edad de emancipación de los jóvenes*, Barcelona: Centre de Cultura Contemporània de Barcelona.

Moran, M. P. (1991) 'Las Mujeres y el Empleo en España 1987-90', *Revista de Economia y Sociologia del Trabajo*, 13-14: 88-103.

Muñoz Pérez, F. (1991) 'Les naissances hors mariage et les conceptions prénuptiales en Espagne depuis 1975', *Population*, 4: 463-473.

OECD (1994) *The OECD Jobs Study – Facts Analysis, Strategies*, Paris: OECD.

Oppenheimer, V. K. (1994) 'Women's rising employment and the future of the family in industrial societies', *Population and Development Review*, 20: 293-342.

Reher, D. (1998) 'Families ties in Western Europe: persistent contrasts', *Population and Development Review*, 24 (2): 203-234.

Simó, C., Golsch, K. and Steinhage, N. (2000) 'Entry into first parenthood in Spain and the process of globalization', GLOBALIFE Working Paper No. 08, Faculty of Sociology, University of Bielefeld.

Simó, C., Castro Martín, T., and Soro-Bonmatí, A. (2001) 'Changing pathways in the transition to adulthood in Spain: labor market, marriage and fertility patterns of young people in the last decades', GLOBALIFE Working Paper No. 18, Faculty of Sociology, University of Bielefeld.

Sommer, T., Klijzing, E., and Mills, M. (2000) 'Partnership formation in a globalising world: the impact of uncertainty in East and West Germany', GLOBALIFE Working Paper No. 9, Faculty of Sociology, University of Bielefeld.

Tamames, R. (1995) *La Economía Española, 1975-1995*, Madrid: Ediciones Temas de Hoy, S.A.

Thurow, L.C. (1975) *Generating Inequality*, Oxford: MacMillan Press.

Van de Kaa, D.J. (1987) Europe's second demographic transition, *Population Bulletin*, 42: 1-57.

16 Ireland and economic globalization

The experiences of a small open economy

*Richard Layte, Philip J. O'Connell, Tony Fahey
and Selina McCoy*

INTRODUCTION

In this chapter we reflect on two basic assumptions of the globalization literature: first, that as economic globalization increases, the power of the state to influence national labor markets and institutions decreases (Ruggie, 1982), and second, that globalization necessarily leads to a trend of increasing uncertainty in both labor markets and fertility decisions. On the contrary, using recent Irish history as an example, we argue that states are important agents in shaping the impact of globalizing forces and that it is these choices - good or bad - in combination with the business cycle that shape both labor market and fertility patterns.

Today, Ireland stands as a good example of a small open economy that has embraced and prospered from globalization, a stance originating in policy decisions made in the 1950s. After the achievement of political independence from Britain in 1922, the new Irish state sought to achieve economic and social autonomy by erecting industrial protectionism, encouraging self-sufficiency and pursuing cultural isolationism. Yet, by the 1950s, this policy of self-sufficiency had proven to be an unmitigated disaster, yielding lower standards of living and slower industrial development than the rest of Europe, a failure that was most evident in the mass emigration of 400,000 people from a population of 3 million.

In response to this crisis, industrial policy shifted in the mid-1950s to the development of an open economy that was fully integrated into the international economy and which encouraged foreign investment. By the mid-1990s Ireland had the fastest growing economy in Europe and a standard of living approaching that of the EU average. Using the initial failure of Irish economic development and belated success as an example, we want to argue here that contrary to much literature on globalization, the policies of nation states have a large bearing on the impact that globalization has on an economy and society at the macro level. We show how the economic policies adopted by the Irish state after 1960 helped alter the balance of industrial sectors and in so doing increased levels of employment, decreased insecurity and brought about a more sustainable demographic situation. Moreover, using data on labor market transitions we show that the structure of labor market regulations adopted by states has impacts on certain risks at the micro level, irrespective of the uncertainty in the labor market itself, though we also show that the economic cycle remains an important influence.

The chapter proceeds as follows. In the section 'The rise of the developmental state' we briefly detail the move to an open, outward looking economy in the 1950s that laid the foundations for the extraordinary growth of the 1990s. This section argues for the importance of the state as an actor in the development of the 'globalized state' by outlining the policy decisions that influenced the nature of Irish industrialization and the Irish experience of recession and economic growth. The importance of the state is also highlighted through the labor market regulations in the Irish context that have led to the inequitable distribution of social risks in the form of unemployment and employment precarity.

These risks are the subject of the section 'Globalization and transitions in the labor market' that clarifies several hypotheses about labor market risks and how these might be related to globalization and labor market regulation. These hypotheses relate to two competing theories about the changing distribution of risk once in the labor market. On the one hand, the 'segmentation' argument (Breen, 1997; Layte et al., 2000) holds that employers will seek to defer the risk of uncertain markets onto their employees, but this deferment will not be uniform across the workforce. Instead, employers will tend to differentiate according to the type of contract held. On the other hand, German theorists and researchers (Beck, 1992; Leisering and Leibfried, 1999) have argued that the labor market instability brought by globalization has actually reached higher into the non-manual classes, a process they label 'transcendence' or 'individualization'. Here we argue and show that segmentation is the norm in the Irish labor market, but the nature of this segmentation has as much to do with state policy as it does with the employment policies of employers. (For a critique of the 'individualization' thesis in the case of Italy, see Bernardi and Nazio, this volume.)

In the section 'The data source' we outline the data used in this chapter: two waves of the School Leavers' Survey and follow-ups from 1987 and 1993. These large surveys give us a cross-section of those leaving the educational system with which to test theories of changing cohort experience during a period of recession and one of growth. In the section 'Analysis one: entering the labor market' we then turn to an empirical test of the hypotheses outlined above.

In the section 'The impact of economic policy on fertility patterns' we return to the importance of state policies for both economy and society by examining the impact of the changing performance of the Irish economy on patterns of fertility and marriage in Ireland in the course of the 20th century. We argue that the expansion of economic opportunity in Ireland after the adoption of more outward looking policies increased security of lifestyle and made possible a more sustainable demographic performance.

THE RISE OF THE DEVELOPMENTAL STATE

It is frequently argued that increasing globalization as reflected in financial flows and investment decisions means that the power of national governments to implement policy and intervene in the economy is decreasing (Ruggie, 1982). Yet, in Ireland the state has played a crucial role in shaping the exposure of the economy to globalizing forces. In fact the state has played a central role both in Ireland's long-run industrial transformation and in the more recent about-turn in Irish fortunes. Many would argue that Ireland's economy has been open and outward looking for at least 150 years in the sense that emigration to Great Britain and the US provided an outlet for excess labor supply at home and agriculture was based on exports to the UK. But, when we speak of the rise of globalization in this chapter we refer to the adoption of policies that did not attempt to shield indigenous business from overseas competition and explicitly courted foreign direct investment. Responding to the failure of protectionist policies in the 1950s, the Irish state adopted a very active role in seeking to promote economic growth and development through closer integration with the international economy, and in attracting foreign direct investment. The adoption of this developmental role was complemented by an expansion of the distributive role of the state, ushering in an era of economic and social progress in the 1960s.

Perhaps the most far-reaching change was that the state became the key actor in attracting foreign direct investment (FDI) and creating a 'world class' location for mobile investment, a position unchanged for the following forty years. The body responsible for this task, the Industrial Development Authority (IDA), was very successful and throughout the 1960s foreign investment grew rapidly, with the proportion of gross output accounted for by these firms rising from 2.3 percent in 1960 to 15.9 percent in 1973 (O'Malley, 1989). Irish political and economic institutions were radically reshaped through the 1970s to the same end. The structure of state finances was transformed to reduce taxes on capital and profits, thus leaving the state heavily reliant on income taxes.

While it could be argued that the policies of the Irish state after 1960 were characteristic of a globalized economy, we would argue that successive governments were doing more than creating a comfortable environment for FDI. The role of the IDA was extended and by the 1990s this body worked closely with managers of transnational subsidiaries in Ireland to define the character of Irish industry without attempting to define the specific strategies of firms (Ó'Riain and O'Connell, 1999). The state also contributed to growth through investment in the education system. Free education was instituted in 1967, which, together with a university construction program would yield large numbers of well-educated young people for the emergent industries of the 1980s and 90s.

From depression to growth

Closer integration with the international economy initially generated a spurt of economic development in the 1960s. However, the international recession in the 1970s revealed the structural weaknesses in the Irish economy, as traditional indigenous industry contracted in the face of international competition. By the 1980s, with mass unemployment and renewed emigration, Ireland was in the throes of economic and fiscal crisis.

The world economic slowdown of the late 70s and early 80s meant that the decade of the 1980s was particularly severe for the Irish economy. The numbers at work declined by about 1½ per annum over the first half of the 1980s, while the size of the labor force increased due both to natural population growth and rising labor force participation by women. The contraction in employment was partly fuelled by the belated decision to remove protection from inefficient indigenous firms in areas such as textiles. Once exposed to the world market, these firms could not compete. Contraction in employment combined with labor force growth resulted in an increase in the unemployment rate from just under 10 percent in 1981 to a peak of almost 17 percent in 1987. This negative side of globalization was compounded by the fiscal crisis that ensued from governments attempting to maintain high levels of spending in the face of falling tax revenues. It was in dealing with this fiscal crisis that the first 'social partnership' deal was struck in 1987 between government, unions and employers, and it was this institutional innovation that laid the final foundation of the conditions that would lead to growth in the 1990s. The state took the lead in brokering the new partnership arrangements, and for the last decade and a half it has underwritten growth by exchanging tax cuts for wage moderation in an effort to boost Ireland's international competitiveness. Thus, at each stage in an uneven process of industrial transformation and development, the state in Ireland has played a key role. The prominence of the state in Ireland is at odds with globalization approaches that argue for the progressive retreat of the state with increasing globalization.

Table 16.1 shows trends in numbers at work, unemployed, and the labor force, as well as net migration over the years 1987-1999. While impressive growth was achieved over the decade as a whole, the rate of growth was in fact unevenly distributed according to the following three sub-periods:

1   Recovery, 1987-90. A period of recovery with strong growth in investment and exports and curtailment of public spending, which generated a brief employment boom between 1989-90 when total employment increased by 4 percent and unemployment fell to 13 percent.

Table 16.1   Numbers at work, unemployed, labor force and net migration, Ireland, 1987-1999

Year	At work	Unemployed	Labor force	Unemployment rate	Net migration
	(1,000)	*(1,000)*	*(1,000)*	%	*(1,000)*
1987	1110	226	1336	16.9	-23
1990	1160	172	1332	12.9	-23
1993	1183	220	1403	15.7	0
1999	1591	97	1688	5.7	19

Sources: Central Statistics Office, various years, Labor Force Survey and Quarterly National Household Survey.

2 Sluggish growth, 1991-93. A downturn in international activity that coincided with increases in interest rates and an exchange rate crisis meant that growth in Ireland faltered. Employment declined in 1991 and 1992 so that continuing growth in the labor force led to increased unemployment, which reached almost 16 percent in 1993.

3 Very rapid growth, 1993-99. Stimulated by both accelerated export growth and increased domestic demand since 1993, the Irish economy has expanded very rapidly, with annual rates of growth in excess of 8 percent. This growth has resulted in a rapid and dramatic improvement in labor market conditions. In the six years from 1993 to 1999, total employment grew by about 400,000 or 33 percent, whereas the unemployment rate fell to 5.7 percent (April 1999).

Flexibilization

We have argued that the Irish economy was already substantially globalized by the mid-1970s and that the incentives offered to transnational companies in the form of low corporate tax rates and other fiscal advantages were put in place to make Ireland an attractive location. However, as also argued, these developments initially led to high levels of unemployment, as indigenous industry was opened to competition. The development of industrial policy in Ireland also left a legacy of flexible labor market regulation - similar to that of the United Kingdom - that has encouraged the growth of atypical employment. As in the United Kingdom, however, there is no statutory control of part-time contracts so contracts of any length and number of hours can be offered, but part-time workers are afforded the same statutory protections as full-time workers. Although legislation does limit the use of serial fixed-term contracts, this is not enforced in practice. On the other hand, trade union density in Ireland is higher than in the UK and due to their involvement in the partnership agreements (see above) trade unions tend to have rather more influence than in the UK. Nonetheless, rather low levels of redundancy payments and weak judicial control of employers decisions means that employers have a great deal more flexibility and control over the use of labor in Ireland than they would in countries such as Italy, France or Germany.

The increased internationalization of economic activity is believed to lead to an increase in labor market flexibility, particularly in terms of working hours and contractual arrangements, giving rise to a greater incidence of atypical working. Table 16.2 shows the incidence of both part-time and temporary working by gender from 1983 to 1997. Part-time working increased from less than 7 percent of total employment to over 12 percent between 1983 and 1997. The incidence of part-time working is far higher among women, who account for over 70 percent of all part-time workers. In these respects, Ireland participates in a widespread international trend towards increased part-time working by women. O'Connell (2000), however, notes that despite this recent increase the incidence of part-time working in Ireland - 12 percent in 1997 - remains substantially lower than the European average (17 percent).

Table 16.2   Part-time and temporary work as a share of total employment, Ireland, 1983-1997

	Men	*Women*	*All*
Part-time as a share of total employment (%)			
1983	2.7	15.3	6.7
1990	3.3	16.8	8.0
1993	4.8	21.1	10.8
1997	5.4	23.1	12.3
Temporary as a share of total employment (%)			
1983	4.7	8.5	6.0
1990	6.6	11.0	8.4
1993	7.3	11.8	9.2
1997	7.1	12.2	9.4

The numbers working on fixed-term temporary contracts also increased in recent years, from 6 percent in 1983 to 9 percent in 1997, with a higher incidence among women than men. Here, again, O'Connell (2000) argues that while the extent of temporary working in Ireland has increased, it still lags behind trends elsewhere in Europe.

With regard to both part-time working and temporary contracts, Ireland has participated in a common European trend towards increased flexibility. However, while Ireland has followed this trend, the rate of flexibilization of employment in Ireland has been slower than the average in the European Union, and the extent of both part-time and temporary working in the latter half of the 1990s remained lower than the average in the European Union.

If Ireland is very much a globalized context and, moreover, if it has encouraged or at least not hindered the flexibilization of labor, then this undoubtedly has implications for one of the main analytical foci of this volume - the transition into the labor market. In the following section we outline several hypotheses about the effect of globalization on labor market transitions and try to contextualize these within the Irish environment.

GLOBALIZATION AND TRANSITIONS IN THE LABOR MARKET

The last section has outlined the dramatic and far-reaching changes that have occurred in the Irish economy and society over the last thirty years. As discussed, many of these developments are dimensions of the process of 'economic globalization' as described in the introduction to this volume, i.e. the growth of foreign direct investment and the presence of transnational corporations, although their effects are highly influenced by the Irish context. The 'open' nature of trade and investment policy has meant that Ireland is an interesting context within which to examine the effects that these processes may have on patterns of transition to adulthood.

The type and quantity of foreign direct investment that has occurred in Ireland is important, but it has also interacted with the late industrialization of Ireland to produce an economy which has a high reliance on information and communication industries. In fact, even the growth in manufacturing industry from the late 1980s was based upon the growth of high technology manufacture, primarily in the form of micro-chips, computers and pharmaceuticals. These types of industries are highly mobile and intrinsically more 'uncertain' in their outlook than, for instance, large-scale heavy industry and traditional manufacturing. Uncertainty may be exhibited in the stability of the enterprises themselves with redundancy being more probable, but it may also be visible in the use of part-time, fixed-term or short-term contracts. The literature on 'flexibilization' holds that employers will use these forms of contract in an attempt to provide numerical and temporal flexibility to labor power (see e.g. Kurz *et al.*, this volume).

However, there are two contradictory hypotheses about the consequences of this growing uncertainty for different types of workers. On the one hand, researchers such as Breen (1997) hold that the rising economic risks associated with globalization lead to a growing *segmentation* of the labor market, expressed in social class terms as a greater experience of both atypical contracts and unemployment among those on 'labor-type' contracts such as manual workers and particularly unskilled manual workers. The *individualization* thesis (Beck, 1992; Liesering and Leibfried, 1999), on the other hand, holds that growing uncertainty means an increasing *equality* of risk of experiencing atypical work and unemployment, as the structuring force of social class wanes in the face of a proletarization of all employees and other risks associated with life course transitions. As argued above, however, we would maintain that state employment regulation has just as much importance for labor market patterns as does the growth of internationalization and product market uncertainty. Certainly, if we compare Irish labor market regulation to that in countries such as Italy where employment protection is high, it is clear that employers are far more able to differentiate among employees.

All these hypotheses, however, come from the international literature and do not take into account the particular conditions of the Irish economy over the last twenty years, i.e., the transition from a depressed economy with high unemployment to one with the highest growth rates in Europe and an extremely tight labor market. In these conditions it may well be that many of the effects of growing uncertainty will be diluted by the fact that the economy is booming and employers need labor.

The hypotheses

What hypotheses can we identify from the brief discussion above and from that in the introduction to this volume, that we can examine using Irish evidence on transitions into the labor market? Unfortunately, we do not have data in the Irish context that would allow us to look back before the globalized period, i.e. before 1960, but we do have data from the 1980s and 90s that allow us to examine the effects of 'globalized' labor markets on transitions in both a period of recession and one of boom. Given this restriction, we examine the following hypotheses:

Increasing uncertainty – atypical contracts

From the foregoing discussion we would expect that temporary contracts are now a more common feature for entrants to the labor market, but we have conflicting theories in the form of the *segmentation* and *individualization* hypotheses about how widely such atypical contracts will be distributed among workers. On the one hand, the segmentation theory suggests that we should see a significant difference between those looking for 'service-orientated' work compared to those looking for 'labor-type' work in the probability of being offered a temporary contract and making the transition from such a contract to a permanent position. Similarly, there should be a big difference between these two groups in terms of their chances of experiencing subsequent unemployment when in the labor market. The individualization hypothesis, on the other hand, posits that we should see no differences between social class groups in terms of these risks. This pattern may very well be similar to what one would expect from strong economic growth, which - as the discussion above indicated - was the case in Ireland from 1994 onwards. However, the individualization hypothesis also suggests that - declining class differentials notwithstanding - we should still see increasing unemployment and use of atypical employment, which is the opposite of what would occur in a strong economic growth scenario.

Increasing uncertainty – unemployment

The globalization literature further holds that unemployment will be a common experience because of the increasing uncertainty of world trade and markets. But as with the transition to a permanent contract, one may ask: is this risk structured by social class cleavages or is it not?

THE DATA SOURCES

The section 'The rise of the developmental state' described two very different periods in recent Irish economic experience that we can label the 'pre-boom' and 'boom' periods. In the former, economic growth was at a low level or negative and inward investment in the economy was very small-scale. In the second, on the other hand, the economy had the fastest growth rates in Europe on the back of large amounts of foreign, mostly US investment. To allow us to examine changes over time in labor market transitions, this chapter uses two different but related data sources: the Irish School Leavers' and Follow-up Surveys of 1987-93 and 1992-98, respectively. The fact that these surveys cover the period from the late 1980s to the late 1990s is important, as this coincides with the pre-boom and boom periods. Using data from across this period we can analyze the impact that these changes had on patterns of transition into the labor market.

The 'School Leavers' Surveys' have been carried out every year in the Republic of Ireland since 1980 and are based on a stratified sample of those leaving full-time second-level education. A representative sample of school leavers are interviewed approximately 9-12 months after leaving their final education (thus, those leaving in May 1986 were interviewed in April/May of 1987). Using a common sampling approach, a standardized design, weighing, imputation and data adjustment[1], the School Leavers' Surveys offer data that are truly comparable across time.

However, as the one-year follow-up period of the School Leavers' Surveys does not offer a very long period of observation, we also make use of two 'Follow-up' Surveys that were carried out on selected cohorts approximately five to six years after the original School Leavers' Surveys. As with the questionnaires for these surveys themselves, changes to the follow-up questionnaires were kept to a minimum in order to maximize the comparability across time offered by the merged database.

The 1992 Follow-up Survey was based on the 1985-86 cohort of school leavers as interviewed in 1987. Of the original 2,090 school leavers, 1,659 were re-contacted in 1992, giving a response rate of 79 percent. The 1998 Follow-up Survey revisited the 1991-92 cohort of school leavers as interviewed in 1993, with an initial sample of 1,396. Of these, 996 were retraced, giving a response rate of 71 percent. However, the 1993 survey was not a random sample of the school leavers population, as it did not interview those who went directly from school to third-level education in the year in which they graduated. To compare such a sample with the complete sample of school leavers as interviewed in 1987 would present difficulties, thus here we have made the decision to confine the analyses to those in both years who did not go on directly to third-level education. This brings down the available number of respondents in 1987 to 1,075 and means that these analyses cannot be seen as representative of all those making the transition into the labor market in these two periods. Nonetheless, the analyses should be very revealing about general changes in patterns of transition.

Definitions and measures used

The standardized structure of the School Leavers' Surveys allows us to create common variables across the data sets for analysis. 'First job' was defined as the first position that respondents took following their completion of full-time education, irrespective of the status of permanency of the job. This means that any part-time or vacation jobs that respondents took whilst engaged in full-time education are ignored. However, a small minority of respondents who subsequently enrolled in a third-level course did not go onto this course immediately after completing their second-level education, but on average one year later. If this period was one year or less, the point of entry into the labor market is taken as the end of the third-level education rather than the time of exit from the second-level institution.

Both the social class and education variables used in this chapter are coded using the classifications employed in the CASMIN study (König *et al.*, 1988).

The variables for both the respondent's class and that of their father are coded using a collapsed, seven-class version of the original eleven-class CASMIN schema.

Education in the CASMIN schema (König *et al.*, 1988) distinguishes between eight categories according to level and - to some degree - the type of schooling involved. However, we have chosen to disregard some of the distinctions that are meaningless in the Irish context and thus collapse the eight categories into a four-fold classification. Thus categories 1a, 1b and 1c (inadequate, completed and basic vocational elementary education) are combined into a primary or incomplete secondary category. It makes no sense in the Irish context to separate those leaving the junior cycle early and those leaving without qualifications. Similarly, 1c (elementary education plus vocational training) does not exist in the Irish school system. Since category 2a (general intermediate plus specific vocational training) does not exist in Ireland, lower and intermediate secondary education (CASMIN 2a and 2b) are combined to form a single lower secondary category.

The closest approximation to this is apprenticeship training that usually follows completion of general intermediate education. Apprenticeships are almost exclusively taken by men and the numbers involved are small and have been declining. Category 2c is retained as a higher secondary category, while lower and higher third-level education (3a and 3b) are combined to make a single tertiary education category.

Though relatively few of the respondents either had children or became married during the period of observation up to the follow-up survey, we nonetheless employ time-varying measures of these variables in the transition rate analyses presented later in the chapter. Combining non-marital and marital cohabitation in a single variable expresses the effect of having a partner on transition processes. Similarly, the time-varying number of children is entered as a covariate where appropriate. (However, because of the small numbers, we abstain from modeling partnership and parenthood as dependent processes themselves.)

Unemployment after entry into the labor market may be an important determinant of the speed of transition into a first job and moreover of subsequent success in the labor market (De Vreyer *et al.*, 2000; Layte *et al.*, 2000). As such we use a variable to represent the number of months spent unemployed.

ANALYSIS ONE: ENTERING THE LABOR MARKET

Here we want to examine the hypothesis that the globalized economy impacts on entry into the labor market by increasing the experience of atypical forms of work such as part-time work and temporary employment. However, as the section 'The rise of the developmental state' made clear, the period covered by the data is that in which Ireland experienced unprecedented growth and transformation of the labor market from around 16 percent unemployment to less than 6 percent. If there is a process of increasing uncertainty in the labor market, it may be that this is less noticeable in an economy that is already at close to full capacity both in terms of labor and capital.

Table 16.3 gives the proportions from our two cohorts experiencing a temporary contract on entry into their first job and makes for interesting reading. As discussed earlier on, first job here refers to that job taken immediately after leaving full-time education, although if the respondent subsequently returned to education within a year, the next job thereafter was used. For all social class groups apart from the routine non-manuals there is a decrease between years in the proportion receiving a temporary contract, the fall being particularly large among the service class employees.

Table 16.3   Proportion gaining a temporary first contract by year and social class, Ireland, 1987-1993

	1987	1993
Service	28.6	16.7
Routine Non-Manual	30.6	35.7
Technical/Supervisory/Skilled	28.9	21.3
Semi-Unskilled	38.4	34.0
All	32.6	28.3
N	306	185

Such descriptive analyses do not take account of the confounding effects of other variables such as sex or qualifications, thus in Table 16.4 we show the results of three logistic models of receiving a temporary contract in one's first job.

The last coefficient in column one of Table 16.4 confirms the finding of the descriptive analyses in it shows a decrease in the prevalence of temporary contracts between the cohorts, suggesting that the better labor market situation for the 1993 cohort aided their transition into the labour market. But there are characteristics that increase the probability of receiving such a contract.

Across both cohorts, having spent a longer period unemployed before gaining one's first job increases the probability of receiving a temporary contract, as does having less than upper-secondary education, or gaining an unskilled job. However, all these risk factors except the previous experience of unemployment become insignificant in the second period when economic conditions picked up and the labor market became tighter. As already discussed, the waning of the segmenting effect of social class could suggest that we are seeing here evidence of the individualization hypothesis, but the decline in the risk of gaining a temporary contract does not chime with this interpretation.

Given this, the logistic analysis implies that economic growth decreases the ability of employers to offer temporary contracts. However, it is also clear that in worse economic times the use of such contracts was segmented among employees: those in unskilled manual occupations were far more likely to receive them.

Table 16.4   Logit model of whether to receive a temporary contract in first job after leaving education in Ireland

Variable	Effect and significance		
	All	Cohort 1	Cohort 2
Constant	-0.66**	-0.84**	-0.14
Female	-0.05	-0.11	0.06
Months unemployed before 1st job	0.42***	0.39**	0.53*
Education primary			
Intermediate certificate	0.09	0.29	-0.25
Leaving certificate	0.54**	0.80**	0.16
Vocational qualification	0.63**	0.80*	0.47
Own class unskilled			
Service	-0.88**	-1.07*	n/a
Routine non-manual	-0.34*	-0.52*	-0.57
Technical and supervisory	-1.01	-0.24	0.00
Skilled manual	-0.63***	-0.61**	-4.70
Father's class unskilled			
Father service	-0.06	-0.07	-0.67**
Father routine non-manual	0.17	0.38	-0.08
Father petty bourgeois	-0.04	-0.01	-0.50
Father farming	-0.07	0.12	-0.25
Father technical and supervisory	0.17	-0.01	-0.25
Father skilled manual	-0.03	-0.07	0.13
1987 Cohort			
1993 Cohort	-0.22		
Log likelihood	1637.139	1025.954	597.936
N	1307	812	495

Notes
# $p < 0.1$
* $p < 0.05$
** $p < 0.01$
*** $p < 0.001$

Moving to a permanent contract

The uneven distribution of atypical contracts suggests that there are segmenting processes in the labor market, as argued by Breen (1997). The question is, however, does this segmentation also affect the movement of those who enter on temporary contracts to a more permanent position? In the following analyses we use the sample of those who gained a first job during the six-year observation period of the follow-up surveys on both cohorts, but restrict the analysis to those who did not obtain a permanent contract in their first job. Furthermore, rather than losing the respondents in the two samples who did not know if they had a contract in their first job, we label this group as having no contract and enter them into the analysis as reference group.[2]

Here we test the competing hypotheses of segmentation and individualization discussed earlier. Given that we want to examine the tendency to move into a permanent contract over a set (and censored) observation period, the appropriate methodology is some form of transition rate model. We use the most flexible form of parametric hazard rate models, the piecewise constant exponential model to analyze this transition. In this model the baseline hazard is taken to be exponential within each of a set of arbitrarily long time periods. Our time periods are six months long up to a final time period of 60+ months. Using this structure we can examine the estimates for a number of other covariates that are important in terms of the hypotheses outlined earlier. Some of these covariates are entered in time-varying format allowing us to examine whether their changing states affect the rate of transition.

In Table 16.5 we show the results for three such models, one using data from both cohorts and two models confined to each single cohort. Turning first to the term that represents the difference between the two cohorts we can see that, contrary to the findings in Table 16.4, being in the later cohort makes the transition to a permanent position significantly less likely. This finding may seem surprising but it should be kept in mind that the general increase in temporary contracts during the period covered by the data (see Table 16.2) is largely among those employees who are already in the labor market rather than new entrants. As we can see here, controlling for other factors, in the later period such workers were less likely to make the move into a permanent position if they had not done so already.

Table 16.5 shows furthermore that those who experienced unemployment prior to entry are less likely to subsequently enter a permanent position. Other evidence in favor of the hypothesis of segmentation is that those in routine non-manual or skilled manual classes are far more likely to move into a permanent position than those in unskilled manual positions. (As one would expect, being self-employed has a strongly negative effect, although the small number of respondents in this class makes the estimate insignificant.) Unlike in Table 16.4, however, this segmenting effect does not decline in the later period, suggesting that even when the labor market is constrained employers continue to segment different types of employees.

Interestingly, the estimated effect of being female is negative in all three models in Table 16.5, indicating that women are less likely than men to make this transition. Although the cohort-specific estimates are barely statistically significant, they increase in the second period, thus women may well be at a disadvantage relative to men.

Lastly we come to the effect of being on a temporary contract rather than no contract. Though receiving a temporary contract slows the transition for both cohorts, it is only significant in the second, and of larger magnitude. This suggests that the transition may have become more difficult in this second, more buoyant period. This last analysis - as the one on entry into the labor market - makes clear that a subsequent transition into a permanent position is heavily segmented. Thus, if one enters the labor market on a temporary contract, it is less likely that a move into a permanent contract will occur.

Table 16.5 Piecewise constant hazard rate model of moving from a temporary or no contract to a permanent employment contract in Ireland

Variable	Effect and significance		
	All	Cohort 1	Cohort 2
Female	-0.18*	-0.16#	-0.24#
Married/cohabiting	0.04	0.12	-0.18
Months unemp before 1st job	-0.40***	-0.43***	-0.36*
Number of children	-0.23	n/a	-0.20
Education primary			
Intermediate certificate	0.08	0.12#	0.02
Leaving certificate	0.20	0.28	0.02
Tertiary	-0.19	0.08	-1.20*
Vocational qualification	-0.01	-0.06	-0.04
Own class unskilled			
Service	0.63***	0.86***	0.06
Routine non-manual	0.52***	0.44***	0.69***
Farmer	0.11	0.01	0.05
Technical and supervisory	0.82	-8.28	
Skilled manual	0.43***	0.38**	0.50**
Self-employed	-7.04	-7.99	-8.13
Father's class unskilled			
Father service	-0.24	-0.26	-0.30
Father routine non-manual	-0.08	-0.05	-0.30
Father petty bourgeois	0.04		0.00
Father farming	-0.04	-0.03	-0.19
Father technical and supervisory	-0.10	-0.35	0.37
Father skilled manual	0.08	0.08	0.12
No contract			
Temporary contract	-0.21*	-0.19#	-0.38*
1987 Cohort			
1993 cohort	-0.61***		
Log-likelihood	-4205.65	-2590.18	-1294.38
Total number of events	1612	947	665
Total number of periods	1708	1023	685

Notes
# $p < 0.1$
* $p < 0.05$
** $p < 0.01$
*** $p < 0.001$

An increasing experience of unemployment?

Having looked at entry into the labor market and the experience of atypical employment in the form of temporary contracts, we now turn to the analysis of whether unemployment is spread evenly across the respondents in our data, or whether certain characteristics make it more likely. As we have already seen in Table 16.1, the decrease in the unemployment rate from 1994 onwards in Ireland was truly remarkable, thus this may have a large bearing on these analyses, with the latter cohort being far less affected.

As in the last analysis, here we want to examine the tendency to move into unemployment while taking account of the fact that the observation period is censored, thus once again we use the piecewise constant exponential model. Results from such a model are shown in Table 16.6.

Looking first at the dummy variable representing membership of the latter cohort, we can see that, as expected, the probability of unemployment fell quite considerably between the two periods. However, Table 16.6 also shows that certain characteristics make the experience of unemployment more likely. Across both cohorts being female makes one less likely to experience unemployment, but this effect is only significant (and then only at the 10 percent level) in the overall model. On the other hand, having experienced unemployment before entering one's first job leads to an increase in risk across both cohorts. It is clear also that being on a temporary contract has a significant positive influence on experiencing subsequent unemployment, again an effect that increases between the cohorts.

Do we see a degree of segmentation among the social class groups in terms of their risk of unemployment or are all groups as likely to experience unemployment, as suggested by the individualization hypothesis? Table 16.6 shows almost all social class groups are less likely to experience unemployment than the unskilled manual class, though the net effect is only significant for the service, routine non-manual and skilled manual classes. The effect for level of education is less clear: lower- and higher-secondary qualifications (intermediate and leaving certificates) are positive in the first cohort but negative in the second.

THE IMPACT OF ECONOMIC POLICY ON FERTILITY PATTERNS

In the section 'The rise of the developmental state' we argued that the economic and social policies adopted by the Irish state in areas such as foreign investment and education significantly influenced the type of industrialization experienced in Ireland and the impact that globalization has had on this. In this final section we argue that these policy decisions also influenced the development of fertility patterns in Ireland by shaping the level of life course uncertainty experienced by Irish people from the 1950s to the late 1990s.

As outlined earlier, in the 1960s Ireland switched from a policy of resistance to globalization (aiming at inward looking self-sufficient development) to an enthusiastic embrace of globalization (aiming at export-led economic growth based on an open trading regime and high levels of foreign direct investment). Although it

Table 16.6   Piecewise constant hazard rate model of experiencing a spell of unemployment after gaining a first job in Ireland

Variable	Effect and significance		
	All	Cohort 1	Cohort 2
Female	-0.17#	-0.16	-0.23
Married/cohabiting	0.19#	0.20	0.21
Months unemp before 1st job	0.56***	0.55***	0.67***
Number of children	-0.59	n/a	-0.59
Education primary			
Intermediate certificate	0.30*	0.42*	0.00
Leaving certificate	0.18	0.43*	-0.41#
Tertiary	0.01	0.18	-0.41
Vocational qualification	-0.35#	-0.14	-0.72*
Own class unskilled			
Service	-0.73*	-0.62#	-0.99#
Routine non-manual	-0.26*	-0.21	-0.49*
Farmer	0.43	-0.34	0.89
Technical and supervisory	0.71	0.33	1.15
Skilled manual	-0.23*	-0.23#	-0.21
Self-employed	-0.77	-0.41	-1.15
Contract permanent			
No contract	0.03	-0.07	0.27
Temporary contract	0.55***	0.45***	0.76***
1987 Cohort			
1993 Cohort	-0.34***		
Log-likelihood	-3470.81	-2343.87	-1114.29
Total number of events	1612	947	665
Total number of periods	1742	1038	704

Notes
# $p < 0.1$
* $p < 0.05$
** $p < 0.01$
*** $p < 0.001$

seemed for a time in the 1980s that this shift was failing to deliver the social and economic advance it promised, the longer-term picture has been positive. By the end of the 1990s, having full employment, rapid economic growth, booming exports and strong exchequer surpluses, Ireland was in a position of greater economic security than at any other time in its history. For the first time ever, workers were faced with the pleasing situation where demand for labor exceeded supply and the threat of unemployment had therefore eased to an unprecedented degree. While it would be excessive to say that economic uncertainty has thus disappeared off stage in Ireland, one could say that the Irish economy has emerged from a long history of extreme uncertainty into a period of much greater security and confidence. It thus represents the reverse of the malign trajectory often associated with globalization, as shown in many other chapters in this volume.

Given that the Irish economic trajectory is so at odds with the negative imagery of globalization, it becomes of particular interest to ask if demographic and family change is similarly at odds with patterns elsewhere. The answer depends very much on the precise terms in which the issue is posed, that is, the details of what is defined as the standard pattern. In some respects, Irish trends in fertility and marriage have shown the same tendencies as elsewhere and should, therefore, be subject to the same patterns of destabilization and growing diversity of family life. Fertility has declined (from a total fertility rate of 4.0 in 1960 to 1.89 in 1999), the share of births occurring outside marriage has soared (reaching 32 percent in 1999) and marital breakdown has steadily increased over recent decades, although only to the level found in the low-divorce countries of Southern Europe such as Spain and Italy. Marriage rates have also declined from the historically high levels recorded in the 1970s.

However, these aspects of Irish trends do not tell the whole story. There are other respects in which the underlying direction of Irish developments is quite distinctive. This is particularly so when recent Irish experience is placed in the context of Ireland's longer-term history of family life and demographic development. In the 1950s, as the 'baby boom' and post-war demographic expansion was well underway in most of the developed world, Ireland's demographic situation was unrelievedly gloomy. The country seemed stricken by an inability to keep up, much less increase its population numbers. Crippling waves of emigration and economic insecurity meant that non-marriage reached very high levels by the 1930s and remained so into the 1960s, with a quarter of all women aged over 50 having never married in 1961. Thus, whereas most other European countries were enjoying a marriage and fertility boom in the 1950s, Ireland's depressed economy and high levels of unemployment and poverty led to a declining population and birth rate.

The radical turnaround in economic policy undertaken in the early 1960s was in part prompted by desperation arising from the relentless and apparently intensifying demographic decline in the 1950s. Large areas of the West of Ireland were experiencing depopulation to alarming levels. It was hoped that economic openness might reverse these population trends in a manner that the earlier policy had not. In the event, this hope was fulfilled, although with some halts and reverses. Population decline was turned into modest, but nevertheless real growth (at an annual rate of 0.7 percent from 1960 to the mid-1990s). Apart from a brief resurgence during the crisis years of the late 1980s, emigration declined and in recent years has turned into substantial net inward migration. Moreover, marriage and fertility rates tracked the growth of the economy that occurred in the early 1970s when the FDI made itself felt. The marriage boom of the 1970s led to a baby boom of the late 1970s and early 1980s that provided a large cohort of young workers for the growth period of the 1990s. Although both marriage and fertility rates subsequently declined during the recession years of the 1980s, the period since 1994 has witnessed a resurgence of household formation and first births to unprecedented levels.

Interestingly, Ireland still has one of the highest total fertility rates among developed nations and the highest in Europe, but the make-up of this fertility has changed markedly since the 1950s. In 1960, 32 percent of all births were of the fifth or higher child in the family and first and second births made up only 39 percent, by 1980 this balance had switched to 15 and 53 percent, respectively, and by 1995 to 5 and 71 percent. The high average number of births to married women before 1960 was balanced in part by the large number of women that never married and thus remained childless (rates of illegitimacy were low). Yet after 1970, not only did the rate of marriage increase, but the average number of births per woman decreased, a process linked to the large increase in educational attainment among women after the introduction of free education in 1967 and a trend toward increased employment participation among women. The pattern of high fertility in the earlier period was thus of a very different nature compared to that of the latter part of the century.

These developments have lent substance to the image of Ireland as a modernizing, developing nation and as a major beneficiary of globalization. Where demographic decline up to the 1960s had been a sign of national backwardness and stagnation, the demographic recovery since then and its consolidation in the 1990s has signaled a new vibrancy and has helped to justify the positive rhetoric that now dominates the political discourse about Ireland's socio-economic performance and prospects. Furthermore, the marked pace of Ireland's demographic upswing in the 1990s like its economic growth coincides with an incipient sluggishness in the demography of other western countries, as reflected in the rapidly ageing populations of countries like Germany and Japan.

CONCLUSIONS

In this chapter we have argued that the idea put forward in much globalization literature that economic globalization leads to the erosion of the power of the state to intervene with social and economic policy to shape outcomes is simplistic at best and, in the Irish case, the opposite of the true process. After three decades of under-development and recession, the dismantling of protectionism and the embracing of globalization by Irish policy makers in the 1950s laid the foundations for the extraordinary growth that occurred in the 1990s. By the end of the 1960s Ireland was already a recognizably globalized state with a large proportion of total output coming from foreign-owned firms that were attracted into the Irish context by a regulatory and tax system tailor-made to the inflow of international capital. However, contrary to the basic assumption of much globalization literature, this investment was not in unskilled jobs in low-value-added processes. Because of the IDA policy of targeting high technology and pharmaceutical companies, investment was instead in high productivity processes staffed by skilled professionals and technical workers.

Though the opening-up of the economy and the end to protectionism initially led to the destruction of up to a quarter of indigenous Irish manufacturing in the recession of the 1980s, the policy of encouraging FDI and open trade paid off in the mid-1990s with high rates of growth. We can see then that the state played a crucial role in guiding the development of the Irish economy and was not over-powered by the anonymous face of global capital and market forces.

Similarly, we also saw that the nature of employment regulation has shaped the distribution of risk in the labor market, as shown by the analyses of labor market transitions in this chapter. Whether we looked at the first job after entering the labor market, the transition to a permanent contract or the experience of unemployment, it was clear that disadvantage and risk were not spread evenly across the population. Contrary to the individualization thesis, the unskilled manual working class experienced a far higher level of risk compared to those with higher levels of skills or more service-type occupations.

In the last section we pointed out that positive effects from economic global-ization could also be traced in the evolution of demographic patterns over the past 50 years. Prior to 1960, Ireland's population history had been marked by long-term weakness and unsustainability, reflected especially in massive emi-gration and population decline. As the economy opened up, demographic stabili-zation set in. Today Ireland's demographic performance, as indicated by fertility and population growth is among the strongest in Europe. This further indicates that positive effects of globalization can be found in various aspects of social life, even in small peripheral countries. Here also, as in earlier sections, we saw the importance of state policy and economic conditions in shaping behavior. As discussed in the introduction to this volume, this relationship is linked to the pattern of uncertainty in the economy throughout this extraordinary period in Irish history.

In many ways Ireland has been fortunate to have had the right economic policies in place for a sufficient amount of time to reap the benefits of develop-ments in particular industrial sectors and the sustained period of growth which many countries, but particularly the UK and US, have experienced in the 1990s. Although state intervention was crucial in providing the right conditions, Ireland has nonetheless been fortunate to be in the right place at the right time to reap the positive aspects of mobile capital. As we have described, this has transformed Ireland from an under performing economy with chronic unemployment to the so-called 'Celtic Tiger' with double digit growth rates. This does not mean how-ever that Ireland will not see the darker side of economic globalization. The Irish Industrial Development Authority will need to continue to connect Ireland into growth sectors of the world economy and government will need to ensure that Ireland remains competitive when attracting mobile investment if development is to be sustained.

NOTES

1 All the surveys have been carried out by The Economic and Social Research Institute (ESRI) in Dublin.
2 Such a lack of knowledge on this subject is quite common in Ireland and the United Kingdom where a large minority of workers, particularly in manual occupations, do not know if they have a contract or not. In law they are required to receive one after a relatively short period but employment protection in general is so weak in these countries that such contracts often have little practical benefit in reality.

BIBLIOGRAPHY

Beck, U. (1992) *Risk Society. Towards a New Modernity*, London: Sage.
Breen, Richard (1997) 'Risk, Recommodification and Stratification', *Sociology*, 31(3): 473-489.
De Vreyer, P., Layte, R., Wolbers, M., and Hussain, A. H. (2000) 'The Permanent Effects of Labour Market Entry in Times of High Unemployment', in D. Gallie and S. Paugam (eds) *Welfare Regimes and the Experience of Unemployment in Europe*, Oxford: Oxford University Press.
König, W., Lüttinger, P., and Müller, W. (1988) *A Comparative Analysis of the Development and Structure of Educational Systems*, Mannheim: Institut für Sozialwissenschaften, Universität Mannheim.
Layte, R., Levin, H., Hendrickx, J., and Bison, I. (2000) 'Unemployment and Cumulative Disadvantage', in D. Gallie and S. Paugam (eds) *Welfare Regimes and the Experience of Unemployment*, Oxford: Oxford University Press.
Leisering, L. and Leibfried, S. (1999) *Time and Poverty in Western Welfare States: United Germany in Perspective*, Cambridge MA: Cambridge University Press.
O'Connell, P. J. (2000) 'The Dynamics of the Irish Labour Market in Comparative Perspective', in B. Nolan, P. J. O'Connell, and C. T. Whelan (eds) *Bust to Boom? The Irish Experience of Growth and Inequality*, Dublin: Institute of Public Administration.
O'Malley, E. (1989) *Industry and Economic Development: The Challenge for the Late Comer*, Dublin: Gill and Macmillian.
Ó'Riain, S. and O'Connell, P. J. (1999) 'The Role of the State in Growth and Welfare', in B. Nolan, P. J. O'Connell, and C. T. Whelan (eds) *Bust to Boom? The Irish Experience of Growth and Inequality*, Dublin: Institute of Public Administration.
Ruggie, J. G. (1982) 'International Regimes, Transactions and Change: Embedded Liberalism in the Postwar Economic Order', *International Organistion*, 36: 379-415.

17 Becoming an adult in uncertain times

A 14-country comparison of the losers of globalization

Melinda Mills, Hans-Peter Blossfeld and Erik Klijzing

INTRODUCTION

This chapter provides a short summary of the key empirical findings from the 14 countries included in this study. It confronts our expectations and theoretical assumptions as outlined at the onset of this volume.

Four general findings emerge. First, youth in all countries are clearly exposed to more uncertainty in the course of globalization. Yet uncertainty is unequal, as risk appears to accumulate in certain groups, generally those at the bottom of the social ladder. Second, in support of our general hypothesis, uncertainty has consequences for family formation, with those in more precarious positions more likely to postpone or forgo partnership and parenthood. Third we describe how youth develop rational responses to this uncertainty, which we identified in the form of diverse behavioral strategies. Strategies include remaining in the education system, postponing family formation, taking on multiple roles or engaging in flexible partnerships. A notable result is that young men and women are affected and respond differently to uncertainty, resulting in an unmistakable gender-specific strategy, particularly in the male-breadwinner societies. Fourth we show overwhelming support for the expectation that nation-specific institutions serve to shield or funnel this uncertainty in unique ways and to particular groups of youth. The chapter concludes with a summary of major findings, the contribution of this study to the field of youth studies and globalization research and the added value of this approach.

THE EMERGENCE OF UNCERTAINTY

The first central finding is that in a globalizing world, *youth are increasingly vulnerable to uncertainty across all countries,* which supports our life course hypothesis elaborated upon in the introductory chapter. This materializes in increasingly more precarious and lower-quality employment such as fixed-term contracts, part-time or irregular work hours, or lower occupational standing (see Table 17.1). This in turn bestows the youngest labor market entrants with a more uncertain future. Youth, who have less labor market experience and who are not yet shielded by internal labor markets, are more greatly exposed to the forces of globalization, which makes them the 'losers' of globalization. As our second volume (Blossfeld, Mills and Bernardi, forthcoming) illustrates, there are indeed some groups such as mid-career men, who generally surface as 'winners' in the globalization process. As insiders, mid-career men are to a large extent shielded by labor force experience, internal labor markets and existing power structures. The forces of globalization are therefore shifted to outsiders such as youth.

The 14 country studies provide evidence for youth's increased exposure to globalization in diverse ways. For example, the youngest cohorts in Italy took more time to find a first job and had fewer chances to transform a fixed-term contract into a permanent one (Bernardi and Nazio, this volume). Young Spanish workers were similarly affected by fixed-term contracts and high unemployment, with British and Hungarian youth increasingly more likely to start their employment career in non-standard temporary jobs or as self-employed workers. In comparison to previous cohorts, the occupational prestige of the first job for Dutch youth plummeted for those born in the 1960s (Liefbroer, this volume). The post-socialist cohorts entering the Hungarian labor market in the 1990s had difficulties not only finding a job, but when they did, it was much more likely to be on a fixed-term contract, particularly for men (Róbert and Bukodi, this volume). Even in Sweden, where youth are largely protected by the social-democratic welfare system, youth took progressively longer to find a job that fit their educational qualifications (Bygren *et al.*, this volume). As Table 17.1 demonstrates, out of the 14 countries, there was only one exception. Due to globalization, Ireland experienced an unprecedented economic boom that actually reduced uncertainty for youth. Compared to previous historical periods, recent Irish cohorts were in fact better off. The increased certainty generated by the Irish 'economic miracle' shows the positive side of the globalization process, an aspect we will return to in our discussion of institutional filters.

INEQUALITY OF UNCERTAINTY

In Chapter 1, we hypothesized that globalization may accentuate or even cultivate inequality, a hypothesis that was confirmed. Not only has uncertainty intensified, but also a clear segmentation process comes about among youth (Breen, 1997). Certain groups of youth are disproportionately impacted, with the risks of globalization being accumulated at the bottom. In support of our employment relationship hypothesis, this insider/outsider split was even more evident in societies with a closed employment system where uncertainty was channeled to labor market outsiders much more intensively (see Bernardi and Nazio; Simó *et al.*, this volume). Our expectations regarding open employment systems were also confirmed. Here the relative shielding of workers was much less prevalent, with risk spread over a wider base, leaving youth to rely much more on their own human capital. Yet in support of our human capital hypothesis, even though uncertainty was more pervasive, inequality still accumulated disproportionately in certain groups such as blacks or visible women, and those with less human

Table 17.1 Summary of main results: Rising uncertainty in the labor market and impact on partnership and parenthood behavior

Welfare regime and country	Rising uncertainty in early life course				
	Uncertain labor market position for younger cohorts	Impact of employment uncertainty on hazard of:			
		Partnerships		Parenthood	
		Men	*Women*	*Men*	*Women*
Conservative					
Germany	↑	↓	↑	↓	↑
Netherlands	↑	↓	↑	↓	↑
[France]	↑	↓	↑/ ↔	↓	↑/ ↓
Social-democratic					
Sweden	↑	↓ / ↔	↓ / ↔	↓	↓
Norway	↑	↓	↓	↓	↓
Post-socialistic					
Hungary	↑	↓	↓	↓	↑
Estonia*	↑	↓ / ↔	↓ / ↔	↓ / ↔	↓ / ↔
Liberal					
Britain	↑	↔(c) ↓(m)	↓(c) ↔(m)	↔	↑
Canada	↑	↓	↓	↓	↓
United States♀	↑	-	↓	-	↓
Family-oriented					
Mexico♀	↑	-	↔	-	↔
Italy	↑	↓	↑	↓	↑
Spain	↑	↓	↑	↓	↑
Ireland	↓	-	↔	-	↔

Notes
↑   Increase in hazard.
↔   No significantly observed effect.
↓   Decrease in hazard.
-    Not examined.
♀   Only women examined.
(m) Marriage.
(c) Consensual union.
*   Analysis was not divided by gender.

capital (see Francesconi and Golsch; Berkowitz King; Mills, this volume). These differences are apparent when we examine which types of youth experience economic, temporal and employment relation uncertainty.

Recall that *economic uncertainty* was operationalized by factors such as the caliber of precariousness of youth's employment and educational activity, as measured by activity status, occupational class, benefits, and earnings. All countries showed an increase in the amount of economic uncertainty, confirming our expectation that youth experience more uncertainty in the employment sphere. With respect to occupational class, it was the manual, un- and semi-skilled workers that were the most impacted by the recent changes, particularly in the closed employment systems. For example, youth in lower occupational classes showed a higher risk of: being employed in temporary contracts (e.g., Spain, Germany, Italy, Ireland, Britain), becoming or remaining unemployed (e.g., Spain, Italy), remaining entrapped in insecure positions (e.g., Italy, Ireland), or having no pension benefits (e.g., Canada).

In Italy and Spain, youth with lower levels of education were actually more likely to find a first job. In these employment systems, highly educated youth need to get a high-quality job match when entering the labor market. If they obtain a job below their qualification level, it is much more difficult to get back on track. This is in stark contrast from the 'stop-gap' job circuit that youth from open employment systems undergo, where lower-level jobs have comparatively less of a 'scarring' effect on their long-term careers. Due to the importance of a good job match in closed employment systems, youth with higher education are very selective and thus have a longer search period. This translated into higher unemployment rates in these societies (see Klijzing, this volume), often of the highly skilled who then must rely on the support of their families. The irony is that fixed-term contracts are used to hire individuals in lower-skilled occupations, thus it is these disadvantaged groups of youth that are the most affected (see Simó *et al.*, this volume). In Germany, there was clear and significant stratification in the type of youth that experienced unemployment from the mid-1980s to the end of the 1990s. Educational qualifications, class position, sex, region (East versus West) and migrant status made a difference in whether youth experienced unemployment or not (Kurz *et al.*, this volume). Findings in Britain and Canada showed that there was a larger amount of heterogeneity across workers in non-standard or precarious work, thus supporting our expectation that labor market flexibility is more widespread among various social groups (Francesconi and Golsch; Mills, this volume).

Particularly in the closed employment systems, uncertainty took the form of *employment relation* or *temporal* uncertainty. In these countries, insiders are especially protected. The only way to introduce flexibility into the system is by shifting it to outsiders who have not yet secured employment protection. The youngest and least qualified workers were increasingly in precarious, fixed-term contracts in Hungary, the Netherlands, Ireland, France, Germany, Spain, Italy and Britain. The use of fixed-term contracts has skyrocketed in many countries. In the Netherlands, for instance, there has been a clear drop in the number of youth who hold a permanent contract and a rise in those with temporary or training contracts (Liefbroer, this volume). Even Irish youth, who were witnessing the best economic upsurge in recent history, had a higher probability of having a temporary contract (Layte *et al.*, this volume). Younger cohorts in Estonia reported a lower level of control and lack of confidence for the future, thus exemplifying clear temporal uncertainty (Katus *et al.*, this volume).

One type of work that results in both lower economic and employment relation uncertainty is part-time employment. The move by many countries to cut the social benefits for part-time workers (e.g., in France, United States, Canada, Britain) made it advantageous for employers to use this labor market flexibility measure to hire two or more part-time workers for each full-time regular position. In these countries, part-time work is synonymous with job insecurity, non-standard working times, lower skilled jobs and lower earnings. The accumulation of experience in part-time jobs in the United States actually hindered young women's transition into full-time work due to the fact that it was not the 'right' kind of experience (Berkowitz King, this volume). In Germany, part-timers were twice as likely to work on a fixed-term basis in comparison to their full-time counterparts (Kurz *et al.*, this volume). In Britain, temporary workers, the self-employed, and seasonal/casual workers were systematically more likely to be in part-time jobs (Francesconi and Golsch, this volume).

We also found support for our expectation that *human capital* would be an important asset to protect youth against uncertainty, particularly in the more liberal welfare regimes. Empirical findings for Britain, for instance, show that education and labor market experience protected youth from falling into unemployment (see Francesconi and Golsch; Berkowitz King; Mills, this volume).

CONSEQUENCES OF UNCERTAINTY FOR FAMILY FORMATION

The impact of increased uncertainty on the lives of youth is clear – it impedes their transition to adulthood, providing clear support for our primary hypothesis outlined in Chapter 1. As we will elaborate upon shortly in our discussion of gender-specific strategies, *economic uncertainty*, particularly for men in male breadwinner societies, postponed family formation. Youth in Estonia, who reported high temporal uncertainty in terms of lack of control and self-confidence, were significantly less likely to enter into partnerships and parenthood (Katus *et al.*, this volume).

Bad economic cycles also appeared to impact family formation. In Mexico, for instance, the relatively stable economic conditions that followed a major economic crisis resulted in an increase in union formation (Parrado, this volume). In Spain, the higher the unemployment rate when youth entered the labor market, the lower the rate of entry into parenthood (Simó *et al.*, this volume). Increases in the female unemployment rate meant a slower transition to first birth for American women, whereas increases in manufacturing wages accelerated progression to first job, marriage and birth (Berkowitz King, this volume). In Britain, entry into unemployment was more likely to occur during the downturn of the business cycle in 1992-93 (Francesconi and Golsch, this volume), and students in Canada were significantly more likely to work in precarious positions for involuntary reasons during a bad economic cycle (Mills, this volume).

The *educational and labor market activity status* of youth also had clear consequences for family formation. The lowest rate of entry into fatherhood in Spain was for men in the most uncertain position of all – the unemployed (Simó *et al.*, this volume). In the Netherlands, young adults without employment delayed union formation compared to those with a permanent, full-time position in the service class (Liefbroer, this volume). As Table 17.1 illustrates, there were mixed findings of the impact of uncertainty for Sweden. Unemployment (after labor market entry) in Sweden had no effect on union formation and parenthood, which supports our welfare regime hypothesis that social-democratic systems with their generous benefits can cushion economic uncertainty for youth. Swedish youth without any attachment to the labor force yet (students or those between school and first job) had somewhat lower propensities to start a first union (Bygren *et al.*, this volume).

Another clear finding across all of the countries was that those enrolled in education were the least likely to enter a first partnership and especially to have a child. The role of a student remains firmly incompatible with the role of a spouse or parent. Some analyses also showed that if students did form a union, it was more likely to be non-marital (e.g., the Netherlands). Whereas in Estonia there was a clear and fascinating diffusion process of cohabitation from the rural and lower educated youth to the urban and higher educated over time (Katus *et al.*, this volume).

The amount of security youth held in their *employment relationship* and degree of *temporal uncertainty* also had real consequences for family formation. The impact of having a fixed-term contract was expected to result in higher temporal and employment relation uncertainty, a hypothesis which generally gained strong support, particularly for young men. The consequence of holding a fixed-term contract for young French men strongly reduced their entry into a first union, an effect that was not found for their female counterparts. However, more extreme levels of employment insecurity (measured by subsidized jobs, training-for-work schemes, unpaid training) impacted both sexes greatly (Kieffer *et al.*, this volume). The German study found only partial support of the impact of type of contract on further transitions to adulthood. The authors suggest that the main reason for this divergence is the heterogeneity of temporary contract positions that consists of both people who are trainees on the job such as physicians and regular fixed-term contracts, a comment echoed in the Hungarian case (Kurz *et al.*; Róbert and Bukodi, this volume).

We found mixed support for our expectation that the public sector is a more secure type of employment, which is clearly due to major institutional differences. In the open and liberal system of Canada, public sector workers were protected and significantly less likely to be in the temporally uncertain positions of irregular shifts (Mills, this volume). In Norway, women were over-represented in the public sector, which had low wages but high job protection and flexibility. Working in this sector allowed them to make an easier work/family linkage (Nilsen, this volume). German men working in the public sector had a higher transition to family formation, with Hungarian public sector workers more likely to have fixed-term contracts. Self-employment for youth rose in countries such as Hungary (particularly for women) and Britain, but had mixed impacts on family formation. In France, for example, the impact of being self-employed on entering into a first union was low for men and non-significant for women (Kieffer *et al.*, this volume).

In summary, as Table 17.1 illustrates, out of the 14 countries several patterns of the impact of uncertainty on family formation are apparent. First, there are clear gender-specific effects in Germany, the Netherlands, Italy, and Spain and to a lesser extent in France, Hungary and Britain. Young women and men seem to be generally affected in the same manner in the social-democratic and liberal regimes, with mixed findings for Estonia, Sweden, Britain and France. The impact of uncertainty on family formation in the post-socialist regimes places them somewhere in-between the conservative and liberal regimes, a fascinating finding in itself.

Second, only Mexico and Ireland found marginal impacts of labor market uncertainty on family formation, albeit for very different reasons. In these family-oriented regimes, partnership and fertility remained as bastions of security. Due to the relatively better economic situation brought about by globalization, young Irish youth actually opted to form unions and have children more so than before (Layte *et al.*, this volume). As a rational reply to uncertainty in the Mexican context, women often worked in order to diversify the source of income and spread uncertainty over a larger base in order to support the family. They engaged in these precarious jobs in order to achieve family goals (Parrado, this volume). Mixed findings in Sweden and France are related to the stronger welfare state support that cushioned youth by providing social benefits to the unemployed, but which also promoted the combination of work and family. The mixed findings in Britain likely reflect the different mindset and lack of real long-term consequences for workers in precarious positions and unemployment in this mobile and open employment system.

RATIONAL RESPONSES TO UNCERTAINTY: THE DEVELOPMENT OF STRATEGIES

Our expectation that youth will develop rational responses to uncertainty within their own institutional context is also supported. These strategies include postponement of entry into adulthood (remaining in the education system, postponing labor market entry and family formation), taking on multiple roles, and entering more flexible partnerships. We also witnessed a clear gender-specific strategy, which is discussed in more detail below.

The first strategy is *general postponement of the transition to adulthood*, illustrated by behavior such as remaining in the education system, entering the labor market later and postponing family formation. There was a clear postponement in the entry into parenthood. There was an extraordinary delay in the onset of childbearing in Spain, which may be the result of educational expansion and entry of women into the work force. In Hungary, only 45 percent of younger females had become parents by the age of 25 in comparison to 70 percent of women 10 years earlier (Róbert and Bukodi, this volume).

Remaining in school is a rational response to the growing insecurity generated by globalization for two principal reasons. First, it confirms our alternative role hypothesis that in a worsening, ever-changing and uncertain labor market with prospects of unemployment or precarious work, youth seek shelter in the educational system. A second motivation to remain or return to school is the growing importance of knowledge in the era of globalization and the subsequent need to obtain more qualifications. By seeking educational refuge, youth temporarily avoid unemployment or precarious work while upgrading their credentials and enhancing their chances in the future labor market. An exception was observed in Mexico where family formation remained at the same ages (Parrado, this volume), and in Sweden and Estonia where there were trends towards earlier non-marital cohabitation (Bygren *et al.*; Katus *et al.*). Due to the relative ease by which these types of unions can be stopped and started and their general cultural acceptance, youth appeared to develop their own rational reply to the situation by reaping the economic and social advantages of living together without a binding commitment.

Regardless of the reasons, there are several consequences of postponement. One is that youth remain either economically dependent on their parents or other financial sources for a longer period of time. For instance, the parental resources of youth had an impact of postponement, with American youth coming from parents with more resources remaining longer in the parental home. This subsequently delays entry into the labor market. Liefbroer (this volume), for instance, shows a remarkable historical increase in the median age at entry into first job in the Netherlands, from 15.4 years for the cohort born in 1901-10 to 20.1 years for the cohort born in 1961-70. The Mexican case provides a twist on the postponement argument. Here women's income became an important resource to their family of origin who pressured them to remain in the parental home as a contributor to the family income (Parrado, this volume).

Another strategy is for youth to *take on multiple roles* such as combining school and work. Many countries showed that the transition from school to work has become progressively more complex. Combining educational enrollment and part-time employment is a way for youth not only to finance their prolonged stay in educational institutions, but also a means to smoothen entry into the labor market. This is particularly the case of liberal countries with an organizational education system, which lack a vocational system with practical training so that youth do not gain an easy foot in the door of the employer. However, this phenomenon has also spread to countries such as Hungary and the Netherlands. Taking on multiple roles served as a protective strategy in Spain, with those who combined education and work being significantly less likely to fall into unemployment. In Mexico, a rational household strategy for Mexican families was to add more individuals to the labor market in order to spread the uncertainty, resulting from recurrent financial shocks. This meant that young married women from the middle classes also had to combine a work and family career (Parrado, this volume). In Canada, youth that combined school with precarious work were significantly more likely to do so for involuntary reasons. This suggests that taking on multiple roles may not merely be an individual choice, but a rational response to gain more skills to get a better job. However, in a country where secondary education has become increasingly more expensive, in addition to student loans and family support, combining school and work may be the only means for some to get better qualifications (Mills, this volume).

A third strategy reflects the *shift from more permanent marital unions to non-marital cohabitation*. In many of the countries, such as Sweden, Norway, the Netherlands, Britain, United States, Canada, and more recently and radically in Hungary and Estonia, there has been a large shift among adults born in and after the 1960s to choose unmarried cohabitation as opposed to marriage. This supports our flexible-partnership hypothesis, which argued that when there is growing uncertainty about behavioral outcomes and the implications of long-term commitments, a rational reaction for youth is to choose a relationship that has less of a binding obligation. For young Swedish women born in 1964, 92 percent choose a consensual union as their first partnership, a pattern that continued to increase (Bygren *et al.*, this volume). Within the United States, a clear division in union formation emerged, with whites and Hispanics more likely to marry in comparison with blacks (Berkowitz King, this volume). This is similar to results in Hungary and Estonia, where cohabitation was concentrated among individuals in less advantageous positions (Katus *et al.*; Róbert and Bukodi, this volume). However, there appeared to be two general groups who have a higher propensity to cohabit across the countries for very different reasons. One was youth with high amounts of human capital and good labor market prospects, who likely saw it as a flexible and non-binding commitment that did not clash with their careers. The other group was disadvantaged youth who used it as a strategy and rational reaction to uncertainty to combine resources in the face of uncertain future labor market success.

The final striking finding was clear support for our gender hypothesis, with *gender-specific strategies emerging in the male breadwinner societies*. As Table 17.1 illustrates, uncertainty in the employment sphere impacted men in a negative way and women in the opposite manner in countries that had a male-breadwinner model. This split between the sexes was particularly evident in Italy, Spain, Germany, the Netherlands, and to a lesser extent in Hungary and France.

The first gender-specific finding is that uncertain men opted to postpone family formation. A precarious employment status or lack of human capital for men had a negative impact on entry into partnership and especially parenthood, a finding that was exaggerated in the male-breadwinner nations. For instance, being unemployed had a strong negative effect for men entering a marriage in Spain, whereas young Spanish men who had the highest security of being employed and working full-time had the highest rate of fatherhood (Simó *et al.*, this volume). In Italy and the Netherlands, both economic and employment relation insecurity clearly reduced the rate of first union formation and fatherhood for men (Bernardi and Nazio; Liefbroer, this volume). Unemployment after a first low-paid job impacted French men's entry into a first union in a significantly negative way (Kieffer *et al.*, this volume).

When we examine the findings for women, two tactics to reduce uncertainty emerged which had opposite consequences for entry into a partnership. We can clearly identify two types of young women, which are family- versus career-oriented types. Particularly in male-breadwinner societies and conservative and family-oriented welfare regimes, certain types of women tended to enter into a marriage and have children faster. Here family formation and taking the domestic role of housewife and/or mother is one type of strategy for young women with less human capital in order to reduce uncertainty. This provides further support for our welfare regime hypothesis outlined in the introductory chapter. Several studies found that women who were employed part-time (e.g., Spain, Germany, the Netherlands, Britain), at a very low starting pay (e.g., France, Hungary), or inactive or unemployed (e.g., Spain, Italy, the Netherlands, France, Britain) were more likely to enter a union (often marriage) or have a child. In Germany, for instance, the temporal uncertainty of a fixed-term contract did not work as an impediment to having a first child for women, and in Hungary it even resulted in a 20 percent increase (Róbert and Bukodi, this volume). In Spain, even the youngest cohort of non-employed women was more likely to enter into a first union.

Three reasons underlie the above findings. First, lower quality jobs have very few prospects for career advancement. This prompts women to opt for motherhood to reduce their own insecurity or as a way of giving meaning and structure to their lives. Second, these women may have already been less attached to the labor force and found domestic life more appealing in the first instance. Being a homemaker is a valued position in some nations and even seen as a luxury in others. Third, following the uncertainty reduction theory of Friedman *et al.* (1994), being married and having children could serve as one strategy to reduce uncertainty, particularly among those who have limited or blocked alternatives to reduce uncertainty in another way. According to this theory, a stable and successful career is an important source of certainty for some, and thus it lowers their likelihood to form a family. Those with marginal career prospects opt for certainty in the family realm, a strategy that may be particularly relevant for women from male breadwinner societies.

The second group of women adopted a very different tactic and sought to obtain more individual human capital and invest in a career, which depending on the institutional context either enabled or constrained them to form a family. In support of our expectations, women with higher education were either less likely to enter into partnerships and parenthood or to experience both transitions later in countries where interdependent careers were institutionally impeded (e.g., Germany, the Netherlands, Spain). In Spain, for instance, highly educated women from the youngest cohorts were significantly less likely to form a partnership or become mothers. Our results provide a spin on Becker's (1981) theory of increased female economic autonomy, which states that women who possess higher human capital are less likely to enter a union with a traditional division of labor and forgo motherhood. We find that this is true, but only in countries where the interdependence between family and work careers is incompatible.

This division in the gender-specific impact of uncertainty did not hold in liberal and social-democratic regimes where the dual-earner model prevails (see Table 17.1). In Canada, part-time work, educational enrollment and a precarious labor market activity status significantly reduced entry into marriage for men, and the likelihood to become first-time parents for both sexes (Mills, this volume). In Sweden, economic self-sufficiency has long been recognized as an important factor to increase union formation for both men and women (Bracher and Santow, 1998). The high level of security afforded by the Swedish welfare state allows youth, particularly mothers, to combine work and fertility, resulting in strong labor market attachment coupled with high fertility rates.

We conclude that it is not the accumulation of human capital that is important for many women, but rather the incompatibility of employment or educational and domestic roles. In many countries entry into marriage and labor market participation does not appear to present a conflict for many young women (Blossfeld, 1995). This is likely due to the fact that the domestic division of labor does not change after entry into marriage, but rather after the birth of the first child. Furthermore, highly educated women do not seem to have in general a lower rate of *overall* entry into motherhood. Rather, as Blossfeld and Huinink (1991) argue, they simply postpone it. In Sweden and Norway, for example, men and women with the highest levels of education also had the lowest propensity to enter a first union, yet still showed comparatively high first-birth rates after entry. In Mexico, highly qualified women employed in commercial or professional activities did not delay union formation relative to non-working women. But in contrast, all types of employment strongly reduced the likelihood of having a child.

A further finding that contradicts Becker's (1981) theory was that Dutch, Swedish, Norwegian and Canadian men with more educational qualifications also postponed family formation. In Canada, both women and men with university education were less likely to enter into marriage (Mills, this volume). Liefbroer (this volume) cites two possible reasons: homogamy (i.e., higher educated males and females marry) or higher educated males are more individualistic and thus postpone binding family commitments (see also Blossfeld and Timm, 2003). An additional argument is that obtaining education is a strategy to attain more human capital and thus certainty in order to form a family or a preference to replace family formation.

Finally, the transition to first marriage and first birth are endogenous processes in most of the countries (Blossfeld and Mills, 2001). Being married was often a key variable in explaining the transition to first child, but particularly so in the family-oriented and conservative regimes. In the Mexican, Spanish, and Italian case, marriage played a deterministic role and was clearly a prerequisite for entering parenthood.

NATION-SPECIFIC INSTITUTIONS AS FILTERS OF UNCERTAINTY

The last central finding is that the extent to which youth experience the consequences of globalization depends largely upon the nation-specific institutions that exist to shield, or conversely, funnel uncertainty to them.

The findings generally supported our expectations outlined in the employment relation hypothesis regarding the impact of open and closed employment systems. When forced to restructure and meet the competitive demands of globalization, nations with closed systems actively targeted new flexibility and restructuration measures at new labor market entrants. In the insider/outsider market in southern Europe, youth entering the labor market met not only high levels of unemployment, but also precarious jobs. In support of our labor market flexibility hypothesis, we found that flexibility measures were targeted at labor market 'outsiders', which are youth and, as we explore in our third volume, women (Blossfeld and Hofmeister, forthcoming). Due to the protection of labor market insiders in the closed system, numerical and temporal flexibility in the form of fixed-term and temporary contracts were used. In countries with open employment systems, flexibility pervaded in more forms, such as temporal flexibility in the form of irregular work shifts and wage flexibility related to lower pension benefits (see Mills, this volume).

Several of the countries in this study underwent extreme shifts in the type of employment relations, which impacted youth's labor market experiences. Ireland, for instance, experienced unprecedented growth and a radical transformation of the labor market in recent decades (Layte *et al.*, this volume). The Irish case is a textbook example of how a state can shift from active resistance to enthusiastically embracing globalization by becoming internationally competitive, seeking to promote economic growth, stimulating an open trading regime, and attracting foreign investment. The legacy of the globalization period left both the possibility and a trail of flexible and atypical employment arrangements, even in the face of a relatively strong union presence. Yet it is an economy that operates at full capacity both in terms of labor and capital, thus somewhat limiting employers' ability to offer fixed-term contracts in relative comparison to other European countries in this study. With virtually full employment at the end of the 1990s, Ireland is one nation in this study that shows how globalization can actually reduce uncertainty in an economy. Since the mid-1990s, it has witnessed a resurgence of entry into marriage and fertility to unprecedented levels. This is in sharp contrast to Ireland's economic depression, high unemployment and poverty in the recent past. A basic conclusion is that globalization can have positive or negative consequences depending on the specific historical situation or influences in a country. Whereas Ireland demonstrates a positive impact, Mexican youth had a more negative experience.

Since the early 1980s, Mexico became extremely vulnerable to the globalization process and felt the 'random' economic shocks via severe economic crises. It is a ruthless case of privatization of state firms, high labor market flexibility and orientation to exports and outside markets (Parrado, this volume). The absence of any unemployment insurance and the fact that around one million individuals lost their jobs after the economic crisis of 1994 led to high levels of poverty and extreme uncertainty. The internationalization of markets signaled the spread of the 'maquiladora' industry, which was a technique to attract foreign investment with cheap Mexican labor and lower costs. The target group for this industry is young single women, often contributing to the family household.

Estonia and Hungary likewise experienced radical shifts in the 1990s as they changed from post-socialist societies with a closed employment system to more open liberal market societies in a rapid period of time. Other examples include Italy and Spain, where we see clear differences between the cohorts who were protected in eras of high regulation and those thereafter.

Educational systems in the different countries impact youths' labor market entry, providing support for our expectations. The dual (vocational) training system alleviates the amount of uncertainty that youth experience in the transition from school to work. In Germany, for instance, the training system feeds into the labor market, with youth able to develop a network of contacts and have a foot in the labor market, which is reflected by the overall lower unemployment rates in Germany (Klijzing, this volume). Furthermore, the implementation of the 'emplois-jeunes' policy of 5-year fixed-term contracts in France, which meant a shift from theoretical to vocational on-the-job training, has been a decisive policy in reducing youth unemployment in the late 1990s (Kieffer *et al.*, this volume). Finally, in the organizational educational systems, we found that youth indeed entered 'stop-gap' jobs before finding a job that would match their educational qualifications. This was the case in Canada, for example, where many youth worked in precarious first jobs as opposed to waiting for a better job match (see Mills, this volume). The lack of 'scarring' that these low level jobs have on youths' entire employment careers in this context permits this type of behavior and is a stark contrast from youth in closed systems.

The type of welfare regime, family system and related support that was provided for youth to combine family and work emerged as another fundamental aspect. In support of our welfare regimes hypothesis, our study demonstrates that the youth who are the hardest hit by uncertainty are the ones living in nations that lack safety nets in terms of unemployment benefits, education grants, housing subsidies (e.g., Italy), and family-related policies that support parenthood. A clear example of how a welfare regime can mitigate the transition to adulthood was shown for the Swedish case. Whereas increasing employment uncertainty tended to dramatically postpone family formation elsewhere, this was generally not the case in Sweden where youth had a comparatively secure social safety net to fall back on. Swedish policy likewise created and reinforced incentives for youth to combine paid work with childbearing and rearing. In fact, over 80 percent of Swedish women with children under the age of seven are active in the labor force (Bygren *et al.*, this volume). This was also the case for Norway, which has a family policy aimed at bolstering female labor force participation via generous maternity leave arrangements, strong protection against dismissal during maternity leave, and ample provisions for subsidized childcare.

Another striking finding was that compared to the conservative welfare regimes (Germany, the Netherlands), France's recent public family policies set it apart.[1] Day care, full-time nursery schools from age two, parental leave for mothers and fathers, and fiscal benefits for childcare have reduced the barriers for women to combine family life with a professional career. This has translated into more full-time female employment, and only a minority of young females choosing full-time homemaking after leaving the educational system. In fact, complete non-participation of young women in the French labor market is rare and the traditional family model for young French youth is clearly a thing of the past (Kieffer *et al.*, this volume). Finally, the strong view in many family-oriented regimes that the family is a vital source of security in the face of economic insecurity was also important, particularly in Ireland and Mexico.

CONCLUDING REMARKS

We now summarize the major findings of this volume, followed by a description of how this study contributes to the field of youth studies and globalization research. We conclude with the added value of our approach.

This comparative study examined the impact of globalization on the early life course of youth in 14 countries. A central finding was that youth have experienced increasingly higher levels of uncertainty, which has a tangible impact on their transition to partnership and parenthood. We first sketched the mechanisms that connected the globalization process to rising uncertainty in the lives of youth. Globalization was characterized by the internationalization of markets, rapid intensification of competition based on deregulation, privatization and liberalization, accelerated diffusion of knowledge and new ICTs and the rising importance of markets and their dependence on random shocks. Together, these elements generated an unprecedented level of uncertainty that directly impacts the life course of youth. But rising uncertainty is institutionally filtered, with some groups more directly exposed to it than others. Institutions pertinent to transitions in the early life course include employment relations, educational, welfare regime and family systems. We then examined the micro-level or individual response to these developments and found that youth develop context-specific strategies via rational decision-making under conditions of uncertainty. Youth react by developing various strategies such as postponement of life events, remaining in school, engaging in flexible relationships, or taking on multiple roles. In the male breadwinner societies, young men and women are not only impacted differently by the uncertainty that globalization brings about, but they develop different coping strategies. Youth have increased economic, temporal and employment relation uncertainty in their early labor market career, which enters into their decisions to form a family.

This comparative study demonstrates that youth experience increasing uncertainty in different ways dependent on their own human capital and institutional context. The changes brought about by globalization in the 1990s served to exacerbate inequalities along many lines. Youth become the outsiders in many countries, or were divided within nations between the employed and unemployed, or higher and lower occupational classes or educational levels. Although there was increased heterogeneity of the spread of risk across different groups in the liberal welfare regimes, uncertainty generally gathered at the bottom. In response to globalization, many countries implemented flexibility measures to deal with the very serious problem of youth employment. Yet these labor market flexibility measures were often experienced by youth with the lowest human capital. Thus the paradox is that although youth with less human capital were the first to benefit by having a job in these high unemployment areas, since the jobs were generally on a fixed-term basis, their advantage was short-lived. The gap between the excluded 'losers' and the 'winners' of globalization can only widen further. Due to higher uncertainty in the workplace, these youth become even more excluded as they encounter difficulties in establishing a family.

This study therewith contributes to both youth studies and globalization research. The majority of studies that examine the transition to adulthood focuses on either one or at most two careers and do not view the transition to adulthood in its entirety as an interdependent process. This study synthesizes the entire transition to adulthood from entry into the labor market through to partnership formation and parenthood. By virtue of this approach we learn about the interdependence between the employment, partnership and fertility careers of the early life course.

Our approach also deviates in several crucial ways from existing work in the field of globalization. First, it takes an *empirical approach*. Among the vast amount of globalization literature in sociology, there are few attempts at constructing testable hypotheses or systematic empirical examinations of how these overarching changes impact the life course of individuals. The principal enterprise of globalization theory has been based on conjectures rather than substantive evidence. The result is speculation that may in fact be an exaggeration of the empirical extent and novelty of globalization. Sociologists such as Beck (1997/2000) and Giddens (1990; 2000) ask us to accept that there is an effect of a 'runaway world' or 'risk society'. For example, Giddens (2000: 12) argues: "Globalization isn't only about what is 'out there', remote and far away from the individual. It is an 'in here' phenomenon too, influencing intimate and personal aspects of our lives." Yet, we are provided with little empirical evidence or an attempt at generating testable hypotheses, mechanisms or causal paths as to how globalization impacts our lives. Our study, on the other hand, outlines mechanisms that connect globalization to the life course and generates clear hypotheses and empirical evidence about how it impacts the lives of youth.

A second difference is that we *bring the individual back into globalization*. A significant strand of the globalization literature is empirical work conducted by economists and political scientists. This work often remains at the macro-level (e.g., trade, foreign investment) and focuses on proving or disproving the existence of a converging global economy (Fligstein, 1998; Hirst and Thompson, 1996), an approach which echoes theories that paved the way for globalization, such as Wallerstein's (1974) World Systems Theory. An approach that examines economic convergence is clearly too limited for a sociological account of changes in the life courses of modern societies. This study shows that it is essential to combine individual-level models of action with institutional explanations (see also Mayer, 1997; 2001).

The third deviation is our placement of the nation-state in the form of *nation-specific institutions as central to globalization*. Previous theorists have proclaimed that globalization undermines the authority or heralds the fall of the nation-state. Ohmae (1990; 1993: 78) maintains that: "the nation state has become an unnatural, even dysfunctional, unit for organizing human activity and managing economic endeavors in a borderless world." Beck (2000: 20) also attacks the idea "that we live and act in the self-enclosed spaces of national states and their respective national societies." In our empirical analyses, however, we have found that nation-states have not lost their significance, but are facing a more general transformation (Sassen, 1996) and that the crucial aspect of how globalization is 'experienced' is rooted within institutions (Hurrell and Woods, 1995). By virtue of our comparative approach across 14 different countries, we witnessed how youth in different nations responded to similar global pressures given institutional, structural and cultural differences.

The final disparity is that *we empirically studied whether globalization results in persistent inequality and stratification* within industrialized nations. Here we deviate from the majority of previous work in two ways. First, due to the theoretical development of globalization from authors such as Wallerstein (1974), literature has tended to focus on inequalities between developing/developed countries, north/south or periphery/core regions (e.g., Wood, 1994). Our work examined inequality of individuals living *within* industrialized nations. A second important deviation is that our results challenge proponents of globalization who argue that established social divisions of class, gender, ethnicity and nation are fragmenting and re-forming (e.g., Beck, 1992; 1997/2000). Our study clearly shows that globalization accentuates differences. We found that inequality emerges in the form of uncertain employment, which is generally concentrated on youth and within this group at the bottom. Our position on globalization and inequality is thus unequivocally different from Beck's (1992: 88; 1997/2000) and to some extent Giddens' (1994; 2000) who predict that globalization will result in an increasingly 'classless society' characterized by the weakening of class ties.

Finally, globalization offers a supplementary explanation of changes in fertility and family formation to previous theories such as the widely used second demographic transition theory (Lesthaeghe and Van de Kaa, 1986; Van de Kaa, 1987; Lesthaeghe, 1995). This theory focuses on changing social practices, values, and the breakdown of many class, gender, and age-based constraints that previously structured demographic events (see Mills, 2000). Central changes according to this theory are educational expansion, increased female labor force participation, creation of the welfare state, and shifts in the economic and political structure. A further element is how economic developments mirror the ability and will of individuals to make long-term binding decisions (Van de Kaa, 1987).

Although there are clearly similarities between the two approaches, our globalization hypothesis offers several new insights. First, the theory of the second demographic transition explains change largely in relation to changes in values via the theory of 'ideational shift'. For example, Lesthaeghe's work on fertility examines the acceptability of fertility and the perceived social and economic circumstances that reduced fertility poses for couples. For a reduction of fertility, there must be an appropriate ideational context that directs individual preferences to warrant the feeling of individual control over fertility and the desire to have a smaller family. Using the work of Maslow (1970) and Ingelhart (1977), the theory of the second demographic transition assumes that personal needs are increasingly important, which leads to a tendency of individualization that in turn impacts fertility behavior and more liberal and secular values. In contrast, our globalization hypothesis explains change as connected to structural shifts in increased uncertainty, with institutions at the center of this process. In our approach, change is thus not described as one general trend among societies.

Second, the theory of the second demographic transition and its building blocks were largely developed in the 1980s, which was a period at the end of an economic boom in many countries and the beginning of educational expansion and significant changes in the role of women. Our theory reflects changes in the aftermath of the mid-1980s. By virtue of this, it can offer additional insight into why more and more youth postpone fertility. For instance, although many young people report that they want to have more children, they often do not achieve this goal (see for instance Noack and Østby, 2002; van Peer, 2002). Why is this the case? The answer is, we believe, that although we see that living standards have increased over time, the gains are disproportionately channeled to certain groups such as the labor market insiders and those who have acquired rights. It is these groups that have the luxury of catering to their higher personal needs and engaging in individualistic behavior. The unprotected either do not experience increases in living standards or do so on a weaker level. Instead of a shift to individualization, they experience increased uncertainty and thus postpone fertility due to their disadvantaged position.

The concept of globalization has an added value to understand changes in the life course. It forces us to develop a multi-level conception that links global transformations to its impact at the institutional and individual level. It also allows us to include countries that often fall outside of the traditional welfare state or comparative work in this field, namely the eastern European countries of Estonia and Hungary and the oft-forgotten member of North America, Mexico. Different experiences and behaviors in these countries led to several interesting findings. Finally, we concede that the impact of globalization on the life course must be specified through more precise theories of its mechanisms. Due to the sheer complexity of causal mechanisms that work their way through institutions and labor markets to the individual level, there has so far been an absence of empirical research in this area. It is our hope that this first attempt will stimulate discussion, modifications and new approaches to study these complex and drastic transformations in society.

NOTE

1   For this reason, France has been put in square brackets in Table 17.1. Often placed within the conservative welfare regime, it has many features in common with countries from a social-democratic welfare regime.

BIBLIOGRAPHY

Beck, U. (1992) *Risk Society*, London: Sage.
Beck, U. (1997, 2nd edn. 2000) *What is Globalization?*, Cambridge: Polity Press.
Becker, G.S. (1981) *A Treatise on the Family*, Cambridge, MA: Harvard University Press.
Bernardi, F., Blossfeld, H.-P., Mills, M.C. (forthcoming) *Globalization, Uncertainty, and Men in Society*.
Blossfeld, H.-P. (ed.) (1995) *The New Role of Women*, Boulder (CO): Westview Press.
Blossfeld, H.-P. and Hofmeister, H. (eds) (forthcoming) 'Globalization, uncertainty and women in society', unpublished book manuscript, Bamberg University.
Blossfeld, H.-P. and Timm, A. (eds) (2003) *Who marries whom? Educational systems as marriage markets in modern societies, European Studies of Population*, Dordrecht: Kluwer Academic Publishers.
Blossfeld, H.-P. and Huinink, J. (1991) 'Human capital investments or norms of role transitions? How women's schooling and career affect the process of family formation', *American Journal of Sociology*, 97: 143-168.
Blossfeld, H.-P. and Mills, M. (2001) 'A causal approach to interrelated family events: A cross-national comparison of cohabitation, nonmarital conception and marriage', *Canadian Studies in Population Special Issue on Longitudinal Methodology*, 28(2): 409-437.
Blossfeld, H.-P., Mills, M. and Bernardi, F. (forthcoming) *Globalization, Uncertainty and Men in Society*.
Bracher, M. and Santow, G. (1998) 'Economic Independence and Union Formation in Sweden', *Population Studies*, 52: 275-294.
Breen, R. (1997) 'Risk, Recommodification and Stratification', *Sociology*, 31(3): 473-498.
Fligstein, N. (1998) 'Is Globalization the Cause of the Crises of Welfare States?', European University Institute Working Paper SPS No. 98/5, San Domenico, Italy.
Friedman, D., Hechter, M. and Kanazawa, S. (1994) 'A Theory of the Value of Children', *Demography*, 31(3): 375-401.
Giddens, A. (1994) *Beyond Left and Right*, Cambridge: Polity Press.
Giddens, Anthony (1990) *The Consequences of Modernity*, Cambridge: Polity Press.
Giddens, Anthony (2000) *Runaway World. How Globalization is Reshaping our Lives*, London: Profile Books.
Hirst, P. and Thompson, G. (1996) *Globalization in Question*, Cambridge: Polity Press.
Hurrell, A. and Woods, N. (1995) 'Globalization and Inequality', *Millennium. Journal of International Studies*, 24(3): 447-470.
Inglehart, R. (1977) *The Silent Revolution*, Princeton: Princeton University Press.
Lesthaeghe, R. (1995) 'The second demographic transition in Western countries: An interpretation', in K.O. Mason and A.-M. Jensen (eds) *Gender and Family Change in Industrialized Countries*, Oxford: Oxford University Press.

Lesthaeghe, R. and van de Kaa, D.J. (1986) 'Twee demografische transities?' [Two Demographic Transitions?], in D.J. van de Kaa and R. Lesthaeghe (eds) *Bevolking: Groei en Krimp* [Population: Waxing and Waning], Deventer: Van Loghum Slaterus.

Maslow, A.H. (1970) *Motivation and Personality*, New York: Harper and Row.

Mayer, K.-U. (1997) 'Notes on a Comparative Political Economy of Life Courses', *Comparative Social Research*, 16: 203-226.

Mayer, K.-U. (2001) 'The paradox of global social change and national path dependencies: Life course patterns in advanced societies', in A. Woodward and M. Kohli (eds) *Inclusions and Exclusions in European Societies*, New York: Routledge.

Mills, M. (2000) *The Transformation of Partnerships. Canada, the Netherlands and the Russian Federation in the Age of Modernity*, Amsterdam: Thela Thesis Population Studies Series.

Noack, T. and Østby, L. (2002) 'Free to choose – but unable to stick to it?', in E. Klijzing and M. Corijn (eds) *Dynamics of fertility and partnership in Europe: Insights and lessons from comparative research*, New York/Geneva: United Nations.

Ohmae, K. (1990) *The Borderless World*, New York: Harper Business.

Ohmae, K. (1993) 'The Rise of the Region State', *Foreign Affairs*, 72(2): 78-87.

Sassen, S. (1996) *Losing Control? Sovereignty in an Age of Globalization*, New York: Columbia University Press.

Van de Kaa, D.J. (1987) 'Europe's Second Demographic Transition', *Population Bulletin*, 42(1): 1-59.

Van Peer, C. (2002) 'Desired and achieved fertility', in E. Klijzing and M. Corijn (eds) *Dynamics of fertility and partnership in Europe: Insights and lessons from comparative research*, New York/Geneva: United Nations.

Wallerstein, I. (1974) *The Modern World-System: Capitalist Agriculture and the Origins of the European World-Economy of the 16th Century*, New York: Academic Press.

Wood, A. (1994) *North-South Trade, Employment and Inequality: Changing Fortunes in a Skill-Driven World*, Oxford: Oxford University Press.

Subject Index

Author Index

Printed in the United States
76429LV00001B/14

9 780415 357302